The Wines of Greece

The Wines of Greece

by Konstantinos Lazarakis

MITCHELL BEAZLEY

First published in Great Britain in 2005
by Mitchell Beazley, an imprint of
Octopus Publishing Group Limited,
2–4 Heron Quays, London E14 4JP.

Copyright © Octopus Publishing Group Ltd 2005

Text copyright © Konstantinos Lazarakis 2005

Greece map copyright © Octopus Publishing Group Ltd 2005

Regional maps copyright © John Flower 2005

A CIP catalogue record for this book is available from the British Library.

ISBN: 1 84000 897 0

The author and publishers will be grateful for any information which will assist them in keeping future editions up-to-date. Although all reasonable care has been taken in the preparation of this book, neither the publishers nor the author can accept any liability for any consequences arising from the use thereof, or the information contained therein.

At the time of writing, the author of this book would like to declare a commercial relationship with the wine-producing companies of George Skouras and Nico Lazaridis.

Printed and bound in England by Mackays, Chatham.

Contents

Acknowledgments

This book could be dedicated to all those people that it kept me away from, for more than a year. Having wonderful people missing you is the ultimate compliment and I know I do not deserve it. However, this book is dedicated to all Greek wine producers. Remembering where you started is always so important. It is these people and their wines that persuaded me to change my life beyond my wildest dreams. And to Theodora. I am so sorry for not being there – just to say thank you and goodbye… But not to worry, I am sure I will tell you all about it one day.

This book would not have been possible without the precious help of numerous people. On the Greek side of this endeavour, any attempt to put on paper all those that helped me acquire stamina, information, facts, and figures is bound to fail – the number of these friends is so great that I will always leave someone out. I am sure that everyone who belongs to that group knows it – and saying "Thank you" is simply not enough.

Equally important are the team from Mitchell Beazley: Hilary Lumsden, Julie Sheppard, Margaret Rand, Susanna Forbes, and Samantha Stokes. I am sure that working with me made them redefine words like "patience", and "time-keeping". I would like to thank them for their tolerance and endurance, as well as for transforming my coarse text into something much, much prettier. Nothing that could be written here could fully express my gratitude.

Map of Greece

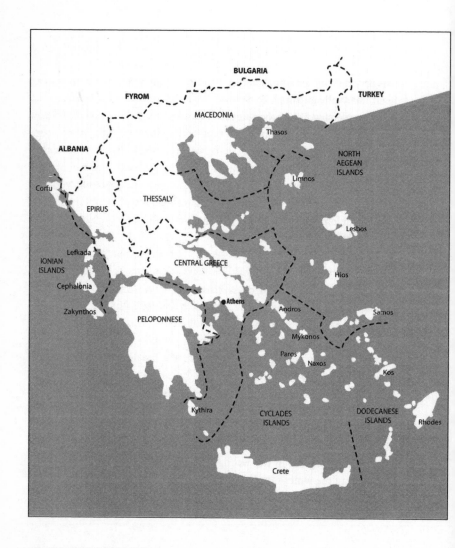

Introduction

It is very difficult for a book about the wines of any one country to be both good and totally impartial. To be good, it should be written by someone with a deep understanding of the subject. An outsider will have an independent point of view but, at the same time, might have problems appreciating where the country and its people come from, why, and where they are heading to. Wine is not a still life or a photograph – it is about dynamics. The more you become involved with any subject, the more your background, personal tastes, and experiences are bound to be influential, if only at a subconscious level. Therefore, impartiality is out of the window, even if the writer goes to great lengths to prevent this.

But is impartiality really needed in a book like this? It is certainly required in matters of judgment, where comparing and finding the best necessitates a well defined decision-making process and a set of exact criteria. Many wine books include all different kinds of star ratings and scores as a guide for readers. Guidance is needed for a complex topic like wine and the majority of wine-drinkers cannot spend significant amounts of time or money getting acquainted with the huge range of wines from around the world. Even so, with such guides there is an underlying risk that individual tastes can become substituted for a collective one – that of the most influential critic. Exchanging personal opinion for a ready-made assurance is an easy but dangerous way to negotiate the intricacies of wine. In addition, it is too tempting for someone to pick up a glass – especially if they are in the wrong frame of mind, having a bad day or pre-judging the wine – and say "this is a bad wine". In my opinion it is not fair to judge a wine by giving it a window of opportunity of less than a minute, three sniffs, and two sips.

Beyond such matters of personal taste, people brought up in traditional wine producing regions find it extremely hard to judge wine based only on what it is in the glass. In countries like Greece, wine has a social dimension that must be taken into account. Agriculture is, most of the time and for most people, a decent kind of poverty. Behind every artisan wine is an immense amount of effort, which has been applied in the hope of creating something worthwhile. Most producers try to make the best they can, according to their preferences, culture, and education. Such attempts are not a part of a marketing strategy but a matter of survival, of struggling for a better future, either for one's self or one's family.

It can be argued that these "behind the scenes" factors do not concern the average punter and that what is important is how the wine in the glass meets the expectations of the final customer. However, many wine-lovers do have a respect for the people that make a living out of wine-growing. They appreciate that there is more at stake than a small tasting note in a book or magazine: "The fruit is not complex, the finish is a bit dry, and it scores seventy-five points out of 100".

Therefore, this is not a book about ratings. It is about a country's visions and disillusions, dreams and traumas, problems and solutions, defeats and triumphs. And since Day One, Greeks have always had a most wonderful way of dealing with these.

Part I

The Background

1

Overview

With a population of some eleven million people, Greece covers an area of 131,944 square kilometres (50,945 square miles) and sports an impressive coastline of about 15,000 kilometres (9,321 miles). One of the most striking features of Greece is the sheer number of islands that encircle the mainland. Out of more than 3,000 islands, only sixty-three are inhabited. The main island groups are: the Ionian islands to the west, the Cyclades to the south, the Dodecanese to the southeast, the Sporades to the northeast and the North Aegean to the northeast of the Sporades. There are also two larger islands: Crete, forming the southernmost point of the country, and Evia, just a few hundred metres off the east coast of the central mainland. The total surface area of the islands is 28,827 square kilometres (11,130 square miles), with their coastlines making up slightly less than half of the total.

GEOGRAPHY AND GEOLOGY

Greece lies between the 34th and 42nd parallels of the northern hemisphere, forming the southern edge of the Balkan peninsula. It ends in the eastern part of the Mediterranean Sea, with its own family of seas surrounding it: the Aegean on the east, the Ionian on the west, itself part of the Adriatic, and the Libyan sea to the south. The division of seas goes on into ever-smaller units – for example, the northeastern part adjacent to Thrace is the Thracian Pelagos (*pelagos* being the Greek word for sea), while the area between the Cyclades and Crete is the Cretan Pelagos. On its northern boundaries, from west to east, Greece borders Albania, the former Yugoslavian Republic of Macedonia, Bulgaria, and Turkey.

Greece is very mountainous, with low-lying land only to be found in areas close to the coasts. There are only three significant plains: Thessaly in

Central Greece, and Macedonia and Thrace in the north. Its mountain ranges are an extension of the Alps of Central Europe, and the body that forms the spine of Greece's mainland is called the Pindos range. In general, the west side of the Pindos is higher than the east, although Mount Olympus, Greece's highest peak, is situated close to the Aegean Sea in the east. The mountains run from northwest to southeast, until they reach the Corinthian Gulf, the long but narrow strip of sea that all but cuts the Peloponnese off from the rest of the country. After this brief interruption, the mountains continue south of the Gulf to the end of the Peloponnese, where they form the three peninsulas ending in the Capes of Maleas, Tenaro, and Akritas. The ranges then continue offshore, creating in their highest points all the islands of the southern Aegean.

Most of the soils of Greece, in both the mountains and the islands, are primarily composed of limestone and sandstone sedimentary rocks. The only significant difference is the northern boundaries, where igneous rock assumes greater importance. In most cases the soils are shallow and poor, often revealing the underlying rock. The notable exceptions are the three main plains, which are deep, more fertile, and have a higher proportion of clay. The areas closer to the sea also have richer, mainly alluvial soils, while some of the islands, like Santorini, can be volcanic with soils that are extremely deficient in nutrients. As a result, loam, schist, chalk, sand, and many other types of soils can be found in Greece.

Greece has very few rivers, and most are small and tend to dry up during the summer months. Only rivers originating further north in the Balkan peninsula, like the Evros which starts in Bulgaria and divides Greece and Turkey, have any significant presence in the summer. This lack of major rivers and their seasonality is the main limiting factor for irrigation of any sort in Greece. Lakes are also limited and mostly confined to the northern part of the country. Most are basins created by the wearing away of the underlying limestone rock, and once again, many of these disappear during the summer months. As a result, their use for irrigation is restricted.

Most of the naturally occurring vegetation consists of heat-loving plants well adapted to the relatively arid climate. Forests that used to cover a large part of the country's surface have been largely destroyed by deforestation or extensive summer fires. Any evergreen forests that have survived are found in northwestern Greece. Despite the relative infertility of soils and the fact that less than a third of the country's surface is cultivated, Greece is predominately an agricultural country. Self-sufficient in most crops, its main exports are all agricultural products, making agriculture the main source of income.

CLIMATE AND WEATHER

The climate of Greece is typically Mediterranean, with ample sunshine throughout the year, long, dry summers, relatively short, mild winters, and brief springs. With its dramatic topography – the alternation of sea and land, and the rapid variations in altitudes – there are of course deviations from this mellow Mediterranean norm.

From a purely climatic point of view, the typical year can be divided into two parts: the cool and wet period, running from the second half of October until the end of March, and the warm, dry months, from April until mid-October. During the first period, the colder months are January and February, where the average minimum temperature is 5–10°C (41–50°F) on coastal regions, 0–5°C (32–41°F) further inland, and below 0°C (32°F) in high altitude regions. Islands in the Ionian and Aegean seas have much milder winters. Rainy and cloudy spells are frequent but never last more than a few days. Springs are short-lived, since winters are late, and the typical summer weather starts in mid- to late-May.

During the warm phase, the weather is remarkably stable with almost permanent clear skies, apart from a few brief storms. The hottest part of the year is usually the last ten days of July and the first ten of August, when the average maximum temperature is between 29–35°C (84–95°F). The mediating effect of the various seas together with the cool northern winds that are common in the Aegean Sea during August make the heat less intense in the coastal zones. Autumn is usually long and warm, lasting right up until December in some southern regions.

Rain is concentrated during the cool period, but can vary widely. The east is the driest, with more rain as you move either to the north or the west. Attica, just south of Athens, is one of the warmest and driest regions of the country, with an average annual rainfall of 414 millimetres (sixteen inches). Alexandroupolis in the northeast has 553 millimetres (twenty-two inches), and Corfu in the Ionian Sea reaches 1,097 millimetres (forty-three inches). During the vine's summer growing period, only Macedonia and Thrace have any significant rain, exceeding the sixty millimetre (two-and-a-half inches) mark during June, July, and August. However, bearing in mind that the average rainfall in Bordeaux for August alone is higher than the total for this three-month period in Greece, the level is still relatively low. Other Greek regions are drier, with even the verdant Ionian Islands receiving less than forty millimetres (just over one-and-a-half inches) during the same time frame. Nevertheless, early autumn rains can cause problems in viticulture. Precipitation levels rise sharply in October and later-ripening varieties in cooler areas, such as Moschofilero in the high plateau of Mantinia, can have difficulties reaching full maturity.

VITICULTURE

Viticulture is an important part of Greek agriculture, accounting for almost 70,000 hectares in 2000 and producing 355,800 tonnes of wine grapes. The gross profit of the grape-growing sector for 2000 was fifty billion Greek drachmas, which equates to 146.7 million euros.

It is interesting to note that the production of the 2000 harvest was almost identical to that of 1961 (363,000 tonnes), although the surface area dedicated to wine grape production was almost double at 133,825 hectares. The most intense period of uprooting was between 1988 and 1996. Between 1961 and 1989, the average yield was 18.9 hectolitres per hectare, while for the 1990s it had risen to 35.7 hectolitres per hectare. Several factors contributed to this, including a growing focus on high-yielding varieties, better cultivation and trellising techniques, replanting of old vineyards and replacement of dead vines, increasing use of irrigation, together with the availability and affordability of healthier planting stock, and chemical treatments and fertilizers. Nevertheless, yield figures can be misleading, since the grape-growing sector can be divided into two main categories. Those growers that make a living out of the vineyard, either working with a wine producer or selling to a cooperative, can routinely produce around seventy to eighty hectolitres per hectare, and sometimes a lot more than that. On the other hand, amateur growers, keeping their old, lightly planted vineyards just to satisfy their own consumption needs, can crop as low as twenty hectolitres per hectare.

Greece's agricultural base is made up mainly of small landowners, with all the resulting drawbacks that such a scale implies, most notably a lack of profitability and an impaired ability to invest, renovate, and adapt to new technologies and know-how. As well as the steep costs, the legal system makes it difficult for wine companies to buy up smaller plots in order to expand. Even in the less prestigious regions, a producer may snap up the first plots of land cheaply, but as soon as neighbouring landowners realise what is happening, prices tend to rise exponentially.

If site consolidation is difficult, then planting new vineyards can be nearly impossible. Developing new vineyards is prohibited and a producer wishing to do so must team up with an agronomist who already has certified vineyards. The agronomist must then transfer the "rights for vineyards" from the initial region to the area in question, uproot the old parcel, and establish the new one – a process that is both time- and money-consuming.

Greek viticulture, in its traditional form, has many things in common with other Mediterranean vine-growing countries. Gobelet training used to be the norm, where bush vines are unsupported by a trellis and pruned to short spurs. Before the invasion of phylloxera during the first half of the twentieth century (see page 27), planting densities were high, sometimes reaching up to 10,000 vines per hectare. Newer vineyards are far less dense, with most plantings being between 2,500 and 4,000 vines per hectare. This is partly due to the increased use of trellising, such as the popular Cordon de Royat system, and partly because of the rising cost of buying grafted stock. Common rootstocks are those preferred for their tolerance to drought, mainly the 41B and 110 Richter, followed by the 1103 Paulsen.

It is fair to say that most Greek vineyards have been organic since almost before the term was devised, with animal manure and sulphur being the main applications used by growers. Weeds were eliminated by ploughing, especially in regions where water competition between plants was intense.

But the last three decades have brought important changes to Greek viticulture, with the increased use of agrochemicals, such as fertilizers, herbicides, fungicides, and insecticides. Other forms of chemicals, like plant growth regulators, are not used either for table or wine grapes. At the same time, the last fifteen years have seen the emergence of a number of organic growers – called "biological" in Greece – and this is currently one of the most important trends in grape-growing. This development is aided both by consumers moving towards organic products and by the simple fact that organic cultivation in Greece is relatively easy and risk-free. Many people cite European Union (EU) funds as the prime motivation for converting the mode of cultivation, but this cannot be the full story: the EU supports would-be organic growers with 650 euros per hectare per year for between three to five years. Bearing in mind that compared with conventional farming, organic cultivation increases costs by roughly five to ten per cent, the financial help provided is practically insignificant. In any event, the increase in cost is about more man-hours and a slight loss on crop levels due to the less vigorous treatment of diseases and pests.

Working in the vineyard remains largely a manual job, with very little mechanization. Greek viticulture, and agriculture in general, has been helped immensely by the increasing numbers of workers coming from other Balkan or Eastern European countries. It is doubtful if the ageing and shrinking population of the Greek countryside on its own could support the wine-producing sector long-term.

THE QUESTION OF IRRIGATION

As expected, irrigation is a burning topic for Greek producers. Following the general EU approach, irrigation is not permitted, except for newly planted vines, but many growers do practise it on the quiet. Some of them are doing so in a very careful way, but others are just aiming to produce as much fruit as possible. The annual rainfall required by the general climatic/viticultural models, bearing in mind Greece's mean temperatures and sunshine hours, is around 700 millimetres, a level attained by only a small part of the country. Most areas are hot and arid during the final weeks of the vintage, stressing the plants and inhibiting fruit maturity. If global warming becomes a permanent part of the equation, then the water availability of the 1960s – when the EU law was created – will be totally different from the expected rainfall of the coming decade.

Irrigation can be employed to relieve water stress on a plant by supplying carefully controlled amounts of water to attain higher quantities of superior quality fruit. However, if irrigation were to become widely permitted, some growers might use it to produce high yields of diluted fruit. One must not lose sight of the whole picture. The fact that a few, high-profile growers and producers, with clear quality objectives and a good understanding of plant physiology, claim that they would produce better wines if they could irrigate, does not mean that a total legalization of irrigation would solve rather than create problems. To make such a measure work in favour of quality, two criteria must be met. First, the Greek government must be able to control yields in a very strict manner, and the penalties for misuse of irrigation must be severe. Second, a pricing structure should be put in place, whereby growers are paid not per kilogram of grapes, but by the hectare, with an additional bonus for quality. This policy should be practised by the majority of wine producers and grape buyers of an appellation, including of course the local cooperative – often the Achilles' heel of such plans. Since both measures are unlikely to be introduced in the foreseeable future, I believe it would be wise to keep the formal ban on irrigation, at least in Greece's quality-wine appellations (*see* Appendix 1).

VINICULTURE

Given the lack of large private companies, it has been the semi-professional *vignerons* who have preserved wine production and its related traditions for the last few centuries. Most of the time, the sole aim behind making wine was to produce enough to sustain the family through the year. A small proportion could be sold, but that was rarely the main source of income for the household. This way of working – and drinking – bred a certain sense of insularity; most producers spent all their lives tasting very little apart from their own wine.

The winemaking philosophy was extremely straightforward. The grapes, either freshly gathered or sun-dried, were pressed in small wooden vertical presses or by foot. Macerations, when desired, were brief; in most cases the juice was allowed to settle overnight with skins and stems, and drained the next morning. Longer macerations were avoided, so most artisan wines were white or rosé. The must was fermented in large barrels, made from chestnut or oak, either Greek or imported. Used barrels from the Cognac region were highly esteemed because they imparted a distinctive flavour in the wine and, having been soaked with a high-strength spirit, there was less chance of developing microbe-or bacteria-related problems. At the end of fermentation the wine was racked off the gross lees and sealed around the bung with plaster or dough. The length of maturation depended on the needs or the patience of the owner, but rarely exceeded six months. Bottling was not practised, apart from filling up *damijanes* (demijohns) to empty last year's produce from the barrel and get it ready for the new vintage. Just as in ancient times, occasionally *damijanes* or even whole barrels were buried underground to be reserved for a special event, such as the wedding of the first-born son.

The development of cooperatives and private companies between the 1950s and the 1970s required a totally different approach to winemaking. Pressing was originally done in large, wooden, vertical presses, but from the 1960s, these were replaced with continuous presses. Oak casks remained important, but cement, enamel, and epoxy resin vats were used for both fermentation and ageing. During the 1980s, "pneumatic presses", "stainless steel vats", "refrigeration units", and "winery hygiene" became buzzwords for all self-respecting Greek wine producers. These developments, along with an influx of trained oenologists, led to a significant rise in wine quality, especially in whites.

A QUESTION OF OAK

In terms of stylistic progress, the most significant changes happened during the 1990s. Customers wanted extremely aromatic whites and deep, oaky reds. These "new" whites were achieved by selecting new varieties (mainly Sauvignon Blanc), and by using cool fermentation, ultra-clean musts, and improved yeast strains that favoured aromatic expression. The demand for new-style reds persuaded wine producers to invest substantial amounts of money in the latest extraction techniques and, most importantly, in brand new French barriques. The smell of new oak became a sure sign of quality, although a common "fault" of many reds produced in the 1990s – and, arguably, some of those produced in the 2000s – was the excessive use of new barriques. By 1995, Greece must have been one of the top spenders in French *tonnelleries*, at least in relation to her production volume. Alliers was the most popular wood, followed by Nevers, Limousin and Tronçais. American oak was introduced in the second half of the decade and Eastern European barriques a few years later. Around the same time, alternative oak products, like staves or chips, were introduced for lower-priced blends.

Alongside the aromatic whites and oaky reds, there was an emergence of oak-aged whites. The first examples came from Sauvignon Blanc and Chardonnay grapes, but Greek varieties, like Assyrtico, followed almost immediately. The first attempts at influencing white wines with oak were made by maturing the young wine in barrel, rather than fermenting it in barrique. Even if lees contact was practised to enrich flavour and texture, there appeared to be a lack of synergy between the oak and the rest of the wine. Malolactic fermentation in oak can often be a way of adding complexity to white wines. However, Greece's warm climate leaves very low levels of malic acid in mature grapes, and thus malolactic fermentation is either brief or impossible. This absence partly accounted for the relative lack of depth in such wines.

These days, Greek oenologists are very much in line with the rest of the world in terms of winemaking techniques and winery equipment. Methods like micro-oxygenation, skin contact, lees contact for reds, cutting-edge presses or extraction/maceration vats, are all widely applied. Producers are gaining more experience in getting the balance right, such as using less new oak or letting the wine spend less time in barrel. They are also becoming more adventurous, trying cold soaks or long post-fermentation macerations, for example. What is truly new is the way they approach innovation. Getting over-enthusiastic about a new technique and allowing it to completely dominate a wine is thankfully a thing of the past. Everything is carefully evaluated and prudently incorporated within the existing wine styles.

There are already signs of the next steps for Greek wine. Viticulture has traditionally lagged behind viniculture, following modern developments elsewhere from a distance. So there is a need to apply the same state-of-the-art approach in the vineyards as in the wineries. In winemaking, it will be interesting to see whether oenologists adopt a "back to tradition" philosophy, especially since Greece has one of the richest heritages in the world. For example, it is discouraging that only a very few modern producers are willing to experiment with natural yeasts, while only a few kilometres away, their fathers, or even grandfathers, are still doing just that.

What can be taken for granted is that Greece has finally resolved all the issues regarding the "hardware" of the wine sector. Ideally in the future, the only constraints will be the potential of her terroirs and the imagination of her producers.

2

The history of Greek wine

To tackle a subject like wine in Ancient Greece is a complicated endeavour. There is an amazing wealth of material describing its appearance, role, and relevance, ranging from the seventh century BC to modern times. In the last two centuries, a large number of books have been published dedicated entirely to the subject. The main reason behind the existence of so many sources is that wine has always been inextricably interwoven into the fabric of everyday Greek life. The Greeks developed an entire philosophy of life in which wine played a dominant part – it was not just a drink, but a celebration of the cultivation of the vine, an appreciation of life itself, and a catalyst in the establishment of rapport between people and countries. Wine has always been looked upon as a means to lift everyday life out of the ordinary, and has been associated with philosophy, with something divine, and with perfection itself.

ANCIENT GREEK WINE
There is no clear evidence to show exactly when the cultivation of the vine began in Greece. Numerous sources indicate that wine production and consumption began in around the seventh century BC, but many people speculate that wine could have been made in Greece as far back as the third millennium BC. Crete was the cradle of the Minoan civilization, and finds suggest that wine was consumed on this island in the second millennium BC. The Babylonians in Mesopotamia and the Ancient Egyptians also made and drank wine during the same period, although, for the latter, wine was mainly a luxury item.

With the Minoan civilization's close links to Egypt, it is logical to assume that Crete could have imported the culture of wine from there. In palaces and villas on the island, archaeologists have found what could be the remains of wine presses and jars whose larger, taller shapes suggest that they were used for the storage of wine rather than olive oil. In addition, even with its limited range, the early hieroglyphic script, Linear A, had a symbol for wine. At the time, the island of Thira (Santorini) had strong trade ties with Crete, meaning that cultivation of the vine and wine production could have moved on to Thira quite quickly and from there to Mycenae on the Greek mainland. However, viticulture and wine were probably passed on by a variety of routes. Vines could have arrived via the coast of Asia Minor and the islands of the northeastern Aegean Sea, as well as travelling south from the lands to the north of Thrace.

Ample evidence exists that wine had already been established as an integral part of Mycenaean culture between about 1600 and 1150 BC. The remains of wine residue, pips, and what could have been pressed grapes have been found, as well as numerous artistic impressions of grapes and wine, mainly on pots and vases. One impressive find was a cellar at Pylos containing more than thirty-five pots, some of them labelled as containing wine. In Linear B script, the more sophisticated successor to Linear A, symbols for wine, vineyards, and possibly even wine merchants have been identified. Wine merchants certainly existed in Mycenae, and it appears that business was flourishing, since Mycenaean pottery has been found in Egypt, Cyprus, and Sicily. Traders also imported wine, as wine jars have been found in Mycenae from other wine-producing regions such as Canaan (across the Mediterranean, along the coast of what is now Syria, Lebanon, and Israel).

The god of wine

Wine was so important to Ancient Greeks that they worshipped it in the form of a god, Dionysus (known as Bacchus to the Romans), one of the twelve major Greek deities. Regarded as one of the most human of the gods, his temperament was in many ways close to that of the people. After all, he was the son of the god Zeus and a mortal, Semeli. Dionysus was involved in numerous major mythological stories, as were his disciples, Selinus and the "satyrs", all demi-gods. Dionysus' constant companions, they spent much of their time drinking wine and enjoying themselves.

According to legend, Dionysus planted a vine at the graveside of his best friend Ampelos, who died young. *Ampelos* is Greek for grapevine, and wine is said to be "the child of Ampelos".[1] Dionysus then shared the secret of winemaking with Oeneas, king of Kalydon, in northwest Greece, who was apparently the first to press grapes and taste their juice.[2] Dionysus met and married Ariadne on the island of Naxos, and among their children were twins named Staphylos ("grape") and Oenopionas ("winemaker"). On his travels, Dionysus was often accompanied by the "maenads", fervent female followers who were often overcome by their passion for wine.

Rituals and *symposia*

Wine became an important part of religious rituals. The word "libate" comes from the Greek root, *leibein*, "to pour forth". Originally a libation was a liquid offering, where wine was brought to the altar and poured with care from a full *oenohoi* (a special vessel for holding wine) as an offering to appease the gods. Wine was widely used in prayers and at sacrifices, and was offered to men going to war for strength.

Wine festivals were partly religious and partly cultural events. A strict programme of these was observed in Athens during the fifth century BC. Developed over the previous two centuries, Athenians celebrated the different facets of vine cultivation and winemaking during these feast days. In October the Oschoforia were held to celebrate the vintage, the Dionysia took place in December to celebrate growth and fertility, and the Anthestiria were observed in February, when the jars containing the recent vintage were opened and the new wine sampled. Surprisingly, there is no evidence of harvest wine festivals. Perhaps this was because it was a busy time of the year, even for high class Athenians. There were numerous other festivals, most importantly the Panathenaea, during which wine drinking featured strongly, although it was not directly related to Dionysus.

Apart from wine festivals, *symposia* were regular social events centred on wine – semi-formal occasions celebrating social and family successes, mainly confined to the upper classes of society. Women were not forbidden, but the vast majority of *symposia* were men-only events. Certain procedures had to be observed when participating in a *symposium*. Before eating, guests drank a *propoma*, a cup of wine flavoured with herbs. During the course of

1. Tsiforos, N, *Greek Mythology*, Ermis Editions, 2000.

2. Gellie, T, "Grapes, Games, and Gods", *Wine International*, September 2004.

the meal guests could drink wine, although this was not obligatory, but at the end of the meal a cup of undiluted wine was served to all present in order to honour all the good deities. The tables were then removed, guests washed their hands, and the *symposium* began.

Presiding over the events was the *symposiarch* (master of ceremonies). He was responsible for diluting the wine in a *krater* (a large, ornate bowl used exclusively for this purpose), in the proper ratio – usually one part wine to two parts water. A fifty-fifty mix was considered insane, and drinking undiluted wine throughout the *symposium* was looked upon as barbaric. The resulting drink of wine and water was called *krasi*, the modern Greek word for wine. It is difficult to determine its exact strength, but estimates suggest that it was somewhere between 3.5 and eight per cent alcohol, about the strength of modern beer. That said, the effects of a typical amount of three or more litres of krasi during a *symposium* should not be taken lightly. The *symposiarch* had other duties. Together with his assisting *oenohoous* (the modern Greek word for "sommeliers"), he ensured that cups were kept full and spirits were high. He proposed toasts, introduced appropriate topics of conversation, and regulated the rate of wine consumption so as to maintain a general atmosphere of euphoria and controlled intoxication. It was his responsibility to encourage someone to drink more, or to stop drinking for a spell if people became aggressive. Heavy drunkenness was not considered socially acceptable, although there is evidence to suggest that guests of successful *symposia* were often in a haze by the final stages of the event.

Given the popularity of *symposia*, several remedies to counteract the ill effects of overindulgence were formulated, as mentioned by the second-century writer, Athenaeus.[3] Moreover, many medicines themselves were based on wine, due to its antiseptic and "restorative" properties. Wine was used to wash wounds, to dissolve other drugs, and as part of the diet during recuperation. It was known that drinking wine was highly unlikely to cause any kind of food poisoning, making it generally safer to drink than water. In expeditions abroad, wine was added to suspect water in order to render it harmless. It was also believed that the application of specific preparations to vines would result in wines that had specific medical properties. For example, it was thought that spreading ashes in the vineyard would help to produce a wine to make people braver, and that wine made in Troizen in the Peloponnese could render men sterile.

3. Athenaeus, *Deiphosophistes*, Kaktos Editions, 1999.

Ancient literature

Some of the earliest references to wine come from the poetry of Homer, in which it is presented as an essential part of life.[4] Greeks and Trojans both drank wine, a fact that he believed made the two peoples equal in culture. Even the Cyclops drank it. The gods, apart from Dionysus, were not that interested since they had access to their own, exclusively reserved nectar.

But the first person to write in detail on the subjects of viticulture and vinification was Hesiod in the seventh century BC. He wrote that harvest on Hios in the North Aegean Sea should be made when "Orion and Sirius [the constellations] are in mid-sky and when the dawn sees Arcturus [the constellation]", thus placing the vintage well into September. The grapes should not be pressed immediately but "left to dry in the sun for ten days, then in the shade for five, and then pressed". In his *Works and Days*, there is a discussion regarding proper storage conditions for wine. Wine should retain its "heat", or its good qualities, and for that the opposite, *i.e.* coldness, was needed. This was regarded as particularly relevant when the containers were not full. It is clear that the negative effects of oxidation, as well as the importance of temperature, were already beginning to be understood.[5]

Several manuscripts in the fourth and fifth centuries BC deal with topics such as vine propagation, site selection, site and variety matching, ampelographical analysis of vine varieties, marking-out the specific origins of certain wines, and analysis of the main characteristics of the resulting wines. The scope and depth of these works show that viticulture and oenology were considered important scientific disciplines. Theophrastus, a fourth-century BC philosopher from Lesbos, could claim to be the father of wine writers, since he was the first to pen whole works dedicated to the vine and its fruits. Two of his most important works are *Concerning Odours* and *Enquiry into Plants*. The former covers a variety of topics, including: wine and the addition of spices to it; terroir, covering subjects like the importance of water bodies close to a vineyard and their effect on ripening times; soil, with advice such as "clay gives heat to the vine"; the weather during the growing period, and the personality of the winemaker. In *Enquiry into Plants*, possibly the first botanical work ever, he takes great pains to put into words the tastes of the various roots and fruits. The interaction between plants, the

---

4. Tsakiris, *Elliniki Oinognosia*, Psihalos Editions, Athens, 2003.
5. Hesiod, *Works and Days II*, 609–17.

soil, and the sun, as well as the relationship between roots, trunk, branches, leaves, and fruit is analysed in great detail.

Early wine legislation

The notion of linking wine to its origins was well established in Ancient Greece. Homer gives examples in his poetry, such as *"pramnios oinos"* – Pramnian wine coming only from the village of Oinoi on the Aegean island of Ikaria.[6] Although regions or cities that were well known for their wine production existed throughout Greece and Asia Minor, it seems that the extremely successful "first growths" of the time were the wines from the islands of the Aegean. Hios was supposed to be the best, followed closely by Lesbos and Thassos. Based on Homer, it is believed that the first place made famous because of its wine was the *"pramnia petra"* site near the village of Oinoi. Since Homer's works were written before the seventh century BC, Pramnian wine must have already been famous by that time. According to Athenaeus, writing in the third century AD, Pramnian wine might have originated in Ikaria, however by the fourth century BC, the title was employed as a generic name for austere, alcoholic wines, in the same vein as the term "Chablis" was once used in California, or "red burgundy" in Australia.

Given wine's great economic significance, legislation was developed in many states in order to prevent fraud, to protect reputations, and to maximize tax revenues. A marble slate discovered on Thassos in the North Aegean, dating from the fifth century BC, details laws governing the wine trade. According to this, *amphorae* carrying wine were sealed by the state's regulators to guarantee authenticity. These containers had to be of a specific size and shape. Citizens of the island were not allowed to import foreign wine, and for that reason ships carrying wine could not approach the island's port. These laws applied not only to the trade in wine, but also to its production and identity. For example, Thassos wines should have a distinct floral character, which was to be achieved mainly by the addition of rose petals during the maturation phase, although the expression of fruit on the nose and palate was expected to be leaning in this direction anyway.

There is enough evidence to support the claim that the wine laws of Thassos are the oldest in the world of wine. Given the importance of the wine trade and the fact that by the fifth century BC a number of other Greek

6. Homer, *The Odyssey*, Book X; *The Iliad*, Book XI.

states like Hios and Maronia had become famous for their wine production, it is logical to assume that these regions also introduced their own wine laws. Nevertheless, to date there are no archaeological or other findings to support such an assumption.

Spreading the wine

Wine exports were important not only because local people could not consume all that was produced, but also because wine fetched higher prices abroad. Within Greece, Athens was the richest and largest importer, and was therefore considered to be the premium market. Yet numerous finds in Egypt, around the Black Sea, in the Danube (from its delta in the Black Sea almost all the way to Austria), in Porticello (southern Italy), and in Etruria (modern Tuscany) illustrate how far the vinous exports travelled. Wine was mainly transported by boat. In the *Iliad* Homer refers to cellars full of wine that has arrived from Thrace on the ships of the state of Achaia.[7] While more recently, wine jars have been found in shipwrecks discovered along the regular trade routes of the era.

Vines were also exported to several regions around southern Europe, with the introduction of viticultural knowledge seen as an important part of the process of colonization. Thus vines had arrived in Sicily by the eighth century BC. Although the Etruscans also played a large role in expanding vine cultivation from their base in Tuscany, it is believed that the Greeks introduced wine production to a significant proportion of Italy. Indeed, when Hannibal invaded Italy in the late third century BC, viticulture was already an integral part of the local agriculture. Further to the west, the Greeks founded Massalia, today's Marseille, around 600 BC and vineyards were rapidly introduced across the Mediterranean coast. During this expansion, the Greeks came in contact with Celts, who were in turn responsible for the development of wine culture further north.

Containers, cups, and *kraters*

Any account of the history of wine in Ancient Greece would be incomplete without a description of the vessels used to transport, store, mix, pour, and drink wine. The complex, numerous uses of wine led to a high degree of sophistication in the manufacturing of these items. The first containers and cups were designed purely for functionality, but developments in pottery

7. Homer, *The Iliad*, Book IX.

allowed artisans to become artists, and wine containers from top manufacturers became status symbols of wealth. The art of decorating these vessels attained a high point in Attica between the sixth and fourth centuries BC.

Understanding the development of wine containers in Ancient Greece can be confusing. Many names used today are derived from archaeological convention, with the most complete accounts of these conventions coming from Roman and Byzantine sources, although few vessels are described in detail. Synonyms were used throughout Greece so that, for example, an *amphora* in Athens was called a *stamnos* in the rest of Greece, complicating historical references. Finally, early finds were unearthed at a time when the understanding of Ancient Greek pottery-making was limited, and they were assigned names that now conflict with present-day evidence. Nevertheless, these terms have been used for so long that any changes now would cause confusion in modern-day research.

The first container that grapes would come into contact with was a *linos*, a large vat for crushing the berries and draining the must. The juice was immediately moved for fermentation to large *pithoi*, clay barrels about 1.5 metres (five feet) tall. The must was transferred from the *linos* to the *pithoi* in wine "skins", usually made from goat hide. The Greeks were well aware that the goat skins imparted a very distinct smell to the liquid, and therefore only used them at this stage of wine production or for transporting the liquid very short distances. They also knew that carbon dioxide produced during fermentation created a real danger of asphyxiation to anyone entering a closed space full of *pithoi*. Thus access to these rooms was permitted only after the first, most intense phases of fermentation had been completed.

Amphorae were the most common type of wine vessel used in Ancient Greece and were used to transport wine over long distances. The earliest such vessels were found in Canaan and date to the fourteenth century BC. Just as today, distinctly shaped bottles indicate that a wine comes from the Mosel, Burgundy, Bordeaux, or Châteauneuf-du-Pape, for example, so the *amphora* shape differed from region to region to denote origin. An *amphora* either had a distinct neck, or the neck and body were a single piece (called a "belly" *amphora*). These containers could hold between twenty and forty litres of liquid, and handles were added for ease of carrying. The seal of origin and other information, such as the date of bottling, were marked on these handles. The bottom was pointed so that the *amphora* could stand in sand and be easily stacked in vertical piles.

Wine had to be diluted with water before it could be drunk, making mixing vessels necessary during *symposia*. The oldest known is a *lebes*, a luxury piece of pottery that was round with a low rim, and rested on a base. However, it was cumbersome to handle and transport, leading to the development of the *krater*, around the eighth century BC. There were many different types of *krater*: a "column" *krater* had very short handles; a "volute" or "Laconian" *krater* had spiral handles rising over the rim; a "calyx" *krater* resembled the shape of a calyx flower, with handles on the lower part of the body and a "bell" *krater* had a body in the shape of a bell, but handles closer to the mouth, making carrying much easier. The last two styles became increasingly popular since they had rims that were wider than their body, making the mixing and drawing of wine that much easier.

Kraters were made from either clay or metal, with the latter considered luxury items. Very few metal *kraters* survive today, partly because people melted them down to make new ones, but primarily because they were plundered by looters of antiquities throughout the ages. The most famous example found to date is the "Vix Krater", discovered in 1953 near the village of Vix, on the upper Seine in France. This large, impressive *krater* was probably from Laconia or from a Laconian colony in southern Italy, then called Magna Grecia. It is 1.6 metres (5.3 feet) tall, 1.27 metres (4.2 feet) in diameter, weighs 209 kilograms (461 pounds), and has a capacity of over 1,200 litres.

During the summer, wine drunk at *symposia* had to be chilled, and *amphorae* were usually placed in wells. Sometimes vessels containing wine were placed in large *kraters* full of water or, for the rich, hail and snow. After it was mixed and cooled, wine was decanted into *oenohoes* for servants to pour into drinking cups. There was a large variety of these cups, the most important being the *skyfos*, the *kantharos*, and the extremely popular *kylix*. Although coming in different shapes and styles, all these drinking vessels were short, with two handles, and sometimes a stem and a broad rim.

The *kylix* resembled today's soup plate. During winter, a *kylix* with a stem was used so that drinkers were able to hold the main body of the cup with one hand, while using the stem for additional grip and stability. In this way, chilled wine was allowed to warm up, very much in the way cognac balloon glasses are used today.

There is evidence that the low-cup and broad-rimmed shape of popular drinking vessels was favoured because it allowed a wider flow of wine into the mouth, stimulating the taste-buds along the edges of the tongue. This increases the perception of tartness – an important factor considering that wine in Ancient Greece typically lacked sufficient acidity. Such cups therefore made wine appear more flavourful and balanced. In keeping with their highly developed sense of aesthetics and passion for worldly pleasures, there is every reason to believe that Ancient Greeks were as sophisticated wine drinkers as these details suggest. It is possible that Georg Riedel, with his twentieth-century demonstration of how the shape of a glass can alter the taste of a wine, was not so much an inventor as a good classical scholar.

Flavourings and additives

Adding flavourings to wine was a crucial process in winemaking. Spices, honey, flowers, herbs, or aromatic oils were used to stabilize the wine by making it less sensitive to contact with oxygen and, when oxidation did occur, these additives would cover any volatile acidity. In *Concerning Odours* Theophrastus goes into great detail about the preparation of blends of spices and other flavourings. For example, he cites that resin produced from pines grown on certain sites must be matched with the product of vines grown on similar types of soil.

Resin is possibly the most important of all additives, since the practice survives to this day in the form of retsina (*see* page 29). There are accounts of Ancient Greek winemakers taking extreme care while producing the resined wine, treating it in a way that reminds one of the ageing of top quality white burgundy. The wine would be kept in large containers with the correct amount of lees – not too much, not too little – with frequent attention being paid to topping-up to ensure air was excluded, coupled with the occasional stirring of the lees, a task often performed during the first few months and less so as time went by.

THE ROMAN AND BYZANTINE EMPIRES

All levels of wine production, trade, and appreciation reached a peak simultaneously between the sixth and fourth centuries BC. After this golden age, the entire sector progressively declined. The conquest of Greece by the Romans in 146 BC marked the end of an era, and Athens ceased to be the most powerful city in the Mediterranean. Soon, trade centres shifted from Greece to Rome, mainland Italy, and southern France. Although the Romans had known about viticulture from the Etruscans of their Tuscan homeland, it was Greek know-how regarding vine-growing and winemaking that was assimilated and disseminated to all corners of the Roman Empire. Greek wine was still highly prized above others in the first century AD, and the Emperor Tiberius was known to present it to his top army officers as a sign of his deepest gratitude.

However, the new political regime adversely affected Greek wine, as established producers and regions now had limited access to new and emerging markets. During the second and third centuries AD, the image of Greek wine faded and commercial possibilities became scarce. Local wine industries were geared for exports and their production could not be absorbed by limited regional consumption. Wine lost its prestige in the new social system and its commercial appeal waned. It was just a matter of time before standards of quality followed the same decline.

With the rise in power of the Byzantine Empire, Christianity became the main focus of the new emperors. A common theme and a strong bond between their citizens was needed and the spreading of the new religion, coupled with an exclusion of all others, was the perfect umbrella under which to unite the new empire. Romans were accused of idolatry and all Ancient Greek gods came under attack. Eventually, any form of worship of these gods was banned. Dionysus was no exception, and under the Byzantines people could be punished for so much as uttering his name during harvest or winemaking.

The transformation of the Roman Empire into Byzantium began in 330 AD with the foundation of Constantinople (today called Istanbul). This immediately became the new imperial capital, but the Byzantine Empire, the empire of a thousand years, was not simply a new name for the Roman Empire. While the western regions of the old Roman Empire disintegrated into numerous feudal kingdoms, this was a new entity in the east.

During the Byzantine era, which ended with the invasion of Constantinople by the Turks in 1453, viticulture was practised by private individuals and monks. The top quality wine regions continued to be in the Aegean and Maronia in Thrace. At that time, the church was gathering power and wealth at an impressive rate. Vineyards were either donated or sold to monasteries, and monks were able to build extensive holdings, source excellent fruit, and produce wines of high quality, as detailed in the scripts found in the Byzantine monastic libraries of Mount Athos. The seventh century saw the appearance of the first shops dedicated to selling wine for consumption either on or off the premises. These were known as *taverna* or *kapilia*.

However, the shift of power from Rome to Constantinople did not have the expected effect of improving Greece's wine trade. As early as the eleventh century AD, Alexius I Comnenus granted Venice wine trading rights throughout the Byzantine Empire, and Venetian shippers were permitted to sell wine without paying duty. This made imported wine cheaper than any Greek product, especially as the quality was often on a par with the best wines coming from the Aegean islands. The great wines of the Veneto, mainly Amarone and Recioto from Valpolicella which were made from sun-dried red grapes, were possibly produced to emulate the popular styles of Hios, Samos, and Crete.

Finally, in 1361 the Byzantine government tried to support the empire's wine producers by persuading the Venetians to separate wholesale and retail trading. The former remained duty-free but the latter required duty to be paid, thus increasing the retail price of imported wines as a result. The Byzantine government also decided to impose taxes on their own imports in the fifteenth century, even if the tax revenue was paid to Venice rather than Constantinople. However, it was too little too late. Having suffered through four centuries of intense and possibly unfair competition, Greek wine producers could not make a comeback; the catastrophe was irreversible. Crete and Cyprus still dominated wine exports, but they were already under Venetian rule.

CHANGING TIMES

During the Byzantine era, viticulture almost stood still, while in contrast, the production and consumption of wine changed significantly. The use of wooden barrels – a practice that had been popular in Western Europe for at least 400 years – was introduced in the seventh century AD. Although small quantities of spices were occasionally still added, other flavourings became less widespread and certainly less sophisticated, the only notable exception being resin. The use of sun-dried grapes for making sweet wines increased. Byzantine wine drinkers were also the first to stop diluting *oenos* (wine) with water (the ancient method of creating *krasi*), but they continued to use the word *krasi* for the undiluted form of wine – a habit that has survived to modern times. Although serving cold krasi was a sign of prosperity in Ancient Greece (ice being expensive), drinking warm wine was the only "upper-class" way in Byzantium.

One bestseller of the time was *Monemovassios oenos*, named after the port of Monemvasia in the southeastern Peloponnese. The style originated here, but later became a generic name used for wines produced in Santorini, Crete and, of course, Monemvasia. *Monemovassios oenos* was exported to France, Germany, and England right up until the eighteenth century. The increasing popularity of this product required ever larger ships to load more wine barrels. Monemvasia, being a small port, could not accommodate these ships and so Crete and Cyprus again won the lion's share of the trade. This led to a decline of the southern Peloponnese as a producer and exporter of high-quality wines.

After the fall of Constantinople in 1453 to the Ottoman Turks, wine exports were halted, but surprisingly, viticulture was not restricted. The Turks were quick to spot the dynamic relationship that the Greeks had with both vine and wine and decided to exploit it to the full. A strict taxation system was introduced that governed all facets of wine, from production through to trade. For example, growers were not permitted to deliver grapes to a winery, even if they owned both, unless all taxes due had been paid in full. This system swelled the coffers of local authorities, but many families were financially ruined when they were unable to satisfy the greed of the occupiers. A final blow was dealt to Greek viticulture when the retreating Turks destroyed most cultivated lands in the aftermath of the 1821 revolution.

The wine trade was allowed to expand in a far more liberal way in regions of Greece that were fortunate enough not to come under Ottoman occupation. Wines made in Crete and certain Aegean islands were exported to most parts of Western Europe. The Ionian islands of Cephalonia and Zakynthos enjoyed close trade-ties with Venice, Livorno, and Genoa, and many Greek merchants traded in wine with Poland and Russia. Nevertheless, in the early seventeenth century, the main shipping routes were increasingly dominated by the English and the Dutch, and the concentration of trade shifted to their colonies at the expense of the eastern Mediterranean, which became more of a receiver than a shipper.

FROM INDEPENDENCE TO PHYLLOXERA

The first decades after the foundation of the modern Greek nation in 1830 saw much unrest and extreme poverty, with the population struggling to afford the basic necessities of food, clothing, and shelter. It soon became clear that cultivating the land could help both upgrade living standards and improve the financial situation. Abandoned vineyards began to be replanted, but as good planting stock was difficult to come by, this took place in a very haphazard manner. An exception to this was the propagation of vines for the production of Corinthiaki, a variety used for the production of raisins, called Stafida in Greek. In the coming decades and up to the end of the century, plantings of Corinthiaki almost quadrupled, while in the same period the acreage dedicated to other wine grapes only doubled.

The devastation of French vineyards by phylloxera in the late nineteenth century came as a blessing for Greek Corinthiaki growers. Exports of dried Corinthiaki grapes (raisins) to France both for consumption and the production of wine increased exponentially. The demand was so high that in several parts of Greece people uprooted other wine grapes, olives, and fruit trees to make way for new Corinthiaki vineyards.

However, France managed to recover from phylloxera in the early twentieth century by introducing American rootstocks. Within a few years French wine production from local grapes resumed, duty became obligatory on imported raisins, and a ban was imposed on wine made from dried grapes, imported or otherwise. To make matters worse, competition in European markets increased dramatically with the introduction of other varieties suitable for raisin production from Australia and California. In a short period of time, the most valuable export product of Greek agriculture had become redundant and prices plummeted. This raisin crisis drove much of the agrarian population to abandon the countryside and seek a better life either in urban centres or in other countries. In some areas, such as the Peloponnese, this crisis resulted in severe social upheaval.

The first known incidence of phylloxera in Greece occurred in 1898 in the northern region of Pilea near Thessaloniki. The spread of the disease in Macedonia was rapid and devastating. Although vineyard planting reached an all-time high in 1916 with 200,000 hectares under vine, vineyards began to shrink significantly after 1920 as a direct result of the spread of phylloxera. Another important development in the first two decades of the twentieth century was the introduction of a new Sultana variety.[8] This was

8. Sultana: although best known for its use as a table grape (*e.g.* Thompson Seedless) and in its dried form as raisins, the Sultana varietal has a long history in winemaking, dating back to ancient times, as a common source material for wines made from dried grapes. Without the concentration brought about by drying, the Sultana grape produces relatively bland wines.

again used for raisin production. The planting of new vineyards accelerated after 1916, mainly in Corinth and Crete.

As early as the mid-1700s, attempts had been made to establish wine companies in Greece. In 1858 two wine companies were established in Patra and Cephalonia, but they did not last. By the end of the nineteenth century there were only ten companies making products derived from grapes, mainly distillates, although wine was also sold in bulk as a sideline. Although some of these companies did manage to win a few medals in international wine competitions, the rest of Greek wine was made using primitive methods and sold in bulk. Stability was poorly understood, and oxidation was prevalent. The only way to make this wine barely drinkable was to add pine resin, giving rise to retsina. The quality of retsinas served in wine tavernas, still called *kapilia* in the big cities, was so low that it drove many people to drink beer instead.

THE TWENTIETH CENTURY

The last 100 years have probably been the most eventful in Greece's long and colourful history. The character of the state has been deeply affected, and most importantly, the lives of the Greek people have been greatly altered. After almost 400 years of an unchanging, miserable way of life for most, things began to change – but not without paying a price. As well as the Balkan Wars of 1912–13, Greece was heavily involved in both World Wars, and its own devastating civil war in the 1940s. There were also many minor clashes with Turkey or some of the northern Balkan countries. It is often said that the first-ever generation of Greeks not called upon to bear arms to defend the nation were those born since 1960. After every conflict the economy of the country emerged in a poor situation, but the Greeks, with an optimism that must be infused in their DNA, saw every problem as a potential opportunity. While the public sector was in many cases more concerned about its own survival than running the country, private companies flourished for most of the second half of the twentieth century. The history of Greece gave locals plenty of experience to help them become some of the most seasoned businessmen in modern Europe.

Rise and fall

The second decade of the twentieth century saw a significant enlargement of the Greek state. After the addition of the Ionian islands in 1864 and

Thessaly in 1881, the size of the country remained stable for close to thirty years. Then, in 1913 and 1914, Epirus, Macedonia, and the Aegean islands, including Crete, officially became part of the Greek state. Six years later, Thrace and the small islands of Imvros and Tenedos were acquired, although the two isles and the eastern part of Thrace had to be returned to Turkey just two years later. This expansion of Greece was by no means an easy road to travel, but it was a way of gathering significant momentum for further economic and social progress.

These continuous land additions make following the significance of viticulture and the rate of new plantings quite difficult. By the middle of the nineteenth century, there were about 50,000 hectares of Greek vineyards. About three decades later, French buyers turned to Greek wines and grapes when their phylloxera-troubled vineyards could not keep up with demand. The response was immediate and vineyard plantations pushed the overall acreage above the 100,000 hectares mark in just a few years. This situation lasted just two decades, until Western European countries re-established their traditional supply channels, mainly in Italy and France.

Strangely, this did not seem a good enough reason for Greeks to stop expanding their vineyards. By 1916, the area under vine reached around 200,000 hectares, but thereafter expansion came to a halt. The main reason was problems with phylloxera that started cropping up in many parts of Greece, especially in Macedonia and Epirus in the northwest. The introduction of American rootstocks provided a much-needed solution and plantings started to increase once more, especially in central Greece and the Peloponnese. Nevertheless, the vineyard area never reached the level of 1915–16 again, eventually falling short of approximately 150,000 hectares.

The principal difference between the frantic growth of the late nineteenth century and the development of new vineyards in the first decades after the phylloxera invasion was a lack of export demand. Between 1925 and the start of World War II, there was no corresponding requirement from either foreign or local markets. Landowners started cultivating more and more vines mainly because there was little else to plant on the infertile land. They also possibly thought that the glory days of Greek wine exports were not over. They couldn't have been more wrong.

Strength in numbers

The *deus ex machina* solution came in the form of cooperatives. Soon after the overproduction problems became apparent, the Greek government decided to found a number of agricultural co-ops. The main aim was to support the agricultural sector, rather than adding value or creating a competitive advantage for it. Thus buying the grapes of growers (all the grapes of all the growers, regardless of quality) was more important than producing, let alone selling, the wine. This is not to imply that there were no cooperatives doing a good job anyway. Many knowledgeable winemakers and marketeers involved in these production units tried hard to make them profitable and successful, as epitomized by the Agricultural Union of Samos, a wine-producing co-op that crafts some of the best sweet wines to be found around the globe.

However, the worst consequence of the cooperative philosophy was to break any link between grape quality, hard work in the vineyard, and income. The only thing that really mattered was quantity, the number of kilograms per *stremma* (the Greek unit of land surface, equivalent to one tenth of a hectare). Any grower trying to achieve higher quality by careful vineyard management and lower yields was committing financial suicide. If Greek viticulture had been developed in a more competitive environment, the quality of today's wines could have been a lot higher than it already is. Nevertheless, such an environment could have been too hostile for the long-term survival of a significant fraction of growers.

A new dawn

Much of what escaped devastation during World War II and the years of Nazi occupation was ruined during the Civil War – possibly the cruellest form of war a nation can go through. It left lasting scars on the souls of all Greeks, but it is extremely fortunate that, nowadays, younger generations seem determined to put tensions and hard feelings behind them. After almost ten years of financial chaos, political turmoil, and substantial losses in human lives, the Greek nation entered the 1950s with a kind of reserved optimism – the only way was up. Large parts of the population started moving into urban centres which had become the "lands of opportunity". It was a time when clever, experienced, and able people could quickly become prosperous or move up the social ladder.

The rapidly improving standard of living had a major impact on wine production. For the first time, small segments of local markets could support and encourage the production of bottled wines. Still, "village" wine represented a large part of the national wine consumption. In fact, many traditional drinkers were initially extremely sceptical about bottled wine – they believed that only a homemade product could be pure and all bottled *krasi* was either artificial or "full of chemicals". Nevertheless, a growing part of the urban population had limited access to village produce and the only solution was some form of packaged wine. A better financial situation allowed some of them to study and travel abroad, exposing them to foreign cultures and tastes, and turning them into more sophisticated and demanding consumers. Visitors to Greece requesting bottled wine also played a crucial role in the improvement of standards.

The wine market in Greece during the 1960s was closer to that of Eastern European wine-producing countries than other Mediterranean or Western European nations. Wine sales were dominated by bulk wine produced either by local, small volume and, most of the times, low-quality *vignerons*, or supplied by the large private companies or co-ops. The bottled market was fairly limited and dominated by a small number of high volume players, providing cheap, branded wines, mainly sold in bulky (one litre or larger) formats or in 500 millilitre bottles sealed with a crown cap – the standard 750 millilitre bottle is a relatively new commodity in Greek wine production.

On the other hand, there were very few, if any, small producers who were bottling a part of their production and enjoying national distribution and a prestigious standing among knowledgeable consumers across the country. In most cases, the best and most skilful wine growers were selling their wares from the cellar doors; they had to be highest quality to be known even as far as the next village. This is a section of the nation's wine history that will remain lost forever – a great pity, since there is plenty of evidence that Greece had her fair share of true artisans. These people had a deep understanding of and an exquisite feel for their vineyards, vines, and wines, but their interest was not in becoming rich or famous. Everything was about enjoying the best wine they could produce with the best friends they had.

The same period witnessed the rise of retsina. Wine with added resin has been made and exported from Greece for more than twenty-four centuries. Retsina has been consumed in the *kapilia* of Athens since the late nineteenth century, but it became the national drink during the tourist boom of the 1960s. At that time, Athens was the main tourist attraction, and for many, visiting the islands was almost an afterthought. The main restaurants of Athens were serving mostly retsina, apart from some top class ones. In addition, the development of bottling made retsina widely available in all the tourist resorts around the country. By the end of the 1960s, the phrase "Greek wine" unfortunately equalled retsina around the globe.

The next decade was of prime political importance, especially the years after the end of the military junta which lasted from 1967 to 1974. Modern Greece was, for the most part, taking its present form. Wine consumption continued its upward spiral, moving slowly but steadily away from bulk, village wine into bottles. Still, what could be called good quality wine was a minuscule part of the market.

The development of the wine sector over the last three decades has formed the perfect basis for the appearance of a few large producers, focusing on high-volume, low-price bottled wines. The companies that were already present in the market and able to take advantage of the situation included Achaia Clauss, Kambas, Kourtakis, and Boutari, followed by Tsantali. All these wineries focused on highly branded products, leading to the most consolidated phase of Greek wine production. The struggle for volume and market share had been fierce and, therefore, no sector of the market could be neglected. In the last years of the 1970s, these five big families of Greek wine started to address the needs of the top-end consumer. With a little help from these producers, plus assistance from a number of friends around the country, Greek wine was ready to set sail on its voyage through its own sea of change.

3

A new era beckons

If Greek wine has already seen a new dawn, one thing is for sure: it is just the beginning. New wineries, new faces, and new ideas crop up at every harvest and at an ever-accelerating pace, making Greece one of the most vibrant wine regions in the world. It is exciting to see that one of the oldest wine-producing nations still has the ability to reinvent itself afresh. According to modern theories of evolution, progress is never achieved through a steady rate of growth or a continuum. There seems to be a long period of inactivity, or stasis, where nothing much is apparent but invisible growing tensions build up. Then, a sudden event can bring unforeseen changes in a very short amount of time. If there is one person who pushed Greek wine out of stasis, that person is Stavroula Kourakou-Dragona, a woman with an impressive CV and many international credits, including a presidency term in the International Organization of Vine and Wine.[1]

In the late 1960s and early 1970s, Kourakou-Dragona was the main force behind drawing up Greek wine appellations legislation. Greece was about to apply for membership of the European Community (renamed the European Union in 1993), so she wanted the new legislation to be as "European" as possible. Kourakou-Dragona had the daunting task of taking the European, i.e. the French, wine laws of the time and adapting them to both the terroir and the reality of the Greek situation. However difficult or, some would argue, premature this project might have been, it made the Greek wine sector realize that modernization was not simply an option, but the only route to survival. Being aware of what was happening in the more

---

1. Organization Internationale de la Vigne et du Vin (OIV): an inter-governmental body based in Paris with forty-seven members who oversee technical and scientific aspects of wine production.

developed wine-producing European countries – and catching up – was absolutely crucial.

As stated above (*see* page 30) in the 1970s, four big players dominated the bottled-wine market: Achaia Clauss, Kambas, Kourtakis, and Boutari. Tsantali, another family owned company, joined this group a few years later. These producers were initially focused on high-volume, low-price wines, but as the market developed, they became more saturated and competitive, each business trying to find new ways of increasing its share. Greek wine, as a whole, benefited enormously from this process.

Achaia Clauss was a long-established, historic house, linked both with a whole region – Achaia, in the northern Peloponnese – and a particular wine: Mavrodaphne of Patras. It was also the first producer to invest in and succeed in creating a national Greek brand: Demestica.

Kambas and Kourtakis were the main companies that persuaded Greeks to buy, drink, and trust bottled wine. In particular, their retsinas even conquered the bastions of "pure, natural village wine" – *kapilia*, tavernas, and coffee shops.

The wines of Boutari showed that the step beyond brands was the new appellations introduced in the mid-1970s (*see* Chapter 4). Its range fully capitalized on the newly created legislative framework. To address this new mode of production, Boutari created a group of peripheral wineries in different regions, pushing the concept of a large Greek producer to a new level.

Finally, Tsantali reminded Greeks how important wine had been for them through the ages. It created products with highly evocative packaging that borrowed heavily from visual images of past Greek glories, spending considerable effort and money to develop patented neo-classical wine bottle moulds. Tsantali was also one of the first Greek wine producers to try and understand consumer preferences and shape product concepts around them.

THE BIRTH OF THE BOUTIQUE WINERY

All of these producers foresaw that high quality wines could only increase in importance and tried to meet the needs of this sector in various ways. This move was not just instinctive – higher-priced, low-volume products from small, boutique wineries had already started gathering momentum. Evangelos Averof had planted some Cabernet Sauvignon vines in Metsovo in the 1950s and his Katogi wine became Greece's first "cult" wine. In 1966, Ioannis Carras started Domaine Carras in Halkidiki, bringing in consultants of the calibre of Emile Peynaud to craft wines that could "compete with the best of the world, not with the best of Greece".[2] The 1970s saw a group of people including Dimitris Hatzimichalis, Thanasis Parparoussis, Dimitris Katsaros, and George and Ann Kokotos starting small-scale, mostly low-tech wineries. They practically created the term "small wine-grower"; up to that point, wine production had all been about large companies, cooperatives, or village growers. Although for this group wine began as a hobby, they rapidly found out that there was a market for premium-priced wine, and soon converted their artisanal set-ups to serious commercial ventures.

The pioneers of the 1970s opened the floodgates for a big rush in the 1980s. The profile of wine was raised and viticulture became the most prestigious form of agriculture. Being a wine producer – that is, a small wine producer – was desirable, esteemed, and profitable. Many families around Greece that had been involved in wine and vineyards for decades, or even generations, had every reason to set up small businesses. The number of wine labels on the market rose exponentially and demand from consumers easily absorbed most of this growth.

The expansion of the number of small producers can only partially be attributed to people with a long-standing relationship with land and vines. Affluent individuals with substantial capital coupled their interest in wine with a sharp eye for investment prospects and created some of the most impressive wineries and estates Greece has ever seen. A number of wine professionals believed that these outsiders had no true links with wine and were merely trying to exploit the product. That might have been true on a few occasions but, even then, Greek wine was going through a period that desperately needed such investors. It needed people to devote serious amounts of money to the purchase of cutting-edge technology and to the introduction of serious winemaking and marketing expertise. Companies that did not just want to capture market share from other wine producers, wanted to increase the wine market as a whole instead.

STARTING SCHOOL

As more people became involved in wine production, top quality, qualified, and experienced oenologists became increasingly scarce. Before 1985, there were some optional oenology classes in agricultural or chemistry degree

2. Konstantinos Carras, presentation of Domaine Carras M Grande Bretagne, Athens, 1995

courses at the universities of Athens and Thessaloniki, but there was no oenology school in Greece. After graduation, alumni had to pass an oral exam, normally lasting less than an hour, and, if successful, they were "licensed to practise the profession of oenology". This approach resulted in significant gaps in knowledge beyond the basic principles of oenology, and a total absence of hands-on experience. Such limitations were widely recognized by the "licensees" who, in the early 1980s, formally proposed the foundation of an oenology department within the Athens Technical Educational Institute or TEI (*see* Appendix 4). The proposal was accepted in 1985 and, two years later, the profession of oenologist was officially recognized by the Greek government. Every year since then, the teachers of the Athens TEI have provided the industry with an injection of enthusiastic, well-trained new blood.

This steady stream of TEI students has been reinforced by oenology graduates from around the globe, particularly France. Greek wine professionals have always considered Bordeaux to be the Mecca of wine knowledge. The first Greek to study in Bordeaux was Stamatis Valezis back in 1837, but the new wave of Greek graduates from French universities began to emerge in the early 1960s. Since then, there has been no looking back. The first Bordeaux-trained winemakers, like Evangelos Gerovassiliou or Argiris Tsakiris, helped immensely in improving cleanliness in wineries, in understanding new techniques and equipment and, finally, in upgrading wine quality. These people have been to Greece almost what Emile Peynaud was to France – they put science at the heart of winemaking.

By the late 1980s things were far easier, with the TEI providing a solid base of knowledge. It was more affordable to study in Athens for three years and then to go overseas just for postgraduate study. Bordeaux ceased to be the only destination, with Montpellier, Dijon, Germany, Italy, and even Adelaide and California entering the picture. Currently, there is a sizable proportion of Greek oenologists with foreign experience. This group is important not because there is much of a difference in their technical know-how or abilities, but for quality standards. They provide a calibration of where Greek wine stands among the giants of the wine world.

The 1990s were a different but equally exciting period for the Greek wine world. The mavericks and innovators of the last decade reached a level of maturity, gaining in volume, image, and market-share. The void created by small producers moving up in size was swiftly filled with new growers.

Although the market was very competitive, it was no longer unknown territory; experience could be gathered with substantially fewer mistakes. This is also when the first "winemaker wineries" started to appear. These were ventures founded by seasoned oenologists like Gerovassiliou who, after years of working for other producers, wanted to be free either to express themselves by trying new, adventurous ideas, or to dedicate their efforts to one region. Some attention-grabbing wines, that simply could not have been produced ten years before, have been released from these wineries. Greek wine was not just growing bigger, but becoming more complex as well.

THE REVOLUTION CONTINUES

The new age of Greek wine should not be viewed as one major renaissance but as numerous small revolutions. Every producer introducing something new, or a fresh interpretation of something old, was adding a meaningful touch to the greater picture. Hatzimichalis introduced Greek wine lovers to varietal wines and specifically to French cultivars, like Cabernet Sauvignon, Chardonnay, and Merlot. The Boutari group created Kallisti in Santorini, one of the first popular examples of modern, barrique-fermented whites that benefited from bottle age. In Nemea (Peloponnese), Athanassios Papaïoannou started to work with Agiorgitiko – previously only considered suitable for soft, quaffable reds – and crafted full-bodied, serious, ageworthy wines. George Skouras used the same variety and added a small percentage of Cabernet Sauvignon to create Megas Oenos – the first Super Nemea. As Super Tuscans did in the 1970s, this wine introduced drinkers to an indigenous grape by blending it with a better-known one.

Yiannis Boutaris, of Ktima Kir Yianni winery, is a particularly influential figure. He became the Angelo Gaja of Naoussa when he took the Xinomavro grape – which traditionally gave pale, thin, acidic, and aggressively tannic wines – and turned it into his serious, modern and dense Ramnista, which combined charm with varietal character. Visionaries are never abundant, but in the last couple of decades, every Greek region or Greek variety has had its fair share of creative, forward-thinking producers.

A catalyst and inspirer for many of these small revolutions was the Athens-based Wine Institute (*see* Appendix 4), founded in 1937, two years before the start of World War II. It stayed inactive for about two-and-a-half decades, but truly got into gear in the 1960s with the creation of the first drafts of Greek wine legislation. The Wine Institute did, and continues to do, a lot of background work on important and diverse fields, but its prime objective these days is studying, evaluating, and preserving the rare indigenous vine varieties and yeast strains of Greek vineyards. The Wine Institute works closely with the Vine Institute (*see* Appendix 4), another important organization based in Athens that is pushing the issue of native cultivars a step further. Grape varieties are assessed in various regions throughout the country in an attempt to identify the most promising combinations of lesser cultivars and terroirs. There is significant research addressing the correlation of particular vine cultivation techniques and fruit composition – again with specific reference to native varieties – and the development and isolation of better clones. These two institutions form an invaluable reserve of knowledge and guidance for growers and producers.

The present state of Greek wine production is, overall, exceptionally healthy. It is the only agricultural sector of the country that is totally self-financed. In addition, there is a remarkable balance between the various sectors of the industry. Large, medium-sized, and small producers have diversified roles and positioning in the market and in-fighting between them is unusual. Producers increasingly show the ability to work together for the common good, as shown by the impact of informal groupings for the development of wine tourism. A relatively recent development is the "Wine Roads" of Greece, an initiative promoted by the Associations of Wine Producers of Northern Greece, Attica, and the Peloponnese.[3] The National Interprofessional Organisation of Vine & Wine (*see* Appendix 4), founded in 2000 and fashioned along the lines of the French *comité interprofessionnel du vin*, was a first attempt to unite all sides with an interest in wine, from vine-growers to wine retailers. Last but not least, the quality of Greek wines has never been higher and there is every sign to indicate that the best has yet to come.

THE CHALLENGES AHEAD

This is not to say that the Greek wine industry has reached a peak. There are many problems still to be resolved. For example, a large number of growers must become more familiar with modern viticultural methods, like canopy management or trellis systems. The importance of low yields, ways to attain them, and how they can potentially lead to higher quality grapes, are

3. Stokes, S, "In the footsteps of Dionysus", *Wine International*, May 2004. For more information visit the website: www.wineroads.gr/en/wineroads.asp

poorly understood or misunderstood by many – some *vignerons* will discuss low production at length, before revealing that their idea of "low yields" is anything below eighty hectolitres per hectare. This would no doubt be different if the first professional, quality-oriented growers had chosen to run vineyards as separate business entities, as happens in parts of California. They would have invested in cutting-edge practices, farming top quality fruit, and marketing it to buyers as a premium product at a corresponding price, rather than simply selling it to the local co-op.

However the key problem for Greek wine is not related to making the product, but selling it, or in terms of today's global market, exporting it successfully. A wine-producing country like Greece has to go through three distinct phases: get the quality right, make this quality known to wine professionals and wine lovers around the world, and, finally, achieve sales. The last two phases are quite separate, as has been shown by the Austrian wine industry. Over the last decade, Austria has made its claim to being a top-quality wine producer. Yet even if top sommeliers and wine writers were aware of the quality, sales to most export markets in Europe and Northern America remained stubbornly unimpressive until recent years. Greece is now reaching that same stage.

Most wine professionals now recognize Greece as a source of very good, if not excellent, wines. While it is true that more work is needed on communication and marketing, this can be accomplished. The specialist retail chain Oddbins (that introduced Greek wines to the UK in the late 1990s) and people like Mary Pateras, who runs Eclectic Wines (a Greek import and distribution business in the UK), and Sofia Perperas, the woman behind All About Greek Wine (a US promotional body for over twenty top producers), have proved that Greek wine can be successful even in the most aggressive markets (*see* Appendix 4).

It is easy to equate the recent industry developments with the latest advances in Greek wine in general – however, the former is only a part of the story. The final product, the wine, involves not just growers and producers but everyone who is making a living out of it. It is impossible to significantly upgrade Greek wine without advancing every link of the chain – from vineyards to cellars, distribution warehouses, retail shops, restaurants, and even the press and broadcast media. Fortunately, a reassuring kind of osmosis seems to work across the sector, but on the other hand, everyone must take some responsibility for building a better future.

The wine trade in Greece is becoming increasingly sophisticated and competent – more of a business and less of a lifestyle. A crucial factor is the escalating presence of imported wines in Greece, since, for the first time in 2003, imports exceeded exports in value. High-quality imports set benchmarks and form new trends, both at the production and consumption ends.

Wine traders are also beginning to treat bottled wine like a food product and pay attention to its storage conditions. In today's climate, where heat damage can be a widespread problem, this is crucial since otherwise excellent bottles can be turned into the worst ambassadors of Greek – or any other – wine.

THE ROLE OF THE CRITIC

Two other factors contributing to the new era of Greek wine are journalists and sommeliers. It is encouraging to note that all major lifestyle publications dedicate at least one page to wine, and all food magazines promote the relationship between fine dining and fine wine. The Union of Greek Wine Journalists – the brainchild of Dinos Stergidis – was established in 1994 and has done a good job in giving substance to and raising awareness of the profession of wine writers. Good quality press coverage is invaluable in helping the public associate wine appreciation with culture and a higher standard of living. Beyond that, Greek journalists have a daunting task ahead: to make wine producers develop one of their most refined abilities, that of accepting criticism in a constructive way. Being exposed is never easy, but in the end always brings about improvement.

Sommeliers first appeared in Athens restaurants in the early 1990s, but initially remained a rare breed. Enough momentum was gained by 1997 to justify the establishment of the Association of Greek Sommeliers (*see* Appendix 4). Currently there are more than 120 members, although not all of them are, strictly speaking, earning their entire living as sommeliers – the rules of the association allow membership for people involved with wine in the on-trade on a more general level, like restaurateurs or hotel food and beverage managers. The most notable achievement for the movement so far has been its organisation in 2004 of the Sommeliers' World Championship in Athens under the presidency of Kostas Touloumtzis. Culminating in an event that named Italy's Enrico Bernardo as the world's best sommelier, the national champions, finalists, association presidents, and leading journalists from over forty countries spent a week in Santorini and Athens, being presented with excellent Greek food and top-quality Greek wine. This is a prominent example of international exposure, but sommeliers have been doing much more for Greek wine. They have convinced restaurateurs that the wine list is one of their establishments' main attributes and, if properly chosen, provides a competitive advantage. They have helped everyone, not just wine lovers, to think of wine as a premium product rather than just a commodity. And these wine waiters remain instrumental in introducing new labels, new regions or varieties, new levels of quality, and different approaches to the appreciation of wine.

Finally, Greek wine owes much to Greek consumers. The wine renaissance happened because of them and their developing standard of living. In essence, the primary source of income poured into the largely closed circuit of the Greek wine industry is the disposable income of all of these customers. Producers must bear in mind that it is these ordinary, wine-loving people who could well dictate the heights Greek wine will finally reach.

The Greek wine community is a paradox. It has the longest tradition in Europe, but still faces a steep learning curve. It enjoys an enormous cultural history, while the prospects for the future appear endless. The potential is so breathtaking that it makes me wonder whether the next new era of Greek wine has already started.

4

Wine legislation and labels

The need to create wine legislation was first recognized by forward-thinking wine-growers and Ministry of Agriculture officials in the early 1950s.[1] It took almost twenty years to reach the first drafts in the late 1960s. Up to that point there were no specific wine laws. Products related to grapes and wine were governed by general rulings dealing with consumer goods, with the main aim of creating "honest" and "safe" products for the end-user.

THE EEC BLUEPRINT

The European Economic Community (EEC, which became the European Community in 1967 and later the European Union, see page 31), of which Greece was not a member at the time, started developing a wine-related policy in 1962. French wine laws were used as a blueprint, since they were considered the most complete and most relevant to the majority of European wine-producing countries. Greece was already a member of the North Atlantic Treaty Organisation (NATO) and the majority of those in government believed the next logical step was to join the EEC. To make that easier, many aspects of government structure, the public sector, society, and, of course, the legislational framework, were steered towards conforming with Brussels. This included wine production.

The daunting task of creating an appellation system in Greece for the first time since the laws of antiquity was placed on the shoulders of the Wine Institute, an organization functioning within the Ministry of Agriculture (see Appendix 4). Established in 1937, the Wine Institute had been virtually inactive for at least fifteen years. The wine laws were developed mainly

1. In 2004 the Ministry of Agriculture was renamed the Ministry of Agricultural Development and Foods. For simplicity the former name is used throughout this book.

between 1968 and 1973, and the driving force behind them was Stavroula Kourakou-Dragona, the "Iron Lady" of Greek wine. Kourakou-Dragona is a woman of international stature who fought hard to promote the wines of her nation worldwide, as well as bringing them into the twentieth century. Within all the constraints of the time, she did the best job she could.

Once again, the French wine laws – which Kourakou-Dragona was very familiar with – were used as a rough draft. The first step was defining the broad aspects of the different wine types, such as colour (white, rosé, red), sweetness (dry, semi-dry, semi-sweet or sweet; all accurately described and related to residual sugar levels and, in the case of dessert *vin de liqueur*, alcohol and sugar levels), and finally, carbon dioxide levels and method of production (still, semi-sparkling, sparkling; with the latter being divided into naturally sparkling and carbonated).

THE BIRTH OF GREEK WINE LEGISLATION

Following the EC laws as established in 1970, the newly born Greek wine legislation divided wines into two broad quality segments, "quality-wines" and "table wines" (*see* Appendix 1). Quality-wines had to be separated into two levels, as in France, which has *vin de qualité produit dans une région déterminée* (VQPRD) as its upper tier and *vin délimité de qualité supérieure* (VDQS) as the lower. Kourakou-Dragona decided that the upper level should be dedicated to sweet Greek wines, the sector perceived as requiring the most protection. These famous sweet wines – Mavrodaphne from Patras and Cephalonia, and the Muscats of Patras, Rio of Patras, Cephalonia, Limnos, Samos, and Rhodes – were the pride of Greece. Since protection was the main objective and criterion, this quality-wine division was named *oenoi onomasias proelefseos elenhomeni* (OPE), (wines of appellation of controlled origin), *i.e.* an identical title to the French *appellation d'origine contrôlée* (AC).

The French model for a lower level of quality-wines was followed as well. Thus, *vin délimité de qualité supérieure* was translated to *oenoi onomassias proelefseos anoteras poiotitas* (OPAP; wines of appellation of origin of higher quality). In this rank, the Wine Institute included all regions that showed potential for quality-wine production and where viticulture had a strong local significance. In the decrees of 1971 and 1972, twenty-one regions were awarded OPAP status and four more were added in the following decades. The focus was on dry styles of all colours, but leeway was left to accommodate semi-dry, semi-sweet, sparkling or semi-sparkling styles.

Unlike in France, however, where VDQS accounts for a minute proportion of total wine production, in Greece, the OPAP sector is substantial.

Laws on OPE and OPAP cover demarcation of region, grape variety or varieties, yield, alcoholic strength, and viticultural and winemaking practices. The zones of production usually follow civil boundaries of prefectures or counties, and sometimes include whole islands. This is a key deviation from the French mould, where borders are defined by the vineyard areas themselves. Such a methodology could not be used, however, as Greece lacked a viticultural register with a complete account of vineyards within the county's vine-growing areas.

Of course, following municipal rather than viticultural restrictions results in the inclusion of parcels of land inappropriate for viticulture, let alone high-quality viticulture. Certain regions do impose a minimum altitude, like the OPAP of Robola of Cephalonia, which stipulates that the wine must be produced from vineyards sited at least 300 metres (984 feet) or higher above sea level. In theory, soil, sub-soil, and factors that can influence meso-climates were considered when the rules were drawn up, but studies conducted during the 1960s could have been a lot more detailed and therefore restrictive. Once again, politics must also have played a part in the decision-making process used to define the demarcated areas.

VITICULTURE AND VINICULTURE

Each department, prefecture, or region has a number of grape varieties that are permitted, along with a core "recommended" list. The records of these varieties are drawn up by the Ministry of Agriculture and constitute the most flexible part of the Greek wine legislation. Any grower wanting to experiment with a different varietal is able to have it added to the records. OPEs and some OPAPs are quite strict on varietal composition however, stating a 100 per cent figure from one or more varietals, while other OPAPs allow a small percentage of other "recommended" or "permitted" grapes.

Yields in Greece are calculated in kilograms of fruit per *stremma*, one *stremma* being equal to 1,000 square metres (a tenth of a hectare). Hectolitres per hectare can be calculated by multiplying the kilograms per *stremma* figure by 0.07, taking as given that 100 kilograms of grapes give 0.7 hectolitres of grape juice. The permitted limits are quite generous, mostly being in the region of seventy hectolitres per hectare, and even those are often exceeded. A grower going above the legal limit must declassify his or her total grape production, but there are no known cases where such a penalty has been given.

Alcoholic strength restrictions are straightforward, underlined by the fact that chaptalization and other forms of enrichment are not allowed in Greece. Thus, alcohol levels have to be attained naturally by winemakers. The levels are easily achievable, ranging from eleven to twelve per cent, but in most cases these are naively low. Many of the varieties have to mature to higher potential alcohol levels than those stated by law to achieve full ripeness in terms of flavour or tannins. This means that there are examples of underripe but perfectly legal OPAP wines available in the marketplace.

Viticultural practices dictated by law include training systems, vine density, methods of pruning, fertilization, and irrigation. Most of these regulations are completely outdated, but on the other hand, a vineyard has never been denied OPAP status because of the wrong training system. In addition, a set policy can be valid for the more fertile parts of an appellation, but will be totally irrelevant to the more infertile hillside sites. Implementation of the rules is complex and sometimes hazy, especially in regions where the wine producer is different from the vine-grower. It is presumed that the former, who will be applying for the appellation, has to check the liability of the latter.

Winemaking practices are supposed to form a part of the OPAP and OPE regulations, but in practise are limited to a ban on chaptalization, rules on length of oak ageing, plus approximate dates for when a vintage can be released. Production has to be carried out within the appellation (an exception is Robola of Cephalonia), while bottling can be done outside the appellation. The most relevant point of this legislation to winemakers is the length of ageing, and these decrees went through an important restructuring in 2005 (*see* below).

AMENDMENTS AND REVISIONS

Under the old regime, an OPAP Nemea wine had to be released after twelve months of ageing in oak barrels. So, in practice, a Nemea producer who wanted to create a lighter, fresher wine from Agiorgitiko, for example, would have had to go for the broader "regional wine appellation" of the Peloponnese. Within this framework, the consumer could not differentiate between various styles of Nemea.

The 2005 amendment of the OPAP wine category with specific reference to compulsory length of ageing was therefore an important development for Greek wine legislation. Under the new rules, a red OPAP wine can be released the February after the vintage. If a producer wants to market a *nouveau* style, this is now possible and it is declared on the label by the term *neos oinos* or *nearos oinos*, both meaning "young wine". A *neos oinos* OPAP can be sold before December 10 following the vintage and "it is recommended" that it is sold-out by the end of the following April.

In white or rosé OPAPs, there is no six month legal limit for the standard bottlings, but wines sold before December 10 must be under the *neos oinos* umbrella. Furthermore, the 2005 modifications re-define or establish a number of label terms, discussed below. This revision could well be one of the very few instances where laws have been created to cover the existing and well-documented needs of producers. Many people hope that this will not be an isolated incident but will signal a new era for Greek wine laws.

A popular debate among producers regards any further augmentation of the existing OPAP rules to incorporate a "Super OPAP" status or "OPAP *crus*". It is vital that any future alterations should be carefully thought-out and implemented – the correct approach can be the difference between brand expansion and brand dilution of the appellations, especially for exports. The future of the Greek wine industry depends on its international standing: to survive, it must treat grapes and appellations as brands and successfully promote them to a large number of export destinations. These markets are only just starting to be aware of what Greek wine is all about, and there is a long way to go before significant results are likely to be achieved. Thus, there is a risk that any alteration of the existing outline of OPAP laws, by adding more complexity, will undermine the attempts to make regions, like Naoussa or Nemea for example, internationally famous in their own right.

TABLE WINES

The bottom tier of the quality structure is "table wine" or *epitrapezios oinos* (EO) designation. The laws concerning EOs basically ensure that the final product is fit for consumption and that overproduction is discouraged. This is the least stringent of all wine categories and, because of that, the most flexible. It is supposed to be the ultimate weapon of European wine producers to changing market conditions, allowing them to design products from scratch, while higher ranks are dedicated to preserving tradition and heritage. There are some excellent EOs produced in several regions, although what happened in Italy, where a number of *vini da tavola* have completely turned the wine industry around in the last two decades, has yet to occur in Greece. Usually, an EO is a winery's cheapest, highest-volume product, and the only way to succeed commercially is either to heavily brand and promote the wine, or to have a very skilful selling team.

A sub-category of EO is devoted to traditional, distinctive wine styles: the *oinoi onomasias kata paradosi* (OKP; wines of appellation by tradition). The regulations deal with the main character of the wine and geographical limitations are less relevant. For example, OKP Retsina can be given to wines produced anywhere in Greece, provided that their colour, aromas, and flavours fall within the vaguely defined parameters of a resinated wine. Apart from retsina, Verdea from the Ionian islands is the only other OKP.

RECOGNITION FOR THE REGIONS

The most significant breakthrough in the Greek wine laws took place in 1989, with the introduction of *topikos oinos* (TO; regional wine designation). Following the EU regime, a TO is technically viewed as an EO, but is allowed to be specific with regard to region, varietal and vintage. Rather like with *vin de pays* in France, the decrees regulating viticulture and vinification are much more relaxed than those of OPAP and OPE, but a bit stricter than EO. Grape varieties have to be taken from the recommended/permitted list, but the style of wine is not specified. In addition, under the 2005 adjustment of wine laws, the sub-category of *neos oinos* is applicable to TOs as well.

There are three levels of TO, corresponding to the size of the region in question. The largest TO encapsulates a whole geographical department, like Macedonia or the Peloponnese, consisting of several prefectures. The next level up in quality terms is the prefectural TO, covering one prefecture. The most specific TO refers to one county only, but a TO can include several.

The more specific a TO, the stricter the legislation, while a departmental TO is treated almost as an EO. Nevertheless, there is a very strict structure in place to ensure that specific, small TOs will never pose a threat to any quality-wine appellations. For example, a producer just outside the limits of a red wine-producing OPAP is allowed to apply for the smallest TO only if the varieties used are different to those cultivated within the neighbouring appellation. If the producer insists in using the "wrong" varieties, then the only legal option is going two levels down, to the largest relevant TO.

Immediately after the TO ruling was voted in by the Greek Parliament, the category became incredibly popular with producers. At the outset in 1989 twelve TOs were passed, nine were added in 1990, just three in 1991, ten in 1992, eight in 1993, ten in 1995, and it seems like there is no end in sight. The current rate of new TOs being generated makes certain that any relevant record is bound to be outdated by the time this book is published.

Nico Manessis, author and leading authority on Greek wines, claims that, "the more you submerse yourself in the fine-print of the Greek wine laws, the more you will be confronted with contradictions or a lack of logic". He explains: "They are stuck in 1970s French appellation blueprints, which they were based on. Market conditions have since changed. They need to be liberalised and follow for example, the IGT [the *indicazione geografica tipica* system], which has served the Italians so well. A winemaker should be using all his or her energy to create and excel, not to deal with legislation." It would be interesting to see laws respecting Manessis' visionaries for a change, rather than making their lives more difficult, as they are the ones to thank for the recent leaps ahead in the Greek wine industry.

THE GREEK WINE LABEL

All accounts of wine laws must include an analysis of the impact of legislation on wine labels; this is a key point relevant to consumers and, therefore, traders. The way provenance and quality status are expressed on a label can instantly help someone choosing a bottle, while geographical boundaries, planting densities, and permitted or recommended varieties have to do with, primarily, the *typicité* and, secondly, the quality of what is in the bottle. The relationship of law, appellation, label, and wine style to consumer awareness, desires, and expectations is an extremely complex one. In an ideal world, the wine label is the link that makes this correlation a bit simpler.

Quality-wine labels

Laws governing wine labels are broadly in line with the EU agenda. The label of a quality-wine – either OPE or OPAP – has to state: the name of the appellation; the full title of the category they belong to (*onomasia proelefseos elenhomeni* or *onomasia proelefseos anoteras poiotitas*); alcoholic strength; the volume of wine in the container, and finally, the name and address of the bottler. Wine type (colour, style) and vintage can be written but are not obligatory. A producer making a quality-wine can use the designation as the main name of the product or use a brand, or both. Only quality-wines have this option. The law specifies a minimum font size for the name of the appellation, to ensure that the wine's origin remains a distinguishing and vital part of its presentation. (Numerous wines have been rejected by the Thessaloniki International Wine Competition, Greece's only wine show, because the size of font used for the appellation was a millimetre too small.)

A distinctive feature of the OPAP and OPE wines is the obligatory paper strip (red for the former, blue for the latter) placed between the top of the bottle and the capsule. The tapes are provided by the Ministry of Agriculture and the amount supplied corresponds to the declared quantity of wine produced and the expected mix of container sizes the producer intends to use. There are also restrictions on the general packaging. Quality wines can only be bottled in glass containers with a capacity of a litre or less, and until 2005 only natural corks could be used to seal the bottles.

Quality wines can use two label terms that specify length of ageing, namely *réserve* and *grande réserve*. *Réserve* is often translated in Greek as *epilegmenos*, meaning "selected", and *grande réserve* is *eidika epilegmenos*, or "specially selected". White *réserve* wines are released after one year of ageing, with a minimum of six months in oak and three months in bottle. Red *réserves* have to spend two years in the producers' cellars, with a minimum of twelve months ageing in oak and six months in bottle. Following the same lines, *grande réserve* whites are released after two years, with a minimum of one year in oak and six months in bottle. *Grande réserve* reds have as their minimum requirements eighteen months in oak and a further eighteen in bottle, with release on the market being after a total maturation period of four years. The barrel size is not specified for red wines, but whites have to be matured in casks with a capacity of 600 litres or smaller.

A larger number of label terms signifying lengths and styles of ageing were introduced with the 2005 amendments. Reds that have been in oak for six months and are released a year after the harvest can state: *orimasse se vareli*, "the wine was matured in oak". This can be followed by *gia eksi mines*, "for six months". Oak-aged whites and rosés have to spend three months in oak and be released after a total of six months to be called *orimasse se vareli,* possibly followed by *gia tris mines* ("for three months"). When a white or a rosé is not only aged but also fermented in oak, the above designations can be altered to *oinopoiithike kai orimasse se vareli* ("vinified and matured in oak"). If the above minimum requirements of time in oak are exceeded, then the latter part of the label term can be changed accordingly.

These ageing terms are not confined to quality-wines and can be used for TOs as well. In the case of OPAP wines, these age descriptions can be used concurrently with *réserve* or *grande réserve*. Therefore, a red OPAP that has spent two years in oak and two in bottle can have a label stating *grande réserve – orimasse se vareli gia dio xronia*, "matured in oak for two years".

Table wine labels

The information allowed for regional wines, TOs, is significantly less than that permitted for the quality-wine level, but the all-important geographical designation, that literally puts the wine on the map, can be stated. The compulsory information for a TO label is: origin as described by the selected TO; the words "*topikos oinos*"; the name of the producer; the place of bottling, and alcoholic strength and volume. In addition, TO bottles must have a code-number starting with two letters that correspond to origin and ending with the two last digits of the vintage year. For example, a TO from Drama from the 2003 vintage must have a code-number starting with "DR", followed by five or six digits and then "/03". The vintage can also usually be stated on the label, beyond its mention in the Code Number.

The obligatory information on EO labels is minimal, which leaves room for branding and product development (according to the lawmakers). But, most producers – especially those with no possibility of branding or product development – this can leave consumers in the dark about what is actually in the bottle. An EO label must state the name and address of the bottler, alcoholic strength, and volume. Vintage, grape variety, and geographical descriptions are not allowed.

The terms *réserve* and *grande réserve* cannot be used in EO wines, but the word *cava* declares an aged table wine. White cavas are aged for one year, with a minimum of six months in oak and six in bottle, making cava the equivalent designation of an OPAP *réserve*. Cava reds are released after three years, with at least a year in oak and a year in bottle.

A wealth of label terms is used to signify quality, including *ktima* ("estate" or "domaine"), *ampelones* ("vineyards"), *oreinoi ampelones* ("mountainous vineyards") or descriptions such as *monastiri* ("monastery") and *pyrgos* ("château"). The words "château" and "domaine" can appear in their French form but not alone – the Greek words *pyrgos* and *ktima* have to be printed as well. Consumers have developed an appreciation of these terms, which are a positive influence.

Constructing detailed legislation to govern the use of such expressions is naturally difficult, but the general notion is that these words should not mislead the consumer. Thus, if a wine is named *pyrgos*, there must be a building within the estate that resembles a château. For the terms *ktima* and *ampelones* to be used, it is mandatory that vineyards and winery are in the same commune. The production facility and fifty per cent of the vineyards must all be owned by the same company, which is named as the producer of the wine. Improper use of these two words has been the reason behind many heated debates and even legal actions in the courts. However, these battles were between producers, while legal authorities, so far, have not been actively pursuing such trials.

As with other consumer goods, there is a directive with regard to wording used to name products. Terms that signify greatness, superiority or quality should not be a part of the branding of a product. In addition, trademarks must not include specifics of "public places", such as villages, communes, rivers, mountains, and so on, with the obvious exception of what is permitted by the relevant appellation and quality level. For example, a producer can use the word Nemea for an OPAP – "Nemea wine" – but not "Asprokampos" or "Koutsi", which are villages in the Nemea designated area.

TOs have officially been the only category that can cite a varietal on the label. For OPE wines this was not such a problem since most appellation names, excluding Samos, include the variety, for example "Mavrodaphne of Patras" or "Muscat of Limnos". Originally, OPAPs could not state the grape they were made of, but in the last few years the rules have been relaxed, with more and more OPAP wines stating their variety on the label. In most of these cases, because of the immense commercial success of varietal wines in Greece, the variety is printed in a far larger font than the appellation.

A lot of producers believe that most labelling regulations are irrelevant. For them, a New World approach would be preferable, since Greece lacks a history of labels and typical or standardized styles, as is the case with France. This reasoning is not wholly unfounded, but sometimes excellence has more of a chance to emerge out of discipline than anarchy.

5
Grapes

Indigenous grape varieties are a potentially invaluable treasure trove for producers and consumers alike. Greek producers are increasingly investing in native vine varieties and beginning to experiment with both established cultivars and those on the verge of extinction. One thing is for sure: the most complex and interesting Greek wines are still to come.

Experts disagree on the exact number of indigenous vine varieties that exist in Greece. Some claim that there are more than 350, but a more realistic figure would be somewhere around 200. This disparity arises from the fact that the same variety can appear under several names in different regions. The confusion isn't helped by the fact that two vines with the same DNA can show remarkably distinct ampelographical characteristics when grown in different terroirs. Of all Greek varieties, perhaps fifty are used on a substantial scale, with less than thirty being well known to connoisseurs.

It is as yet unclear whether or not indigenous varieties can give Greece a sustainable marketing advantage. They may be the way forward, but it will surely be an uphill struggle, not least because many of these varieties have names that are very difficult to pronounce for non Greek-speaking consumers. In addition, although Greek producers and quite a few journalists like to claim that wine drinkers are getting bored with the international grape varieties, extensive research suggests that this is only true in a few sectors of the market. Knowledgeable wine lovers do search out new tastes and so would seem to be a prime target for Greek producers, but it is this very inquisitiveness that makes them less likely to stick to any one region or wine. In sharp contrast, the average wine drinker has far more consistent buying habits, and is therefore more attractive in terms of revenue.

Bearing in mind the popularity of the international varieties, producers decided to tread the middle ground, and the late 1980s and early 1990s saw the creation of blends that married local varieties with international ones. Marketing aspirations aside, this resulted in some truly successful combinations: Cabernet Sauvignon adds backbone and structure to the softer Agiorgitiko, while Merlot rounds out the sometimes aggressive tannic structure of Xinomavro.

Some might say that producers have failed to exploit the full marketing potential of wines from imported varieties, mainly as far as exports are concerned. They have been unable to settle on a set style of wines from these grapes and to create a benchmark for Greek wines, even if it was based on an international grape, in the same way that New Zealand has with Sauvignon Blanc, Barossa with Shiraz, and Chile with Merlot. In Greece, the style of a Cabernet, Merlot, or Chardonnay can vary considerably. So far, the taste of these wines depends more on the producer than the region or any other factor. That said, Sauvignon Blanc from Drama and Kavala, as well as Cabernets from the south-western Peloponnese, are showing signs that they may develop their own regional identities.

Later on in this chapter we will consider the main international varieties planted in Greece. New vineyards of non-native varieties now include ever-more exotic offerings, such as Negroamaro, Tempranillo, Schioppettino (from northeast Italy), and Grecanico Dorato (from Sicily). Viognier has attracted quite a following and features in the core commercial portfolio of more than half a dozen producers. However, although most vineyards are carefully planned these days, some varieties have been chosen without taking into account the extremes of the Greek climate. Sylvaner, for example, has been misguidedly planted in some of the hottest areas of Crete.

A QUESTION OF IDENTITY

Using advanced DNA identification techniques, the Agriculture University of Athens has begun projects to compare the genetic make-up of Greek grape varieties with those of their more famous French or Italian cousins, but so far no links have been found. Given that viticulture spread to continental Europe from Ancient Greece, the predecessors of European grape varieties must have existed in Greek vineyards at some point. Yet with *Vitis vinifera's* habit of mutating so easily, two plants of the same variety in the fifth century BC could by now be seen as two distinct varieties. For example, until the eighteenth century, Malvasia was one of the best-known Greek wines to be exported to Europe, giving rise to the belief that the various varieties now known as Malvasia growing in most Mediterranean countries, from Italy to Spain and even Madeira, must be essentially Greek. However, recent analyses have shown beyond any doubt that these varieties are not related to their indigenous namesake. The same is true for Ribolla Gialla of Friuli and Robola from Cephalonia. Ultimately, however, striving to create some of the world's finest Cabernet Sauvignon or Chardonnay in Greece is more important than proving that these varieties originated there.

Indigenous vines are increasingly being placed under the microscope and many nurseries are concentrating on producing healthy planting material, as the availability of virus-free stock is vital to the future of Greek vineyards. As a result, modern propagation projects are often quick to discard varieties susceptible to viruses that are difficult to eradicate. For example, research on Agiorgitiko clones has been suspended, since it was proving difficult and costly to achieve a virus-free status. However, viruses are not always detrimental. While some can result in the destruction or death of a vine, others can help reduce vigour, lowering yields, and raising quality by delaying ripeness. This increases the hang-time, giving the phenolics more of a chance to mature, and affecting the texture of the tannins in particular.

This is the case with many varieties, but especially true for vines producing grapes with aggressive tannins or low colour, like Xinomavro. If it were possible to produce totally healthy Agiorgitiko vines, there is a high probability that the resulting wines would differ in character from what is now looked for in the variety. In other words, the characteristics recognized as those of Agiorgitiko are partly an expression of its DNA, but also an equally important expression of its virus infections, the most important being the leaf-roll virus.

CLONES AND THE QUEST FOR QUALITY

Virus side-effects aside, clonal selection is not only important for the creation of healthy propagation material, but also for quality, as shown by Italy's Chianti Classico 2000 project. In the Tuscany region during the 1990s, a number of quality-oriented producers became concerned with the calibre of Sangiovese clones available from nurseries. At that point, available clones were selected for their ability to produce higher yields, or because they were easy to graft, while the quality of the final product was almost secondary. These producers, together with leading academics, nurseries, and local viticultural institutions, started Chianti Classico 2000 with the aim of identifying clones or lesser varieties of the region with the highest quality potential. According to many wine-growers, this project has provided useful results, even if the process of finding the best Sangiovese clones is still ongoing.

This has taught Greek producers an important lesson. Currently, national universities and private companies such as Ampeloiniki and Vitro Hellas are working on identifying promising clones for about fifteen of the most important Greek varieties. In certain cases, such as that of Roditis, what were believed to be clones of the same variety had genotype differences higher than one per cent; they therefore had to be reclassified as distinct varieties. Conversely, clones of Xinomavro with distinct and consistent differences in the vineyard were shown to have identical DNA. Research has already moved on to the next stage, where micro-vinifications of varietal clones are being undertaken to see what conclusions can be drawn with regard to potential quality. It is often said that using just one clone gives one-dimensional wines, but it is necessary to plant, cultivate, harvest, and vinify clones separately to assess their character and potential. Blending to achieve complexity must come later, and even then, different clones can only be planted and harvested together if they ripen at the same rate. This can be done with varieties like Assyrtico for example, but is not possible for clones of Moschofilero.

In the end, however, it would be a mistake to concentrate on identifying the clones of just a handful of varieties at the expense of lesser-known, but potentially important, distinct varietals. These could prove profitable in terms of quality and marketing, while currently being in danger of disappearing. For example, the Papas from the Soufli region in eastern Thrace, near the Turkish border, seems to have an intense, aromatic character and a unique style. Preliminary results from studies of the Dopio variety from Metsovo (Ioannina, Epirus) and the Vlachico and Bekari grapes from Zitsa (Ioannina), are promising, while in the Velvendos region in southern Macedonia, an excellent grape variety has been identified that produces wine in a style akin to a variation on the Cabernet/Merlot theme.

When discussing the use of micro-vinification programmes to rate clones and varieties, it is important to understand the criteria that are being used. In modern research facilities across the world, a good clone or variety is defined as one with average to high yields, average to high (but not excessive) sugar levels at ripeness, and moderate to moderately low acidity.

Red grapes should have good colour and high to moderately high levels of tannins, while white grapes should have a good aromatic profile and low phenolic levels. The wines are mostly vinified in stainless steel and evaluated when young. These criteria require grapes with no extreme characteristics, and if used exclusively, may well result in the rejection of varieties such as Nebbiolo and Xinomavro – both have the ability to achieve balance and great character, but do not conform to the restrictive measurements outlined above. The same can be said of grape varieties like Chenin Blanc that need a considerable amount of time in bottle to develop their true potential. On the contrary, the varietals that would be deemed valuable, according to the criteria, are those that give moderately intense, easy-drinking, fruity wines. But the world of wine does not need more Cabernet or Chardonnay look-alikes. If anything, it needs a bit more drama.

Varietal and clonal selection is further complicated by variables such as cultivation methods, yield, climate, site, and soil, while in the winery, modern vinification and ageing techniques are now becoming varietal-specific. For example, Savatiano has always been regarded as a low-quality varietal with a distinct lack of character. However, recent analysis of its aromatic precursors suggests that Savatiano is one of the most fragrant Greek varieties, but the vine, in order to express this characteristic must be restricted to yields as low as forty hectolitres per hectare. Savatiano currently averages in excess of 120 hectolitres per hectare.

For various reasons, the white Vidiano from Crete is considered merely average, but viticultural consultant and expert, Haroula Spinthiropoulou, believes that this vine suffers in the dry, hot climate of the region it is grown in today. If planted in cooler climates, she says it has the potential to become one of the great Greek varieties.[1] The permutations seem endless, and a touch of luck is probably also needed to strike gold in terms of identifying a grape of interest that also behaves in an "ideal" fashion.

HARVEST, RIPENESS, AND POTENTIAL ALCOHOL

A prime concern for all Greek viticulturalists is the timing of harvest and how this can be manipulated for expressing established varieties in a new and possibly unpredictable way. Traditionally, most Greek wine-growers started their harvest around a set date, not worrying how ripe the fruit was. In the last thirty years, more people have realized that observing vintage variations and establishing stricter criteria for fruit ripeness can be beneficial. Their prime concern became sugar levels and the target was set, almost unanimously, at about 12.5 per cent potential alcohol, regardless of region, variety, or desired style of wine. Leaving the fruit on the vine any longer was considered undesirable for various reasons, including the fear that high sugar levels would lead to stuck fermentations and that the acidity would fall too low (even if acidification was frequently practised). Additionally, alcohol above thirteen per cent was regarded as a defect and winemakers feared that fruit flavours would get "too cooked" or "too jammy". It is possible that Bordeaux- or Dijon-trained oenologists of past decades influenced this opinion, as they were educated about vine-growing in far cooler climates than Greece.

Since 1990, producers have became more adventurous, realizing that higher ripeness allows many varieties to display different but equally exciting facets of their character. Riper Assyrtico has all the minerality of the variety, but higher extract and the potential to absorb oak more confidently. Xinomavro picked at 13.5 degrees Baumé still has firm, but not aggressive, tannins and a rounder palate. Agiorgitiko at fourteen per cent alcohol retains a freshness of fruit while building up a dense, impressive structure.

It is slightly strange that Greek growers have started to explore later harvests at a time when many of their New World counterparts working in warm climates are getting over their obsession with "extra hang-time" and heading for less alcoholic, more elegant wines. Nevertheless, viticulturalists must gain experience with these vines, even if it is just to find out that their original approach was the best. One way or another, higher maturity for these varieties is not just a matter of leaving the grapes on the vine for longer while other aspects of cultivation remain unchanged. The vines must be treated in a different manner, from pruning through to trimming. Having said that, everything that persuades people to consider new options and to gain a fresh insight is, in the long run, a positive development.

GREEK WINE GRAPES

White varieties

AIDANI

Aïdani probably originated in Asia and today is widely planted in the Cycladic islands, especially Santorini, Paros, and Naxos. It is well suited to these hot and arid islands, since it is highly resistant to water stress. The vine is susceptible to both powdery and downy mildew, although the latter is not as frequent as the former in these climates. Aïdani is easy to graft and compatible with all major rootstocks available in Greece. Despite being regarded as a vigorous vine, its vegetative vigour is moderate, but it does produce large bunches of grapes, exceeding 500 grams each. With every fruitful shoot giving one to two bunches, yields per vine can be excessive. Average yields of thirty hectolitres per hectare may seem low, but this is due to low planting densities (less than 3,000 vines per hectare) or lack of water, while individual vines may actually be overcropped.

One of the few commercially available wines made purely from Aïdani is produced by the cooperative of Santorini, Santo Wines. Otherwise, it is mainly used in blends to round off and soften the steely, austere, acidic, and sometimes alcoholic, Assyrtico.

ASSYRTICO

Arguably the finest Greek white grape variety today, Assyrtico has the rare ability of balancing breadth and power with high acidity and steely austerity. A pH below three and a total acidity above 6.5 grams per litre as tartaric is not uncommon in the wines of Santorini. The flavours of this variety have a crystalline intensity and a moderate level of fruit that is never too sweet, raisiny, or confected, while the body combines extract with lean structure. In short, the best Assyrtico is akin to the finest Muscadet on steroids – remarkable, considering that it is grown in some of the hottest, sunniest, driest vineyards on earth.

The Assyrtico vine is resistant to most diseases; vigour is moderate to high. When not stressed, it can produce more than sixty hectolitres per hectare. It is extremely resistant to drought, and its hard wood protects it from the intense winds that buffet the Aegean islands during the summer. Assyrtico also shows a remarkable ability to adapt to different soils and climates. This potential was quickly recognized by producers across the country, making it one of the most transplanted Greek varieties today. Apart from its major role in the Santorini OPAP, Assyrtico is also listed in the Côtes de Meliton OPAP in Halkidiki, Macedonia, and there are few regions where this variety is not planted to some extent. Varietal Assyrticos across Greece do not have the same minerality and breed as those from Santorini, but they have more aromatic intensity, higher levels of fruit, and more breadth on the palate.

As expected, scientific research is focusing on the clones of Assyrtico.

Traditionally, growers on Santorini have maintained that there are three clones: the "proper" Assyrtico, FlaskAssyrtico, and Arseniko. Recently it was proved that FlaskAssyrtico is a totally different variety and that Arseniko is a virus-infected Assyrtico. No major differences were observed between the three in the vineyard or in micro-vinifications, and all shared Assyrtico's big disadvantage – its tendency to oxidize rapidly.

Assyrtico does not need cask ageing to display great character and its affinity with oak is questionable, notwithstanding its tendency to oxidize. There are some outstanding examples of oak-aged Assyrtico – such as the partially-oaked Ktima Argyrou (Santorini) and the full-oaked version from the same producer – but the majority lack a good synergy between oak and fruit. On the other hand, extended oak ageing of the *vin santo* produced from sun-dried Assyrtico, Athiri, and Aïdani grapes, plays a major role in creating top quality dessert wines that have the complexity of an oloroso sherry with the bite of a Tokaj.

ATHIRI
Athiri, one of the oldest varieties of the Aegean islands, was traditionally planted in the Dodecanese and the Cyclades, and was reasonably important in Crete. It is still widely grown in those regions, but has been transplanted to a large number of prefectures around Greece, bringing the total of its vineyard area close to 1,000 hectares. The popularity of the variety can be explained by its cultivation characteristics as well as the style of wine it produces. Athiri is a vigorous vine, tolerant of arid conditions, and very resistant to most diseases, apart from powdery and downy mildew. It can adapt and give good results on a variety of soils, although light, calcareous, or argilo-calcareous soils are the best. It ripens relatively early, before the end of August, so it escapes possible early autumn rains. The timing of harvest is important because natural acidity drops quickly in the final stages of ripening. Finally, Athiri responds well to high yields, producing ripe and flavourful grapes even at 100 hectolitres per hectare or higher.

Apart from the ease of cultivation, Athiri produces a very commercial style of wine. Excluding some excellent examples from the highest vineyards of Rhodes, the variety is rarely able to achieve intensity, character, or great complexity. Nevertheless, in stainless steel, cool-fermented, and reductively handled, Athiri is suitable for fresh, fruity wines, with moderate to high alcohol, medium body, and soft acidity. Athiri's combination of high yields and a clean personality is a useful tool in producing pleasant, high volume brands that hit the right price-points, as proved by the very successful and charming varietal wine of Tsantali in Halkidiki, Macedonia.

Athiri is one of the three main varieties of Santorini, together with Assyrtico and Aïdani. Of these, it is the lowest in acidity and therefore lends suppleness and softness to the more angular Assyrtico. Santo Wines, the Santorini co-op, produces an interesting single-varietal Athiri, but the finest expressions of the grape come from Rhodes – in particular, from vineyards above 450 metres (1,476 feet) altitude. Here cool temperatures and a long growing season can produce elegant, high-pitched Athiri. Beyond that, the variety is grown in most departments of mainland Greece. In Macedonia, it is included in the varietal blend of Domaine Carras' Côtes de Meliton OPAP, where, in the early 1990s, Evangelos Gerovassiliou made some exquisite Athiri: full of finesse, crisp, and almost cool climate in definition.

In the Cyclades, mainly on Santorini and the vineyards of Manolis Moraitis on Paros, there is a red-skinned version, called Athiri Mavro (Black Athiri) that reaches higher acidity and alcohol levels. Thrapsathiri, a variety cultivated in Crete and other parts of southern Greece, was considered a clone of Athiri, but this was found not to be the case.[1]

DEBINA

Debina is the most important indigenous white variety grown around Zitsa in Ioannina in Epirus. One of Debina's key exponents, Lefteris Glinavos from the Zitsa Monastery winery, does not believe that it is a native variety, but that it was imported from Italy or northern Epirus in Albania. In their search for "new" grape varieties, many producers from Thessaly to the Peloponnese have planted new vineyards with Debina; plantings are scattered throughout northern Epirus and into Albania.

Debina is vigorous, has moderately high yields (seventy hectolitres per hectare) and, although it is mildly susceptible to water stress and botrytis, grey rot presents the greatest threat. In the cool, high-altitude (500 metres/ 1,640 feet and above) limestone vineyards of Zitsa, Debina buds late and ripens slowly. Harvest usually takes place in late September or early October and, in the final stages of ripening, Debina rapidly loses acidity without any significant improvement in its aroma profile.

1. Spinthiropoulou, H, *Oinopoiisimes Poikilies tou Ellinikou Ampelona,* Olive Press Publications, Corfu, 2000.

Debina wines are usually low in alcohol, reaching around eleven to twelve per cent only in hot vintages. Acidity levels usually surpass 6.5 grams per litre, while the aromas and palate structure suggest a cooler climate terroir than that prevailing in Zitsa. Despite its distinctive lemony aroma, it cannot be considered an aromatic variety. Indeed, among native grapes, only Lagorthi reaches full aromatic expression at lower sugar levels. Debina produces the OPAP wines of Zitsa, which can be dry or semi-sparkling (dry or semi-sweet). The effervescent examples can be excellent.

LAGORTHI

Although a few Lagorthi vineyards exist in the northern Peloponnese and on some of the Ionian islands, Lagorthi is far more famous than its modest acreage would suggest. The late, pioneering Constantinos Antonopoulos recognized the grape's potential in the late 1980s and established its name – at least among serious wine-growers. Today fewer than ten producers crush significant quantities of Lagorthi, but some of the bottlings, such as the single-varietals from Oenoforos winery in Eghio, Domaine Spiropoulos further south in Mantinia, and the Adoli Ghis blend of Lagorthi, Asproudi, and Chardonnay from Antonopoulos, are extremely promising and have attracted a loyal following.

Lagorthi has a moderate aromatic intensity and a relatively low fruit level. It rarely exceeds 12.5 per cent alcohol by volume and has crisp acidity. It is elegant and its structure is so indicative of a cool climate that, when tasted blind, it is hard to believe that this wine has been produced in such a hot region. Growers are now starting to plant it further north, in Macedonia, to assess Lagorthi's reaction to cooler terroirs. This move towards northern latitudes is logical given Lagorthi's sensitivity to water stress. The vine is vigorous and has a moderate to moderately high resistance to most vineyard diseases. It is a late ripener, reaching full maturity towards the end of September, sometimes even later. It has a thick skin and a relatively low juice percentage. A peculiar feature that denotes Lagorthi's ability to fully mature at very low sugar levels is that its cane-wood and pip-wood maturation is already advanced at ten degrees Baumé, while the canes of some other Greek varietals don't mature until well after harvest.

MALAGOUSIA

Malagousia has one of the most interesting histories of all Greek grape varieties. In the mid-1970s Professor Logothetis from the Agricultural

University of Thessaloniki rented a small plot from Yiannis Carras, then the owner of Domaine Carras in Halkidiki, to plant some rare grape varieties that he had encountered on his trips around Greece. There he planted Lagorthi, Hopsathiri, Latino, Debina, and the then unheard of Malagousia, which he had spotted in Etoloakarnania in western Central Greece. Initially, these grapes were simply harvested and vinified together, without truly evaluating the wine quality potential of each individual variety.

It did not take long for Evangelos Gerovassiliou, then winemaker at Domaine Carras, to realize that Malagousia was a truly distinctive variety with an intense and idiosyncratic aromatic profile. He propagated it and the increased volume resulted in the first barrique-aged varietal bottlings in the early 1990s. The results were stunning. The wine had the power of a Chardonnay, the extract of a great Semillon, a great affinity with oak, and an aromatic character that could only be described as unique. It hints at Muscat, although it is not as sweet, profound, or floral. The primary fruit level is high, showing ripe peaches and apricots, coupled with hints of fresh green pepper.

Malagousia became an overnight success. Shortly after, Domaine Carras entered turbulent times and, sadly, the Malagousia wines produced today by Domaine Carras and others, although distinctive, lack something of the complexity and finesse of those earlier bottlings. Very few properly stored bottles of the Carras Malagousia 1993 or 1994 exist today. But, when tasted in the late 1990s, these wines showed excellent development and enough vivacity for further ageing potential – something unprecedented for a dry Greek white wine.

Gerovassiliou planted Malagousia on his own estate in Epanomi near Thessaloniki and, utilizing both his perfectionist approach and substantial resources, he continues to explore the limits of this variety. The vine is not resistant to drought and one or two careful periods of drip-irrigation can help to advance ripeness. Through ampelographical observations, Gerovassiliou believes that he has isolated two clones. One has smaller berries and appears to be more aromatic than the larger-berried clone. Many rootstock trials have attempted to increase acidity and limit yields, because Malagousia is a vigorous vine: SO4 had a low success rate, accentuating the need for water; 41B gave some good results in parcels with high stone content; however in other soils, 110R and 140R gave the most promising results; new trials with 161-49 and 1103P have yet to be concluded.

Grapes harvested at various ripeness levels have shown huge differences in aromatic potential. When harvested below 11.5 per cent potential alcohol the variety shows few aromatic properties. Findings indicate that optimum aromas can be obtained when the grapes are harvested between 12.5 and 13.5 per cent potential alcohol. If Malagousia gets overripe, the level of terpenes rapidly increases, giving the wine an almost Muscat-like character. Gerovassiliou believes in limiting yields using natural means, and that intense pruning or green harvesting can lower the yields per hectare (although the average yield per fruitful bud would increase). Currently he struggles to keep yields below fifty-five hectolitres per hectare, but as the vines get older he could get well below this. He believes that the secret of the first Carras Malagousias was that the poor, schist soils of the domaine's Malagousia vineyards had an intense suppressing effect on vine vigour, resulting in low yields of twenty-four hectolitres per hectare.

Malagousia is now planted in various regions, although again, public awareness of the variety belies the extent of its vineyard acreage. Wineries in Attica, Drama, Mykonos, and, of course, Malagousia's homeland of Etoloakarnania, are producing distinctive wines with high alcohol levels, moderate to low acidity, high phenolic content, high extract, and a full palate. The availability of planting stock is somewhat limited as Malagousia suffers significant virus infections, but it seems that this will not be enough to prevent Malagousia from becoming one of Greece's most important indigenous varietals in the decades to come.

MONEMVASIA

Monemvasia probably originated in the eponymous port in Laconia in the Peloponnese and was used to make Malvasia, for centuries Greece's best-known exported wine. With the decline in trade, however, vineyards in the region were abandoned until very recently, when Theodorakakos, Batistas, and Katogi's Monemvasia Winery began replanting the variety with promising results. It is now known that the Monemvasia grape is not related to the Malvasia varieties, although this was a common assumption in the past. It is therefore sad that more Greek producers today vinify Malvasia than they do Monemvasia.

The cultivar is now mainly planted on the Cyclades islands, a few other Aegean islands, and Evia, with the majority being on the island of Paros, where it produces the OPAP wines. With his decades of experience, Paros' Manolis Moraitis is regarded as patriarch of the variety.

Monemvasia is a vigorous vine, easy to graft, with moderately high yields. It ripens early, and higher, cooler altitudes assist the vine in achieving a better alcohol and acidity balance at harvest, normally around mid- to late-August. It is very resistant to water stress and most major vine diseases, the wines easily exceed twelve per cent alcohol by volume, and acidity is often relatively low. It has a moderate aromatic intensity with an intriguing spiciness, a high level of fruit, and a faint Muscat-like character. Monemvasia does not have a great affinity with oak, and the must should be handled carefully, since it has a tendency to oxidize. It will be interesting to see how Monemvasia performs in the cellar when harvested at a ripeness exceeding fourteen per cent alcohol, even if the acidity subsequently has to be corrected by the winemaker.

MOSCHOFILERO (FILERI)

In the early 1990s there was a huge rush towards this pink-skinned variety. Producers from Mantinia – the Peloponnese OPAP of Arcadia that has to be at least eighty-five per cent Moschofilero – together with winemakers from the rest of the Peloponnese, became very enthusiastic. There was a widespread feeling that a "Greek Chardonnay" or, even better, a "Greek Gewurztraminer" had finally been discovered. The ever-innovative George Skouras was even persuaded to match his ground-breaking Megas Oenos red, a pioneering and impressively structured blend of Agiorgitiko and Cabernet Sauvignon, with a Megas Oenos white – a pure Moschofilero. It is telling that recently Skouras rechristened Megas Oenos white as plain Moschofilero.

The variety can produce excellent, fresh, highly aromatic, light-bodied, crisp white wines. However, it seems that Moschofilero will never achieve the levels of complexity or depth of a great Assyrtico – although excellent producers like Tselepos and Antonopoulos are trying hard to prove this assertion wrong.

Moschofilero is the blanket name for a varietal with widely varying clones. The most important are Asprofilero (White Fileri), Xanthofilero (Blonde), and Mavrofilero (Black). The vineyard behaviour of these clones is quite distinct, both in ampelographical characteristics, like leaf shape, growing habits, bunch shape, and grape colour, as well as technological specifications, such as harvest timing, sugar, and acidity levels, and aromatics. For example, Asprofilero and Xanthofilero mature much later than Mavrofilero and have lower sugars and aroma compounds together with much higher acidities, giving a lesser wine. Nevertheless, even Mavrofilero has two sub-clones, with similar harvest times and levels of acidity, but sugar levels that can vary by as much as twenty grams per litre, or as much as one per cent potential alcohol. Most of this variation is due to problems with viruses.

Genetic instability, the pink skin colour, the intense terpene and Muscat-like aromas, together with the fact that the word "Moscho" is derived from Moschato, meaning aromatic, led many to speculate about a genetic link between Fileri and Muscat or Gewurztraminer. However, modern DNA analysis has proved that the Moschofilero family is separate from these two varieties. As a vine, Fileri is fairly vigorous and relatively high yielding, although in fertile vineyards with very high vigour, bloom disruptions and berry-set failures are noticeable. Harvest times range from late September to late October according to clone and climate.

The Moschofilero variety is planted throughout the Peloponnese and on many of the Ionian islands. It is extensively used as a blending component, lifting the aromas and acidity in Roditis and Savatiano. However, the glory of Moschofilero is Mantinia OPAP, at an altitude of more than 550 metres (1,804 feet). The Blanc de Noir Mantinias from the best growers is a cross between the spicy, floral, rose-petal nose of a Muscat and the crisp, light, lean palate of a Sylvaner. Some producers macerate the grape skins for forty-eight hours to get a lively, spicy rosé, such as Meliasto from the Spiropoulos estate.

Antonopoulos carried out an interesting experiment, letting very ripe Moschofilero undergo a shorter maceration leading to a Gris de Noir. Named Gerontoklima Rematias and bottled only in 500 millilitre bottles, it was an instant success. Apart from dry still whites or rosés, Mantinia has a significant history of using Moschofilero to produce Charmat-method sparkling wines, although Yiannis Tselepos is getting good results in his Villa Amalia using the *méthode traditionnelle*. In addition, sweet wines from dried grapes are already on the market, like Idistos from Spiropoulos. The various facets of Moschofilero have yet to be fully explored and the surprises might not be over yet – a lot of growers have been talking about the possibility of Greece producing Botrytis-affected dessert wines. If there is one place in Greece that could do this, it is Mantinia with Moschofilero.

MUSCAT OF ALEXANDRIA

Muscat of Alexandria is not technically a native Greek variety. It probably originated in Africa as part of the large Muscat group, members of which were among the earliest varieties of *Vitis vinifera* to be cultivated. It is now cultivated the world over for wine, raisins, and table grapes. In Greece it is not as widespread as Muscat Blanc (*see* below). It can be found on the island of Limnos, and to a lesser extent, in Central Greece, around Thessaloniki, Rhodes, and on some of the Ionian islands.

The vine is vigorous and its susceptibility to fungal diseases, as well as *coulure* and *millerandage*, somewhat limit its potential in northern climates. It has a tendency to overcrop as each fruitful shoot can produce up to three bunches, each exceeding 450 grams. Muscat of Alexandria produces the dry OPAP white wines of Limnos, as well as the island's sweet OPEs. The dry style is light and refreshing, with surprisingly crisp acidity. The *vins de liqueurs* can be balanced, charming, and full of fruit aromas.

MUSCAT BLANC A PETITS GRAINS

White Muscat is the oldest and the finest of the Muscat family. It is grown throughout the world and in Greece is used in the production of excellent dessert wines in many regions, such as the famed OPE wines of Samos Muscat (north Aegean), Muscat of Rio (northern Peloponnese), Muscat of Patras (northern Peloponnese), Muscat of Cephalonia (Ionian), and Muscat of Rhodes (Dodecanese). It is also blended with other grapes, since as little as five to ten per cent Muscat Blanc in a blend can give a substantial lift to aroma and fruit.

The vine is moderately vigorous and yields are lower than those of other Muscat varieties. Muscat Blanc is mildly resistant to water stress but highly susceptible to a wide variety of vine diseases. It is very prone to developing water shoots – the fruitless spurs that can emerge near the base of the vine which must be eliminated during spring to direct vigour and reserves from the root system to last year's buds. The vine starts the season early, but the grapes need a long hang-time so are harvested in early to mid-September. Once ripe, there is a narrow window when aromatic character is at its optimum, and if the vines are harvested either too early or too late, the enormous terpenes potential is lost.

The dry wines are refreshing, with a lower acidity than those made from Muscat of Alexandria, but with an outstanding complexity of rose petals, fruit, and bergamot flavours. The sweet wines are considered finer than those made from other Muscats, and although they can be delicious when young, they retain fruit on the palate even after substantial time in oak or bottle. Mature Samos Muscats are definitely some of the finest examples of this variety in the world.

It should be noted that other members of the Muscat family are cultivated in Greece, though to a lesser extent, and with less impressive results. Muscat of Hamburg is the most important, together with Black Muscat. In the regions of Spina and Masa on Crete, two different clones (or perhaps varieties) have been identified: Muscat of Spina and Muscat of Masa. The differences are minor between these and Muscat Blanc, although their skins do appear somewhat thinner.

The Muscat vine has a propensity to adapt to new terroirs so well that in some instances it is difficult to determine whether a group of vines consists of a single variety, two or more clones or a number of different varieties. For example, the Caïr viticulturists on Rhodes believe that Muscat di Trani is a distinct variety, and they list its vineyards separately from those of Muscat Blanc. Haroula Spinthiropoulou, however, maintains that Muscat di Trani is simply another synonym for Muscat Blanc.[2]

ROBOLA

Is there a true Robola cultivar? According to Michalis Boutaris, son of Yiannis Boutaris, Robola could just be the generic name of a wine made in Cephalonia from local varieties. DNA fingerprinting in California identified Robola stock as the Thiako grape. The same analysis in Athens on the vine material available there suggested that their Robola was the Goustolidi grape – and beyond any shadow of a doubt, the variety was different to that available in California. The name of this variety led some to believe that there was an association between Robola and Ribolla Gialla, the Italian grape variety from Friuli. However, ampelographical differences belie this. Identification problems aside, what most modern viticulturalists consider to be Robola is the finest white grape variety of the Ionian islands, and one of the best in Greece

Robola is used as a single varietal in the Robola of Cephalonia OPAP, but growers in other parts of Greece, recognizing its potential, have begun

2. Spinthiropoulou, H, *Oinopoiisimes Poikilies tou Ellinikou Ampelona*, Olive Press Publications, Corfu, 2000.

planting it elsewhere. One of the most expensive wine grapes in Greece, Cephalonia wineries pay up to 0.80 euros per kilogram to their growers.

Robola is best when grown at high altitudes (above 300 metres/985 feet), on sloping, well-drained, gravelly soils that are poor in organic matter. The ground is so rocky in the Cephalonia OPAP zone that the Venetians named the wine "*vino di sasso*" (wine of stone). The vine is fairly vigorous, but sensitive to water stress and is susceptible to powdery mildew, botrytis, and several vine viruses. Bunches are relatively small, loose, and berries are small. Robola is compatible with most rootstocks available in Greece today, but it is still predominantly an ungrafted variety, grown as a bush vine.

In the cellar, Robola is sensitive to oxidation and minimal handling from vine to pressing is essential. The best results are achieved using the latest technology: small pneumatic presses and whole-bunch pressing. Even then, the pressing must be very slow. There are many people who believe that the true Robola character can only be tasted on Cephalonia – even getting a bottle across the mainland apparently leads to a loss of aromas.

Grapes grown on this terroir have the potential to produce aromatic, fresh wines of exceptional quality that are characterized by delicate citrus and mineral aromas, balanced, crisp acidity, and medium body. It is one of those Greek varieties that do not have a distinct Greekness to them – Robola possesses a firm elegance that is rarely encountered in Greek, even Mediterranean whites. The best examples of Robola of Cephalonia OPAP wines can be superb and show interesting results when aged for a couple of years in bottle. Some growers pick the grapes too early, as they are afraid of losing acidity. However, some higher strength examples (13.2 per cent alcohol by volume or higher) show that higher grape ripeness can give Robola extra depth and complexity.

RODITIS

Roditis is cultivated throughout mainland Greece, from Thrace in the north to Laconia in the south, with the exception of Epirus and the west of Central Greece. It is one of the oldest indigenous varieties and known by several names. Some are likely to be clones, while others will be distinct varieties; research projects are currently trying to determine which is which. But it is certain that however many varieties may have been grouped under the Roditis name, the principal variety is multi-clonal, and terroir affects not only the morphology of the vine, but also its maturity profile at harvest.

Roditis is a very vigorous vine, resistant to drought but highly sensitive to powdery mildew. When grown in fertile soils it is susceptible to *coulure* and *millerandage*. Nevertheless, even when it is grown on less productive sites, it still has the potential for high yields, surpassing 120 hectolitres per hectare in some areas, and the resulting wines are light and dilute, with little aromatic intensity. Where Roditis is grown at high altitudes (300 metres/984 feet and above) and in light, calcareous, infertile soils, the vines lose some of their vigour, average bunch weight falls below 450 grams and ripening slows. The wines then have high levels of fruit – often reminiscent of ripe melon – intense aromas and flavours, and a broad, dense structure on the palate. In some well-made examples, a touch of Sauvignon Blanc-like nuances is found. Alcohol can approach thirteen per cent with moderate, but balanced acidity.

Roditis is used alone in the OPAP wines of Patras (Peloponnese), with Savatiano in Anchialos (Thessaly), and with Athiri and Assyrtico in the Côtes de Meliton OPAP. Several regional denominations also allow Roditis, most notably the TOs of Macedonia, Thessaly, and Attica. It is also considered suitable for the production of retsina, especially in the low-lying and high-yielding vineyards, while the best grapes from the northern Peloponnese are used to produce top varietal white wines or good quality blends.

Producers are constantly experimenting to make the ultimate Roditis, and different clones are playing a major role in this quest. Gaidouroroditis ("donkey Roditis") is heavily criticized as uninteresting and high yielding. Because of the latter characteristic, it is highly popular with growers where quality is not the aim and their sole income is directly related to kilos of grapes produced. Nevertheless, Gaidouroroditis can be used to produce low price, but still decent, flavourful, and clean, everyday wines.

Anestis Babatzimopoulos in Thessaloniki released his Galanos (Sky Blue) Roditis in the late 1990s, with its rich, fruit character and excellent depth. The Kanellatos (Cinnamon) Roditis and the Roditis from the Megara area in Attica have been singled out for further study, but most growers in the Peloponnese regard Alepou (Fox) Roditis as the epitome of the variety. Alepou has dark red berries, smaller clusters, and ripens earlier. It is said that the grapes are so sweet and tasty, with such a high terpene content, that foxes prefer them, hence the name. This clone is low yielding – Gaidouroroditis can produce up to 350 hectolitres per hectare while Alepou can be an eighth of that – so the only way that it can survive is by being supported by top quality producers. Currently the wineries of Oenoforos, Skouras, and Antonopoulos are investing heavily in Alepou and the results have been excellent. The "classic" Roditis must not be overlooked, however. It is a moderately late ripener with a cylindrical grape bunch of modest size and medium berry weight. Its grapes turn a dark pink colour easily, even without the aid of sun exposure.

SAVATIANO

Savatiano is the most commonly planted indigenous grape variety in Greece, covering more than 18,000 hectares. It is mostly seen in Attica, the island of Evia, and Viotia (Central Greece), but extensive vineyards can be found on the Cyclades islands, in Macedonia, and the Peloponnese. It is also planted on Cephalonia (Ionian islands) where it is known locally as Perahortiko. It is a variety used in the Anchialos OPAP with Roditis and in several regional wine designations. Yet the bulk of Savatiano is used for the production of retsina and other table wines.

The vine is moderately vigorous and is resistant to powdery and downy mildews and water stress. Bunches are large, sometimes weighing up to 500 grams and, if cultivated in flat, fertile, irrigated vineyards, yields can exceed 250 hectolitres per hectare. As with other varieties that tend towards high yields, Savatiano grapes give more promising results when grown in cooler climates and on dry, moderately infertile soils. In addition, carefully cultivated, old vines, such as those in Roxanne Matsa's Attica vineyards, can strike a good balance between alcohol, acidity, and extract.

Many Greek cultivars are harvested too early, since growers are afraid of losing acidity, but it has been shown that grapes allowed to mature a little longer often develop a more complex character. The reverse is true in the case of Savatiano. In dry, hot regions where September rains are uncommon, Savatiano vines are allowed to develop huge quantities of fruit which is then left on the vine for as long as possible to allow sugar levels to soar. In the Koropi area of Attica, sugar levels in excess of fifteen per cent potential alcohol, and pH levels above 3.7, are common.

High-yielding Savatiano gives very dull, bland wines. Careful additions of tartaric acid, the use of selected yeast strains for alcoholic fermentation, reductive handling to maintain a level of dissolved carbon dioxide in the final wine, and restrained alcohol levels can result in an excellent, easygoing style of wine such as the value-for-money Lac de Roches from Boutari. The wines can be further improved by the addition of small quantities of more aromatic, crisper varietals such as Assyrtico or Moschofilero. Savatiano has the potential to give wines with aromatic intensity, high fruit levels, and a balanced, broad structure on the palate, but only if grown on appropriate sites, with yields kept below seventy hectolitres per hectare, and if harvested at the right time. Of course, it is questionable whether growers would be willing to plant Savatiano on these sites at the expense of other more refined and potentially more commercially valuable varieties.

VILANA

Although red grapes dominate Crete, Vilana is the island's most important white variety. Most vineyards are located in the counties of Heraklion and Lasythi. Vilana is very vigorous, with a tendency to overcrop, an important consequence being the vine's susceptibility to fungal diseases due to the lack of air circulating in the dense canopy. A short pruning system is used to try to decrease vigour, but this stimulates foliage growth and results in a very crowded canopy. Providing that it is planted on non-irrigated hillside vineyards in soils with a high sand content, that it is trellised appropriately to allow larger canopies to develop, and planting density is kept below 3,000 plants per hectare, Vilana can give extremely interesting results.

Vilana is used to produce two of the best Cretan wines: the Peza OPAP which is 100 per cent Vilana, and the Sitia OPAP which is a blend with Thrapsathiri. The best examples have a moderate to high alcohol content, a balanced, though by no means crisp, acidity, and a moderate to intense floral aromatic profile. Vilana is best when vinified reductively since it oxidises very easily but, in competent hands, it has the ability to display high levels of spicy, rich primary fruit flavours and a most refreshing palate.

Red varieties

AGIORGITIKO

Agiorgitiko will probably be the most important red Greek variety in terms of international recognition – it could be what Carmenère is for Chile, Pinotage is for South Africa, and Shiraz is for Australia. The style of wine is distinct and serious, but still a benchmark for modern, crowd-pleasing reds. The colour is deep, the nose has red fruit aromas and sweet spices, there is an excellent affinity with new oak, and the palate is rich and fine-grained without being too tannic, alcoholic, cloying or fat. It is very hard to dislike a well-made Agiorgitiko.

This is a variety that Greeks call "polydynamic", describing the ability to produce wines in a large assortment of styles. Actually, the term could have been invented for Agiorgitiko: fresh and crisp rosés; vibrant *nouveau* wines showing a successful expression of carbonic maceration; medium-bodied and extremely soft reds; up to the most concentrated, tannic, and ageworthy monsters. Yiannis Paraskevopoulos and Leon Karatsalos of Gaia Wines in Nemea (Peloponnese) are champions of the latter, but are not afraid to go one step beyond, sun-drying the variety and ageing the *recioto*-like sweet wine in oak for more than four years.

Agiorgitiko is extremely sensitive to viruses and attempts to identify promising clones came to a halt when it was revealed that a virus-free form of the vine could not be found. It is possible that what growers consider to be Agiorgitiko may not be a distinct variety at all, but rather the virus-infected version of another variety – which may not have been as aristocratic if it had been cultivated and developed.

The vine has average vigour, but can produce high yields. It is extremely susceptible to powdery mildew and sensitive to downy mildew, potassium deficiency, and water stress. Agiorgitiko needs stress to produce good quality and overcome its tendency to overcrop. The best conditions are dense (by Greek standards) plantations, at 5,000 vines per hectare or higher, plus non-irrigated, infertile soils, together with competent canopy management. All this helps the vines to produce fewer but more concentrated grapes, while a long growing season is essential to reach full maturity of phenolics and aromatics, and higher sites are preferred. Agiorgitiko ripens after mid-September and usually has quite a prolonged harvesting period, so vintages can be important. It also has moderately small bunches that are difficult to cut, while its berries are small and thick-skinned.

Agiorgitiko, cultivated in the Nemea OPAP as well as across Attica, and the central and northern Peloponnese, is used as the backbone of many cross-regional EO blends. Indeed, some think that historically Nemea Agiorgitiko sold in bulk was always an important blending component in cross-European table wines, particularly in the 1970s. Growers wanting to try their hand at such a successful grape might grow it sporadically in several regions. Nemea may lead the way, producing high volumes of widely varying styles, including some premium contenders, but regions like Macedonia, with the superb varietal Areti made by Evangelos Gerovassiliou and Vassilis Tsaktsarlis on their Biblia Chora estate, give the Peloponnese growers food for thought.

KOTSIFALI

If someone wanted to illustrate a typical "hot Mediterranean" red wine, a pure Kotsifali would be a good example. Wines from this variety are high in alcohol, intense but sometimes coarse in aromas, and very low in acidity. Colour is difficult to extract from the thin skins and is highly unstable, turning rapidly brown and pale. It is easy to understand these shortcomings when you compare the percentage of grape solids by weight. In Kotsifali, pips and skins are just 3.3 per cent of the total weight of berries, while in Agiorgitiko they represent 9.2 per cent, and in the deeply coloured Vertzami over fifteen. Under this light, Kotsifali needs a blending partner to add colour, acidity, and tannins, and traditionally Mandilaria has fulfilled this role, although Crete's Sotiris Lyrarakis produces a very harmonious, complex Kotsifali/Syrah blend. On the other hand, Kotsifali can add quality and character to a blend – it can be aromatic in an individual and interesting way. The level of primary fruit is not high or excessively sweet, but spices, herbs, and hints of flowers do add a very complex patina.

Kotsifali is a vigorous, high-yielding vine, very resistant to the majority of diseases, apart from botrytis and downy mildew, both of which are fortunately rare in Crete. It prefers deep, well-drained, argilo-calcareous soils, ideally with a small proportion of pebbles. It ripens in late August or early September and potential alcohol levels at harvest can easily exceed thirteen per cent. More work is needed on clonal selection as there are some variations, and the most promising have yet to be identified, propagated, and made commercially available.

The variety is grown all over Crete, but is most popular on the eastern end of the island, in Heraklion and, to a lesser extent, Lasithi. Together with Mandilaria, it is the blend of Archanes and Peza, two of the OPAPs in Heraklion. It can also be included in the larger TO of Crete, and the prefectural TOs of Heraklio and Lasithi. It is rarely grown outside Crete.

LIATIKO

Until now Liatiko has been best known for being incorrectly linked to the Italian Aleatico variety than for the superb sweet wines it produces in Crete. Aleatico, a red grape of Lazio and Puglia, is reminiscent of Muscat in its aromas and is likely to be a red mutation of Muscat Blanc. Sometimes called Leatico, it produces sweet wines in the island of Elba. Yet dissimilarities became noticeable after the two varieties were compared genetically.

The Greek Liatiko is a vigorous, highly productive vine, moderately resistant to downy mildew and aridity, but very sensitive to acid rot. It favours deep, argilo-calcareous soils, and short pruning down to two buds is required for a favourable canopy microclimate in the following season. It ripens early – before the end of August in most areas. There are three Liatiko versions identified in Crete: Psilorogo (small-berried) Liatiko that looks like a cross between Liatiko and Stafida vines; Araiorago (loose-bunched) Liatiko has an inconsistent berry size, and finally, Kotsifoliatio, with lighter coloured leaves and berries than standard Liatiko.

Liatiko is used in the production of both dry and sweet wines. Although some producers craft interesting dry examples of the variety, Liatiko displays more character and flair in sweet wines. Fresh Liatiko grapes are low in anthocyanins, high in sugars and aromas, and moderate in acidity. When sun-dried – the basic method for producing sweet wines from the variety – the colour gets even paler, but the acidity increases due to the concentration, and the balance of the resulting style is first class. The best sweet examples are produced in the Dafnes OPAP in Heraklion and, with about twenty per cent Mandilaria, in the Sitia OPAP, also in Heraklion. In both appellations, the legislation allows dry styles as well. Liatiko is also a blending element in most of the island's TOs, like Crete, Heraklion, and Lasithi.

LIMNIO

Limnio is the first varietal explicitly named by ancient historians and therefore a likely candidate for being not just the oldest cultivated variety in Greece, but the oldest in the world. Hesiod mentions it, while Polydefkis refers to "*Limnia stafili*", a grape from Limnos, one of the northernmost islands of the Aegean.[3] There was also a Limnio producing the popular Maronia reds in Thrace. It is tricky to say for sure whether or not the ancient *Limnia stafili* is the same vine that modern Greek viticulturalists identify as Limnio, but it has been proved that the current form is the same Limnio that was used for the production of the famous Mount Athos monastery wines of centuries past, like the *Monoksilitis oinos*.

The Limnio vine has moderate vigour, is prolific, and quite hardy; it is exceptionally resistant to water stress and most diseases, excluding downy

3. Polydefkis was a Sophist, writing at the end of the second century AD. He was born in Egypt but lived in Athens. He wrote books on numerous subjects, but only *Onomastikon* has survived to the present day.

mildew. It is well adapted to most types of soil, even though the best quality results are usually found in dry, infertile, and gravelly sites. It is a relatively late ripener, usually reaching full maturity after mid-September. Bunches are very tight and difficult to remove from the vine. Medium-sized bunches seem to reach maturation at widely differing times – some will be shrivelling while others will be close to *veraison*.

Unfortunately, Limnio is not as illustrious today as in the past. Even the island of Limnos has not been granted an appellation, and justifiably so. Reds of the variety seem thin and angular, with the possible exception of those produced from Hatzigeorgiou. Apart from Limnos (where it is also known as Kalambaki), Limnio is mainly cultivated in Macedonia and Thrace, with good results, suggesting that the variety could thrive in cooler climates. It offers a style that is moderately high in alcohol and moderate in most other aspects, such as tannin, colour, body, and acidity. What makes a difference is the aromatic profile – full of fresh herbs and small-berried red fruits – while the overall structure on the palate is lean, but not at all sharp.

Limnio can be included in a variety of TOs in northern Greece, but is usually blended with international varietals, like Cabernet Sauvignon or Merlot, adding some nuances, but diffusing any real varietal character. When considering the potential quality that a top Limnio from Macedonia can show, then, once again, Domaine Carras' apogee in the first half of the 1990s comes to mind. The excellent varietal bottling of the estate took Limnio into a different league and was a benchmark for Greek wine: understated, not overly fruity, but full of personality. It is a sad fact that this high point has not been reached again since, yet it remains a valuable yardstick.

MANDILARIA

Mandilaria is one of the most deeply coloured varieties in Greece, and surely the most popular of these. Because of this, vineyards are being planted far beyond its southern Aegean birthplace. Even the most extracted Cabernet Sauvignon can improve in colour with the addition of just ten per cent of Mandilaria. In the red OPAP of Paros, twenty per cent Mandilaria grapes are co-macerated with the white Monemvasia to produce a red wine deeper in colour than some traditional Xinomavros – the only occasion in Greece when blending a red and white grape for the production of a red wine is permitted. Unfortunately, varietal Mandilaria will never be Greece's answer to late-harvest Shiraz from Australia, since intense colour sums up most of its character.

Mandilaria is moderately low in acidity, thin in palate structure, and lacks intensity in aromas and flavours, while harvesting above 12.5 degrees Baumé is either the result of very hard work in the vineyard or an exceptional terroir.

The vine is very vigorous and productive, although it prefers vegetative growth over excessive fruit loads. Having originated in Crete, the Cyclades, and the Dodecanese, it is resistant to dry conditions, but sensitive to acid rot, botrytis, and downy mildew. Controlling soaring vigour in Mandilaria is vital. Planting densities above 5,000 vines per hectare lead to overlapping canopies between plants and highly shaded fruit. Sites have to be infertile and dry to restrain growth, or warm and low-altitude to help sugar accumulation. Finally, pruning has to take into consideration the plant's capacity in the vineyard concerned, since too few buds can lead to high water shoot growth, while too many will leave the vine unable to mature the whole crop.

Mandilaria acts as Kotsifali's colouring agent in many blends from Crete, with the most famous being the OPAPs of Archanes and Peza in Heraklion. It is found in Santorini, producing most of the local red wine, although in terms of quality it is totally eclipsed by the much rarer Mavrotragano – the former is usually lean and dry while the latter can be Greece's answer to Mourvedre. The only OPAP that gives Mandilaria a chance on its own is Rhodes (where it is known as Amoriano). But the rosés produced on the island are much more convincing in their freshness and elegance than most of the reds. Finally, Mandilaria is used for its colouring abilities in many TOs around the Aegean Sea.

MAVRODAPHNE

Assuming that Muscat varieties cannot be classified as exclusively Greek, Mavrodaphne is the best known native variety, both within the country and on the export market. Apart from retsina and Samos, most people who have holidayed in Greece have had at least some contact with the sweet reds of the variety, probably in their Mavrodaphne of Patras OPE version. Fortunately, Mavrodaphne has been in the careful hands of one of Greece's most famous – and most competent – wine companies for almost 150 years. Achaia Clauss was founded in 1861 and from its early days has been almost synonymous with the grape. Because wine was not enough of a claim to fame on its own, the Achaia Clauss team was quick to turn its exceptionally beautiful winery into a tourist attraction in its own right – still one of the most successful cases of agro-tourism in Greece.

Given the popularity of the grape and its potential as a brand name, it is surprising that winemakers have not tried to exploit Mavrodaphne further or adapt it to the new trends on the market. The variety is mostly associated with a pale, tawny red style of sweet, fortified wine. Although it is a deeply pigmented, tannic grape, most commercial Mavrodaphnes are silky, fine-grained, faintly tannic, and without any generous concentration. This is due to both the extraction strategies employed by winemakers and the somewhat oxidative and prolonged ageing in oak, adding spices and botanical nuances to the ripe, sweet primary fruit. This approach can be exquisite, and old Mavrodaphnes from the best producers have impressive complexity and rare personality, on a par with the likes of the greatest sweet Grenaches of Roussillon in Banyuls and Rasteau. The wine world needs these unique and individual genres, but as the renowned critic and writer Hugh Johnson puts it, they are "a declining speciality".[4] At this stage, Greece cannot afford to have one of her best ambassadors as a declining speciality.

Mavrodaphne can produce modern styles of sweet wines, far closer to the more extracted, fruity, and voluptuous ports or port look-alikes from the New World, as shown by the efforts of producers like Antonopoulos and Spiliopoulos. In addition, the varietal can be used for admirable dry reds – an expanding sector – instead of a shrinking share of the sweet wine market. The variety has been used as a blending component for some time, as in the exceptional Château Clauss Cabernet Sauvignon/Mavrodaphne blend, and Ktima Mercouri's Refosco/Mavrodaphne, Nevertheless, these were branded, while Mavrodaphne was a minor and therefore less visible part of the product's personality and image. It will be interesting to see market reactions, both at home and abroad, to the concept of dry varietal Mavrodaphne. The first attempts have already taken place in Cephalonia and results, at least on the quality level, look promising.

The Mavrodaphne vine is moderately vigorous, productive, very sensitive to dry conditions and downy mildew, but less so to powdery mildew. High yields produce dilute wines, so deep, fertile soils, intense fertilization or irrigation, and other cultivation schemes that promote high fruit loads have to be avoided if high quality is the objective. It ripens in mid- to late-September and the thick-skinned grapes grow in relatively loose bunches. Mavrodaphne shows some genetic instability, with the Regnio clone in

4. Johnson, H, *Pocket Wine Book 2004*, Mitchell Beazley, London, 2003.

Achaia having tighter bunches and different leaf shapes, while Tsigelo has smaller berries. In Cephalonia, local growers believe they work with a higher quality clone of the variety, which is very close, if not the same, as Tsigelo. On the same island, a variety called Thiniatiko is also associated with the Tsigelo Mavrodaphne.

Mavrodaphne was traditionally grown in the northwestern Peloponnese and on many Ionian islands, where it produces the only two red Greek OPEs of the nation, Mavrodaphne of Patras and the long-forgotten but currently re-emerging Mavrodaphne of Cephalonia. Total acreage is around 650 hectares, but new plantations are on the rise, with more growers now wanting to experiment with the variety.

NEGOSKA

Negoska originated from Naoussa and many people believe that this is where it took its name – in Slavic, Naoussa was called Negush. It is also called Popolka Naoussis and Negoska Popolka. Although it can be found in most regions of Macedonia, the most important Negoska presence is in Goumenissa. As a vine, it is vigorous, productive, resistant to most major diseases, and prefers deep, calcareous soils with good drainage. It starts its annual growth cycle at the same time as Xinomavro, in the first half of April, and the two varieties are harvested together, after September 20. Negoska has all the elements needed to cover some of the weaknesses of Xinomavro: it has deep colour, high sugar levels, soft tannins, and only moderate acidity.

VERTZAMI

In terms of total plantations, Vertzami is almost insignificant. But in terms of quality it seems to be a rising star. Furthermore, unlike Limniona, Tsapournakos, and other gifted but low-acreage varieties, it is already creating a commercial following. Vertzami is Mandilaria's counterpart in western Greece. In the western Peloponnese, western Central Greece and in the Ionian islands it is used to add colour to multi-varietal blends. It is a deeply coloured varietal and even forty-eight hours of intense maceration is usually enough to obtain an impressive degree of extraction. Colour aside, Vertzami has intense red fruit aromas, a high level of gentle tannins, and a good balance between the high alcohol and the moderate to high acidity – a far more complete wine than a pure Mandilaria.

The vine is vigorous, productive, and resistant to most diseases, apart from downy mildew. It needs sites with low water stress and gravelly, infertile soils. It ripens after mid-September, but has to grow on relatively warm sites. In cases of cooler climates or higher altitudes, sugar accumulation is slowed down and it is possible that maturation will stop before reaching 12.5 degrees Baumé. In vintages and vineyards where Vertzami can reach thirteen degrees or higher, there is a full expression of the character of the grape, together with a most striking colour.

Vertzami is thought to have originated in Italy, but a popular synonym is Lefkaditiko, suggesting a homeland in Lefkada in the Ionian Sea. Apart from Lefkada, it is found in Agrinio (Etoloakarnania, Central Greece) and Preveza (Epirus). The producer that put the variety on the map is Antonopoulos Vineyards in Achaia, sourcing it from excellent vineyards in Lefkada and masterfully blending it with either Cabernet Franc or Mavrodaphne. The results should convince more growers to pay greater attention to Vertzami.

XINOMAVRO

Xinomavro is the exact opposite of Agiorgitiko. While the latter is relatively easy to grow, not capricious in the winery, and amazingly charming to drink, Xinomavro is an erratic diva. It is difficult to grow, since it is sensitive to arid conditions, powdery and downy mildew, as well as botrytis. It needs light to moderate soils and calcareous sites with excellent water retention capacities. It is very sensitive to potassium deficiency, a problem that is always reflected in extremely high levels of acidity in the grape, often exceeding 7.5 grams per litre. There is a narrow range of planting densities, around 4,000 vines per hectare, for achieving optimum results, while the same is true for fruit-load per vine, degree of pruning, and de-leafing. Canopy architecture is most important, favouring the vertical shoot positioning system. Even when expertly handled, Xinomavro's sugars and tannins can both fail to reach maturity, especially in cooler vintages or vineyards.

Clonal selection is most important for the variety. There are a number of clones available, all differing significantly in most characteristics, from flowering and ripening times, bunch and leaf sizes and shapes, berry colour and size, to wine quality features like colour stability and aromas. Five clones in particular have been identified, with the Velvendos clone, named after the eponymous lake in Kozani, Macedonia, at one extreme and the Gianakohori clone at the other. Velvendos needs cooler climates since it is the first to ripen, and gives a softer tannic structure and good fruit aromas. Gianakohori, isolated at the Ktima Kir Yianni winery (in Naoussa, Macedonia), is a complete contrast, being tannic, powerful, and aromatic, although not very fruity. The current mode of thinking suggests that it is difficult to find an ideal Xinomavro clone, and the best solution is to have a mix. Interplanting clones is an interesting concept, but can be practised only with clones maturing at the same rate, which limits possibilities.

In the winery, it is difficult to achieve sufficient colour without losing its characteristic, dry, angular, and unforgiving tannins. During ageing in oak or in bottle, Xinomavro's colour is relatively unstable, lacking depth and moving quickly into tawny. Recent experiments with pre-fermentation maceration, especially at Kir Yianni, have shown promise – a water-based, non-alcoholic solution with high levels of sulphur dioxide can help to extract riper tannins and more stable anthocyanins than macerating the grape solids in a fermenting, and therefore alcoholic, must. The traditionally made wines are often pale and advanced in colour, lacking sweet, fresh primary fruit on the nose and moving towards an eccentric spectrum of tomato, garbage, and dried plums, while acidity can be protruding on a tight, lean, and tannic palate. Still, Xinomavro is one of the noblest grape varieties of southern Europe.

Many Greek wine lovers consider Xinomavro to be the country's answer to Pinot Noir. Although there are similarities in the high acidity, pale and fast developing colour, together with a distinctive aromatic profile, Pinot Noir can be extremely charming when young, displaying an exotic, light, red berry, and fruit salad nose. To my mind, Xinomavro is closer to being the Greek Nebbiolo, having a similar tannic structure, as well as an absence of sweet and fresh elements in its aromas and flavours. Nevertheless, as is true with the best Barolo and Barbaresco, Xinomavro can give wines with a wonderful depth, complexity, and character. As proved by bottles of Boutari's Naoussa from the early 1970s, Xinomavro is not only capable of greatness, but is arguably the most ageworthy Greek red varietal, producing wines that not only develop, but improve over a period of several years, if not decades. In addition, the best wines of the 1990s, let alone the 2000s, will age far more gracefully than their predecessors, promising even more exciting wines in thirty years or so.

As with Agiorgitiko, Xinomavro is another polydynamic varietal, capable of producing wines in a variety of styles, as exemplified by the lovely rosés of the Amyntaio OPAP in Florina, Macedonia, which can be dry, medium-dry or medium-sweet, sparkling or still. The region also produces some excellent *blanc de noirs*. The second OPAP that consists of Xinomavro is Naoussa, in neighbouring Imathia, where the grape evokes the Italian connection. Many Naoussa growers are taking up the challenge, even if Ktima Alfa and Hatzis in the cooler Amyntaio region are already making a bid for excellence. In the Goumenissa OPAP of Kilkis (central Macedonia), Xinomavro is blended with the deeper-coloured but less noble Negoska. Together with the Stavroto and Krassato varieties, Rapsani in Thessaly is the fourth OPAP that contains Xinomavro – the only non-Macedonian OPAP, it is the warmest, being the most southerly. In addition, Xinomavro is widely planted all over northern Greece and therefore present in numerous TOs.

In a world where the most fashionable reds are the wines that look, smell, and taste like new-oak-aged Cabernet Sauvignon or Merlot, regardless of whether they contain the varieties or not, Greece will have a difficult job in promoting Xinomavro. A challenging task – but also a rewarding one.

This chapter has mentioned just a few of the Greek grape varieties. Numerous others exist, but are more or less localized and are therefore discussed in more detail in the chapters covering their respective regions.

INTERNATIONAL WINE GRAPES

White varieties

CHARDONNAY

Chardonnay first appeared in Attica in the mid-1960s, followed about a decade later by Dimitris Hatzimichalis' plantings in Atalanti, Central Greece. Diogenis Harlaftis planted Chardonnay in the early 1980s, but it wasn't until the early 1990s that Hatzimichalis made a significant commercial impact with the variety. Since then, it has proved as popular in Greece as elsewhere around the world. In less than two decades, the number of wineries crushing Chardonnay has risen to over 100, almost a third of the total, and the variety is found in more than half of the nation's wine regions.

Chardonnay gives the best results in cooler sites. Since the vine is not particularly drought-resistant, careful irrigation is important. It is one of the first varieties to bud in Greek vineyards, around mid-March, thus sites susceptible to spring frosts must be avoided. Most growers in Greece prefer the Dijon clones that ripen in late August or early September, although a few have chosen the earlier-ripening Champagne clones. These can be harvested in early August, in an attempt to expose the fruit to less total heat and therefore to get a more elegant character and faster flavour development.

Chardonnay is used as a blending component for large volume labels, where it is usually mixed with Greek varieties that need roundness on the palate. It is a permitted variety in many regional wine appellations across the country. Varietal Chardonnays can come in a number of guises. Some are fresh and simple, with or without any oak overtones, and are quite similar to the style of southern France. Many producers are using blends of oak-aged and stainless-steel matured Chardonnay, trying to avoid the heaviness of a totally oaked wine. The oak-aged examples, only a portion of which are barrel-fermented, rely heavily on new French oak. Malolactic fermentation is difficult, due to the low levels of malic acid present in the new wine, apart from in some cool areas in northern Greece.

It seems that there is some hesitation about top-drawer examples, with some wines being lean and reserved, and only very few going for the full-throttle, warm-climate style as illustrated by Californian examples. It is indicative that most Greek Chardonnay is around 12.5 per cent alcohol, a level attained even in the cool Chablis region, while few are above 13.5 per cent. Coincidentally, a top example of the variety in Greece, Antonopoulos Vineyards, is possibly the only one to regularly exceed fourteen per cent. Although several Greek Chardonnays develop well over two to three years, none have proved to be worth ageing more than that – apart from Skouras' Dum Vinum Sperum 2001, the first Stelvin-capped Greek wine. At the time of writing, this is still youthful and in need of more time to develop complexity.

GEWURZTRAMINER (TRAMINER)
There are very few hectares of Gewurztraminer in Greece and less than seven producers cultivate it on a noteworthy scale. This is fairly logical, as Gewurztraminer adapts to cool climates and high altitudes, so suitable vineyards are limited. Yet good Gewurztraminer is so seductive that every producer is tempted to try it out.

Gewurztraminer is grown in Arcadia (Peloponnese), Ioannina (Epirus), Imathia, and Florina (both in Macedonia), in sites where spring frosts are not the norm. The Katogi winery (now merged with Strofilia) insists on plain Traminer, the less aromatic clone, but most producers work with Gewurztraminer. It ripens in early September and, again, growers are extremely conservative with ripeness levels: in the much cooler Alsace region, the variety never fully develops its flavours before reaching twelve degrees Baumé (equal to about twelve degrees alcohol), with the best examples reaching fourteen degrees or more, while their Greek counterparts mostly stay around the 12.5 per cent alcohol mark.

Bearing that in mind, it is perhaps not surprising that most Greek Gewurztraminers lack the intense aromatic profile and the lusciousness of the palate encountered in the better illustrations of the variety worldwide. Nevertheless, a well-made Greek example can still be a good wine with wide appeal. Tselepos probably leads the way, while Katogi produces a good dry Traminer and a much better, late-harvest, semi-sweet version. Kir Yianni and Boutari use Gewurztraminer in blends, while Samartzis and the emerging Lalikos winery in Kavala, eastern Macedonia, are crafting some clean, spicy, and aromatic varietals. Greek Gewurztraminers are not expected to age, although it will be interesting to see how the late-harvest bottling from Katogi develops.

RIESLING
Only three Greek wineries declare any plantings of Riesling: Château Pigasos, Oinoforos, and Boutari, with only the first two producing varietal versions. The noblest white variety in the world dislikes too much heat and Greek examples lack the grace of wines produced in Alsace, Germany, Austria, or even cool climate Australia. The wines are usually harvested in late August and at around 12.5 degrees Baumé, where flavour development is limited to some fresh, moderately intense, lemony flavours. On the palate there is plenty of acidity and a relatively angular structure. The two single varietals produced so far come from cool sites, but Château Pigasos Riesling from the much cooler Naoussa region in Macedonia is broader and more forward than the Oinoforos version from the north Peloponnese. It would be interesting to have the Oinoforos Riesling harvested at much higher Baumé. Both will develop in the bottle for up to four years, although it is questionable whether they will improve significantly.

Judging from the national sales of the few hundred bottles of Greek or imported Riesling, it is logical to assume that promoting the variety to locals might be a difficult job. Greek wine drinkers get excited either by oaky and rather heavy styles such as oaked Chardonnay, or more flamboyant and aromatic whites, like Gewurztraminer. High acidity will always be a problem and, therefore, Riesling is likely to remain more of a curiosity, reserved for a small sector of the market.

SAUVIGNON BLANC

While Riesling is unlikely to make waves in the Greek market, Sauvignon Blanc is possibly the most influential addition to Greek vineyards, at least as far as white varieties are concerned. The number of producers crushing Sauvignon Blanc (around seventy) may not be as high as for Chardonnay, but the impact on tastes of producers and consumers alike is incomparable. One factor limiting the number of people growing the variety is that plantings are heavily tilted towards the north, while the warmer south shows a bit more resistance. In northern and cooler regions, Sauvignon is harvested in late August, usually around 12.5 degrees Baumé, but some producers are delaying harvest up to an additional degree.

Sauvignon Blanc, usually called just Sauvignon in Greece, was initially cultivated at Domaine Carras, in Halkidiki, Macedonia, and used to add aromas to some of the blended bottlings. A few years later, Nicos Lazaridis started using it further north at his winery in Drama. Lazaridis and winemaker Bakis Tsalkos blended it with Semillon, Assyrtico, and Ugni Blanc in Château Nico Lazaridi, but the style was more textured than profoundly aromatic, closer to an unwooded Semillon-dominated white Bordeaux than anything else. In the early 1990s, Nicos' brother, Kostas, and his oenologist, Vassilis Tsaktsarlis, created Amethystos. The blend was close to Château Nico Lazaridi but the approach was totally different: Sauvignon Blanc-dominated; stainless-steel fermented with carefully selected yeast strains; very aromatic, somewhere between the chalky notes of the Loire and the exotic fruit of the New World; fresh, light, and crisp, but very round on the palate. Amethystos was a whole new kind of wine for Greeks, and became an instant success. A number of producers and wine drinkers accused the new style of being "closer to cologne than wine", but many tried to emulate the character while using other varieties, or simply copied the blend.

While some producers favoured the aromatic, grassy, and fresh Sauvignon Blanc style, others developed premium oak-aged wines, calling them Fumé.

The aromas were toned down but enriched by wood, while the palate was broader and denser. There was opulence without the heaviness of an oaky Chardonnay. The term Fumé became very successful, but also controversial. Some people used it as a pointer for oak-aged whites from any variety, while others thought that Fumé should only be employed for barrel-aged Sauvignon Blancs. They suggested that a link could be drawn between Pouilly-Fumé – where Fumé implies a flinty and smoky character to its Sauvignon Blancs – and the toasty character of the oaky Greek version, without considering that most Pouilly-Fumé wines receive no oak treatment. Debates became so fierce that there were attempts to take the subject to court. Currently, the term is used by producers on both sides and there is no legal directive relating to its use. Generally, neither the Fumé nor the fresher versions are wines to keep for more than three years. However, the blended Château Nico Lazaridis or the same producer's varietal Magiko Vouno (Magic Mountain) have a proven track record of ageing more than five years without losing fruit or freshness.

SEMILLON

Semillon is another grape that, in a Greek context, seems more important than it is. There is limited hectarage, all belonging to estates rather than co-ops: Château Nico Lazaridi in Drama (Macedonia); Biblia Chora in neighbouring Kavala; Hatzimichalis (Central Greece), and Iassos on the Aegean island of Hios. All except Kostas Lazaridis are blending Semillon with other varieties, mainly to give depth and extract to Sauvignon Blancs. In Kostas Lazaridis' Château Julia Semillon, the grape is allowed to shine on its own, possibly illustrating that it could be a great alternative to Greek Chardonnay – it can have as much depth and extract without the heaviness, it is high in fruit flavours but not overly sweet, and most importantly, it has an exquisite affinity with oak.

It is difficult to see why the style and quality of great Barossa Semillons could not be emulated in several Greek cellars. A step in this direction was Ovilos, released in 2002 by Biblia Chora. A Semillon/Assyrtico blend, barrel-fermented and then barrel-aged for six months, Ovilos is released more than a year after harvest. The quality of Ovilos, as well as Rahes Galanou White, a Sauvignon Blanc/Semillon blend from Domaine Hatzimichalis, are clear signs of better things to come.

Semillon ripens a few days later than Sauvignon Blanc and some skin contact is allowed, to a varying extent, by most producers. It is relatively slow to develop flavours, but those waiting for 12.5 degrees Baumé or higher are richly rewarded. Semillon-based wines could prove to be some of the longest-living Greek whites.

TREBBIANO (UGNI BLANC)

The Trebbiano entry could easily be included in its entirety under the Château Nico Lazaridi entry. It is widely cultivated all over Greece and more than twenty wineries use it for the usual reason: Trebbiano is famous for its ability to produce high yields while achieving respectable sugar and acidity levels. It is easy to grow on most soils and most climates, especially on hot, fertile valley floors. Provided the vine receives plenty of potassium, a producer can harvest more than fourteen hectolitres per hectare in late September at 12.5 degrees Baumé and around 6.5 grams per litre of acidity. The wine is quite bland in character, but this can be turned into an advantage. In a judicious blend, Trebbiano augments the quantity, leaving smaller amounts of more temperamental grapes to dominate the personality.

In a move full of commercial stubbornness, Nicos Lazaridis and his son Federico became infatuated with the idea of creating a top quality varietal Trebbiano from their vineyards in Drama. Yields of around forty hectolitres per hectare, brief skin contact, ageing, plus lees contact in old French and American oak for six months followed by at least six months in bottle, led to the creation of Agora, later to be re-named plain Trebbiano. Despite spending over a year in the Lazaridis cellar, the wine remains a little unforgiving on release, and is dominated by oak. Given the chance to age for three years, it blooms, becoming nutty, rich, and complex, not unlike a white burgundy. It is undeniably one of the few Greek whites that can improve for five years and stay alive for a decade.

The winery also released an unusual late-harvest but dry Trebbiano Opsimo in 1998. The best Trebbiano parcels of the estate were left on the vine for three more weeks and the wine was fermented and aged for nine months in one hundred per cent new French oak. Opsimo has one per cent more alcohol, more oak flavours but, at the same time, the fruit is sweeter and more intense. It might be too early to truly evaluate its ageing potential, but the first vintages are still youthful and developing well.

VIOGNIER

Viognier is the most popular of the "minor" varieties and it already has a loyal following among both producers and consumers. There are around a dozen producers that deal with Viognier, most of whom are making varietal bottlings. There are, as expected, high-profile, premium offerings, again commanding more attention than their quantities justify. Evangelos Gerovassiliou in Macedonia and George Skouras in the Peloponnese, a personal friend of Marcel Guigal, planted the first vines in the early 1990s.

Apart from its tendency to give low yields, Viognier can easily grow in most of the cooler parts of Greece, and is usually harvested in late August or early September. The styles of Greek Viognier vary. Some producers are harvesting the grape at just 12.5 per cent potential alcohol, while Viognier is famous for needing very high levels of sugar ripeness to develop its typical, exotic aromatic character. Other wines are dominated by oak, mostly new and French. The third genre is high alcohol Viogniers, above 13.5 per cent, but with a lack of fruit concentration and depth. The most textbook-like Viognier is from Titos Eftihidis, but that does not mean there are not others that are equally good if a bit more idiosyncratic. For example, Kostas Lazaridis produced a good late-harvest, semi-sweet version, while Skouras' Cuvée Eclectique, made from grapes partially dried on the vine, is possibly one of the most peculiar Viogniers in the world.

Red varieties

CABERNET FRANC

Cabernet Franc in Greece has always had an identity crisis. It was initially planted because a number of producers wanted to create a fine "Greek Bordeaux", so the first violin of Cabernet Sauvignon was to be accompanied by Cabernet Franc and Merlot. Merlot managed to convince winemakers that it was worthy of being a soloist, but not Cabernet Franc – the reason must be more related to image than anything else, since it is easier to plant and grow than most high quality French varieties that have been imported into Greece. Cabernet Franc is less sensitive to arid conditions than Cabernet Sauvignon, it can grow on lower and warmer vineyards, and it ripens more than two weeks earlier. In general, Cabernet Franc is very reliable, year-in, year-out.

Even as a blending component, the variety adds complexity and its characteristic herbaceousness to many Bordeaux blends, especially those coming from Macedonia. In most wineries the blends are made before the barrel-ageing period, so it is difficult to single out the characteristics of pure

Cabernet Franc, but in general, French oak is preferred and justifiably so. Colour, tannins, and primary fruit intensity are usually lower than those of Cabernet Sauvignon, while acidity varies significantly from region to region.

Although Cabernet Franc in single varietal mode has yet to appear, at least in commercial quantities, two producers have created wines with a strong Cabernet Franc character: Antonopoulos Vineyards and Domaine Hatzimichalis. Antonopoulos has two wines that are not predominantly Cabernet Franc, but do display some of the distinctiveness of the grape: Cabernet Nea Dris, a very Australian-like effort with seventy per cent Cabernet Sauvignon and thirty per cent Cabernet Franc, and the elegant Gerontoklima Rematias Vertzami/Cabernet Franc, where the proportion of the latter is forty per cent. The wine closest to a varietal Cabernet Franc is Raches Galanou Red from Hatzimichalis, with fifty per cent Merlot added. The inaugural vintage, which was 2003, was put on the market in late 2004 and was one of the most interesting new releases of that year. From a legislational perspective, the variety is included in many regional appellations and, most importantly, in the OPAP blends from Côtes de Meliton on the Halkidiki peninsula in Macedonia.

CABERNET SAUVIGNON

Noted fine wine merchant and critic Jasper Morris MW once said that every dry white wine should be called Chardonnay. Then the back label could say: "This Chardonnay is seventy per cent Sauvignon Blanc and thirty per cent Semillon". If "red" and "Cabernet Sauvignon" were used instead, then his comment could describe how deeply fond of this grape Greece is. The variety is widely viewed as an archetype for high quality red wine. Many producers place their Cabernets at the top of their portfolios and most consumers are prepared to pay top dollar for Cabernet wines, regardless of whether they are made from the grape or not. The depth of colour, the intensity of ripe fruit, and the richness on the palate are, for the average Greek wine drinker, simply irresistible.

The first vines of Cabernet Sauvignon in Greece were planted in the early 1960s in Metsovo, Epirus, by the pioneering founder of Katogi winery, Evangelos Averoff, followed by around ten other producers during the 1970s. Most of them were using it as a part of a blend and bottling it under a brand name. Dimitris Hatzimichalis was the first to create a varietal Cabernet Sauvignon in the mid-1970s. It took half a decade to achieve success, but the impact of his wine was tremendous. In one stroke it made the variety almost a household name and introduced the concept of varietal wines to the market. The wine was relatively soft and very approachable, but still had enough varietal *typicité* and ageing capacity. Since then, Cabernet Sauvignon has been widely planted in all Greek wine-producing regions, to be used either alone or to boost Greek varieties, most notably Agiorgitiko. It is impressive how even a twenty per cent addition leads to a noticeable "Cabernetization" of a wine.

Cabernet Sauvignon in Greece is far more erratic than Cabernet Franc or Merlot. It is susceptible to most diseases and extremely sensitive to water stress, so it has to be confined to cooler and wetter areas with deep, relatively infertile, and well-drained soils. It is one of the best examples a Greek grower can use for persuading anyone that irrigation in Greek regions can significantly improve quality. In cases where the site is not perfect, the final ripening stages may be continuous if uneven, but development is full of stops and starts. Thus, the grower must be very observant and able to harvest the fruit within a very narrow window of opportunity. Despite the popularity of Guyot training in France, Cordon Royat is mostly preferred in Greece. The vine needs a healthy uptake of magnesium and, in initial plantings, rootstocks like SO4 created problems. Cabernet Sauvignon is harvested in early September and most producers look for potential alcohol levels around thirteen degrees Baumé, although an increasing number are aiming for higher ripeness, following the examples of Konstantinos Tsolis at Tsolis winery and Antonopoulos Vineyards (both in the Peloponnese).

Cabernet Sauvignon is permitted or recommended in almost half of fifty-two prefectures around the country, and close to 140 producers use it. The majority definitely lean towards the Old World style. It could be described as being similar to a warm-vintage Bordeaux, slightly fruitier and without reaching the same level of austerity. The best examples of such wines can age for up to a decade, but it is still rare for a wine to do more than just survive. The grape is included in the historic OPAP of Côtes de Meliton and in numerous TOs.

CARIGNAN

Carignan is one of the lesser-known, low-profile foreign varieties cultivated in Greece. Despite many imported counterparts, Carignan is perfectly suited to the hot and dry climate of the country. In fact, if planted in higher altitude sites or in northern slopes, it fails to ripen. It is cultivated in many regions of

Greece and is included in some appellations, as well as being recommended or permitted in more than fifteen prefectures. Carignan's most prestigious showing is as a component in the Mesenikolas OPAP in Thessaly.

The vine is vigorous, very productive, sensitive to botrytis and downy mildew, and extremely resistant to water stress. It adapts easily to a variety of soils, provided that these are warm and rich in potassium. Harvest takes place in mid- to late-September. Although Carignan can produce very good quality if yields are kept below forty hectolitres per hectare, most growers use it in a completely different way. Since it is easy to grow, and easy to achieve a good colour and thirteen degrees Baumé, it is used to help native varieties by adding alcohol and depth. There are no varietal bottlings and even finding pure Carignan *cuvées* in Greek barrel-ageing rooms is extremely rare.

CINSAULT

Cinsault was one of the first French varieties cultivated in Greece. It was planted before World War II, mainly in Macedonia and Thrace, but never became a popular choice. Today's plantings have shifted further south, and are for the most part in Crete and the Dodecanese islands.

As a vine, Cinsault is very well adapted to many Greek regions. Moderately vigorous, it is very productive, but sensitive to powdery mildew and botrytis. It dislikes sites that are humid, especially during spring, preferring dry, warm, sandy, and infertile soils. It is harvested during the first half of September. Cinsault responds very badly to high yields, producing grapes with low levels of sugars, phenolics, and acids. At fifty hectolitres per hectare, it improves in quality, but still lacks character. The very few (less than ten) producers that crush the variety usually macerate it with other grapes, like Grenache.

GRENACHE ROUGE

Grenache is a variety that Greek producers should pay more attention to. It is ideally suited to the terroir of numerous regions around the country and it can be used for a variety of wine styles, including excellent rosés, soft young reds, and even more extracted styles, either as a varietal or in a blend. More than forty producers use it, but mainly in blends, adding broadness on the palate and warmth to the fruit expression. The majority of Grenache plantings are less than twenty years old, so as the vines age and, hopefully, more producers become interested in working with lower yields, more promising results should be expected.

The vine grows on most soils, although dry, gravelly, warm sites give the best results. It is very vigorous, very productive, resistant to dry conditions, but sensitive to downy mildew and botrytis. The bud-break of Grenache is early, in mid- to late-March, and sites that might be susceptible to early spring frosts must be avoided. Windy areas in the spring are also problematic, since the variety is prone to poor fruit-set, although tipping – removing ten to twenty centimetres (three to eight inches) of the shoot tip – just after the start of flowering improves its success rate. It is sensitive to magnesium deficiency, so low magnesium-uptake rootstocks like Fercal can cause problems with chlorosis. It easily achieves thirteen degrees Baumé or higher and is harvested in early to mid-September. It oxidizes quickly and so lengthy maturation in barrel is to be avoided, except when blended with less fragile varieties, such as Syrah.

Evangelos Gerovassiliou in Macedonia and the Dougos family in Thessaly are possibly the only two producers that have created blends where the Grenache character comes across with clarity, depth, and concentration. Legally, these blends are permitted by the appellations of the Dodecanese, Thebes in Central Greece, and Epanomi near Thessaloniki.

MERLOT
The history of Merlot in Greece is much longer than most people might imagine. The variety was introduced together with Cabernet Sauvignon by pioneers like Yiannis Carras, Dimitris Katsaros, and Evangelos Averoff, who wanted to create Bordeaux-like blends. The variety stayed in the shadow of Cabernet for decades, until the early 1990s when Dimitris Hatzimichalis released a varietal Merlot. This first solo appearance was a serious attempt, being extracted, dense, and very oaky. The wine was aged for more than a year in new French oak – a rare and very expensive practice at the time.

Hatzimichalis' Merlot was also the first Greek wine that tried to convince consumers about its high quality and high price, not just by taste, but by packaging as well. Compared to what was available then on the market, the presentation was dramatic: a tall, heavy, thick black bottle with a very long neck, the company logo embossed on the wax capsule, a large, imposing label, and the longest cork ever seen in the Greek wine industry. The success was so impressive that most producers and consumers supposed that Merlot had to be at the very top of any product portfolio, only matched by the most expensive Cabernet Sauvignons.

More than a decade later, the image of the grape has expanded, from many soft, high volume varietals via the classic Bordeaux blends up to the ultra-premium Merlots. A blend that has proved popular is Xinomavro/ Merlot, with the latter giving body, fruit, colour, and softness to the more angular indigenous variety. Although the number of producers making these wines is not quite as high as those working with Cabernet, the proportion achieving a good level of quality is substantial. For the top *cuvées*, ageing in French oak is a major component of the style, and winemakers often prefer the more aromatic kinds of oak, like Limousin. Alcohol levels and maceration times have been raised over the years as more and more producers gain confidence with the variety. It is a part of many regional appellations, but mainly in northern Greece.

By Greek standards, the vine is not very vigorous or high-yielding and it needs a steady water supply throughout the growing season. There is a marked sensitivity to downy mildew and botrytis. Merlot needs cool, mountainous sites and deep, cool, clay-dominated soils. High vigour soils promote the incidence of *coulure* and poor fruit-set, especially with the Merlot clones preferred in Greece. The same problems arise in areas where rainy and cool weather is common around flowering. It starts its vegetative cycle very early, in mid-March, and is picked by early September.

MOURVEDRE

Officially, there are only two producers cultivating Mourvedre in Greece, Ktima Mercouri and Boutari, but other growers are trialling the varietal in Halkidiki and Crete. As a high-quality, truly Mediterranean variety, it is expected to be of increasing interest to Greek *vignerons*. The results so far are on a very small scale, but it seems that low-yielding Mourvedre vines grown on deep, calcareous, warm soils can result in wines with rich colour, alcohol exceeding thirteen percent, acidity close to six grams per litre, and a high level of tannins. Mourvedre could be a first-rate addition to many Greek blends.

The vine is vigorous and moderately productive, but sensitive to arid conditions, as well as powdery and downy mildew. It requires high levels of potassium and any deficiency is rapidly apparent. It is a late-ripening variety, starting the season in mid- to late-April, while harvest takes place after mid-September. Early autumn rains can create problems in the last stages of maturity, so it is important to avoid rootstocks that delay or prolong the growing cycle, like 420A.

REFOSCO

Refosco is one of the low-acreage but high-profile varieties in Greece. Despite hailing initially from northeastern Italy, in Greece it is always linked with Ktima Mercouri in Pyrgos, western Peloponnese, since it has been growing there for more than a century. The association is so strong that Refosco vines planted in the local area are called Mercoureiko (literally "belonging to Mercouri"). Even Haroula Spinthiropoulou, in her seminal *Oinopoiisimes Poikilies tou Ellinikou Ampelona* ("Wine Grape Varieties of the Greek Vineyard") includes Refosco under the "Greek Varieties" chapter and not under the "International Grapes cultivated in Greece". A handful of other producers have planted Refosco, but so far none has matched the haunting aromatic elegance and grace of Mercouri. The estate itself is releasing a semi-experimental bottling from the red-stem, small-berry clone, called Refosco dal Peduncolo Rosso, which is a totally different style from the standard bottling. Even though elegance takes a secondary role, it has a whole new dimension of depth, power, and fruit.

The vine is vigorous, moderately productive, and sensitive to powdery mildew. Budbreak takes place around mid-April and a quite long life-cycle ends with full maturity in early October. Alcohol levels are around 12.5 per cent, with moderately deep colour and acidity exceeding 5.5 grams per litre. The variety is included in the Mercouri tailor-made TO of Letrinoi, as well as in the nearby TO of Côtes de Petrotou.

SYRAH

Syrah was cultivated at Ktima Carras in Halkidiki for a number of years before it was decided to bottle it as a single varietal in the early 1990s. Carras' Syrah 1993 and 1994 were extremely promising wines, very close to the style of a northern Rhône. The quality of these efforts persuaded many producers to explore the potential of this variety. Currently, growers' interest in Syrah is accelerating at a remarkable pace, with more than seventy wineries crushing it in the 2003 vintage, even though the area it covers still lags some way behind Cabernet Sauvignon and Merlot. Nevertheless, many viticulturalists suggest that Syrah is far better suited to Greek vineyards than any Bordeaux variety.

The plant is vigorous, moderately productive, and sensitive to arid conditions, botrytis, and wind, since the young shoots break off easily. The sensitivity to dry conditions led many Greek growers to use the drought-tolerant 110R rootstock, but that increased the incidence of chlorosis. Syrah needs sites that are not prone to early spring frosts and that have deep, granite, or schist soils with good water retention capacity. Site selection is further complicated because low water stress tolerance is coupled with an aversion to high humidity. Its cultivation is quite demanding. For example, pruning systems are clone-specific and multi-clonal trials require a high level of skills from the vineyard workers. In addition, the phase between *veraison* and full maturity is very short so growers have to be vigilant. Harvest is in late August or early September, taking into account that most growers do not want to leave the fruit on the vine for much longer.

Excluding the first vintages of Carras, the style of Greek Syrah was initially indeterminate, with moderate alcohol levels, coarse or very short extractions, and excessive levels of new oak. By the late 1990s a steep and impressive learning curve had most people moving confidently towards a more New World style. There is higher alcohol, elevated but not aggressive extraction, and evident but not overwhelming oak (skilful blends of French and American wood), while fruit is polished, yet sweet, ripe, and intense. Greek varietals do develop for a number of years, but most reach their peak within the first five years. In certain ways, Syrah can boost local varieties in a much more interesting and complex manner than Cabernet Sauvignon, as illustrated by some Xinomavro/Syrah *cuvées* in Ktima Alpha in Amyntaion (northwestern Macedonia) and in Sotiris Lyrarakis' exceptionally distinctive Kotsifali/Syrah from Crete. The variety is included in some appellations, such as Adriani or Epanomi in Macedonia, and in the Mesenikolas OPAP in Thessaly.

This chapter has mentioned just a few of Greek vine varieties. Numerous others exist but are, more or less, localized and therefore discussed in more detail in the chapters in their respective regions. *See* Appendix 2 for a list of all other main indigenous grapes featured in this book.

Part II

The Regions

1

Thrace

Up in the east of the mainland, bordering Turkey and Bulgaria, Thrace is one of the most geographically remote regions of Greece, and socio-economic development was slow during the twentieth century. Poverty was a major problem, not only in the smallest villages but also in the relatively larger cities of Xanthi, Komotini, Alexandroupoli, and Soufli. The lack of a strong financial centre in the region was, and probably still is, evident. Local people are quick to admit that successive governments have put insufficient effort behind supporting private enterprise and pouring funds into the area – they often speak of a "forgotten Thrace". In the last few decades, the young generation has injected capital into the area, either during military service in one of the numerous camps here, or when studying in the newly founded universities. Still, this has only helped a small part of the population, and any local diffusion of money has been slow. So far in the first decade of the twenty-first century, the standard of living in Thrace is improving – getting closer to the national average in some sectors – and it should catch up with the rest of Greece before too long.

Books discussing the wine production of Greece do not usually devote a separate chapter to Thrace, normally including it with Macedonia. This underlines the small scale of production and the low importance placed on viticulture by the local community. In fact, Bellas winery in Soufli in the prefecture of Evros, established as recently as 1994, can lay claim to being one of the first producers in Thrace to make, bottle, and sell wine beyond the local market.

Yet wine production in Thrace has an illustrious past. Throughout Classical and well into Byzantine times, wine produced in the area was famous, especially in the town of Maronia, southern Rodopi, and could

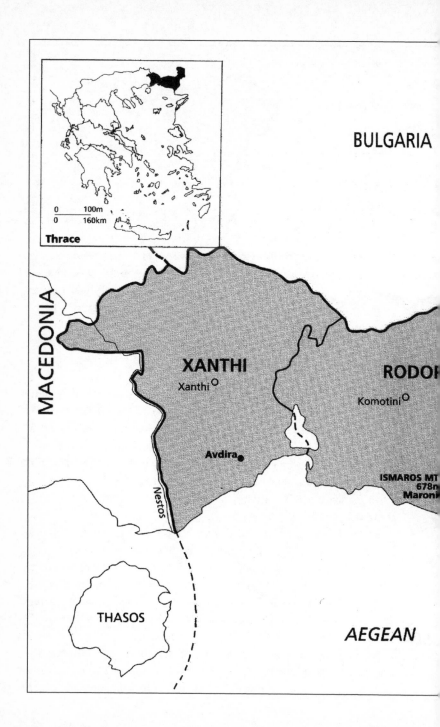

BULGARIA

MACEDONIA

Thrace

0   100m
0   160km

XANTHI

Xanthi ○

RODOF

Komotini ○

Avdira●

Nestos

ISMAROS MT
678n
Maroni

THASOS

AEGEAN

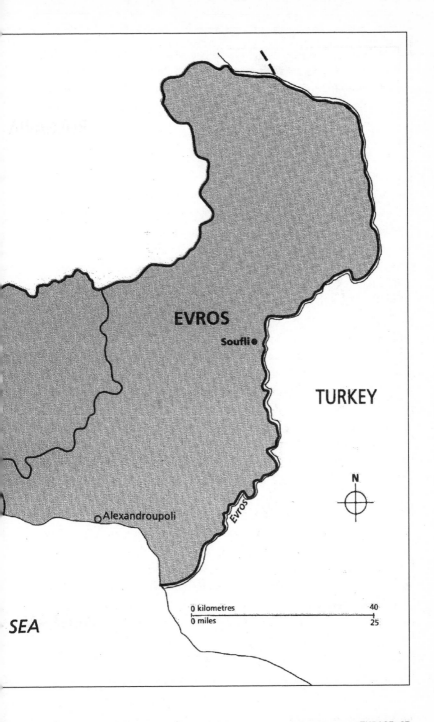

EVROS

Soufli●

TURKEY

N

oAlexandroupoli

Evros

0 kilometres   40
0 miles   25

SEA

demand high export prices. After all, this was supposed to be the wine that Odysseus used to fool Polyphemus, the most famous Cyclops, by getting him drunk so that he could escape.[1] Mythology aside, there is a wealth of archaeological evidence showing a thriving wine industry, and *Maronios Oenos*, wine from Maronia, and *Ismarios* from the eponymous mountain standing on the east of town, were the first wines in Ancient Greece to become famous.

The decisive move away from viticulture happened during the second half of the nineteenth century. Local landowners realized that the lack of any substantial wine businesses nearby was making table- and wine-grape production financially unfeasible. Instead, tobacco, sugar cane, and cotton were the products that could guarantee significant returns, and certain sites in central Xanthi and Rodopi proved particularly suitable for the production of top-quality tobacco. High demand for these products, plus a strong local Muslim population, pushed viticulture into the shadows.

Vines for wine-grape production continued to exist, but only on a small scale and mainly for domestic consumption. From the 1920s onward, the first waves of refugees from eastern Thrace – where vine-growing had been a major part of the culture – slightly reinvigorated wine consumption. Nevertheless, the impact was far less evident than the boost these people gave to wine further west in Macedonia. Quantities produced were low and minute volumes were traded, since the relatively insignificant demand was satisfied with wines from the nearby islands of Thassos and Bozcaada (Turkey), from Asenovgrad (in Bulgaria), Kirklareli (in Turkey) and, to a lesser degree, from Kavala in Macedonia. Another factor limiting the expansion of wine culture was the fact that the Muslim population preferred Ouzo to wine or grape-related distillates.

From the 1970s, the tobacco, cotton, and sugar-cane crops favoured by growers around Thrace ceased to be popular among national traders, who could find alternative and cheaper sources in Eastern Europe. Consequently, demand decreased. People started evaluating other ways of using their land and vineyard plantations emerged as one option. However, at that time the big companies of central Macedonia were not interested in buying fruit from Thrace; meanwhile producers in Kavala and Drama were small, so their needs were met by relatively local vineyards. In addition, building a new

1. Homer, *The Odyssey,* Book IX.

modern winery, with its high initial capital and heavy running costs, proved out of reach for all interested parties – particularly since the possibility of EC funding was remote.

A NEW BEGINNING

However, the situation was set to change. In the the early 1990s, established wine producer Evangelos Tsantalis decided to move into Thrace. In the Maronia region it established a joint venture with a local businessman Apostolos Tassou. The new venture, Maronia AE, needed a legislational framework within which to work. This was soon after the laws governing regional TOs had been introduced (*see* Appendix 1), so the required paperwork was swiftly submitted in order to apply for the first TOs of Thrace. By early 1997, the TOs of Thrace, Ismaros, and Avdira were in place.

To ensure Tsantalis had enough fruit, Maronia AE began collaborating with other local landowners. Tsantalis provided the funds, but most importantly, his chief viticulturalist, Giorgos Salpigidis, and his hugely experienced team supplied the know-how. Great efforts were expended in conducting workshops for potential growers, offering extensive seminars on vine cultivation, integrated pest management, and the exact variety-specific standards Tsantalis used to evaluate, price, and buy grapes. The first Maronia AE wines were warmly received in a number of export markets as well as by Greek consumers, and booming sales created a strong demand for local grape production. More and more people were persuaded to switch from other crops to vines and, in just a few years, twenty-five hectares of vineyards were under contract to the company. These developments in the Maronia region vividly illustrate how a large wine company can influence the fate of a poor agricultural region and its people.

NEW FACES AND OUTSIDE INFLUENCES

Currently, the growth of new plantings and new production units gathers momentum by the day. It is inevitable that, increasingly, more people will be attracted into viticulture and more grape-growers will be keen to start their own enterprises instead of selling on their harvest, especially while the public status of wine producers continues to rise. For example, the Zgouridis family has made substantial investments in vineyards close to the village of Avdira in south Xanthi. They believe that building a winery can wait until the vines reach maturity, so their cellar is still unfinished, but will be ready to receive the 2006 vintage. Meanwhile the wines are made in Fountis winery in Naoussa.

In the same region, Lazaros Avramidis has been making a living out of wine for many years – not producing it, but selling it through his excellent shop in the town of Xanthi. After the establishment of the Avdira TO in 1997, Avramidis felt more secure about acquiring three hectares and started planting vines himself. In early 2004, at least four wineries were planned or under construction near Xanthi, something that, even ten years ago, would have seemed unthinkable.

Progress is made not only in new ventures but by putting into use available know-how. Melina Tassou, daughter of Apostolos Tassou, decided to start her own wine enterprise in Komotini, Rodopi. Her impressive CV – viticultural studies in Thessaloniki, oenology studies at the University of Bordeaux, harvest work in Bordeaux, Burgundy, and at Brown Brothers in Victoria, Australia – could have guaranteed her a job in any Greek winery. However, she believes that top-quality wine can be produced in Thrace and has established Kikones winery five kilometres (three miles) from Komotini. There are plans for ten hectares of vines; the initial plots are planted with French varieties, but some Greek grapes will follow. The small winery is fashioned in a Burgundian style and volumes will be kept low, since manual destemming and *pigeage* are considered vital. The first vintage was 2004, so by the time this book is published, we will be able to try the Kikones wines for ourselves.

Even on such a small scale, this unique mix of wine-related influences, mainly from the north and the east, has created a strong identity for Thrace. This is shown by the selection of grape varieties that appear throughout the region, even though there may be some confusion about what is being grown in some old vineyards.

Mavroudi of Thrace, for example, the tannic, intense, small-berried, low-yielding local strain of Mavroudi, is believed to be closer to the Mavrud found in Asenovgrad, near Plovdiv across the border in Bulgaria, than other clones found in the Peloponnese, Attica, Central Greece, Macedonia, or even Albania. The white Zoumiatiko, found also in Macedonia, is Bulgaria's Dimiat, the country's most planted indigenous white variety, as well as Yugoslavia's Smederevka. The important pink-skinned Pamidi, sometimes called Pamiti, is Bulgaria's major indigenous variety Pamid. A key difference is that most of the Pamid production in Bulgaria is geared towards soft, indifferent reds, because of the variety's very low level of phenolics, while most producers in Thrace harvest Pamidi with higher sugar levels and use it as a blending component, mainly but not exclusively for rosés. Bulgaria's influence extends still further, as the Cinsault found in Thrace was probably imported from there.

Melnik is a powerful, ageworthy, tannic red grape grown around the ancient town of Melnik, Bulgaria, close to the border, so it seems certain that at least a few Melnik vines must exist in some of Thrace's established vineyards. Interestingly, the noted writer and critic, Jancis Robinson MW, says that Melnik wines "taste more Greek... than typical of modern Bulgaria".[2] So far, however, growers have done little work on identifying whether the local vines are actually Melnik – a pity, given the excellent track record of the variety in producing the most ageworthy Bulgarian wines just a few kilometres away.

Viticulturalists believe that there are methods by which someone can "sense" the way a specific terroir will "accept" vine-growing, even if there has been no previous vine-related history. One of the best clues is the percentage of newly planted young vines that fail to survive the two first winters. The quality of vines acquired from the nursery, soil preparations, and worker skills do play a part, but once these issues and irrigation are taken into account, soil, climate, and weather are the most important factors. Failure rates that exceed ten per cent can be a sign that, for some reason, the area has a limited affinity for viticulture. Levels close to six per cent can be considered normal. From the outset, plantings in Ismaros (Rodopi) and Avdira (Xanthi), a surprisingly encouraging success rate of ninety-eight per cent or higher was observed. Even if Thrace has not been exploited by wine producers for centuries, it seems that its terroir has great potential for the future.

VITICULTURE

Soils across the region vary widely, with the majority able to support vine-growing. Vineyards near the Aegean coast have deeper soils, but there is more sand and the drainage is excellent. Further inland there is more clay and the fertility is higher, while the higher sites of Rodopi are less productive and more gravelly. The area around Evros is the most fertile, since the Evros River on the border with Turkey has created deep layers of rich alluvial soils that are high in organic content.

2. Robinson, J, *The Oxford Companion to Wine,* Oxford University Press, 1999.

On the southern slopes of Rodopi and the plains of Xanthi and Komotini, rainfall is the limiting factor for grape production. Here, cold air currents flowing down from the north mix with the warm, humid streams coming in from the Aegean – known locally as the Samothrakeotis wind since it originates from the island of Samothraki. This sudden drop in temperature causes a build-up of humidity, resulting in high levels of rainfall throughout the year, especially during the crucial summer period. Therefore achieving maturity is problematic, apart from specific sites with drier meso-climates, such as the village of Iasmos, twenty-five kilometres (almost sixteen miles) west of Komotini. Only a small strip of land by the coast, running east from Kavala (over the border in Macedonia) to Maronia in southern Rodopi and extending inland for up to ten kilometres (six miles), has a summer level of rainfall that allows grape-growing. The shoreline itself is very arid and can receive as little as ten millimetres (0.4 inches) of rain between May and September, making irrigation crucial.

High humidity causes frequent problems with fungal diseases, and Thrace is one of the most susceptible areas in all of Greece for downy mildew. But careful vineyard work and the use of open canopies can prove sufficient to avoid trouble in most cases and most vintages. Most of the vineyards near to the coast benefit from relatively low summer/winter and day/night temperature differences.

The Maronia vineyards on Ismaros Mountain boast a slightly different terroir. Just one to four kilometres (0.6–2.5 miles) from the coast, plantings are at an average altitude of 350 metres (1,148 feet). This ensures a mean summer temperature that is at least 2°C (3.6°F) lower compared with vineyards at sea level, and therefore slightly higher acidity overall and far better anthocyanin levels in red varieties.

RECENT CHANGES

Viticulture in Thrace has changed significantly over the last ten years. Traditionally, the vines were free-standing, with the trunk rarely exceeding seventy-five centimetres (2.5 feet) in height, and planting densities ranged between 3,000–4,000 vines per hectare. Spur pruning was preferred and canopy humidity could be a problem in sites with high humidity or high rainfall. The most common treatment was, and still is, dusting with sulphur.

Wine-growers in Thrace were not very willing to take risks, so the varieties planted were harvested before the end of September. The levels of maturity sought were quite conservative, rarely exceeding 12.5 per cent potential alcohol, while yields regularly exceeded eighty-four hectolitres per hectare (twelve tonnes per hectare).

The arrival of Tsantalis in the early 1990s was widely considered a milestone, and soon new private ventures began investing in the area. The viticultural approach started changing, even for long-established growers. New plantings embraced the Cordon de Royat training system, and although planting densities remained the same, the trunks became shorter. This helped improve the air circulation within the canopy, and while yields stayed the same, ripeness was improved. Drip irrigation is now widely practised in the regions where summer rainfall is low, such as the coastal zones.

WINE REGIONS

Although Thrace does not have any quality wine appellations of its own (OPEs/OPAPs), it does have three regional wine appellations (TOs). The largest of these is the TO of Thrace, covering the whole region and all styles of still wine. Permitted varieties are a mix of Greek and French cultivars, very much based on the commercial attractiveness of these grapes and not on what has been grown traditionally.

The TO of Ismaros has been tailor-made to the needs of the Tsantalis and Maronia AE winery. The start was a bit shy and the base of the varietal mix was Zoumiatiko, Roditis, Limnio, and Grenache, but revisions have been and will be made, since Tsantalis' focus on the Maronia venture is the production of varietal wines. The Avdira TO is the least open to French varieties and Zoumiatiko, Roditis and Pamidi have to be at the heart of any Avdira TO wine.

Thrace TO

White still: dry; semi-dry; semi-sweet.
Rosé still: dry; semi-dry; semi-sweet.
Red still: dry; semi-dry; semi-sweet.
White varieties: Assyrtico; Athiri; Chardonnay; Malagousia; Moschomavro; Sauvignon Blanc; Roditis.
Red varieties: Cabernet Sauvignon; Carignan; Grenache Rouge; Limnio; Limniona; Merlot; Syrah.

Ismaros TO, Rodopi prefecture

White still: dry; semi-dry; semi-sweet.

White varieties: Zoumiatiko and Roditis must be at least fifty per cent of the blend, the balance being other local recommended and permitted grape varieties.

Rosé still: dry; semi-dry; semi-sweet.

Rosé varieties: Roditis and Grenache Rouge must be at least fifty per cent of the blend, the balance being other local recommended and permitted grape varieties.

Red still: dry; semi-dry; semi-sweet.

Red varieties: Limnio and Grenache Rouge must be at least fifty per cent of the blend, the balance being other local recommended and permitted grape varieties.

Avdira TO, Xanthi prefecture

White still: dry; semi-dry; semi-sweet.

White varieties: Zoumiatiko and Roditis must be at least fifty per cent of the blend, the balance being other local recommended and permitted grape varieties.

Rosé still: dry; semi-dry; semi-sweet.

Rosé varieties: Pamidi and Roditis must be at least fifty per cent of the blend, the balance being other local recommended grape varieties.

Red still: dry; semi-dry; semi-sweet.

Red varieties: Pamidi must be at least fifty per cent of the blend, the balance being other local recommended grape varieties.

EVROS

The final zone of grape production in Thrace is the eastern prefecture of Evros. It has yet to be awarded a TO, due either to a lack of strong local interest, or perhaps a lack of capital with which to pursue such a quest with the Ministry of Agriculture. Nevertheless, the area between Soufli and Orestiada, some fifty kilometres (thirty-one miles) further north, is not insignificant in terms of grape production, with more than 500 hectares of vineyards.

Viticulture in Evros can be divided into two distinct regions. The area closest to the coast and around Alexandroupoli shares a common climate with other coastal parts of Thrace, although here the inland plain is not as deep as in Komotini and Xanthi. The other viticultural region, along the Evros River following the border with Turkey, is a flat area where the altitude rarely exceeds seventy metres (230 feet) above sea level. This part, one of the most northern wine-growing districts in Greece, is not as cold as one might expect, since the close proximity of the Evros River does moderate any extremes of temperature. In general, the mean temperatures during the vine-growing season are around 3°C (5.4°F) lower than in Maronia or Avdira in Rodopi, while other areas further west on the same latitude, in the northern part of the Drama prefecture, are the coldest parts of Greece. In Soufli and Orestiada, grape sugar levels are lower than those achieved in regions closer to the coast, and in cold years with late vintages, a large proportion of the late-ripening varieties, like the Opsimo of Soufli, will struggle to achieve ripeness and to mature properly. Wines above thirteen per cent alcohol are difficult to produce.

A fresh style

It is too early to try and define a specific style of wine produced in Thrace. There is only a handful of wineries in the region, most of which are relatively recently established, and their *modus operandi* can vary hugely. In the 1970s, the few wines produced were either very light reds and rosés, lacking fruit, extract, and structure, or dilute, non-aromatic, and slightly coarse whites. Nowadays, the character of a wine is more likely to display the ability or approach of the winemaker than any notion of a "Thracean terroir". What modern wines do have in common is a freshness of fruit that is usually not found in the warmer regions of Greece such as Crete or the Peloponnese. Nevertheless, the lack of a regional *typicité* has not been an obstacle for the best producers to craft some exciting and most promising wines.

PRODUCERS

BELLAS WINERY
Thessi Profitis Ilias, Soufli, Evros, 646 00.
Tel: +30 255 402 4041; Fax: +30 255 402 4042.
Vineyards owned: 12ha; under contract: 50ha; production: 2,000hl.
A relatively small family venture that started in 1994, Bellas was the first organized attempt to establish a winery/distillery in the Evros region. The Bellas brothers, Grigoris and Thanassis, first focused on the production of tsipouro, the distillate from pressed grapes and stems, which was an instant success in the local market. Although wines were added to the company product range just a few years later, Bellas Tsipouro is still the most popular

line and one of the very few grape-related products from this part of Greece to be found in Athens.

The Bellas family cultivates several rare and local varieties, along with Cabernet Sauvignon, Damiatis, and a Soufli Muscat. These include Neroproimia ("the early ripeness of water"), Karnahalades (a group name for a family of varieties), Mavroudi of Thrace, and Opsimo, "the late ripener" of Soufli. The last one is probably the most noble of these, but it is difficult to decide if there is any real potential.

The style of wines produced is both individual and a bit old-fashioned – light in colour and body, with reserved aromas and a relatively low level of light fruit. The Bellas range is straightforward, with three blends, White, Rosé, and Red, finishing off with a rich, traditional but quite stylish, Retsina.

CELLARS OF EVROS
Winery: Marassia Trigonou 680 07.
Head office: Evritika Kellaria AE, PO Box 102, Orestiada, Evros 682 00.
Tel: +30 255 208 5501; Fax: +30 255 208 5201; Email: ebritiko@otenet.gr
Vineyards under contract: 7ha; production: 1,500hl.
Evritika Kellaria was established in 2003 in Orestiada, "the town of Orestis", which lies in the northeast of Thrace, some fifty kilometres (thirty-one miles) north of Soufli. The winery lies at an altitude of fifty metres (164 feet), just 300 metres (984 feet) from the border with Turkey and 1.5 kilometres (9.3 miles) away from Adrianoupolis. The winery is a joint venture between Vassilis Harovas, a mechanical engineer from Macedonia, and three members of the Arvanitidis family: brothers Alexandros and Stavros, and their cousin Vassilis. The Arvanitidis family has a thirty-five-year history of producing tsipouro and other spirits and liqueurs, but the first time they produced wine under the Cellars of Evros brand was in 2003. The quantity produced at first was 1,500 hectolitres, which rose to almost 2,000 hectolitres in 2004, and the final target is set at 3,000 hectolitres. Harovas believes that, even with such a small-scale production, expanding sales beyond the local market and, if possible, developing an export business are key priorities.

With the export market in mind, the vineyards have been planted with Chardonnay, Sauvignon Blanc, Merlot, and Cabernet Sauvignon. In order to ensure top-quality stock, young plants have been imported directly from France. Some local varieties, like Pamidi, will be planted in the future, but at this initial stage, they are not seen as crucial. The yields range between sixty and seventy-five hectolitres per hectare, depending on the variety and vintage, although the vineyard's low planting density has to be taken into account when evaluating grape load per vine – narrow tractors were not readily available in the region, so the vineyard design had to accommodate a required row-to-row distance of 2.5 metres (8.2 feet), which resulted in a vine density of around 3,000 vines per hectare.

The climate is generally dry during summer and autumn, and the levels of rainfall are so low that irrigation is needed. The drip-irrigated vineyards that supply the Cellars of Evros lie between the Evros River and its smaller neighbour, the Arvos, so relative humidity is high. Despite that, downy mildew and other fungal problems are rare and therefore organic cultivation is not only feasible, but reasonably trouble-free. Nevertheless, there are no plans at the Cellars of Evros for conversion to organic status. Harovas believes that organic cultivation, and especially the organic accreditation system, is nothing more than a marketing trick.

The wines from the Cellars of Evros are straightforward, well-made, and possess a good varietal definition with an added touch of elegance. The value-oriented line, named after the winery, consists of two single-varietals, a Merlot and a Sauvignon Blanc, both vinified and matured for a few months in stainless steel. The top tier wines, a stainless-steel-fermented Chardonnay and a Merlot aged in new oak for six months, are called Sta Vimata tou Orfea, meaning "in the steps of Orpheus". An oak-aged Cabernet Sauvignon will be a late reserve bottling, but a brand name has yet to be decided.

DOMAINE VOURVOUKELI

Domaine Vourvoukeli, Avdira, Xanthi.
Tel: +30 254 107 5098; Fax: +30 254 106 9216;
Website: www.domaine-vourvoulkeli.gr; Email: info@domaine-vourvoulkeli.gr
Vineyards owned: 7.5ha; production: 150hl.

Fyssis Ampeloessa was one of the first wine producers to be established in Avdira, with the first harvest in 2002. The annual production is less than 20,000 bottles and there are no plans to increase it significantly in the future. Instead, there is a determination that this will stay a boutique venture. Fruit is sourced mostly from owned vineyards that are about as close as one could get to the sea. Four hectares are located three kilometres (1.86 miles) from the shore, while the other 3.5 are just 500 metres (1,640 feet) from the beach. With such proximity to the coast, there are fears that salinity could be a problem in the long run, but so far no significant effect has been observed.

The organically cultivated vineyards are predominantly planted with Greek varieties, plus Sauvignon Blanc, Syrah, Merlot, and Cinsault. Assyrtico was brought in from Santorini and a Roditis clone came from the Peloponnese (rather than the nearer vineyards of Macedonia). Zoumiatiko plantings are noteworthy, but Pamidi is the most widely used local variety. Pamidi is valued for its ability to reach high sugar levels, fourteen degrees Baumé or higher, but it is always blended with other, more flavourful varieties. The yields here are much lower than those in the Ismaros TO in Rodopi. Excluding Pamidi, which can reach sixty hectolitres per hectare, the usual yield is thirty-five hectolitres per hectare or lower, and owner Nikos Vourvoukelis – who runs the winery with his sister Flora as the general manager – believes that this level is too stressful for the vines. An increase of up to thirty per cent would prove beneficial to both quality and, of course, quantity.

There is a commitment to local grape varieties, but in Thrace, this comes at a price. Cuttings from Zoumiatiko and Pamidi have been painstakingly gathered from old vineyards in the region and sent to Italy for nursery grafting – a process that has taken months and cost far more than simply planting with readily available varieties. Following this philosophy, the most remarkable part of the vineyards is a small section that constitutes a local viticultural archive. Vourvoukelis' father originally planted about 100 vines from local but unidentified varieties that he found in old vineyards planted long before cuttings from other parts of Greece were introduced on a large scale. This plot is cultivated in a uniform way: harvested in one pass and all grapes are poured into one of the larger blends. The current situation prohibits closer research into what exactly is planted in this mixed plot, but hopefully this will change. The underlying idea is that lesser-known varieties could be the key to success. There seems little point in producing another Sauvignon Blanc in Greece, even if it is a good one – an emphasis on local or rare cultivars is possibly the only way forward.

The first crop of any commercial significance was in 2003. At the moment, the wines are made in the Mavromatis winery in Kavala, Macedonia, but an Avdira cellar will be ready for the 2006 harvest. Christos Kanellakopoulos, head winemaker of the Santorini Cooperative, was initially hired to design the new winery and is now working as a consultant winemaker. Kanellakopoulos acknowledges that making wine in rented space within another winery is not easy. The available resources and equipment are divided between two different winemakers, and most of the time, two different, if not contrasting, philosophies. In these circumstances, an oenologist has to play safe. There is less room for experimentation, while control, reassurance, and reliability become prime concerns. Both Kanellakopoulos and Vourvoukelis believe that the Avdira winery will be instrumental in fine-tuning the styles of the existing products and beginning work on more exciting projects, such as producing single-varietals from the rarest native varieties, or a blanc de noir from Pamidi.

The wines of Fyssis Ampeloessa are well-made and clean in style, although the fruit is not emphasized. There are two brand names used: the upmarket Lagara (meaning "pure liquid") and Avdiros. Lagara White is a blend of seventy-five per cent Sauvignon Blanc and twenty-five Assyrtico, co-fermented when the maturity of each variety allows. Lagara Red is aged for ten months in new French barriques. It is mainly Merlot, although up to fifteen per cent of the blend is Pamidi and Cinsault. In the Fyssis Ampeloessa vineyards, Cinsault is very close to Pamidi in flavour profile, and both cultivars have a very pale colour. However, Cinsault is a very late ripener that is harvested well into October and, even at that stage, the sugar level rarely exceeds 11.5 degrees Baumé.

The Avdiros range is simpler in style. Avdiros Red is mostly Limnio, with a small addition of Pamidi and Cinsault, and is aged for eight months in American oak, half of which is new. An interesting Avdiros Rosé is mainly Pamidi along with fifteen per cent Syrah for colour and spice. The range also includes a straightforward white called Thracekos Roditis.

TSANTALI/MARONIA AE

Maronia, Rodopi, 694 00.
Tel/Fax: +30 253 302 1503; Website: www.tsantali.gr.
Vineyards owned: 50ha; under contract: 25ha; production: 5,300hl.
See also Tsantali entries on pages 139, 162, 213.

It is clear that a large company like Tsantali would never start a project in a region with no recent viticultural history if there was no evidence of significant potential. Wines from Maronia and Ismaros were extremely successful in ancient times, and this solid past was a perfect match for Evangelos Tsantalis' plans to develop modern wines destined to compete in foreign markets. For this he required an underdeveloped, and therefore cheaper, region. The project began in the early 1990s with Maronia AE, with

Tsantalis and Apostolos Tassou as the founding partners, on an eighty/ twenty share split. In January 2004, Tassou sold his stake to Tsantalis, apart from 1,000 shares which he kept for sentimental reasons.

With an average altitude of 350 metres (1,150 feet) and a location less than two kilometres (1.2 miles) from the sea, the vineyards in Maronia have an unusual terroir. These south-facing hills of Ismaros form an amphitheatre overlooking the Aegean Sea, receiving an average of 1,750 hours of sunshine between April and October, together with cooling breezes from the sea, as well as the Samothrakeotis wind. These factors cause considerable day/night temperature variations that delay ripening to a substantial degree. Often, varieties that have already been harvested and fermented in the Tsantali Aghios Pavlos winery in Halkidiki still need a few more days hang-time on the vine in Maronia. The upper part of the hill, where the soil is both stony and high in limestone content, is planted with white grape varieties. In the lower vineyards the temperatures are, on average, a full degree higher at 14.5°C (58°F), and the soils are heavier. Here the sugar and anthocyanin levels increase faster, making red varietals the grapes of choice in these plots.

Initially, the scope of Tsantali's Maronia venture was to make varietal wines, with a large percentage of them aged in oak. The average age of the vines is still low – the first plantings were only in 1992 – but as the plants grow older, reserve wines will start being produced. The focus is on international grape varieties, mainly Chardonnay, Viognier, Sauvignon Blanc, Merlot, Syrah, and Grenache Rouge, together with some plantings of Malvasia, Roditis, and Limnio, together with the local Ermogennitiko. The latter variety, grown almost exclusively by Tsantali, produces fruit with a vivid, violet-red colour, and good levels of acidity and sugar content, suggesting that it has the potential to produce wines of very good quality. Nevertheless, current acreage and the youth of the vines allows only micro-vinifications at the moment, so it will be a few years before we see the first bottlings of Ermogennitiko varietals.

Malvasia was still relatively rare in Greece, so planting it in Thrace was a controversial move. *Malvasios oenos* or *Monemvassios oenos* was one of the most famous wine in Greece's viticultural past (*see* page 24) and it has long been associated with the town of Monemvasia in Laconia, Peloponnese, although a lot of exported Malvasia wine was made in Crete, Santorini, and other Aegean islands. It is not clear if the wine was produced from certain vine varieties, if it was a wide-ranging, ill-defined blend, or if the name was used to declare an origin or just a style. In the country's recent viticultural history, no varieties called Malvasia have been found, despite an impressive web of numerous Malvasia varieties across southern Europe, from Collio in Italy to Colares in Portugal and Madeira, well into the Atlantic.

Whatever the situation, Greek authorities believed that Malvasia had to stay linked with the Laconia region, especially Monemvasia or Crete. Therefore, plantings in Thrace were strongly discouraged, even if cuttings destined for all Greek regions, including Laconia, were being imported from Italian nurseries. Quite a few producers faced strong resistance when they decided to plant Malvasia, including Babatzimopoulos in Macedonia and Hatzimichalis in Central Greece, but the team at Tsantali managed to succeed in creating a framework that allowed Malvasia to be produced.

Currently, harvested grapes are transported in small crates to the main Tsantali winery in Aghios Pavlos, Halkidiki, Macedonia, but there are plans for a winery in Maronia. Selection by the harvesters and maintaining low temperatures during transportation ensures that the quality of fruit is not compromised. In addition, the wines produced from Maronia grapes, such as Chardonnay, Viognier, and even the highly aromatic Malvasia, can tolerate a degree of extraction and skin contact. All whites undergo some oak ageing. The highest-volume white, Chardonnay, is fermented half-and-half in small oak casks and stainless-steel vats. A small production of two varietal wines from Viognier and Malvasia is grouped under the brand name Vine and Oak and aged in mostly new 300-litre oak casks. There is a quite distinctive, intense character here, although the oak is a bit overpowering, at least during the first few months after release.

The only red wine from Maronia available in commercial quantities is the Ismaros TO Syrah. It has been by far the most successful, with the UK retail chain Oddbins listing it almost on release. It shows clear varietal character and a well-defined but balanced oak presence from ageing for eight months in 300-litre new Alliers oak casks. The tannic structure is moderately dense but soft and charming. Taking into account that the vines are young – not yet a decade old – that grapes are harvested at a modest thirteen degrees Baumé, and macerated for only seven days, the Tsantali Ismaros TO Syrah has a remarkable depth of character, and excellent ageing potential. It seems that future bottlings can only add to the excitement.

2

Macedonia

The northern borders of Macedonia are framed by Albania, the Former Yugoslavian Republic of Macedonia (FYROM), and Bulgaria, with Thessaly to the south, Epirus to the southwest, and Thrace further east. Southern Macedonia meets the Aegean Sea, with the Halkidiki peninsula extending into it, but – with the exception of Thassos, off the Gulf of Kavala – Macedonia's coastline is unusually island-free.

The department is divided into three sub-segments: western Macedonia with the prefectures of Kastoria, Florina, Grevena, and Kozani; eastern Macedonia with Kavala and Drama; and the remaining seven prefectures in central Macedonia. The general topography of Macedonia is much more gentle than the rest of the mainland, with scenery reminiscent of the coastal regions of Bulgaria. However, Macedonia is a large department and there are variations. Similar to Epirus further west, western Macedonia is extremely mountainous; it contains part of the Pindos range which includes several of Greece's highest peaks, such as Mount Olympus (2,917 metres; 9,570 feet). Grevena, Kastoria, and Kozani have very few areas, if any, lower than the 500 metres (1,640 feet). The only significant gap in the high altitude is found north of Thessaloniki, in the valley between the Paiko Mountains in the west and Kerkini in the east. The rest of the district has many small mountains, alternating with low-altitude plains, most notably one in the centre and another to the east in the triangle defined by Serres, Kavala, and Drama.

CLIMATE AND AGRICULTURE
Macedonia's climate is variable and differs from the rest of the country. Inland at 200 metres (656 feet) altitude, Naoussa has a mean average temperature of 24.7°C (76.5°F), whereas the figure for Kavala on the coast is 26.3°C (79°F).

Although rainfall in general is only slightly higher in Macedonia than most parts of Greece, it is the pattern that differs. For example, although Ahaia in the northwest Peloponnese and Florina in western Macedonia both have an average rainfall around the 650 millimetre mark (25.6 inches), Ahaia has 4.6 millimetres (0.2 inches) in July and 118 millimetres (4.7 inches) in November, while Florina has thirty-four millimetres (1.3 inches) and sixty-nine millimetres (2.7 inches) over the same months.

Agriculture is a major source of income in the area. The only significant urban centre is Thessaloniki, and tourism is not that important, except in a few areas such as Halkidiki and Thassos. Some industrial plants exist and there are a number of small, specialized artisanal businesses. Viticulture is key only in specific spots or prefectures, and in some cases, wine production is secondary to tsipouro, a grape distillate popular in several parts of the region. Viticulture in Macedonia is relatively easy, since the land does not experience the extremes of other Greek regions. Water is generally available, the Pindos range and other surrounding mountains guarantee a steady supply of water through numerous rivers and lakes, and most producers who want to or need to irrigate have no problems. Soils vary widely, from the highly fertile to the relatively infertile and across many different types and depths.

WINE PRODUCTION

In this predominantly red region, the most important traditional grape is Xinomavro. Macedonia has a noteworthy group of native varieties, but most are only found in a few prefectures. Before phylloxera's invasion, the story was very different, as estimates suggest that sixty per cent of the varieties were lost. In Siatista in Kozani, research on vines that survived phylloxera found many varieties, but none that were promising. Another change since phylloxera is vine-planting densities, which used to be up to 10,000 vines per hectare, but subsequently fell to 3,000 – the main reason being financial, as young vines that used to be free suddenly had a price.

The central European influence on the region is reflected in the general styles of wines produced here. Macedonian wines lack the heat and Mediterranean character of many regions further south, and certain areas like Amyndeo in Florina make wine with a distinctly "cool-climate" feel to them. Whites from international varieties, like Sauvignon Blanc, are leaner, fresher, and more lifted than examples found in, say, Central Greece.

Macedonia has been producing wines since antiquity and there is more

MACEDONIA

0 kilometres 40
0 miles 25

N

MACEDONIA

0 160km
0 100m
Macedonia

Axioupo
Goumeniss

FLORINA
Florina○
Aghia
Pandeleimonas
Amyntaion●

PELLA
Edessa○
Pola Nera
Gianitsa●
Marina
Ge

ALBANIA

Kastoria○
KASTORIA

Yianakochori●
Episkopi
●Naoussa
Stenimachos● ●Trifolo
Veria○
IMATHIA

KOZANI
Siatista● Kozani○
Velvendos●

PIERIA
Katerini○

Grevena○
GREVENA

MT OLYMPUS▲
2917m

Krania ●
Rapsani ●Py
Goni ●

Metsovo
EPIRUS

THESSALY

BULGARIA

DRAMA

Mikrochori●

Kokinogia

SERRES

⊙ Drama
Adriani●
Agora

⊙ Serres

KAVALA

.KIS

○Kilkis

●Kavala

MT PANGEO▲
1956m

●Amisiana
●Eleutheroupli
Nea Peramos

Ossa●
MT. VERTISKOS▲
1103m

Platanotopos

●Eleochori

ea Mesimvra

nchialos
ghia
anasios
essaloniki

THESSALONIKI

●Kariani

THASOS

Neoi
Epivates
● Nea Michaniona
●K. Sonolari
nomi
●Aghia
Pavlos

○Poligiros

HALKIDIKI

MT. ATHOS
▲ 2033m

Thermaikos

MT. SITHONIA
▲ 817m

Gulf

Neos
Marmaras●

AEGEAN SEA

evidence with every new archaeological expedition. With the troubles of the early twentieth century, however, many young people moved away and many vineyards were abandoned. A fresh impetus came from an unexpected source in the early 1920s. At the time, the Greek nation was living through what was later called the "Asia Minor Catastrophe". After wars and diplomacy failed, some Greek cities on the coast of Asia Minor become part of Turkey. Locals had two choices: either to stay and lose their nationality and identity, or to evacuate places like Constantinople and Smyrni, becoming refugees. Macedonia, and particularly Thessaloniki, were a major reception point for these *mikrasiates*. These people had a very close relationship with the vine, even if distillates were the product of choice rather than wine. One of the first acts of many *mikrasiates* in their attempt to establish a new life was to plant a vineyard.

This series of events meant that the Macedonian wine industry developed in a very different way to the rest of Greece. There are only two cooperatives in the whole region, as large private companies, like Boutari and Tsantali, became the big players. Instead of the protective environment of a co-op, people had to adapt to a competitive environment, which resulted in a great improvement in the whole viticultural sector, making it one of the best in Greece. Out of the thirteen prefectures of Macedonia, only four do not have any registered wineries, though all have some vineyards. In terms of volume of production, the leader is Florina, followed by Halkidiki and Kozani.

CLASSIFICATION

Macedonia has no OPE quality-wine appellations, but does have the red wine OPAPs of Naoussa in Imathia, Amyndeo in Florina, Goumenissa in Kilkis, and Côtes de Meliton in Halkidiki. There are a number of TOs in the most important regions and more will be added in the near future. If Greek legislation were as flexible as Italian, this area would have been festooned with at least three new OPEs by now.

Macedonia TO

White still: dry.
Rosé still: dry.
Red still: dry.
White varieties: Assyrtico; Athiri; Chardonnay; Malagousia; Roditis; Sauvignon Blanc.
Red varieties: Cabernet Sauvignon; Limnio; Moschomavro; Merlot; Syrah.

The producers of Macedonia tend to be both sound and innovative, even adventurous. The Union of Wine Producers of Northern Greece's Vineyards has been active over the years, organizing events and tastings as well as the nation's only International Wine Competition. The Wine Roads of Northern Greece project, encompassing not only Macedonia but Thessaly, Thrace, and Epirus, has been successful in developing wine tourism.

WESTERN MACEDONIA

KOZANI

Situated in western Macedonia and bordering Thessaly on the south, the central area of the Kozani prefecture is a plateau surrounded by mountains. The most striking feature is the Aliakmonas Reservoir – an area artificially flooded to build up water reserves for general use. Apart from specific batches, soils in Kozani are mainly gravel and relatively infertile. The climate is quite cool for Greece, with the average temperature being less than 24°C (75°F) in the summer and a few degrees above zero in winter. Rainfall is not ample but is evenly spread throughout the year – the driest month is August, with thirty millimetres (1.2 inches), and the wettest is November with double that. Hail can be a problem throughout the year, especially at higher elevations.

The main varieties of the region are Xinomavro and Moschomavro. The latter is a local black variety that is vigorous, productive, relatively resistant to aridity but sensitive to botrytis. Late-budding and late-ripening, its cycle starts in mid-April and finishes in early October. Moschomavro became famous with Tsantali's mono-varietal wine, showing fresh acidity, medium colour, and a very intense, sweet nose with more than a few Muscat nuances. Moschomavro can be a highly individual, light, and extremely charming wine. Other varieties include Stavroto, one of the grapes of the Rapsani OPAP in Thessaly, and Vergioto – a vigorous, productive red variety that is generally sensitive to diseases. It yields large bunches with large grapes, producing wines of pale colour, high alcohol, but very low acidity.

Kozani has 942 hectares of vineyards fairly evenly spread throughout most communes. The traditional heart of viticulture is Siatista, on the slopes of Mount Askio, where viticulture has been present since at least the fifteenth century. Wine producers enjoyed a brief spell of export success to France in the late nineteenth century. Now there are around 100 hectares, with some sites going up to 500 metres (1,640 feet) altitude. The main grapes are Xinomavro and Moschomavro, and red, rosé, and white wine styles are made, the latter often appearing as Xinomavro blanc de noirs.

A traditional sweet wine is made from Xinomavro and Moschomavro grapes, either left for ten to fifteen days to dry in the sun, or dried in the shade or indoors before being aged in large, used oak barrels, sometimes for many years. Some producers practise a kind of *solera* system to keep their barrels topped up. The wine is around 15.5 per cent alcohol with more than ninety grams per litre of residual sugar, and a low level of colour and tannins. The wine can only be bought locally since it is not bottled.

Siatista and Velvendos are Kozani's two TOs. The latter was created to accommodate the needs of Vogiatzi Estate, the only producer in the area.

Siatista TO

Rosé still: dry.
Red still: dry.
Varieties: Xinomavro can be up to eighty per cent of the blend, the balance being other local recommended grape varieties.

Velvendos TO

White still: dry.
White varieties: Batiki; Chardonnay; Malvasia Aromatica; Roditis; Xinomavro.
Rosé still: dry.
Rosé varieties: Xinomavro; Moschomavro; Merlot; Cabernet Sauvignon.
Red still: dry.
Red varieties: Xinomavro; Moschomavro; Merlot; Cabernet Sauvignon.

PRODUCERS

SIATISTA AIFOROS WINERY

1st km Palaiokastrou, 503 00 Siatista. Tel/Fax: +30 246 502 1049.
Vineyards owned: 15ha; under contract: 1.5ha; production: 100hl.
The only registered winery in the general area of Siatista, established in 1999. The vineyard holdings of Yiannis Tioukalias, the owner, are organic and include mainly Xinomavro and Moschomavro. Only one wine is released: the dry red Aiforos Argyros.

VARDAKA WINERY

2nd km Kozanis – Aianis, 501 00 Kozani.

Tel: +30 246 102 6214; Fax: +30 246 103 4527.

Production: 7,000hl.

The largest wine producer of the prefecture, with about three decades of solid dominance in the region. The winery crushes Xinomavro, but only rosé and blanc de noirs wines are made, sold under the Vardakas name, while bulk wine makes up the lion's share of sales.

VOGIATZI ESTATE

504 00 Velvendos. Tel/Fax: +30 246 403 2283;

Email: yiannis.voyatzis@boutaris.gr

Vineyards owned: 3ha; production: 200hl.

Yiannis Vogiatzis is the Bordeaux-trained production director of Boutari and one of the most quick-witted winemakers in Greece. He makes wines with *typicité*, precision, and grace in a style that is never over-extracted, over-oaky or over-alcoholic. Working at Boutari and its six wineries has given Vogiatzis good experience in most of the key Greek wine-producing regions.

Vogiatzis, together with his brother Nikos and his father Harisis, decided to create a boutique winery in his homeland, Velvendos. In the organically cultivated vineyards, they exploit the potential of the terroir, as well as of new varieties. Plantings include a mix of French and local varieties, together with a small "vine lab" where they planted as many local varieties as they could find. The vine density is high, at 4,500 plants per hectare, in an attempt to get "more terroir" into the grapes and increase competition between root systems. The estate also researches rootstocks and clones, and has managed to isolate a Velvendos Xinomavro clone.

The wines of Vogiatzis have a Rhône feel to them, especially the reds. The Ktima Vogiatzi Red, a Xinomavro/Merlot/Cabernet Sauvignon blend, has a remarkable depth without any hard edges. The Xinomavro/Moschomavro rosé is light and crisp and the Vogiatzi white, an unoaked Chardonnay/Roditis/Batiki blend, is rich but not heavy. The most recent addition is an expressive Malvasia Aromatica, which must be one of the best in Greece.

GREVENA

The Grevena prefecture, nestling in the Pindos mountain range, has only 172 hectares of vineyards. Despite the presence of a TO focusing on rosés and reds, there are no registered wineries in this area.

Grevena TO

Rosé/Red still: dry; semi-dry; semi-sweet.
Rosé/Red varieties: Cabernet Sauvignon; Merlot; Moschomavro; Roditis; Syrah; Xinomavro.

FLORINA

Florina is in northwestern Macedonia, near the borders with Albania and FYROM. Mostly above 500 metres (1,640 feet), the region is dotted with lakes, but there are no major rivers, only a few minor creeks. Florina is the coldest major wine-producing region in Greece. Its climate is close to being Continental, with cold winters and relatively cool summers. The maximum average temperature for July is 23°C (73.5°F), close to the Bordeaux figure for the same month, while the lowest average in January is 0.5°C (33°F). During winter there is considerable snowfall.

Florina is a demanding place for *vignerons* – they have to look for the warmer spots because cool sites can be too cool. Alluvial soils prevail, but fertility varies widely. Selected spots have high levels of sand, making them immune to phylloxera. The region has 1,236 hectares of vineyards, half of which are within the demarcated appellation of Amyndeo. The *mikrasiates* refugees did the first major plantings after phylloxera, although there is evidence that vines were grown as far back as the thirteenth century BC.

Amyndeo OPAP

Rosé still: dry; semi-dry; semi-sweet
Rosé sparkling: dry; semi-dry.
Red still: dry; semi-dry; semi-sweet.
Red/Rosé varieties: Xinomavro.

Amyndeo, in eastern Florina, is the prefecture's one OPAP, awarded in 1972. Amyndeo is the cooler edge of Greek viticulture. Vintages are important here, site selection is vital, and viticulture needs attention to detail. Amyndeo demands and rewards competence. Most of the vineyards are found between the lakes of Petron and Vegoritidas, and altitudes range between 570–750 metres (1,870–2,460 feet). The climate of the area follows Florina's general pattern, except for the northern winds, which blow all year round, and serve to cool the vines rather than stress them. Soils close to the lakes are rich in organic matter and high yields – over 105 hectolitres per hectare – can be achieved. The yields are important, but not just for quality reasons, as high cropping vines have delayed maturity, reaching well into late October, when the weather can get too cold for further development.

The appellation is devoted to Xinomavro and it expresses the grape in far more ways than other Xinomavro OPAPs in Macedonia. OPAP wines can be red or rosé. The locals make some excellent blanc de noirs from Xinomavro, but since these have been left out of the OPAP framework, they have to be traded as Florina TOs. These *vins gris* can blend depth with freshness, while keeping the true aromatic qualities of Xinomavro surprisingly intact. Most OPAP reds are dry.

Amyndeo Xinomavro compares with Naoussa Xinomavro to the east in the same way that Côte de Beaune Pinot Noir compares with Côte de Nuits. Amyndeo is usually lighter, not as tannic, but more floral. Good growers can add ripeness and concentration to their fruit, creating a style close to Naoussa, but without the same levels of power and firmness.

Amyndeo is the only OPAP in Greece where rosé is important, and one of the few that produces significant quantities of sparkling wines. Most sparkling wines are made with the Charmat method and it is debatable whether or not a traditionally-made sparkling Xinomavro would lose more in charm than it would gain in complexity.

Florina TO

White still: dry.
White varieties: Chardonnay; Roditis; Sauvignon Blanc; Traminer; Xinomavro.

PRODUCERS

ALPHA ESTATE

2nd km Amyndeo – Agiou Panteleimona, 532 00 Amyndeo.
Tel/Fax: +30 8 602 4077; Email: evaggelos@the.forthnet.gr;
Website: www.alpha-estate.gr
Vineyards owned: 37ha; under contract: 10ha; production: 3,000hl.
Angelos Iatridis is a relaxed, softly spoken man with some strongly held views. "There is no such thing as a vague definition of wine quality," he says. There is no artistry when making wine, no instinct. Everything can be measured, every aspect can be quantified. If you know what you are doing, what you are looking for, and how you monitor it, the quality will be there." A radical viewpoint, yet tasting his wines makes it difficult to refute.

In the mid-1990s, Iatridis and a highly qualified team of experts created Ampelooiniki, a small, well-equipped research centre. The company offered consulting services around the country, collaborating successfully with producers, nurseries, universities, and laboratories at home and abroad. In 1998, all this expertise resulted in a thirty-three-hectare vineyard in Amyndeo, named Ktima Alpha. Viticulturalist Makis Mavridis and Iatridis, together with vineyard consultant Dr. Stephanos Koundouras, leave nothing to chance in Ktima Alpha. The vineyard has eleven varieties, including Pinot Noir, Tannat, Montepulciano, and Negro Amaro. The best parcel of sandy soil, about 4.5 hectares, was dedicated to ungrafted Xinomavro. Complete bud and grape removal was used in the first four years to help vines grow in the required shape. Since the establishment phase, there has been a strict policy regarding green harvesting and leaf and shoot thinning, while Koundouras put in place one of the first specialized drip-irrigation regimes in Greece.[1]

The same painstaking approach goes into winemaking and maturation. Oak is considered a vital element, and Iatridis travels widely to find the best barrels for his wines. Oak maturation is relatively short: "Everything that oak can impart to wine and all the changes that it has to go through, happen during the first six to eight months," he believes. "Beyond that, you just destroy the wine and its ability to age long term in bottle – it might get softer, but not better."

The two basic reds are both made with a pre-fermentation cold soak at 8°C (46°F), careful temperature control during maceration, *sur lie* ageing with regular *bâtonnage*, eight months' maturation in American oak, and bottling with no fining or filtration. The main wine is Ktima Alpha Red, a blend of mainly Syrah with twenty per cent each of Merlot and Xinomavro. The wine has a reserved tightness that would be difficult to place in Greece.

Ktima Alpha White is a Sauvignon Blanc picked very ripe and aged in stainless steel *sur lie* for three months. The overall texture is so rich that one almost expects to find oak, but the clarity and power are pure expressions of the grape.

1. Regulated Deficit Irrigation is a drip-irrigation scheme where plants are monitored and supplied with regulated amounts of water to be kept under constant but mild stress. RDI controls and greatly improves maturation of grapes, even if, at yields of twenty to thirty-five hectolitres per hectare, Alpha Estate grapes should not have any problem in reaching maturity.

The most exciting wine of the portfolio is the Amyndeo OPAP, made from ungrafted Xinomavro, with great density, fruit, and a big, tannic structure. From the initial 2003 vintage, this wine almost redefined what Xinomavro could be, bringing in a new level of power and a New World personality, even at the expense of finesse. It will be interesting to see this wine developing in bottle. The estate also makes small batch bottlings from other varieties, occasionally releasing some cases, like the Alpha No.1 Tannat, which had more than a touch of Madiran's Château Montus to it. Finally, half a hectare of Gewurztraminer is left to overripen to make an attractive sweet wine.

COOPERATIVE OF AMYNDEO

1st km Amyndeo-Florinas Road, 532 00 Amyndeo.
Tel: +30 238 602 2258; Fax: +30 238 602 3879; Email: winemyn@otenet.gr
Vineyards under contract: 350ha; production: 9,800hl.

Amyndeo was one of the later cooperatives founded in Greece, appearing in 1959. It has 400 member growers working almost exclusively with Xinomavro. For years, it was the sole player in the appellation. The co-op has a large portfolio. There are three whites based on Xinomavro: a pure Amyntas; a Xinomavro/Sauvignon Blanc called Minthi; and a very good Chardonnay and Xinomavro blend, Drenios, with just a hint of oak backing up a complex fruit character. Rosés are important and made in all permutations. The sparkling wines are well-made – simple, fresh, crisp, and fruity.

The reds are the most serious part of the range, and the top offering is the Amyndeo Epilegmenoi Ampelones, made from selected vineyards. These non-irrigated, earmarked parcels on the highest parts of the appellation are vinified separately every year, but they are bottled only when the vintage is considered excellent. A reliable wine that is produced five times every decade and can age for at least eight years.

HATZI WINERY

1st km Amyndeo – Ag. Panteleimona, 532 00 Amyndeo.
Tel/Fax: +30 238 602 4215.
Vineyards owned: 1ha; under contract: 7ha; production: 440hl.

The Hatzis family has an impressive history of involvement with wine going back to the early nineteenth century, but it was in 2000 that Yiannis Hatzis built his own winery and started producing small quantities of Xinomavro wines. A qualified chemical engineer, Hatzis learns fast and adapts quickly to new situations.

Currently only still wines are made, but there are plans for sparkling wine using the Charmat method. His approach to Xinomavro is totally different to that of Ktima Alpha – far less extracted, with more spice and a marked elegance. The two whites are blanc de noirs Xinomavro, one oak-fermented, the other vinified in stainless steel, with the latter being a top-quality example of a clean, white Xinomavro. Hatzi Rosé fully exploits the grape's high acidity, as well as its light colour – the must is macerated for two days to get the colour densities that Agiorgitiko gives in twelve hours. Thus more flavour precursors are extracted, leading to a higher aromatic intensity and a more typically "red-wine" nose.

However, it is the Hatzis reds which are most notable. There is an OPAP Amyndeo bottling and a varietal Syrah, both aged in French oak for a year, with a small proportion of new oak. The pure Xinomavro is tight, with a definite "cool climate" fruit-feel, that tastes as if it could age for at least a decade. The Syrah contains fifteen per cent late-picked Xinomavro (harvested in mid-October, while most Xinomavros ripen a week earlier). This has an extra touch of ripeness and an additional degree of alcohol, making it a bit more forgiving in its youth, but perhaps not as ageable as pure Xinomavro. Overall, this is a compact, high quality range.

KIR-YIANNI ESTATE
532 00 Ag. Panteleimon Amyndeo.
Tel: +30 238 606 1120; Fax: +30 238 606 1185.
This is basically a crushing and vinification facility for the Kir-Yianni Estate (for full details, *see* Kir-Yianni entry on page 136) and it is used for about three months every year. The main winery is dedicated to premium reds, but the company wanted to have some whites as well as more affordable lines. Yiannis Boutaris had been working with Florina grapes for some time and was persuaded that white wines had great potential. Moreover, local Xinomavro grapes could be used for that Greek rarity, an OPAP rosé, as well as some easy-drinking reds. With this in mind, Kir-Yianni founded the Vegoritis winery, later fully incorporated in the Kir-Yianni Estate.

Four wines are crushed, fermented, and blended in Amyndeo. The major line is Samaropetra, a popular blend of Roditis, Sauvignon Blanc, and Gewurztraminer that is ripe, soft, and full of fruit,with a charming note of spice. Tesseris Limnes (Four Lakes) is a fuller, less aromatic white, made from Xinomavro, Chardonnay, Roditis, and a touch of Gewurztraminer, that began production in 2004. All varieties have some skin contact, except the

Xinomavro. Akakies is the OPAP rosé, firm and full of fruit. The only red produced here, the vivacious Paraga, is not an OPAP but a TO of Macedonia, since as well as Xinomavro it also has small percentages of Syrah and Merlot.

CENTRAL MACEDONIA

PELLA

Pella is northwest of Thessaloniki. Its capital is Edessa to the east, while Yiannitsa is an important province just northwest of Pella. The western and northern sides of Pella touch on the Vermio, Kaimaktsalan, and Voras Mountains, but much of the remainder is part of the main Macedonian plain, the exception being Mount Paiko, which stretches from the FYROM border south through Goumenissa and Yiannitsa. The climate is warmer than Florina and similar to that of other low altitude areas of central Macedonia.

Much of the soil is fertile, mainly of the argilo-calcareous type, and high in organic matter. Between 1928 and 1936, a large centrally located lake was drained, leaving a highly fertile plain. This fertility, along with phylloxera, pushed many growers into other more profitable forms of agriculture, but viticulture always persisted. The first evidence of wine production dates back to the reign of Philip II, father of Alexander the Great. Today, the total acreage is around 600 hectares, mainly confined to the slopes of the surrounding mountains.

Pella has no quality appellations, but one prefectural TO created relatively late in 1995. Under the regulations, whites have to be predominately Roditis and rosés and reds mainly Xinomavro, illustrating the major varieties of the area. There are some minor varieties, but very few can be considered as a local exclusivity. An exception is the rare vine Opsimo Edessis (late-ripening Edessa). It seems to be a very promising variety, having a long growing season, an aromatic character, and excellent levels of acidity. The vine is in a "grey zone" of ampelographers, with most information about it being largely anecdotal, but there is interest from the viticultural team of Katogi & Strofilia; therefore, more news is expected in the future.

Pella TO

White still: dry; semi-dry.
White varieties: Roditis can be up to seventy per cent of the blend; Chardonnay; Sauvignon Blanc; Ugni Blanc.

Rosé still: dry; semi-dry.
Red still: dry.
Rosé/Red varieties: Xinomavro can be up to sixty per cent of the blend; Cinsault; Merlot.

PRODUCERS

LIGA ESTATE

1st km Yiannitson – Arhontikou, 581 00 Yiannitsa. Tel/Fax: +30 238 202 4421.
Vineyards owned: 6ha; under contract: 10.5ha; production: 800hl.

Having gained considerable experience with Tsantali and the Naoussa Co-op following his oenology degree in Montpellier, Thomas Ligas established his estate in 1985. Despite his strong affiliation with Imathia, he decided to settle in Pella, becoming the first commercially significant producer of the prefecture.

Ligas runs his own estate under an organic regime and is pleasantly surprised that growers he buys from are more than willing to follow his approach. He produces four wines. Ktima Ligas White is a fresh blend of Sauvignon Blanc, Roditis, and Chardonnay, but it is the varietal Roditis bottling that is the better of the two. Ligas Roditis is one of the cool-climate examples of the grape, but it still has spicy, sweet fruit. Red varieties are Xinomavro and Merlot, and a clean, blended rosé is produced from both grapes. The Ktima Ligas Red, a blend of fifty-five per cent Merlot and forty-five per cent Xinomavro, is one of central Macedonia's most stylish reds, with understated oak and fine-grained tannins.

IMATHIA

Imathia is in central Macedonia, but has coastal access via the Aliakmonas River delta. The capital is Veria, with Naoussa the second most important city. Topographically, there is a significant difference between the west and east sides. While the east is part of the central Macedonian plain, the west is at a much higher altitude. Mount Vermio separates Imathia from Florina and Kozani. This difference in altitudes is reflected in the soils and climate. The slopes of Mount Vermio are much less fertile and cooler than the area nearer the sea, while there is also a marked variation in sunlight hours, with the mountainous side being much more overcast than the rest of the prefecture.

Naoussa OPAP

Red still: dry; semi-dry; semi-sweet.

Red variety: Xinomavro.
Communes of note: Gastra; Yianakohori; Fitia; Pola Nera; Ramnista; Strantza; Trilofos.

Imathia TO

Red still: dry.
Red variety: Xinomavro must be up to sixty per cent of the blend, the balance being other local recommended and permitted grape varieties.
White still: dry.
White varieties: Roditis; Priknadi; Xinomavro.

When discussing wine production in Imathia, we start with Naoussa. Apart from being the only OPAP quality-wine appellation in the prefecture, Naoussa dominates the vineyard acreage. Out of 781 hectares, just 100 are outside this appellation and even those are relatively near to it.

Naoussa overlooks the plain of central Macedonia, at altitudes ranging from 150 to 400 metres (492 to 1,312 feet). There are nine villages in the appellation, including Naoussa, and the soils are a patchwork of limestone, loam, sand, and clay. The climate is cooler than the lower areas of Imathia, but not as cold as Florina. Northern winds can be an inhibiting factor, not because of their severity but because of their chilling effect, sometimes resulting in spring frosts. The prefecture of Thessaloniki has stronger winds in comparison, but in Naoussa the highest winds happen during April and May, when vine growth is young, while further east the most intense winds are during the summer months. Growers try to select sheltered sites, usually with a southeasterly aspect.

Naoussa is a mono-varietal appellation, dedicated entirely to Xinomavro. This is the region where the variety excels, producing some of its best wines. Clonal selection is important, with most Naoussa stock delivering more tannin and fruit than, for example, the early maturing clone of Velvendos. In Naoussa, harvest starts at the end of September, but the complete harvest across all parts of the region spans around three weeks. October has three times as much rain as September, making late-ripening vintages a problem.

Vintage variations aside, Xinomavro responds badly to high yields, producing a very low level of anthocyanins and aggressive tannins. The legal limit of the appellation is seventy hectolitres per hectare, but quality-oriented producers wishing to make styles with good extract have to go for no more than half that. Xinomavro in Naoussa is often compared with Pinot

Noir in Burgundy, but the occasionally fierce tannic structure of this OPAP makes Nebbiolo and Barolo a far better comparison. There is a lack of colour, which browns quickly, a lack of sweet primary fruit aromas and flavours, a firm structure, with high acidity, often angular tannins, and a lack of fatness and softness on the palate.

If made well, Naoussa is one of the great Greek wines, offering an amazing depth, breathtaking complexity, and possibly the longest ageing potential of any dry Greek wine. The Boutari winery has preserved some significant stocks from vintages going back to the early 1970s, which illustrate how Naoussa can not only survive but also improve over at least two decades. However, this style of Xinomavro is not so easy to sell. Naoussa needs food, which is fine for old-school wine-lovers, but they are diminishing, and younger drinkers demand softer, more accessible wines that can be drunk on their own, without drying the mouth, such as the more approachable Agiorgitiko wines from Nemea.

At the moment, Naoussa wines come in a variety of styles. The first is the traditional Naoussa: moderately pale in colour, turning to tawny after a few years; low in primary fruit, but intense, spicy, and animal-like on the nose; medium in body, with firm tannins and high acidity. The second style is a more ambitious version of the first: longer extractions; higher tannins, but not necessarily deeper in colour or higher in alcohol.

Another type is an attempt to present a more modern Xinomavro by muting the most aggressive elements of the variety. Winemakers opt for an easy style that is slightly fuller in body and slightly reduced in acidity, while whole-berry fermentation is used to give ruby-red colour and softer tannins. Small amounts of Merlot round off the palate and add sweetness and fruit on the nose. In theory, this Merlot addition downgrades the wine to Imathia TO status, but producers seem able to include up to about ten per cent Merlot – not legally allowed, but not hugely unjust to the appellation. A milestone of the soft approach was the basic Naoussa from Boutari in the 2000 vintage, an electrifying wine that made many wonder how was it possible for Xinomavro to be so sexy. The last style of Xinomavro is dense, extracted, tannic, and oaky, but a lot more commercial than a typical Xinomavro. All these approaches offer successful, serious wines for their respective target markets and price segments. As is the situation with Barolo, the modern styles receive some criticism, but arguably it is they that will, hopefully, bring new wine drinkers closer to Naoussa and Xinomavro.

The combination of a capricious variety, a cool climate (by Mediterranean standards), and a relatively complex terroir produces a variety of possible permutations. This has been vividly illustrated by ongoing discussion about the "*crus*" of Naoussa, their differences in character and the possibility of encapsulating them within a new legislational framework. Naoussa is the prime OPAP where such a debate is taking place, with Nemea being a close second. There are seven favoured communes. Trilofos, one of the low-altitude vineyards, for instance, has rich soils and a hotter meso-climate, so the grapes are low in colour and extract, while the sugar levels are usually high. Fitia, close to Trilofos, is much higher, and is a later-ripening region, giving potentially the most lifted character. Pola Nera, in the north, at an altitude of around 250 metres (820 feet), is almost as late-ripening as Fitia, but produces wines with less fragrance. The communes of Yianakohori (350 metres; 1,148 feet), Strantza (250 metres; 820 feet), and Ramnista (200 metres; 656 feet) have closely linked terroirs, very close to Naoussa itself, and it appears that the higher the region, the higher the level of sweetness on the primary fruit. Wines of Gastra, south of Ramnista but at about the same elevation, are a tannic, unforgiving Xinomavro benchmark. Apart from altitude, differences in soil and aspect among these areas and within each area also play a part.

However, it is rare to be able to compare wines from different producers from the same village, or to find comparable examples from a variety of vineyards, producers, and vintages. Single-vineyard wines usually come from small-scale wineries that dominate one area. For example, there are very few, if any, pure Yianakohori *cuvées* apart from Kir-Yianni's. Producers that make bulk blends occasionally present single-vineyard tanks or casks, but not finished, let alone aged, wines. In contrast to Burgundy, Barolo, and Bordeaux, where many wineries produce single-village wines and extensive tastings can yield meaningful results, it is difficult to reach a proper conclusion with the existing producers' structure in Naoussa.

Yiannis Vogiatzis, the production director of Boutari, is in a good position to discuss this. His winery gathers fruit from most areas, and Vogiatzis goes to great lengths to keep parcels separate, at least in the initial stages. He believes vine-growing techniques and yield are without doubt the most important factors: "There is a grower in Trilofos, a village that many consider a source of low-quality grapes, that delivers the best fruit, year-in, year-out," he says. "It is not the soil, not the aspect; it is just him understanding his vines and guiding them towards producing the most concentrated grapes." On the other hand, it is clear that if one producer was able to grow parcels in all communes, differences would emerge. It seems that Naoussa, Gastra, and Pola Nera need a bit more time.

PRODUCERS

BOUTARI

592 00 Stenimachos Naoussas.

Tel: +30 233 204 1666/7; Fax: +30 233 204 1240;

Email: naoussa.winery@boutari.gr

See also Boutari entries on pages 144, 150, 232.

The Boutaris family began one of the important Greek wine dynasties when it started bottling wine in Macedonia back in 1879. Boutari has been developing business in the Thessaloniki prefecture since 1906, but the heart of the company, as well as its fame, has always been firmly connected with Naoussa. Boutari has been key in making the Naoussa appellation known throughout Greece. Moreover, Boutari, together with Tsantali and the Vaeni Cooperative, has done much to keep Naoussa growers interested in viticulture, providing them with a great deal of know-how and helping to raise general standards.

This is especially true for Boutari, where a large team has been helping Naoussa growers to get a better idea of how better Xinomavro grapes can be produced. The main aim is to delay sugar ripeness in the best sites, so that the phenolic maturity is higher at harvest. This is achieved by better handling of irrigation, shorter pruning, and pushing vines to grow higher and develop a larger leaf area. Yields are also important, with an optimum fruit load per vine of between two and 2.5 kilograms. Production director Yiannis Vogiatzis claims that below 1.8 kilograms of grapes per vine (about fifty hectolitres per hectare), there is no noticeable improvement in quality.

Boutari has also been at the forefront of Xinomavro winemaking. Currently, there is much discussion about cold-soaking Xinomavro, *i.e.* macerating it at low temperatures before initiating fermentation, but this method has been evaluated in the Boutari cellars since 1991, the year Vassilis Tsaktsarlis, the winemaking prodigy of Biblia Chora and Domaine Costa Lazaridi, completed his degree thesis on the subject. Winemaking here is very fragmented, with more than forty-five lots handled separately from reception to the end of the barrel-maturation period.

The style of Boutari Xinomavro is elegant, fine-grained, and silky – Vogiatzis is an opponent of show-stopper Naoussas. There are three pure Xinomavro wines, the top of the line being the Grande Réserve, which has been produced since OPAP Naoussa came into being in the early 1970s. It is aged in oak barrels, half of which are usually new, for two years. The barrel size used to be 500 litres but now there is a preference for 400-litre barrels, especially with wide-grained Nevers wood. There are a few barriques, mainly from the tighter-grained Alliers oak. Consistently one of the best Naoussas, especially when price is taken into account, Grande Réserve's proven ageing track record is enough to make many expensive Greek Cabernet Sauvignons blush.

The Boutari Xinomavro Réserve takes a more modern approach. Still elegant, it has more of a focus on new oak. Finally there is the higher-volume, lower-price Naoussa, which does not state variety on the label. This wine used to be an archetype for Xinomavro, with all the positive as well as the less forgiving aspects of the variety. In the 2000 vintage, there was a major change in extraction philosophy: very light crushing; cold but fast start of the fermentation (around 10°C; 10°F), and a slow warming-up of the must accompanied by short but frequent pumping-over around the clock. The result is one of the most forward and appealing expressions of Xinomavro seen in Naoussa, and a new style that could make the variety much more successful commercially. Boutari also makes a soft Xinomavro/Merlot that has been flourishing since the early 1990s.

Boutari might not produce the flashy, ultra-premium Xinomavros that could potentially make Naoussa world-famous one day, but this winery provides the essential groundwork that can efficiently support the more flamboyant wines.

BYZANTINE VINEYARDS
G.Kirtsi 11, 592 00 Naoussa. Tel/Fax: +30 233 202 4986.
Head office: G'Parodos Vasileos Konstantinou 7, 592 00 Naoussa.
Tel: +30 232 205 2290; Fax: +30 232 205 2291; Email: arabatz2@otenet.gr
Vineyards owned: 9.2ha; under contract: 27ha; production: 200,000hl.

A large producer, focusing on bulk wine, Retsina and Nama holy communion wine. On a négociant basis, he trades two OPAP Amyndeo wines. The winery's most interesting wine is the Byzantine Vineyards Cabernet Sauvignon.

CHATEAU PEGASUS

592 00 Pola Nera Naoussis. Tel: +30 697 670 5976.
Head office: Thesi Elies Petridi, 592 00 Naoussa. Tel: +30 233 202 7262;
Fax: +30 233 204 4971; Email: markovitis.trifon@klonatex.com
Vineyards owned: 10ha; production: 510hl.

A relatively small winery that does well on the export market, especially in Japan, the USA, and Germany, but whose presence in the national market rests somewhere between the cult and the obscure.

Innovative brothers Trifon and Dimitris Markovitis established Château Pegasus in 1980, well before the latest wave of boutique wineries in Greece. It was one of the first estates to go fully organic and is now experimenting with Biodynamic cultivation. There is no official accreditation yet, since Dimitris is keener on having the freedom to explore the results than being limited by a regulatory body. The vineyard in Pola Nera, offering a unique blend of Xinomavro, Riesling, and Chardonnay, is meticulously kept, with vines dating back to early 1970s producing small quantities of fantastic quality fruit. Winemaking is traditional but backed up with a high level of technical knowledge.

Despite the quirky feel of the estate, Château Pegasus Naoussa could not be closer to a template of the appellation. The style is firm, if not a bit lean, while the colour shows age relatively fast. However, the nose is full of fragrance, with a complex spice and floral personality. The ageing ability of Pegasus Naoussa is noteworthy, with most vintages being at their prime almost ten years after the harvest. The estate's whites are a lot more eccentric, with Pegasus Chardonnay being more reserved than most Greek examples, while Pegasus Riesling is a rich and broad example of the variety. Both whites are produced in tiny quantities and are difficult to find.

CHRISOHOOU ESTATE

592 00 Strantza Naoussis. Tel: +30 233 204 5080; Fax: +30 233 204 5081;
Website: www.chrisohoou.com; Email: info@chrisohoou.com
Vineyards owned: 10ha; under contract: 32ha; production: 2,300hl.

This is another old private Naoussa estate, established in the late 1940s. Kimis Chrisohoou currently runs the business, which includes a substantial number of owned or collaborating vineyards. The portfolio of products is quite diverse, but most lines rely on marked residual sugar levels and rather jammy fruit aromas and flavours. Chrisohoou Naoussa is on the light side,

Ktima Chrisohoou Naoussa, from the estate's own fruit, is denser and shows more new oak, and Chrisohoou Kava is a decent blend of Merlot and Xinomavro. The first wine is aged in oak for a year, while the other two stay in wood for eighteen months in total, with additional time in bottle. Mavro Chrisohoou (Black Chrisohoou) is a more recent addition, made from Xinomavro, Cabernet Sauvignon, and Merlot in a more modern style than the rest of the winery's reds. To date, however, it is not very convincing and seems fairly heavily manipulated.

The most intriguing wine is Prekniariko, possibly the only varietal wine from the grape of the same name. The vine has several synonyms apart from Prekniariko, such as Prekna, Preknadi, or the more usual Priknadi. It prefers calcareous soils and is vigorous, productive, and sensitive to botrytis but resistant to drought. It starts the season quite late, close to mid-April, and is harvested during the first ten days of September. Wine made from Priknadi is high in alcohol, oxidizes easily, and is supposed to be mildly aromatic. However, Chrisohoou Prekniariko, which is aged in oak for two months, seems broad, rich, and more textural than aromatic. It is an individual wine that can develop some complexity if kept in bottle for a year after vintage.

DALAMARA WINERY
Grigoriou Kirtsi 31, 592 00 Naoussa. Tel: +30 233 202 8321.
Head office: Vasileos Konstantinou 30, 592 00 Naoussa.
Tel/Fax: +30 233 202 6054; Email: dalamaras@alphanet.gr
Vineyards owned: 3ha; under contract: 3ha; production: 300hl.
Yiannis Dalamaras is another serious Naoussa producer, crafting small quantities of tannic but very aromatic and age-worthy Xinomavro. The Dalamaras family has one of the longest wine-producing histories in the region and there is evidence of a Yiannis Dalamaras first buying a vineyard back in 1840. Today, the family-run vineyards are organic and the grapes are used to produce Tsipouro as well as wine. Viticulturalist Haroula Spinthoropoulou works as a consultant, also identifying promising clones of Xinomavro, and winemaker Kostas Sdoukopoulos completes the team.

Dalamaras produces two whites with identical Roditis/Priknadi/Malagousia blends – Dalamara White is unoaked and Dalamara Kapnistos White (*kapnistos* means smoked) is the barrel-aged version. They offer a good balance between Malagousia aromatics, Priknadi texture, and Roditis broad flavours and palate. The oak version is remarkably low-key, even after more than eight months in barrel – Dalamara wines are always judiciously oaked. Ampelonas Dalamara is a blend of Xinomavro with twenty per cent Cinsault to round off the tannic, acidic edges of the native variety. The top wine – and a very good OPAP – is Palaiokalias Naoussa, capturing all the *typicité* and intense, old-fashioned but charming facets of the appellation. Old vintages are rare but can be stunning.

FOUNTIS ESTATE
592 00 Strantza Naoussis. Tel/Fax: +30 233 202 2256.
Vineyards owned: 5ha; production: 1,800hl.

Fountis Estate is one of Naoussa's medium-sized wineries and has been commercially active since 1990. Originally from eastern Thrace, the Fountis family relocated to Naoussa in the early twentieth century. Initially, the family sold its grapes to the major négociants, but Nikos Fountis was finally persuaded to start producing his own wine. Today he runs the business, helped by nephew Dimitris Ziannis, a Dijon-trained oenologist and winemaker for Katogi in Metsovo.

Most of the production is based on Xinomavro, even the white wines. There is a simple but fresh blanc de noirs, and a white called Trigias, again a Xinomavro, but this time fermented and aged over lees in new French oak. Trigias starts a bit lean and closed in fruit, but a year in bottle opens up to the more typical Xinomavro nose, which balances the wood aromas. Fountis Rosé is a well-made pink Xinomavro, which is very soft on the palate.

The reds start with Olganos, a French oak-aged fifty-fifty blend of Xinomavro and Merlot. OPAP Naoussa is represented by two bottlings, coming from two different communes of the appellation. Naoussaia is produced from Ramnista fruit, while Ktima Fountis fruit is sourced from Strantza. On release, the Naoussaia has more tannins while the Ktima shows a higher level of primary fruit, being richer and sweeter but also less concentrated and slower to develop. The Fountis reds are traditional in style, showing a lot of barnyard aromas. They are quite reductive with a structure that often lacks density on the mid-palate. With some ageing, they develop a very spicy, animal-like personality.

The Fountis Estate is also used by the Katogi & Strofilia company (*see* page 194) to source good-quality Xinomavro wines for a variety of products, including the Katogi & Strofilia OPAP Naoussa Porfyri Ghi, an Agiorgitiko/ Xinomavro blend, and the Katogi Rosé.

KARANATSIOU VINEYARD SELECTIONS

1st km Naoussas 3–5 Tria Pende Pigadia, 59200 Naoussa.

Tel/Fax: +30 233 205 2223; Email: karanatsios@nao.forthnet.gr

Vineyards under contract: 5ha; production: 350hl.

This is a small winery in Tria Pende Pigadia, established in 1999, that sources local fruit. There are two products: a very ripe, textured OPAP Naoussa called Plagies Vermiou and a white blend of Roditis and Sauvignon Blanc. Karanatsiou is also experimenting with Sangiovese and Syrah. It would be interesting to have a blend of the two made in Naoussa. Karanatsiou is most definitely a winery to watch in the future.

KARYDA ESTATE

Thesi Ano Gastra, 592 00 Naoussa; Head office: Byronos 6, 592 00 Naoussa.

Tel/Fax: +30 233 202 8638.

Vineyards owned: 2.1ha; production: 120hl.

Karyda Estate is one of the smallest Naoussa estates and one of the best. Konstantinos Karydas and his son Petros run the venture in a very hands-on manner, not unlike the finest and smallest domaines in Burgundy. In the winery there are no tricks or gimmicks, just the essential equipment. By contrast, all the work goes into the 2.1-hectare vineyard in Ano (Upper) Gastra, an early ripening spot used to produce quite an alcoholic Xinomavro, almost always harvested in late October and with a potential alcohol of 13.2 per cent or above.

The vineyard was planted in 1979 on a sandy-calcareous parcel of land; a drip-irrigation system has recently been put in place to help with dry vintages. Yields are kept below fifty hectolitres per hectare, sometimes much lower, and about a third of the fruit is green-harvested at the beginning of *veraison*. Much attention goes into de-leafing and other methods of canopy management, trying to keep vines with enough active leaf surface to promote ripening and to protect the fruit from sunburn, while at the same time controlling vigour. For example, leaves are primarily removed from the east-facing side, so that the early morning sun can dry off the condensation on the fruit caused by night mist, while the thicker shade on the west-facing side protects the fruit the intense late-afternoon sunshine.

Karyda produces two wines in very small quantities – less than 1,000 bottles per year. Ktima Karyda White is a blend of Malvasia Aromatica and Assyrtico, which has eight-hour skin contact with dry ice, is fermented in stainless steel, and bottled relatively fast. As expected, this clean white is more Malvasia on the nose and more Assyrtico on the palate. Ktima Karyda Red, sometimes referred to as Syllektikon (Collectable), is sixty per cent Xinomavro and forty per cent Cabernet Sauvignon. Aged for two years in 100 per cent new French oak barriques, most of which are heavily toasted, the wine shows a surprisingly integrated oak presence, even if toasty flavours do get through, and the end result is rich, tannic, and serious, needing a few years in bottle to integrate its elements.

The basic product of Karyda – and the one that its fame is based upon – is its straight Naoussa. The grapes are macerated for eight days, and although this is not a cold soak, the temperature never exceeds 25°C (77°F). Yeasts are inoculated, but the malolactic, which takes place in epoxy-lined cement vats, is natural. Karydas believes in long oak ageing, so his Naoussa is kept in used French oak barriques for almost two years. Karydas' Naoussa is a bit riper than most wines of the appellation, showing *typicité* but also good, high-pitched fruit. Both on the nose and on the palate, there is a floral, complex dimension that reinforces any Barolo/Naoussa comparison. Although it undoubtedly has significant ageing potential, it is, on release, at a very complex stage of development. This is a fine example of "premier division" Naoussa and one of the best-value wines in Greece.

KIR-YIANNI ESTATE

Yianakohori 59200 Naoussa; Tel: +30 233 205 1100; Fax: +30 233 205 1140. Head office: 3 Victor Hugo Street, 546 25 Thessaloniki; Tel: +30 231 052 0650; Fax: +30 231 052 4430; Website: www.kiryianni.gr; Email: info@kiryianni.gr Vineyards owned: 45ha (Naoussa), 15ha (Amyndeo); under contract: 55ha; production: 5,000hl.

See also Kir-Yianni entry in Florina section on page 126.

To fully understand the connotations of the name "Kir-Yianni", one has to know some facets of Greek language, society, and the history of the Boutaris family. In Greek, a form of address known as the "plural of courtesy" is widely used, especially between people of different ages or social standing. A man is addressed as Kirios (Mr) followed by his surname. Using Kirios together with the first name, for example "Kirios Yiannis", is still quite formal. The "Kir-Yianni" mode of address denotes a close relationship where even the singular could be used, although the person concerned is of such standing that, no matter how close, he still commands respect, without even asking for it. Yiannis Boutaris is such a person – he is one of the most influential figures in his sphere, while also being a totally relaxed, approachable, almost bohemian personality. Yiannis Boutaris is the "Kir-Yianni" of Greek Wine.

Yiannis is a member of the important Boutari wine dynasty – he is named after the company's founder. Yiannis and his brother Constantinos became involved in the family business, and while Constantinos was steered towards the commercial side, Yiannis started managing production. From the early days, he was not afraid of controversy. For example, while overseeing the initial vintages of the Boutari winery in Santorini, he was also trying to persuade small growers to stop selling their grapes to Boutari and start their own wineries. In the 1960s, he bought a forty-five-hectare vineyard in Yianakohori, the highest point of the Naoussa appellation, without his father Stelios being aware of it. When Stelios found this out, he was furious. "Boutaris are wine producers," he said. "What the hell do they have to do with vine-growing?"

Meanwhile, the Boutari company went from strength to strength and established itself as a market leader, particularly in the mid-price, high-volume sector. Unfortunately, the two brothers disagreed on a number of vital strategic matters and a split became inevitable in the second half of the 1990s. Yiannis decided to leave, taking with him almost none of the company assets or copyrights on the use of the Boutari name. The only thing he insisted on having was the Yianakohori vineyard and the choice of the new name was obvious. Today, Kir-Yianni's Yianakohori is, undeniably, one of the great estates of Greece.

The work carried out in the Yianakohori vineyards is remarkable by any standards. The soils have been carefully analyzed and divided into thirty-two parcels. As well as Merlot and Syrah, most have been planted with Xinomavro at an average density of 4,200 vines per hectare, far above the Naoussa average of 3,000. The pattern of parcels, varieties, rootstocks, and training systems is highly complex, but every single decision is backed up by scientific evidence. Greek varietal expert, Haroula Spinthiropoulou, has devoted significant amounts of time to working on the clonal selection of the Xinomavro parent material found on the estate and there are now more than five separate clones being isolated and evaluated. Every parcel is cultivated under its own regime and up to fifty per cent of the potential crop is green-harvested just after *veraison*.

This painstaking work continues in the winery, with many small-batch vinifications. Despite the high quality of fruit at harvest, four people man the sorting table to remove any poor berries. The first wines of the Kir-Yianni era, from 1996 to 1999, were vinified by Angelos Iatridis, followed by Mihalis Boutaris, the UC Davies-educated son of Yiannis. The approach was quite Burgundian, with three days of cold soaking, no crushing, and very gentle extractions. Cultivated yeasts are used for the primary fermentation, but malolactic is natural. The oak treatment is a different story, with experiments including several types, sizes, makers, and toastings of barrels, both French and American.

The current team of Kir-Yianni is impressive at all levels of the business, and includes many young people working for their postgraduate degrees in viticulture or oenology. Thomas Karanatsios, a man with an impeccable knowledge of Yianakohori's terroir, has long been the vineyard manager. Yiannis and Mihalis are also aided by Stelios, Mihalis' brother, who looks after commercial matters, having worked at major wine companies in Europe and the USA.

Yianakohori produces only red wines, since whites are vinified in the Florina winery. Its Merlot and Syrah are among the best examples found in Greece, both being powerful, rich but tannic, age-worthy, and with plenty of backbone. Merlot is aged for a year in French barriques, while Syrah is matured for six months in used French oak 500-litre barrels and then transferred into newer barriques for an additional six months. Yianakohori is the basic wine and the estate's main breadwinner. It was one of the first trend-setting blends of Xinomavro and Merlot, with the latter adding much charm to the former. Naoussa OPAP is represented with two wines.

Ramnista is a Xinomavro with an above-average ripeness, aged in 500-litre oak barrels for a year. An excellent illustration of what Naoussa can achieve, it needs more than five years to unfold its personality. In 2002, Kir-Yianni released a single-vineyard Xinomavro from the oldest plot of the estate, and with Mihalis' technical dexterity on full display, this wine was unlike any Xinomavro made in Greece before. If Naoussa is Barolo, then this is a single-vineyard wine from Gaja. One can only speculate on the staying power of such a wine, a fact well understood by the Kir-Yianni team. Single-vineyard releases had been discontinued shortly after the inaugural vintage, but will now resurface with six or seven years of age as Ramnista Réserve. There is every reason to anticipate greatness.

MELITZANI WINERY

Agra 14, 592 00 Naoussa. Tel: +30 233 202 2742; Fax: +30 233 202 5312.

Vineyards owned: 4ha; production: 250hl.

The Melitzanis family has been making a living out of wine since at least 1918, when a small winery and retail shop were established in Naoussa. The shop is now a major part of the business. The Melitzanis brothers, Andonis and Agamemnonas, currently produce a lovely Tsipouro, some Retsina, a fresh and simple Roditis white called Epainos, and even, as a négociant, an OPE Mavrodaphne of Patras. However, the strength of the wine portfolio is to be found in the Xinomavro wines, sourced from a very good four-hectare parcel in Gastra. Melitzani's style is charmingly old-fashioned, with minimal oak intervention and an acid-tannin structure that is full of grip and cries out for food. There are two versions of Xinomavro: Melitzani Naoussa is briefly aged in large, old oak barrels for six months, and shows ample fruit, coupled with animal-like undertones; Melitzani Kava is a pure Xinomavro again, but sold as an EO rather than a Grande Réserve OPAP Naoussa. This shows clear signs of oxidation, but has enough richness beneath it to make this an element of its character, rather than a fault.

TSANTALI

Railway Station, 592 00 Naoussa. Tel: +30 233 204 1461.

Vineyards owned: 20ha; under contract: 100ha.

See also Tsantali entries on pages 109, 163, 213.

Tsantali has a major investment in Naoussa, with a winery, a private non-irrigated vineyard in Strantza, and long-term contracts with more than 100 vine-growing families. The company's able viticultural team ensure that the sourced fruit meets Tsantali's exact criteria, even in the most difficult of vintages. Xinomavro is an important variety in the Tsantali portfolio, forming the spine of many regional blends, but the Naoussa winery crush is dedicated mainly to making the OPAP bottlings.

From the four OPAPs that include Xinomavro, Tsantali does not produce any Amyndeo or Goumenissa. Of the remaining two, Naoussa is a complete contrast to the Rapsani wines, produced in Thessaly on the slopes of Mount Olympus. Rapsani bottlings are extremely modern, from the wine through to the packaging. On the other hand, Tsantali Naoussa is all about tradition and Xinomavro *typicité*: a pale colour, an intense nose full of wild flowers, sweet spice, and a very elegant oak presence. The palate is medium-bodied, with some Xinomavro tannins that are more lace than steel. Although the lightness of structure might be misleading, the Tsantali Naoussa develops beautifully over the course of a decade, which is quite a feat for a modestly priced wine.

Apart from the basic Naoussa, Tsantali produces a Naoussa Réserve. The best parcels from each year are kept separately, macerated for nine days (three more than the traditional *cuvée*), aged in Alliers barriques for a year, plus two more in bottle. Tsantali's Naoussa Réserve is very close to the style of the basic Naoussa, but does have an additional layer of complexity on the nose and extract on the palate. Overall, a very good, small, but well-targeted range.

VAENI NAOUSSA WINERY

592 00 Episkopi Naoussis. Tel: +30 233 204 4274/4597; Fax: +30 233 204 4598.
Vineyards owned: 2.3ha; under contract: 200ha; production: 11,500hl.

Fifty per cent of all Naoussa production is crushed in the region's co-op, which is named Vaeni. It was only established in 1983, but hard work from its 200 members has already made it one of Greece's most successful co-ops. This success cannot only be measured by pure sales, but also by export figures and Vaeni's brand recognition around the country. As found with many examples of nationally successful organizations, a network of retail outlets in major cities has proved invaluable.

The production team, led by Thomas Maras and Katerina Tsamis, puts a great deal of effort into making the best-possible wines, even though the equipment available is not exactly cutting edge. The packaging of many wines is possibly the most imaginative of any Greek co-op's portfolios. The basic line is a series of EOs called simply Vaeni, made in dry or semi-dry versions and in all colours. There are two Xinomavro blanc de noirs, a decent Imeros, and a much more flavourful Dogmatikos. The is also a red Imeros: a half-Xinomavro, half-Syrah non-vintage blend, made in a very soft style. There is a pure Syrah bottling, which is enjoyable but not very typical of the variety. Vaeni's top rosé is called Salammbó and points toward a local taste that prefers semi-dry pink wines.

Vaeni produces four OPAP Naoussa labels, three of which use the different styles of ageing, as described by legislation. Vaeni Naoussa is aged in mainly used French barriques for twelve months, Vaeni Naoussa Réserve ages for eighteen months in oak and two years in bottle, while Vaeni Naoussa Grande Réserve spends two years in barrel and two in bottle. All three are traditional and well-made – possibly not the very best examples of Xinomavro but pleasant and representative of both appellation and variety. In addition, even the more upmarket bottlings are sold at good value prices.

Finally, Vaeni is releasing an individual limited production Naoussa, called Damaskinos. This Xinomavro is made from the ripest berries selected from each harvest and spends a total of eighteen months in oak, with the final six in new, high-toast French barriques. The wine can be shockingly toasty on release, showing little sign of development in bottle, even after ten years. Damaskinos is purely a matter of personal taste, but deserves at least a try from all fans of Xinomavro.

KILKIS

Kilkis is the northern part of the great Macedonian plain, bordering Pella on the west, Thessaloniki on the south, Serres on the east, and FYROM on the north. Kilkis is the only significant low altitude gap in the mountain ranges that form the natural boundaries between Macedonia and its northern neighbours, so is vital in connecting most of the Balkans with Thessaloniki and the Aegean Sea. Apart from the Vardaris River (also called Axios), there is an important highway that starts from Thessaloniki, travels through the whole of the Kilkis prefecture, and finally reaches the national border and beyond. The capital of the prefecture is Kilkis, with Goumenissa being the second-largest provincial town.

Although most of Kilkis is at sea level, the eastern and western parts of the region are on the slopes of Mount Vertiskos and Mount Paiko, respectively. However, most of this higher land is in the form of rolling hills rather than steep, aggressive slopes. This gentle topography allows the Aegean Sea's influence to reach well into the region, ameliorating any weather extremes throughout the year. From a viticultural perspective, the most important part is the west side, taking in most of the east-facing slopes of Mount Paiko – Goumenissa OPAP is located here.

There are 328 hectares within the Goumenissa appellation and 263 hectares nearby. The demarcated region includes the Paiko slopes, between 150–250 metres altitude (492–820 feet), an area with a relatively reliable climate for grape production, at least when compared with other OPAPs found in the western parts of Macedonia. On average, Goumenissa is around 0.8°C (1.4°F) warmer than Naoussa, humidity levels are significantly lower, and sunshine hours are up to fifteen per cent higher.

With Goumenissa as the main reference point, Kilkis has a history of wine-growing that stretches back to antiquity. In the early decades of the twentieth century, the area accepted a large number of refugees from eastern Thrace, people who brought fresh ideas and new techniques to the local wine-producing traditions. Unfortunately, phylloxera destroyed all the vineyards in 1918 and replanting started in the following decade. For a number of years well beyond World War II there was no significant development in viticulture, at least on a commercial level. This had to wait until the mid-1970s, when Boutari took an interest in Goumenissa and started sourcing large quantities of fruit from the region. Most importantly, Boutari promoted the local wines via its nationwide distribution, making them popular in most important cities around Greece. Goumenissa wines were successful enough to persuade Boutari to build a winery within the appellation in 1985.

The area already had some producers before Boutari became interested. For example, Titos Eftihidis established his winery in 1974 and Hristos Aidarinis followed just four years later, but these producers sold their wines primarily within Kilkis and Thessaloniki. Boutari not only raised national awareness, but also helped viticulture to retain financial appeal. In addition, the experienced Boutari team was instrumental in winning over the regulatory authorities which granted OPAP status to Goumenissa in 1979.

Goumenissa is one of the four Xinomavro OPAPs of Greece, but here the variety has to be complemented by at least twenty per cent Negoska. The maximum allowed yield is about seventy hectolitres per hectare. The law requires that the varieties are co-macerated and co-vinified, while the wine must be aged in oak for at least twelve months. Goumenissa wines are always compared with the great Xinomavros of Naoussa, even if the altitude is generally lower, the climate is warmer, the aspect less variable and less important, and the soils slightly coarser. If Naoussa wines are elegant, floral, and firm, Goumenissa's are broader, softer, and with a higher level of primary fruit aromas. In many examples, this fruit dimension is expressed in a slightly rustic way, showing raisiny characters and barnyard undertones, which are sometimes attributed to Negoska. However, the best wines of the appellation seem to forego this array of aromas.

Another important point is alcohol levels. Despite the warmer terroir of the region and the inclusion of Negoska – a grape that can push ripeness levels higher than pure Xinomavro – local growers have been reluctant to go for later harvest dates. While in Naoussa, more and more producers are releasing wines close to or above the 13.5 per cent alcohol mark, most Goumenissa labels are one degree lower. However, it has to be noted that there are only five or so OPAP Goumenissa wines on the market. On average, the quality level is high and this can be considered one of the most reliable red quality-wine appellations in Greece. Apart from Xinomavro and Negoska, other varieties found in the general region include Roditis, Grenache Rouge, and Merlot.

Goumenissa OPAP

Red still: dry.
Red varieties: Negoska must be at least twenty per cent of the blend; Xinomavro.

PRODUCERS

AIDARINI HRISTOU WINERY

1st km Eparxiakis Odou Goumenissas – Kilkis, 613 00 Goumenissa.
Tel: +30 234 304 2555. Head office: Platia 23rd Oktovriou, 613 00 Goumenissa;
Tel: +30 234 304 1293; Fax: +30 234 304 3513; Email: aidarini@sparknet.gr
Vineyards owned: 5ha; under contract: 12ha; production: 900hl.

It seems that the first Aidarini winery was built more than a century ago, but the wine-producing business of Hristos Aidarinis was established in its present state in 1978. Bulk wine sales are still over four-fifths of the annual production, but there is an ongoing attempt to improve the portfolio of bottled products. Quality was static during most of the 1990s, when the winery started a national distribution network – the wines were closed and lacking in charm or depth. However, the twenty-first century has brought about change, both stylistically and qualitatively, and now Aidarini is crafting some of the most exciting bottles of Kilkis wine.

An average Roditis/Sauvignon Blanc blend was replaced with a pure, ripe, stainless-steel fermented Sauvignon Blanc that could be mistaken for an unoaked cool-California varietal. Aidarini Rosé is a crisp, sweet-scented Xinomavro, which is softer than most Imathia examples, as well as riper, less tannic, and with a stylish touch of French oak. Aidarini Goumenissa has thirty per cent Negoska and is the most modern wine of the appellation. Highly polished, rounded, and well-defined, this is not the most age-worthy wine of the OPAP, but in the first five years of its life it is a very charming introduction to Goumenissa.

ARHONTAKI VINEYARDS

614 00 Aksioupoli. Tel: +30 234 303 1859; Fax: +30 234 303 2232.
Vineyards owned: 6.5ha; production: 400hl.

Established in 1999, Arhontaki Vineyards is the only Kilkis winery that is not producing any OPAP Goumenissa wine. The estate's initial steps have been ambitious, including building a serious production plant and setting up some excellent vineyards. In the first few years, an Ampelooiniki team was hired to fine-tune techniques in both vineyard and cellar. However, the last few years has seen Iosif Arhontakis focusing on the bulk wine sector.

There are still some bottled wines that show good potential. The white wine, Polidroso, is a Roditis/Sauvignon Blanc blend, showing a very clean expression of the latter grape. The Arhontaki Red is a typical Cabernet Sauvignon, with a small addition of Cabernet Franc, while Dreveno Red is a broad-structured Xinomavro/Merlot blend.

BOUTARI

613 00 Goumenissa. Tel: +30 234 304 1989;
Fax: +30 234 304 1598; Email: goumenissa.winery@boutari.gr
Vineyards owned: 7ha.
See also Boutari entries on pages 130, 150, 232, 385, 449.

As was the case in many wine regions that lacked a commercial critical mass, the presence of Boutari in Goumenissa acted as a much-needed catalyst. Boutari saw in Goumenissa a user-friendly alternative to Naoussa, still based on the flamboyancy of Xinomavro, but in a less piercing style. Even in the mid-1970s, Naoussa land and grapes were much more expensive than in Goumenissa, where competition from other companies was less fierce. On the one hand, Boutari had a good commercial reason to invest in Goumenissa, while on the other, the Goumenissa name had a chance to reach many markets, nationally and internationally.

Following its usual policy, Boutari built a winery in the appellation within less than a decade of its initial interest in the region. In order to gain control over the fruit, a 6.6-hectare estate was established. The mono-parcel Ktima was located in the Filiria commune and was simply named Ktima Filiria. The estate is at the lower altitude of the appellation, between 171 and 187 metres (561 and 613 feet). Vine-planting density is at 4,000 vines per hectare instead of the usual 3,000, recalling the Yianakohori approach in Naoussa. The focus is mainly on Xinomavro and Negoska, while a 0.4-hectare section is dedicated to experimental plantings of Agiorgitiko, Malagousia, Cabernet Sauvignon, and Athiri.

Boutari produces only two wines from this OPAP. Boutari Goumenissa is the basic bottling and the highest-volume wine of the appellation. In some vintages it can be a bit austere on the palate and lacking in fruit aromas, but it is still good value. Ktima Filiria is on a different level, with much more fruit extract, density, and structure. It has a sweet oak character and some hallmark Xinomavro flesh, and both characteristics are balanced with opulence and intensity. In the Boutari Wine Library, some Goumenissa bottles from the mid-1980s are looking deceptively like old Naoussas, even if development has been faster. However, Ktima Filiria vintages do seem to age at a much slower rate, and some fine bottles should be found when the initial vintages reach their third decade.

EFTIHIDI ESTATE
Thesi Megalo Potami, 613 00 Goumenissa. Tel: +30 231 304 3228.
Head office: Ermou 12, 54 624 Thessaloniki. Tel/Fax: +30 231 027 3620.
Vineyards owned: 6ha; production: 230–250hl.

Titos Eftihidis has been a wine producer for more than thirty years, but his wines have only become known to Greek wine-lovers over the course of the last decade. He has been one of the most forward-thinking figures in Goumenissa and has remained determined to keep volume below 40,000 bottles annually.

Ktima Titou Eftihidi Goumenissa is a wine that clearly belongs to the modernist side of the OPAP, with clean primary fruit and a well-focused oak presence. It will be interesting to see how recent vintages develop over the next decade or so. Beyond this OPAP wine, Eftihidi releases some unusual EOs. Tavros tis Paionias (the Bull of Paionia) is a varietal Cabernet Sauvignon, showing that the variety has potential in the Kilkis terroir, while moving towards a restrained, Old World style. Limnio Eftihidi is simple and pleasant, possibly hitting the exact spot Titos Eftihidis wanted it to hit. Finally, Ktima Titou Eftihidi Viognier has gained an almost cult following among top sommeliers in Athens and Thessaloniki, being one of the most best examples of the variety in Greece. It has the peachy Viognier *typicité* on the nose, supported by rich oak undertones, while the palate is not full-blown, coarse, hot or heavy. Not a dead ringer for Condrieu, but certainly comparable with California examples.

TATSI ESTATE
Bizaniou 4, 613 00 Goumenissa.
Tel: +30 234 304 2936; Fax: +30 234 304 1053; Email: ktimatatsis@aias.gr
Vineyards owned: 3.5ha; under contract: 4ha; production: 250–300hl.
This small, family-run Goumenissa winery was established in 1997. Despite being the youngest venture in the appellation, the focus is traditional for all aspects, from winemaking and wine style to packaging. There is a low-key approach, but all the elements and *typicité* of Goumenissa wines are there. Vineyards are certified organic, much effort goes into vineyard management, and yields are routinely kept below fifty hectolitres per hectare.

Tatsi White is based on Roditis, with some blanc de noirs Xinomavro and Cinsault. Tatsi Rosé is a rare, varietal Negoska, and is surprisingly crisp and intense. Tatsi Red is mainly Limnio: a simple, soft, easy-drinking wine. Tatsi Goumenissa is spicy and floral on the nose with some shades of leather, but the palate is a touch softer than one might expect. The most intriguing wines of Tatsi are grouped under the brand Premno. Premno White is a dry-farmed Roditis, with ultra-clean, cool-fermentation aromas, while Premno Red is a fresher, younger mode of a Xinomavro/Negoska blend.

THESSALONIKI
The prefecture of Thessaloniki in central Macedonia holds a strategic location between central Greece, Thrace, and the Balkan countries. It is the country's second-largest port after Piraeus and offers access to all of the Aegean Sea. The city of Thessaloniki is a cultural, financial, trade, and social centre and has been crowned the "co-capital" of Greece. The region boasts one of the world's longest recorded histories and the people of Thessaloniki have long been dictating, rather than following, any new developments.

Thessaloniki borders Imathia to the west, Pella, Kilkis, and Serres to the north, and connects two gulfs: Thermaikos on the west, and Orfanos, southeast of Serres. This strip contains two major lakes, Koronia and Volvi, and separates the Halkidiki Peninsula from the rest of Greece.

The topography varies significantly. The western part of the prefecture, home to the city itself and a small section to the south where Epanomi is located, is fairly flat and has a low average altitude. The scenery is more varied and complex on the western side of the region, with the imposing presence of Mount Hortiatis just west of Thessaloniki at 1,200 metres (3,940 feet), and Mount Vertiskos, close to the borders with Kilkis and Serres. Although altitude and aspect play a major role in a site's meso-climate, overall the climate is heavily influenced by the proximity of the sea.

The importance of the prefecture of Thessaloniki in viticultural matters is two-fold. In terms of acreage, Thessaloniki is the fourth-largest prefecture in northern Greece (after Florina, Halkidiki, and Imathia), with 759 hectares of vineyards. In addition, Thessaloniki is the second-largest city in Greece, as well as the administrative centre of Macedonia. Many large wine companies have therefore established head offices or large production plants in the area and these producers play a significant part in the development of viticulture in Thessaloniki and the general region of Macedonia.

Phylloxera destroyed most of the vineyards in the early twentieth century, a fact underlined by the relative lack of indigenous and exclusive varieties. Much of the revival in vine-growing came before the World War II, due mainly to commercial ventures launched by the refugees from eastern Thrace who brought with them a strong tradition of producing distillates like ouzo and Tsipouro. It can be said that Thessaloniki, and to a certain degree Macedonia, emerged only recently as a major wine-producing area. However, local people have done well to at least catch up with the rest of the nation.

Currently, viticulture is not limited to particular areas. In fact, there are few sites where no vines are found. Soils vary widely, but are generally young, quite fertile, and many coastal sites are quite sandy. However, styles depend above all on the producer. There are no quality-wine appellations and the four TOs that are present have been tailor-made to cover the needs of specific wineries rather than to promote traditional styles or varieties.

Epanomi TO

White still: dry.
White varieties: Assyrtico; Chardonnay; Malagousia; Sauvignon Blanc.
Red still: dry.
Red varieties: Grenache Rouge; Merlot; Syrah.

Messimvria TO

White still: dry.
White varieties: Zoumiatiko can be up to twenty-five per cent of the blend; Roditis.

Côtes de Vertiskos TO

Rosé still: dry.
Rosé varieties: Athiri; Assyrtico; Xinomavro.

Sohos TO

White still: dry.
White varieties: Chardonnay.
Red still: dry.
Red varieties: Cabernet Sauvignon; Merlot; Syrah.

PRODUCERS

ARVANITIDI VINEYARDS

Askos, 570 16 Thessaloniki. Tel: +30 239 506 1626; Fax: +30 231 045 0263.
Vineyards owned: 4ha.

This is a recent enterprise whose first few hundred cases were released onto the market in 2004. The vineyard was set up in 1999 by viticulturalist Thanassis Arvanitidis, his wife Maria Netsika, and his brother Giorgos. Netsika, a qualified winemaker, spent many years with Boutari and set up her own PR and wine communication company, Wine Plus, in Thessaloniki. With such a talented team, it is clear that the current wines, however good, have yet to display the estate's full potential.

Initial plantings covered one hectare with the aim of growing to six hectares over the next decade. The site selected was in Sohos, on the slopes of Mount Vertiskos, and Arvanitidis worked hard to ensure that the selected plots were not overly fertile. Cultivation is organic and yields are kept below fifty hectolitres per hectare. Apart from the estate's major varieties of Chardonnay, Cabernet Sauvignon, and Merlot, Arvanitidis has planted Malagousia, Syrah, Barbera, Nebbiolo, Agiorgitiko, Montepulciano, and Koiniariko – a rare local red variety, originating in Asia Minor that is very vigorous and resistant to most diseases, but moderately productive. It buds in the first half of April and is harvested in early October. Early results suggest that Koiniariko can produce wines with rich colour, moderate alcohol and acidity but quite good aromatics.

At the moment, Arvanitidi Vineyards has two products: a Chardonnay and a fifty-fifty Cabernet Sauvignon/Merlot blend. The white is stainless-steel fermented and aged for three months in new French oak and on fine lees. The red is aged for a year in French oak, half of which is new. Both wines are reserved in style, and fashioned in a restrained, French-like manner. They are definitely not showy, but full of fruit, balanced, and elegantly structured.

BABATZIMOPOULOU ESTATE

570 00 Anhialos Thessaloniki. Tel: +30 231 072 2309.

Head office: Arkadioupoleos 17, 546 32 Thessaloniki.

Tel: +30 231 051 9705; Fax: +30 231 051 1465; Email: info@babatzim.gr

Vineyards owned: 25ha; under contract: 18ha; production: 2,450hl.

Anestis Babatzimopoulos is one of those larger-than-life figures in the Greek wine world. You could listen to him discussing history, vine-growing, and winemaking and be fascinated for hours. The details wouldn't concern technicalities, though, for Babatzimopoulos is a spiritual sort – everything is about human lives, love, feelings, and expectations. He is at complete peace with himself and his profession, so much so that making a profit seems almost irrelevant. Babatzimopoulos does not see things the way others do. For example, rather than take the plane, he still uses the train to get from Thessaloniki to Athens, since he "needs those six hours of isolation, just to put thoughts on paper" and "get close" to himself.

With such a personality, it is easy to think that he is an entrepreneur, starting a business from nothing. Yet the Babatzimopoulos company was established in Constantinople (now Istanbul) in 1875, re-founded in Thessaloniki in 1932, and now the Babatzimopoulos Estate is co-owned by Babatzimopoulos and Konstantinos Vavatsis. Babatzimopoulos' field of expertise is not winemaking but vine-growing and distilling. He is one of the world's best producers of distillates. His products include honey distillates, grape and wine distillates from a large number of different varieties, and young and barrique-aged spirits. For this alone, Babatzimopoulos deserves to be far better known.

In the past, the wines of Babatzimopoulos have been less successful than his distillates, possibly because his initial winery in Anhialos was very low-tech and tried to cater for both spirit and wine production. Now the company has a new winery in Ossa, a separate distillation plant, and some excellent vineyards, which are a major plus for any future development. On the southwest side of Mount Vertiskos and at 600 metres altitude (1,968 feet), they have a complex, slightly humid meso-climate that is quite demanding but very promising. Signs of a changing style appeared with the wines from the

2003 and 2004 vintages: the whites had fruit and definition, the reds became better extracted, while the oak handling acquired a certain grace.

The white wines regularly perform better than his reds. The portfolio includes a very clean, aromatic but dense Malagousia, a rich Malvasia di Candia and a Galanos Roditis. Galanos (light blue) Roditis is a clone of the variety with less pink skins that turn a pale shade of blue before *veraison*. This clone was introduced into Macedonia by Tsantali but Babatzimopoulos is the only producer that makes a varietal, or mono-clonal, bottling that is full of the melony *typicité* of good Roditis.

The Babatzim Rosé is a crisp Xinomavro with a lifting touch from some Muscat. Babatzimopoulos Chardonnay, Merlot, Xinomavro, and Cabernet Sauvignon varietal wines are all well-made, typical of their respective varieties, and expected to achieve higher levels of complexity in the coming vintages.

BOUTARI

Head office: Nea Monastiriou 134, 563 34 Eleftherio Thessalonikis;
Tel: +30 231 077 7900; Fax: +30 231 070 6411;
Website: www.boutari.gr; Email: info@boutari.gr
Vineyards owned: 100ha; under contract: 550ha; production: 150,000hl.
See also Boutari entries on pages 130, 144, 232.

Boutaris is one of the most important families in Greek wine and it is responsible for a wine-producing company that, together with Tsantali, Kourtaki, and a few others, has shaped the past of the sector and looks likely to play a role in its future.

Yiannis Boutaris started his wine producing enterprise in Naoussa back in 1879. A winery was built in 1906 and the company began activities in Thessaloniki. The organization arrived at a turning point in the late 1960s, when the two sons of Stelios, then the managing director, took over the business. Konstantinos became involved with management and marketing, while Yiannis Jr looked after production. From a business perspective, Boutari had two additional milestones: in 1987, it was listed in the Athens Stock Exchange, a ground-breaking move for a wine company; and in 1991 the company absorbed Cambas, an historic family-owned brand name and one of the oldest and largest wine producers in Attica.

In the late 1990s the two brothers decided to go their different ways. Konstantinos, being the most business-oriented of the two, remained at the head of the large Boutari company, while Yiannis, far more artistic in nature, departed and focused on his Yianakohori boutique estate (*see* page 136). Boutari is one of the country's most vibrant business entities and a major force in promoting Greek wine on the export market. Its range is reliable, offers good value for money, and has enough volume to back up important customers. Above all, Boutari remains a family firm, having welcomed the fifth generation on board, represented by the open-minded, high-spirited Marina Boutaris.

The Boutari strategy is well laid out. The centre of attention is mainly Greek quality-wine appellations and native varieties. In order to exploit fully the possibilities of each region, Boutari was quick to establish production plants in what were considered the key OPAPs. Over the course of three decades, the company has created wineries in Goumenissa, Santorini, Arhanes in Crete, Mantinia in the Peloponnese, and Attica, as well as the ongoing Naoussa and Thessaloniki businesses.

Boutari wanted to establish its own vineyards, too. The creation of a few estates, most notably in Goumenissa, Santorini, and Crete, provided greater control for the vine-growing, so that a few premium products could be made from the respective appellations. In addition, some parcels were designated as experimental plots so that the winemaking team, managed by the gifted Yiannis Vogiatzis, could try out new ideas and new methods. These experimental wines are difficult to find beyond the visitors' centres at the Boutari wineries, but they can offer some of the most exciting and esoteric examples of the tradition – and the future – of Greek wine.

This tight focus continues throughout the company's portfolio. Boutari wines are about varietal *typicité*, primary fruit, and drinkability, but also about structure and texture. The wines are never heavy, overextracted, or over-oaked. From a commercial standpoint, Boutari never wanted to create show-stopping, premium wines that would impress the world with their density and complexity. The target was the medium- and lower-priced segments of the market. Apart from the name of the company, it doesn't rely on brand names – an exception being Lac des Roches, possibly the most successful, non-resinated Savatiano in Greece.

The basic products consist of a Retsina, a Meliritos semi-sweet white and semi-sweet red, a very successful rosé, and a TO of Crete. The first line of OPAP products includes Santorini, Paros red, Nemea, Goumenissa, and Naoussa. Above that, there is another OPAP range, this time traded as varietals and offering extra depth of character, with Assyrtico, Moschofilero,

Xinomavro, and Agiorgitiko. Boutari was also a champion in trading high-volume varietal wines from French varieties – mainly Syrah, Cabernet Sauvignon, Merlot, Chardonnay, and Sauvignon Blanc – or blends like Cabernet Sauvignon/Agiorgitiko, Xinomavro/Merlot, and a white Roditis/ Xinomavro. In addition, Boutari is one of very few Greek producers that still makes an EO nouveau (*see* Appendix 1).

Kava Boutari, a blend of Xinomavro from Naoussa and Agiorgitiko from Nemea, deserves a special mention. The wine is aged mainly in old oak barrels for a year, spends a further year in stainless-steel vats, and finally, another year in bottle, resulting in a developed, soft, individual, and very appealing wine at a good price. Finally, Boutari has been careful to keep some old vintages of Kava, Naoussa, and Goumenissa in decent quantities. Although these are fragile wines and there is some variation, some fantastic bottles are occasionally encountered.

GEROVASSILIOU ESTATE
575 00 Epanomi Thessaloniki. Tel: +30 239 204 4567/4543; Fax: +30 239 204 4560; Website: www.gerovassiliou.gr; Email: ktima@gerovassiliou.gr
Vineyards owned: 41ha; production: 1,700–2,200hl.

Evangelos Gerovassiliou is regarded as one of the best winemakers in Greece and arguably one of the finest in Europe. Many oenologists consider him to be the best and few can deny the "Gerovassiliou Midas Touch". His personal and business decisions always turn out to be the best possible choices taken at the optimum time.

After fifteen years in the market, Gerovassiliou wines still always sell out at premium prices and at a very conservative discounting policy, across the whole wine trade. Retailers, sommeliers, and consumers have been queuing up for additional stocks of Gerovassiliou white or red for the last fifteen years, no matter how the wines change and evolve – in varietal composition, in style, even in production method. There is no recipe here, just a continuous refinement of every aspect of the product.

Gerovassiliou studied at the University of Bordeaux under the supervision of the father of modern oenology, Professor Emile Peynaud. When Peynaud was hired as a consultant at Domaine Carras (*see* page 160) and it became clear that a resident winemaker was needed, Gerovassiliou was the obvious choice. While still with Carras, he started his own estate in Epanomi, about forty kilometres (24.8 miles) south of Thessaloniki.

The first vines were planted in 1981, the first vintage took place in 1986, and the first small-scale commercial releases were three years later. Initially released under the name of Beau Soleil, the name was swiftly changed to Ktima Gerovassiliou (Gerovassiliou Estate) after a couple of vintages. By the mid-1990s, Gerovassiliou started developing his vineyards and winery with greater urgency, possibly foreseeing the up-and-coming problems at Domaine Carras. After Domaine Carras went bankrupt in 1997, he devoted himself to his estate, creating a perfect miniature domaine – including a world-class corkscrew collection.

In Gerovassiliou Estate few things are left to chance. All the grapes are from the estate's 40.7 hectares on sandy soil and at 300 metres (984 feet) altitude. There is a meteorological station and sensors measure humidity at three levels – on the ground, at a height of fifty centimetres (1.6 feet), and in the soil at a depth of thirty-five centimetres (one foot). The data is constantly analyzed and matched with observations in the vineyard. Using this data, a disease pressure forecast is drawn up, together with a plan for precautions and preventative actions. Vine stress and rate of photosynthesis are closely monitored and drip irrigation is practised independently at each plot and according to each variety – for example, Sauvignon Blanc regularly needs more water than Assyrtico. Integrated Pest Management has been used for the last five years, and organic cultivation has been in place for over a decade. However, the vineyards are not certified. "I drive to the estate from my place and I see it is a spraying day for many growers. As I reach my vineyards and walk through the vines, I cannot see them spraying, I cannot hear them, but I can smell them. How on earth can I go and call my vineyards organic?" he asks. It would be interesting if a few Burgundy producers who claim to cultivate half a row of vines Biodynamically in the middle of Montrachet responded to this comment.

For Malagousia, more than six different rootstocks are used, from the popular SO4 and 110R, to the more esoteric choice of 161-49, in an attempt to reduce the vigour of this prolific vine. Planting densities range from 3,000 to 5,000 vines per hectare and even 10,000 vines-per-hectare parcels have been planted. Unfortunately, this resulted in extreme competition between plants and created high levels of stress. Yields are regularly below fifty hectolitres per hectare, while Chardonnay, Assyrtico, and Syrah are kept below thirty-five hectolitres per hectare. Bud removal, de-leafing, and green harvesting and are used in an effort to get ripeness right at harvest, while the weather patterns of the present and past year are also taken into account. Apart from sugar levels, the phenolic ripeness of red varietals is considered of prime importance. The ionization method is used to determine the proportion of phenolics that have been ionized and are thus more stable and potentially softer.

In the winery, Gerovassiliou does almost everything that can be done by a winemaker: skin contact for whites, apart from the Assyrtico; cold soak for reds; different degrees of clarification for every variety, with higher cloudiness being important for Chardonnay and Malagousia; and a large array of extraction methods, including *delestage* and *pigeage*. Maceration times differ widely from grape to grape – reaching up to sixty days for small batches of the oldest Syrah – and oak maceration vats were introduced in 2004. Whites are not inoculated with artificial yeast, while the higher-alcohol reds are. All estate wines get a certain amount of oak treatment and new French oak is used liberally, but the wines take up the new wood in a very integrated way.

The style of Gerovassiliou Estate wines is extremely commercial, with all the positive meanings of the word – a connoisseur will find the wines complex and serious, a winemaker will consider them thought-provoking, while ordinary consumers will just fall in love at first sip. Gerovassiliou White is a blend of Malagousia and Assyrtico that receives just a kiss of oak for two months. It has a typical nose, full of fresh green peppers and peaches, and is considered by some to be the best aromatic white wine made exclusively with Greek grapes. Export markets receive tiny quantities of a varietal Malagousia, again with a faint touch of oak. The barrel-fermented whites are more structured and full of varietal character: Gerovassiliou Fumé is a grassy Sauvignon Blanc; the Chardonnay is very Burgundian and develops nicely over three to five years; and the Viognier is a heavy, oaky expression of the grape.

Gerovassiliou Red is eighty per cent Syrah, fifteen per cent Merlot, two per cent Grenache Rouge, and three per cent experimental Greek varieties. It is extremely charming on release, usually one-and-a-half years after the harvest, but it does not respond to bottle age. The reverse is true for the monumental Gerovassiliou Syrah, which is close in style to some of the best Tuscan Syrahs. If this wine were made in Italy by a famous producer, it would cost ten times its current price. The final wine, again reserved mainly for export markets, is Avaton, an esoteric blend of Mavrotragano, the obscure but top-quality grape of Santorini, local Mavroudi, and some Limnio. It's a complex, graceful wine, proving that the possible permutations of lesser Greek varietals can yield impressive results if the producer is capable and knows what he wants. And Gerovassiliou certainly does.

KECHRI WINERY

Thesi Olybou, 570 09 Kalohori.

Tel: +30 231 075 1283; Fax: +30 231 075 1372; Email: hkech@tee.gr

Vineyards under contract: 10.5ha; production: 2,200hl.

This family company, established in 1954 near Thessaloniki, works with collaborating vineyards from Messimvria, north of Thessaloniki, and from the general area of central Macedonia. A major part of the business is the popular Doriki line of liqueurs, but the wine side has been constantly developing under the guidance of Dijon-trained Stelios Kechris.

His positioning has been remarkably down to earth, with good pricing policies across his portfolio. His bestselling line is Retsina Kehribari, which leans towards a richer expression of the style. The two Genesis blends, a Xinomavro/Merlot and a Roditis/Sauvignon Blanc, are the lighter lines, while the varietal bottlings of Xinomavro, Cabernet Sauvignon, Sauvignon Blanc, and Roditis, are straightforward but more structured.

MANDOVANI WINERY

V.Gavriilidi 37, 570 19 Neoi Epivates.

Tel: +30 239 202 8319; Fax: +30 239 207 5033.

Vineyards owned: 4ha; under contract: 4.5ha; production: 350hl.

Angelos Mandovani, originally from Italy, decided to create a small family winery and vineyard in Neoi Epivates, near Thessaloniki airport, in 1994. The current annual production is relatively small, with most of it consumed in northern Greece, but occasionally some stock can be found in Athens.

Mandovani White is a blend of Ugni Blanc, Roditis, and Chardonnay. The rosé is a Xinomavro with good varietal definition. Mandovani Rosso is mainly Muscat of Hamburg and is light, with a touch of dry tannins. Finally, Mandovani produces two different Traminers, the lighter Oinopoiima and the heavier Orimo Traminer Vareli. Oinopoiima is a pleasant white, but lacks intensity. Orimo Traminer Vareli means "ripe and oaky Traminer" and this describes it exactly: spicy, oaky, and rich, but possibly a bit heavy. Overall, Mandovani deserves more national recognition then he presently receives.

TSAMTSAKIRI ANASTASIA

575 00 Kato Scholari Epanomis. Tel: +30 239 209 1149; Fax: +30 239 209 1821.
Vineyards owned: 3.7ha; production: 550–600hl.

Anastasia Tsamtsakiri started in Epanomi at about the same time as Evangelos Gerovassiliou in the early 1980s. The winery generated interest in the late 1980s and early 1990s, but the wines have been making far less of an impact, at least on a commercial basis, in the last decade. The wine looks and tastes like it has been made in Drama – elegant and very "French" in approach. The two best wines are made from estate fruit and are called Château Anastasia. The white is made from Assyrtico and Athiri, while the red is Cabernet Sauvignon and Limnio.

HALKIDIKI

The capital of Halkidiki prefecture is Poligiros in the heart of the region, but many administrative activities take place in nearby Thessaloniki. Apart from its northern borders with the prefecture of Thessaloniki, the rest of the region is surrounded by sea. Halkidiki is one of Greece's most distinguished landshapes: a "hand" of three peninsulas extending into the Aegean Sea. These are, from west to east, Kassandra, Sithonia, and Athos, otherwise known as Aghion Oros. The land that joins Halkidiki to the rest of the mainland is dominated by Mount Holomondas (1,166 metres/3,825 feet). Kassandra is fairly flat but the middle peninsula of Sithonia has its eponymous 817-metre (2,680-feet) mountain, and Athos has the imposing presence of Mount Athos, with its peak of 2,030 metres (6,660 feet), at its southernmost tip.

A unique institution, the Aghion Oros, or "Holy Mountain" has been the heart of the Eastern Orthodox church for over a thousand years. The peninsula is comprised of twenty large monasteries and is scattered with *skites*, religious cottages where the monks live. The Greek state practically considers Aghion Oros to be a separate country, and monks are subject to religious laws rather than those voted by the Greek parliament. Aghion Oros is considered sacred and only men – and male animals – are allowed to enter the area. It is a place of stunning natural beauty and visiting it, for those who can (a special permit is required), is an unsurpassed experience. The area has been respected throughout the centuries, and some believe that the amount of knowledge, ancient artefacts, and treasures gathered in the monasteries are on a par with those found in the Vatican.

Climate and history

The climate of Halkidiki is ideal for viticulture – it is essentially maritime, escaping the hot spells found further south or inland. Very few areas of Halkidiki do not have direct eye contact with the sea and, wherever one stands, the coast is only a few kilometres away. The combination of the area's topography and the sea's proximity means that there are plenty of sites benefiting from both the positive influence of the sea and a relatively high altitude. There is little threat of disease, and organic viticulture has always been practised here.

In ancient times Halkidiki probably made some of the most celebrated wines of Greece, with the historic towns of Mendi and Skioni in Kassandra having particularly notable histories. Viticulture has remained important over the years and vine-growing and winemaking owe a lot to the monks of Aghion Oros. In some ways, the monasteries of Athos have acted as an ark, preserving the culture, experience, and know-how gathered over the centuries. Wine was particularly tightly woven into the monks' lifestyle, being a major activity and possibly the only luxury they were allowed. Vine-growing was kept at a high standard and wine was always treated with the utmost respect, being regarded as one of the most valuable assets the monks had. The inhabitants of Aghion Oros had a very special relationship with wine and it was used for sacramental, spiritual, and even healing purposes – each monk had a certain daily allowance for wine, which was doubled every time he fell sick.

Regions and classifications

Halkidiki is second only to Florina in Macedonia in terms of vineyard coverage, with 912 hectares. Porto Carras has over a third of these (311 hectares) and over half of the remaining vineyards are found in Aghion Oros. Kassandra is the least important area. As with many Macedonian regions, there are not many local varieties, with most land dedicated to Assyrtico, Athiri, Limnio, Xinomavro, and Grenache Rouge.

Halkidiki has one OPAP, the Côtes de Meliton, an appellation covering both red and white wine, tailor-made for the needs of the former Domaine Carras. Initially only the varieties were dictated by legislation, but in 1989 their relative proportions became regulated too. Currently, Côtes de Meliton white has to be fifty per cent Athiri, fifteen per cent Assyrtico, and the balance Roditis; while the red must be thirty per cent Cabernet Sauvignon, together with Limnio and Cabernet Franc.

The prefecture also has a number of TOs: a general TO of Halkidiki; another in Sithonia to accommodate Malagousia whites and Syrah reds from Domaine Carras; plus an Agioritikos TO, a regional wine of Aghion Oros. The term "Agioritikos" was, in a way, a forerunner to the TOs. In 1981, about eight years before the official introduction of regional wines in Greece, Agioritikos was approved as a legal label term. It was the first time that a geographical designation could be stated on packaging, without being an OPAP or an OPE. Fortunately, the competitive advantage this conferred took only eight years to be understood by the law-makers.

Côtes de Meliton OPAP

White still: dry.
White varieties: Athiri fifty per cent; Roditis thirty-five per cent; Assyrtico fifteen per cent.
Red still: dry.
Red varieties: Cabernet Sauvignon thirty per cent; Limnio and Cabernet Franc seventy per cent combined.

Halkidiki TO

White still: dry; semi-dry; semi-sweet.
White varieties: Athiri; Assyrtico; Chardonnay; Malagousia; Muscat of Alexandria; Roditis; Sauvignon Blanc; Ugni Blanc.
Rosé still: dry; semi-dry; semi-sweet.
Rosé varieties: Roditis; Xinomavro; Cabernet Sauvignon; Grenache Rouge; Syrah.
Red still: dry; semi-dry; semi-sweet.
Red varieties: Cabernet Sauvignon; Grenache Rouge; Limnio; Merlot; Syrah; Xinomavro.

Agioritikos TO

White still: dry; semi-dry.
White varieties: Assyrtico; Athiri; Chardonnay; Roditis; Sauvignon Blanc; Ugni Blanc; Xinomavro; Zoumiatiko.
Rosé still: dry; semi-dry.

Rosé varieties: Grenache Rouge; Limnio; Roditis; Xinomavro.

Red still: dry; semi-dry.

Red varieties: Cabernet Sauvignon; Grenache Rouge; Limnio; Syrah; Xinomavro.

Sithonia TO

White still: dry.

White varieties: Malagousia must be at least sixty per cent of the blend, the balance being other local recommended and permitted grape varieties.

Red still: dry.

Red varieties: Syrah must be at least sixty per cent of the blend, the balance being other local recommended and permitted grape varieties.

PRODUCERS

MYLOPOTAMOS WINERY

Iero Keli, Aghiou Eftathiou, Karyes, Mt Athos.

Tel: +30 237 702 3774; Fax: +30 237 702 3932.

Website: www.mylopotamos.com; Email: info@mylopotamos.com

Vineyards owned: 5ha; production: 480hl.

Mylopotamos Winery is a brave venture by the monks of Aghios Efstathios in Aghion Oros. Aghios Efstathios is made up of a temple and a *metohi* (monastery dependency). Mylopotamos was founded in 973 AD and the first vineyards were allegedly planted shortly afterwards. Viticulture continued uninterrupted until World War II, when phylloxera and financial difficulties took their toll. In 1990, the local monks decided to inject a new lease of life into the deserted Mylopotamos and fresh plantings followed in 1992. Three years later, the Mylopotamos wine-producing company was the first to bottle wine within Aghion Oros and to market it within Greece and beyond. The current general manager, *monachos* (monk) Epifanios, is helped by a team of gifted wine professionals including winemaker Professor Apostolos Matamis and Thanos Fakorelis, the well-known and highly regarded Bordeaux consultant, who oversees production.

The wines would have been noteworthy whatever the quality. Fortunately, the people behind Mylopotamos have put much effort into making this project work. The style is not the polished and highly defined approach found in the Aghion Oros wines of Tsantali, but there is depth, richness, and extract. The Roditis-based Mylopotamos White is soft but reserved in aromas. The reds of the estate are better. Mylopotamos Red, the basic line, is predominantly Cabernet Sauvignon. A straight Limnio proves that the variety gives its best expression in the general area of Halkidiki. The top wine is a Merlot, having the Fakorelis influence all over it. Finally, a semi-sweet Nama communion wine is produced, which, unsurprisingly, is mainly consumed in the locality.

PORTO CARRAS ESTATE

Porto Carras, 630 81 Neos Marmaras. Tel: +30 237 507 1381;
Fax: +30 237 507 1229. Head office: 20 Solomou Str, 174 56 Alimos.
Tel: +30 210 994 9809; Fax: +30 210 994 9457;
Website: www.portocarraswines.gr; Email: wines@portocarraswines.gr
Vineyards owned: 473ha; production: 5,000hl.

The story of Porto Carras is one of the great stories of Greek wine. It began in the early 1960s, when the wealthy ship owner Yiannis Carras decided to buy a large area in the Sithonia Peninsula, just off the coastal village of Neos Marmaras. The plan was to develop the property in two distinct ways: as a luxurious tourist resort and as a premium wine estate that could compete with not just the best in Greece, but the best in Europe. From day one, Carras was aware that he was aiming high and that he should find the very best expertise. Professor Logothetis, from the University of Thessaloniki, was hired to study the variations in terroir and meso-climate in order to suggest the optimum variety for each parcel of land. Even the renowned oenologist, Professor Emile Peynaud, was brought in from the University of Bordeaux. Peynaud never vinified wine at Domaine Carras as many people thought, but he did supervise the establishment of the vineyards, and in particular the French varieties. Evangelos Gerovassiliou, a former student of Peynaud, became resident oenologist, and by the mid-1970s Domaine Carras was in full bloom. At the time, the estate was the largest private viticultural enterprise in Europe and it still is one of the biggest organic vineyards in the world. By any standards, it was an extremely ambitious endeavour.

The fine detail of the vineyards was and still is breathtaking. Petite Syrah, Cabernet Franc, and Cabernet Sauvignon were planted in the northern part of the estate, where conditions are slightly cooler and more humid. Merlot, Limnio, and Sauvignon Blanc were planted in another cluster at a lower altitude and in a drier spot. On parcels overlooking the resort and the winery, Assyrtico and Roditis were planted, topped up with more Cabernet

Sauvignon on the higher parts. In all three groups, stripes of Athiri separated plots of the other varieties. In 1976, Logothetis requested permission from Carras to use a small plot of land in order to plant some rare indigenous varieties like Lagorthi, Thrapsathiri, Liatiko, Debina and, in particular, Malagousia. In the schist soils of Domaine Carras, Malagousia yielded less than twenty-four hectolitres per hectare, which was possibly a reason for the outstanding quality of the resulting wines. Currently, the legal limit is fifty-six hectolitres per hectare, the lowest in Greece except for Santorini, but the vineyards rarely yield as much.

In 1982, a few years after the initial vintages of Carras started making waves in the Greek market, the region was awarded OPAP status. It was the first time in Greece that the authorities had conferred this classification on a private business, and it is likely that the Carras family's social standing, plus some important friends, were key elements in this achievement. At the time, however, Domaine Carras was making the best wines in Greece, a position only challenged in the 1990s. For many Greek wine-lovers, Château Carras 1993 is the best dry red wine ever produced in the country, with 1990 and 1975 lagging not too far behind. The Porfyrogenitos bottlings, a special selection from the best vintages released after more than a decade, suffered from huge bottle variation, but the best were on a par with Bordeaux *grand cru classé* châteaux. When Domaine Carras presented the first commercial vintage of its Malagousia in the prestigious Grande Bretagne Hotel in Athens, the audience was astonished. The Syrahs from 1993 and 1994 are still yardsticks for Greek winemakers. Beyond these exclusive products, the Athiri/Assyrtico Melissanthi, the varietal Limnio, and a blanc de blancs were all stunning examples of their respective genres.

Unfortunately, in the late 1990s, financial problems ensued. Some unlucky business moves hurt the credit rating of the estate, which was swiftly confiscated by the banks. After a long series of discussions and negotiations, the Stegos family took hold of the complete property, from the winery, vineyards, and brands to the hotels and the marinas. Yet two years of turmoil had left the winery – especially its vineyards – in an abandoned state, and the new owners had to invest vast amounts of money just to make the environment workable.

The current management is working hard to develop modern, fresh lines like Five Rings, Ambelos, and Hellenic Portraits. At the premium level, a Porfyrogenitos has been released from the 1993 vintage that does not exactly show the grace of Château Carras from the same year and as expected its price tag is absurd (200 euros per bottle). Malagousia is produced in an oaked and an unoaked version, with the latter offering more varietal *typicité*. The Melissanthi and the Château Carras are returning to form, while Syrah is now clearly the flagship of the estate. However, it is difficult for anyone who has been exposed to the previous glories of Domaine Carras to be objective in any critique of these efforts. Hopefully, the Stegos family will realize the true potential of Porto Carras Estate before too long.

TSANTALI

638 00 Agios Pavlos Halkidiki. Tel: +30 239 907 6100/8; Fax: +30 239 905 1185; Website: www.tsantali.gr; Email: export@tsantali.gr
Vineyards owned: 260ha; under contract: 1,250ha; production: 160,000–200,000hl.
See also Tsantali entries on pages 111, 141, 213.
Tsantali is one of a small number of families that has been vital in the development of modern Greek wine and there is every indication that this pivotal role will continue. Tsantali has been active in promoting Greek wines far beyond the national borders, while success at home always came from products that have been built on good value.

Due to their geographical proximity, many people compare Tsantali with Boutari, the two grand wine families of Macedonia. Both are very able, major players, producing value-for-money wines, but the philosophy behind these wines could not be more diverse. While Boutari has faith in the major appellations and in charismatic indigenous varietals, Tsantali's products try to rediscover the past and (possibly lost) glories of Greece. For example, Tsantali rejuvenated OPAP Rapsani, the wine made in the shadow of Mount Olympus in Thessaly, while Maronia in Thrace, the ancient equivalent to today's Bordeaux, is already providing Tsantali with useful tools to conquer even more export markets. The company single-handedly brought the amazing, ancient, and mystical terroir of Aghion Oros to the forefront of modern Greek wine production, simultaneously creating one of the most popular wine labels of the last twenty years.

This does not mean that Tsantali does not use modern major appellations – there is a winery and major investment in Naoussa, the company buys wines from Patras, Limnos, and Samos on a négociant basis, and oversees winemaking in the Cooperative of Nemea.

Tsantali originated in eastern Thrace, and the family's main interest was the production of ouzo and tsipouro. The company and its staff were transplanted to Macedonia and wine increasingly became a much more important part of the business. Today, the volume of distillates produced is about a quarter that of wine, although it makes slightly more revenue.

Tsantali is a professional company employing high-calibre experts. The president is Ioanna Tsantalis, but the day-to-day running of the company is the responsibility of Giorgos Tsantalis, an energetic person with a highly hands-on approach, who handles the German market – Germany absorbs sixty-five per cent of all its exports. Managing director Angelos Dimitriadis is in charge of strategic planning, Pavlos Argyropoulos is the winemaking director and one of the most experienced and multi-faceted oenologists in Greece, and last but not least, viticultural director Giorgos Salpigidis is equally indispensable.

The general philosophy is based on strong viticultural assets, including the development of totally new or underperforming regions. Salpigidis is an extremely busy man, organizing seminars and workshops for more than 1,200 growers and vineyard workers who are associated with the company. These people learn how to cultivate their vineyards organically under an "Integrated Vineyard Management" regime. Tsantali's viticultural team lays out a whole set of criteria that are specific to each site, grape variety, and projected wine style. Most importantly, there is a complex pricing policy for grapes that relates to how the above criteria are met, as opposed to being purely related to sugar levels.

A special mention is reserved for two vineyards in Halkidiki: Chromitsa and Aghios Pavlos. The vineyards of Metohi at Chromitsa, owned by the Panteleimon Monastery, cover eighty hectares on the slopes of Mount Athos. Most are fully terraced and in deep, infertile, sandy-clay soils. Agioritikos TO wines have been made since the 1980s and have been a phenomenal success. The white is currently an Assyrtico, Athiri, and Roditis blend, while the off-dry rosé is Limnio, Roditis, and Xinomavro. In the 1990s, Tsantali decided to go a step further and crafted a premium white and red that are possibly the company's best products. Chromitsa is an oak-aged blend of Chardonnay, Assyrtico, and Athiri, full of fruit and extract, while Metohi is a dense, structured but fine-grained Limnio and Cabernet Sauvignon blend.

The scale of things in Aghios Pavlos to the west, around the company's head offices and main winery and distillery, is rather different, with twenty hectares owned by the company and 230 growers supplying fruit from 400 closely monitored hectares. Here the climate is slightly hotter than at Aghion Oros while the soils are lighter but equally deep. Ampelones Aghiou Pavlou

White is a popular and crisp Roditis with a lifting touch of Sauvignon Blanc, while the same area produces a very good varietal Merlot.

Given the sheer quantity of wine produced, Salpigidis is providing Argyropoulos with first-rate fruit. Argyropoulos manages a chameleon-like winemaking style, always taking into account market needs. For example, Tsantali championed the idea of producing entry-level wines for the national market with four to seven grams of residual sugar per litre, which has repeatedly been proved successful. In the upper range of wines, there is a very sensitive use of oak, underlying and supporting but never masking the fruit. Finally, all Tsantali wines, from the cheapest to the most expensive, only reach the market when they are ready to drink – some could improve, but none are too young to be drunk straight away.

As might be expected, Tsantali produces a vast array of products. At the basic level, Makedonikos white, rosé, and red are excellent value and a good introduction for younger wine-drinkers. Moschomavro is a charming summer red, with an intense Muscat nose, a fresh and light palate, and just a hint of tannin. At the upper end, Kava Tsantali, a blend of Xinomavro and Cabernet Sauvignon, is full of spicy complexity.

SERRES

Serres is one of Macedonia's largest prefectures. Its shape almost mirrors the outline of the Strimonas River valley, running from northwest to southeast, with its delta located in the Orfanos Gulf, halfway between Halkidiki and Kavala. The Strimonas River flows from Kerkini Lake, close to the tri-national borders point of FYROM, Bulgaria, and Greece, and is pivotal for both agriculture and almost all the trade of the region. The Strimonas Valley is located between the Vertiskos Mountains in the west and the Vrontous, Menikio, and Pangeo mountains in the east, and is relatively fertile for northern Greece.

Viticulture in Serres has a long history, much in line with its western neighbour, Thessaloniki. Today about 400 hectares are dedicated to vineyards, most of which are on the slopes, although the sub-areas all have some vines. The area has a low profile, at least as far as quality wine production is concerned. There are no registered winemaking companies, and most local production takes place either in home cellars or for use by large Macedonian producers for multi-regional blends. However, there is one TO appellation in the area, relating to white wines made predominantly from Zoumiatiko, together with smaller additions of Muscat of Alexandria and the local Asproudes (*see* Glossary).

Serres TO

White still: dry; semi-dry; semi-sweet.
White varieties: Zoumiatiko must be at least fifty per cent of the blend, the balance being other local recommended and permitted grape varieties.

KAVALA

Kavala, together with Drama, forms eastern Macedonia, separating the rest of the mainland from Thrace. Kavala is a coastal prefecture, reaching from Serres and Drama in the north to the northernmost part of the Aegean in the south. The Nestos River forms Kavala's eastern borders. The main plains within Kavala are located primarily around the Nestos Delta, in the coastal areas, and in the strip of land that connects the cities of Kavala and Drama. Much of the land is at low altitudes, except for the two main mountains: Pangeo, east of Kavala City, which forms a natural border with Serres, and Lekanis, located northeast of the capital, at the meeting point of Kavala, Drama, and Xanthi. Thassos Island is opposite Kavala city and is dominated by Mount Ipsario at 1,205 metres' altitude (3,950 feet).

Kavala is the capital city of the prefecture and its port is a major economic centre for all of northern Greece – and has been for at least three centuries. It is a key Aegean outpost for a large part of the Balkan Peninsula, and a meeting point between east and west. This prime location favoured the development of a mercantile elite in the area, and the existing wealth, with the exception of Thassos, somehow inhibited the development of a strong tourism sector, despite the area's natural beauty and historical interest. By way of illustration, top Bordeaux growths have been on sale in Kavala since the early twentieth century.

Climate

The climate of Kavala and the area around Mount Pangeo is particularly noteworthy. The combination of topography and prevailing wind directions form a heat trap in the Kavala region. Southeast- and south-facing slopes receive plenty of sunshine, while being sheltered from cold, northern winds. These vineyards overlook the Aegean Sea but are not as influenced by sea breezes as, for example, Maronia in Thrace. The latitude of the area, close to

41°, still guarantees a cooler meso-climate than regions in Thessaly, Central Greece, and further south. However, by Macedonian standards, it is still quite warm: the average mean temperature of the hottest month, July, is 26.5°C (79.9°F), which is 0.7°C (1.3°F) higher than Alexandroupoli and 2.4°C (4.3°F) than Amyndeo. Only Thessaloniki is comparable, but there is a big difference in average wind speed: 5.5 knots compared with 4.1 in Kavala. There are two rainfall peaks during the year, one around April the other November, while the driest months are August and September, with average rainfall of 17.5 millimetres (0.7 inches) and 10.4 millimetres (0.4 inches) respectively.

Regions, grapes, and classifications

The whole region, especially the slopes of Mount Pangeo, is a significant viticultural area providing high-quality fruit to both local and other producers. Table grapes are important, but with 630 hectares currently planted, wine grapes are growing in importance, driven mainly by an increasing demand for international varieties. Greek grapes feature, but instead of there being any particularly notable local grapes, most of them are selected from the popular Greek choices such as Roditis or Assyrtico. Sauvignon Blanc, Chardonnay, Cabernets Sauvignon and Franc, Merlot, and Syrah are the major focus for most new plantings. The wines of Kavala generally have a brightness of fruit and warmth that is not found in many Macedonian wine regions.

In general, Kavala has been viewed as an attractive location for viticultural investments – as well as its pleasant meso-climate, there are several higher-altitude sites yet to be exploited. And the soils are relatively fertile, so that healthy yields of ripe fruit can be attained easily. Apart from the Mavrommatis and Protopapas wineries that have been around for several decades, most of the wineries have been established since the late 1990s. Two are investments from successful producers from outside the area: Biblia Chora, co-founded by Evangelos Gerovassiliou from Epanomi in Thessaloniki and ex-Domaine Costa Lazaridi winemaker, Vassilis Tsaktsarlis; and Mackedon Winery, set up by Drama's Château Nico Lazaridi. More wineries are on the way, such as one from the Lalikos family.

Due to its recent emergence, Kavala's wine industry remains relatively under-regulated, although bearing in mind that most developments have happened in recent years, this is understandable. The only regional TO, established in 1995 and called Pangeoritikos, relates to the slopes of Mount

Pangeo and covers all wine colours. White TOs enjoy an array of varietal options, since regulations are more concerned with keeping the percentages of Roditis, Assyrtico, and Ugni Blanc under certain levels than the actual make-up of the wine. The reds of the area are Bordeaux-influenced, with Cabernet Sauvignon taking a minimum of fifty per cent of the blend and Merlot following with fifteen per cent.

Pangeoritikos TO

White still: dry.
White varieties: Roditis up to thirty-five per cent of the blend; Assyrtico up to ten per cent; Ugni Blanc up to ten per cent; the balance being other local recommended and permitted grape varieties.
Rosé still: dry.
Rosé varieties: Cabernet Sauvignon at least fifty per cent of the blend; Limnio at least fifteen per cent; the balance being other local recommended and permitted grape varieties.
Red still: dry.
Red varieties: Cabernet Sauvignon at least fifty per cent of the blend; Merlot at least fifteen per cent; the balance being other local recommended and permitted grape varieties.

PRODUCERS

BIBLIA CHORA ESTATE

Kokkinohori, 640 08 Kavala. Tel: +30 259 204 4974; Fax: +30 259 204 4975; Email: oinopedion@anc.gr
Vineyards owned: 15ha; under contract: 10ha; production: 1,550hl.
Established in 2001, Biblia Chora caused a stir within a year of its wines first appearing in mid-2002. It might not have the brand recognition of some of the older wineries, but it does have fanatical friends who make sure that every restaurant's allocation is swiftly sold out. Among its peers in price terms, Biblia Chora is one of the hottest names in Greek wine.

This success was no surprise, since the winery was the brainchild of two high-profile – and already highly successful – winemakers: Evangelos Gerovassiliou and Vassilis Tsaktsarlis. As well as being responsible for some of the most impressive Domaine Carras wines, Gerovassiliou had already proved that he could create something quie substantial out of nothing at his Epanomi estate. Tsaktsarlis is the winemaker behind the inspiring initial vintages of Domaine Costa Lazaridi in Drama, and the man who introduced a New World style of aromatic whites, especially Sauvignon Blanc, to the Greek wine-drinking public.

As far as wine production essentials are concerned, the winery has been established very swiftly, and the more decorative, less functional parts of the building will be installed over the course of the next years. The situation in the vineyards is in a similar phase: while new vineyards are constantly being established in an area of fifteen hectares, at an altitude of 350 metres (1,148 feet), there are ten hectares' worth of growers supplying fruit to cover ongoing needs. The standards in the vineyard and in the cellar are at least as high as at the Gerovassiliou Estate.

Both Biblia Chora and Gerovassiliou wines are made in a very modern, ultra-clean, highly reductive style: very charming, intense, and commercial without lacking depth. However, Biblia Chora wines have an extra degree of varietal clarity and power, while the Gerovassiliou wines show more subtlety and underlying complexity.

The basic line, simply called Biblia Chora, forms the majority of the estate's production and sales. Biblia Chora White is often described as "the Amethystos of the 2000s" (Amethystos was an extremely successful label for Domaine Costa Lazaridi in the 1990s). Made from sixty per cent Sauvignon Blanc and forty per cent Assyrtico, the nose is dominated by the Sauvignon, with the most New Zealand-like aromatic character to be found in any Greek wine. It is stainless-steel fermented with a few months on fine lees. Biblia Chora Rosé is a pure Syrah, crisp and light but full of red berry fruit flavours. Currently this is the only Syrah wine produced by the estate, since the young vines are not deemed ready to produce the quality needed for a rich, extracted red wine. However, there are substantial plantings of the variety and, in the future, a Biblia Chora Syrah is likely to appear. Biblia Chora Red, a fifty/fifty blend of Cabernet Sauvignon and Merlot aged in new French oak for a year, is brimming with ripe, juicy fruit and sweet oak, while the tannin structure is velvety but dense.

This line of wines is augmented by three others, all of which are small-volume, premium-priced wines. Ovilos is a white that raised more than a few eyebrows with its inaugural 2002 vintage. It is fifty per cent Assyrtico and fifty per cent Semillon, aged in new French oak for eight months. This is another typically Tsaktsarlis, trend-setting style, with broadness, richness, intense oak and ripe fruit, while the nose is so grassy that it is reminiscent of a very ripe California Sauvignon Blanc. The first vintage came from quite a difficult year, so it is possibly not the best expression of the wine, but from 2003 onwards it will be very interesting to see how Ovilos develops in bottle. The last two wines are called Areti and have also caused a stir, especially the red. It is the only Agiorgitiko wine produced in northern Greece and proves that the variety has world-class potential in a range of terroirs. It is tighter in character than most Nemea wines, both in structure and in flavour profile, but the character of the variety is all there, enveloped in density and intensity. Areti White is an Assyrtico, not as pioneering as its counterpart, but a relatively aromatic expression of the grape.

The portfolio of Biblia Chora is by no means complete and there are fresh ideas for additional wines from the coming vintages, such as Olivos Red, a pure Cabernet Sauvignon. One way or another, Gerovassiliou and Tsaktsarlis look set to keep their fans happy and busy.

FELLAHIDIS WINERY

PO Box 5, Agios Andreas, 640 07 Kavala. Tel: +30 259 402 2457;
Fax: +30 251 022 4270; Website: www.fellahidis.gr; Email: fellahidis@otenet.gr
Vineyards owned: 2.2ha; under contract: 10ha; production: 600–800hl.

This is one of the smaller wineries in the region, established in the early 1990s with the wines released onto the market several years later. Savvas Fellahidis, the man behind the venture, has always been fully committed to organic viticulture and was the first producer in the region to seek organic accreditation. Much effort goes into the cultivation of his 2.2 hectares, as well as keeping his contracted growers up to speed.

The wines of Fellahidis have a traditional feel to them, and almost all are aged in used oak. The basic range is Kourvoulo, meaning "vine plant". Kourvoulo Red and Rosé are from Cabernet Sauvignon and both are aged in oak for three months, the latter being a rare style of a semi-dry rosé with oak treatment. Kourvoulo White is a reserved Roditis, given a lift by a dash of Sauvignon Blanc. The two top dry wines, labelled "Organic Vineyards of Savvas Fellahidis", are a Chardonnay aged in oak for three months, plus a complex blend of Cabernet Sauvignon, Merlot, Syrah, and Limnio matured in barriques for six months, and clearly the best from this winery. Fellahidis also makes a rare Vin de Liqueur Contessa with Roditis from Thassos Island. It is aged in oak for just three months and overall is quite a reserved wine. His Fellahidis Makedonissa Retsina is a decent example of the style.

LALIKOU FAMILY WINERY

Palaia Kavala, 65 500 Kavala. Tel/Fax: +30 251 083 6938.

Vineyards owned: 12.8ha; production: 1,000hl.

This new venture has a very good vineyard already in place and its new winery was completed just before the 2005 harvest. Kostas Lalikos has impressive landholdings in some of the highest parts of Mount Pangeo, at 750 metres' altitude (2,460 feet), planted only with French varieties. All his vineyards are in the process of being certified organic.

There have been some releases of Lalikou wines, made in rented facilities and in an old Lalikos family winery, which were interesting but more suggestive of potential for the future. The exotic whites, a Viognier aged in oak for six months and a Gewurztraminer, are full of spice and very typical of their varieties. The whites are completed by a Sauvignon Blanc and an oak-aged Chardonnay. Lalikou reds are soft and fruity, and the varietal Merlot is a touch better than the Lalikou Red, a Cabernet Sauvignon with twenty per cent Merlot. Some other reds are in the pipeline as young vines mature – possibly a Syrah as well as a much-anticipated Petit Verdot.

MACKEDON WINERY

Platanotopos Piereon, 640 08 Kavala. Tel: +30 252 108 2050; Fax: +30 252 108 2047; Website: www.mackedon-winery.gr; Email: mackedon_winery@yahoo.com

Vineyards owned: 6.5ha; under contract: 25ha; production: 1,260hl.

See also Château Nico Lazaridi entry on page 177.

Established in 1999, Mackedon is the sister winery of Château Nico Lazaridi in Drama. With the success of the Drama winery, the Lazaridis family felt that the market could sustain an expansion. However, Federico Lazaridis, Nicos' son and company managing director, felt that further growth for the existing château might dilute both image and quality. He felt that new products were needed and, possibly, a brand new winery. So attention moved to Kavala – an easier place than Drama in which to launch a new project – and the Mackedon Winery was born.

With a large number of good-quality vine-growers already in the area, there was no need to develop substantial vineyard holdings. The approach was to be totally different from Château Nico Lazaridi, and the identity of Mackedon has been built up on more modern, obviously varietal wines, both in packaging and style. If the Lazaridi Drama wines were French-inspired, then the Kavala products have more than a twist of New World vivacity.

Cabernet Sauvignon, Merlot, Syrah, Chardonnay, and Sauvignon Blanc grapes have all been sourced. Apart from long-term contracts with some of the best Pangeo *vignerons*, Lazaridis and the Bordeaux-trained Bakis Tsalkos, the skilled oenologist behind all Lazaridi projects, decided to create a 6.5-hectare vineyard around the winery. This could be used to develop a core of high quality fruit for most of the Mackedon portfolio, as well as to experiment with certain varieties in the new terroir. Two lines of products have been developed: Mackedon and Lion d'Or (or Hrysos Leon). Mackedon wines are the cheapest products, a Sauvignon Blanc/Roditis/Assyrtico and a Cabernet Sauvignon/Merlot produced in small volumes and aimed largely at the local Kavala market.

The Lion d'Or range used to comprise four varietals, all aged for at least a few months in French barriques: a Chardonnay, a Sauvignon Blanc, a Syrah, and a Cabernet Sauvignon. However, since 2003, Nicos, Federico, and Bakis decided to redefine the level of synergy between the two wineries, leading to a reshuffling of product styles and labels. The Mackedon line has been retained intact, being simple but very straightforward, clean, and soft. The Lion d'Or Chardonnay and Cabernet Sauvignon also stayed, the former showing hints of oak and broad but not full structure, and the latter having good blackberry fruit and velvety tannins. Lion d'Or Syrah was re-branded as Nico Lazaridi Syrah and labelled close to the style of the Lazaridi Merlot from Drama. This Syrah is much more restrained than other Macedonian examples of the grape, closer to France in character. Lion d'Or Sauvignon Blanc was replaced by a sixty per cent Semillon, forty per cent Sauvignon Blanc blend, aged in oak for six months – once again showing a leaning towards Bordeaux.

MAVROMMATIS WINERY
7km Kavala–Thessaloniki Rd, 641 00 Amisiana.
Tel: +30 051 032 6265; Fax: +30 051 032 6207;
Website: www.mavrommatis-wines.gr; Email: mavrowine@cav.forthnet.gr
Vineyards under contract: 30ha; production: 3,000hl.

The oldest and largest winery in Kavala by a long way, established in 1906; this historic venture did a lot for the survival of viticulture in the region, as well as keeping the Kavala winemaking flag flying high for many decades. Today Giorgos Mavrommatis is both general manager and oenologist. There are no vineyards owned, so the fruit is sourced from collaborating vineyards and local growers. Currently, Mavrommatis wines have a limited presence outside of the general Kavala region.

The Mavrommatis style is quite tight and reserved, aiming for structure over flavour, more spices and herbs than primary fruit. The best wines are Aisthitos, a Sauvignon Blanc; Rarum Vinum, a barrel-aged Chardonnay; the age-worthy Porfyros, made from predominantly Cabernet Sauvignon and smaller proportions of Merlot; and Mavrommatis Merlot.

PROTOPAPAS WINERY
Kariani–Kavala 640 08. Tel: +30 258 204 4888; Fax: +30 259 204 4902;
Website: www.protopapaswines.com; Email: info@protopapaswines.com
Vineyards owned: 20ha; under contract: 30ha; production: 200hl.

One of the pioneers, if not the mavericks, of Macedonian wine production, Thanassis Protopapas was introducing new ideas long before they became mainstream, but only rarely is he credited for them. A chemical engineer by profession, Protopapas has been producing varietal wines since his Cabernet Sauvignon appeared in 1985. New varietals have been regularly introduced ever since. He was one of the first producers to strike long-term contracts with the vine-growing monasteries in Mount Athos (*see* page 156), to vinify them *in situ*, and to bottle them in Kavala. Finally, he was the first wine producer to offer bottle-storage and ageing facilities for his clients.

However, Protopapas never became mainstream or particularly well known. Apart from a brief spell of popularity during the 1990s, mainly due to his Mount Athos Demi-Sec Rosé, these wines have been considered a curiosity rather than trend-setters. The small quantities produced and the company's apparent commercial shyness must account for much of this, as well as the style of the wines: relatively light, not ultra-clean, not extracted, and yet full of flavour.

The whites do not see any oak, but all the reds are routinely matured in a blend of French, American, and Russian oak for a year, plus an additional year in bottle before release. Varietal offerings include Sauvignon Blanc, Chardonnay, Syrah (labelled "Sirah"), Merlot, and Cabernet Sauvignon. There are two basic TO Pangeoritikos wines: a very crisp white blend of Chardonnay and Sauvignon Blanc with just a touch of Roditis, and a fine-grained red made from Cabernets Sauvignon and Franc, Merlot, and Syrah.

The specialized products, like the Agioritikos appellation wines, offer a more interesting style. The Mount Athos vineyards are plots where several varieties are interplanted, and the average vine age exceeds sixty years. Three wines are produced from these sites and all are less commercial, less polished, but much more complex and individual than the basic Agioritikos range from Tsantali. All three colours are blends of many varieties, more than six for each colour, vinified together. The principal grapes for the red are Limnio, Cabernet Sauvignon, and Xinomavro. The same together with Fokiano, dominate the *demi-sec* rosé, while the white has Assyrtico, Chardonnay, Athiri, Sauvignon Blanc, and up to six additional varieties. Finally, the most individual wine is Thassoinos, a red wine produced from Georgina grapes from pergolas in Panagia, a small village in northeast Thassos. Georgina is a very rare variety and Protopapas is the only producer that deals with it, let alone produces a varietal wine. Thassoinos is a red wine verging on the rosé, since Georgina gives extremely light colour, alcohol of around eleven per cent, and a very light tannin structure. Nevertheless, Thassoinos has a surprising aromatic complexity – full of fresh strawberries and ripe, sweet cherries – that makes it irresistible. Protopapas claims that this wine is at its best five years after the harvest, but it is difficult to see any important reasons for waiting that long.

SIMEONIDIS WINES

Eleohori Neas Peramou, 640 07. Tel: +30 259 409 2789; Fax: +30 259 408 2440; Website: www.simeonidiswines.gr; Email: info@simeonidiswines.gr
Vineyards owned: 5ha; under contract: 20ha; production: 1,000hl.

One of the youngest Kavala wineries, this was established in 2001 by Polihronis Simeonidis. He owns some vineyards, but Simeonidis is well-connected in the local vine-growing community – three generations of the family have been involved with wine production – so access to good-quality fruit from other growers is relatively easy. Low yields are very important for Simeonidis, who prefers yields of less than sixty hectolitres per hectare.

The overall presentation of the portfolio is very much influenced by the Drama school of labels (*see* page 175), while the style of wines is more about primary fruit than anything else. Whites are cool-fermented and do not receive any oak treatment, while reds get just a three-month-long kiss of oak. Iliostalaktos Red and White are the multi-varietal blends, both having a small proportion of Muscat of Alexandria to lift flavours. Idipnoos White, from the premium range, is a simple Sauvignon Blanc/Roditis blend, while Idipnoos Chardonnay and Idipnoos Sauvignon Blanc show much more character.

Idipnoos Red is a straightforward Cabernet Sauvignon and Merlot blend, while the varietal Idipnoos Merlot is soft, round, and easy to drink.

DRAMA

Drama is land-locked in the northern half of east Macedonia, bordering Bulgaria to the north, Thrace to the east, Kavala to the south, and Serres to the west. The capital is the town of Drama, located at the centre of the region. The prefecture is sheltered in the north by the impressive Rodopi Mountain range, while the lower-altitude Menikio, Falakro, and Lekanis mountains form a complete umbrella within the region, running from west to east. The only low-altitude land is the area around the capital itself and the strip of land that connects Drama with Kavala.

Despite good protection from northern winds, the climate of Drama is cooler than that found in Kavala or Serres. The average summer temperature is 0.8°C (1.4°F) lower than that of Kavala, there is less sunshine, and there is a difference in rainfall and overall humidity. Mount Menikio on the west stops the rain clouds, and since the coast is over thirty kilometres (almost nineteen miles) away, the Aegean Sea's influence is not important.

In economic terms, Drama presents a complete contrast to Kavala, with a large part of the population facing significant economic difficulties. This was not always the case – Drama used to be a relatively wealthy area, with many clothing manufacturers providing the main source of income. However, as other Balkan countries and China started to offer cheaper labour costs, so Drama was abandoned by external investors, leading to high rates of unemployment. Today, most employment relates to agriculture, mainly grain and corn production in the fertile soils of the Drama Valley. Marble mines are also important – Drama marble is extremely popular with architects around the world, but the industry is extremely centralized.

The development of viticulture in Drama over the last three decades has certainly been dramatic and fascinating. Despite archaeological evidence of a strong wine-producing sector in the area, especially close to Adriani, there have been no substantial vineyards in the region for at least four centuries. There are no specific viticultural reasons – just a combination of cultural and economic factors. This changed in the late 1980s when the Lazaridis brothers, Nicos and Kostas, decided to start a winery. One of Europe's largest marble producers, the Lazaridis family has been one of the region's most affluent. With no existing plantations, the Lazaridis duo invested heavily in vineyards, making a boutique winery set-up the only option. In just a few vintages, Château Nico Lazaridi produced some of the best and most expensive wines in Greece. By the early 1990s, the two brothers, both strong personalities and extremely energetic, decided to part company. As a result, Kostas started Domaine Costa Lazaridi in 1992.

This parting of the ways, however unfortunate on a personal level, was one of the most fortunate events in the history of Greek wine in the 1990s. By 1994, both Lazaridis ventures were extremely successful, establishing Drama out of nowhere as one of the most up-and-coming – and upmarket – wine-producing regions of Greece. The two estates had much in common: the name; extraordinary wineries full of luxurious marble; substantial vineyard holdings; Bordeaux-inspired varieties and blends; pricey but very successful wines; and finally, Château Mouton Rothschild-inspired labels. The wineries both promoted Drama wine and gave an identity to the area. However, the styles of the two wineries could not have been more different, with Kostas going for intense aromas and a crisp style, while Nicos opted for texture and structure.

This success was like an electric shock to the Greek wine industry. Suddenly there were imitators of the Lazaridi products everywhere; many small landowners in Drama began to plant vines, and investment in the region increased. In 1995, Yiannis Papadopoulos and Yiannis Kalaitzidis established the Wine Art winery. A year later, Giorgos Manolesakis and Pavlos Pavlidis founded their respective estates. As a result of this interest, today Drama is one of the best-known regions among Greek wine-lovers. In many ways, it is the New Zealand of Greece. With only 350 hectares of vineyard and just five wineries that craft some superb wines, the region's image and commercial importance far exceed its true significance in terms of volume. In terms of the quality of wine per bottle produced, Drama is one of the top prefectures in Greece.

However, the late development of viticulture in Drama has left it outside the current quality classification system. There are only three TOs, mostly developed to cater for the needs of the two Lazaridis wineries: a prefectural TO of Drama; a TO of Agora, close to Château Nico Lazaridi; and a TO of Andriani, for Domaine Costa Lazaridi. The varietal mix of the vineyards is dominated by red and white Bordeaux varieties, together with Ugni Blanc, Assyrtico, Roditis, Chardonnay, and Syrah. The wines of Drama are regularly compared with those of its neighbour, Kavala. It is difficult to generalize and there are many contrasting styles within both areas, but if Drama is Left Bank Bordeaux, then Kavala is Right Bank, or, if Drama is France then Kavala is South Africa: the former is firmer while the latter is slightly more exuberant, but both are potentially exhilarating.

Drama TO

White still: dry.
White varieties: Sauvignon Blanc at least forty per cent of the blend; Semillon at least fifteen per cent; Assyrtico; Roditis; Muscat of Alexandria; Chardonnay; Ugni Blanc.
Rosé still: dry.
Rosé varieties: Cabernet Sauvignon at least fifty-five per cent of the blend; Roditis; Grenache Rouge; Merlot.
Red still: dry.
Red varieties: Cabernet Sauvignon at least forty per cent of the blend; Merlot at least fifteen per cent; Limnio; Cabernet Franc; Syrah.

Agora TO

White still: dry.
White varieties: Ugni Blanc at least fifty-five per cent of the blend; Roditis; Muscat of Alexandria; Chardonnay; Sauvignon Blanc.
Rosé still: dry.
Rosé varieties: Cabernet Sauvignon; Cabernet Franc; Grenache Rouge.
Red still: dry.
Red varieties: Merlot at least fifty-five per cent of the blend; Cabernet Sauvignon; Cabernet Franc.

Andriani TO

White still: dry.
White varieties: Semillon at least forty per cent of the blend; Assyrtico at least ten per cent; Chardonnay; Ugni Blanc.
Rosé still: dry.
Rosé varieties: Cabernet Sauvignon; Merlot.
Red still: dry.
Red varieties: Merlot at least forty per cent of the blend; Syrah at least ten per cent; Cabernet Sauvignon; Cabernet Franc.

PRODUCERS

CHATEAU NICO LAZARIDI

PO Box 101, Agora, 661 00 Drama. Tel: +30 252 108 2049/50; Fax: +30 252 108 2047; Website: www.chateau-lazaridi.gr; Email: n-lazaridi@otenet.gr

Vineyards owned: 52ha; under contract: 30ha; production: 3,950hl.

This is the winery that started the new viticultural era for Drama, starting trends that went far beyond the limits of this prefecture. Marble magnate Nicos Lazaridis created a superlative winery that became a model for many wine producers, particularly in the way the wines are labelled. The extensive family collection of paintings was used to decorate the bottles, giving a Mouton-Rothschild-like look to the wines. Currently, there are over fifty Greek wines either copying or being influenced by Nicos' approach.

Château Nico Lazaridi has never felt the need to produce as high a volume as Domaine Costa Lazaridi, and the winery has flouted other commercial trends, too. In a Greek market where the younger the white the better, and where producers join a race after harvest to be the first to release the new vintage's whites, Château Nico Lazaridi waits almost a year to release some of its whites. Indeed, the winery is possibly the only one in Greece with a proven track record of age-worthy whites, even the basic, totally unoaked Château Lazaridi White. In a time where the more aromatic and flamboyant a wine is, the better, these wines are quite muted but very extracted and dense. Despite the popularity of varietals, only three out of ten of the portfolio are varietally labelled. Even these are not the ever popular Chardonnays or Sauvignon Blancs, but a Merlot and two different versions of Trebbiano. In order to follow a more commercial path, the Lazaridis family established the Mackedon Winery in Kavala (*see* page 170) and invested in a joint venture with Mykonos Winery (*see* page 370–1).

The heart behind this creative stubbornness is Federico Lazaridis, Nicos' son, who has been running the estate for several years. Since the estate began, Federico's essential companion has been Bakis Tsalkos, a Bordeaux-trained oenologist and one of Greece's great wine stylists. On a table full of glasses, a Tsalkos white or red wine can always be spotted easily. The winemaking approach is very traditional – no wizardry, no infatuation with reductive handling, just basic techniques making the most of the concentrated fruit harvested from the estate's excellent, organic vineyards.

Château Nico Lazaridi is the portfolio's main line. The white is a stainless-steel fermented blend of Sauvignon Blanc, Semillon, and Ugni Blanc, creating a very Bordeaux-like character. In good vintages it can develop in the bottle for more than eight years, and Tsalkos enjoys surprising audiences with vertical tastings of this, the winery's cheapest white wine. The red, made from Cabernet Sauvignon, Merlot, and Cabernet Franc, although not tight is extremely reserved on release and regularly needs three to six years in bottle to unfold. There is also a very clean and focused Cabernet Sauvignon Rosé.

In the 1990s the Nico Lazaridi team became fascinated by Ugni Blanc, putting a lot of work into making some of the most unusual wines of Greece. The basic Ugni Blanc is aged in older French and American barriques for six months. When young, it seems dominated by the wood and traces of an oxidative character appear, but three years in bottle bring balance, while seven years unveil an admirable complexity. The second Ugni Blanc is a dry, late-harvest version which spends eight months in new oak. At 13.5 degrees alcohol, this has fuller fruit and a much denser structure, but perhaps surprisingly, is much easier to understand. The third varietal label is a Merlot which changed its style in 2002 towards a lighter, fresher, and fruitier expression of the grape.

The top wines of Château Nico Lazaridi are called Magiko Vouno ("magic mountain"). The white is a barrel-fermented Sauvignon Blanc and the red is a stunning Cabernet Sauvignon aged in new French oak for a year followed by three more years in bottle – this red could age for more than two decades. Both Magiko Vouno wines have achieved cult status in Greece – they are never seen openly for sale, you have to know the right person to obtain even a single case. The winery could easily sell ten times the amount produced, but quantities remain low and strictly on allocation, since scarcity preserves both quality and image.

In the partly organic vineyards and in the HACCP-accredited winery, there is a lot of experimentation, much of it with a distinctly Italian theme.[2] For example, Greco di Tufo, Grecanico, Angelota, Ansonica, Aglianico, and Tempranillo vines are grown, with the latter two making excellent partners. Semillon trials are fermented and aged in acacia barrels bought from an Austrian cooperage suggested by leading Austrian winemaker Willi

---

2. HACCP (Hazard Analysis of Critical Control Points) is an internationally recognized quality-control system in use throughout the food and drinks industry.

Bründlmayer, arch-innovator and self-educated oak expert. Out of such experiments two sweet wines have emerged, both made from sun-dried grapes and aged in oak for eighteen to twenty months and in bottle for at least two years. Melissourgos is a Merlot, sun-dried for two months and Moushk is a Muscat Blanc, dried for half that time. Despite eighty grams per litre of residual sugar left on these wines, there is a phenolic structure and firmness that makes both seem less sweet than they are. Their ability to age is remarkable, often with exquisite results.

DOMAINE COSTA LAZARIDI

Adriani, 661 00 Drama. Tel: +30 252 108 2348/2231; Fax: +30 252 108 2320; Website: www.domaine-lazaridi.gr; Email: info@domaine-lazaridi.gr
Vineyards owned: 200ha; under contract: 50ha; production: 9,500hl.

Domaine Costa Lazaridi is one of the major players in the premium segment of the Greek wine industry. This was the second winery of Drama, after Château Nico Lazaridi, but in terms of success and commercial visibility it is an equally important name. Kostas split from his brother, Nico, a few years after the establishment of Château Nico Lazaridi. Much effort has gone into establishing the vineyards, and today Kostas Lazaridis is one of the largest organic vineyard-holders in Greece. Without no wine background himself, Kostas wanted a highly skilled winemaker, and Vassilis Tsaktsarlis was hired. Just back from oenology studies at Bordeaux University, this appointment was a key element in the winery's swift success. Tsaktsarlis put into practice all the knowledge he had acquired to create very aromatic, Sauvignon Blanc-dominated blends in a way that was unprecedented in Greece, plus distinctive, rich, serious Cabernet blends. The wines appeared under the brand name of Amethystos and were an instant success. One of the strongest brands of the 1990s, Amethystos still performs very well.

By 1999, Lazaridis and Tsaktsarlis had developed different ideas about how the estate should be run, and the latter decided to leave and join forces with his long-time friend and mentor Evangelos Gerovassiliou, creating the Biblia Chora winery in Kavala (*see* page 167). Yiannis Oxizidis, who had been Tsaktsarlis' assistant for several years, was promoted and for the first few years carried on the earlier styles before developing his own ideas. Just as legendary Loire winemaker Denis Dubourdieu had advised Tsaktsarlis in the 1990s, so Kostas wanted to provide Oxizidis with some additional help. After much searching, Michel Rolland was appointed winemaking consultant, overseeing production of the winery's reds, the first time such a high-profile advisor has been linked with a Greek winery. The first reds made under Rolland's guidance came from the 2004 vintage.

Although the style of many of the wines has fluctuated, the main threads behind the domaine's portfolio remain the same. Amethystos White is a Sauvignon Blanc blend, together with Assyrtico and some Semillon. During the late 1990s, the amazing success of Amethystos had led to an over-reliance on bought-in grapes – the wine had to be changed from a TO of Drama to the more general TO of Macedonia, with a corresponding, albeit minor, dip in quality. In recent years though, with smaller sales and more Lazaridi vineyards coming of age, Amethystos is back on form. The rosé version, a blend of Syrah, Merlot, and Cabernet Sauvignon is one of Greece's top pink wines. Amethystos Red, made from Cabernet Sauvignon, Merlot, and Limnio, had a dense, extracted style in early vintages, but it has been slowly moving to a less oaky, much softer, easy-drinking form.

Changes in Amethystos wines would have been tricky without the emergence of another line, called Château Julia. There are two Château Julia Chardonnays: one is stainless-steel fermented and the other, Driino, spends six months in new French barriques. Both are well-made wines, but for me the oak-fermented Château Julia Semillon wins top honours for the whites. There is also an Assyrtico, one of the firmer and more acidic examples to be found outside Santorini, bordering on the austere. As for the reds, Château Julia Merlot is not very extracted, but clearly one of the best Merlots in Greece.

Domaine Costa Lazaridi also has a vibrant range of small-volume or experimental wines. A dry, oak-aged Viognier has enough varietal character, while a late-harvest, sweet version may lack a bit of substance. Domaine Costa Lazaridi Syrah is oaky, big, tannic, and definitely ageworthy. The flagship wine, Amethystos Cava, is a pure Cabernet Sauvignon, extracted for more than two weeks, aged in new French oak for eighteen months, and then in bottle for two further years.

Aside from wines, the company is expanding with other products. For example, an oak-aged, grape distillate called Cigar has been released in tiny quantities, while a vinegar is also on the way. Kostas Lazaridis has made substantial investments in Kapandriti in Attica, creating vineyards, a new winery, and a striking function centre that should make an impact on the local community. The first vintage from the Lazaridi Kapandriti Estate is 2005.

MANOLESAKI ESTATE

Adriani, 661 00 Drama. Tel: +30 252 108 2010/2033; Fax: +30 252 108 2015; Website: www.domaine-manolesaki.gr; Email: info@manolesaki.gr

Vineyards owned: 14.8ha; under contract: 5ha; production: 1,000hl.

Giorgos Manolesakis has been involved with vine-growing since 1989 and started to produce wines on a commercial level almost a decade later. By that time, substantial vineyards had been developed, but success meant that additional fruit had to be sourced from growers within the prefecture or around Mount Pangeo.

Manolesakis aims for fresh, youthful whites and reds that verge on the oaky side, even if only a third of the cellar's barrels are renewed each year. Genima Psihis White ("offspring of the soul") is a Sauvignon Blanc/Chardonnay blend, while the red is a blend of Cabernet Sauvignon, Merlot, and Syrah, and the rosé is pure Cabernet Sauvignon. A Roditis/Sauvignon Blanc blend made with fruit from Kavala vineyards is a simple white. There are also three varietals: Fumé Chardonnay, Cabernet Sauvignon, and finally, the Manolesakis Merlot, the estate's best wine, being round, full of *typicité*, and replete with velvety extract.

PAVLIDIS ESTATE

Kokkinogia, Drama 661 00. Tel: +30 252 105 8300; Fax: +30 252 105 8310; Email: info@ktima-pavlidis.gr

Vineyards owned: 40ha; production: 300hl.

Pavlos Pavlidis is another major Drama marble producer who decided to become involved with wine, showing a serious, dedicated approach. The viticultural research organization Ampelooiniki designed the two main vineyards from scratch, making sure that the full potential of the sites was exploited. One parcel is located in Kokkinogia, with red clay soils, and the other is in Menikio Oros, with richer *terra rossa* soils in the lower parts and limestone on higher elevations. Much care has been taken deciding what to plant where, and density is 5,000 vines per hectare, to increase competition between roots. Some vines – such as Agiorgitiko, Assyrtico, Malagousia, Syrah, and Mavrodaphne – are planted in both sites to increase blending opportunities, while Tempranillo, Sauvignon Blanc, and Chardonnay have only been planted in Kokkinogia. The same painstaking care has been taken in creating the estate's cellar, another spectacular Drama winery, designed by cutting-edge architect Panagiotis Hatzinas, an avid wine collector himself.

The wines are very polished, very clean, and with enough structure to support their intensity. Pavlidis Estate White is a Sauvignon Blanc/Assyrtico blend, precise, defined, grassy, and crisp. A barrel-fermented Chardonnay stays on its lees in American and French oak for six months. Even if Ampelooiniki is not consulting any more, the Chardonnay has more than a touch of Angelos Iatridis' style – Iatridis being co-founder of Ampelooiniki and the acclaimed Alpha Estate. Pavlidis Red has equal parts Cabernet Sauvignon and Merlot, plus twenty per cent Limnio. Each variety is vinified separately, with macerations of up to three weeks for the French varieties. Malolactic fermentation takes place in oak – French and American – where the wine spends a further year. Pavlidis Red matches power with elegance and is enjoyable on release, but will develop for up to eight years.

Maturing vines should play an important part in the future quality of the Pavlidis range, and new products will give the winery an opportunity to continue to develop distinct identities. For example, the first vintages of Assyrtico are admirable, matching minerality and austerity with fourteen degrees alcohol. The same is true for Tempranillo, which seems to have good potential in the Drama area. Pavlidis Estates is a promising producer that is bound to go higher in quality terms with every new vintage.

WINE ART ESTATE
Mikrochori, 661 00 Drama. Tel/Fax: +30 252 108 3626;
Website: www.wineart.gr; Email: winepap@dra.forthnet.gr
Vineyards owned: 10ha; under contract: 8ha; production: 800hl.

Yiannis Papadopoulos and Yiannis Kalaitzidis started their Drama vineyards in 1993, with a brand new winery two years later. The partners are two of the most low-profile Greek wine producers; both are softly spoken and unpretentiously kind. They don't belong to the marble-trading community of Drama, instead they are qualified mechanical engineers, but they do have an affinity with art. Thus they decided to name their estate Techni Oinou, or "Wine Art", and embellish their wine labels accordingly. Currently, there are plans to expand the vineyard holdings and to increase the proportion of organically cultivated parcels.

The most popular line of wines is Techni Alipias. The white, a Sauvignon Blanc/Semillon blend, is full of the character that has become a Drama speciality. Techni Alipias rosé is Cabernet Sauvignon with Grenache Rouge, and finally, the red is a Cabernet Sauvignon/Merlot blend aged in French barriques for a year. The latter has a soft structure and a moderately intense nose, full of spices and herbs.

The Idisma Drios range is several quality levels above, with oak becoming a much more important stylistic element. The first release was a Chardonnay, fermented and aged in Alliers oak for five months. The wine has a well-integrated oak presence and is quite crisp, but could possibly benefit from some additional hang time on the vine. Idisma Drios Assyrtico is made in the same way, apart from three additional months in barriques. Even if the oak shows much less, this is possibly the best wine from Wine Art. The range concludes with a Merlot that is forward and round.

There are a few other varieties, like Syrah, Agiorgitiko, and Sangiovese, and occasionally small-production wines are released. For example, in 2001, 300 bottles of a Nebbiolo emerged at a price that most good-quality Barolos retail for in Athens. Notwithstanding the price, the wine comes from young vines that need more age to show a typical, unaggressive structure. The following vintages were made in a much more experimental style and since 2003, it seems that good results could well be just around the corner.

3

Epirus

The Epirus department is made up of four prefectures: Thesprotia, Arta, Preveza, and Ioannina. Thesprotia and Preveza border the Ionian Sea to the west, and Arta, with the Arachthos River as its main spine, faces the Amvrakikos Gulf. The prefecture of Ioannina is inland, bordering Albania on the northwest and the departments of Macedonia and Thessaly to its east. Apart from certain, small areas – like the plain of Arta, including Arachthos, a plain just to the north of Igoumenitsa in Thesprotia, the delta of the Acheron River, close to Parga, and the shorelines – Epirus is a very mountainous area, of which a large proportion is at an altitude of 700 metres (2,300 feet) or above. In the prefecture of Ioannina the lowest point is still higher than 350 metres (1,150 feet).

CLIMATE AND VITICULTURAL HISTORY

This high average altitude is one of several factors that contribute to Epirus' relatively humid and cool climate. To the west, the Ionian Sea influences the coastal regions with breezes, and its moderating effect limits any weather extremes. As a result, winters and summers are mild. The Pindos range is found in the west, a solid body of mountains that continues on to form the spine of mainland Greece. Volumes of water evaporating from the Adriatic Sea join westward-moving clouds and often break across the Pindos Mountains, which act as a natural barrier. This increases precipitation across Epirus, although the quantity of rainfall and its timing within the year rarely pose a significant problem for viticulturalists.

The climate of Epirus, combined with its mainly clay soils, which have a moderate to low lime content, means that there is enough soil moisture

throughout the seasons and, in an average year, irrigation is not needed. There is a distinct difference between vineyards on the slopes and those downhill or on the valley floors. The latter tend to benefit from richer soils, so there is hardly – if any – water stress. Hillside soils are less fertile and drier, although not excessively so.

The prefectures of Thesprotia, Arta, and Preveza have no commercially significant wine producers, although there are a number of amateur vineyard owners making wine for their own consumption, and some bulk wine companies that cater for local demand. The prefecture of Ioannina is the viticultural heart of Epirus and includes Metsovo and Zitsa, the two areas with organized, large-scale wineries with national distribution. But this has not always been the case. Before World War II, viticulture in Epirus – although mainly geared towards amateur wine production for home use – was far more widespread, and not just around the city of Ioannina. After 1945, however, huge numbers of people left Epirus, affecting the region financially and leaving a large number of semi-deserted villages with poor, elderly populations. In the 1950s and 1960s, neglected vineyards were easy prey for phylloxera.

It is clear that areas like Arta or Preveza, where the soils are excellent for vines and the summers and autumns are far warmer than in Zitsa and Metsovo, show a lot of potential. Before too long, the viticulture revival experienced in Thrace could well be seen in Epirus.

GRAPES

A fact that underlines Epirus' comparative remoteness is the relatively small number of native varietals found in the region, especially when you consider the varietal complexity of the Ionian islands, just a few kilometres away. In Epirus, particularly in the north, the main concern in varietal choice is planting early-ripening varieties to avoid the early autumn rains. Strangely enough, however, roughly six times out of ten the important Debina grape will, if given a chance, ripen well into October.

International varieties have not proved popular in Epirus and, excluding Metsovo and some vineyards in the Ioannina prefecture, are insignificant in commercial terms. In the Katogi vineyards in Metsovo, red Bordeaux varieties and Gewurztraminer produce impressive results, while Cabernet Sauvignon is widely used as the backbone of many local red blends of Ioannina's TOs. With regard to white grapes, Chardonnay and Riesling receive some attention, while Sauvignon Blanc plantings are rare – although the general terroir could help produce interesting examples, possibly closer to the Loire style than mainstream Greek Sauvignon.

Debina is the most popular white variety, not just in the general region of Ioannina and Zitsa, but also in the rest of Epirus. Roditis and Malagousia are the only varieties to be recommended right across Epirus, but both have a much lower profile than Debina.

The most important red grapes, Bekari and Vlahiko, are mainly confined to the area around Ioannina, but can be found throughout the region. Both varieties ripen at roughly the same time, in early September and the Debina harvest starts after the red must macerations have finished. Some suggest that Bekari can reach higher levels of maturity than Vlahiko, producing wines above 12.5 per cent alcohol, instead of twelve per cent or lower. Nevertheless, Vassilis Vaimakis, production manager at the Ioannina Cooperative, believes that "the difference in sugar levels between these varieties – in fact, between any two varieties – simply do not exist, provided that terroir, cultivation, and yield level are identical". But all wine-growers agree that Vlahiko has a lifted aromatic complexity, a vibrant acidity, but a low level of phenolics. Fortunately, Bekari can be a good blending partner, with its deep colour but relatively muted flavour profile.

A SPARKLING TRADITION

With particular emphasis on the general province of Ioannina, Epirus is one of the very few Greek regions that can claim a tradition in sparkling wines, together with Rhodes and Amyntaio in Florina – although only those from Rhodes have a substantial presence across the country. In Epirus, a range of sparkling styles can be found. The wines are mainly whites, from very pale green-yellow to moderately pale gold. There are a few rosés, ranging from onion-skin to deep pink in colour, with the most famous example being Kyra Frosini from Glinavos Winery in Zitsa. The style ranges from fully sparkling to semi-sparkling, *pétillant*, or slightly *perlant*, and the wines can be dry (although very rarely are they bone dry), off-dry or *demi-sec*. Production methods vary widely, from the OPAP Zitsa wines made in the traditional method to cheap, carbonated wines.

The best sparkling wines from Epirus deserve to be far more popular in the rest of Greece. Most Greek people drink sparkling wine only at weddings, and not as an apéritif but served with the wedding cake, so the *demi-sec* bottlings are, or should be, preferred. On occasions like these, a Champagne-shaped bottle and a foreign – if possible, French-sounding – name on the label are all that matter. Only a small percentage of wine drinkers view sparkling wines beyond this cliché, and this is a sector still dominated by Champagne. If more Greek people start to consider good-value sparklers as a valid choice at any hour of any day, the sales of Epirus wines could flourish, and deservedly so.

It would be interesting if producers tried to create some *prestige cuvée* bottlings of sparkling Debinas through prolonged lees contact in bottle prior to disgorgement. Could this variety stand the test of time, keeping its freshness while marrying with, for example, a decade's bottle-age and aromas from extended lees contact? And if this was sufficiently successful and marketed at a carefully selected price tag – high, but not too high – it might well attract the attention of knowledgeable consumers and wine journalists across Greece and, hopefully, further afield. With the significant exception of CAIR, the forward-looking Rhodes co-op, and its excellent ten-year-old Cair Rosé Brut Reserve, sparkling winemaking in Greece is mainly about adding sparkle to a fresh and vibrant still wine. Nuances of development, presence of autolytic character, and creaminess of texture are usually considered beyond the needs of the marketplace.

WINE APPELLATIONS

Epirus and, in particular, the prefecture of Ioannina, has the advantage of an all-encompassing OPAP appellation. The Zitsa OPAP was established in the first wave of regulation in 1971–2. Given Zitsa's relative geographical isolation, small acreage and, in commercial terms, almost non-existent wine production, it is almost bizarre and incredibly fortunate that an OPAP was awarded to this remote northwest corner of Greece.

The principal type of soil in Zitsa is limestone, which favours elegance and high acidity. The climate is influenced by its high altitude, at an average of around 700 metres (2,300 feet), and its proximity to the Kalamas River. Winds blowing inland from the Ionian Sea and through the Kalamas Valley have a moderating effect on any weather extremes, lowering temperatures in the hot summer months while warming the region during winter. To benefit from this, the actual demarcated region of this OPAP is strategically placed on the slopes of Zitsa as the land comes down to the river.

It is often said that, even if one takes into account the detailed pattern of meso-climates in Zitsa and the particulars of the Debina grape variety, the maximum allowable yield of 1,000 kilograms per *stremma* (seventy hectolitres per hectare) is too high. Even if "high" means within the values permitted, since Debina responds badly to high yields, quality-oriented growers have to at least go below fifty hectolitres per hectare to achieve some concentration and character.

In cases like Zitsa it is easy to discern a different, somewhat elusive, but extremely important role for European legislation regarding appellations: the preservation of styles, varieties, and heritages. The other OPAPs of Greece will easily find a place in the country's vinous future. In Nemea, Rapsani, Paros, and Meliton, for example, modern, seductive, rich, charming wines can be produced that could become alternatives for people who enjoy modern Cabernet-like wines. Naoussa could be developed as the Piedmont of Greece – not necessarily mainstream, but with a complex and sophisticated presence that will be alluring for wine connoisseurs. Given the time and a fair chance, Cephalonia, Mantinia, and Santorini will stun the world with concentrated and steely Assyrticos, fragrant Moschofileros, and flowery, ethereal Robolas.

In Zitsa the situation is totally different. The grape variety here is Debina, a variety known to be present in the region since at least the seventh century AD. It is sensitive to grey rot, very sensitive to water stress, and responds badly to yields above sixty to seventy hectolitres per hectare. Zitsa is the northern cultivation limit for Debina. In this region, at an altitude of 600–700 metres (1,970–2,300 feet), the Debina harvest starts in the last ten days of September, carrying on well into October. The local weather is notoriously unreliable after September 15 and, in around four vintages out of every ten, maturity problems arise.

Debina wines are low in alcohol, rarely reaching above 11.5 per cent and more usually around eleven per cent. They are high in acidity, almost always above 6.5 grams per litre, and usually light in body, and lacking in density, texture, and intensity of aromas. Wines from Zitsa have traditionally focused on semi-sweet and off-dry, sparkling, semi- or mildly sparkling styles, all of which are currently falling out of fashion. Nevertheless, Debina in Zitsa can make some of the most elegant Greek wines, with stylish aromas, a some-what muted but well-defined character closer to Austrian than other Greek light whites – an amazing freshness on the palate, and sheer drinkability. Zitsa OPAP certainly adds something unique to Greek wine production, but it is likely that, without its own legislation to protect it from market trends, it could now be facing extinction.

Epirus TO

White still: dry; semi-dry; semi-sweet.
White varieties: Malagousia; Roditis.
Rosé still: dry; semi-dry; semi-sweet.
Rosé varieties: local recommended and permitted grape varieties.
Red still: dry.
Red varieties: local recommended and permitted grape varieties.

Zitsa OPAP, Prefecture of Ioannina

White still: dry; white sparkling: dry; semi-sweet.
White varieties: Debina must be at least sixty per cent of the blend, the balance being other local recommended and permitted varieties.

Ioannina TO

White still: dry; semi-dry.
White sparkling: semi-sparkling; sparkling.
White varieties: Debina must be at least sixty per cent of the blend, the balance being other local recommended and permitted varieties.
Rosé still: dry, semi-dry.
Rosé sparkling: semi-sparkling; sparkling.
Rosé varieties: Vlahiko and Bekari must be at least fifty per cent of the blend, the balance being other local recommended and permitted varieties.
Red still: dry.
Red varieties: Cabernet Sauvignon must be at least sixty per cent of the blend, the balance being other local recommended and permitted varieties.

Metsovo TO

Red still: dry.
Red varieties: Cabernet Sauvignon must be at least sixty per cent of the blend, the balance being other local recommended and permitted varieties.

PRODUCERS

GLINAVOS WINERY

PO Box 45444, Zitsa.
Tel: +30 265 802 2212; Fax: +30 265 802 2261; Website: www.glinavos.gr
Vineyards owned: 7ha; under contract: 30ha; production: 5,500hl.

The formal name of this company, Glinavos-Monastiri-Zitsa SA, points to the existence of an old monastery (*monastiri*) close to the estate. In the sixteenth-century this building was dedicated to the Prophet Elias and monks have been producing wine here since its early days. During the years of the Ottoman occupation, the monastery was one of the official purveyors to the governor, Ali Passas. At that time, its fame was such that Lord Byron was a visitor on more than one occasion.

The winery began by sourcing thirty hectares-worth of native varieties – Debina, Bekari, and Vlahiko – from local growers. It proved difficult to persuade these growers to reduce yields, and quantities produced from these plots were, predictably, higher than desired. Thus the need to have access to low-yielding vineyards became ever more pressing. The purchase in 2002 of a seven-hectare parcel was just the beginning, and there are plans for further development. The aim is to reduce yields to fifty hectolitres per hectare or lower with the Debina plantings.

The new vineyards contain Chardonnay, Malagousia, Riesling, and Roditis vines. Chardonnay was planted to explore the potential of the variety in this terroir and is bottled as a single varietal. In sharp contrast, the other three white varieties will be used to add complexity to Debina – Riesling and Malagousia for a higher level of aromas and fruit, and Roditis for body, extract, and riper fruit character. This could mean an expansion not only in new Ioannina TO wines but also in Zitsa OPAP labels, since sixty per cent of these must be Debina, with the balance including permitted varieties.

Thomas Glinavos is the general manager and his brother, Lefteris, is the president and winemaker, although, being a typical Greek family business, job titles mean little and both are involved with all aspects of the business. Both look after customers and help promote the wines, especially in their home town of Ioannina – the local market absorbs more than sixty per cent of their annual production, a fact that makes things rather easier for them. They consider themselves very fortunate that Ioannina has a large, dedicated group of people who enjoy life, good food, and good wine – not always the case in smaller cities around Greece.

The most striking feature of the Glinavos range of wines is the sheer wealth of different Zitsa OPAP labels. Even more impressive is the ease with which Lefteris can explain what distinguishes each of the nine wines produced and how this is reflected in the glass. Primus is the top label (the words *protos oenos,* "first wine", appear under the name of the wine).

Made from ripe Debina grapes harvested from selected vineyards in the appellation, only the first forty per cent of the free-run juice is included in this stainless-steel-fermented *cuvée*. While Primus is the most refined and elegant version of Glinavos' Debinas, local taste demands more body and extract, so the rest of the range includes at least a small percentage of press wine. The other wines are more than noteworthy, with a slightly higher level of phenolics making them a little bit rustic without taking away any charm or personality. Fygos is the organic label, while Lithinos is aged in new French barriques for six to eight months.

The two sparkling Zitsa wines are both available in brut and *demi-sec* versions. Byron is made using the Charmat method, and Poème (following the trend for Greeks to seek French-sounding names) is *méthode traditionnelle* and aged on lees in bottle for about a year. This is supported by the Glinavos style, which aims for riper Debinas than anyone else in the appellation and, thus, pushes alcohol levels to twelve per cent and above. A speciality of the Glinavos Winery is the Kyra Frosini EO, a semi-sparkling rosé blend of Debina and Vlahiko bottled with thirty grams per litre residual sugar. It is quite traditional in style, again to suit local tastes, and may seem a bit heavy, but at the same time its rich and fruity complexity can be very good.

Red wines tend to be less popular in this region, but the winery is putting a lot of effort behind its reds. There is a Cabernet Sauvignon, aged one year in stainless steel and then six months in oak, that would benefit from a bit more maturity, especially in terms of phenolics. Glinavos also markets some Nemea OPAP, which is well-made but quite simple. Kokkino Veloudo ("red velvet") EO is a far better, more complex effort, showing a successful match between Vlahiko, Bekari, and Agiorgitiko sourced from Nemea. Aged in used oak for ten months, Kokkino Veloudo is one of the most popular labels of the winery. The top red is Dryades, where Cabernet Sauvignon is given more complexity with the addition of twenty-five per cent Bekari and Vlahiko, all co-macerated for ten days. The blend is rounded off with up to fifteen per cent Agiorgitiko and aged in new French oak for a year. A rare wine produced only in exceptional years, Dryades averages out at less than 4,000 bottles per year of production and about six vintages a decade. Although not necessarily age-worthy, it is nevertheless full of character and individuality.

IOANNINA COOPERATIVE

Zitsa 440 03; Head office: H. Trikoupi 38, Ioannina 453 32.

Tel: +30 265 107 0961; Fax: +30 265 107 7941; Email: uacioan@otenet.gr

Vineyards under contract: 150ha; production: 10,000hl

For many people who deal with Greek wine, the Ioannina Cooperative is one of the very best in Greece. With such institutions it is difficult to put that reputation down to just one reason or one person. Usually, just one weak link is enough to bring the quality down within a wine-growing organization, while success can only be guaranteed if everyone involved has the desired degree of competence. Ioannina Cooperative is fortunate enough to be linked to a terroir where quality-oriented grape-growing is favoured more highly than extremely high yields and industrial-scale production. It is one of the most advanced co-ops in terms of available technology and equipment – but, if one were forced to single out a reason for the exceptional quality of its wines, it would have to be Vassilis Vaimakis, the general manager of the co-op, as well as the production manager and chief oenologist.

It is always important that the person who takes the majority of the decisions understands all the procedures shaping the final product. Vaimakis is a passionate, intelligent, and highly knowledgeable man, sometimes with quite set views. "Vlahiko is far more complete that Bekari. Its wine is much better and more complex," he says. "If I had a chance, I would never use Bekari." Not only is Vaimakis one of the key reasons for the co-op's excellent range of wines, he is also the main impetus behind developing this portfolio and bringing it into the twenty-first century.

Although the name of the co-op suggests it covers the whole region of Ioannina, the core of the production relates to Zitsa OPAP and its wines. The range is not vast, with three main OPAP bottlings and three other wines that are of Epirus TO status (which therefore go under the slightly more specific designation of Ioannina TO). The main bottling, Zitsa Classic, is a pure, typical, and, as the name suggests, classic expression of the Debina grape: floral, elegant, charming, and light. Alcohol is usually around 11.5 per cent and acidity is relatively high, giving a crisp, refreshing palate. For local tastes, this combination of acidity, dryness, plus a lack of sweetness due to the higher levels of alcohol can be considered excessively acidic and angular.

This was the main reason behind the creation of the second Zitsa OPAP wine, which is semi-dry, semi-sparkling, and trades under the name Zitsa Vin Blanc Pétillant. By a combination of chilling the fermenting musts and making the vats airtight, fermentation is slowed and finally stopped. Thus, the wine is left with ten grams per litre of residual sugar while the carbon dioxide emitted in the final stages is trapped and creates a light sparkle. The acidity is actually slightly higher in the Petillant than in the Classic, at about 0.5 grams per litre, but the residual sugar makes the palate rounder and masks the acidity, while the effervescence diminishes the impression of sweetness, creating an excellent summer wine style.

The last Debina is Zitsa Hilion Margaritation ("Zitsa of a thousand pearls"), which is a simpler offering somewhere between Petillant and Classic in approach, with a rounder feeling on the palate. Low levels of carbon dioxide do not qualify it as semi-sparkling, but do add a certain amount of freshness.

The trio of Epirus TO wines offers a possible glimpse of the future for the co-op, if not for the whole Ioannina region. Orion Dry White is a blend of Chardonnay and Debina. The Debina fruit used for this bottling has to be concentrated and relatively high in ripeness, so it comes only from selected vineyard sites which are primarily judged on yields. Chardonnay adds ripeness and sweet fruit expression, alcohol (which still stands at a modest twelve per cent), roundness, and body. Seirios, a blend of Vlahiko, Bekari, and Xinomavro, is a rosé full of fruit, crisp acidity, and good aroma and flavour definition. Arktouros is an oak-aged red, consisting of locally grown Cabernet Sauvignon, along with Vlahiko and Bekari. The local grapes tend to embellish the character of the Cabernet rather than create a synergy. Slightly higher levels of ripeness could make this wine more modern and allow more emphasis on the fruit.

KATOGI & STROFILIA WINERY

Metsovo 442 00. Tel: 30 265 604 1684; Fax: 30 265 604 2397; Website: www.katogi-strofilia.gr; Email: katogi@met.forthnet.gr Vineyards owned: 15ha, plus 20ha on lease; under contract: 80ha; production: 9,000hl.

(*See also* entry for Katogi & Strofilia on page 239.)

Evangelos Averoff was a leading intellectual and one of the most prominent twentieth-century Greek politicians. He was personally responsible for transforming much of the Metsovo region, and among those developments was the founding of the Katogi winery in 1959. The trigger was some sixteenth-century documents he found in the nearby St Nicholas monastery, clearly describing a flourishing system of wine production. As a politician, he was intelligent, exceptionally forward-thinking, open-minded, and very pro-European. He believed that the most secure future for Greece was to be found in the embrace of Europe: to be specific, in Western Europe. So, in a move full of politcial meaning, he decided not to grow any native vines, but rather Cabernet Sauvignon – in doing so, he was possibly the first to introduce this variety to Greece.

Metsovo was not the easiest place to grow vines, so establishing Katogi winery was practically akin to financial suicide. For others, the cost of establishing and cultivating remote and inaccessible vineyards at an altitude of 1,000 metres (3,280 feet) would have been simply unthinkable, but Averoff was famous for never giving up. He kept investing until the first profits appeared in 1990. After the initial harvest in 1962, Averoff proposed the foundation of a cooperative for the local community. He would have been responsible for supplying the vines and producing the wine, all free of charge, while the growers involved would have been shareholders of the company – one share for each vine planted. There was no take-up, however, either because locals failed to see the potential or because of scepticism, and so, after three years of fruitless attempts, Averoff decided to continue alone.

The wine was made in his *katogi* (basement) until 1973, when a proper winery was built. By then, Katogi Cabernet Sauvignon was only sold locally but had already acquired a nationwide cult status. Retailers of the region fortunate enough to stock it insisted on an extremely strict "two-bottles-per-customer" policy. In Athens, Katogi Cabernet could only be found in two places: the Grande Bretagne, then the most prestigious hotel in Greece, and Alpha-Beta Vassilopoulos Deli.

When it became a little easier to find outside Metsovo, Katogi Cabernet emerged as the first example of an icon wine in Greece: expensive, made in small quantities that could hardly satisfy demand, and produced by a small boutique wine-grower involved with all aspects of the production. During the 1970s and early 1980s, Katogi remained the most exclusive Greek wine, to be found only on the finest tables around the country.

The style of Katogi until 1984 was very lean, needing at least five years to become approachable. The use of barrels made from local oak that was slightly rustic and a touch aggressive was another factor that made early Katogi in need of bottle-age. Nevertheless, bottles from the 1973 vintage tasted in 1990 were remarkably youthful and still firm. The winemaking in these wines may seem a touch old-fashioned and low-tech, but taking all things into account, this is not surprising. To make it rounder – though increasing the quantities must also have played some part in the decision – the varietal composition moved from 100 per cent Cabernet Sauvignon to a blend of sixty per cent Cabernet and forty per cent Agiorgitiko bought from

Nemea. As an experiment in 1985, half the Cabernet production was blended with Agiorgitiko and the rest was bottled as a single-varietal Katogi. The results were promising, and since 1986 the whole production of the wine has been a blend called Katogi Averoff. The first releases of this new style Katogi were very different, but the quality was still exceptional. These vintages aged gracefully well into the 1990s, when the local Metsovo oak barrels were replaced with French barriques. Currently the wine is made mainly in Nemea, with a small proportion of Metsovo Cabernet Sauvignon added in. The personality of the wine is remarkably consistent and the quality is good, given that production figures approach half a million bottles a year, although it is debatable whether the ageing ability of current vintages will match those of the last three decades.

In 1994 Sotiris Ioannou, the managing director of the estate and Averoff's son-in-law, decided together with the winemaker, Sotiris Sotiropoulos, to recreate the original Katogi as a brand new label: Ktima Averoff. This Cabernet, with up to five per cent Merlot and five per cent Cabernet Franc, is vinified in a classic, straightforward way: macerated for twenty-five to thirty days, malolactic fermentation in barrel, and ageing in new French oak for a year followed by an additional year in bottle. This wine is what Katogi used to be – firm, intense, and tannic – but with a whole new dimension of flavours, elegance, extraction, and a very sensitive use of oak.

Katogi's Traminer, also planted in 1994, was first made commercially available in 1998. The original version was a straightforward, stainless-steel-fermented dry wine, with some balancing spicy character. Those who thought that this would be an explosive, Alsatian-like "Gewurztraminer-made-in-Greece" were somewhat disappointed. The grapes do receive a few hours of skin contact, but one suspects that the relatively low level of ripeness at harvest (the finished wine has 11.5 per cent alcohol and just under four grams of residual sugar per litre), influences the rather restrained character. A few vintages after the first release of Katogi Traminer, a late-harvest Traminer, called Meliphron, was produced. It is made from overripe grapes, with a proportion being left to dry on the vine but without any botrytis. The alcohol content of the final wine is the same as the dry version, but the residual sugar is around seventy grams per litre. This added level of ripeness makes it significantly more intense on the nose, and the palate is sweet but not cloying. It would be interesting to see a Traminer harvested at a ripeness level somewhere between the two styles and fermented dry or off-dry. The portfolio of white wines is completed with a barrel-fermented Chardonnay and a Katogi white.

There has been a marked expansion in the red selection available from Katogi, especially when you consider that only one red was made in the first thirty-five years of the winery's existence. Apart from Ktima Averoff, there is Floghero, a blend of Cabernet Sauvignon with a bit of Merlot that has the same philosophy as the Ktima, but comes from contracted vineyards in Metsovo with yields averaging forty-five to fifty hectolitres per hectare. The maceration is shorter, up to twenty days, making it a lot more approachable in its early life.

Porfyri Ghi is a wine that, strictly speaking, falls into the Katogi portfolio but is a blend of Xinomavro from Naoussa, made in the Fountis winery, and Agiorgitiko from Corinth. After blending, the wine is aged for over a year in 300-litre barrels and the resulting wine has a more traditional feel to it when compared with Floghero or Ktima Averoff. A small quantity of Xinomavro rosé is also made, which is traded as Katogi Rosé.

In the late 1990s Katogi got together with Strofilia in Attica, Mercouri in Ilia, and Antonopoulos Vineyards in Achaia, to found the Octana winery in Nemea. Most of these companies were producing Agiorgitiko varietals or blends, and a production unit in the heart of the Agiorgitiko area would offer impressive economies of scale and greater control over quality. The initial idea was that the four producers would eventually merge, or work separately, but with a high degree of synergy. However, Antonopoulos Vineyards and Mercouri decided to withdraw, and in 2001, Katogi & Strofilia was created. From day one, the two teams displayed a remarkable degree of cooperation and common vision. There is no doubt that Katogi & Strofilia is currently one of the major medium-sized wineries in Greece.

4

Thessaly

Thessaly is in the heart of mainland Greece and has been a crossroads for people, conquerors, goods, and cultures over the millennia. With the Pindos mountain range circling the entire region, Thessaly is almost isolated from the west, with two narrow passages, known as the Gates of Thessaly, controlling access to the central province. In the north, Mount Olympus touches on both the Thermaikos Gulf and Mount Ossa a few kilometres further south. In the south, Mount Othris leads to the Pagasatikos Gulf, leaving a slightly larger gap between the Maliakos Gulf and the town of Lamia. Between these two "gates" lies the great plain of Thessaly, extending inland for almost 150 kilometres (ninety-three miles) beyond the towns of Trikala and Kalambaka.

Thessaly is the largest single site of highly productive soil and therefore one of the most fertile parts of Greece. Indeed, it is often referred to as *O Kambos* ("The Plain"), as if it were the only plain of note. Thessaly is one of very few areas where the economy is largely based on agriculture. Average income is one of the highest in the country, as is the standard of living. The major land-owning families of Thessaly have long been regarded as among the most important and influential in Greece, and this wealth was one of the main reasons why the Ottoman Empire went to such lengths to control and exploit the district.

The largest part of Thessaly is devoted to what agronomists call "large cultivations", meaning grain and cotton. Vine-growing is not widely practised because to date, the other possible options have been far more lucrative. Vineyards have only been planted on the periphery of the area and the mountain slopes, which has ensured good grape quality, as the soils on the plain are extremely heavy and rich in organic matter. Water availability is not a problem as a number of rivers, like the Pinios, can be used for irrigation, and snow from surrounding mountains lasts well into the spring. For the Kambos vineyards, yields of 250 hectolitres per hectare are not unusual.

In addition to rich soils, the lower parts of Thessaly are extremely humid. The vertiginous girdle of mountains forms a wind shield in all directions, and acts like a humidity trap, retaining the moisture from fogs and rivers and making fungal diseases a serious concern.

IN WITH THE NEW

Apart from a few isolated spots, viticulture has been almost irrelevant for the people of Thessaly, but the future may well see some change. Eastern European countries have hit the grain and cotton trade hard, with good prices and quality to match. Industries involved in the cotton trade, like cloth manufacturers, have been shifting their focus away from Greece to Bulgaria and Slovenia, as well as China and India. EU funds – a great support over the years – will be switched to the newer members of the European community. This all means that over a relatively short period of time, crops which were profitable have become hard to sell. As many viticultural consultants in Thessaly will testify, an increasing number of land-owners are seeking advice about establishing vineyards. Far from being a lifestyle choice for hobbyists, wine production is increasingly being viewed as a way of guaranteeing a better future.

The latest vineyard developments in the lower parts of Thessaly might well yield some interesting results. New methods of vine cultivation – such as large, open-canopy trellis systems, alongside advanced irrigation methods – can achieve good-quality grapes from highly vigorous, fertile vineyards. Moreover, the best terroirs of Thessaly have yet to be fully exploited. Areas such as Elassona, just north of Tyrnavos on the southwest side of Mount Olympus – which used to have a good, commercially active cooperative – currently have no substantial winery.

The village of Kalipefki is another of Thessaly's viticultural secrets. Just uphill from the Rapsani OPAP, Kalipefki is situated at an altitude of 1,000 to 1,100 metres (3,280–3,608 feet) The soil is light and the meso-climate is exceptionally dry, sunny, and cool. There is no evidence that vines have been grown here before, but it could turn out to be an outstanding terroir just waiting to be discovered.

GRAPES

The recommended varieties are Assyrtico, Roditis, and Limnio, along with Cabernet Sauvignon and Syrah. Cinsault and Batiki are on the permitted varietals list, the latter being one of very few that could be called local, even if it is found occasionally in Evia, Macedonia, and Thrace. Batiki is a white variety that is extremely sensitive to all kinds of mildew and, therefore, difficult to grow on many Thessaly plots. Both sugar levels and acidity are low, but Batiki can give wines with substantial structure. Local growers think that the negatives outweigh the positives, and total acreage is decreasing.

The reverse has happened with another grape, the red Limniona. A few years ago, this variety, called Limniona by some and Limnio by others, was identified in a number of locations by the Wine Institute, an Athens-based organization whose primary purpose is to evaluate and preserve indigenous varietals. It was clear from the start that the variety was not associated with the Limnio cultivated in many other Greek wine regions. Observations in the vineyard, microvinifications, and local experience suggested a top-quality varietal, with high fruit aromas and flavours, a dense red-black colour, high levels of rich but not astringent tannins, and high dry extract. Many people believed that this grape could prove exceptional, being able to give modern yet distinctive, age-worthy reds, and thus Limniona was rushed into the "recommended varieties" lists of many regions, especially in the south.

REGIONS AND CLASSIFICATIONS

Thessaly is made up of four prefectures: Larissa and Magnissia on the eastern seaboard, Trikala and Karditsa further west. Given the limited popularity of wine production, finding three quality-wine appellations is surprising, but the local co-ops and the agricultural sector have proved a powerful combination. The OPAPs include Anhialos in Magnissia, Rapsani in Larissa, and Messenicola in Karditsa. Anhialos is a white-only OPAP, and the other two are purely red. All three were, until recently, seriously under-performing and available only locally.

There is a general TO for Thessaly, while Larissa has two TOs: Krania, tailor-made for the producer Ktima Katsaros, and Tyrnavos. Some names, such as Rapsani, have become better known than others, thanks to the efforts of the producer Tsantali, who in the space of ten years has turned it from a forgotten village on Mount Olympus into one of the most vibrant names in modern Greek wine.

According to the latest agricultural census, the total wine-grape acreage for Thessaly is 4,408 hectares. Magnissia has 449 hectares, of which fifteen are dedicated to the Anhialos OPAP and Larissa has 2,417 hectares, including 190 in the Rapsani OPAP. Trikala has 704 hectares of vineyards and Karditsa 838 hectares, with the Messenikolas OPAP taking ninety-three of these.

Thessaly TO

White still: dry; semi-dry; semi-sweet.
Rosé still: dry; semi-dry; semi-sweet.
Red still: dry; semi-dry; semi-sweet.
Varieties: Assyrtico; Cabernet Sauvignon; Limnio; Roditis; Syrah.

MAGNISSIA

Magnissia has the spectacular Pagasitikos Gulf in the east, and the even more impressive Mount Pilion, a picturesque holiday destination, filled with romantic, small villages. The main city, Volos, was traditionally the most industrial part of Thessaly as well as an important commercial port, but today both these sources of income have dried up.

Magnissia is fairly flat and most of the soils are rich, full of clay, fertile, and heavy. The sea's proximity has a cooling effect during the summer, but the climate is still fairly hot. The main varieties are Savatiano and Roditis, both of which respond to the region's meso-climate with high yields. Magnissia can produce good-quality wines, provided technical dexterity is exercised in both the vineyard and the cellar. What is missing in viticultural terms is a sense of character, of uniqueness – a sense of place. Magnissia could be a good *tabula rasa* for producing value-oriented wines with as few constraints as possible. Instead of that, Magnissia was granted an OPAP – Anhialos – named after the town of Nea Anhialos on the coast.

Magnissia is an example of an appellation being granted to a sole co-op. At the time of its creation, other local growers were relatively insignificant. The varietal blend was confirmed as Roditis and Savatiano, with proportions that seemed to change constantly. A few years ago it was eighty-five per cent Roditis, but now the figure stands at fifty per cent. In order to curtail overproduction, regulations have banned the use of cordon-trained vines, allowing only the fruit from unsupported plants. The possibility of open canopies to decrease canopy humidity or the use of large trellis systems to increase quality and ripeness of fruit while keeping yields higher, were not considered. Still, the legal yield limit stands at a hefty eighty-four hectolitres per hectare. In addition, Anhialos OPAP rules forbid both skin contact – since colour extraction from Roditis is considered a fault – and ageing in oak, in order not to mask the primary flavours of the varieties. What adds to the absurdity is the total lack of control over these aspects, under the cooperative *modus vivendi*.

It is fortunate that a group of forward-looking producers has decided to try and redefine the wines of Magnissia, either within or outside the regulations.

Anhialos OPAP

White still: dry.
White varieties: Savatiano fifty per cent; Roditis fifty per cent.

PRODUCERS

APOSTOLAKI FAMILY WINERY

371 00 Krokio Almyrou. Tel: +30 242 202 9160;
Fax: +30 242 202 9163; Email: argowine@otenet.gr
Vineyards owned: 15ha; production: 1,000hl.
The Argo Company was founded by the Apostolakis family in 1954, initially to produce ouzo and spirits for export markets like Germany and what was then the USSR. In 1970, the Apostolakis brothers, Apostolos and Andreas, decided to start buying wine from around the region for bottling and then exporting. With time, the need for a production plant and their own vineyards became ever more pressing, so Apostolos' son Dimitris went to study oenology in Germany, and the brothers began building a winery in Krokio village, within the Anhialos OPAP. Apostolos tragically died in 2002, but the vision he and his brother shared lives on.

Today Dimitris is in charge of production while his sister Katerina, a designer, takes care of packaging and the winery's interior design. Apostolos Jr, Andreas' son, looks after sales. The HACCP-certified (*see* footnote on page 178) winery and the surrounding organically-cultivated vineyards make the Apostolakis family one of the most substantial investors in vertically integrated winemaking operations during the last decade.

Initially, the Apostolakis family had a few problems working within the Anhialos appellation. Dimitris and Apostolos were not keen on producing OPAP wines, believing that it would be better to add Assyrtico to the blend in place of Savatiano. This decision disqualified Apostolaki Blanc from OPAP status, but at the same time, it was impossible to apply for a lesser local white regional wine appellation, a TO, since the wine would be the same colour as Anhialos. The only alternative was the departmental TO of Thessaly that is very close to the anonymity of an EO.

Regarding red varieties, Grenache, together with Merlot, Syrah, and Xinomavro, was planted in 1997, when the first vineyards were established. Although Grenache was allowed at the time of planting, it was excluded from the list of permitted varieties in 2003. Merlot is currently forbidden in the region and the local Office of the Ministry of Agriculture resists all applications for a Merlot or Syrah TO of Krokio. In this case, regulations appear to defend a questionable tradition and promote an unclear *typicité*, so aspirations for quality mean disregarding them.

The winery is currently financed by sales of excellent tsipouro, made from Tyrnavos Muscat, very good ouzo, and well-priced bag-in-box table wines (tsipouro production always goes hand-in-hand with the production of high-volume, but not premium, wines). A complete focus on bottled wine would have been unviable, given the relatively neutral image of the region around Greece. Nevertheless, the commitment is there. Apostolaki White is mainly Roditis, with Assyrtico and a small amount of Ugni Blanc. No skin contact or wood-ageing, just a month of lees contact, giving fruit, density, and roundness. Apostolaki Rosé is a clean and crisp Roditis, with forty per cent Grenache co-macerated for four days.

There are two reds in the portfolio: a basic Apostolaki Red and a straight Syrah. The former is thirty per cent Xinomavro, fifty per cent Syrah, and twenty per cent Grenache, each macerated separately. Dimitris makes no compromises in his quest for differential phenolic extraction. Xinomavro is macerated for three to five days in an autovinification tank, with the emitted carbon dioxide causing very gentle pumping over. Grenache is fermented on the skins for six days, with classic pumping over, and Syrah has the most intense maceration, spending five days in a vat with a vertical propeller, vigorously mixing must and skins. There is a danger of extracting harsh pip tannins with this style of maceration, but the vat has an inclined base so, on the second day of the process, a large proportion of seeds are removed. After fermentation, the different parcels and varieties are blended and aged for eight months in young, but used, Vosges oak barriques. The final product has a surprising elegance and silkiness, with Xinomavro adding a fine patina to the Syrah. The best parcel of Syrah is harvested later than the rest, vinified separately and aged for a year, again in young but not new oak. The Apostolaki Syrah packaging is finished with a striking label, more Californian than Greek in style. Apostolakis wines may have yet to settle on their final style, but the available know-how and determination suggests that some excellent wines will be crafted in the near future.

DIMITRA, COOPERATIVE OF NEA ANHIALOS

40km, Anhialos–Mikrothivon Rd, 374 00 Nea Anhialos. Tel: +30 242 807 6210/6140; Fax: +30 242 807 7276; Email: apsa-dimitra@vol.forthnet.gr
Vineyards under contract: 250ha; members: over 600; production: 3,000hl.

Dimitra is the co-op of Nea Anhialos and, for almost a century, was the sole wine crusader in Magnissia. With over 600 members, Dimitra is primarily focused on Tsipouro production, very popular in the *tsipouradika* (tsipouro and *mezes* restaurants) found along the coast. Another big seller is wine sold in bulk, which comes in most formats, from bag-in-box to large plastic vats. Head winemaker Panayiotis Tomaras is a skilled professional and, with all the shortcomings of both region and the co-op's structure and philosophy, he manages to achieve a sum that is far greater than its parts.

A small part of the production is bottled and is of a perfectly acceptable quality. Dimitra has never claimed to produce top-quality wines – just honest, good-value products. Nevertheless, Dimitra Red, from the local Sikiotis variety, is worth highlighting.

HOLEVA VINEYARDS

374 00 Nea Anhialos. Tel: +30 242 807 6245/6781; Fax: +30 242 807 6245.
Vineyards owned: 2.5ha; under contract: 5ha; production: 700hl.

This recent family enterprise in Nea Anhialos was founded in 2000. The vineyards are certified organic and between them Hrisa Gatou Holevas and Nikos Holevas have planted a fascinating selection of varieties. Apart from Roditis and Savatiano, there are Cabernet Sauvignon, Merlot, Syrah, Xinomavro, Hamburg Muscat, Muscat Blanc, and Mavrodaphne. The family has made a serious effort to exploit the potential of two local varieties, Sikiotis and Fraoula Kokkini ("strawberry red") and preliminary results seem to justify the interest. Sikiotis is a red variety, also found in Macedonia and the island of Evia (Central Greece). The vine is vigorous, moderately prolific, and ripens in mid-September. It can produce deeply coloured wines with relatively high alcohol levels. In contrast, Fraoula Kokkini is very productive and gives less colour but a higher aromatic intensity.

Holeva has also problems with the regulations. It produces a varietal Savatiano table wine (EO), a varietal Roditis EO, but no OPAP blend of the two. The winery's range is made up of EOs, with dry and semi-dry whites and rosés, as well as a multi-varietal red. Development of the red wine portfolio may yield a few surprises in the future.

TIMPLALEXI ESTATE
37 100 Mikrothivai, Almyros.
Head office: Mihopoulou 12, 371 00 Almyros; Tel/Fax: +30 242 202 3716.
Vineyards owned: 4.5ha; production: 450hl.

Dimitris Timplalexis has always been a true believer that the Anhialos OPAP can produce interesting, good-quality wines. Two prerequisites were a small-sized set-up and hard work in the vineyards. Established in 1996, the Timplalexi Estate is still the region's smallest winery, producing less than 100,000 bottles a year. The estate's own vineyards cover most of its needs and Timplalexi is proud to demonstrate the peculiarities of its soils – not overly fertile and full of seashells.

Although plantings of Merlot and Xinomavro suggest a red wine addition to the range soon, the Timplalexi Estate currently has just two white labels. The Anhialos OPAP Savatiano/Roditis blend, when released for the first time in the late 1990s, redefined most wine lovers' perception of the appellation, being broad, textured, and full of juicy fruit. Kokarella is a pure Roditis and develops the theme of the basic bottling a lot further. It is legally only an EO, but for me shows more character and complexity than the OPAP. A most skilled grower that deserves more recognition.

LARISSA

Although fairly flat for the most part, the prefecture of Larissa includes Mount Olympus in the north and Mount Ossa in the northeast. It is a wealthy district with a steady influx of people moving from Athens in search of a more relaxed lifestyle. The city of Larissa is the most important in the region.

Rapsani is the only quality wine appellation (OPAP) of the prefecture, located on the lower foothills of Mount Olympus. Of course, "lower Olympus" does not signify low altitude, as Greece's highest mountain reaches 2,917 metres (9,570 feet), so vineyards reaching up to 700 metres altitude (2,300 feet) are still on the lowest part of the slopes. Nevertheless, the appellation starts a lot lower. Vineyards from the valley floor up to 100 metres altitude (328 feet) are the warmest and most fertile. Parcels up to 250 metres (820 feet) are in loess soil but the yields are still high. The upper parts are better, where the soils are a lighter, rocky, ferric-schist type, and the cooling effect of Olympus night breezes are more noticeable. The legal yield limit is seventy hectolitres per hectare, and although often exceeded in the lower parts, it is rarely achieved in the higher plots.

The region of Olympus has great sentimental value for all Greeks, and Rapsani wine was an integral part of this image – it was the nectar of the gods. The region's co-op produced excellent wines in the past, as proved by some rare bottles surviving today in the cellars of some Larissa connoisseurs. Although different to the current Tsantali style – they were in fact closer to Naoussa, less rich and broad, but equally impressive in complexity – these wines were undeniably of an exceptional quality, but the co-op's commercial approach was flawed, and financial problems followed. The Greek Agricultural Bank repossessed the winery, but the cooperative, as the union of vine-growers, survived. In 1991, when the pioneering producer Tsantali decided to focus on Rapsani, it bought the production plant.

The varietal composition of Rapsani OPAP is defined as equal amounts of Xinomavro, Stavroto, and Krassato. The latter is the local part of the blend, Stavroto is grown further south and Xinomavro further north. Rapsani is the fourth OPAP, after Naoussa, Amyndeo, and Goumenissa, where Xinomavro features. Stavroto is difficult to grow – by the time it reaches 11.5 degrees Baumé it is usually half-rotten. It is also called Ampelakiotiko Mavro or, in a virus-infected version, Ampelakiotiko Galano ("Sky Blue from Ambelakia Village"). It has low sugar levels, moderate acidity, and tannins can be harsh. Krassato is totally different in character. Relatively deep in colour, it is high in sugar and rich in dry extract. It is doubtful whether Stavroto imparts any meaningful elements to Rapsani, while on the other hand, some *cuvées* from half Xinomavro and half Krassato can be exquisite.

The Rapsani demarcated region used to include four villages: Krania, Pyrgetos, Ambelakia, and Rapsani itself. Under the OPAP regulations Krania could not produce a TO red wine, since the Rapsani wine was of the same colour (*see* Part I, Chapter 4). For the innovative Katsaros Estate, the only available option – apart from abandoning red wine – was a broad regional wine classification, a Thessaly TO. Applying much effort and skill, the owner, Dr. Dimitris Katsaros, managed to exclude the commune of Krania from the OPAP-covered region, and a red Krania TO was granted for his Cabernet Sauvignon/Merlot blends.

Another strong viticultural centre is Tyrnavos, northwest of the city of Larissa. More than 30,000 tonnes of grapes are crushed annually and many wine producers throughout Greece buy large quantities of must or wine from the area to cover their table wine (EO) needs. Beyond wine, Tyrnavos is famous for its Tsipouro, making some of the country's most distinctive grape distillates. Part of the fertile Thessaly plain, the yields are predictably high, yet overall Tyrnavos and the neighbouring Damassi village deliver some good-quality grapes.

The main varieties of Tyrnavos are Hamburg Muscat and Roditis, though before World War I and phylloxera the varietal composition of the vineyards was much more complex. It is certain that a large number of varietals have been lost for ever. While setting up the wine legislational framework in the late 1960s, the "Iron Lady" of Greek wine, Stavroula Kourakou-Dragona, was particularly aggressive towards Hamburg Muscat, wanting to ban it altogether. It is a dual-purpose variety, giving both edible and wine grapes, and is usually regarded as the lesser of all Muscats. Nevertheless, as proved by various Tyrnavos wines, Hamburg Muscat can yield a number of simple but aromatic and perfectly enjoyable wines. This excludes the occasions when producers overextract for colour, getting pip tannins which leave the wine astringent. The region's other important variety is often called Damassi Roditis. It is a high-quality Roditis, full of extract together with high acidity, making Damassi one of the top destinations for the occasional Roditis buyer.

Rapsani OPAP

Red still: dry.
Red varieties: equal parts of Krassato, Savroto, and Xinomavro.

Krania TO

White still: dry.
White variety: Chardonnay.
Red still: dry.
Red varieties: Cabernet Sauvignon; Merlot.

Tyrnavos TO

White still: dry.
White varieties: Roditis seventy per cent; Batiki thirty per cent.

Red still: dry.
Red varieties: Cabernet Sauvignon must be at least fifty per cent of the blend, the balance being other local recommended grape varieties.

PRODUCERS

COOPERATIVE OF TYRNAVOS

1st km Tyrnavos–Larissa Rd, 401 00 Tyrnavos. Tel: +30 249 202 2002/4771;
Fax: +30 249-202 2230; Email: info@tirnavoswinery.gr
Vineyards under contract: 550ha; production: 60,000hl.

The Cooperative of Tyrnavos produces some of Greece's best Tsipouro, based on Hamburg Muscat, a most fitting grape for the purpose. Rare, barrel-aged examples can be compared with top-quality grappa. Hamburg Muscat is also used to produce large volumes of easily quaffable, mostly off-dry rosé. A large part of the production is sold in bulk and, one suspects, might reappear as "local artisan wine" in many tavernas across Greece.

The good value, bottled wines are clean and have enough fruit to be enjoyed over an informal summer holiday lunch. The co-op's Retsina is considered to be one of the best traditional examples to be found today.

DOUGOS WINERY

400 04 Itea Gonnon. Head office: Xilokastrou 3, 413 35 Larissa.
Tel: +30 241 062 0621; Fax: +30 241 053 0992;
Website: www.dougos.gr; Email: dougos@otenet.gr
Vineyards owned: 5.4ha; production: 350hl.

Dimitris and Thanos Dougos have entered their winery's second decade full of hope for the future. Both are innovative, with an attentive ear and a sharp eye. Above all, they want to create new wines without losing sight of tradition. Although they already craft good wines from French and Greek varieties, their main priority is to create a Rapsani OPAP. The vineyards are situated in one of the area's best parcels, at 600 metres (1,968 feet), with high limestone content and yields of less than forty hectolitres per hectare. Nevertheless, the winery is just half a kilometre from the current OPAP boundaries. There have already been many discussions with the local agriculture office, but Thanos remains optimistic. "All difficulties will be dealt with," he says. "A Dougos Rapsani wine will happen soon." However, Thanos is not totally happy with the Rapsani regulations and criticizes Stavroto. "It adds nothing to the blend and it is so difficult to grow. When it is ripe it is rotten, and when it is healthy it is below eleven degrees Baumé." He prefers Krassato, which provides both colour and structure.

Methystanes White is the basic, revenue-earning label of the winery, and the only wine made using bought grapes and not bearing a "made from organically grown grapes" label. It is mainly Roditis, with fifteen per cent Assyrtico and some Batiki. Dougos Winery White is more complex and concentrated on the nose and palate. Its varietal make-up is identical to Methystanes but Chardonnay substitutes Batiki. The top white, Methymon, is Roditis from the high Rapsani slopes, close to 500 metres altitude (1,640 feet) and aged in French oak for three months.

The Dougos reds are slightly more expressive than the whites. Methystanes Red is the one earmarked to be upgraded to Rapsani OPAP. It is a stunning example of the appellation, being lighter than the Tsantali example, without its crystal clear fruit definition, soft tannin, and highly polished oak, but with a brilliant, low-key complexity of spices and dark fruits. The blend does not follow the OPAP equal-parts rule for the three grapes: Xinomavro is up to fifty per cent; Krassato up to forty per cent; and Stavroto makes up the remainder.

The best Dougos wine – and one of Thessaly's finest – is Methymon. The intriguing blend consists of seventy-five per cent Cabernet Franc, Syrah, and Merlot, plus ten per cent of Grenache, with a bit of Cabernet Sauvignon, ten per cent Limniona, and five per cent Batiki. The white Batiki is harvested well in advance of the red varieties and vinified as a red grape, macerated for up to a week. The Batiki "red" wine has a deep golden straw colour and notable structure on the palate, but extremely low acidity. Bottled alone, it would need some serious acidification and would still shock many consumers. Nevertheless, it would be one of Greece's most idiosyncratic wines.

In 2001, a small proportion of vines from all seven varieties was allowed to overripen and a barrel of late harvest Methymon was made, totally dry but with 15.1 per cent alcohol. Possibly the most Châteauneuf-du-Pape-like wine ever produced in Greece, the success of the experiment was quickly noticed, and all vineyards of Methymon are now pushed towards higher sugar levels, creating a much more interesting wine.

KARIPIDI VINEYARDS

Thesi Vounaina, 430 62 Larissa. Tel: +30 241 098 1087; Fax: +30 241 098 1088; Website: www.karipidis.com; Email: karipidi@otenet.gr
Vineyards owned: 19.2ha; production: 1,000hl.

In 1985, brothers Lazaros and Pantelis Karipidis started a hobby winery in Vounaina, pretty much *terra incognita* for viticulturalists. The climate of the region, with its gentle hills on the Thessaly plain and its free-draining soil, promised trouble-free vine cultivation and, at that point, nothing else was required. There were no aspirations for high-quality wine production, just something interesting to do at the weekend. After a few years it became evident that the vineyards had some serious potential. In addition, it was the 1990s, when numerous small wine producers were joining the market every year and so in 1997, the brothers decided to start a commercially oriented business.

Since the general area had no long-standing tradition and no dominant classic vine varieties, varietal selection for Karipidi Vineyards was interesting from the start. Consultant winemaker at the time was Vassilis Emmanouilidis, a young and talented Bordeaux-trained oenologist. He reasoned that it would be wise to plant well-known varietals in this unknown terroir. The initial choice comprised Sauvignon Blanc, Cabernet Sauvignon, and Merlot, plus a bit of Syrah. In the late 1990s, with the market flooded with Greek examples of these varieties, Pantelis and Lazaros thought that they needed a point of difference, so they also planted a trio of famous Italian varieties – Sangiovese, Primitivo, and Nebbiolo.

Sauvignon Blanc is released in two styles. A basic, stainless-steel version is grassy, lifted, and strikes a good balance between the vivacity of the grape and the heat of Vounaina. A Fumé Sauvignon Blanc is fermented and aged in French barriques for eight months and shows a good integration of oak and fruit, leaning more towards firmness than fatness.

The estate's reds all receive a year of oak-ageing, totally French but from a variety of forests and with a range of toastings. All wines see some Alliers oak with the Vosges reserved for Cabernet, Syrah, and Sangiovese, and the Nevers goes to Nebbiolo, Primitivo, and Merlot. Cabernet is blended with twenty per cent Merlot for a touch of softness and is bottled as the basic red. The best parcels of Merlot and Syrah are bottled separately. These wines are restrained, tannic, not flashy, and seem to benefit from some time in bottle.

Although an interesting commercial proposal, when the Italian varietal trio was released in 2002, the wines themselves were not overly attractive. They were quite aggressive, lean, and relatively fruitless. It seemed as if there has been a lack of understanding about the grapes' characteristics. For example, all the alcohol levels were around 12.5 per cent, while the varieties in question really need to be harvested above 13.5 degrees Baumé to achieve fruit and phenolic ripeness.

Determined not to be put off, in 2003 the Karipidis brothers hired Ampeloiniki, Greece's top viticulture and viniculture consultant, to further develop the style of their products. Although Ampeloiniki always starts in the vineyards, there is already a noticeable change in the reds, with more fruit, more extract, a lot more depth, and a better feel for each variety. If an experimental vinification of Cabernet/Merlot in 2003 captured in a few magnums is a marker for the future, then we can expect the Karipidis wines to be even more dense and voluptuous.

KATSAROS ESTATE

400 07 Krania Pyrgetos. Tel: +30 249 504 1666.
Head office: Panagouli 6, 412 22 Larissa. Tel/Fax: +30 241 053 6811.
Vineyards owned: 7.5ha; production: 250hl.

During the 1990s, Katsaros Estate was the quintessential boutique winery, and aspiring competitors in the twenty-first century will have no less difficulty in keeping up. Dr. Dimitris Katsaros set up a small vineyard and winery in the late 1970s in the middle of the Rapsani appellation. His aims were clear from the start: to craft small quantities of age-worthy wines. Wine was first bottled from the 1981 harvest, with the initial commercial release being in 1989, where a thousand bottles of the 1987 vintage sold in a matter of weeks at a record price of 800 drachmas (2.35 Euros). Almost twenty years later, the winery still produces only 15,000 bottles of red and 20,000 bottles of white Katsaros Estate.

The Katsaros vineyards were initially located inside the OPAP Rapsani area, but unhappy with the prescribed varietal selection, Katsaros managed single-handedly to get the Krania village excluded from the appellation so that a red Krania regional wine (TO) classification could be created for Cabernet/Merlot blends, and a white TO for Chardonnay. The choice of French-only grapes was not rash; the local varieties were studied for several years before being abandoned.

The vines are planted on a light, stony soil with exceptional drainage and, at an altitude ranging from 650 to 800 metres (2,130–2,620 feet), the mean temperature during the growing season is 7–8°C (12–14°F) lower than on the plain. Cultivation is organic and usually trouble-free, even with light summer rains. The vineyards are separated into twenty-two plots and each is harvested separately. Yields are below forty hectolitres per hectare, even though the planting density is high by Greek standards, at 4,800 vines per hectare. Severe green harvesting takes place, leaving four bunches per vine, or one bunch per shoot.

The winemaking is fairly traditional and straightforward. Evangelos Gerovassiliou advised during the 1990s, and now the estate is advised by Kiriakos Kinigopoulos, a consulting winemaking prodigy with a CV that includes many high-profile projects, from top Burgundy estates to Antinori in Italy, as well as wineries in Chile and Argentina.

Katsaros Estate Red is eighty per cent Cabernet Sauvignon and twenty per cent Merlot. It is co-macerated for three weeks, aged in oak for a year, bottled unfiltered, and released after an additional year in bottle. The white version first appeared in the late 1990s and is a Chardonnay aged in oak for eight months. The proportion of new oak, which was quite dominating in early vintages, is on the decrease now, standing at sixty-five per cent for the red and fifty per cent for the white. Both wines are impressive, even though the white is tight, unforgiving, and lacks an expected degree of opulence. The red needs ageing, and finding older vintages, especially in magnum, is a treat.

Even though some experimental plots of Assyrtico, Agiorgitiko, and Pinot Noir have been planted, Katsaros has no plans for expansion. The only thing he is waiting for is the vines to get older, adding more dimensions to his wines.

LELLIS WINERY
400 03 Dimitra Lakereias. Head office: Filellinon 81, 412 21 Larissa.
Tel: +30 241 053 3772; Fax: +30 241 053 2471;
Website: www.hermes.gr/lelis; Email: lelis@hermes.gr
Vineyards owned: 1ha; under contract: 1.7ha; production: 200hl.

A family venture founded in 1990 and driven by Stelios Lellis, the winery's annual production is close to 25,000 bottles and is spread across five labels. The brand name of the range is Pithigia, which is the name of the Ancient Greek celebration in Anthestiria, signifying the opening of new barrels with the new wine.

Pithigia White is a simple Roditis with a splash of Chardonnay. In good vintages an oak-aged Chardonnay from the winery's own vineyards is produced. Cabernet Sauvignon, Merlot, Syrah, and Xinomavro make up the blend for the Pithigia Red, aged in Greek and French oak. A Cabernet Sauvignon/Merlot blend aged totally in French oak is also bottled as a limited-release Pithigia Paleothen, and a rosé completes the portfolio.

TSANTALI

125th km EO Athinon–Larissa, 400 08 Rapsani.

See also Tsantali entries on pages 109, 139, 162.

Rapsani is one of the most impressive success stories for Tsantali, if not for the whole of Greek wine. An appellation with a rich history, an exceptional terroir, and three native varieties formed the perfect platform for Tsantali to develop a strong brand name. Its achievement was twofold. Firstly, commercial success for Tsantali's Rapsani wines amplified demand for local grapes, giving a sense of purpose for people from the surrounding areas – in the late 1980s, the villages of Rapsani were veering towards the poverty line, but Tsantali provided a large part of the population with a significant money-generator. And secondly, Rapsani spearheaded one of the most successful attempts to promote Greek wines to the wider world. By combining classic images of Greece with a wine that is uniquely native but still amazingly international in style, Tsantali came up with a product that drinkers around the world could relate to and still feel undeniably charmed by.

The Tsantali operation started with the buy-out of the local co-op's winery from the Agricultural Bank in 1991 (*see* page 206). As ever, the essentials begin in the vineyard, so the Tsantali viticultural team worked hard to ensure that grapes from local vineyards were of high enough quality. Plots were replanted or re-trellised, disease problems were treated, and drip-irrigation systems were introduced. Great care was taken to raise levels of knowledge among local growers. For example, different varieties were interplanted in the fields, and the workers had to learn how to recognize each one and the different pruning and harvesting requirements of each.

Xinomavro and Krassato are harvested first and Stavroto follows a week later. Each variety is harvested and vinified separately. A key ingredient of the Rapsani wines is extraction – transforming the unforgiving Xinomavro and Krassato grapes into a velvety wine of almost Merlot-like softness. Maceration takes place in wooden vats, each parcel is carefully monitored, and there are no norms or formulae, just an analytic approach. Ageing of the wine is simple: a year in 300-litre Alliers oak, half of which is new, followed by a year in bottle.

There are four versions of Rapsani, two of which are rarely available to the public. The higher-volume Olympus Rapsani is the lighter of the range, with the usual Xinomavro character displayed in firm tannins, light body, and refreshing acidity. A selection from higher vineyards, vats, and barrels, plus some additional time in oak produces a Rapsani Epilegmenos ("reserve", *see*

Appendix 1): a serious model of modern Greek wine, showing balanced oak, ripe but not overly sweet fruit, low-key herbs, silky tannins, extract, and presence. This is the wine that put Rapsani back onto the world wine map.

For most connoisseurs of Tsantali wines, these are the only Rapsani bottlings, but chief oenologist Pavlos Argiropoulos keeps two other wines well-hidden in the main Tsantali cellars in Aghios Pavlos, Halkidiki. The first, Private Collection, is along the same lines as the Epilegmenos, except that selection standards are higher at all stages of production, meaning that concentration and extraction are elevated to a higher plane.

The last Rapsani wine is made only in certain years when the summer Livas – a hot, severe wind – blows through the higher vineyards causing the grapes to naturally dehydrate. A careful selection of these concentrated grapes is used to make a few barriques of Rapsani Livas Cuvée, an opaque wine, approaching the fifteen per cent alcohol level that amplifies the Rapsani style to almost Australian proportions. First produced with the 2000 vintage, this is a curiosity that vividly demonstrates the unknown possible permutations that could still be hidden in the Greek terroirs.

VASDAVANOS WINES
415 00 Giannouli Larissa. Tel: +30 241 059 1166; Fax: +30 241 059 1620; Website: www.vasdavanos.gr; Email: vaswin@panafonet.gr.
Vineyards owned: 0.5ha; under contract: 50ha; production: 10,000hl.

Vasdavanos is by far the biggest private winery in Thessaly and the only private winery functioning in Tyrnavos. Hamburg Muscat, Savatiano, and Roditis are the main varieties crushed, followed by Ugni Blanc and small quantities of Debina. Nevertheless, the Vasdavanos family believes that Hamburg Muscat is an important tool in developing commercial high-volume brands which still retain some character.

The winery recently invested in its own vineyards, mainly in order to start experimenting with varieties that are rare in the area. Merlot, Cabernet Sauvignon, Syrah, and Agiorgitiko have been planted, mainly to decide which might be a good blending partner for Hamburg Muscat. A longer-term project is the development of some premium products, thereby entering the company into a smaller but more prestigious, faster-developing and potentially more profitable market. For a company like Vasdavanos, the technicalities should not be a problem; achieving the right image might be more of a challenge.

TRIKALA

The city of Trikala is located on the western end of the Thessaly plain, but most of the prefecture's area extends north and west of Trikala, well into higher altitudes. This district, one of the most mountainous in Greece, is surrounded by mounts Tzoumerka, Lakmos, and Hasia. The Pinios River runs through Trikala, creating a small but striking valley around the town of Kalambaka. The breathtaking beauty of Meteora, the community of Byzantine monasteries built 600 years ago on gigantic perpendicular rocks, is found on the left bank of the river.

Viticulture in Trikala is somewhat limited, although Meteora used to have extensive vineyard land, and wines from the region have mainly localized importance and appeal. There are no regional wine classifications (TOs), let alone appellations of higher quality ranking, so the available choice is EO (table wine), or the most general TO of Thessaly designation. Some local producers are trying to create a basic framework, either a TO of Trikala or Meteora, and although they have not yet succeeded, there is no reason why they should not gain these regional descriptions in the future.

PRODUCERS

PAPAVASSILIOU ESTATE

422 00 Kastraki Kalabakas. Head office: Thiramenous 16, 122 42 Aegaleo.
Tel/Fax: +30 210 591 2336.
Vineyards owned: 2.5ha; under contract: 2.5ha; production: 300hl.

This producer is the only commercial winery in the historic Meteora area. The Papavassiliou family is the main drive behind efforts to create a Meteora TO classification. Roditis, Muscat, and Batiki, together with Cinsault, are the main varieties crushed. The winery produces a Meteoritikos range and a higher-priced Kastrakinos white and red. Eklisiastikos is a sweet red communion wine.

TSILILIS WINERY

421 00 Raksa Trikalon. Tel: +30 243 108 5885; Fax: +30 243 108 5381.
Vineyards owned: 5ha; under contract: 15ha; production: 2,000hl.

Ouzo and tsipouro take precedence over wines at Tsililis. Since Konstantinos and Efthimis Tsililis started in 1989, the brand name Tsililis has become one of the most dynamic in the local spirits market. The Tsililis wine business is restrained by comparison, though owned vineyards are being developed and the aim is for quality. Roditis and Hamburg Muscat are of prime importance, followed by Xinomavro, Merlot, Cabernet Sauvignon, as well as Assyrtico and Chardonnay. Askitiko White and Red are the basic products and fruit from the family vineyards is used for the Ampelones Tsilili White and Red.

KARDITSA

Karditsa lies below Trikala, on the southern part of the Thessaly plain. More than half the district is on high mountain slopes, but Karditsa still enjoys some of the benefits of the fertile Kambos. The Tavropos Lake is an important feature, reassuring growers and landowners that water is swiftly accessible. Apart from Tavropos, there is a large number of small rivers and creeks flowing down from north-facing slopes, going through the eastern side of the prefecture and finally into the Pinios River. There are very few districts in Greece that are so self-sufficient in terms of water.

The main grape varieties of the area are Hamburg Muscat, Batiki, and Savatiano, planted here in post-phylloxera times after World War II, together with the local Rosaki, a rare, pale red variety, able to produce light rosés or whites with moderate body and simple aromas, and Fraoula.

Messenikola was one of the latest additions to the list of quality wine appellations (OPAPs) in 1994. Myth surrounds the name of the appellation, as well as the village. It is said that during the Ottoman occupation, a certain Monsieur Nicolas arrived from France and helped the local community to develop new commercial ventures. One of the most important projects was viticulture, and Nicolas introduced a grape variety, thereafter called Mavro Messenikola ("Black Messenikola"). Many people have been quick to suppose that Mavro Messenikola could have been a French varietal that was transplanted in Greece in this way and possibly lost in its motherland after phylloxera. However romantic this may seem, there is no evidence of a French provenance for the grape. Although notably lighter, it is more likely to be a variety related to Xinomavro.

The demarcated region of Messenikolas ranges between altitudes of 250–600 metres (820–1,970 feet) and includes three villages: Moschato, Morfovouni, and Messenikolas. The appellation technically goes up to Lake Tavropos, at 800 metres (2,620 feet), but the quantities of grapes produced there are not significant. Soils are light and gravelly with some red clay spots and high water-retention capacities. This characteristic keeps vine vigour and productivity high. The permitted yield is eighty-four hectolitres per hectare. Higher yields are the norm, while Mavro Messenikola must reach at least fifty-five hectolitres per hectare to give some character and density.

The varietal composition of the OPAP is seventy per cent Mavro Messenikola and the rest must be Carignan and Syrah. Carignan is included because of ease of cultivation but it is debatable whether it adds to the final blend in terms of quality. Syrah, on the other hand, is a perfect addition to Mavro Messenikola – indeed, the *cuvées* that bypass the rules by being fifty-fifty blends of Syrah and Mavro Messenikola are exceptional. It is a great pity that, legally, these grapes could not be the only ambassadors of the Messenikola OPAP. The style of these wines doesn't just mimic Syrah with a few nuances of Mavro Messenikola thrown in, but is truly distinctive, scented, and fine-grained on the palate.

Currently, most people encountering a Messenikolas red will find a light, almost rosé wine, lacking in tannin structure, extract, and depth. This is underlined by the fact that, under the old legislation, Messenikola was the only red OPAP of Greece with no restrictions regarding maturation time before release – it needed more freshness than ageing. If this situation continues, then it is unlikely that Messenikolas wines will gain popularity beyond Karditsa and Thessaly.

Messenikola OPAP

Red still: dry.
Red varieties: seventy per cent Mavro Messenikola, thirty per cent Carignan and Syrah.

PRODUCERS

KARAMITROU WINERY

430 67 Messenikolas, Karditsa. Tel: +30 244 109 5250; Fax: +30 244 107 0871;
Website: www.messenikolaswines.com; Email: giorgoskaramitros@yahoo.gr
Vineyards owned: 4ha; under contract: 3ha; production: 500hl.

Giorgos Karamitros established this notable new venture in the Messenikola OPAP in 2000, and it is already clear that its wines will give a new breath of life to the image of the appellation. Messenikola Karamitros is a modern wine, from packaging to product, full of fruit and full of character. Although most Messenikolas wines are released onto the market as soon as possible after the vintage, Karamitros is not in a hurry to get his wine bottled. It is too early to tell, but Messenikola Karamitros might well benefit from some short-term ageing, which, given the appellation's general image, is impressive in itself.

Karamitros, interestingly, focuses only on dry wines, forgoing the general trend of the region. The basic range is called Polihnis, available in white, rosé, and red, as well as a soft Karamitros White. This is an extrovert, modern venture that promises interesting things for the future.

KARDITSA COOPERATIVE

Tauropou 72, 431 00 Karditsa. Tel: +30 244 102 2976.
Head office: Grigoriou Lambraki 10, 431 00 Karditsa.
Tel: +30 244 102 8832/7811; Fax: +30 244 102 6112.
Vineyards under contract: 1,000ha; members; 20,000+; production: 11,500hl.

The largest producer of Karditsa and second only to Tyrnavos Cooperative in Thessaly, the Karditsa Cooperative consists of 162 primary agricultural cooperatives and more than 20,000 growers. Following the norm in this region, a large proportion of production is sold in bulk rather than bottled. Although the winery releases dry wines of all colours and some off-dry reds, the highlight of the portfolio is the OPAP Messenikola bottling. This is possibly ninety-five per cent of the appellation's bottled production and is very light in both colour and structure. Retsina Gioma is another popular label. The wines of Karditsa Co-op are rarely seen outside Thessaly.

KOTOULA WINERY

Terma odou Filikis Etairias, 431 00 Karditsa. Head office: Hatzimitrou 47, 431 00 Karditsa. Tel: +30 244 102 2321; Fax: +30 244 104 2820.
Vineyards owned: 1.6ha; under contract: 0.9ha; production: 3,000hl.

Sotiris Kotoulas is an important personality in Thessaly. He was one of the first trained oenologists in Greece and, during the 1970s, one of the most important. His efforts to upgrade the standards of wine production were remarkable, both for his own winery, which began in 1974, and on a far more general level. It is a shame that the style of his wines seems to have stayed in the 1970s – but with a loyal clientele that supports the winery and its products, this is not a big problem.

There are only dry EO wines and no OPAP labels. The three white varietals, crushed in the winery, are bottled separately. There is an Epilektos Roditis ("selected Roditis"), a rare and flowery Epilektos Debina, fatter than the Zitsa OPAP style, and an Epilektos Batiki, showing the variety's body and structure but also its lack of acidity. The only red variety, Mavro Messenikola, is bottled as an *epilektos nouveau* (*see* Appendix 1).

5

Central Greece

The Greek name for this province, *Sterea*, means "Solid" Greece and it is the name used for the southern part of the mainland, excluding the Peloponnese. The province borders the Ionian Sea to the west, Epirus and Thessaly to the north, and the Aegean Sea to the east. To the south lies the Corinthian Gulf, a thin strip of water that separates the Balkan Peninsula from the Peloponnese. Central Greece is home to the most populated area of Greece, Attica, which includes the nation's capital, Athens. The sizeable island of Evia is also classified as part of Central Greece.

TOPOGRAPHY AND REGIONS

With the Pindos range of mountains stretching south to the very edge of the Corinthian Gulf, the central parts of Central Greece are some of the country's highest. The main flat areas are located on the west side, around Mesologi and Agrinio in Aitoloakarnania, and on the east, in Attica and Thebes. Overall, the west of the region has a much higher average altitude than the east. The soils vary widely and include some of the richest and poorest sites in Greece. Some of the high parts in the central heartland are unsuitable for any form of cultivation, including vines; while the flat area around the city of Thebes in Viotia is particularly fertile and most plants grow with ease.

This complex topography results in a wide range of meso-climates. The west of the region is humid, high plots in the centre are extremely cold, and Attica is the driest and hottest place in Greece. Water availability is not limited, since several important rivers stem from the Pindos mountain range. In addition, there are numerous lakes, some of which are man-made, that sustain reserves around the year. Since over a third of the total Greek population lives in the eastern part of Central Greece; the infrastructure that is in place to accommodate their needs can also be used for agricultural purposes to provide irrigation where necessary.

The contrasts found across Central Greece extend to its economy. Villages in Aitoloakarnania and the central areas are some of the poorest in Greece and are constantly abandoned by young people – as happens with the most remote areas of Thrace or Epirus. By contrast, the eastern part is the financial and trade centre of Greece and has been for fifty years. It dictates trends and offers opportunities for the younger generation. Yet, living in the financial heart of the nation does not guarantee a high standard of living – Athens and its inhabitants are similar to those of all major European cities, coping with a frantic everyday routine and moving away from the typically stress-free and relaxed approach to life that the Greeks historically followed.

The most important viticultural region, Attica, is split into a number of prefectures for administrative reasons: Athens; Piraeus (the port); Western Attica; and Eastern Attica. The other six prefectures that make up Central Greece are, from the west, Aitoloakarnania, the small Evritania to the north, Fokida and Viotia, both of which border Fthiotida to the north, and finally the island of Evia. The whole of Central Greece has about 21,000 hectares planted with wine grapes, which is about twenty-eight per cent of the entire Greek vine acreage. The concentration of vineyards is much greater than it looks at first sight. Evritania is one of the few prefectures in Greece with no vineyards registered, while Fokida has 400 hectares, Aitoloakarnania 762 hectares, and Fthiotida 820 hectares. That leaves an area of 19,000 hectares – about the size of the entire vineyard area of New Zealand – to be divided between Viotia (3,437 hectares), Evia (3,942 hectares), and Attica (11,540 hectares).[1]

THE RISE AND FALL OF RETSINA

A large part of the modern vinous history of Central Greece, possibly excluding the last three decades, can be encapsulated in one word: retsina. The retsina phenomenon was created in this region and then taken up by other areas such as Macedonia and islands in the Aegean. Tree resin was used in a number of ways – for example, to seal clay *amphorae* and to create a film on the surface of the wine to minimize air contact – and its presence in wine was mainly viewed as a preservative and a flavouring agent, making

1. All figures are taken from the latest nationwide survey for the Greek Ministry of Agriculture and relate to 2001.

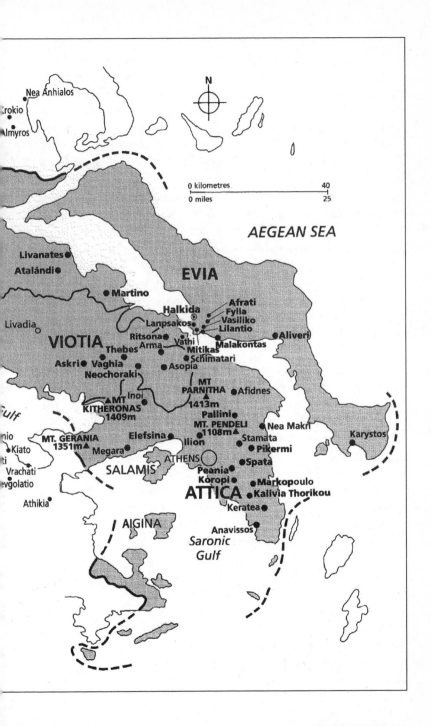

N

0 kilometres 40
0 miles 25

AEGEAN SEA

Nea Anhialos

rokio

lmyros

Livanates
Atalándi

EVIA

Martino

Halkida
Livadia   Lanpsakos
            Ritsona   Vathi
VIOTIA   Arma
        Thebes   Mitikas
Askri Vaghia   Schimatari
    Neochoraki   Asopia

Afrati
Fylla
Vasiliko
Lilantio
Malakontas   Aliveri

MT
PARNITHA   Afidnes
1413m

Inoi
MT
KITHERONAS
1409m

Gulf

Pallini
MT. PENDELI
1108m
Stamata   Nea Makri

Karystos

nio
Kiato
ti
Vrachati
vgolatio

MT. GERANIA
1351m
Megara

Elefsina
Ilion
ATHENS

SALAMIS

Pikermi
Spata

Peania
Koropi

Markopoulo
Kalivia Thorikou

ATTICA

Athikia

AIGINA

Keratea

Anavissos

Saronic
Gulf

the wine less prone to oxidation and to mask any off-flavours developed during winemaking or storage. It is curious that this wine style was widely found two millennia ago, spreading throughout Greece to southern Italy, yet two centuries ago it was confined to Attica, Viotia, and Evia. All regions making retsina today have followed the success of Central Greece.

Retsina was traditionally made by adding resin to wine. The resin would be left in the barrel until all the wine had been drawn off, or until the wine was racked off the lees and resin sludge as soon as the desired intensity of flavour was attained. Pine trees abound in the region, and the finest resin comes from the Aleppo pine. Over the years, the typical amount of resin added has been decreasing, possibly reflecting improvements in winemaking. In the late eighteenth century wines with resin concentration of 7.5 per cent were encountered, while in the early twentieth century up to the 1960s, most retsina contained about five per cent resin. During the 1960s, commercial and bottled retsina become available, usually made with much lower resin additions of one to two per cent. A common problem was very low acidity and too much or too little alcohol.

Today retsina has a legal definition restricting the resin presence and demanding a more balanced wine. Resin must be between 0.15 per cent and one per cent of the final product, minimum acidity must be 4.5 grams per litre, and the alcohol has to be between ten per cent and 13.5 per cent. The same is valid for Kokkineli, a rosé retsina made from macerated Roditis. Current practices are also different, with the resin added to the must instead of the wine, and the new wine left on its lees for just a week after the end of fermentation. Modern retsina can be extremely fresh, charming, and full of fruit, together with a much more delicate presence of resin.

The modern popularity of retsina started to grow in the late nineteenth century, and Athenian *kapilia* (notorious drinking holes) became prime destinations for horse carts carrying barrels full of young wine or must. With Athens' influential position as a trade and cultural centre, and the increasing ease of communication and transportation, the trend developed rapidly, spreading throughout the land. After World War II, when tourists started flooding into Athens and many of the Greek islands, retsina's popularity increased. Producers like Kourtaki and Cambas boosted sales by bottling retsina and shipping it to tourist resorts. However, changes in consumer tastes, the increasing sophistication of local customers and visitors, and, it has to be admitted, bad wine, has stalled the progress of retsina. Today the average quality of the product is higher than ever and sales are still strong, but a mere shadow of what they were in the 1960s.

Wine production in Central Greece has now moved decisively out of the retsina era and there are many wineries that can compete with the best. Sadly, it seems that many of the negative connotations from the 1980s still linger on. Much of the excitement generated in the last twenty years about modern Greek wine has been focused on other regions and Central Greece has been considered almost irrelevant. When local producers made progress and caught the attention of wine-lovers around the country, it tended to be considered an isolated incident. Meanwhile, little was done to upgrade the image of the broader area, while in contrast, the first successful producers from Drama and Kavala in Macedonia significantly raised the awareness and image of their districts.

GRAPES AND CLASSIFICATIONS

Savatiano is the king of Central Greece. In Attica it makes up more than ninety per cent of the total volume, in Viotia the figure is close to fifty per cent, and in Evia it is about eighty per cent. The rest of the vineyards are planted with Roditis. It is often thought that the predominance of Savatiano is closely linked to the past glories of retsina, but this is not entirely true. Traditionally, Savatiano was just one of many varieties used for retsina and in many regions it was not the most important. Instead, Roditis was believed to make the finest examples of the genre. However, phylloxera changed all that. In the years after its arrival between the World Wars, there was an urgent need for new parent stock, preferably for a variety that could be grafted easily, could withstand the hot and arid conditions of the region, and, finally, could provide very high yields. The choice of Savatiano, for authorities and landowners, was obvious.

There is no tradition for producing rosé or red wines, so the first attempts are less than thirty years old. So far Cabernet Sauvignon has been the most popular red variety and it still dominates newly established plots. Nevertheless, as the number of adventurous and open-minded growers increases, plenty of other varieties are arriving in Central Greece. Favourite white varieties include Assyrtico, Athiri, Chardonnay, and, to a lesser extent, Sauvignon Blanc and Malagousia. As for red grapes, Grenache Rouge and Carignan have been used as workhorse red grapes, while some producers have been producing good Syrah and Merlot. It is clear that the replanting strategies after the arrival of phylloxera limited the diversity of indigenous varietals in the region, making it currently one of the most homogeneous in Greece.

Despite the sheer size of the vineyard acreage, Central Greece has no quality wine appellations, neither OPAP nor OPE. In the first wave of OPAP designations in 1971, two such appellations were granted, one to Halkida in Evia and the other to Kantza in Attica, but following minimal interest, both were suspended. However, what Central Greece lacks in quality wine appellations it makes up for in regional appellations, its TOs. There are, in total, more than twenty-two TOs in Attica, Viotia, Evia, and Fthiotida, plus a generic one for Central Greece, and there are more in the Ministry of Agriculture's legislational pipeline. Just like the vibrant *vins de pays* scene in the south of France, these TOs illustrate the changing dynamics of the region, with more and more producers seeking new wine styles, alternative choices of varieties, and – finally – ways out of the retsina epoch.

Central Greece TO

White still: dry.
White varieties: Athiri; Assyrtico; Malagousia; Roditis; Savatiano; Sauvignon Blanc.
Rosé still: dry.
Red still: dry.
Red/Rosé varieties: Cabernet Sauvignon; Carignan; Merlot; Syrah.

ATTICA

Attica is the southeastern tip of Central Greece, ending at the beautiful Cape Sounio, with western coastlines around the Corinthian Gulf, southwestern coastlines around the Saronic Gulf, and eastern coastlines along the southern Evoikos Gulf. It borders the prefecture of Viotia in the north and the Peloponnese to the west. Administratively, Attica extends just west of Megara, close to Mount Gerania. Athens, Greece's largest city, and its suburbs take up a large part of Attica's surface area.

All Attica's borders with other prefectures are essentially geographical limits imposed by mountains: Mount Gerania in the west, and mounts Kitheronas, Pateras, and Parnitha in the north. Two mountains exist solely within Attica – mounts Pendeli and Imitos – and these define the capital's boundaries. This natural cover cuts off breezes from the north while the flat sections of Attica are exposed to warm winds coming from the south. The sea does exercise a moderating effect on coastal areas, but the majority of the region has one of the driest and hottest climates in Greece – from May to September, there is an average of 17.8 days of rain and the average temperature over the summer months is 27°C (82°F). Ancient Greeks had more than a few good reasons to establish Athens where they did.

Viticultural hotspots

There are three distinct areas where vine-growing is important. The first is Megara, on the western side of the prefecture. Most vineyards are located in a flat stretch between the mountains of Gerania, towards the Corinthian Canal, and Mount Pateras. The broad shape of the region – like a corridor connecting two gulfs – generates a gentle but constant breeze that exerts a welcome cooling effect. Megara had very few producers who could be regarded as quality-oriented until the establishment of the Evharis Estate in 1985. But the grapes of the area were regularly bought by Attica's larger producers, and the local co-op was, and still is, an important supplier of bulk wine for wine companies, retail shops, and restaurants.

The second area is the flat plain of Mesogia, which includes most of the land lying south of Pendeli and east of Athens. Coastal areas, like Anavissos, are slightly cooler and have a less extreme meso-climate, but in general this is the hottest and driest place in Greece. The soils are mainly limestone but relatively rich, although not as fertile as many plots in Megara. Natural levels of rainfall are hardly enough to sustain growing vines, so irrigation, if practised wisely, can increase both quality and quantity of grapes. Currently, the vineyards are about fifty per cent dry-farmed and fifty per cent irrigated, mainly to produce higher yields. Savatiano, the main grape, gives quite high crop levels in the area. The best parcels produce about seventy hectolitres per hectare, while irrigated plots easily reach three times that. Maturity is not a problem; fourteen degrees Baumé is attained in most later-harvested vineyards.

The Mesogia plain near Athens used to be an important vine-growing area, but due to urbanization, this may become no more than a distant memory. The new Athens National Airport was finalised in the 1990s, and to provide access a new national road was built connecting Mesogia to several parts of Athens and bringing many vineyard areas within a forty-minute drive from the centre of Athens. In the process, many vineyards were claimed by the Greek government to make space for the airport and the new roads. Most importantly, many department stores and other businesses moved next to the airport, and property prices rose sharply. In addition, many Athenians with land in the region decided to make it their permanent home, as reaching the northern suburbs of the capital can be quicker from Mesogia than from downtown Athens. Thus property development became a much more attractive financial proposition than growing vines. People like Roxani Matsa, who stuck with her nine-hectare Matsa Estate at a time when prospective buyers were offering her unfeasibly high amounts of money for it, were either committing financial suicide or an act of passion.

The third viticultural area is northern Attica, which includes Mount Parnitha and much of the Pendeli Mountains. This is the higher, cooler, and most infertile, arid part of Attica. Even if sunlight hours are as high as in the lower regions, cold nights and cool days arrive early in the autumn. This means, for example, that Savatiano in Stamata only reaches twelve degrees Baumé in the better years. Yields can occasionally reach 110 hectolitres per hectare, but on average they are much lower.

Classifications and wine tourism

At present, Attica's higher vineyards are thought to have the highest quality potential, but this has not always been the case. Growers from these areas used to have great difficulties selling their grapes. Buyers only purchased them in times of shortage and when they were confident that they could blend away the flowery, crisp, fresh character of the fruit. The trend was towards rich, alcoholic, low-acid wines and the hotter regions of Attica, mainly Mesogia, were considered the top sources.

Attica's wine producers have been particularly busy over the last two decades establishing no fewer than fourteen regional wine appellations (TOs) in the region (*see* Appendix 1). The oldest and more general, like the TOs of Spata or Markopoulo, are white wine-related and refer mostly to Savatiano and, less frequently, to Roditis, Assyrtico, Chardonnay, and even Sauvignon Blanc. There are also a few red wine appellations, like the Attica and Vilitsa TOs, which are used for Cabernet Sauvignon. It is hard to discuss terroir differences between these TOs, since the majority were established for the needs of only one producer, making comparison difficult – the style, philosophy, and type of products vary so widely.

Meanwhile, the Attican Vineyards Wine Producers' Association has been working hard to promote wine tourism throughout the region. The Wine

Road of Attica has been set up, and there are many wine-related events throughout the year. With its many historic and beautiful buildings, and given the proximity of Athens, Attica can be used for both business and social events – surely a great way of introducing new people to the modern wines of Attica.[2]

Attica TO

White still: dry.
White varieties: Savatiano; Roditis; Assyrtico; Athiri.
Red still: dry.
Red variety: Cabernet Sauvignon.

Anavissos TO

White still: dry.
White varieties: Savatiano; Roditis; Assyrtico; Ugni Blanc.

Côtes de Kitherona TO

White still: dry; semi-dry; semi-sweet.
White varieties: Savatiano; Roditis; Assyrtico; Athiri; Chardonnay; Sauvignon Blanc.
Rosé still: dry; semi-dry; semi-sweet.
Red still: dry; semi-dry; semi-sweet.
Red/Rosé varieties: Roditis; Cabernet Sauvignon; Carignan; Grenache Rouge; Merlot; Syrah.

Côtes de Parnithas TO

White still: dry; semi-dry; semi-sweet.
White varieties: Savatiano; Roditis; Assyrtico; Athiri; Chardonnay; Sauvignon Blanc.
Rosé still: dry; semi-dry; semi-sweet.
Red still: dry; semi-dry; semi-sweet.
Red/Rosé varieties: Agiorgitiko; Cabernet Sauvignon; Carignan; Grenache Rouge; Merlot; Syrah; Roditis only for rosé.

---

2. Attican Vineyards Wine Producers' Association, Eleftherios Venizelos, 19019 Spata. Tel: +30 210 353 1315; Fax: +30 210 353 2310; Website: www.enoaa.gr; Email: enoaa@ath.forthnet.gr

Gerania TO

White still: dry.
White varieties: Savatiano; Roditis; Assyrtico; Chardonnay;
Sauvignon Blanc.
Rosé still: dry.
Rosé varieties: Roditis; Robola; Agiorgitiko; Carignan; Grenache Rouge.
Red still: dry.
Red varieties: Agiorgitiko; Carignan; Grenache Rouge; Merlot; Syrah.

Ilion TO

White still: dry.
White varieties: Savatiano and Roditis must be at least fifty per cent of
the blend, the balance being other local recommended grape varieties.

Koropi TO

White still: dry.
White variety: Savatiano must be at least eighty per cent of the blend, the
balance being other local recommended grape varieties.

Lilantio Pedio TO

White still: dry.
White varieties: Savatiano, Roditis can be up to twenty per cent of the blend.

Markopoulo TO

White still: dry.
White variety: Savatiano must be at least eighty per cent of the blend, the
balance being other local recommended grape varieties.

Paiania TO

White still: dry.
White varieties: Savatiano 100 per cent or Savatiano eighty per cent and
Assyrtico twenty per cent.

Pallini TO

White still: dry.
White varieties: Savatiano; Roditis; Assyrtico; Sauvignon Blanc.

Spata TO

White still: dry.

White variety: Savatiano must be at least eighty per cent of the blend, the balance being other local recommended grape varieties.

Vilitsa TO

Red still: dry.

Red variety: Cabernet Sauvignon.

Vories Côtes de Pentelikon TO

White still: dry.

White variety: Chardonnay must be at least eighty per cent of the blend, the balance being other local recommended grape varieties.

PRODUCERS

ALLAGIANNI WINES

27th km Paianias–Markopoulou Rd, 190 03 Markopoulo.

Tel: +30 229 904 0261; Fax: +30 229 904 0892; Email: allagw@otenet.gr

Vineyards owned: 5ha; under contract: 5.7ha; production: 1,000hl.

A relatively young winery established in 1995 by Dimitris Allagiannis. The project has quite a fresh feeling from the wines to their packaging. The estate's own vineyards have gone beyond Savatiano and now include Assyrtico, Cabernet Sauvignon, Mandilaria, Mavrodaphne, Moschofilero, and even Grenache Blanc. The most interesting wine of Allagianni is its Melistalakto, a sweet, Mavrodaphne-inspired red.

ANAGNOSTOU WINERY

69 Andrianou St, 194 00 Koropi. Tel: +30 210 662 4242; Fax: +30 210 602 0715; Website: www.anagnostou.com.gr; Email: chanagn@ath.forthnet.gr

Vineyards owned: 6ha; under contract: 8ha; production: 1,800hl.

Established in 2001, the Anagnostou Winery soon grew to a good size and has made a successful impact commercially. The portfolio created by general manager Christos Anagnostou sticks to traditional Koropi styles. There are three pure Savatiano whites, including a clean retsina, an upmarket Ampelones Anagnostou, a crisp rosé, and a soft red from Agiorgitiko. All are well-made, but relatively simple.

ATHANASSIADIS WINERY
See the entry for Domaine Harlaftis, page 233.

BESBEAS ESTATE
16 Tzavela, 152 35 Vrilissia. Tel: +30 210 6137181; Fax: +30 210 6137103.
Vineyards owned: 2ha; production: 230hl.

A small high-altitude Stamata estate focusing solely on one wine, the Besbeas Estate Red. It is mainly Cabernet Sauvignon, with a small amount of Merlot, and is aged in oak for about a year. The wine is put on the market five years after the vintage and its elegant, forthcoming, spicy characteristics are already creating a stir in top Athenian restaurants.

BOUTARI
20km Leoforos–Marathonos Rd, 190 09 Pikermi.
Tel: +30 210 660 5200; Fax: +30 210 210 603 7980;
Website: www.boutari.gr; Email: attica.winery@boutari.gr.
Vineyards owned: 2ha; production: 230hl.

See also Boutari entries on pages 132, 146, 152.

Production at the Boutari winery in Attica was officially suspended in 2004 and all lines except for the Cambas wines (*see* below) were moved to the Boutari winery in Thessaloniki. However, this facility was responsible for producing one of the company's most important brands and one of Greece's most successful wines: Lac des Roches. Even if the name was borrowed from "Limni Petron" ("lake of stones"), in Macedonia, this wine was always based on Savatiano, and its current designation is TO of Central Greece. The Lac des Roches phenomenon started in the 1980s, garnering huge success in all major markets around the country. The pace slowed, however, and by the mid-1990s the label had faded into oblivion.

After a few quiet years, Boutari decided that there was still room for the brand and so invested heavily in an ambitious relaunch and revamp of Lac des Roches. The sales may not have rebounded to previous heights but the wine has a very healthy presence in its sector. Today, Lac des Roches is the epitome of a high-volume everyday wine brand in Greece, expressing Savatiano in a charming, bright, and defined way.

The winery had also been used for producing the Cambas wine range. One of Attica's great wine dynasties, the Cambas family had been producing wine since 1869. A major trend-setter during most of the first half of the twentieth century, it focused on wineries in Attica and Mantinia

(Peloponnese). Wines such as Imetus, one of the first heavily branded Greek wines, and the white Cava Cambas, a pioneering cask-aged Savatiano, have been yardsticks for many contemporary producers. The Cambas brand name and properties were sold to Boutari in 1991, the Kantza winery was closed, and after the closure of Boutari's Attica winery, most lines have moved either to the Cambas winery in Arcadia or Thessaloniki.

DOMAINE HARLAFTIS

11 Stamatas Avenue, 145 65 Athens. Tel: +30 210 621 9374;
Fax: +30 210 621 9290; Website: www.harlaftis.gr; Email: wines@harlaftis.gr
Vineyards owned: 12ha; under contract: 3ha; production: 5,500hl.
See also Domaine Harlaftis entry in Corinth, Peloponnese, page 305.
This winery is known under two names: Athanassiadis Winery and Harlaftis Wines. The company was started in 1935 by Nicos Athanassiadis, but two decades later, his daughter Adda and her husband Diogenis Harlaftis inherited the management. The company name and the basic lines of the winery retained the Athanassiadis brand while newer premium products were developed under the name Harlaftis. For some consumers, there is still some confusion about how these two names relate to one another.

Athanassiadis was one of Central Greece's pioneering producers and it is a shame that more people did not follow his example in the 1980s and 1990s. Right from the start, Athanassiadis was able to supply the prestigious Grande Bretagne Hotel of Athens with his bulk wine, and after 1949, with bottled products – quite a rarity in those days. Since 1955 the company has adopted an estate approach, a route that was atypical by the prevailing standards of the time, when most producers had to source fruit from other vineyards. In the late 1970s, Harlaftis was one of the first producers to plant a trellised vineyard, and he pioneered Cabernet Sauvignon in Attica. The Stamata estate today is still very focused on specific grape varieties: Cabernet Sauvignon, Savatiano, Chardonnay, and Assyrtico. Panos Zoumboulis, a competent, talented Bordeaux-trained professional, has been winemaker for many years, presiding over a widening range of products. In 1997, Harlaftis established a winery in Nemea in the Peloponnese in order to include some OPAP Nemea wines in his portfolio, as well as to secure access to good Agiorgitiko for his cheaper blends. Thanos Fakorelis was retained as consultant in the late 1990s, primarily to develop the Nemea winery.

The basic Athanassiadi King range is excellent value for money. The two

TO cavas, also well priced, are among the best examples of their type.[3] The red is mainly Cabernet Sauvignon with forty per cent Agiorgitiko, aged for two years in barrels, half of which are new. The white, a fifty/fifty blend of Assyrtico and Savatiano, aged in oak for six months, and released after two years, is a bold statement as an aged and developed – rather than fruit-focused – white. Both cavas are full of personality, even if wine-drinkers keen on modern wines might find them a bit challenging.

The aged whites notion is taken a step further with the complex, extracted Harlaftis Fumé, a Chardonnay/Assyrtico blend. Aged for six months in new Nevers oak and about a year in bottle, this could develop further in the short term after release. Harlaftis produces a barrel-fermented Chardonnay along the same lines, which perhaps lacks the personality of the Fumé.

The top product is Château Harlaftis, a wine made from the best Cabernet Sauvignon from the estate's oldest parcels. Yields are below fifty hectolitres per hectare, with extensive green harvesting in the middle of the growing season. Château Harlaftis shows the credentials of Zoumboulis, being a subtle rather than a flashy, rich Cabernet, with excellent ageing potential. Its good price and a relatively low profile make it a bargain for those who know it.

DOMAINE VASSILIOU

26km Lavriou Ave, 194 00 Koropi. Tel: +30 210 662 6146; Fax: +30 210 662 6870; Website: www.vassilioudomaine.gr; Email: info@vassilioudomaine.gr
Vineyards owned: 25ha; production: 2,250hl.
See also Domaine Vassiliou entry on page 307.

Over the last twenty years, Giorgos Vassiliou has been one of Attica's most significant advocates. While his prices, product styles, and philosophy have remained firmly grounded as his business has developed, at the same time the volume involved has increased sufficiently to give him the critical mass needed to make an impact on the marketplace. His wines have always been made in an honest, straightforward way, aiming for a food-friendly style that is not exotic or overly aromatic. A turning point for the business was the establishment of a winery within the OPAP Nemea demarcated region. Vassiliou had been producing a Nemea wine as a négociant for a number of years, but the need for a winery in the region was evident. The first vintage

---

3. "Cava" for EOs is the equivalent of "reserve" for OPEs and OPAPs, denoting extra time ageing before release. *See* Appendix 1, and Part I, Chapter 4, Wine legislation.

produced from the new facility was 2003 and signalled a new era in wine quality. Aided by the consultant Thanos Fakorelis, the first release was quite a revelation – longer extractions and high levels of phenolic ripeness, producing one of the most New World-like Nemeas.

The Vassiliou portfolio is a lot more reserved than the 2003 Nemea might suggest. The core product – and the one that made the brand Vassiliou known – is Ampelones Vassiliou White, a very soft, light, refreshing Savatiano with a small proportion of Moschofilero. Vassiliou's winemaking studies in Dijon are hinted at in his Fumé Savatiano, with its elegant, almost understated oak presence. Vassiliou Rosé is simple, fruity Cabernet Sauvignon, while Vassiliou Red, an Agiorgitiko from Nemea with twenty per cent Cabernet Sauvignon, is quite a tight wine.

Vassiliou also releases a Mantinia, a Santorini, a retsina, and a Savatiano. The latter comes from a twenty-five-year-old parcel that yields less than twenty-five hectolitres per hectare. This is by far the most exotic wine of the estate. Exploding with flavours, it clearly suggests that the current, widespread uprooting of many old Savatiano parcels is a huge loss.

EVHARIS ESTATE
Thesi Pefnekeas, Mourtiza, 191 00 Megara.
Head office: Lagoumitzi 24, 176 71 Athens. Tel: +30 210 924 6930;
Fax: +30 210 924 6931; Website: www.evharis.gr; Email: evharis@evharis.gr
Vineyards owned: 15ha; under contract: 10ha; production: 1,000hl.
Tourism entrepreneur Haris Antoniou and architect and regional planner Eva-Maria Boehme founded Evharis Estate near Megara in 1984, using the first syllable of their names to christen their estate. The idea was not just to create a wine-producing company, but to expand the business into tourism and a venue for events. Although Megara had a long history of producing bulk wine, Evharis was the first attempt to create a quality-wine project in the region. The area used to establish Evharis vineyards had not been replanted after phylloxera. The aridity, and factors such as the northern aspect of many slopes, dictated a careful selection of varieties, rootstocks, and cultivation techniques. Out of thirty hectares, only fifteen were finally selected. Initially, mistakes were made with planting techniques, such as trellising and canopy management, and the first wines that appeared on the Greek market in the mid-1990s showed a lack of proper fruit ripeness.

Antoniou recognized these shortcomings and in the late 1990s hired the leading wine consultant Ampeloiniki to help in getting the vineyards as well as the cellar in order. Much work was directed towards a more balanced vine-growth throughout the season, with the main objective being higher ripeness, higher phenolics, and longer extractions for the reds. Currently, the wines of Evharis are at least one per cent higher in alcohol than the vintages made a decade ago. But, more importantly, there is a whole new dimension of fruit, density, and charm to all the products.

The basic Ilaros line consists of a white and a red, convincingly made, for sale at a lower price point. A step up is Evharis Estate White, an Assyrtico blend with twenty-five per cent Chardonnay, and Evharis Estate Red, predominantly Syrah, macerated for two weeks, with smaller amounts of Merlot and Grenache Rouge, both of which clearly show the Ampeloiniki influence. Melapus is a good Bordeaux blend, half Cabernet Sauvignon and half Merlot, aged in oak for eight months. A quartet of varietal wines are typical, modern examples of their varieties. The Assyrtico is aged in oak for six months and is one of the best interpretations of this variety outside of Santorini. The Chardonnay, again aged in oak, is a touch lighter in structure. The reds, a Merlot and a Syrah, are made in a rich, almost exotic style, and the latter especially shows impressive layers of fruit and concentration.

Finally, Evharis offers some more individual products, like the top Moschofilero-based sparkling wines, Eva and Boehme. The Charmat-made, off-dry Eva is very light, flowery, and simple. Boehme, aged *sur lie* in bottle for a year, is more complex, and the high alcohol (13.5 per cent) blends well with the acidity of the variety.

FRAGOU ESTATE

21 Kosti Palama St, 190 04 Spata. Tel: +30 210 663 3940; Fax: +30 210 663 2087; Website: www.fragou.com.gr; Email: asimina@fragou.com.gr
Vineyards owned: 7.5ha; under contract: 8.5ha; production: 750hl.

The Fragou Estate has been around since 1934, but it was only in the early 1990s that Asimina Fragou decided to take a more commercial direction. The buildings in the estate were completely renovated, but manage to retain the charm of their heritage, making it one of the most beautiful wine estates in Attica.

When the first "new era" wines from the estate appeared on the Greek market, Fragou was at the forefront of the wine revolution. However, since then, the wines have not moved on much in a market that is changing rapidly. Overall, the wines are good. The fruit for some wines is sourced from the Peloponnese. There is a fresh Savatiano, a slightly heavy Chardonnay, and a light Grenache Rouge, suitable for summer drinking. The best wines are the two Cabernet Sauvignons and the tannic, austere Cava Fragou.

GEORGA FAMILY WINERY

6 Riga Feraiou, 190 04 Spata. Head office: 12 G.Georga, 190 04 Spata.
Tel/Fax: +30 210 663 3345; Website: www.geowines.gr; Email info@geowines.gr
Vineyards owned: 4.3ha; under contract: 3.7ha; production: 260hl.

The wines of the Georgas family are likely to be increasingly discussed in the coming years. Dimitris Georgas, a Didier Dagueneau look-alike, not only shares Dagueneau's approach, but also his philosophy, being one of Greece's keenest followers of Biodynamism. All of his wines are now made from organically cultivated grapes and his vineyards are heading slowly but steadily towards full Biodynamic cultivation. His position is difficult, with almost no experience or sources of information available in his region. Nevertheless, he is determined to stick to his decision and become one of the first fully Biodynamic estates in Greece.

Georgas believes that above all his wines must be an expression of the character of the fruit. He uses minimal intervention in his winemaking, using only natural yeasts, with no filtration or fining. However the winery is surprisingly high-tech, full of stainless-steel vats and computer-controlled refrigeration systems, since, according to Georgas, "You need control over temperatures and hygiene if you want to leave the wine with no additives." All his wines are bottled with zero or minimal sulphur addition.

The Georga Retsina of Mesogia is possibly the only wine of this type made from organic grapes. The Biodynamic Georga Family White, a TO of Spata, is arguably the most dense, rich, and extracted Savatiano of Greece. The Georga Family Seira No.1 Red is a *nouveau*-style Syrah with just ten per cent Merlot. The portfolio finishes with two sweet wines made from overripe grapes and aged in French oak for a year: a white from Savatiano, and a red, made from a co-extraction of Syrah, Merlot, and Savatiano, called Seira No.2.

GOSMAS VINEYARDS

1 Eleftherias, 145 64 Kifissia. Tel: +30 210 675 5678;
Fax: +30 210 677 4747; Email: kazazaki@otenet.gr
Production: 120hl.

A very small, almost underground producer, Giorgas Gosmas releases only white wine, but merits special attention for his Ramnousios Palia Ampelia ("old vines"): a very well made oak-aged Savatiano. Beyond this, there is

Spithari, a Savatiano/Assyrtico/Malagousia blend, and Ampelones Gosmas Red, made with Grenache, Syrah, and Cabernet Sauvignon.

GREEK WINE CELLARS (KOURTAKI WINES)
20 Anapafseos Ave, 190 03 Markopoulo. Tel: +30 229 902 2231;
Fax: +30 229 902 3301. Website: www.kourtakis.com; Email: kourt@otenet.gr
Halkida winery: 20km Thivon–Halkida Rd, Ritsona, 341 00 Halkida.
Vineyards owned: 56ha; under contract: 1,350ha; production: 300,000hl.

Greek Wine Cellars is the new name for Kourtaki Wines, reflecting its expansion over recent years and its investment in a number of other wineries and regions. The Kourtakis family is one of Greece's most significant wine dynasties. Vassilis Kourtakis, one of the first Greeks to study winemaking, founded the company in 1895. During its first few decades, it focused primarily on retsina, with Kourtakis investing heavily both in marketing and cultivation and production techniques. At the time, most Kourtaki retsina was sold in bulk and shipped to a large number of destinations around Greece. Vassilis' son, Dimitris, who studied winemaking in Dijon, started selling branded retsina in half-litre, crown-capped bottles. The Kourtaki name became synonymous with bottled retsina and the ease of transporting this new product made it instantly successful in tourist resorts around the country. Sales took off in the 1960s, reaching a plateau in the 1970s, when Retsina Kourtaki sold about sixty million bottles annually.

Luckily, just before retsina's star started to fade, Vassilis Kourtakis, Dimitris' son, joined the company after studying and working for several years in Burgundy. Vassilis wanted to see Kourtaki Wines develop beyond retsina, and so began establishing new facilities in the Ritsona area of Halkida, on the island of Evia, together with new brands. Thus Apelia was launched. A pioneering series of low-priced EO table wines, Apelia was based on cool fermentation, selected yeast strains, relatively low acidity, and low residual sugar level, an approach that made it extremely accessible. With Apelia, Kourtaki managed to shift sales from mainly on-trade into the off-trade as well. Around the same time, Kourtaki developed close links with another successful label, Calliga in Cephalonia, later buying the brand.

Since then, the company has developed further, for example introducing OPAP and OPE products into its portfolio, and investing in facilities in regions like Crete. When the Kouros range – consisting of a Nemea Agiorgitiko and a Roditis Patras – were listed by Lufthansa, they became the first Greek wines to feature on a non-Greek airline's wine list. The Kourtaki portfolio has stayed deliberately small in terms of the volume produced. The introduction of Vin de Crete wines pushed the company to new export heights, with a range designed for major foreign markets which managed to achieve listings in numerous major supermarkets. The next step was the launch of four varietal bottlings, an Athiri, an Assyrtico, a Moschofilero, and an Agiorgitiko, plus a Cabernet Sauvignon/Grenache Rouge blend – the first Kourtaki wine from non-Greek grapes.

Greek Wine Cellars is one of the country's most powerful producers whose presence has influenced the whole sector. The largest producer and bottler of Greek wines, it is a major player on the export markets, selling half of its 3.2 million cases to foreign markets. With its fortunes in capable hands, it has created strong brands and underpinned them with fresh, charming, easy drinking wines that offer good value for money.

KATOGI & STROFILIA – ANAVISSOS WINERY

Mikras Asias, 190 13 Anavissos. Tel: +30 229 104 1650;
Fax: +30 229 103 8850; Website: katogi-strofilia.gr; Email: strofilia@otenet.gr
For full details, *see* Katogi & Strofilia entry on page 194.

Strofilia was among the leaders of the Greek wine revolution in the 1980s, bringing with it one of the most innovative approaches the country had ever seen. Yiannis Maltezos and Achileas Lampsidis decided to make use of the Maltezos family vineyards in Anavissos in 1981. With no wine training between them (both had trained as mechanical engineers), Maltezos and Lampsidis were far from typical wine producers. Young and full of energy, they wanted to make wine for the fun of it. If someone had told them that in twenty years time they would be part of one of Greece's largest premium wine producers, they would have burst into laughter.

Strofilia was pivotal in persuading young Greeks that wine could be hip and non-conformist. It achieved this not only with its styles of wines, but also through its Strofilia wine bar, which opened in 1985 in central Athens, just a few blocks away from the Greek parliament. Strofilia brought about a breakthrough in attitudes towards wine-drinking. Up to that point, wine had been viewed either as a commodity or as a fine but formal product. In Strofilia, young Athenians learnt that Greek wine was a rapidly developing sector and that everyone could play a part in its fascinating progress.

Maltezos and Lampsidis never tried to make their wines look or taste overly serious, flashy, or sophisticated. Instead, Strofilia wines have always been easy-drinking and food-friendly, hence the absence or very cautious use of oak and the relatively conservative alcohol levels (rarely above 12.5 per cent). The winery's portfolio was remarkably stable for its first fifteen years, with just Strofilia white, red, and rosé. However, after 1995, the team began creating new labels, sometimes just for a few vintages, such as Nafsika – a stunning blend of Assyrtico and Savatiano which was possibly the best white ever produced by the winery – and a massively structured Strofilia Assyrtico. Unfortunately, both wines are no longer in production.

The new product development was aided by the addition of vineyards at Aigialia in Ahaia, northwest Peloponnese, a top-quality site at 750 metres altitude (2,460 feet) and dedicated to Roditis, Chardonnay, Viognier, and Syrah. A new winery was built in Anavissos and in 2001, Strofilia merged with the groundbreaking Katogi winery, creating Katogi & Strofilia, which meant extra resources for both companies – and one more winery in Nemea.

The top selling Anavissos wine is Strofilia White, a blend of sixty per cent Roditis and forty per cent Savatiano. Although it's a very decent wine given its production volume, Strofilia Giinos, a pure Roditis, has more character. The clean Strofilia Rosé, which is also sometimes called Rosé tou Fegariou ("moon's rosé"), is a varietal Agiorgitiko that is macerated overnight prior to fermentation. Strofilia Red is possibly the most underrated wine of the whole portfolio. A blend of seventy per cent Agiorgitiko from Nemea and thirty per cent Cabernet Sauvignon from the original Anavissos vineyards, it is a very classy wine, very low-key and full of flesh.

Newer additions to the portfolio include Mikri Strofilia and Rogostamo. Taking a different approach to Agiorgitiko, Mikri Strofilia (sold as Katogi Fresco on the export market) is made in a fresh, almost *nouveau* style, aged for two months in older oak. It can be enjoyed chilled. Rogostamo is a pure, stainless-steel-fermented Chardonnay that is surprisingly full, but vivacious and fruity. It's good to see the Strofilia portfolio changing and maturing while the people behind it preserve a youthful attitude towards the business.

MARKOU VINEYARDS

1st km Peania–Markopoulo Ave, Peania, Attika 19002.
Tel: +30 210 664 4711; Fax: +30 210 664 4123;
Website: www.markouwines.gr; Email: info@markouwines.gr
Vineyards owned: 20ha, 10ha in Attica, 10ha in Nemea; under contract: 35ha; production: 3,000hl.

The Markou brothers, Spiros and Kostas, come from an Attica family that has been involved in wine for over a century. The modern era of Markou

Vineyards began in 1983, when the brothers built a new winery and replanted ten hectares of the family property. Apart from Attica, the Markou brothers own ten additional hectares of Agiorgitiko in Nemea, while they source fruit from a number of regions in Peloponnese, like Mantinia and Trifilia.

The winery's portfolio is structured into three groups: the Epilogi (Selection) line is the basic range; Domaine Markou wines come from fruit produced on the family's property; and the Syllogi Collection is a series of limited-release products. Domaine Markou White is a crisp Savatiano/Roditis blend, while the red is an Agiorgitiko Nemea OPAP with good varietal definition despite being on the lighter side. Syllogi Cabernet Sauvignon from Trifilia is fairly evolved, having spent two years in oak, and the Syllogi Chardonnay shows a marked oak presence. Syllogi Fumé is a Savatiano aged for a year in oak and six months in bottle. Again it shows quite a developed style – not fruity, but rich.

MATSA ESTATE

61 Leontariou, 153 51 Pallini.

Tel/Fax: +30 210 665 9058; Email: matsarox@otenet.gr

Vineyards owned: 9ha; production: 600hl.

Established in 1875 by the Cambas family, another important Greek wine dynasty, this was the company's flagship estate; an alliance through marriage brought about the name change from Cambas to Matsa. The Cambas family always had good links with the Boutaris family and the Matsa wines are now an integral part of its portfolio, having been sold under the Boutari banner since the mid-1980s.

Roxani Matsa has been running the estate since 1982. A larger-than-life figure, she was voted Wine Personality of the Year by the Union of Greek Wine Journalists in 2001, as much for her work in the vineyard as in the cellar. It was Matsa who signed-off the official termination of the Kantza OPAP in 1992. The presence of a white wine OPAP had posed great problems in the establishment of new Savatiano regional wine appellation (TO) for local producers. Matsa was the only producer making a Kantza OPAP, but she felt that helping numerous other growers was more important than fighting for an exclusive appellation.

Matsa has been one of the few producers willing to share planting stock of rare varieties. "To make good wines from a variety, you need to accumulate experience, and I cannot do that on my own," she says. For that reason, Matsa gives away more than 50,000 buds of Malagousia every year to other vintners or leading vine nurseries like Vitro Hellas.[4] She has made headlines for her refusal to sell her vineyards, which are located in the much sought-after area near the new international airport. She could easily earn enough money to afford ten times as much land in a top-quality area in almost any OPAP of Greece, but she explains that with no husband or children, investing is not an issue. She is happy as long as she can support her everyday life.

The Matsa Estate used to be one of the prime sources of top-quality Savatiano from old vines, bottled as Matsa Estate Vieilles Vignes. The wine was one of the finest examples of this variety, but due to Savatiano's poor image, it could not secure a decent price point. Although it was a hard decision to make, in 2003, Matsa and the Boutari team changed the varietal composition of the Matsa Estate wine to equal parts of Sauvignon Blanc and Assyrtico. The estate is gradually being replanted, with half a hectare of Savatiano uprooted each year. Several varieties have been tried on the site, including Athiri, Grenache Blanc, Muscat of Spina, Chardonnay, and Viognier, with most being field grafted to the most promising Assyrtico and Malagousia vines.

Malagousia is a vine that Matsa has worked with for years in the vineyard, and she believes it is capable of great things. It was planted in 1990, with the first vintage in 1997. Initially, Matsa pruned it short and the plant was producing a small number of large, compact bunches – as a result, the grapes often burst before they arrived at the winery. So she converted to long cane pruning and the bunches became smaller and less tight, allowing the fruit to reach full maturity. Malagousia Matsa is the best wine of the estate so far, while the first release of an experimental Syrah, the first Matsa red, is eagerly awaited.

MEGAPANOS WINERY

1st km Pikermiou-Spata Avenue, 190 09 Pikermi. Tel: +30 210 603 8038;
Fax: +30 210 603 8037; Website: www.megapanos.gr; Email: info@megapanos.gr
Vineyards owned: 1.2ha; under contract: 2ha; production: 1,500hl.

Softly spoken but very firm in his beliefs, Alexandros Megapanos is one of the most distinctive characters in the Greek wine world. He is also one of very few native winemakers who have studied and worked in France – including at Château Margaux – but he has been happy to put his French

4. Vitro Hellas, Niseli, Naoussa, 593 00 Imathia. For more information,
Tel: +30 233 302 7281; Website: www.vitrohellas.gr; Email: vitro@alfanet.gr.

experiences to one side in order to start again from scratch in an attempt to understanding Greek wine production in its own context.

As an example, Megapanos is a true believer in Greek oak, seeing it as half choice and half duty to try to exploit the full potential of this type of wood. (Evangelos Averoff at the pioneering Katogi winery traditionally used Greek oak in Metsovo, but it was abandoned as being too coarse.) Megapanos oak-aged wines do have a very distinct wood influence – not as aromatic as American oak, and possibly lacking the finesse of the best French oak barriques; nevertheless the wood character supports the fruit and adds complexity. If a wine has to be about fruit and not about wood, then Greek oak can be promising, at least in the hands of Megapanos.

One of Megapanos' best wines is his *grande resérve*, which is aged for two years in oak and eighteen months in bottle before release. Called Palaio Kellari Red ("old cellar red"), this Nemea OPAP is very different from most other Nemea wines – it is full of spices, herbs, and notes of dried fruits. The palate is full but not aggressive, and layered with fine-grained, melted tannins. Palaio Kellari Red is generally ready to drink on release, but could develop over the short term. The other top Megapanos wine is his straight varietal Savatiano, from an old vineyard yielding less than thirty-five hectolitres per hectare. Far from the typical Savatiano wine, this is quite extracted, rich, and broad.

MEGARA COOPERATIVE

Pachi, 191 00 Megara. Tel: +30 229 608 0412; Fax: +30 229 608 0601;
Email: gerania@gerania.com.gr
Vineyards under contract: 800ha; members: 750; production: 25,000hl.

The oldest co-op in Greece, Megara was established in 1910 and is, by current standards, only moderate in size. The winery sells large quantities of bulk wine, mainly supplying other producers and retailers. So far, any efforts to enter the market as a commercial entity have been limited or not very successful. There are some bottled wines but they are hard to come by, with the possible exception of the co-op's retsina.

PANAGIOTOU ESTATE

6 Mihail Dritsa, 190 03 Markopoulo. Tel/Fax: +30 229 602 5363.
Vineyards owned: 15ha; production: 500hl.

Vassilis Panagiotou is one of the smaller Attica producers, releasing fewer than 2,500 cases per year. His family has been involved with wine since

1860 and there are many illustrations of this heritage around the winery. The equipment on the premises is pretty basic, proving that cutting edge technology is not essential to make good red wine in this region.

Honest, good-value, bag-in-box wines and bulk sales make up most of the winery's turnover, but three bottled products are sold under the brand name Vassilis Panagiotou. The white is mainly Savatiano, with small amounts of Assyrtico and Sauvignon Blanc; the rosé is fresh and very light; and the red, Merlot with less than ten per cent Cabernet Sauvignon, is stunning. Made with very ripe grapes, this wine is extracted for a week, aged in partially new French oak, and reaches alcohol levels of 14.5 per cent or higher. The result is possibly the most concentrated red in Attica, with a high level of tannins and amazing depth. Closer to warm climate Australia than Markopoulo, appreciating its richness is perhaps a matter of personal taste. However, when I spoke to him during a visit to Greece in 2002, Marcel Guigal proclaimed it the most impressive wine he had tasted that week.

PAPAHARALAMBOUS WINERY

Thesi Tsalmeza, 190 02 Paiania.
Head office: 1 Mihail Stamati, 190 02 Paiania. Tel/Fax: +30 30 210 664 3377.
Vineyards owned: 15ha; production: 1,000hl.

Established in 1972, this estate was the first to plant Cabernet Sauvignon in a collaboration with the Athens-based Wine Institute. The original plot still exists and has been added to significantly since then. The Papaharalambous Cabernet Sauvignon is a TO of Vilitsa, a classification used exclusively by this producer. It is honest, but with a slightly old-fashioned character.

PAPAGIANNAKOS ESTATE

2 Papagiannakou St, 190 03 Markopoulo.
Tel: +30 229 902 5206; Fax: +30 229 902 2354;
Website: www.papagiannakos.gr; Email: info@papagiannakos.gr
Vineyards owned: 7ha; under contract: 35ha; production: 3,500hl.

The Papagiannakos family has been making wine since the early twentieth century, with the current director, Vassilis Papagiannakos, involved over the last twenty years. The wines are extremely well made and delightfully fresh, even if not as cutting edge as the charming, innovative labels they sport. The last two decades have seen much development – not into new wines, but further refinement of existing products.

The whites are based on Savatiano, with a very good retsina, a good Savatiano Papagiannakos, and a much better Papagiannakos Estate. The philosophy of the Savatiano focuses on the fresh, fruity side of the grape, while the Estate comes from family plots and is as light as the varietal version, with an additional lift on the nose. The Papagiannakos reds are made from Peloponnesian grapes, the Papagiannakos Red being mainly Agiorgitiko from Nemea with about twenty per cent Cabernet Sauvignon from Pylos to the southwest in Messinia. The producer's top wine, a varietal Cabernet Sauvignon from Pylos and nearby Trifilia, is aged in oak for a year and is in a warm but not overripe style.

PYRGOS VASSILISSIS ESTATE
67 Dimokratias Avenue, 131 22 Athens. Tel: +30 210 238 0404;
Fax: +30 210 231 3129; Email: serpieri@otenet.gr
Vineyards owned: 5ha; production: 290hl.

Pyrgos Vassilissis is an idiosyncratic wine producing company. The estate belonged to the Greek royal family until the mid-nineteenth century, and its name, which translates as "the queen's tower", or *Tour de Reine* as many people know it, was inspired by its original visionary, Queen Amalia. Nowadays it is completely surrounded by apartment blocks, although an official decree dictates that the land must remain an agricultural area. Wine production is a small part of the activities, which include breeding livestock and making olive oil.

The estate became part of an agricultural school and is now owned by the Serpieris family, with Freddy Serpieris at the helm. The modern revival began in 1990, when a small production facility was built and the vineyards were replanted. The wines came on the market in 1995, but despite their high quality, are not often seen. Perhaps the family's prestigious network of supporters will continue to buy the vast majority of the 40,000 bottles produced each year, reinforcing the aristocratic feel of the estate.

The whites are aromatically low-key, but well-structured, with consultant Alexandros Magapanos being a decisive influence. Pyrgos Vassillissis White, a Savatiano/Chardonnay/Roditis blend, is the simplest wine. Swapping Saviatiano with Sauvignon Blanc, Serpieri Estate is crisper and slightly more open. A fumé version uses more Chardonnay and has a well-balanced oak presence. A Bordeaux blend of both Cabernets and Merlot is aged in American oak and has a perfumed, spicy, yet fresh Cabernet character.

SEMELI WINERY

1 Semeli St, 145 75 Stamata. Tel: +30 210 621 8119; Fax: +30 210 621 8218;
Website: www.semeliwines.com; Email: kokotos@semeliwines.com
Vineyards owned: 7.5ha; production: 2,000hl.
See also Domaine Helios entry on page 306.

George and Anne Kokotos have a gift for investing in new places and
turning them into something special. They were the first to start up a hotel
in Elouda, Crete, back then an almost deserted backwater but now one of
the most luxurious resorts in Europe, if not the world.

It was practically the same story with their estate in Stamata, with the
pair starting one of Greece's best wineries from scratch. Head winemaker
Andonis Popolanos, one of the first trained viticulturalists to also practise
oenology, has been key throughout, providing a much needed link between
winemaking and the quality of the source material.

The vineyards are at 450 metres altitude (1,476 feet) in a cool site. Lack of
rainfall is a problem, so an irrigation system was installed in 2001. Minimum
quantities of organic fertilizers are used on the poor, slate and sandy clay
soils, hence yields are kept to around fifty hectolitres per hectare. The
Kokotos estate was one of the first places in Greece where Cabernet
Sauvignon was planted in rows. Despite initial problems, vertical shoot
positioning and Guyot trellis systems have been adopted. Mainly Cabernet
Sauvignon, Merlot, and Chardonnay are grown on the estate today, with
growers in Attica and the Peloponnese on long-term contracts supplying
Savatiano and Roditis.

The two basic lines produced are Amaryllis and Semeli, both of which
are fresh and soft. A Semeli OPAP Nemea and a Thioni OPAP Mantinia
were bottled in the Semeli winery, but these two labels have now been
moved to the new Kokotos winery in Nemea, Domaine Helios (*see* page
306). Roditis used to be represented by an oak-aged version (production
has now ceased) and Roditis *sur lie*, made using fruit from Aigialia in
the Peloponnese. It was aged on lees for up to ten months in stainless
steel, and is now showing ripe, pure Roditis fruit, while on the palate it
has a level of intensity and extract rare for the variety. For the Chardonnay,
a pre-fermentation maceration lasts twelve to fourteen hours and dry ice
is used to keep temperatures low. Since 2002, it has been decided that the
wine should undergo fermentation and six months of maturation in
French oak, achieving better oak integration.

The flagship wine is Château Semeli, a Cabernet Sauvignon with up to ten per cent Merlot, made from vines that were planted in the early 1980s. Both varieties are harvested and vinified together. The cool climate gives Cabernet grapes with firm tannins and high acidity which, in some years, exceeds seven grams per litre. It has impressive freshness of fruit and the alcohol is never too high. Unusually, malolactic fermentation is blocked, making the young wine seem even firmer, while preserving the freshness and vivacity. The wine is aged in 100 per cent new French oak for two years and in bottle for a year. Château Semeli is one of the most expensive Greek red wines – the current vintage retails in Athens with a price tag of thirty euros a bottle or more. It is difficult to say that it is too expensive, since the 8,000 to 10,000 bottles produced every year sell out in a matter of months. It is one of the most ageworthy Greek reds. It can be slightly unforgiving on release, but in early 2004, a tasting of vintages back to 1984 revealed that it needs at least four to seven years to soften and open up, while it can be amazingly charming and youthful at the age of fifteen. Overall, Château Semeli is a top-quality wine that, in terms of style, is much closer to the Médoc than to the majority of other Greek Cabernet/Merlot blends.

VIOTIA

Viotia is just north of Attica, extending further north as well as to the west, and sandwiched between the Corinthian Gulf and the northern Evoikos Gulf. The capital of the prefecture is Thebes, with the second major city, Livadia, located to the northwest. Despite mountains featuring strongly in both Viotia and Attica, the two have totally different topographies. Attica is sheltered from the north and west and gets exposed to southern winds, while the mountains of Viotia have a northeastern exposure. Major peaks that surround the general area are, from east to west, mounts Parnitha, Pateras, Elikonas, and Parnassos. The plain of Thebes, extending to the north of the city and reaching up to the coast, includes Iliki and Paralimni lakes, as well as the large, drained Kopais Lake area. Water resources are thus ample for agriculture and many soils are deep and rich. Overall, the climate of Viotia can be as dry as conditions further south in Attica, yet is significantly cooler, at least in the higher altitudes of the surrounding mountains.

Viticulture here is in competition with other forms of agriculture and is mainly isolated into four distinct parcels. The first is on the north-facing slopes of Mount Parnitha, the highest being at altitudes of up to 500 metres

(1,640 feet). This is also the coolest spot in the prefecture, facing mostly north. Moving to the west, the next important region is found near Mount Kitheronas, at slightly lower altitudes of about 350 metres (1,148 feet). Elikonas, in central Viotia, with altitudes of 200–400 metres (656–1,312 feet), is the warmest meso-climate of the three.

The final area is the only one found on flat land. The Arma region, close to the borders with Evia and east of Thebes, is the warmest and most fertile spot in Viotia, resulting in higher yields. In the past, Arahova, in the west of the prefecture on the slopes of Mount Parnassos, was also important, with some of the highest and oldest vineyards in Greece. The lower plots were infected by phylloxera, however, and these were abandoned after World War II.

Grape varieties in Viotia have traditionally been linked to those found in Attica (*see* page 227), with Savatiano being the most planted and Roditis a distant second. Replanting over the last two decades has increased the presence of other grapes, initially Assyrtico and Roditis and subsequently the French varieties. Mountainous vineyards were dedicated to white grapes, including Chardonnay and Sauvignon Blanc, while the lower areas of Arma supported red grapes. The general trend was towards more Mediterranean grapes, but also higher-yielding varieties, and Grenache Rouge, Carignan, and Syrah prevailed over Cabernet Sauvignon.

Viotia has only two regional wine classifications, listed below. The Thebes TO is the general designation, while the Côtes de Kitherona TO refers to the slopes of Mount Kitheronas, part of which is shared with Attica. Côtes de Kitherona should reflect the cooler climate of the area, but at the moment there are no producers using the designation.

Thebes TO

White still: dry; semi-dry; semi-sweet.
White varieties: Savatiano; Roditis; Assyrtico; Athiri; Chardonnay; Sauvignon Blanc.
Rosé still: dry; semi-dry.
Red still: dry; semi-dry; semi-sweet.
Red varieties: Agiorgitiko; Cabernet Sauvignon; Carignan; Grenache Rouge; Merlot; Roditis only for rosé; Syrah.

Côtes de Kitherona TO

White still: dry; semi-dry; semi-sweet.

White varieties: Savatiano; Roditis; Assyrtico; Athiri; Chardonnay; Sauvignon Blanc.

Rosé still: dry; semi-dry; semi-sweet.

Red still: dry; semi-dry; semi-sweet.

Red varieties: Roditis; Cabernet Sauvignon; Carignan; Grenache Rouge; Merlot; Syrah.

PRODUCERS

CAVIROS WINERY

89km National Rd Athinon–Lamias, 322 00 Thebes.
Head office: Salaminos 9, 142 32 Nea Ionia. Tel: +30 210 253 3881;
Fax: +30 210 251 6738; Email: caviros@acsmi.gr
Production: 2,000hl.

This winery was established in 1965, when Konstantinos Antonopoulos left Achaia Clauss in the Peloponnese to set up his own venture. Currently owned by Konstantinos Mitsis, the brands produced here have remained the same for at least the last fifteen years: two whites, Filerato and Elissar from Moschofilero; a rosé called Cimarosa made with Moschofilero and Agiorgitiko; and two reds, Caviros Red and Resérve, made from Agiorgitiko. Usually the wines lack fruit and clarity.

DOMAINE HATZIMICHALIS

Arma, 322 00 Thebes. Tel/Fax: +30 226 207 2144;
Website: www.hatzimichalis.gr; Email: info@hatzimichalis.gr

For full details, *see* Domaine Hatzimichalis entry on page 260.

Dimitris Hatzimichalis has traditionally been based in Atalandi, where he represents the prefecture of Fthiotida with one of the most prestigious and well-known wineries of Greece. His range of wines has always been priced on a premium level, and justifiably so – this is a boutique set-up with almost three decades of solid and constant investment. When the need for a lower priced wine arose in the early 2000s, Hatzimichalis decided to establish a new winery in a region where good quality, but slightly cheaper grapes were readily available rather than be in danger of depreciating his Atalandi brands. Thebes proved a wise choice, not just because it met the price and quality criteria, but also because it was close to Atalandi.

The winery focuses exclusively on two budget-oriented wines under the Dionyssos Land label, together with providing storage facilities for other

Hatzimichalis wines. The white is a blend of Roditis, Assyrtico, and Sauvignon Blanc, while the red is made from Grenache Rouge, Syrah, and Carignan. The idea behind both wines is for a softer, fruitier wine that is easier to drink on its own than the usual style of Hatzimichalis from Atalandi. The result is remarkably good value for money.

INO WINERY

30km Thivon–Athinon, 322 00 Thebes. Tel: +30 226 202 8781/4; Fax: +30 226 202 8144; Website: www.inowines.gr; Email: inong@inowines.gr Production: 80,000hl.

A vibrant, recent addition to the area of Thebes, INO was established in 2001 with the aim of exploring the potential of Viotia for the creation of high-volume brands. The company was established when Tassos Sabanis and Manolis Skouloudis (*see* page 256) bought the Cooperative of Thebes. The focus has been on low price points and alternative packaging. The range INOpoiimata, sold mainly as bag-in-box, has been an important bestseller of the last few years, particularly in the supermarket segment. Retsina Yortassi is another successful brand. INO also has a range of varietal wines, including Savatiano, Chardonnay, and Cabernet Sauvignon. Likno and plain INO are the brand names of the lower-priced wines. Overall, these wines don't show much character but are competently made and have enough fruit.

SAMARTZI ESTATE

Askri Vagia, Dimos Thespiou, 320 02 Viota. Tel/Fax: +30 226 206 7009; Website: www.ktimasamartzi.gr; Email: info@ktimasamartzi.gr Vineyards owned: 35ha; under contract: 50ha; production: 2,000hl.

A relatively recent venture founded by Panayiotis Samartzis in 2000 and maturing fast. Samartzis has substantial vineyard holdings in the cool area of Askri. He produces about ten different labels using a variety of designations, from TO of Central Greece to TO of Corinth. The most interesting wines are the varietal Gewurztraminer, full of spice and more varietal definition than most, and an oak-aged Cabernet Sauvignon/Merlot red under the Mortero label from Corinth. The style is constantly developing and improving across the product range.

EVIA

Evia is the second-largest island in Greece after Crete and runs parallel to the eastern coast of Central Greece. There is a short bridge linking Halkida, its capital, with the Athens to Thessaloniki highway, and the two ends of Evia are in regular ferry contact with the mainland. Nowadays, many people work in Athens and live in Halkida or vice versa. This proximity is beneficial for the economy and growth in most sectors is better than the national average.

The topography of Evia is complex, with hills and mountains alternating with low fields and plains. There are three main mountain ranges. The lower is found at the northern tip of the island, opposite Livanates in Fthiotida. In the south of Evia, Mount Ochi overlooks the town of Karystos at 1,399 metres (4,590 feet). The third range encircles Halkida from the east to the north and is the highest, with Mount Dirfis standing at 1,743 metres (5,720 feet).

Regions, varieties, and classifications

Viticulture is confined, once again, to three distinct areas. The smallest region – also the coolest – is located at the very northern tip of Evia, just by the entrance to the Maliakos Gulf. The second-largest acreage is found in the south, around Karystos, where the local climate has more in common with the Cyclades than the rest of Evia, being hot, arid, and extremely windy. However, the hottest vine-growing area is found around Halkida and is the largest and the lowest in average altitude. The surrounding mountains shelter Halkida from the north and east and act like a heat trap. However, breezes from the Evoikos Gulf moderate temperatures through most of the summer. The official size of the vineyard surface is augmented by the fact that, administratively, the prefecture of Halkida includes a part of Viotia, including the regions of Avlis, Ritsona, and Vathy.

In terms of grape varieties, Evia boasts a cross between those of the Aegean Islands and Central Greece. Savatiano still covers four-fifths of the total acreage, with Roditis traditionally being present and Assyrtico, Chardonnay, and Sauvignon Blanc being later additions. Aegean varieties such as Aidani, Limnio, Mandilaria, and even Liatiko also make some rare appearances. There are some more unusual vines, such as Karampraimis, a red variety that supposedly came from Asia Minor, and is now found in small quantities in Evia and Paros. It is vigorous, productive, mildly resistant to drought, and ripens in late September, producing grapes with high sugar levels, low colour, and moderate acidity. Another unusual grape is Vradiano, a red variety also found in Fthiotida that the ampelographer Karimbas suggests might come from Bordeaux (without naming any famous relative vines from that area). It is vigorous, productive, and very resistant to drought, while it ripens in mid-September, giving grapes with moderate colour, high sugar levels, and moderate acidity.

Evia has been awarded three regional wine appellations (TOs), which are all exclusively related to white wine – predominantly Savatiano, with the balance being Roditis. Lilantio Pedio and Ritsona Avlidos are central Evia TOs, while Karystos TO refers the southern vineyard area. It has to be noted that, however one-dimensional, the three Evia designations are widely used among the local producers. (Red varieties and red wines from the region have to be sold under an EO or a TO of Central Greece designation.)

Karystos TO
White still: dry.
White varieties: Savatiano at least ninety per cent of the blend; Roditis.

Lilantio Pedio TO
White still: dry.
White varieties: Savatiano; Roditis up to twenty per cent of the blend.

Ritsona Avlidos TO
White still: dry.
White varieties: Savatiano at least ninety per cent of the blend; Roditis.

PRODUCERS

AVANTIS ESTATE
Mitikas, 341 00 Halkida. Tel: +30 222 105 5350.
Vineyards owned: 20ha; under contract: 7ha; production: 700hl.
Previously known as Mountrihas Estate after its owner Apostolos Mountrihas, the winery underwent a name change when Andreas Triantafillou joined as the second partner. Active since 1994, the wines of Mountriha and Triantafillou have been making an impact in the market since 1999. The initial vineyards were in Mitikas, close to Halkida, and with extra demand, the partners added some parcels in Viotia, in Arma and Neochoraki.

Since 2002, Avantis has been one of the best medium-small producers in Central Greece, and its portfolio seems to improve with every vintage. The first attempts were clean and straightforward, but subsequent releases have shown more character and more definition. All vineyards are in fairly hot areas so the style is tilted towards the fuller side.

The fresher products are a Grenache Rouge/Syrah rosé and the Avantis Estate, an Assyrtico/Sauvignon Blanc blend that has good structure and vivacity. Avantis Sauvignon Blanc is subject to prolonged skin contact and oak-ageing, acquiring a distinct *gris* colour. It is more wooded Loire than oaky New World in varietal expression. The best white is Avantis Dryos, an oak-aged Malagousia/Assyrtico which strikes a fine balance between the lifted Malagousia flavours and a sweet oak presence.

The Avantis reds and sweet wines are more exotic and more adventurous than its whites. Both of the two reds are made from Syrah. Avantis Syrah, the higher-volume *cuvée*, is quite ripe and peppery, showing a Rhône influence more than anything else. The Avantis Collection Syrah could not be more different. A dark, rich, alcoholic, tannic wine, it seems to adopt a New World approach, but without the clarity of fruit found in most Australian wines – in a blind tasting, a good guess might be South Africa. It is a barrel selection of a single vineyard in Arma; when the normal Syrah is about to be bottled, the best barriques are chosen, and their maturation is prolonged for a further eighteen months. It will be interesting to see how the initial vintages mature. In addition, this is the only Greek wine where the price changes according to the quality of the vintage. The 2001 vintage was released in Athens at a retail price of thirty-five euros while the 2002 was made available a year later at twenty-five euros.

The same selection process is followed for a pair of sweet, Muscat-dominated wines: Melitis and Melitis Collection. The former is fresh, easy drinking, and full of the rose petal Muscat *typicité*, while the rare Collection bottling is evolved, rich, and full of intensity. A lovely wine, ready to drink on release.

HALKIDA COOPERATIVE
Filla, 341 00 Halkida.
Tel: +30 222 105 4934/1934; Fax: +30 222 105 4934.
Vineyards under contract: 1,000ha; members: 800; production: 5,000hl.
Despite a large surrounding vineyard area, the Halkida Cooperative is comparatively moderate in size. Founded in 1934, it currently has 800 members. Bulk wine makes up the majority of its sales, with the Halkida Retsina being the more popular bottled product.

KARYSTOS-MARMARI COOPERATIVE
Odos Karistou–Halkida Rd, 340 01 Karystos.
Tel: +30 222 402 2782/2282; Fax: +30 222 402 2282.

Vineyards under contract: 600ha; members: 700; production: 25,000hl.

Marmari is a small town, just north of Karystos. Established later than the Halkida Cooperative, and with fewer members and fewer hectares under contract, the Karystos-Marmari Cooperative still manages to produce five times the amount that its counterpart does. The emphasis is again on bulk wines, producing dry whites from Savatiano and Roditis, and dry reds from Merlot, Cabernet Sauvignon, and Agiorgitiko.

LYKOS WINERY

Malakonda Eretria, PO Box 34008, Evia. Tel: +30 222 906 8222;
Fax: +30 222 906 8200; Website: www.lykoswines.gr; Email: info@lykoswines.gr
Vineyards owned: 3.5ha; under contract: 22ha; production: 2,300hl.

The Lykos family was famous for having one of the best, most respected restaurants in the Halkida area – an institution that, alone, was promoting the development of wine culture. With one guaranteed top on-trade outlet Apostolos Lykos decided to move into wine production, and the first wines were made from the 1994 vintage. In character they emulated the style of food served in the restaurant: hearty and opulent. Thus initial vintages were on the heavy side, with oak masking the fruit due to long ageing in new casks and, in some cases, very low acidity. Over the years, the wines were refined, and today they are a class above their early versions.

The basic line is called Panselinos ("full moon") and is made up of an Assyrtico/Sauvignon Blanc blend, a Grenache Rouge rosé, and a red Cabernet Sauvignon. Good Agiorgitiko and Moschofilero are sourced from the Peloponnese for the red and white Kerastis range. Kratistos is the premium red of Lykos, an OPAP Nemea with a far more balanced structure than of old, but still one for people who enjoy the spices and fragrance of new oak. Iliatoras, a supple, barrel-fermented Chardonnay, has a more sophisticated integration of oak, and the very lively Melikos is a sweet fortified Muscat aged in French barriques.

MALAMATINA WINERY

Konstantinou Malamatina 1, 341 00 Faros; Head office: Kalohori, 570 09
Thessaloniki. Tel: +30 231 075 2346; Fax: +30 231 075 2736;
Website: www.malamatina.gr; Email: malamatina@malamatina.gr
Vineyards under contract: 600ha; production: 270,000hl.

Malamatina is one of the largest wine producers in Greece and possibly the most profitable, based on just one product: Retsina Malamatina, a lightly resined, extremely drinkable example mainly sold in crown-capped, 500 millilitre bottles. In the majority of Greek tavernas, this is the only choice. The company has been trading in wine since 1895, but the last two decades, under the guidance of Kostas and Mihalis Malamatinas, have been crucial for its success. The corporation has three production plants in the general region of Evia and Viotia.

MONTOFOLI ESTATE
Palaia Xora, 340 01 Karistou. Tel: +30 222 402 3951; Fax: +30 222 402 6318; Email: genkainv@otenet.gr
Vineyards owned: 1.6ha; production: 100hl.

Not only has the Karakostas family done a lot for Greek wine, it has done much to promote wine in Greece in general. Their Cellier wine shop in Athens has been around for almost a century, educating locals about fine wine and supplying those who can afford it with top-quality bottles like Bordeaux First Growths (www.cellier.gr). When Pavlos Karakostas took over the family business, he introduced many changes. A gifted entrepreneur, Karakostas has been very successful in a variety of sectors, including dairy products and general branded consumer goods. However, wine has always held a special place in his heart, and Cellier is very much a hobby and a labour of love, as well as a business. He expanded the number of shops in Athens, established a wine club, a wine bistro, and most importantly, an import and distribution company called GENKA, with a list of high-calibre agencies such as Gaja, Bollinger, Penfolds, and Torres.

In 1986, Karakostas decided to create a winery in Karystos to focus on a small number of products, to be produced in tiny quantities and hand-sold in his Cellier shops. Captivated by the extreme nature of the Karystos climate, which is far closer to Paros than Halkida, he planted mainly Aegean varieties like Aidani, Assyrtico, and Athiri, together with Liatiko, some Grenache Blanc, and Cabernet Sauvignon.

Right from the start, Karakostas wanted to have an ultra-rare sweet wine as his winery's flagship, possibly emulating the style of Santorini's *vin santo*, even if he also planted a few vines of Pedro Ximénez. The flagship Montofoli Estate is made from Athiri, Aidani, and Assyrtico, picked ripe, at about 13.5 degrees Baumé, and sun-dried for about ten days. The wine is fermented naturally and aged in French 400-litre barrels for three years, bottled mainly in half bottles, and matured for an additional year before release. This wine is quite unlike anything else in Greece or indeed the world – it could be described as a *vin santo* made in Jura. The sweetness is barely perceptible, totally overwhelmed by an extraordinary dry extract, very high acidity, and an intense, flowery minerality. The nose is complex, but lean rather than opulent. The wine develops in bottle at a very slow pace. It is too early to say, but this wine could have one of the longest ageing capacities in Greece. Karakostas keeps aside some barrels of Montofoli from what he considers the best vintages. These barrels are meticulously topped up and small quantities are drawn out for very special occasions and bottled together as a rare multi-vintage Cuvée d'Or.

The Montofoli Estate also has a dry white wine, made from Savatiano and Grenache Blanc, called Myrtilos.

SABANIS WINERY

Ritsona, 341 00 Halkida. Tel: +30 222 103 4860; Fax: +30 222 103 4865;
Website: www.sabanis.gr; Email: info@sabanis.gr
Vineyards owned: 11ha; production: 1,200hl.

Tassos Sabanis and Manolis Skouloudis are partners in the INO Winery (*see* page 250) and a grape concentrate business (*see* Skouloudis Estate below). But Sabanis also has a separate winery substantially larger than the Skouloudis Estate, and in general, far more commercially active. All the fruit is sourced from the estate's vineyards.

The basic line is simply called Sabanis; it consists of a Roditis white, a Grenache Rouge/Cabernet Sauvignon rosé, and a red blend of Grenache Rouge, Syrah, and Cabernet Sauvignon. The most interesting wines are Methistikos White, a very good Roditis from a dry-farmed single-vineyard; Ampelones Sabani, a pure, reserved Sauvignon Blanc; and Palaiomenos Red, a soft, oaky Syrah/Cabernet Sauvignon blend. The portfolio finishes with a Charmat-method Moschofilero called Vin Sabanis, a sweet Eveli Muscat, and a blended Methistikos Red.

SKOULOUDIS ESTATE

Mitikas, 341 00 Halkida. Tel: +30 222 109 2920; Fax: +30 222 103 4865;
Website: www.skouloudis.gr; Email: agroktima@agroktima.gr
Vineyards owned: 8ha; production: 150hl.

Manolis Skouloudis, a Bordeaux-trained oenologist, together with his partner and local winery owner, Tassos Sabanis (*see* above), is the most successful producer of rectified grape juice concentrate in the country. Skouloudis Estate is a hobby sideline for Skouloudis, working on family vineyards in Mitikas and producing small quantities of white, rosé, and red. All wines are made from traditional local varieties and in traditional style.

TSALAS SMALL ESTATE
Thesi Tria Magazia, 341 00 Halkida.
Tel: +30 222 109 2420; Fax: +30 222 109 2268.
Vineyards owned: 2ha; production: 300hl.

A small producer, Kostas Tsalas has been releasing wines since 1993. The current wines are a lot better than average – the basic Small Estate Tsala White is a TO of Lilantio Pedio, followed by a Grenache-dominated rosé, and a pure Cabernet Sauvignon. However, the lower-volume wines are much more interesting. Syllektikos is a Chardonnay/Sauvignon Blanc blend and there is a small Malvasia production, referred to as Malvasia del Chianti, an aromatic, lifted, and charming wine. New plantings of Sangiovese should yield interesting results.

FOKIDA
The prefecture of Fokida lies between Aitoloakarnania to the west, the Corinthian Gulf to the south, Viotia to the east, and Fthiotida further north. Most of its surface is taken up by the Giona Mountains on the east and the Vardoussia range on the west. Most slopes face south, overlooking the Peloponnese. The meeting point of the two land masses is Lake Mornos, west of the capital Amfissa, which is one of Attica's most important water reserves. Low altitude areas are only found near the coast and on a narrow strip of land connecting Amfissa and Itea, again by the Corinthian Gulf. Despite its southern aspect, Fokida is a relatively cool part of Central Greece, due to its high elevation – Mount Giona reaches 2,507 metres (8,225 feet) and Vardoussia 2,495 metres (8,185 feet).

Fokida is of limited viticultural importance and, prior to 2002, there were no declared wine-bottlers in the region. There are no available regional wine appellations (TOs), so the choice is between an EO or a regional Central Greece TO. Vine-growing is difficult, since most plots are either infertile, too steep, or dedicated to other plants. There seems to be potential, however, which could be exploited if the wines are positioned at a premium enough level to cover the high cost of production. It will be interesting to see what Parnassou Vineyards and its owner Nicos Argyriou manage to do in the next few vintages.

PRODUCERS

PARNASSOU VINEYARD

330 51 Polidrosos. Tel: +30 223 402 3544; Fax: +30 223 402 3194.

Vineyards owned: 15ha; under contract: 5ha; production: 800hl.

Nicos Argyriou was the first to establish a winery in Fokida, putting the region on the modern Greek wine map – an adventurous investment, but also one full of excitement and possibilities. The winery is in the northeast of Fokida at Polidrosos on the slopes of Mount Parnassos and belongs to the area of Arahova at the northeast tip of Fokida. Yiannis Flerianos, the highly educated son of Mary Flerianou, herself one of the most influential Greek oenologists of the 1980s, is winemaker. The vineyard was planted with a number of French varieties like Cabernet Sauvignon, Cabernet Franc, Sauvignon Blanc, Merlot, and Syrah, as well as Malvasia and Malagousia. Traditional varieties are sourced from collaborating vineyards.

Currently, the Parnassou Vineyard range is limited to a white, a rosé, and a red, which are all traded under the umbrella brand of Erohos. By far the most intriguing of the three is the Erohos Red, the only varietal Arahovitikos produced in Greece. Arahovitikos, or Mavroudi Arahovas, is the dominant variety of the region. Vigorous and productive, with a relatively deep colour, it ripens in early September and easily reaches sugar levels above thirteen degrees Baumé. Overall, it seems a modern and promising grape. As more varieties become available to Argyriou, so his products should become even better.

FTHIOTIDA

Fthiotida, in the north of Central Greece, borders Thessaly to the north, Evritania to the west, Fokida and Viotia to the south, and the Evoikos Gulf to the east. The capital of the region is Lamia. Fthiotida is a valley basin, which starts from the sea and extends inland towards Karpenisi, totally surrounded by mountains: Oiti and Kalidromo to the south, Othris to the north, and the solid Pindos range to the west. The southern part of the prefecture includes Atalanti, Livanates, and Martino and has a complex topography, with hills, mountains, and low fields. Although this is the northern part of Central Greece, it is almost as warm as Viotia, except for the higher-altitude regions or areas influenced by cool winds flowing down from the Pindos mountains or, further south, from Mount Parnassos.

History, grapes, and legislation

Fthiotida has a long viticultural history, especially around the area of Atalandi, where wine production was present from ancient times until phylloxera arrived after World War II. The shrinking and ageing population didn't take up the challenge of re-establishing such historic vineyards until Dimitris Hatzimichalis arrived in the early 1970s. In one stroke, he revived the vinous side of Atalandi, creating one of the great success stories of Greek wine. Domaine Hatzimichalis was the region's first winery and, in the last ten years, seven new producers have taken root. Terroirs vary widely, from hotter to cooler regions, and from highly fertile to infertile soils. Fthiotida can be very rewarding for any viticulturalist who has a clear idea of what he or she needs.

In Fthiotida, the Savatiano land of Central Greece comes to an abrupt halt. A large number of current plantings have been developed in the "post-Hatzimichalis" era, and therefore non-traditional varieties play an important part in the overall picture. Sporadic older vineyards contain many well known varieties as well as a significant proportion of Mavroudi varieties. (Mavroudi is a blanket name for a number of dark-skinned varieties found throughout Greece, most of the time interplanted with other vines or other types of Mavroudi.) Another variety found in the area – as well as in other regions of mainland Greece – is the white Kontokladi. Possibly originating from Zakinthos, it is a vigorous, highly productive vine producing small bunches of grapes that reach maturity in mid-September. Kontokladi is rich in sugars but low in acidity.

The legislative framework of Fthiotida has been tailored to meet the requirements of Dimitris Hatzimichalis, which was trying to give a place-specific identity to his wines, even on the labels. The three TOs of Koilada Atalantis, Opoundia Lokridos, and Côtes de Knimidos have been designated in that light, and their varietal compositions largely reflect the match of terroir and vines as made by Hatzimichalis. The only exception is Martino, a TO established in late 2004 to help Domaine Dimakis, the sole producer of the area.

Koilada Atalandi TO

White still: dry.
White varieties: Roditis; Assyrtico; Athiri; Robola; Chardonnay; Sauvignon Blanc; Semillon.
Red still: dry
Red varieties: Cabernet Sauvignon; Merlot.

Opountia Lokridos TO

White still: dry.
White varieties: Robola must be at least sixty per cent of the blend;
Assyrtico; Athiri; Chardonnay; Sauvignon Blanc.
Red still: dry.
Red varieties: Cabernet Sauvignon must be at least sixty per cent of
the blend; Limnio; Xinomavro; Syrah; Merlot; Cabernet Franc.

Côtes de Knimidos TO

White still: dry.
White varieties: Assyrtico must be at least fifty per cent of the blend,
the balance being other local recommended grape varieties.
Red still: dry.
Red varieties: Syrah must be at least fifty per cent of the blend, the
balance being other local recommended grape varieties.

Martino TO

White still: dry.
White varieties: Roditis; Malagousia; Athiri; Robola; Chardonnay;
Sauvignon Blanc; Ugni Blanc.
Rosé still: dry.
Rosé varieties: Roditis; Syrah.
Red still: dry.
Red varieties: Syrah; Cabernet Sauvignon; Cabernet Franc; Merlot.

PRODUCERS

DOMAINE HATZIMICHALIS

Atalandi winery: 2km Atalandi–Livanaton, Megaplatanos, 352 00 Atalandi.
Tel: +30 223 302 3172; Fax:+ 30 223 302 3619. Head office: Athens–Lamias
Rd, 145 64 Kifisia. Tel: +30 210 807 5403; Fax: +30 210 807 6704;
Website: www.hatzimichalis.gr; Email: info@hatzimichalis.gr
Vineyards owned: 160ha; under contract: 20ha; production: 15,000hl.
See also Domaine Hatzimichalis entry on page 249.
Dimitris Hatzimichalis is one of the most prominent Greek producers and
one of the most influential figures in the modern Greek wine revolution.
His presence, his wines, and his commercial success have paved the way for
a significant number of today's movers and shakers of the national wine

industry. It was Hatzimichalis who introduced varietal wine and French varieties to the Greek wine-drinking public, most importantly Cabernet Sauvignon, Chardonnay, and Merlot. He was the first to define the term *ktima* (estate) in Greece. He worked hard to reveal ancient traditions, varieties, and forgotten aspects of Greek wine, and to link them with the present and, when possible, the future.

When Hatzimichalis started his own winery and vineyard in Atalandi in 1962, it was the first modern investment of its kind in the area since the phylloxera invasion. However, prior to this, Atalandi had had one of the longest, non-stop winemaking traditions in the country, with evidence of an active wine sector going back as far as the fourth century BC. The initial years were difficult, with wine production proving insufficient to keep the venture afloat. So turkey breeding was used as an alternative source of income; hence the domaine's turkey logo. Sales improved over the years, leading to the small producers' wine boom of the late 1980s – in a way, Hatzimichalis *was* the wine boom of the 1980s. His wines have proved impressively popular, not only in Greece, but also in the major export markets. The company developed as the market evolved, increasing in size accordingly. The initial nine hectares are now close to 160, while the early basic winery has been replaced by one of the most outstanding production and cellaring facilities in Greece.

Before he could exploit it, Hatzimichalis first had to understand the potential of Atalandi, which turned out to possess a very complex terroir. The valley is surrounded by a number of mountains, offering a huge variety of aspects and soils. The lower parts acts like a Bernoulli tube, with breezes from the Evoikos Gulf in the east alternating with cooler winds from higher elevations. There were plenty of trials and a few errors along the way, but attention to detail was always Haztimichalis' strong point. Varieties planted included Robola, Assyrtico, Athiri, Chardonnay, Sauvignon Blanc, Merlot, Cabernets Sauvignon and Franc, Syrah, Xinomavro, and others.

The Hatzimichalis portfolio consists of a large number of wines, which include multi-varietal blends, varietals, and brands. Up to 2002, the white wines have been consistently less impressive than the reds, lacking primary fruit. In some ways, they seemed to be stuck in the 1980s, but recent vintages have been more promising.

Cabernet Sauvignon was one of the first wines produced and it is the hallmark of the winery. Even if more expensive wines have been added, this one remains full of warm-climate varietal character, has excellent ageing potential, and is very good value. The Merlot, the first Greek example and still one of the best, is not as opulent as many but has excellent structure. The Kapnias range – meaning "smoky" – includes a Chardonnay fermented in oak and a Cabernet Sauvignon aged in high-toast oak. The latter is very convincing – tannic on release, but first-rate after a few years in bottle. The two cavas (see Appendix 1), a Cabernet Sauvignon and Roditis/Chardonnay, are among the most complex and individual Hatzimichalis wines. Sauvignon Blanc is planted in a parcel of chalky soil, akin to that of Pouilly and the Loire Valley. The grape is represented by an oaked and unoaked version, both of which have reserved aromas and are firm on the palate. The Hatzimichalis Chardonnay used to be more Hatzimichalis than Chardonnay, but in 2003 a change in style pushed ripeness higher and the varietal character emerged out of the shadow of a very well-structured wine.

Around the same period, Hatzimichalis started evolving new and exciting products. Neologismoi was a series of small-scale varietal wines from Italian grapes that might have had Greek origins. The range had varying success, but as a concept was a breakthrough. The Neologismoi range includes Grecanico, Grechetto, Verdicchio, Schiopettino, Aglianico, and Malvasia, with the three last standing out as the best. Along with these wines, the Rahes Galanou single-vineyard label yielded two wines: a Sauvignon Blanc/Semillon and a Cabernet Franc/Merlot. The involvement of Bordeaux-trained Professor Giorgos Kotseridis in many of these projects signalled a whole new approach: more fruit, more definition, and more elegance.

Presumably, the developments will not stop there. Although not reflected in its portfolio, Hatzimichalis has been doing tremendous work on numerous "*crus*" of Atalandi, matching specific sites with varieties, clones, rootstocks, and cultivation regimes. For example, more than four different parcels of Chardonnay have been handled separately, but blended together in the end. There are intentions to address this by breaking each blend down into the respective components and marketing them separately. In a few years time, the Hatzimichalis portfolio might look very different to how it does today and will certainly be a lot more fascinating.

DOMOKOS WINES

Gerakli, 350 10 Domokos. Head office: 4 Anemomylon, 350 10 Domokos.
Tel: +30 223 202 3232; Fax: +30 223 202 3232.
Vineyards owned: 10ha; under contract: 15ha; production: 370hl.

Domokos is in northern Fthiotida, overlooking the Larissa plain. Domokos Wines is a project devised by three friends – Martha Vassilopoulou, Velissatios Garaganis, and Yiannis Patouridis – who loved wine and were in a position to invest. At some stage this entertaining hobby turned into a good business, since now the winery sells more than 40,000 bottles per year. Most fruit is sourced from the Gerakliou Estate in the Domokos region. The winery produces a pair of quite traditional but very honest labels: Iliopyros, a Sauvignon Blanc/Assyrtico blend, and Filoktitis, a Cabernet Sauvignon/Merlot blend. In addition, some Syrah and Malvasia are grown on the estate, possibly pointing to future products.

KARADIMOU VINEYARDS
Megaplatanos, 352 00 Atalandi. Tel: +30 223 302 2753.
Head office: 14 Aiantos Lokrou, 352 00 Atalandi; Tel/Fax: +30 223 308 0113.
Vineyards owned: 4.5ha; production: 70hl.
A small, totally organic producer that started in 2001, very close to Domaine Hatzimichalis. All fruit comes from an estate vineyard, at 420 metres (1,380 feet), which is dry-farmed. Only one label, Crescendo, is produced, which is a blend of Malagousia, Assyrtico, and Sauvignon Blanc. This has been one of the better new entries in Central Greece, being surprisingly open and exotic, without being either sophisticated or pretentious.

MAVROIDI VINEYARD
350 05 Livanates. Tel/Fax: +30 223 303 1967.
Vineyards owned: 4ha; production: 280–300hl.
Another small, organic estate close to Atalandi. Anestis Mavroidis has been active since 1995 and works exclusively with his landholdings. He used to focus on the local market and bulk wine, but since 2001 there has been a significant change in tactics, coupled with a noted improvement in quality. Currently, the portfolio consists of two labels: Mavroidis Vineyards White is a fresh blend of Athiri, Assyrtico, and Chardonnay, while its red equivalent is a rich and soft Grenache Rouge, Merlot, and Syrah blend. A producer to watch.

AITOLOAKARNANIA
Aitoloakarnania is in the west of Central Greece, bordering Epirus to the north, and Fokida and Evritania to the east, with the Ionian Sea to the west, and the Gulf of Patras to the south. Here the Pindos range slopes towards the sea and there are numerous rivers, most importantly the Aheloos. The

prefecture is covered with a dense network of lakes, with Trichonida being the most important. The lagoon of Mesologi is a significant financial centre for the local community, together with the provincial town of Agrinio. The climate of the region is close to that of the Ionian Islands, with higher rainfall, higher humidity, and less heat than the rest of Central Greece.

Vine-growing has been and still is present in the region, but has never gained a high commercial value. Other sources of income, such as tobacco cultivation, are more attractive, so vineyards are mainly used to cover the home consumption of the landowner. Currently, varieties include a mix of vines from the Ionian Islands and the Peloponnese. Malagousia, a grape that supposedly originated here, is curiously absent, apart from new plantings. The soils and topography of the district, together with an additional interplay of lakes and rivers, make Aitoloakarnania a place where many exquisite terroirs remain to be discovered. A good step forward is the emergence of a handful of "weekend wine producers" who, helping each other, are trying to understand their region and raise the profile of its wines across Greece. Definitely a region to watch.

PRODUCER

KARAGIORGOU WINERY

Periohi Xiromero, 300 06 Astakos. Tel: +30 264 603 8030.

Vineyards owned: 3.5ha.

The first wines from Leonidas Karagiorgos were released in 2004. His organic vineyards are in the Astakos area, on the Ionian coast, where sea breezes moderate the heat. The winery is constantly developing, but initial vintages are being produced mainly on an experimental rather than commercial basis. Taksideftis, a Roditis varietal, is full and melony; Ioannis is a blend of Merlot with thirty per cent Cabernet Sauvignon and has good fruit; and finally, the rich, expressive Malagousia which lacks any Muscat-like overtones. From a previously unknown region, this is a fine first effort.

6

Ionian islands

There are seven islands in the Ionian group, hence the Greek name *Eptanissa*, meaning "seven islands". These are, from north to south, Corfu, Paxos, Antipaxos, Lefkada, Ithaca, Cephalonia, and Zakynthos. There is a different flair in the way Greek culture is expressed on the Ionian Islands and the natives highlight their individuality. You can see it in their local idioms, their temper, and their vivacious approach to life. This can probably be attributed to the history of the islands. Greeks believe that the Ottoman occupation had a negative impact on their standard of living, while other empires, like the French, British, and Italian, invested more in the nations they occupied. The Ottomans were in charge of the Ionian Islands for less than half a century, compared with almost four centuries for the mainland. The Venetians, by contrast, arrived in 1386 and stayed until 1797. After a brief spell of French occupation, the islands became a British protectorate until, in 1864, they became part of the Greek state.

CULTURE AND NOBILITY
Although the Ionian Islands were exposed to four cultures during those years, the Italian influence was the most pre-eminent, followed by the British. The economies of these islands became forward-looking, complex, and geared towards high-quality trade and exports. Societies had a significant degree of sophistication and a well-defined hierarchy. Arts like music and literature developed a prestigious social standing, and artists gained a place within the spiritual leadership of each island. Anything that made life beautiful, like food and wine, was something that deserved dedication and respect.

These social and political developments gave the Ionian Islands a chance not only to become familiar with the notion of aristocracy, but to actually build one

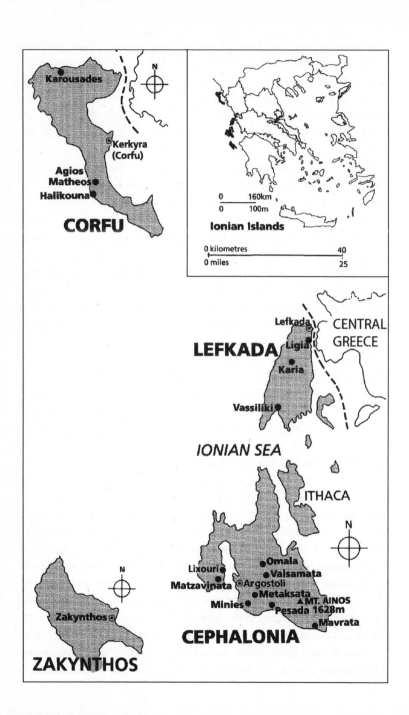

up, something not possible in most parts of modern Greece. Even today, many people confuse *to kratein ton plouto* ("possessing wealth") with *to kratein to ariston* ("possessing excellence"). There is a world of difference between being able to afford the finer things in life and building a lifestyle around appreciating these, in a respectful, uplifting way.

Within this framework, wine could not be left out. Although viticulture always remained a back-breaking, difficult job, wine production became an upper-class, noble occupation. It was not something to cover the annual needs in wine or to make a profit, but a way to infuse life with a deeper meaning. This approach can be found in many wineries around the Ionian Islands today.

The different occupants exploited the Ionian Islands in different ways. A number of French and Italian wine traders constantly capitalized on the islands' vinous produce. Ionian wine was largely exported, although more often than not, it was "baptized" as Italian along the way. On the other hand, Venetians introduced raisin production – the drying of edible grapes – and this played an important role in the development of viticulture. In some cases raisins stimulated vine cultivation, while in others it was so successful that it almost led to the extinction of wine grape-growing. Raisins were either exported as such or used to produce wine at times when western Europe had a shortage of fresh grapes due to phylloxera. This trade was exclusively controlled by the Venetians and the British and, when the Ionian Islands became part of the Greek nation, any export activity came to an abrupt halt. The locals had neither know-how nor brand name to defend.

CLIMATE AND CLASSIFICATION

According to the Ministry of Agriculture, the area dedicated to wine grapes in the Ionian Islands is 3,556 hectares. From a viticultural point of view, Paxos and Antipaxos are of limited interest. The southern part of Ithaca has six hectares of vineyards, most of which are classified as part of the Mavrodaphne of Cephalonia OPE. The figure was 200 times higher 150 years ago. Today, sizeable wine production can be found only in Corfu, Lefkada, Cephalonia, and Zakynthos. Cephalonia has the largest acreage, with a total of 1,105 hectares (including Ithaka), of which 305 hectares comprise the three quality wine appellations of the area. Not far behind is Corfu, with 1,055 hectares, followed by Lefkada (742 hectares), and Zakynthos (654 hectares).

Overall, the climate of the Ionian Islands is lacking in extremes and the maritime influence is obvious. The islands form the western border of

Greece, just after the Adriatic Sea. Weather crashes over the Pindos Mountain range, which is the backbone of mainland Greece, affecting the climate of all islands or regions close to the Ionian Sea. This natural barrier influences both rainfall and winds. Rainfall levels are some of the highest in Greece and high humidity can be a problem in some of the less than perfect vintages. In addition, pockets of warm air cool down when they reach the Pindos range, becoming heavier and flowing downhill, resulting in cold eastern winds that affect all the Ionian Islands lying just a few kilometres off the mainland coast, especially Corfu and Lefkada.

The Ionian islands are quite mountainous, with the exception of Paxos and Antipaxos. The rest are very steep in places with a more aggressive topography than the islands of the Aegean, including a wide variety of aspects and inclinations. This creates a wider variation of soils, with fertile lower vineyards and poorer soils on the hillsides. It also means different meso-climates, from hot sites near to sea level to spots at high altitudes where several varietals fail to reach full maturity. All these elements result in a diversity of terroirs and wine styles.

The vast range of wines is not just due to a fragmented terroir, but also to the number of varieties present. In fact, the two reasons are interrelated – the relative isolation of the islands and the numerous permutations of soils, altitudes, meso-climates, and weather patterns formed a perfect platform for *Vitis vinifera* to exercise its habit of genetic divergence over the centuries. The lists of recommended and permitted varietals on the islands are, in most cases, extremely long, and yet cover only a fraction of the existing varieties. In fact, there is no Ionian Islands regional wine denomination, the only departmental TO not to exist, which indicates that a common denominator across the region could not be found. Once again, it is possible that the finest varietals have yet to be discovered, and committed visionaries will be needed to save them from extinction.

ZAKYNTHOS

Lying at the southern end of the Ionian group, Zakynthos has the warmest climate. There is a higher percentage of low-lying fields when compared with the other Ionian Islands, and although the soil varies, in general it is quite heavy and relatively fertile. The terroir of Zakynthos thus favours less elegant wines than, for example, Cephalonia.

The rise of the raisin

The viticultural history of Zakynthos was influenced by the Venetians to a far greater extent than the other Ionian Islands. In the sixteenth century the island saw the introduction of grapes suitable for raisin production, since Venetians, the world's most sophisticated traders, saw export opportunities. Zakynthos proved an excellent place to produce raisins because of its low average altitude. Success was immediate and impressive and plantations went from strength to strength. Nevertheless, during the lack of European wine due to the phylloxera crisis, a significant proportion of the redcurrant production was vinified and exported to several countries. This situation continued until the last decade of the nineteenth century, when there was finally a ban of *stafiditis oenos*, the name for wine made from raisins. Nevertheless, the Zante raisin – the name the Venetians used for the raisins made from the Corinthiaki grape from Zakynthos – still accounts for much of the island's viticultural sector and still does well on the export markets.

Despite the success of the Zante raisin, however, wine grape production was not abandoned, a fact proved by the impressive mix of varietals available today. Even if the current number of different varietals is less than the sixty boasted of in the nineteenth century, Zakynthos can lay claim to being one of the most multi-varietal islands in the Mediterranean. The major varieties include Katsakoulias, a red, large-clustered variety with a pale colour and relatively high acidity; Avgoustiatis, a vine that withstands arid conditions and provides grapes with extremely high acidity, dense colour, and high fruit level: Skiadopoulo, a white variety that adapts well in most soils to produce fruit with high sugar and moderate acidity levels; Migdali; and Pavlos. The latter ripens in late September, almost a month and a half later than Migdali, but both are vigorous, highly productive white varieties giving high sugar levels while retaining moderate acidity. Skiadopoulo is the base of the OKP Verdea appellation (*see* below). Other varietals include Goustolidi and Robola, plus rarities like Robola Rouge, a red version of Robola not found on Cephalonia, which is rich in colour and very aromatic; Kokkinovostitsa, "the one with red stems", a variety of which only a few hundred vines survive and which is usually co-vinified with other grapes, and Violento, a vine that was originally considered a rich, high-ripeness, local clone of Roditis, but has since been proved to be its own distinct variety – a vigorous, productive vine ripening in mid-September and producing grapes that usually exceed thirteen degrees Baumé but have low acidity.

Zakynthos produces Verdea, one of the two OKP wines of Greece – the other one being retsina.[1] Traditionally, Verdea was a dry, oak-aged wine with extremely high alcohol, sometimes exceeding 15.5 per cent, but, at the same time, with quite high acidity, giving an idiosyncratic balance between body, warmth, freshness, and above all, spiciness. The colour of these wines bordered on pale tawny, but with an intense tinge of green. More often than not, the wine was bottled cloudy and as a result quickly formed a sediment. Although not overwhelming, oxidation was a key part of the style, present on both the nose and palate. Old-style Verdea is a wine that demands understanding on behalf of the drinker – if served blind, it is logical to assume that most international wine professionals would dismiss it as faulty at first sight and sniff. Nevertheless, served as a strong after-dinner drink on a cold winter evening in Zakynthos, Verdea can be a most rewarding alternative to the world's increasing wine standardization.

The style of Verdea is achieved by using a mix of ripe and unripe grapes. There might have been a specific reason for this originally: one of the most highly regarded grape varieties on the island is Goustolidi, which happens to be the first to ripen. (The grape may have been named after *Avgoustos* (August), since it was one of very few varieties to enter the final stages of maturation so early.) Given that vineyards in Zakynthos were multi-varietal, the only available option was to harvest at the time the best grapes were ripe, in early to mid-September, even if harvesting plots in one pass made certain that unripe grapes of Robola, Skiadopoulo, Pavlos, and the ultra-rare and obscure Areti and Korinthi, formed a large proportion of the blend. Legislation suggests that OKP Verdea must include seventy-five per cent Skiadopoulo, but given the complex varietal blends of most vineyards, this is very difficult for growers to control, let alone the authorities. The harvest for Verdea is not unlike the approach taken for Vinho Verde in Portugal – although the tastes could not be more different.

Despite the claims of many Zakynthos wine people that Verdea will always resist market trend, a more consumer-friendly Verdea was created to quench

1. OKP wines are defined as "wines of appellation by tradition", and this classification, a sub-category of table wines EO, is devoted to preserving traditional, distinctive styles. *See* Appendix 1 and Part I, Chapter 4.

the thirst of tourists. Nowadays, most commercially available Verdea is paler in colour, less oxidized, and the alcohol rarely exceeds thirteen per cent.

The island produces small quantities of rosé and red wine, although it is sometimes difficult to distinguish the two, as reds can be relatively pale while rosés can be quite dense in colour and high in tannins. Traditionally, rosé wines were not produced by a short maceration but rather a long one with grapes of low pigmentation. In the last decade, the style of the rosés have been moving closer to what most people would consider as such, being paler, fruitier, fresher, and less tannic.

Verdea OKP

White still: dry.
White varieties: Skiadopoulo must be at least seventy-five per cent of the blend, the balance being other local recommended grape varieties.

PRODUCERS

CALLINICO WINES

6 Kalipado, 291 00 Zakynthos. Tel: +30 269 506 1547;
Fax: +30 269 506 3099; Email: callinico@otenet.gr
Vineyards owned: 1.5ha; production: 5,000hl.

Theodoros Voultsos is the pioneer of new-age Verdea. He developed a style designed to be more approachable to the uninitiated wine-lover spending the summer in Zakynthos. The standard version of his Verdea is still rich, ripe, and high in acidity, but oxidation is minimal, in fact barely noticeable. It has lower alcohol than the usual fifteen per cent, and a refreshing palate, although the nose remains distinctive and includes a certain spiciness. There is a *grande réserve* bottling that follows the more traditional route, which is aged in old oak to impart complexity rather than oak flavours.

The winery's range is not limited to Verdea. Callinico Red and White are semi-sweet, multi-varietal blends. Enetikon Rosé is made in dry and semi-dry versions, with the former being fresher and more focused on clean fruit. Ambeloravdi, the only dry red, is one of the most modern wines of Zakynthos.

COMOUTOS ESTATE

Ktima Agria, 29 100 Zakynthos. Tel: +30 269 509 2285; Fax: +30 269 509 2284.
The most aristocratic winery in Zakynthos, if not the whole Ionian Sea, the

Comoutos Estate is situated within Agria Estate, a property that dates back to 1638, making it the oldest functioning winery in Greece. Currently, the estate is run by Eleni Comoutos and her brother, George Likoudis, and wine production is only a small part of the business.

Comoutos is the winery that, in a certain sense, defined Verdea. Most people came into contact with the traditional style of the wine mainly through Comoutos wines, and these bottles still remain guardians of the genre. In recent decades there has been an attempt to modernize the winery, but current examples suggest more a polishing of the style than a redefinition of it. The Comoutos approach is still focused on extraction, long ageing in oak, breathtaking complexity, and ripeness.

Cultivation is totally organic and the winery relies heavily on estate-grown grapes, especially in key varieties like Robola and Avgoustiatis. For its Verdea, the Comoutos family uses Goustolidi, Robola, Skiadopoulo, Pavlos, and Areti. A small proportion of Pinot Gris completes the blend: a rare planting of the variety that is called "Tokay" here and considered to be a vital element of the final character of the wine. Verdea Grande Réserve is released after five years and is an excellent model of what traditional Verdea can be.

Comoutos Rosé, Rouge, and Grande Réserve Rouge are made mainly with Avgoustiatis and Katsakoulias. The Grande Réserve Rouge is the top of the line label. Intense, oxidative, alcoholic, and full of spice, it is a difficult wine to describe in terms of other wine styles, but for me it is reminiscent of the idiosyncratic aromatic character of old vintages of Castillo Ygay in Rioja. Comoutos wines deserve far wider recognition than they currently enjoy.

SOLOMOS WINES
Bohali, Kydoni, 29 100 Zakynthos. Tel: +30 269 502 7700; Fax: +30 269 502 7711.
Vineyards owned: 7ha; under contract: 12ha; production: 3,000hl.

This is another family-run winery, founded in 1990, and thus a relative newcomer by Zakynthos standards. Together with Comoutos, it is one of the island's smaller wineries. The vineyard holdings are substantial and include some of the lesser-known varieties like Robola Rouge, Violento, and Moschardina, a white grape that, as the name suggests, is reminiscent of Muscat, but is not technically a part of the Muscat family. Consultant Gerasimos Hartouliaris, owner of the small Divino winery in Cephalonia, advises resident winemaker Konstantina Solomos.

The range relies heavily on semi-dry and semi-sweet wines. The standard

Verdea is quite pleasant and the fresh, light Solomos Retsina is possibly the finest to be found on the island. The Cava Solomos is an oak-aged red with relatively low primary fruit flavours, but good complexity.

ZAKYNTHOS COOPERATIVE

10 Stoupathi, 29 100 Zakynthos. Head office: 42 Lomvardo, 29 100 Zakynthos; Tel: +30 269 502 2005; Fax: +30 30-269 502 2268; Email: easzakinthoy@aias.gr
Members: 5,000+; production: 9,000hl.

The cooperative is the largest producer on Zakynthos, gathering the grape production of more than 5,000 growers. Verdea and Retsina are the most important labels, with the former produced in dry and semi-dry versions. It is decent quality and therefore a safe choice in the local tavernas.

CEPHALONIA

The history of Cephalonia is quite similar to that of the rest of the Ionian islands, from antiquity up to World War II. The Venetians and the British left their mark on the culture of the islanders – an influence that has been preserved and highly valued. The most important event in recent decades was the major earthquake of 1953. With thousands of deaths, more than half of the population decided to leave the island. "The 1953 earthquake tore apart the social fabric of Cephalonia," is how top local wine producer Spiros Cosmetatos puts it. Poverty, abandonment, and uncertainty about the future became significant problems affecting every part of the commercial, cultural, and social life of the island.

Despite this, today Cephalonia is the most important of the Ionian islands in terms of wine production. While the other islands may boast a stronger viticultural history, Cephalonia is the most developed viticulturally, and arguably produces the finest and most famous wines. Nevertheless, the future is not secure. Wine production in Cephalonia is by no means financially attractive. There is a widespread lack of vineyard workers, as the tourist industry and immigration are more attractive alternatives to young people. However, most new winery owners on the island approach their ventures not as plain businesses, but as part of an aristocratic, uplifting, truly Ionian lifestyle.

Climate and viticulture

The climate of Cephalonia is lacking in extremes; thus generally, viticulture is not hampered by any weather-related restrictions. Winter and spring rainfall are ample, while the ripening period of the varieties grown on the island is relatively dry. Low rainfall does not mean low humidity, and fungal diseases are the most significant problem, mainly botrytis, and powdery and downy mildew. The disease pressure on the plants is accentuated by the fact that bush vines are the norm. In order to reduce water stress, the canopies of these plants are not opened up and this limits air circulation and sun exposure. Spiros Cosmetatos tried the split- and open-canopy Geneva Double Curtain training system at his Gentilini Winery, but he still faced the same problems. It seems that linear vineyards with vines trained to the Vertical Shoot Positioning system at a height of 0.7 metres (just over two feet) or higher is the best option.

Sulphur and the Bordeaux mixture are used to combat botrytis and mildew, and these are applied in quite a peculiar way practised in several regions across Greece. The sulphur powder, or Bordeaux mixture, is put inside a sock, and the grower, wearing a mask, goes into the vineyard and hits the vines with it. It's a competent solution, even if the control over qualities applied is not that meticulous. Beyond chemical treatments, growers try to keep the canopy of bush vines open by tying shoots of neighbouring vines together. This takes place a couple of weeks before harvest, and apart from minimizing humidity-induced problems, it serves to advance maturity by increasing sunlight penetration.

Even if Cephalonia's relatively large size is taken into account, the island has a wide variety of soils. Those around Mount Ainos are high in limestone, for example, which gives Robola its elegance and minerality. In the southwestern part of the island the limestone is not so pure, and sandy patches can be found. Around Lixouri, where most Moschatella (*see* below), Mavrodaphne, and Muscat is found, there are heavier, clay soils.

Individual vineyards are tiny, rarely more than 0.4 hectares in size, and yields are low, averaging around thirty-five hectolitres per hectare for Robola vineyards and close to forty-five hectolitres per hectare for other local varieties. Two-thirds of the vineyards are to be found on slopes. Terraces were common in the past, to minimize erosion and the impact of cold wind in the spring. Some terraced plots exist today in the Robola OPAP zone, but it is by no means a standard practice any more.

A miscellany of varieties

Cephalonia is home to many varieties, either exclusively or along with a handful of other places. Some varietals grown widely elsewhere are known under different names on the island: for example, Perahoritiko is the local synonym for Savatiano. The local Association of Wine Growers, working in collaboration with the Institute for Plant Conservation at the National Foundation of Agricultural Research in Volo, eastern Thessaly, has set up an experimental plot of vines in the Vallianos Agricultural School in Argostoli to preserve, study, and possibly propagate more than forty-three local varieties.

The most famous variety of the island, if not the whole of Ionia, is Robola. Indeed, Robola of Cephalonia is the only OPAP quality-wine designation of the Ionian Islands. One of the noblest Greek varieties, Robola produces whites of great elegance, full of lemony fruit and fresh acidity, and not lacking in depth or extract. The Robola of Cephalonia OPAP classification applies to specific communes in the southern part of the island, and to vineyard areas with an altitude of fifty metres (164 feet) or higher. There is a great leap in quality for Robola fruit grown at high altitude – from 300 up to 800 metres (984–2,624 feet) – mainly due to cooler temperatures and more infertile soils.

Robola of Cephalonia was put on the modern international map because of the commercial success of a single pioneer: the Calliga Winery. In the 1970s and 1980s, the winery created a strong identity for its Robola, tirelessly promoting its unique packaging: an Alsace-shaped bottle in a rag sack. The local cooperative and the Matzavino winery followed the trend and demand led to booming sales. Today, only the cooperative continues to use this Robola packaging. The Matzavino winery was bought by Theodoros Orkopoulos to create Domaine Foivos (*see* below), while the Calliga brand name was bought by Greek Wine Cellars (*see* page 238). The Calliga Robola label has been discontinued and presently it is unclear if there are plans to re-establish a Calliga Winery in Cephalonia.

Apart from Robola, one of the most important varieties on Cephalonia is Tsaousi, which can be both a table and a wine grape. With big bunches, its potential alcohol rarely goes above 12.5 per cent, and when it does, the acidity falls rapidly. It is full of lemony and honeyed aromas and sometimes has spicy undertones. Supposedly of Egyptian origin, it was first established in Drama, Kozani, and Imathia in northern Greece. In these regions there are vines called Tsaousi, but the link is uncertain. Tsaousi's only other appearance in Ionia is some small batches in Corfu. It can produce up to seventy hectolitres per hectare, an extremely high yield for Cephalonia.

Moschatella is exclusive to Cephalonia. As the name suggests, it is a white grape with a light Muscat aroma, nevertheless it is not associated with the Muscat family. It is a vigorous and productive vine, producing bunches that easily exceed 600 grams each, while the fruit is rich in sugars and full of aromatic, floral intensity.

Other important varieties include Goustilidi, also known as Vostilidi and Goustolidi, a white grape to be found across many Ionian Islands. In Cephalonia it is a late ripener and can be harvested in late September, almost twenty days after the majority of other varieties have been picked and much later than the usual harvest date on Zakynthos. Its wines are high in alcohol, heavy in structure, and in most existing examples, quite rustic in style and flavours. Although Zakinthinos' name suggests a provenance from Zakynthos Island, it is only found in Cephalonia. It is known to give fresh acidity, moderate alcohol, and a moderately low fruit level.

This complex mix of varieties continues over to Ithaca, where white and black Thiako vines are relatively important. Thiako Red, a vigorous, productive vine, ripens in early September and gives high sugar ripeness but low colour. Thiako White is very similar to the red version, apart from berry colour and ripening time, which is fifteen days earlier.

Thiniatiko is a name that causes misconceptions. Many sources suggest that the Metaksata TO must be a blend of Thiniatiko and Mavrodaphne. Others claim that Thiniatiko is not a vine cultivar but a traditional blend of Mavrodaphne, Araklinos, and Korfiatis, the last two varieties being red, producing wines with deep colour, alcohol above thirteen per cent, and good levels of acidity. Both ripen by late September, so can be interplanted, although Korfiatis is extremely vigorous and drought resistant, while Araklinos behaves in the opposite way. Yet DNA fingerprinting techniques show that what some grape-growers know as Thiniatiko is nothing more than Tsigelo Mavrodaphne, a variation with denser, smaller clusters, and smaller berries that ripen more than twenty days later than the Regnio clone to be found in Ahaia, Peloponnese.

Classifications and fine wine

As well as its Robola OPAP, Cephalonia has two other quality designations, again the only ones in the Ionian Islands: Muscat of Cephalonia OPE and

Mavrodaphne of Cephalonia OPE. The Muscat appellation is confined to the western part of the island while the Mavrodaphne-demarcated area is scattered in many parcels, including the southern part of Ithaca. Legislation covers only sweet versions of these wines. A decade ago, only minute quantities of the two wines were produced and almost none was bottled. Since only bottled wine has a right to an OPE or OPAP classification, the two appellations became virtually extinct. Thanks to dedicated producers like Sclavos, Vassilakis, Hartouliaris of Divino Wines, and, more recently, Orkopoulos of Domaine Foivos, both styles have been resurrected in the last decade, and the early examples are extremely promising.

There is no reason why the "retrieved" Muscats and Mavrodaphnes of Cephalonia could not be among the finest in Greece. Terroirs are of high quality, producers show competence, and most of all, the available genetic material is excellent. The local sub-variety of Muscat is the superb Muscat Blanc, and Mavrodaphne plantings are dominated by the Tsigelo clone. The south of Ithaca and the southeastern edge of Cephalonia produce richly coloured Mavrodaphne; maturity is achieved at 12.5 per cent potential alcohol or lower, and the acidity remains at high levels for the variety. This is in sharp contrast with the Mavrodaphne around Lixouri, where fourteen per cent potential alcohol or higher is easily attained.

There are three TOs in Cephalonia, all of which currently have limited commercial value. Côtes de Ainos ("on the slopes of Mount Ainos") is potentially the most interesting. It comprises the co-vinification of Tsaousi, Goustolidi, and a small part of Robola for the white, while the red is predominantly Mavrodaphne. The cooperative is the only producer of Côtes de Ainos TO white. The red Côtes de Ainos TO is currently obsolete. The other two TOs have been tailor-made for the needs of specific producers: Matzavinata TO for Matzavino and Metaxata TO for Caligas. Some of the regulations, especially in the Matzavinata TO, have been amended to facilitate new producers in the region like Domaine Foivos.

A main concern for producers in Cephalonia, in common with other islanders around Greece, and indeed, the world, where road access from the mainland is not possible, is high transportation costs and lack of immediate service support. An technician in Athens can load a car and reach almost every single winery in the Peloponnese or Central Greece within three hours, any time of day or night. For Cephalonia, emergencies – usually at harvest time where every hour counts – can mean fourteen hours just waiting for the next ship from Patras to Argostoli. Indeed, many wineries are obliged to buy each piece of machinery twice, just in case something goes wrong. A side effect of these problems is that wine production is limited to the people already involved in the island. Outsiders are generally not willing to make such large-scale investments in semi-remote places like Cephalonia, where the returns on investment will not be as impressive as elsewhere. Thus, the potential of the region is drastically reduced and the only way forward is for locals to produce top-quality wines and to promote them skilfully. For Cephalonian producers this is not a choice but a necessity.

Robola of Cephalonia OPAP

White still: dry.
White variety: Robola.

Muscat of Cephalonia OPE

White still: naturally sweet (*vin naturellement doux*); fortified sweet (*vin doux naturel*); fortified sweet from selected vineyards (*vin doux naturel grand cru*); sweet (*vin doux*).
White variety: Muscat Blanc.

Mavrodaphne of Cephalonia OPE

Red still: naturally sweet (*vin naturellement doux*).
Red variety: Mavrodaphne.

Côtes de Ainou TO

White still: dry.
White varieties: Tsaousi and Goustolidi must be at least eighty per cent of the blend, the balance being other local recommended and permitted grape varieties.
Red still: dry.
Red varieties: Mavrodaphne must be at least seventy per cent of the blend, the balance being other local recommended and permitted varieties.

Metaksata TO

Red still: dry.

Red varieties: Mavrodaphne must be at least sixty per cent of the blend; Araklino up to twenty per cent; Korfiatis up to twenty per cent.

Matzavinata TO

White still: dry.

White varieties: Goustolidi must be at least forty per cent of the blend; Tsaousi at least twenty-five per cent; Moschatella at least ten per cent, the balance being other local recommended and permitted grape varieties.

Rosé still: dry.

Rosé varieties: Goustolidi must be at least twenty-five per cent of the blend; Thiako at least twenty per cent; Tsaousi at least ten per cent, the balance being other local recommended and permitted grape varieties.

Red still: dry.

Red varieties: Mavrodaphne must be at least fifty per cent of the blend; Araklino at least fifteen per cent, the balance being other local recommended and permitted grape varieties.

PRODUCERS

DIVINO WINES

Pasada Kemamia, 280 83 Cephalonia. Tel/Fax: +30 267 106 9190.
Vineyards under contract: 4ha; production: 300hl.

A venture founded in 1996 by the very active oenologist Gerasimos Hartouliaris. Divino Wines is one of the very few wineries that produce both OPE and sweet wines, Muscat and Mavrodaphne, which are complex and quite developed on release. There is also a notable Robola OPAP.

DOMAINE FOIVOS

Thesi Paliki, Vouni Paliki, 282 00 Cephalonia. Tel/Fax: +30 267 102 9505.
Head office: Knossou 36, 153 44 Gerakas, Attica.
Tel: +30 210 661 7755/6152; Fax: +30 210 661 6153;
Website: www.domainefoivos.com; Email: info@domainefoivos.com
Vineyards owned: 5.7ha; production: 360hl.

Theodoros Orkopoulos bought the historic winery of Matzavino to establish Domaine Foivos in 1999. George Orkopoulos has in his charge some excellent sites planted with Moschatella, Mavrodaphne, Tsaousi, Thiako, Araklino, and Vostilidi, all cultivated organically. The combination of varieties, soils, and meso-climates is demanding and, as the Foivos team admits, a lot is learned every year. Low yields are helping them to get a better understanding of what potential exists.

The philosophy of Domaine Foivos is to focus on rare Greek varieties, and the range of products backs this up. A blend of Tsaousi, Vostilidi, Moschatella, and Muscat is found in different wines, starting with the basic Passe Partout, moving to Asfodelos and up to Miisi White, which is available in two versions: a standard one and an "organically grown". The last bottling is to my mind the winery's top white, better than the Foivos OPAP Robola.

Miisi Red is a complex blend of Thiako, Araklino, and Mavrodaphne, but Methisforos, an all-Mavrodaphne *cuvée*, is more layered. Foivos is one of the new wineries that plans to invest in the forgotten OPE of Cephalonia. Both Mavrodaphne and Muscat dessert wines are being produced or developed, the latter called Stalaktitis.

It is too early to judge the Foivos wines and it would be unfair to try to evaluate their potential based on current releases. Nevertheless, current examples are clean, well-made, and do show individuality and character. If the shy, softly-spoken and low key Orkopoulos sticks to his desire to constantly improve both vineyard and cellar, he could well emerge as one of the Ionian Islands' top wine producers.

GENTILINI WINERY

PO Box 137, Minies, Argostoli, 28 100 Cephalonia. Tel: +30 210 752 1187; Fax: +30 210 752 1346; Website: www.gentilini.gr; Email: gentilini@in.gr
Vineyards owned: 7.5ha; under contract: 20ha; production: 500hl.

After studying and working in marketing in the UK, Spiros Cosmetatos spent a few years in Stellenbosch before deciding on a change of career and starting Gentilini winery in 1984. Having developed his tastes away from the mainstream styles that were being produced in Greece at the time, let alone Cephalonia, he approached the venture with a fresh vision. He immediately recruited winemaker Giorgos Skouras, newly graduated from the University of Dijon, and together they started crafting steely, firm, high acid whites from both local and international varieties.

His groundbreaking approach was evident in the cellar as well as in the vineyard. On an island where bush vines were the norm, he was the first to try the Geneva Double Curtain trellis, a sophisticated, divided canopy-management system. He hired consultant winemakers from Bordeaux and South Africa and experimented with microvinifications of unusual wines which were released at record-breaking prices. For example, his eighty-case batch of Amano 1991, a sweet Muscat, was released in 1993 with a 11,000 drachmas price tag, equivalent to thirty-three euros and more than double the price of the most expensive Greek wine at the time. Gentilini Alto was a steely, age-worthy Sauvignon Blanc from a single, drip-irrigated vineyard. Cuvée Exceptionelle was a blend of twenty-five per cent early-harvest and seventy-five per cent late-harvest, barrel-fermented Chardonnay that combined high acidity and alcohol approaching the fifteen per cent mark. The Animus bottling was pure Robola with eleven per cent alcohol, no residual sugar, and more than eleven grams per litre of acidity.

Even in the late 1980s it was extremely difficult for a Greek wine-lover to appreciate the Gentilini style unless he or she had previously been exposed to the wines of the Loire, Chablis, or other Northern European dry whites. While sales at home proved problematic, this didn't stop overseas success. The wine called "Gentilini" received impressive critical acclaim from abroad and was the first Greek wine to be listed by noted London wine merchant, Justerini & Brooks.

In 1997, Mariana Cosmetatos, the daughter of Spiros, left her career in hotel management in the US to join the family business, together with her husband, Petros Markantonatos. Gabrielle Beamish, a British horticulturalist, was the full-time viticulturalist and winemaker, and this trio led Gentilini into one of the most spectacular transformations ever seen in Greece, not so much in quality, but in style and overall approach. Markantonatos even started buying tired bottles off the shelves in retail shops and restaurant around Greece in order to give the new wines a chance.

The change started in 1998, but the vintage that had the most significant impact was 2000. The wines became less aggressive, less mineral, less acidic, less extracted, more elegant, more flowery, and far more commercial without lacking substance. The "Spiros-era" Gentilini wines had been a bit more idiosyncratic, more individual, and with a few years of careful bottle-age, extremely complex. In some senses, those wines had been years ahead of their time.

Investing in the vineyards was judged as vital. In the plots around the winery, with an impressive quarry just a few hundred metres away vividly displaying the high limestone content of the soil, the Geneva Double Curtain system was abandoned because the soils were not fertile enough to properly support the big vines. The Vertical Shoot Positioning trellis system was adopted instead. The Gentilini vineyards remain one of the few linear plantations on the island.

The viticultural expert Haroula Spinthiropoulou was invited to evaluate existing varieties and clones as well as the potential of the planted sites. Along the way Spinthiropoulou found some unidentified clones of Fileri as well as Asprofilero ("white Fileri"), Mavrofilero ("black Fileri"), and Moschofilero. Even if all the berries on some vines were at the same level of analytical maturity, some of these had significant within-bunch colour differences. It has been suggested that this is a rootstock-scion interface problem, rather than a clonal characteristic. Certain plots of Moschofilero were switched to Syrah, with a few interesting experiments of intergrafting, a form of field grafting made along the way.

Field grafting is a method of changing the fruiting variety of an existing vineyard, where the scion of the new variety is grafted on top of a freshly cut trunk of the American rootstock, with the whole upper part of the original vine being removed. In intergrafting, a small part of the trunk of the previous variety is retained and the scion is grafted onto that, and not directly onto the wood of the American rootstock. It is believed by some people, like California's Randall Grahm of Bonny Doon, that interstocks can have an important influence on quality. The experiments in Gentilini vineyards have not yielded any conclusion regarding quality of fruit – it is early days. Nevertheless, it is certain that leaving a few centimetres of Moschofilero wood between the R110 rootstock and the Syrah buds facilitated the rapid growth and vigour of the scion and the new plant became fully established in just three vintages, while conventionally grafted vines tend to need four to five years. In addition the extra height made weeding around the plants less important for the health of the graft.

The Gentilini team wanted to establish some Syrah vineyards so that the winery's all-white portfolio would be augmented by at least one red wine, preferably a top-quality, premium-price label. Thus, a Syrah was first pro-duced with the 1999 vintage, when twenty crates of grapes gave enough must to ferment in a glass demijohn. From the 2000 vintage, the Syrah grapes have been co-fermented and co-extracted with ten to fifteen per cent Mavrodaphne. The maturity of the varieties differs. In 2000, the Syrah was harvested ripe enough to have a ten per cent berry shrivel, while the Mavrodaphne was close to twelve per cent potential alcohol. The result was a wine with 15.2 per cent alcohol and a relatively low pH of 3.3. Following advice from Rob Easthope from Rustenberg in South Africa, in 2001 the two varieties were vinified separately and total alcohol levels were moved down to 14.5 per cent. This wine proved good enough to become a cult among Athens sommeliers and to be included in the "Top 100" of Tom Stevenson's Wine Report 2004 (Dorling Kindersley). Beyond this Syrah/Mavrodaphne blend, there are plans for a cheaper, non-oaked, fresh red, possibly based on brought-in Agiorgitiko grapes from Koutsi in Nemea.

The Gentilini Robola OPAP fruit is sourced from vineyards on the slopes of Mount Ainos, at an altitude of 600 metres or higher (1,968 feet). Fruit is bought in from a core of ten growers who are paid in cash to secure Gentilini a say in cultivation, especially after *veraison*. Different altitudes (600, 650, and 800 metres; 1,968, 2,132, and 2,624 feet) are fermented separately, with fruit from the highest altitude, terraced, and very steep sites giving wines of stunning elegance. Each "altitude *cuvée*" is split into two, with one batch fermented with *Saccharomyces cerevisiae* yeasts that produce the classic Robola flavour profile, and the rest fermented with *Saccharomyces bayanus* for more complex and intense aromas. The Gentilini Robola is clearly one of the best examples of the variety.

Gentilini Classico, the winery's first label, is a complex blend of mainly Tsaousi, with twenty per cent Robola, ten per cent Sauvignon Blanc, and ten per cent Moschofilero to counterbalance the low acidity of the main component and add complexity. The "new-style" Fumé is fifty per cent Chardonnay and fifty per cent Sauvignon Blanc, but the alcohol is lower, around thirteen per cent, with only twenty-five per cent being barrel fermented. The rest is fermented in stainless steel and aged in one-, two- and three-year-old oak barriques. Only 3,000 bottles are produced from a single vineyard that usually yields around twenty-five hectolitres per hectare.

Gentilini was one of the first wineries in Greece to experiment with plastic corks in the late 1990s, the main reason being the desire to break into the UK market. Oddbins' marketing and buying director Steve Daniel, a big advocate of synthetic closures, strongly recommended that all the whites at least, should be bottled under plastic. The first attempts were on export-only batches since, at the time, the Greek market, especially the crucial Cephalonia restaurant scene, was too conservative. Markantonatos started packing twelve-bottle cases with half-natural and half-synthetic corks on a trial basis for the local restaurateurs. Soon after the initial shock faded, Gentilini began receiving more orders for plastic-sealed bottles, given that returns of these from diners were minimal as problems of oxidation were reduced. Since the 2003 vintage, all the whites and a small-production Moschofilero rosé have been sealed with Supremecorq. Following concerns about the ageing ability of synthetic closures, the next step is now being considered: Markantonatos is promoting Stelvin-capped whites from New Zealand in local restaurants and closely monitoring consumer reaction.

ROBOLA OF CEPHALONIA COOPERATIVE

PO Box 56, Omala, Argostoli, 281 00 Cephalonia. Tel: +30 267 108 6301;
Fax: +30 267 108 6481; Website: www.robola.gr; Email: robola@aias.gr
Vineyards under contract: 300ha; Members: 260+; production: 8,000hl.

The biggest producer of Robola on the island, the co-op produces more than seventy per cent of the Robola of Cephalonia OPAP wines. The co-op – which was formed in 1982, although the winery was not built until 1987 – followed the example of the successful Calliga Winery in dressing its basic Robola bottling in sacking. It still does a great job in producing an enjoyable Robola, particularly when the price is taken into consideration (lower than four euros a bottle retail). It is well-promoted all over Greece as well as many export markets. People within the organization believe that, with the exception of olive oil, Robola is the most dynamic Greek agricultural product on the export markets.

The premium OPAP Robola bottling is San Gerassimo, named after the eponymous monastery of the island's patron saint, just a few hundred metres from the winery. The heavy Bordeaux bottle and imposing label make one expect a rich, intense experience, and the wine doesn't disappoint. The co-op produces a substantial range of EO wines found throughout the basic tavernas in the tourist resorts around the island. A special mention must also be given to the Côtes de Ainou TO bottling. Possibly the most modern wine in the range, it is a blend of Goustolidi, Tsaousi, Robola, and the highly obscure Mothonios, a variety on the verge of extinction.

SCLAVOS WINES

Socratous 10, 282 00 Lixouri, Cephalonia.
Tel: +30 267 109 1930; Fax: +30 267 109 3169.
Vineyards owned: 5ha; under contract: 10ha; production: 260hl.

Evriviadis and Spiridoula Sclavos are two of the first people in Greece to convert their whole estate – where most of the vines are eighty-years-old – to Biodynamic cultivation. It has been organic since 1986, but the couple increasingly felt that organic cultivation was being used mainly as a marketing tool rather than as a route to better quality, so in 1996 they embraced Biodynamism, the no-compromise alternative. The conversion was easy in some respects, since Cephalonia is a place where climate is forgiving, and difficult in others, given the relative isolation, but the fact that Evriviadis was a trained viticulturalist certainly helped.

Nearly a decade after the conversion, the results are considered more than promising. For example, Evriviadis has found that the active calcium in the vineyards – the proportion of calcium in the soil that can actually be used by the vine roots – stands at forty per cent, more than double the previous figure. In addition, varieties like Vostilidi can reach ripeness levels of up to seventeen per cent potential alcohol, even in cooler vintages like 2004.

The focus is totally on local grapes and in presenting them in unique ways, like the 2,000 bottles of white Metagitnion produced annually from ultra-ripe Vostilidi with its usual fifteen per cent alcohol and over thirty grams per litre of residual sugar. The attention to detail is carried over to the winery. There is a low-input winemaking philosophy, using only natural yeasts, with no fining or filtration. The estate wines are made without using any sulphur dioxide. High-quality, healthy fruit is important, and a sorting table is used at grape reception. This winemaking approach demands a certain degree of understanding on behalf of the consumer. "We suggest that our white wines are not consumed cool, but at room temperature," says Evriviadis. "They are full of proteins and, when chilled, create protein haze. Nevertheless, we do not think that haziness or heavy deposit make our wines less good. In addition, we have noticed that our Biodynamic *cuvées* respond better to oxidation – even without the protection of sulphur dioxide, the open bottles develop over several days."

The Robola OPAP produced by Sclavos is sold under the brand name Vino di Sasso (Italian for "wine of stone"), the name used by Venetians for Robola, since the vines are practically growing on stone. It is sourced, when possible, from organic growers within the Robola area, but this is not always easy and never cheap. Other Sclavos dry whites are a lot more adventurous. Moampeles is a clean, ripe, dry Tsaousi. Efranor is thirty per cent Goustolidi and seventy per cent Moschatella; it is stainless-steel fermented and very close in style to a dry, light Muscat.

In addition, enormous effort goes into Mavrodaphne and Muscat wines. Idis is a Muscat of Cephalonia OPE, sun-dried for five days and aged in old oak for up to two years. Orgion is a dry Mavrodaphne made from bought-in grapes and aged in new Alliers oak for one year. Every year, 4,000 bottles are produced from Sclavos vineyards, labelled as "made from organically grown grapes". The standard *cuvée* is of high quality, even if it lacks the extra dimensions of the estate wine.

Sclavos wines are not for those who enjoy forward, fruity wines. The style is complex, multi-faceted, and quite oxidative, making appreciation very much a matter of personal taste. Even if some people are not keen on the style, it is fair to say that Greece needs more people like Sclavos – not charmed by what is popular, but willing to explore new possibilities.

VASSILAKIS WINERY

Valsamata, Argostoli, 281 00 Cephalonia. Head office: Thesi Triklino, Aghios Ioannis, 491 00 Corfu. Tel: +30 266 105 2440; Fax: +30 266 105 2166.
Vineyards owned: 3ha; under contract: 10ha; production: 525hl.
A family company established in 1995, based in Cephalonia but also trading wines from Corfu. There is a vast portfolio of EOs, but the best wines are the Cephalonia Robola OPAP, Mavrodaphne OPE, and Muscat OPE bottlings.

VITORATOS WINERY

Thesi Paliki, Matzavinata, Lixouri, 282 00 Cephalonia.
Tel: +30 267 109 4244; Fax: +30 267 109 2558; Email: vinvit@hol.gr
Vineyards owned: 3.4ha; production: 500hl.
Andreas Vitoratos started this venture in 1993, sourcing fruit mainly from his own vineyards around Matzavinata. There is a good Robola, a white Polismigos from Tsaousi, Vostilidi, and Moscatella, but the most interesting wine is a dry Mavrodaphne.

YIANNIKOSTAS METAXAS ESTATE

Mavrata, 280 82 Cephalonia. Tel: +30 267 108 1292; Fax: +30 267 108 1692;
Website: www.metaxaswinestate.com; Email: metwines@kef.forthnet.gr
Vineyards owned: 2.5ha; under contract: 10ha; production: 350–400 hl.
Yiannikostas Metaxas Estate is the brainchild of both Yannikostas Metaxas and his English-born wife, Martine. The history of the Metaxas family and its involvement with viticulture can be traced back at least two centuries, but the modern renaissance did not happen until the early 1990s. Yannikostas and Martine started a small family wine business as an alternative lifestyle hobby and became so involved that they built a small winery in 1996. The couple

remain the main driving force, with the assistance of the talented consultant oenologist, Efi Kallinikidou.

Metaxas was the first private producer to focus on the creation of a high-quality, premium-price Robola. He wanted to create an identity that was quite separate from what had already been established by Calliga and the cooperative. The Metaxas Robola was extremely promising from 1993 up to 2000, with the wine being one of the finest examples of the period. Kallinikidou played an important role in achieving this quality level and developing the style – clean, full of precision, extracted, and rich, without being angular or old-fashioned. The secret behind this quality could well be the careful selection of growers, most of whom were working with yields below thirty hectolitres per hectare.

The range has been expanded since the early days, with four table wines (EOs). Metaxas buys Agiorgitiko wine from Nemea as the basis for his dry red, Arethousa Krini, and his semi-dry rosé Zefyrou Pnoi. For whites, Metaxas uses only local varieties, sometimes as a blend, like the *demi-sec* Prokris. The last wine of the range is a dry white Elios, which is a rare 100 per cent Zakynthino, full of fruit and freshness.

In the early 2000s, a slight drop of quality was noticed and the whole range has moved towards higher sugar levels, less finesse, and more obvious fruit – moving away from the hallmarks that made the wines of Metaxas critically acclaimed. In 2005, increasing economic difficulties pushed the Metaxas family to seek a buyer for this venture.

LEFKADA

Although just off the northern tip of Ithaca and Cephalonia, Lefkada is closer in viticultural terms to Zakynthos, located further south. Connected to Central Greece by a bridge, the mainland's proximity affects the island's climate, especially during autumn and winter, where cold winds flow down from the Pindos Mountains. As expected, east-facing slopes are affected the most, and this effect is accentuated by the steepness of the island. Lefkada covers a relatively small surface area, but has the second-highest mountain of the Ionians, Elati, standing at 1,182 metres (3,878 feet).

Lefkada is a kind of oxymoron among the Ionian Islands in terms of the size of wine-grape vineyards, raisin production, and varietal composition. Although it is the smallest wine-producing island, it is the third-largest in vineyard area. Yet, even if the proportion of land dedicated to vines is high, wine production is not as important in financial terms as in Cephalonia. There is a corresponding situation with raisin production. The Venetians planted large parts of the island with vines for grapes to dry into raisins, but, despite a relatively successful export business in the nineteenth century, the Lefkada raisin never became as sought-after as that from Zakynthos. This safeguarded the wine-grape vineyards, which have been left almost undisturbed.

Regarding varieties, while Cephalonia, Zakynthos, and even Corfu could be described as ampelographical jungles, the vineyards in Lefkada are surprisingly mono-varietal. The dominating variety here at over ninety per cent is the red Vertzami. A variety of Italian origin, possibly Trentino, Greeks relate it to Lefkada to such a degree that a common synonym is Lefkaditiko. Apart from Lefkada, Vertzami is found in Corfu and on western parts of mainland Greece, like Preveza and Patras.

Vertzami is a deeply pigmented grape with thick skins, small but very dense clusters, and the ability to reach high levels of sugars (*see* Chapter 5, page 76). Since it is a late-ripening variety, it responds badly to high altitudes, at least in the terroir of Lefkada. In vineyards above 500 metres (1,640 feet), ripening is delayed until late September. At that time of the year, the cold winds start blowing and, therefore, sugar accumulation is seriously hindered. In lower sites, Vertzami still takes a relatively long time to mature, but reaches potential alcohol levels above thirteen per cent at least two weeks earlier.

Regardless of the Vertzami dominance, there are small quantities of other varieties that are usually lost in the blends of the local co-op. Some of these have emigrated from the mainland, like Malagousia, Lagorthi, Mavrodaphne, and even Merlot, but other varieties are to be found in few regions other than Lefkada. For example, there are some plants of Vardea, a very neutral, low-acidity white grape (not to be confused with the Verdea OKP classification), Glikopati, a high-sugar, high-acid red grape, Thiako, one of the few vines that can be successfully cultivated at Lefkada's high altitudes; and Chlores. The latter is an old white variety, possibly originating from Zakynthos – very sensitive to drought, but vigorous and fertile. Harvest takes place in late August and sugar levels are high while retaining decent acidity.

Lefkada TO

White still: dry; semi-dry; semi-sweet.
White variety: Verdea.

Rosé still: dry; semi-dry; semi-sweet.
Red still: dry; semi-dry; semi-sweet.
Rosé/Red varieties: Vertzami; Merlot.

PRODUCERS

COOPERATIVE OF LEFKADA

Head office: Golemi 5-7, 311 00 Lefkada. Tel: +30 264 502 2319;
Fax: +30 264 502 5898; Email: taol@otenet.gr
Vineyards under contract: 580ha; Members: 4,000; production: 8,000hl.

With its membership of nearly 4,000, the Cooperative of Lefkada is the major force of wine production on the island. Most wine is sold locally and to tourists. The main variety is Vertzami, although small quantities of Vardea can be found. The top of the line range is called Agiomavritikos, consisting of white, rosé, dry red, and semi-sweet red wines, all of which are soft, reliable and show some fruit.

LEFKADITIKI GHI

Simvros, Vassiliki, 310 82 Lefkada.
Tel/Fax: +30 264 503 9139; Email: robotis@acn.gr
Vineyards owned: 1.1ha; under contract: 0.8ha; production: 1,100hl.

Established in 1999, it has only taken a few years for Lefkaditiki Ghi (meaning "Lefkada's Soil") to be considered the island's best wine producer. This could be due to Dimitris Robotis' serious commitment to developing vineyards, whether his own or under contract. The emphasis in purely on dry styles and focused on just two Lefkada TO wines: the Lefkaditiki Ghi White and Red. Special mention must be made to the white Lefkaditiki Ghi, a rare, pure Vardea that has already won awards in the International Wine Competition of Thessaloniki as "the best wine of the competition produced from a rare Greek variety". Both wines are modern in style, not rich, but quite extracted, and focused. The white might be more well known, but the red gives a good template of what Vertzami from Lefkada should be.

VERTZAMO WINERY

Ligia, 311 00 Lefkada. Tel: +30 264 507 1268; Fax: +30 264 507 1544.
Vineyards under contract: 32ha; production: 3,200hl.

A large producer in Lefkada, but still less than half the size of the co-op, Vertzamo Winery has much in common with the co-op, relying at it does on many vine-growers, quite a few of whom are under contract. Vertzamo is the island's only major exporter, particularly to Germany. The winery produces possibly Lefkada's only noteworthy retsina. The wines are dry and their character is a cross between that found at the cooperative and Lefkaditiki Ghi. The lower-tier range is called Vertzamo, but the two Lefkada TOs, Lefkadios White and Red, are fruitier and rather better.

CORFU

Located at the northern edge of the Ionian Sea, Corfu is the largest of the Ionian Islands. Some parts lie closer to the shores of Albania than Greece, but it is the relative proximity of the Adriatic Sea and Italy that makes Corfu particularly popular with Italian holidaymakers. Indeed, tourism is the main source of income for the island, with the vast majority of young and middle-aged people being involved in this sector. In strict financial terms, abandoning the hospitality industry and getting involved in viticulture makes no sense. It is fortunate that the relatively large size of the island leaves enough space for vineyards to exist harmoniously with hotels, bars, and swimming pools. Nevertheless, it is debatable whether the manpower needed to work these vineyards during the growing season will be available in the future.

There is a distinct topographic variation between the south and the north of the island. The only mountain, Pandokratoras, shields the island from the north, while the rest of the island is relatively flat. Red varieties are mostly planted in the north, where soils are heavier and vineyards are generally planted on slopes. In the southern part, the average altitude is close to sea level, soils are coarser, and white grapes dominate plantings.

The first aspect of the weather on Corfu that springs to mind is humidity. Often the local weather station will record precipitation without any rain actually falling. All year long, damp weather is the norm, to the extent that moisture can affect the health of susceptible members of the population. The same happens to sensitive vines, and it is no coincidence that the prevailing varieties on the island are relatively resistant to high humidity conditions.

The vineyard area is dominated by two varieties, the white Kakotrigis and the red Petrokoritho. *Kako* means "bad", or specifically "difficult" in this instance, and *trigis* means "harvest", telling us that the stems of the variety are hard and removing them from the vine is difficult. Kakotrigis wines are rich in alcohol, moderately high in acidity, and the colour has a green tinge, possibly due to the green colour of the shaded sides of the berries, to be found even in very high levels of maturity. This is a grape that gains enormously in flavours after a certain amount of hang time, but local growers rarely wait as long as they might since Kakotrigis is very sensitive to insect bites. Another kind of within-bunch differentiation, this time concerning ripeness, is seen in Petrokoritho. The vine is extremely vigorous but open canopies favour high sugar accumulation. Nevertheless, a proportion of less ripe berries guarantees a good backbone of acidity and fresh, if not herbaceous, aromas.

Varieties of minor importance in Corfu include opposite-colour versions of the dominating cultivars (red Kakotrigis and white Petrokoritho), where the vines act in a similar way, Robola, White Muscat, Mavrodaphne, Roditis, and Skopelitiko, a moderately vigorous, moderately productive red variety that gives wines with high sugar levels and excellent acidity.

The two most important producers of Corfu, Theotoky and Livadiotis, are really boutique wineries – their annual production is less than 25,000 bottles. At such small ventures, wine-growers manage to achieve great attention to detail, but there is still room for improvement, especially in the cellar. In the vineyard, modern viticultural techniques that would assist understanding and help growers to realize the potential of a variety could improve quality standards significantly. Looking into the habits of each different variety, fine-tuning the trellis and canopy-management systems, and timing the harvest more accurately would be invaluable.

Kerkira TO

White still: dry.
White variety: Kakotrigis must be at least sixty per cent, the balance being other local recommended and permitted grape varieties.

Halikouna TO

White still: dry.
White variety: Kakotrigis.

PRODUCERS

LIVADIOTIS WINERY

Thesi Halikouna, Aghios Matheos, Kastellana, Messi, 490 84 Corfu.
Tel/Fax: +30 266 102 8482.
Vineyards owned: 1.5ha; under contract: 3ha; production: 170hl.

Livadiotis is the second most important winery of Corfu and a total contrast its rival, Theotoky Estate. Sotiris Livadiotis has built a low-profile, but healthy business over the last fifteen years, improving steadily with each vintage. Located in the south, the vineyards focus on white varieties like Kakotrigis, the rare Xipleko, a grape which is full of extract and body but lacks primary fruit and intensity, and the white version of Petrokoritho. The only red grape grown is Skopelitiko. Nevertheless, certain varieties are sourced from nearby vineyards.

The two EO wines, Livadiotis Red and Livadiotis Xipleko, are well made, with the latter being a unique curiosity. The rest of the portfolio is made of two whites: a Livadiotis TO of Halikouna white and a TO of Corfu. Both are full of character, intense, and rich in texture – they stand a league apart from what Corfu was thought capable of. A most promising winery for the future.

THEOTOKY ESTATE
Livadi, Karousssades, 490 81 Corfu. Tel: +30 266 105 1524.
Vineyards owned: 13.5ha; production: 150hl.

If Livadiotis Winery is the low-key venture of an ambitious, young entrepreneur, then Theotoky Estate is a flamboyant piece of the island's history. Although founded as a modern business in 1986, the estate has centuries of history and Count Theotokys is a descendant of one of the most famous and powerful families of the island. The estate is sometimes called Roppa Estate, since it is located in the valley of the same name. Wine is only a side-product of the estate – out of 120 hectares, only 13.5 are dedicated to the vine. The estate's animal farm and its dairy products are famous, as is its exquisite olive oil.

During the 1980s and 1990s, Theotoky wines were under-performing. All labels, including the white and the rosé, were aged in oak for substantial lengths of time, sometimes up to three years. As a result, the fruit was lost and the oxidative character was evident. There was a substantial variation from one vintage to the next, as well as from one bottle to the other, mainly due to erratic cellar management.

A welcome change occurred in 2001, when Yiannis Halikias, owner of the highly regarded Antonopoulos Vineyards (see page 356), took over the management of the winery. In the vineyards, old vines are being retrellised, different pruning systems are being tried out in order to pull the harvest forward, and soil management techniques are being introduced to improve drainage. In the cellar, long periods of oak maturation are now a thing of the past. Stainless steel is used, not because it is supposed to be the best solution in terms of quality, but because it is the best way to understand the grape varieties.

Research is ongoing as regards wine style. For example, in 2002 Kakotrigis was fermented and aged in oak; in 2003 it was just aged in oak; and in 2004 it saw no oak treatment at all. The conclusion was that the grape needs the oak to gain in body. Currently, the winery's red and white Theotoky are reserved and tight in character, but with developing aromas. Theotoky Red is light in colour and structure, while showing elegant oak flavours. It is made from Maltzavi, as Vertzami is called here, Skopelitis, Kozanitiko Red, a vigorous, productive vine that matures in late September, providing grapes with low alcohol and moderate acidity, and a few vines of Cabernet Sauvignon. All varieties are, at present, harvested in one pass and co-vinified, but this is likely to change in the future. The white is fuller in texture and the acidity sometimes goes below a pH of three. It is produced from a single vineyard that is interplanted with eighty per cent Kakotrigis and twenty per cent Robola. Kakotrigis ripeness is used as a guide to harvest time, therefore the faster-maturing Robola provides an extra layer of complexity. If the Theotoky Estate manages to achieve riper Kakotrigis, then the wine will gain a lot more presence and character.

7

Peloponnese

Located at the very end of the Balkan Peninsula, the Peloponnese forms the southernmost tip of mainland Greece. It is almost an island, since its only land connection with Central Greece was breached to create the Canal of Corinth. To the east of the canal lies the Gulf of Saronikos, close to the busy port of Pireaus and Athens. On the west is a long thin strip of sea separating the Peloponnese from Central Greece. Just east of the city of Patras lies the closest point between the two departments: Rio in the Peloponnese and Antirio in Central Greece. In 2004, a bridge was finished, linking the two and marking one of Greece's most important infrastructure works. The stretch of sea beyond Patras towards the Ionian Sea is the Gulf of Patras.

GEOGRAPHY AND CLIMATE

The Peloponnese is shaped rather like a hand, similar to Halkidiki. The "thumb", in the northeastern part touches on the Corinth Canal and includes Nafplio, while the three "fingers" are, from west to east, Messinia, Mani, and Laconia, leading respectively to Capes Akritas, Tenaron, and Maleas. The complex shape and shorelines of the region give it a varied topography. In general, the Peloponnese is a very mountainous zone. Across the whole department, there are seven peaks close to an altitude of 2,000 metres (6,560 feet) or more. Apart from regions near the coast and between the mountains, there are few substantial low altitude areas; one plain on the northwest, between Patras (Achaia) and Pyrgos (Ilia), another around Kalamata in Messinia, and one in Laconia between Sparta and Gythio. Despite there being very few fertile areas where "large" crops can be grown, agriculture is a major occupation for the local population, even if it cannot generate substantial levels of trade and economic growth.

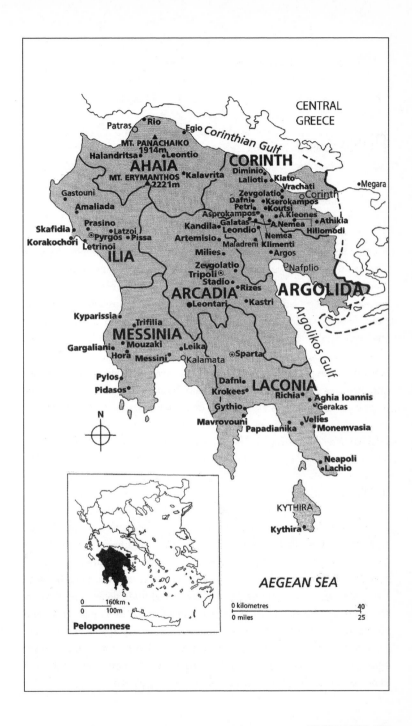

CENTRAL
GREECE

Patras
Rio
Egio
Corinthian Gulf

MT. PANACHAIKO
1914m
Halandritsa
Leontio
CORINTH
AHAIA
MT. ERYMANTHOS
2221m
Kalavrita
Diminio
Lalioti
Kiato
Vrachati
Corinth
Megara
Gastouni
Zevgolatio
Dafni
Kserokampos
Amaliada
Petri
Koutsi
Asprokampos
A.Kleones
Athikia
Prasino
Galatas
A.Nemea
Hiliomodi
Skafidia
Kandila
Leondio
Nemea
Korakochori
Pyrgos
Latzoi
Pissa
Artemisio
Maladreni
Klimenti
Letrinoi
Milies
Argos
ILIA
Zevgolatio
Nafplio
Tripoli
Stadio
Rizes
ARGOLIDA
ARCADIA
Leontari
Kastri
Kyparissia
Trifilia
Argolikos Gulf
MESSINIA
Mouzaki
Leika
Gargaliani
Hora
Messini
Sparta
Pylos
Kalamata
Pidasos
Dafni
LACONIA
Krokees
Richia
Aghia Ioannis
Gythio
Gerakas
N
Mavrovouni
Velies
Papadianika
Monemvasia

Neapoli
Lachio

KYTHIRA

Kythira

AEGEAN SEA

0   160km
0   100m
Peloponnese

0 kilometres   40
0 miles   25

It is especially difficult to generalize about the climate here. Overall, the area is one of the southernmost parts of Greece, falling between the latitudes of 38.15 and 36.17 degrees – only Crete, Rhodes, and a few other Aegean Islands are further south. The climate can be considered broadly Mediterranean, with mild winters, short springs, hot and dry summers, and prolonged autumns. Nevertheless, the Peloponnese is exposed to all sorts of influences: it is affected by the Meltemia winds of the Aegean, unsheltered from either the cold northern winds or the hot Livas blowing from Africa. Since the rain-bearing clouds travel in an easterly direction, the western part of the district is much more humid than the rest. For example, Pyrgos in Ilia receives an annual average of 920 millimetres of rain (thirty-six inches), Mantinia, in the centre, has 780 millimetres (thirty-one inches), and Nemea, less than fifty kilometres further east, just 410 millimetres (sixteen inches).

These vast permutations of altitudes, slopes, and exposures, and the presence or absence of the sea's influence create numerous different meso-climates. For example, overall Tripoli might receive less rain than Pyrgos, but from June to September, it gets ninety-three millimetres (3.6 inches) while Pyrgos receives about forty per cent less, just fifty-five millimetres (2.2 inches). However, over the same period, the average atmospheric humidity of Tripoli is thirty-five per cent lower than Pyrgos.

The Peloponnese is divided into seven administrative prefectures, six of which are located on the periphery of the region, with Arcadia in the centre. Running clockwise from the north, the prefectures are: Achaia, Corinth, Argolida, Arcadia, Laconia, Messinia, and Ilia.

HISTORY

The Peloponnese must surely have been one of the first places on earth to systematically grow grapes and make wine. We know that viticulture has been present for at least 4,000 years – some claim as long as 7,000 years. Although export success came later than for the Aegean Islands and Thrace, it outlasted many of these regions. The high point came during the Middle Ages, when the port of Monemvasia became world-renowned as a source of the famous Malvasia wine. Monemvasia remained vital for the Malvasia trade at least until the sixteenth century, even if, by that time, other Aegean Islands had become equally important. The next two centuries under Ottoman rule were extremely difficult, and viticulture was neglected. People began relocating to the key coastal areas, bringing vineyards with them.

A turning point in the viticultural history of the Peloponnese was the development of raisin plantations just after the end of the Ottoman rule in 1828. These lasted until the end of the phylloxera crisis (*see also* pages 25 and 269). The region of Corinth was home to Corinthiaki, a variety capable of producing excellent raisins. At the time, the Peloponnese and the Ionian Island of Zakynthos had the exclusivity on Corinthiaki production. Thus, booming sales persuaded vine growers to plant more Corinthiaki vineyards. Corinthiaki vine is a difficult plant to grow: it is highly sensitive to all fungal diseases and responds very badly to rich soils, high-capacity sites, crowded canopies, and high crop loads. In essence, Corinthiaki requires top terroir and careful viticulture. Consequently, all wine grapes have been uprooted from the best parcels of land to make room for more Corinthiaki. Even today, a century after the end of Corinthiaki's Golden Age, there is no dilemma in a grower's mind – planting a site with Corinthiaki can be as much as three times more profitable than growing wine grapes, even if the latter attracts top prices. This has been the area's vine-growing curse. It is certain that without Corinthiaki the Peloponnese would have been a different, more diverse wine region.

Despite the difficulties, vine-growing persisted in the Peloponnese. Real growth emerged after World War II, mainly in the centre and the north, in Patras, Mantinia, Nemea, and the Corinthian coast. The south remained involved in wine production, but with a lack of substantial investment and no commercially important wineries – most wine grapes were simply used to cover home consumption. The situation has, however, been changing rapidly over the last twenty years. Currently, the Peloponnese is home to numerous leading producers and several high-calibre, volume-oriented wineries. Even important companies like Boutari and Tsantali from northern Greece have been taking an interest in the region. Wine production is constantly developing in diverse ways, from the expansion of long-established, high-quality appellations like Nemea, to the exciting advances of forgotten regions like Laconia.

REGIONS AND CLASSIFICATIONS

Traditionally, Nemea was the only red grape zone in the Peloponnese, an area otherwise dominated by white- or pink-skinned varieties, like Roditis. The region is dominated by numerous indigenous varieties – a viticultural Noah's Ark, exceeded only by the island of Santorini in terms of the density of assorted vines. Wine grape vineyards total close to 22,000 hectares, and each prefecture has significant vine plantations, making the Peloponnese second only to Central Greece in terms of wine production. Laconia has the smallest vineyard surface area at just 685 hectares. More than half of the Peloponnesian vineyards are located in Achaia and Corinth.

Legislation granted the Peloponnese six quality wine appellations (*see* Chapter 4). Out of these, four are found in the prefecture of Achaia: the OPEs of Mavrodaphne of Patras, Muscat of Patras, and Muscat of Rion Patras, plus the Patras OPAP. Of the other two, one is in Mantinia, Arcadia, and the other in Nemea, split between Corinth and Argolida.

With the exception of Moschofilero wines that display an almost cool-climate elegance, there is a distinct Peloponnese style in most of its wines. The character vividly proclaims the Mediterranean origins, being full of ripe fruit, coupled with herbs and sweet spices, broadness, power, and warmth on the palate, while not being heavy. The producers of the area have traditionally been afraid to harvest their grapes late, so alcohol is modest by the climate's standards, rarely exceeding thirteen per cent. Nonetheless, more and more people nowadays are willing to go for higher ripeness, both with local and international varieties.

Another important aspect is acidity: the wines of the Peloponnese are by no means deficient in acid, even if some grapes, like Agiorgitiko, manage to mask the pH level with their structure. By harvest time, most of the malic acid is already consumed by heat, at least with the red grapes, so local varieties seem to have been selected for their ability to sustain good levels of tartaric acid. Overall, the Peloponnese wines have a lower pH than equivalent wines from Spain or Australia, bringing them closer to southern Italian examples.

Peloponnese wine producers have been very active in promoting their extensive wealth of terroirs, appellations, and grapes, as well as some stunningly picturesque villages and numerous archaeological sites. The local wine producers' union has traditionally been less high-profile than its counterpart in Macedonia, but much ground-work has been done. An important development has been the Wine Roads of the Peloponnese, much in the same vein as the Wine Roads of Northern Greece. There are seven branches, each corresponding to a different prefecture.

Peloponnese TO

White still: dry.
White varieties: Assyrtico; Moschofilero; Lagorthi; Malagousia; Roditis; Robola; Chardonnay.

Rosé still: dry.

Red still: dry.

Red/Rosé varieties: Agiorgitiko; Cabernet Sauvignon; Cabernet Franc; Merlot; Syrah.

CORINTH

Corinth lies at the northeast tip of the Peloponnese, connecting it with the rest of mainland Greece. Its northern coasts touch the Gulf of Corinth while the east reaches the Saronikos Gulf. The prefecture borders Argolida to the south, Achaia to the west, with a narrow corridor, close to Kandila, where Corinth borders Arcadia.

For administrative purposes, there is a small area beyond the Corinth Canal, including roughly half of Gerania Mountains, which belongs to Corinth rather than Attica. The capital is the City of Corinth, with most of the population living along the coasts of the Gulf of Corinth. One reason for this is that the prefecture's low-altitude plains are only found around Corinth and near the shoreline – most of the rest of the area is made up of gentle hills and slopes. To the west, Mount Kyllini's peak reaches 2,374 metres (7,790 feet).

Agriculture is a major occupation and viticulture is extremely important. Corinth is the major red wine supplier of Greece. In northern Greece, when a prefecture includes an OPAP, most vineyard plantings are usually made within the appellation. This is not the case in Corinth, however, or in the other Peloponnese OPAPs. The total vineyard hectares in Corinth is 6,137, out of which about a third, 2,123 hectares, is OPAP Nemea (a small section of the appellation is also in Argolida). There are two main facets to the Corinth wine industry: one is related to Nemea red wine production, and the other mainly deals with bulk wine from Roditis or multi-purpose vines – that is, those that can be used either for table grapes, raisin production, or for wine production. Of course, as smaller, high-quality producers arise every year outside the prime area of Nemea, there are diversions from this summary in most parts of Corinth. Apart from Nemea OPAP, there are no other quality-wine appellations in the area, just two TOs: the prefectural TO of Corinth and the TO of Klimenti.

The reds have it

Nemea and Naoussa in Imathia, Macedonia, are the two most important red wine appellations in Greece, in terms of quality, quantity, sheer number of wineries, and image. In many ways though, Naoussa and Nemea are very different; while the former uses Xinomavro, a variety producing potentially outstanding wines that consumers can find difficult to understand, Nemea is about Agiorgitiko, a grape that is pure charm in all its manifestations.

Taking its name from the old Nemea village of Aghios Georgios, meaning "St George", Agiorgitiko is close to most wine-drinkers' idea of a modern red wine. It has a great, deep, dark-ruby colour, persuading locals to call it "lion's blood", since mythology claims that Hercules killed a lion here in one of his most famous labours. The nose is full of sweet spices and ripe but fresh red berry fruit – sometimes more lifted and other times more extracted. There is a great affinity between the grape and high quality French new oak. The palate of Agiorgitiko is, or should be, soft and relatively full. In rosé wines there is an excellent acidity, while extracted reds can be tannic, but are never aggressive. However, Nemea is developing in many ways. Twenty years ago, a Nemea wine was all about softness and suppleness; nowadays, in the quest for the next "Great Greek Red", it is very difficult to find a serious Nemea that is not tannic. However, all expressions of the variety can, if properly made, be very convincing.

The appellation requests a maximum yield of ninety-four hectolitres per hectare (twelve tonnes per hectare). For the production of easy-drinking reds, Agiorgitiko can give excellent results at such levels but denser red styles require much less than this. Legislation only allows reds to be called OPAP – dry, medium-dry, or medium-sweet, although the last versions are hard to find. Rosés cannot be classified OPAP, which is a shame. The 2005 amendments to the legislation have broadened the ageing options for Nemea producers – previously it was mandatory to age in barriques for a year. As expected from the size of the appellation, there is a significant variation of terroirs, production standards, and finally, wine quality.

Weather and the three zones

The climate of Nemea is typically Peloponnesian: mild winters, summers with several days above 40°C (104°F), and long autumns. However, the harvest is one of the longest in Greece, with some parcels ripening around 20 September and others going well into mid- to late October – impressive for a mono-varietal appellation. Regarding rainfall, there is a big difference between these two months, with September having an average rainfall of 14.3 millimetres (0.6 inches) and October going up to 58.2 millimetres (2.3 inches). Under these circumstances, it is not just the ripeness levels of the grapes that dictate harvest time in Nemea, but also the timing of the heavy autumn rains. Rain-related harvests happen about four times every decade, at least for the later-ripening sites, while rainfall during August and September in 2002 destroyed the complete harvest.

Nemea, like Naoussa, is one of the appellations where special sites – *crus*, or sub-appellations – are fiercely debated. Most producers argue not about their existence – they are taken for granted – but how and if these names can be incorporated within the present legal framework. Nemea's consumers are one step ahead of Naoussa's. Whereas a Naoussa-drinker may be unaware of the significance of the names Trilofos and Gastra, Nemea wine-lovers are already seeking out wines from, say, Koutsi, possibly the champion of all Nemea *crus*, even if the name is only written on the back label.

Nemea includes the communes of sixteen villages and three distinct sub-regions, which are broadly classified by altitude. The first starts from the Nemea valley floor, at about 230 metres altitude (755 feet), going up to approximately 450 metres (1,476 feet). The next is a band of slopes ranging between 450–650 metres altitude (1,476–2,133 feet), while the last consists of the higher parts of the appellation, going up to 900 metres (2,953 feet).

The first zone is by far the hottest and has the richest soils, mainly red clay. Here grapes ripen the fastest and it is relatively easy to achieve fourteen degrees Baumé or above. In fact, the inclusion of sweet wines in the OPAP regulations was mainly because of these very ripe grapes and the possibility of using them in *vin de liqueurs* or other similar styles. The combination of fertile soils, high yields, high temperatures, and fast sugar accumulation leads to slow flavour development, and most vineyards in the area are suited to the production of lighter wines.

The middle zone is regarded as most suitable for modern wines: the "New Nemeas". Sites have a cooler meso-climate and lower water-availability limits yields. Indeed, in some areas vines can be very stressed in certain years and careful irrigation would do wonders in improving quality. Alcohol levels approach thirteen degrees, but some producers go higher through extra work in the vineyard to reduce yields and by taking risks, i.e. harvesting late. The fruit character from these altitudes is well-suited to making extracted and oak-aged wines. However, this zone is by no means homogenous. Aspect and topography can vary widely, as can soils. For example, Gymno and Koutsi are at about the same altitude, but the former has very infertile, stony soils and a steep gradient, while the latter has limestone and a relatively mild ascent.

The last zone relates to the highest parts of Nemea, dominated by the important Asprokambos plain. Standing between 750 and 900 metres (2,460–2,953 feet), Asprokambos is the coolest part of the appellation by far. The soils are mainly argilo-calcaire, and the area's cooler meso-climate has established its reputation as a prime source for rosé, due to high acidity and bright fruit character. However, nowadays many premium producers are becoming more interested in "cool" (by Peloponnesian standards) viticulture and show a renewed interest in premium Nemea. Top examples from Asprokambos show an impressive combination of excellent colour, fresh but deep fruit, velvety yet assertive tannins, and a notable but balanced acidity.

It will not be easy to firmly establish a scientific basis or a sound political framework behind any subdivision of the Nemea appellation. On the other hand, many producers, like Gaia, have already illustrated that there will be commercial advantages in allowing *cru* labelling in the region. Matters will develop regardless over the next decade, but they should leave room for everyone: large production wineries or high-volume blends will benefit from cross-zone blending. In contrast, premium products could work both ways. Single-vineyard wines will, without doubt, add much commercial spice to a grower's portfolio.

Despite the size and the complexity of the appellation, Nemea producers seem determined to promote their region in a unified way. This is extremely important since Nemea, on a collective, commercial, and volume-related level, is the major hope for a great Greek red wine breakthrough in export markets. The pan-Nemea trade tastings, Progefsi Nemeas ("Nemea *en primeur*") are an example of such a strategy. Since the 2003 vintage, growers have shown barrel samples of the new Agiorgitiko wines to all sectors of the trade seven months after the vintage. This event was organized by Nemea producers and Dinos Stergidis, one of the brightest minds in the world of Greek wine. Among other activities, Stergidis has set up Greece's only wine fair, Oinorama, started the first trade newspaper, *Ampelotopi*, and brought most wine writers under the umbrella of the Union of Greek Wine Journalists. So far, Progefsi Nemeas is not really run like the Bordeaux system, since there is no way to pre-buy the stock. Therefore, it is more of an *en primeur* tease than a full *en primeur* campaign, but hopefully it will not be too long before producers get out the order forms. Top Nemea wines certainly deserve to be among the most highly sought-after wines in Europe.

Nemea OPAP

Red still: dry, semi-sweet, sweet.
Red variety: Agiorgitiko.

Corinth TO

White still: dry.
White varieties: Roditis; Savatiano; Asproudes can be up to twenty per cent of the blend; Lagorthi; Assyrtico; Chardonnay; Sauvignon Blanc; Ugni Blanc.
Rosé still: dry.
Rosé varieties: Roditis; Agiorgitiko; Mavroudi; Cabernet Sauvignon.
Red still: dry.
Red varieties: Agiorgitiko can be up to twenty per cent of the blend; Mavroudi; Cabernet Sauvignon.

Klimenti TO

White still: dry.
White variety: Chardonnay must be at least fifty per cent of the blend, the balance being made up of other local recommended and permitted grape varieties.
Rosé still: dry.
Red still: dry.
Rosé/Red varieties: Cabernet Sauvignon must be at least fifty per cent of the blend; Agiorgitiko.

PRODUCERS

COOPERATIVE OF NEMEA

130 Papakonstantinou Avenue, Nemea, 205 00 Corinth.
Tel: +30 274 602 2896/2210; Fax: +30 274 602 3052;
Website: www.nemeanwines.gr; Email: contact@nemeanwines.gr
Members: 2,100+; production: 60,000hl.

The Cooperative of Nemea is one of the most important wine-producing organizations in Greece. Established in 1937, it was instrumental in keeping the viticultural tradition of the area alive and supported local *vignerons* through some of the most difficult times. Apart from its social importance, the co-op has provided many large wine-producers with good-quality bulk red wine at cheap prices, so the quality of many high-volume table wines can easily be attributed to its good practices.

A vital factor in the co-op's success is its head winemaker, Hristos Peppas, one of the most skilled, experienced, and talented oenologists in Greece. In addition, his deep understanding of the Nemea appellation is unmatched. It is remarkable that he succeeds in his job, bearing in mind that such an organization cannot refuse grapes from any of the growers, no matter how bad they may be. Crafting decent as well as excellent wines under such conditions is a true balancing act. Many true admirers of the appellation secretly hope that one day there might be a Peppas Estate.

The Nemea co-op crushes mainly Agiorgitiko, although some white wine is produced from Asproudes, the collective name used for a variety of unidentified white varieties with similar characteristics that are harvested and fermented together. Hercules is the basic line of dry wines, showing good quality for the price. Lais is the *demi-sec* equivalent. The standard Nemea is good, Special Nemea is better, and Reserva Nemea is excellent, a fine example of high-quality Agiorgitiko fashioned in the style that prevailed in the 1980s – though the wine is not at all old-fashioned and is extremely competitively priced. Once, a highly reputable Nemea producer said that it would be financially viable to buy the co-op's entire production of Reserva Nemea, stick his labels on, sell a great wine at his price and make a very decent profit. Maybe he should hire Peppas instead…

DIONYSSOS WINERY

18 Kolokotroni, 200 11 Lexaio Vrachatiou.
Tel: +30 274 108 6217; Fax: +30 274 108 6497.
Head office: 178 Vouliagmenis Avenue, 172 35 Athens.
Website: www.dionyssos-wine.gr; Email: info@dionyssos-wine.gr
Production: 60,000hl.

One of the prefecture's largest producers, matching the Co-op of Nemea in volume, Dionyssos is the oldest private winery in Corinth, founded in 1941. The general manager Yiannis Koutsouros focuses on bulk wine sales, being active in Athens as well as the Peloponnese. Dionyssos is the brand name of the basic products; the middle part of the portfolio feature some TO of Corinth dual varietals, mainly a white Roditis/Chardonnay and a red Agiorgitiko/Cabernet Sauvignon, and there are two OPAP labels, with the Nemea being far better than the Mantinia.

DOMAINE GIOULIS

Thesi Kambos, Klimenti, 200 17 Corinth. Head office: 4 Dimotikou Scholiou, 200 02 Velo. Tel: +30 274 203 3223; Fax: +30 274 203 3791; Email: gioulis@otenet.gr
Vineyards owned: 9ha; production: 300hl.

A small estate in Klimenti, outside the area of Nemea, but in the higher parts of central Corinth at 750 metres altitude (2,460 feet). Since 2005, the complete range is made from organically grown grapes. This domaine was established in 1993 and is the creation of viticulturalist Giorgos Gioulis who runs most aspects, from vine-growing to winemaking and marketing. Gioulis has worked hard to establish a legal framework within which his wines can be classified, something he finally achieved in 1996 with the TO of Klimenti. This encapsulates white wines that have to be at least fifty per cent Chardonnay, and reds made predominantly from Cabernet Sauvignon.

It is interesting to analyze how the high-altitude influences Gioulis' wines. His only white is a Chardonnay/Roditis blend: a fresh, crisp wine, showing less of the Chardonnay characteristics, which is planted at 1,000 metres (3,280 feet), and more of the Roditis. The basic red is a Cabernet Sauvignon/Agiorgitiko – a relatively soft, fruity blend.

The strength of the Gioulis portfolio, though, lies firmly in its straight Cabernet Sauvignon. Harvest takes place after 15th October, a full month past this grape's vintage date in many other Greek regions. Even at that point, the alcohol rarely exceeds 12.5 per cent. This might not be the most dense, intense, or complex example of Cabernet Sauvignon, but it does show an amazing *typicité*, far closer to a medium-bodied, relatively-light Bordeaux than anything else produced in the area. Keeping it for up to five years can add pleasant nuances of spices.

DOMAINE HARLAFTIS

Thesi Achladias, 205 00 Nemea. Tel: +30 274 602 4197;
Website: www.harlaftis.gr; Email: wines@harlaftis.gr

For full details, *see* Domaine Harlaftis on page 233.

This is the second winery of the Harlaftis/Athanassiadis family of Stamata, Attica, established in 1997. Diogenis Harlaftis had long seen Agiorgitiko as an important grape with a number of potential uses, two of which were to give character and quality to the winery's large-volume red and rosé blends, and to create some additional premium wines to match the Château Harlaftis Cabernet Sauvignon produced in Stamata. The move into Nemea was thus logical in order to secure supplies, and Harlaftis understood that to succeed in his quest to produce a top-quality Nemea, the purchase of his own vineyards was imperative.

Apart from the vinification of Agiorgitiko for the general needs of Domaine Harlaftis, the winery now makes two OPAP Nemeas. The first is Argilos Ghi – *ghi* here means "soil", so the name hints at argilo-calcaire soil, the predominant soil type around the winery. Argilos Ghi is a typical Nemea, with a balanced oak presence and a mild tannic structure. However, the wine that attracted most people's attention to the Harlaftis Nemea venture was its Nemea Reserve, an Agiorgitiko aged for more than eighteen months in new French barriques, followed by two years in bottle. The combination of the skills of winemaker Panos Zoumboulis and consultant Thanos Fakorelis gives an idea of the quality to be expected, although stylistically the wine seems more influenced by the powerful Fakorelis approach than the more elegant Zoumboulis touch. First released with the 2000 vintage, the wine is full of density and concentration without being too flashy or full-blown. Harlaftis Nemea Reserve will age gracefully for a decade or more and is undoubtedly one of the best debuts of the region in the last few years.

DOMAINE HELIOS

Semeli Wineries, Koutsi, Nemea, 205 00 Corinth. Tel: +30 274 602 0360; Fax: +30 274 602 0361; Website: www.semeliwines.com; Email: helios@semeliwines.com
Vineyards owned: 20ha; under contract: 90; production: 6,200hl.

For full details, *see* Semeli Winery entry on page 246.

Domaine Helios, or Salasco, as the company is officially named, was founded in 2000 with the first crush completed in 2003. The partners behind the venture are Giorgos Kokotos of the Semeli Winery in Stamata, and Mihalis Salas, managing director of the Piraeus Bank. Right from the start, every aspect of this endeavour has been imposing. The new space age winery was one of the most impressive in Greece, both aesthetically and functionally. It was also fully equipped with several luxurious bedroom suites, giving wine-related tourism in Corinth an unexpected twist. Since day one, Kokotos had a clear vision for Domaine Helios: the aim was to create a winery that could make large quantities of good-quality wines from Greek varieties at a price that could compete on the export markets – in essence, wines that could be considered by supermarket buyers and high-volume retailers around Europe and North America. Traditionally this has been the most difficult field for Greek wines to succeed in.

Domaine Helios wines started appearing in early 2004 and quantities from the first vintages were relatively limited. However, by the 2007 vintage, the winery should be producing more than 1.5 million bottles annually. The volume leading lines are Orinos Helios ("mountainous sun"), comprising an aromatic, floral Moschofilero/Roditis blend, and a straight Agiorgitiko with just four months in oak. Once again, because of the minimum ageing regulations, this has fallen under the Peloponnese TO classification. Orinos Helios OPAP 2003, a clean, fresh style of Nemea, was released in late 2004. The only other product in the pipeline is a Nemea Orinos Helios Réserve, which will be in the market in early 2007. Grapes used for this *cuvée* were harvested from estate-owned Koutsi vineyards. A tasting of barrel samples showed a broad structure and a very skilful extraction.

A notable feature of all Domaine Helios Agiorgitiko wines from the 2003 vintage is the marked presence of oak when fresh on the market, while some time in bottle tones down the woody aspect. This was inevitable, since it was the very first year of production – Semeli could not supply enough used barrels, with Kokotos being reluctant to buy any from other wineries, fearing a possible Brettanomyces infection. Therefore, the only possible option was to buy new barrels, a point appreciated by Nassiakos. In subsequent vintages, the new oak will be more in balance with the older wood.

DOMAINE VASSILIOU
Thesi Karfoksilia, Eparhiaki Odos Nemea-Dafni, Nemea, 205 00 Corinth.
Head office: 26km Avenue Lavrio, 194 00 Koropi, Attica.
Tel: +30 210 662 6870; Fax: +30 210 662 7686;
Website: www.vassilioudomaine.gr; Email: info@vassilioudomaine.gr
Vineyards owned: 10ha; production: 850hl.
For full details, *see* Domaine Vassiliou on page 234.

This is the Nemea estate of Giorgos Vassiliou, the successful wine producer from Attica. Most of Vassiliou's red wines were already heavily dependent on Corinth-sourced grapes, so it was only a matter of time before he set down roots in Nemea too. In 2001, he started a winery totally dedicated to Agiorgitiko. Most importantly, this went along with the purchase of an important domaine in middle-zone Nemea, planted with twenty-five-year-old vines. The site is now registered as organic and yields an average of around fifty hectolitres per hectare.

The domaine will still produce red wine for the Vassiliou Red, but its main focus will be an OPAP Nemea. The inaugural 2001 vintage for this new production facility was a distinct improvement in quality over previous years. However, 2003 was even more impressive. There have been two *cuvées* of this wine. The "standard" one following the style of the 2001, being fine-grained, spicy, and forward, but with extra complexity. The "special" was a fourteen per cent alcohol wine, with plenty of extract and a firm tannic structure, coupled with exotic fruit nuances. If this is an indication of where Vassiliou Nemea will be heading in the future, then we can expect some exciting wines.

DRIOPI ESTATE
Koutsi, 205 00 Nemea, Corinth. Website: www.tselepos.gr; Email: tselepos@can.gr
Vineyards owned: 5ha; production: 1,125hl.
For full details, *see* Domaine Tselepos entry on page 330.
Established in 2003 in the key Koutsi area, this venture has been much in the news for many reasons. Primarily, it was great to see Yiannis Tselepos, one of Greek wine's high-flyers, moving into Nemea. Previously he had been producing an OPAP wine from rented winery space which, although decent, was not on a par with the rest of his portfolio.

The second reason was that the new winery was a joint venture between Tselepos, Paris Sigalas from Santorini (Cyclades islands), and Alexandros Avatangelos – a wealthy entrepreneur who already owned a large share in Sigalas Estate, and was establishing Tiniakoi Ampelones, a pioneering venture on the island of Tinos. Moreover, Tselepos was establishing not just a winery but a fantastic estate, buying a prime cut of Koutsi land full of low-yielding, carefully managed thirty-year-old-plus vines.

Unfortunately, the plot was next door to the Gaia estate (*see* page 309), and it was a site that Gaia's owners, Yiannis Paraskevopoulos and Leon Karatsalos, had wanted to buy for some time. Thus began a heated dispute, the details of which are irrelevant, but which illustrates how top Greek winemakers are increasingly on the look-out for the best terroirs and are willing to fight even for a few additional top-quality hectares.

After the estate's acquisition, the experienced Tselepos team, headed by oenologist Takis Smirniotis and viticulturalist Vassilis Lolis, found that very few things in the vineyard needed fine-tuning; the first crush took place the same year. Nemea Driopi 2003 made its debut in the very first pan-Nemea trade tasting, Progefsi Nemeas (*see* page 302), creating quite a stir with its superb concentration and structure. On its later release the wine was still as extracted, but far more polished and fine-grained after its additional seven months in new oak and almost a year in bottle.

Totally unlike the previous vintages of Nemea Tselepos, Nemea Driopi is possibly the most age-worthy standard Nemea there is. However, Tselepos has another card up his sleeve: crafting small quantities of a Driopi Estate wine. Barrel-sample tastings point to a wine with the same style as the Nemea Driopi, but with several layers of complexity and a sophistication of the tannins. Eventually this wine will surely rank in the very top Greek wine division.

GAIA WINES
Koutsi, Nemea, 205 00 Corinth.
Tel: +30 274 602 2057; Fax: +30 274 602 206.
Head office: 22 Themistokleous Street, 151 22 Athens. Tel: +30 210 805 5642; Fax: +30 210 805 5542. Website: www.gaia-wines.gr; Email: gaiawine@acn.gr
Vineyards owned: 6.5ha; production: 2,250 hl.
See also Gaia entry on page 386.

A leading Nemea winery, established in 1994 by agronomist Leon Karatsalos and oenology professor at the Athens Technical Education Institute, Yiannis Paraskevopoulos. The two partners also have another venture in Santorini, producing equally impressive, ground-breaking wines with Assyrtico grapes.

The Gaia estate is an impressive vineyard in Koutsi, in the upper parts of the middle Nemea zone (*see* page 301) at 650 metres altitude (2,132 feet). The vines are twenty-five years old and yields are kept below fifty hectolitres per hectare. Great emphasis is placed on choosing exactly the right time for the harvest. The strategy is to pick the best grapes as ripe as possible before any increase in sugar levels (for fear of any grape dehydration). Karatsalos, Paraskevopoulos, and the young, gifted production manager, Dimitris Akrivos, meticulously keep an eye on every minute detail in the vineyard and the cellar.

The Gaia winery is predominantly about Agiorgitiko, but the non-Nemea wines should not be overlooked. Notios White is a youthful, light, crisp blend of Roditis and Moschofilero, with both grapes are handled reductively. While only the free-run juice of Roditis is retained, Paraskevopoulos wants an extra dimension from Moschofilero, so he takes its must up to 1.4 bars of pressure during pressing, as opposed to usual 0.2, in order to extract more solids and create a denser texture. The other white is Ritinitis Nobilis, easily the best retsina in Greece. Roditis from

Achaia vineyards yielding around seventy hectolitres per hectare is used to produce an excellent white that, by itself, could easily be one of the best Roditis in the Peloponnese. However, a small quantity, less than 0.5 per cent, of high-quality resin from Halepensis pines is added during the cool fermentation, creating a very clean wine, full of melon and mastic aromas (mastic is a gum from Mediterranean tree bark which is used in varnish and chewing gum, *see* page 425). It's a clever idea which demonstrates that a top-quality resin wine is not an oxymoron.

Beyond these two wines, Gaia is dedicated to showing all the fascinating aspects of the Agiorgitiko variety. The first step is a wine called "14–18 h", a rosé which is self-evidently macerated for fourteen to eighteen hours on the skins, resulting in a refreshing wine, bearing its 13.5 per cent alcohol with grace. The simplest red is Notios, meaning "southern", which shows Agiorgitiko's ability to produce charming, soft, early-drinking reds. The must is only macerated for six to seven days – an extremely short time by Paraskevopoulos' standards. Notios also gets a kiss of oak – just forty-five days – using barriques with a medium-plus toast to make a quick impact, while micro-oxygenation is utilized to soften the tannin structure. All of the Gaia reds get some degree of micro-oxygenization, with Notios receiving most. There is also a basic Nemea in the winery's portfolio, which is simply called Agiorgitiko. This receives full oak-ageing treatment and carries it off with subtlety. It shows a clarity and intensity of fruit that brings Chile to mind.

Gaia Estate is the producer's flagship wine and one of Nemea's icons. The very best parcels of the vineyard are carefully harvested at optimum ripeness, usually above 13.5 per cent potential alcohol. The next stage is crucial in the style of the final wine, especially since Paraskevopoulos is a master of extraction. In order to get the most from his grapes, he was one of the first in Greece to buy wooden open-top fermentors – an expensive but top-quality way of vinifying red wines. The maceration is stretched to its limits, to see how much extraction can take place, with constant vigilance to ensure no increase in coarseness. After three weeks to a month on skins, the wine is racked into new French oak barriques to go through malolactic fermentation and to mature for a year. After that, the wine is bottled unfined and unfiltered. Since its first release from the 1997 vintage, Gaia Estate has been a landmark for Nemea and has inspired many people working with Agiorgitiko to redefine their approach. Without losing any of the variety's character, it is as if it has brought a touch of Australia to Nemea. Despite this winemaking process seeming intense on paper, the wine itself is actually wonderfully elegant and requires ageing – not to acquire softness but to increase complexity. The wine won a red wine trophy in the inaugural *Decanter Magazine World Wine Awards* in the UK in 2004.

But the various manifestations of Gaia Agiorgitiko do not stop here. Karatsalos and Paraskevopoulos have decided to create a sweet wine from sun-dried Agiorgitiko. There are no plans for bottling it so far, but the wines from several vintages rest in oak in Gaia's cellars, with the winemaking team again checking how far they can stretch the various parameters. Greece needs more people like this.

GOFAS ESTATE

8 N Eustathiou, 205 00 Nemea, Corinth. Tel: +30 274 602 4281; Fax: +30 274 602 0045; Website: www.ktimagofa.gr; Email: gofaswines@ktimagofa.gr
Vineyards owned: 7ha; production: 90hl.

Established in 1959 at a time when only the local co-op and Kissas winery were active, the Gofas Estate was one of the region's pioneering private enterprizes. In the past, Konstantinos Gofas has been keeping a low profile, but, today it seems that he is entering a new, more extrovert phase. There are new products, new, more modern packaging, plus a whole new promotional strategy. Nonetheless, the overall size of the enterprise remains minuscule.

Gofas makes six wines: five varietals and one Nemea. His Roditis and Agiorgitiko are both Peloponnese TOs and are the simpler wines of the portfolio. A level up is the Gofas Cabernet Sauvignon and Sauvignon Blanc, with the latter bordering on the side of *demi-sec*. Château Dominique Syrah is a rare example of the variety grown in the Peloponnese, a good wine but possibly without much Syrah definition. The top wine is Gofas Estate, a Koutsi-sourced Nemea, full of power with a focused Agiorgitiko personality.

LAFAZANIS WINERY

Arhaies Kleones, Nemea, 205 00 Corinth.
Head office: 17 Sokratous, 190 18 Magoula, Attica. Tel: +30 210 555 5501;
Fax: +30 210 555 7674. Email: lafazani@otenet.gr
Vineyards owned: 5ha; under contract: 50ha; production: 3,500 hl.

The Lafazanis' involvement with wine began in 1958 in Piraeus, then moved to Magoula near Elefsina in Attica, where an important winery was created. This production site is still active and focuses mainly on bulk wines. Spiros Lafazanis, a qualified oenologist, took charge of the company in 1985 and eight years later started the Nemea winery. Currently, private vineyards are limited, but there are plans to increase them up to ten hectares.

Lafazanis Roditis and Lafazanis Agiorgitiko are the value-oriented wines – both unoaked, simple but very pleasant, and well-presented in their minimal packaging, especially the popular airline quarter-bottles (175 millilitres). The Sillogi Collection Lafazanis White is a well-made blend of Moschofilero and Roditis, while the red is a very good, barrique-aged blend of Agiorgitiko and Cabernet Sauvignon.

Lafazanis Nemea is the estate's most impressive wine, striking an individual stance. Although it is one of the more alcoholic Nemea wines, usually above 13.5 per cent, it shows a restrained oak presence, contrary to most examples of the "riper" school of thought. Lafazanis believes that oak, at least barriques, does not work well with Agiorgitiko, especially as regulations demand that the wine has to be aged for at least a year. Lafazanis abandoned barriques for his Nemea, moved to 300-litre barrels, and then settled for a capacity of 500 litres, achieving a remarkable balance. For his Nemea, Lafazanis is a champion of blending fruit from different parts of the appellation, using grapes from Arhaia Nemea, Arhaies Kleones and the occasional twist of Asprokambos freshness. He seems to be quietly but constantly refining his style. No marketing gimmicks – just real substance.

LAFKIOTIS WINERY

Arhaies Kleones, Nemea, 205 00 Corinth. Tel: +30 274 603 1244/1231;
Fax: +30 274 603 1361; Website: www.lafkiotis.gr; Email: lafkiotis@nethouse.gr
Vineyards under contract: 1000ha; production: 9,000–9,500hl.

Another winery in Arhaies Kleones dating back to 1960, this estate has developed into one of the relatively large private companies in Nemea, but there is a good balance between bulk sales and bottled products. There are no estate-owned vineyards, but quality is assured, thanks to most of the winery's needs being covered by long-term contracts with growers.

The portfolio starts with Kleoni White, Red, and Rosé, based on Roditis and Savatiano for the white and Agiorgitiko for the other two wines. The two OPAP single-varietals, an Agiorgitiko and a Moschofilero, are relatively reserved in style. Rodamo is a blend of Agiorgitiko and Cabernet Sauvignon, aged in French oak for eight months. The top wine, Agionimo, an OPAP Nemea aged in new French oak, shows more power than the other Lafkioti reds.

LANTIDIS VINEYARDS

Xerokambos, Nemea, 205 00 Corinth; Tel: +30 274 602 4056; Fax: +30 210 654 4905; Website: www.lantideswines.com; Email: lantideswines@hotmail.com
Vineyards owned: 5.1ha; under contract: 3.5ha; production: 1,800hl.

Panos Lantidis has been one of the most influential people on the Greek wine scene over the last two decades, helping to shape the character of Greek wine. However, this did not happen because of his wines, but because – together with Yiannis Tselepos of Domaine Tselepos – he became the importer of Nadalie's distinctive barrels from the Médoc (www.nadalie.fr). The company was among the first to import high-quality French oak. The heyday for new wood among local winemakers was the 1990s, and in 1993, seven years after Tselepos started his venture, Lantidis decided to get involved in winemaking himself. Slowly but steadily the Lantidis family worked harder on the raw materials and today quality is much better, especially with the red wine range.

Moschofilero Lantidis, a Peloponnese TO and this producer's only wine not to be aged in oak, has a light palate and a typical, Turkish delight nose. The Nemea OPAP is aged in oak for three more months than required by legislation – barriques are obviously not in short supply at Lantidis – but it does not show excessive oak. Hrysampelos is fifty/fifty Cabernet Sauvignon and Agiorgitiko and is one of the more tannic examples of this blend. Finally, Cava Lantidis, made from sixty per cent Cabernet Sauvignon, twenty per cent Merlot, and twenty per cent Agiorgitiko, stays in new oak for two years, followed by eighteen months in bottle. Not a wine for the long haul, but complex, rich, and ready to enjoy on release.

MARRAS WINERY

Zevgolatio, 200 01 Corinth.
Tel: +30 274 105 0066; Fax: +30 274 105 0222; Email: marras@otenet.gr
Vineyards owned: 5ha; production: 15,000hl.

This is a large producer in Corinth making substantial quantities of simple, easy-to-drink wines. Managing director Fanis Marras was one of the few people in Greece to take up the challenge of starting an intense advertizing campaign in the early 2000s, with hoardings, restaurant promotions, and other rather expensive strategic elements. Despite high sales, the image of the company could be a lot more visible among its peers.

OKTANA

Asprokambos, 205 00 Nemea; Tel: +30 274 105 1240; Fax: +30 274 105 1390.
Vineyards owned: 20ha; production: 3,200hl.
See also Katogi & Strofilia entries in on pages 194 and 239.

This winery, established in 1998, has quite a turbulent history. In the late 1980s and early 1990s, the Greek wine trade witnessed the rising of the Santa Maura star. Santa Maura has been one of the most important distribution networks in Greece, specializing in small and medium-sized wineries. The two owners, cousins Nicos and Yiannis Halikias, have been responsible for the successful introduction of many wineries that are currently among the premier division of Greek wine. By 1996, Nicos and Yiannis had acquired Antonopoulos Vineyards, following the untimely death of Konstantinos Antonopoulos, while the Santa Maura portfolio also included leading boutique producers like Katogi, Strofilia, and the Mercouri Estate.

All these wineries were, to a great extent, boutique wineries, with limited resources and expansion possibilities. However, the market was thirsty for their wines, particularly the reds. The Halikias' initial plan was to set up a large winery in Nemea that could provide Agiorgitiko red and rosé wines for existing or new labels in the partners' portfolios. The initial vintage was 1998, from which an Oktana Red and an Oktana Nemea were made as independent products.

Working out the fine details of such an intricate enterprise proved to be trickier than expected, and at a very early stage the Mercouri Estate pulled out, followed by Antonopoulos Vineyards and Santa Maura a few years later. In the early 2000s, the Katogi and Strofilia wineries decided to merge, incorporating the wineries in Metsovo, Anavissos, and Oktana, as well as starting a new distribution network. Currently, the Oktana winery turns to Katogi & Strofilia for all its crushing. Varieties other than Agiorgitiko, such as Roditis, Moschofilero, Cabernet Sauvignon, and Merlot, make up a significant proportion of the annual production.

PALIVOS ESTATE

Archea Nemea, Nemea, 205 00 Corinth. Tel: +30 274 602 4190;
Fax: +30 274 602 0191; Website: www.palivos.gr; Email: palivos@nethouse.gr
Vineyards owned: 28.5ha; production: 1,800hl.

One of the more low-key Nemea producers, but one who is always striving to improve his existing wines or to create notable new ones, Giorgos Palivos established this estate in 1995. His family has a long winemaking tradition in the area and Palivos mostly relies on his own vineyards to cover his requirements. The Nemea vineyards are found in the lower parts of the middle zone, giving good potential for age-worthy wines (*see* page 301). Great care has been taken in the cultivation of the vineyards, and Palivos is always open to new ideas. For example, he has planted a 1.5 hectare plot on its own roots rather than on American rootstocks, believing that the clay-deficient soil of the site will not allow phylloxera to develop. The first experimental vinification was in 2003 and preliminary results are most interesting, giving a flavour profile of Agiorgitiko that is slightly more exuberant than the other Palivos examples.

Ampelones Red, Rosé, and White are the value-oriented Palivos wines, all unoaked and based on the classic grapes of the region: Agiorgitiko and Roditis. Petrines Plagies ("Côtes de Petrines") is an unusual blend of Malagousia and Chardonnay, showing the aromatics of the former and some broadness on the palate from the latter. Intense *batonnage* in stainless-steel vats is a key ingredient of its style. Palivos Estate is the main Nemea bottling of the estate, belonging to the more elegant, less extracted school of thinking, which is also the approach for the Nemea Réserve, which has been produced since the 2001 vintage.

Conversely, the winery's top labels, the Terra Leone Single-Vineyard Selection, are in a fairly oaky, late-harvest style. There is a varietal Merlot and a Cabernet Sauvignon, from prime Nemea land, harvested in late September at fourteen degrees Baumé or higher, macerated for almost three weeks, and aged in new French oak for thirty-two and thirty-four months respectively. The first vintage was 2001 and these young wines are very difficult to evaluate at this early stage.

The Palivos portfolio concludes with Terra Leone Heliou Techni (the latter two words mean "Art of the Sun" in Greek), where Muscat Blanc grapes from Rio of Patras are sun-dried for ten days and cool-fermented until they reach fourteen per cent alcohol. The wine is surprisingly fresh, but not light.

PAPAIOANNOU VINEYARDS
Ancient Nemea, Nemea, 205 00 Corinth. Tel: +30 274 602 3138; Fax: +30 274 602 3368; Website: www.papaioannouwines.gr; Email: info@papaioannouwines.gr
Vineyards owned: 57ha; production: 5,000hl.

Nemea owes a lot to Thanassis Papaioannou. One of the first pioneers of the region, he started a small estate in 1984 and was one of the people to contribute to Greece's new wave of small wine producers. Unusually, he did not come from an oenological background like most of his counterparts, but he did have plenty of viticultural experience, including a spell working for Katogi (*see* Katogi & Strofilia, page 194). He is widely considered a master of vine-growing, with a strong feeling for terroir, its needs, and the most suitable variety. Evangelos Gerovassiliou says, "When he is in the vineyard, he is absolutely the best."

The largest part of Papaioannou's vineyard holdings is in Xirokambos, but he also has sites in six other villages of Nemea. Papaioannou makes the most of every single one, a fact illustrated when he started replanting some of these with carefully selected non-local vines: Assyrtico, Chardonnay, and even Pinot Noir – not to mention experimental blocks planted with up to thirty different varieties. He could not resist planting Cabernet Sauvignon, highlighting his Katogi connection.

Papaioannou might be a leader in viticulture, but he is a completely self-taught winemaker. That might not have mattered if he was a fan of rich, heavy, extracted wines, but he favoured fresh, intense, clean styles. The level of technical dexterity needed to produce wines of such character was attained when his son Giorgos returned after completing a winemaking degree. Now Thanassis' extreme care in the fields is matched by Giorgos' careful handling in the cellar.

Papaioannou wines are graceful and full of charm; even his two more powerful bottlings, the Fumé and Palaia Klimata, show a winemaking philosophy that aims at minimal intervention. Unexpectedly perhaps, the wines are also very commercial, full of silkiness and clearly defined primary fruit. In some ways Papaioannou is one of the most Burgundian-like *vignerons* in the Peloponnese.

The whites of Papaioannou should not be overlooked. The Ampelones Papaioannou is a firm yet fruity Roditis. Beyond that, there is a pair of Assyrtico wines and a pair of Chardonnays, one aged in oak and the other in stainless steel. The two Assyrtico wines are called Plagies Ai Lia ("Côtes de Ai Lia"). Here Assyrtico shows the firmness of Santorini, possibly without the steeliness and the extract, and is far less exotic than examples from Northern Greece. The wood-aged Plagies Ai Lia receives four months in French oak, partially new, and has often been criticized for being too oaky.

That may have been so in the 1990s, but later years have been more balanced. The unoaked Chardonnay, Poikiliakos, has enough texture that you could question whether or not it has indeed seen wood, while the Fumé is a full, rich, exotic, explosive wine.

Cabernet Sauvignon is also made in two bottlings. Driofilos is released younger, showing notable yet integrated oak without being too tannic. The non-vintage Cava Papaioannou is all about velvety complexity and is ready to drink on release. The Pinot Noir, Pinar, is a rarity in Greece. Provocative and truly enjoyable, it is soft and full of bright red-berry fruit, albeit without any real Pinot Noir character.

Papaioannou's apotheosis is Agiorgitiko, with many labels and quality steps that give Giorgos the ability to select the best grapes for the best use. The Ampelones Rosé leans towards texture rather than aroma. Papaioannou Agiorgitiko is a stainless-steel-aged, simple approach. The best parcels of Agiorgitiko are directed towards Papaoannou Estate, one of the most stylish yet understated Nemea wines.

Since 1996, the oldest parcel, with nearly forty-year-old vines, is vinified, aged, and bottled separately to become Palaia Klimata ("old vines"). Stating "old vines" in Greece was a novelty at the time, even if some producers were making some old-vine selections for top labels. In Palaia Klimata it is clear that intensity comes from the grape, not from any winemaking extraction tricks. When leading Greek wine writers were served Palaia Klimata blind, they thought it was a top-quality Rioja *reserva* – and in style and quality, they were pretty close. Finally in 2005 a small parcel of seventy-year-old vines was released as Mikroklina ("microclimate") Nemea. The inaugral 2001 vintage spent eighteen months in oak and two years in bottle and it looks set to elevate the boundaries of Nemean quality to a whole new level.

PIRGAKIS ESTATE
Asprokambos, 205 00 Nemea, Corinth.
Tel/Fax: +30 274 605 1364; Email: kpwines@otenet.gr
Vineyards owned: 9ha; production: 150–200hl.

The story of Pirgakis Estate is one that is likely to recur more and more frequently in the coming years. The Pirgakis family has been involved with growing table and wine grapes since the 1950s. In the 1970s, Takis Pirgakis moved the focus onto wine grapes, most notably Agiorgitiko. By the mid-1990s they owned an important vineyard in Asprokambos at an altitude above 750 metres (2,460 feet), and Pirgakis started planting additional varieties such as Cabernet Sauvignon, Merlot, Petit Verdot, Assyrtico, Chardonnay, and Roditis. In 1998, the family finally started its own winery, using its own fruit rather than selling it.

Currently, Pirgakis is moving into organic viticulture, with about four hectares already accredited as such. Takis' son, named Konstantinos after his grandfather, is a qualified winemaker and has already brought a new flair to the enterprise. The entire portfolio is made from good Asprokambos fruit, apart from the Moschofilero for the Roditis/Moschofilero blend which hails from Arcadia. Pirgakis Chardonnay is unoaked but has good fatness, possibly coming from extended *batonnage*. The rosé of the estate is a simple Agiorgitiko.

Pirgakis reds have density and broadness, but there is also an Asprokambos tightness and freshness. Spilia is a Nemea OPAP, with an excellent balance between acidity and fatness. The Cabernet Sauvignon/Agiorgitiko blend is soft with clear fruit expression, although the straight Cabernet Sauvignon is far better. A proportion of it is racked off its skins into oak before the end of fermentation. Malolactic then takes place in barriques, where the wine spends a further eighteen months. A wine for the medium-term, but a very good interpretation of the variety in Asprokambos.

RAPTIS WINERY
Leontio, 205 00 Nemea. Tel: +30 274 606 1700/1325;
Fax: +30 274 606 1701; Email: craptis@aias.gr
Vineyards owned: 7ha; production: 1,100hl.

Active since 1998 and managed by Hristos Raptis, the core of this winery's production comes from private vineyards in Nemea, with additional grapes sourced from the general Peloponnese region. The Raptis trio, Roditis, Merlot, and a Cabernet Sauvignon/Agiorgitiko blend, have a soft texture and moderate intensity. Nemea Raptis is the portfolio's best wine, making leaps in quality over the last four vintages.

REPANIS ESTATE
Thesi Kserokambos, Nemea, 205 00 Corinth. Tel: +30 274 602 0450/1;
Fax: +30 274 602 0452. Head office: 30 Harilaou Trikoupi, 174 56 Alimos.
Athens; Tel: +30 210 995 0719/994 2772; Fax: + 30 210 993 1989;
Website: www.repanis.gr; Email: info@repanis.gr
Vineyards owned: 2.5ha; under contract: 20ha; production: 1,000hl.

Nicolas Repanis has been involved with the import, export, and distribution side of wine and various foods since the mid-1980s. In 2000 he made the leap to producer, and Repanis winery, one of the most beautiful new buildings in Nemea, was ready to crush the 2001 vintage. For fruit, his 2.5 hectare vineyard has been registered organic, and he has several strategic partnerships with growers around the Peloponnese, for example, in Achaia, Pylia, and Mantinia. At the time of writing (2005), Professor Giorgos Kotseridis is acting as consultant, helping particularly with the ageing of Agiorgitiko.

Repanis produces three whites – Roditis, Chardonnay, and Moschofilero – one Agiorgitiko rosé, and three Agiorgitiko reds, all carrying a common, quite distinctive packaging theme. The Moschofilero is sourced from Arcadia, while the other two varieties come from Aigialia in Achaia. The best of the three is the Roditis, being reserved and full of elegance.

The reds are a touch better than the whites. Repanis is keen on rich, fruity, intense Agiorgitiko wines, even if they are not aged in oak. There are two Repanis Agiorgitiko labels, one using brought-in grapes, the other made with the estate's own organically cultivated grapes. Both are vinified in an easy, soft style, but the latter has an extra depth of character. Repanis' liking for intense reds is evident in his top wine, an OPAP Nemea. The blend contains parcels from a number of regions around Nemea, since Repanis believes that different sites bring in different facets, giving the blend maximum complexity. Repanis Nemea is a very modern wine: deep, extracted, but full of sweet fruit.

ZACHARIAS WINES

Nemea, 205 00 Corinth. Tel: +30 274 602 2667; Fax: +30 274 6023579;
Website: www.zacharias.com.gr; Email: zacharias@otenet.gr
Vineyards owned: 17.2ha; under contract: 20ha; production: 1,000hl.

Viticulturalist Ilias Zacharias owns the largest private winery in the appellation. Many large producers, like Achaia Clauss, use it to make Nemea OPAP wines. The winery releases about 130,000 bottles under the Zacharias name, while the vat capacity of the facility exceeds four million litres. Needless to say, these large companies would not leave their wine in the hands of someone who was not capable, and additionally Zacharias delivers good value for money.

The Zacharias portfolio starts with the Allegro range, moving up to Zacharias Red and the Fliasios White, and finishes with a Mantinia and a Nemea. The best wines are Nemea and Fliasios, an interesting blend of Roditis, Assyrtico, Sauvignon Blanc, and Sklava. This latter is a relatively rare, pink-skinned variety found in Corinth and Argolida. Speculation suggests a connection with the Italian variety Schiava, while its wine can have more than a touch of Moschofilero. It is vigorous, productive, resistant to drought, and ripens in mid-September.

ARGOLIDA

Argolida lies just south of Corinth, bordering Arcadia to the west. The Gulf of Saronikos lies off its eastern coast, while the Argolikos Gulf lies just off Nafplio, the capital city. Both the gulf and the prefecture are named after its second most important city, Argos. Argolida forms a peninsula, extending southeast into the Aegean towards the beautiful, picturesque islands of Spetses, Hydra, and Poros. A small part of the tip of this neck of land belongs to Attica for adminsitrative purposes. While the northern and western parts of the area are situated on the high-altitude slopes of the central Peloponnese and Corinth, the rest of Argolida is either flat or full of low hills. On a geographical, financial, and agricultural level, the most important plain is the one located around Argos and Nafplio.

Argolida has a long history and its political significance starts in ancient times with Argos, Mycenae, and Epidavros, reaching into the eighteenth century, when Nafplio was selected as the first capital of the newly established Greek state. The local population is relatively affluent, and agriculture is a major occupation for many families. Viticulture is relatively important, but is largely confined to high-altitude areas where other forms of cultivation are difficult. Argolida has a total of 736 hectares of vineyards, out of which 165 hectares are within the limits of Nemea OPAP, making up about seven per cent of the appellation's total acreage.

In terms of climate and terroir, the areas that have notable plantations of wine grape vines can safely be considered an extension of Corinth. Regarding grape varieties, Argolida features all the important vines of Corinth. In addition, there are glimpses of the varietal jungle that is encountered further south, in the form of occasional appearances of rare, and many times unidentified, vines.

Nemea OPAP

Red still: dry; semi-sweet; sweet.
Red variety: Agiorgitiko.

PRODUCERS

AIVALIS WINERY

4th km Eparhiakis odou Nemea-Petriou, Nemea, 205 00 Argolida.

Tel: +30 275 202 9641; Fax: +30 275 202 1175.

Head office: 21 Averof, Nafplio, 211 00 Argolida.

Tel: 275 202 1175; Fax: 275 202 9641.

Vineyards owned: 3.5ha; production: 100–200hl.

The Aivalis style has been a surprise to some of the people who are familiar with Nemea. On the other hand, most developing, high-quality wine regions have a few Aivalis-type pioneers – producers who want to take their appellation or variety to extremes, while at the same time staying loyal to the traditions of the region. Established in 1997 by Hristos Aivalis, this small winery was equipped with the essentials for red winemaking. The final result was low-tech, with a number of small five-tonne stainless-steel vats accounting for most of the expenditure – Aivalis wanted to be able to split up his production into many lots. Scattered in many areas of Nemea, some of the Aivalis vineyards have been in the family for generations, while others have been acquired in the last decade.

The style of winemaking is quite low-input. All the wines are fermented with their natural yeasts and exposed to very long and hot extractions. Aivalis believes that these yeast strains are well adapted to the prevailing high temperatures and, therefore, can work on warmer musts than commercially available cultures. In order to extract more tannins and dry extract, Aivalis ferments all his wines at 32–35°C (90–95°F). Finally, every *cuvée* is bottled unfined, unstabilized, and unfiltered; Aivalis believes such processes to be unnecessary, since long cask-ageing should guarantee the stability of products.

The winery used to produce only red wines, but in 2004 Aivalis produced his first rosé, Anthi Rodon. This is made from must racked almost without any skin contact and fermented at high temperatures, so it is more about body and power than aromas. The first red, called simply Aivalis Nemea, is produced from five to six different parcels across the appellation. The average yield is about fifty hectolitres per hectare, while the age of the vines spans twelve to twenty-one years. There is an eighteen-day maceration, the malolactic fermentation takes place in oak and the wine is aged in new barriques for a year, seventy per cent French oak, thirty per cent American. Overall, a good, full-style Agiorgitiko.

Monopati is the first single-vineyard selection of Aivalis, from a site with thirty-five-year-old vines that yield around twenty-three hectolitres per hectare. Maceration goes up to forty days and the wine goes into oak for fourteen months, a fifty/fifty balance of French and American oak.

Then there is Tessera (Greek "four"), from the top single-vineyard: a four-hectare parcel owned by the Aivalis family for more than a century and not replanted since then. A visiting American viticultural team could not come up with a precise estimate of the vines' age, but did say that their root systems resembled in size those of olive trees rather than *Vitis vinifera*. Is this the Greek Hill of Grace? Possibly the only one exploited, since many parcels in Laconia can lay an equally impressive claim in terms of age.

The Tessera grapes are harvested at about the same maturity as those destined for the Monopati *cuvée*, around 13.5 per cent potential alcohol, but the acidity tends to be higher. Yields are usually below eight hectolitres per hectare, maceration goes up to fifty days, the wine spends sixteen months in new, highly porous American oak, where oxygenation is more intense, and then is racked into French oak, again new, to spend up to twenty additional months – the only Greek wine to receive a "double new oak" treatment.

As you might expect, Tessera tastes very dense, amazingly concentrated, and ripe but not overly so, while the oak is very evident and the tannic structure is particularly firm. Although difficult to understand, at the same time, it would be disingenuous to dismiss it as coarse and overextracted. Possibly, only time in bottle will tell. Finally, although this is a rare, individual, and expensively crafted wine, Four's price tag is on a par with famous Bordeaux classed growths and is, in my view, unrealistic. However, I suppose someone in Greece had to do it.

DOMAINE SKOURAS

Winery One: Gymno, 205 00 Nemea. Winery Two and Head Office:
Malandreni, 10km Argos-Sterna, 21 200 Argos, Argolida.
Tel: +30 275 102 3688; Fax: +30 275 102 3159;
Website: www.skouraswines.gr; Email: skouras@hol.gr
Vineyards owned: 11.7ha (Corinth: 5.7ha, Nemea OPAP: 4ha, Argolida: 2ha);
under contract: 58ha (Argolida: 4ha, Nemea OPAP: 40ha, Arcadia: 10ha,
Messinia: 3ha); production: 7,000hl.

Dijon-trained oenologist George Skouras started his own winery in the Peloponnese in 1986 after working for a few years in Cephalonia, mainly in the Calliga and Gentilini wineries. A vital component of the Greek wine revolution of the 1980s, Skouras executes an impressive balancing act between pushing international varieties and refining local varieties and appellations. This venture has been developing over the years: a small winery in Gymno in 1994; important vineyard acquisitions in the late 1990s; and an impressive new winery in Malandreni in time for the 2004 vintage. This latest production plant is possibly the first where Skouras can be free of logistics and restrictions, so a new Skouras Era might be beginning.

Skouras is a great character and a fine ambassador for Greek wines, but his most important quality could be his people management skills. If Skouras doesn't know something, he knows exactly where to find a person who does. With many decades of experience in the Peloponnese, Aristidis Zouzias acts as viticultural consultant, Nontas Delogiannis keeps operations ticking over with immense accuracy as winery manager, while the young, extremely skilled as well as charming oenologist, Dimitra Trahani, is the production manager.

Skouras has an aversion to full-blown, high-alcohol, overly exotic wines, and his personal taste in wine is illustrated well by his portfolio. Most of the wines are about fruit concentration, not winemaking extraction: "If you have a concentrated grape, then even the first drop of juice is going to be concentrated. You do not have to smash the fruit to get density," he says.

The value wines are simply called Skouras, with a white Moschofilero/ Roditis blend, a soft Agiorgitiko with just five per cent Cabernet Sauvignon, and an exquisite Agiorgitiko/Roditis rosé.

Skouras Moschofilero is not an OPAP Mantinia because the selected, old-vine parcels are outside the appellation. The pink-skinned grapes go through a dry-ice maceration, with very low temperatures leading to a partial cryo-extraction that gives full flavour without any colour. This approach leads to a Moschofilero that shows *typicité* on the nose, but a fuller body and a touch more ripeness than most.

Skouras also makes two different Chardonnays and two Viogniers. The varietal Chardonnay is thirty per cent oak-aged, being fresh, round, and easy-drinking. Dum Vinum Sperum has been produced since 2001 in small quantities – fewer than 2,000 bottles per year. Fermented and aged in new French oak for six months, it is the first Greek wine to be bottled under Stelvin. Initial vintages are developing slowly, so Skouras is releasing it later each year, aiming to eventually have Dum Vinum Sperum on the market when it is about five years old.

Skouras started working with Viognier after long discussions with his friend, Marcel Guigal. His standard Viognier is at a modest (for the variety) 12.5 per cent alcohol, and is again partially aged in oak. It's an enjoyable wine, but lacks the exotic character one might expect from the variety. Viognier Eclectique is a different story: the best bunches of Viognier are retained on the vine but the stem is snapped. Two weeks later, these are harvested when the sugar concentration is not much higher, but the aromatic profile is totally different. The wine is expressive, again only with hints of Viognier aromas, but with a very individual, yeasty nose – what Steve Daniel, the former Oddbins buyer who introduced the UK to Greek wine, once called "a cross between oaky Viognier and fino sherry".

Apart from one varietal Merlot and a Cabernet Sauvignon with some varietal definition, the reds of Skouras are dominated by Agiorgitiko-based wines. Skouras Nemea is an honest, easy-drinking example of the appellation. The premium bottling is Grande Cuvée, coming from four 900-metre (2,953-feet) altitude parcels in Asprokambos. It is an extremely bright, focused, concentrated Agiorgitiko coupled with an acidity level reminiscent of a white wine. A graceful wine, which will age for a long time.

Finally, the flagship of Skouras is Megas Oenos, a blend of old-vine Agiorgitiko and twenty per cent Cabernet Sauvignon. Megas Oenos was first made in 1986, and was one of the pioneering, high profile "Super-Nemea" wines. This is the epitome of the Skouras approach, with firm tannins, muted fruit and oak, and a strictly medium body. In addition, Skouras enjoys playing with elevated volatile acidity levels in this wine, saying, "Volatile acidity is like salt – a bit helps to bring out the flavours, while if you reach a level where its flavour stands apart, then you have a problem." With a few years in bottle, Megas Oenos becomes very Château Musar-like, bar the oxidation, giving some truly memorable bottles.

Currently, Skouras is preparing a range of five single-vineyard wines that will be released onto the market after many years of ageing – possibly signalling a much anticipated Greek version of Vega Sicilia's Unico.

KORONIOTIS WINERY
Panorama, Argos, 212 00 Argolida.
Tel: +30 275 109 1850; Fax: +30 275 109 1359.
Vineyards owned: 3.5ha; under contract: 6ha; production: 1,000hl.
The owner of this venture, Kiriakos Koroniotis, has an impressive academic

track record in viticulture and oenology. Apart from the winery, established in 1998, Koroniotis has a major oenological laboratory in Argos, offering soil and wine analyses to a large number of the region's growers and winemakers. In 2000 he released his first wines: a 1998 Nemea and a 1999 Moschofilero. The winery has a low profile in Greece and it is geared mainly for exports, with major clients in Germany and Holland. Koroniotis wines are not flashy or aromatic, but focused, competently made, and well-structured.

PAPANTONIS WINERY

48 Kanari Street, Argos, 21200 Argolida.
Tel: +30 275 102 3620; Fax: +30 275 102 4719;
Website: www.papantonis.gr; Email: medenaga@otenet.gr
Vineyards owned: 1.5ha; under contract: 8ha; production: 500hl.

This boutique winery is the family enterprise of brothers Kalli and Antonis Papantonis. Most of the stock is sold to private clients, making the wines difficult to find. However, the fact that the winery's main wine, Meden Agan (literally, "nothing to excess") has had significant export success, suggests that Papantonis wines are worth seeking out. Meden Agan was one of the first wines to be listed by Oddbins when the high street chain introduced high-quality Greek wine to UK wine-drinkers in the late 1990s. The winery also has ISO 9002 and HACCP accreditation (*see* footnote on page 178), an expensive process given the small scale of the endeavour, illustrating the Papantonis commitment to quality. Hristos Peppas, production manager at the Nemea Co-op, acts as consultant.

Papantonis has an Agiorgitiko vineyard within the Nemea appellation, but he felt that the OPAP status was almost irrelevant for a wine sold on such a personal basis. Therefore, the Meden Agan is an EO, equivalent to table wine. It is a pure Agiorgitiko aged in French oak for a year, twenty per cent of which is new. The wine has a very elegant character with hints of wood, plus spice and dark fruit. A velvety structure makes it enjoyable on release, while it can mature well for up to seven years. In 2002, Meden Agan, after a decade of being the only commercial Papantonis product, was joined by Lysimelis, a sweet Agiorgitiko. Grapes are left to overripen on the vine and the dense must is left to ferment until it stops naturally at around fifteen per cent alcohol. The sweetness level is in excess of 120 grams per litre, but the wine is balanced and, indeed, quite fresh. A very good example of a sweet Agiorgitiko – unfortunately there are only a few hundred cases each year.

ARCADIA

Although not totally inland – the eastern parts of the prefecture between Corinth and Laconia have coastline on the Argolikos Gulf – Arcadia is in the heart of the Peloponnese. The capital is Tripoli, situated at the centre of the prefecture, while Megalopoli, the second most important town, is in the southwest corner. Apart from the coastline and a small plain around Megalopoli, there are very few areas at sea level. Completely encircled by neighbouring mountains, the region has a high average altitude, with the highest spot being the Menalo range, just northwest of Tripoli, with its peak of 1,980 metres (6,496 feet).

The climate of Arcadia, at least inland, is notably different from other regions of the Peloponnese, the high altitude resulting in cooler temperatures. Humidity is not high in the summer, a common phenomenon on the west of the Peloponnese, although there can be a wide variation between July and December: forty-five per cent and seventy-eight per cent respectively. Nevertheless, Arcadia attracts rainfall, even during the summer. Summer and winter are relatively mild, with maximum July or August temperatures rarely exceeding 32°C (90°F); the minimum temperature in the coldest months, January and February, is around 1°C (34°F).

The specifics of the Arcadian climate make it the last area to harvest in the Peloponnese. Viticulture is important, with a total vineyard acreage of 1,555 hectares. Apart from the region of Mantinia, vineyards can be found in most communes, even if they are only used to cover their owners' needs in wine and are not commercial plantations. White grapes and the pink-skinned Moschofilero dominate the varietal profile, followed closely by the Asproudes (*see* Glossary). The most important Asprouda is Glikerithra, sometimes called Glikasprouda, a variety well-noted for its high sugar levels and low acidity, making it a good partner to Moschofilero, with its crisp, low-alcohol palate.

Classifications and grapes

The only quality-wine appellation is Mantinia OPAP, encompassing 621 hectares. Mantinia is located north of Tripoli, on a relatively flat plateau extending from an altitude of 600 metres upwards (1,968 feet). Here the cooler climate of Arcadia fully reigns, coupled with infertile, clay-rocky soils. Maximum yield is ninety-four hectolitres per hectare, but most of the producers work below this level.

Moschofilero dominates the zone with about eighty-five per cent of the vineyards, the remainder being mainly Asproudes. So legislation wisely states that the varietal profile of any Mantinia wine must be predominantly Moschofilero, with up to fifteen per cent Asproudes. Harvest time varies from vintage to vintage; the more a vintage goes over into October, the more erratic the weather patterns can be. In some years and in the early-ripening spots, harvest can begin in late September, with most of the area being cleared during the first three weeks of October. Cool weather can push the vintage back to early November, while exceptionally cold vintages, as in 2004, will mean some parcels do not reach full maturity at all, with ripeness levels being stalled below ten degrees Baumé.

Beyond occasional maturity problems, Mantinia is a place where vine-growing is relatively trouble-free, and the lack of summer humidity explains the absence of many vine diseases. As a result, Mantinia has become one of the first centres of organic viticulture in Greece, with a number of growers becoming eloquent ambassadors for the movement nationwide, such as Apostolos Spiropoulos. There is also a team of independent *vignerons* evaluating the merits of Biodynamic viticulture.

The combination of cool climate and Moschofilero vines produces some wines that are very un-Greek in style, showing a pale colour, a sweet and floral nose, alcohol that usually stands between at around twelve per cent, a lean and light palate structure, and a crisp acidity that often dips below three on the pH scale. If someone was unaware of the region's style, it would be possible to think that a good-quality Moschofilero was closer to Alsace than anything else. This different character has acted as a magnet for a number of major companies.

Back in the 1970s, an important use of Moschofilero was the production of cheap Greek "Champagne", an approach that did little justice to the grape. Developments in vinification, such as the availability of selected yeasts and refrigeration equipment for conducting cool fermentations, made the creation of a new style of Mantinia possible. These wines won fans among wine-lovers and wine producers alike, and Greek people, traditionally not keen on acidic wines, became curiously fond of the crisp Moschofilero – usually with the help of four or six grams of residual sugar. There followed a commercial explosion of Moschofilero during the 1990s, as it developed into the most high-profile indigenous grape, at least within Greece. Now, it is practically compulsory for every Peloponnesian winery, and most of the large, multi-regional companies, to have at least one Mantinia or one Moschofilero-based wine in their portfolio. More than twenty-five wineries sell a branded Mantinia, second in popularity only to OPAP Nemea.

Despite the hopes of many Arcadian growers, it seems that Moschofilero will have to struggle to produce wines of great quality and complexity. However, it can lay claim to being able to produce the most distinctive, instantly charming dry white wines of Greece. Some producers are looking into oak-ageing Moschofilero, but so far most of these wines are quite coarse, with minimal synergy between oak and grape. The most carefully made wines, like the ones from Domaine Tselepos, Boutari, and Spiropoulos, try to get some fat onto the Moschofilero through *batonnage*, while at the same time toning down the oak level. The results are pleasant and balanced, yet one cannot help but wonder if this is truly a way of making a better wine or simply an attempt to tune into the current trend for oaky whites.

Apart from the Mantinia OPAP there are two TOs. The Arcadia TO allows more freedom for minor varieties, as Moschofilero only has to be half of the blend. The Tegea TO has been created following work by Yiannis Tselepos, to accommodate his fabulous reds based on Bordeaux varieties.

Mantinia OPAP
White still: dry.
White varieties: Moschofilero at least eighty-five per cent;
Asproudes varieties.

Arcadia TO
White still: dry.
White variety: Moschofilero must be at least fifty per cent of the blend, the balance being other local recommended and permitted grape varieties.

Tegea TO
Red still: dry.
Red varieties: Cabernet Sauvignon; Cabernet Franc; Merlot.

PRODUCERS

CAMBAS/BOUTARI WINERY
8th km Tripoli–Pyrgou National Rd, 190 09 Milies, Tripoli, Arcadia. Tel/Fax: +30 271 041 1477. Website: www.boutari.gr; Email: cambas@boutarigroup.gr

Vineyards owned: 70ha; under contract: 10ha; production: 23,000hl.

See also Boutari entries on pages 130, 144, 150, 232, 385, 449.

Andreas Cambas, the founder of one of Greece's most important wine-producing dynasties, set up his firm in the second half of the nineteenth century. Although based in Attica, the connections with Mantinia are strong. In 1927, the company bought a forty-hectare vineyard here and created a winery. By 1930, it was producing a dry Mantinia – a different kind of wine from what had been known as Mantinia up to that time – and a number of distillates, since brandy was a major part of its sales. The company was acquired by Boutari in the early 1990s, revitalized, and the winemaking rights for all the Cambas brands were retained. Today Mantinia-related wines, sold under both names, are important and extremely successful. The Cambas Mantinia still enjoys high sales, together with the basic Boutari Mantinia OPAP, which is traded as a varietal Moschofilero. A TO of Arcadia Cambas and a Boutari Mantinia are also produced solely for export.

While Yiannis Vogiatzis, the head Boutari winemaker, was trying out new methods of production, he produced a Skin Contact Moschofilero as an experimental wine. The intense aromas that resulted from pre-fermentation maceration made Skin Contact almost a legend, and the company added it to its regular portfolio. For this bottling, the winemaking team and the resident winemaker, Mihalis Kartsonakis, were using only fruit from the Boutari vineyards, where the average age of vines exceeds thirty years.

A later addition was Tesseris Epohes ("four seasons"), a barrique-aged Mantinia. Finally, there is Ilida, an exotic blend of fifty per cent Moschofilero, forty per cent Chardonnay, and ten per cent Gewurztraminer. Out of the three varieties, only Chardonnay is barrel-fermented. Ilida is a pleasant wine, full of flowers, sweet spices, and ripe fruit, while being soft and easy on the palate. A unique and interesting approach.

The company's portfolio of Agiorgitiko wines includes a simple, very light Nemea, a rather better Agiorgitiko, the slightly old-fashioned Cambas Nemea, and Cava Cambas, a wine that goes into mud-stained bottles – in 1981, Cambas cellars were flooded and the company decided to sell the cava bottles without washing them. The sales success persuaded the production team to repeat the accident every year, but in a much smaller and more controlled form.

As a part of Boutaris' experimental portfolio, Yiannis Paraskevopoulos vinified some old-vine Nemea wines in the early 1990s that were truly outstanding and years ahead of their time. Very few bottles still remain, but any that do should be surviving with poise.

DOMAINE TSELEPOS

14th km Tripoli–Kastri Road, Rizes, 220 12 Arcadia. Tel: +30 271 054 4440; Fax: +30 271 054 4460. Head office: 9A Mantamadou Street, Maroussi, 151 26 Athens. Tel: +30 210 810 4994; Fax: +30 210 803 0319; Website: www.tselepos.gr; Email: tselepos@acn.gr
Vineyards owned: 25ha; under contract: 15ha; production: 2,200hl.

Yiannis Tselepos was born in Cyprus and educated in Dijon. A winemaking degree in Burgundy left him with a love for the region; he'd like to be a Burgundian in the middle of Arcadia. Together with Spiropoulos, he was one of the pioneers of the 1980s, putting Mantinia on the map as the home of top-quality, boutique wineries. While Spiropoulos expanded significantly, Tselepos has remained relatively stable, at least during the last decade. However, a notable development has been the creation of the Driopi Estate, together with Paris Sigalas and Alexandros Avatangelos (*see* page 308).

The Tselepos portfolio has been remarkably stable since 1997, with nine different wines. Overall, it is a compact, highly reliable, high-quality range. Despite starting at a high level, all wines are constantly improving. The Tselepos style is about flamboyancy and intensity. There are three Moschofilero wines. Mantinia Tselepos is one of the biggest premium-selling wines of the appellation, showing varietal *typicité* in a hyper-charged style. The Mantinia Barrel Fermented stays in mainly old oak for five months and, most importantly, another five months in bottle. By this time, the oak has settled, giving possibly the best example of this style. Finally, Villa Amalia, a sparkling Moschofilero named after Tselepos' wife, is made in the traditional method, staying *sur lie* for two years and giving a wine where the floral side of the grape is in complete balance with the yeast presence.

In his search for vineyards for Cabernet Sauvignon, Tselepos came across Avlotopi, an arid, infertile site full of schist, at 780 metres altitude (2,560 feet). While most of it was perfectly suited to the red variety, Tselepos decided to try Gewurztraminer on two slopes, one of the first Greek outings for this grape. Tselepos was reluctant to go to high levels of ripeness, even with yields below thirty hectolitres per hectare, and harvested at twelve degrees Baumé. Thus in the early days the wine was reserved, leaving Gewurztraminer admirers somewhat disappointed. Since the 2003 vintage, the wine, now rechristened Melissopetra, has been harvested much later and gives out better varietal *typicité*.

The final white is a barrique-fermented Chardonnay sourced from the Kokkinomylos ("red mill") vineyard. This vineyard has been planted with several Dijon clones while yields are kept at around thirty-five hectolitres per hectare. The wine spends six months on fine lees and six more in bottle, being quite Burgundian in character with a slightly overt oak presence.

The Tselepos Nemea will be discontinued to make room for Nemea Driopi. The most approachable red, Tselepos Estate, is made with seventy-five per cent Avlotopi Cabernet Sauvignon and twenty-five per cent Kokkinomylos Merlot. The top grape selection from each of the two single vineyards is treated and bottled separately as Avlotopi Cabernet Sauvignon and Kokkinomylos Merlot, resulting in some of Greece's most impressive Bordeaux varietals. Both are picked overripe, sometimes with a small proportion of shrivelled grapes; maceration lasts for twenty-five days; and ageing in new Nadalie oak barriques takes about eighteen months, followed by another year in bottle. The wines are expensive by Greek standards, but worth buying and keeping in the cellar for at least ten years. Both are equally impressive, but if I had to select one, it would be the Merlot, with its extra degree of exotic complexity.

NASSIAKOU WINERY
Komvos Nestanis, 12th km Tripoli–Nestanis, Tripoli, 221 00 Arcadia.
Tel: +30 271 056 1252; Fax: +30 271 023 4690.
Head Office: 15 Nikitara, Tripoli, 221 00 Arcadia. Tel/Fax: +30 271 024 2931
Vineyards under contract: 28ha; production: 2,100hl.

The historic Nassiakos family has been involved in vine-growing in Mantinia for many decades, as well as buying fruit from growers on long-term contracts. The winery was built in the early 1980s and the whole family is involved in the business. The grandson of the founder, oenologist Leonidas Nassiakos, divides his time between Mantinia and Nemea, where he is the head winemaker at Domaine Helios (*see* page 306).

Most producers who make two versions of Mantinia OPA – one traded as a varietal and the other not – usually sell the latter at a higher price. Nassiakos does the reverse. Nassiakos Moschofilero is clean and floral, while Nassiakos Mantinia is steelier and far crisper. Nassiakos Agiorgitiko is a soft Peloponnese TO, with just seven days' maceration and three months spent in oak. In sharp contrast, the Nassiakos Nemea, a full alcoholic degree higher at around 13.5 per cent, is macerated for a month and gets a full year in new French oak. Coming from carefully selected parcels and areas of the appellation, this is fine-grained, tannic, but not angular.

SPIROPOULOS ESTATE
Artemisio, Ancient Mantinia, Tripoli, 221 00 Arcadia. Tel: +30 279 606 1400/1101; Fax: +30 279 606 1406. Head office: 62 D Solomou, N Ionia, Athens. Website: www.domainspiropoulos.com; Email: arkas1@otenet.gr
Vineyards owned: 60ha; under contract: 35ha; production: 7,000hl.

Spiropoulos Estate is one of the first high-quality estates in Mantinia and a keen advocate of organic cultivation in the Peloponnese. The initial winery dates back to 1860, but the new phase of Spiropoulos involvement with wine began in 1987. Organic cultivation started in the early 1990s, and by 1996, all the family-owned vineyards were officially accredited. The company has been expanding over the years, and is now approaching the one-million-bottle mark, but keeping the same quality standards. Yiannis Paraskevopoulos acted as consultant winemaker for most of the 1990s. Current managing director, Nondas, has served in many high-ranking posts in wine-related associations over the years. His son, Apostolos Spiropoulos, arrived fresh from his winemaking degree at California's UC Davis in 2000. Since then, the portfolio is constantly developing, and Apostolos is never afraid to innovate. The Spiropoulos family has expanded into organic livestock breeding as well.

Moschofilero is the Spiropoulos obsession – no fewer than six versions are produced, all different. Orino is the most basic expression, made from bought-in grapes and left with about four grams per litre of residual sugar to enrich the light but fresh palate. Spiropoulos Estate is a textbook, modern Moschofilero. There is also a Spiropoulos Estate Oak Fermented, where only new French oak is used, mainly barriques as well as some 300-litre barrels. Meliasto is an excellent Moschofilero rosé where, along with the extraction of colour, a whole new density of fruit is revealed: peaches, fresh grapes, spices, rose petals, and Turkish delight – more a cross of Muscat and Gewurztraminer than typical Moschofilero.

Idistos Oenos is, so far, an experiment, where Moschofilero bunches are allowed to overripen on the vine, then sun-dried for just over a week, and finally aged in new French oak for over two years. This produces many challenges, like leaving bunches well into December and harvesting them healthy, so Apostolos is very conservative about its continued production. However, the wine is a very extracted manifestation of the variety. Finally, Ode Panos is a Charmat-method, floral, elegant sparkling wine, possibly an ode to the earlier style of Moschofilero as it was introduced to modern drinkers.

Spiropoulos had started producing a range of varietal wines such as Chardonnay, Roditis, Sauvignon Blanc, and Cabernet Sauvignon, but these are being discontinued. However, Spiropoulos Lagorthi is a rare, top example of this variety, packing very good concentration into just eleven per cent alcohol, and developing well over a course of three years or more.

There are two reds. Dorkas is the Nemea OPAP of the winery, a decent middle-of-the-road effort. In contrast, Porfyros is one of the most stylish reds of the Peloponnese, and could be mistaken for a premium Tuscan Bordeaux blend. It is made from fifty per cent Agiorgitiko and equal parts of Cabernet Sauvignon, Cabernet Franc, and Merlot. All varieties are separately macerated for up to thirty days and the wine is aged for sixteen months in top-quality Alliers and Nevers oak. Surprisingly, the wine tastes like it has been made in a much more restrained way. It is ready to drink on release but the "Apostolos era" vintages are capable of ageing for at least eight years.

LACONIA
Laconia is the southeastern part of the Peloponnese, and includes two "legs" of the department: the eastern "Laconian" peninsula (with Cape Maleas at its tip) and Mani. The prefecture borders Arcadia on the north and Messinia on the west. Just south of Cape Maleas is the island of Kythira. The northern part of Laconia is dominated by the mountain ranges of the central Peloponnese, most importantly Mount Parnonas, which stands at 1,839 metres (6,033 feet) on the west side of Sparta, the prefecture's capital. Mani is also very mountainous, dominated by Taygetos Mountain, the highest in the Peloponnese with a peak of 2,404 metres (7,887 feet). However, around Sparta there is an important plain which spreads from the central part of the district down to Krokees, Gythio, and Papadianika. In addition, the area south of Papadianika and the historic eastern port of Monemvasia is relatively hilly, but by no means mountainous.

The general climate of Laconia is typically Mediterranean, with hot and dry summers, even if the higher-altitude parts do escape some of the summer heat. Humidity and rain are scarce from May to September, and water availability can be a problem. The Evrotas River, running through the Sparta plain, helps regarding irrigation.

Viticulture is oddly significant in Laconia. According to the Ministry of Agriculture, there are 685 hectares in the prefecture, making it the smallest in vineyard acreage compared with other parts of the Peloponnese. However, a large number of vineyards are unregistered, as landowners grow vines only for their own winemaking needs. In Laconia, as well as in many other regions of the Peloponnese, very few local people buy wine from supermarkets or wine shops – usually there is at least one member of the family who will keep them supplied all year round.

History

The region's viticultural record is one of the most important in the history of wine. Laconia and the beautiful port of Monemvasia have been producing Malvasia wine for centuries. What it tasted like, how it was made, and even the grape constituents are questions still being fiercely debated. Local pioneers like Giorgos Tsimpidis of Monemvasia Winery (*see* below) are determined to shed some light on the mysteries of this wine. Sadly, most of the twentieth century saw little commercial wine production in Laconia, with almost no significant wineries. Despite the fast development of Nemea, Mantinia, and Patras, the region remained imprisoned in a kind of backwater. Commercially oriented ventures had to wait until 1990 – all of Laconia's active wineries, except Miragias Vineyards, have been established since then.

Even if Laconia was late getting into the Greek wine revolution, it has been quick to catch up. More and more people are exploring the local viticultural treasures and trying to do their own thing. Some are making substantial investments, such as the Doukas family, owners of a medium-sized, successful supermarket chain in Athens, who have established a new winery in Richia. With a bit of luck and a lot of stamina, Laconia could easily be the Collio of Greece sometime in the next decade. An important asset will be the numerous local varieties and the outstanding old vineyards.

Grapes

The number of indigenous varieties almost exclusive to Laconia is truly breathtaking. Most wineries in the area crush, knowingly, more than a dozen grapes that are unheard of by producers just 100 kilometres (sixty-two miles) away. Many of these rare vines are interplanted in vineyards and it takes a skilled eye to distinguish them. Moreover, Laconia brims with old vineyards and families that have been cultivating them for generations. In most cases, the age of the vines, very low yields, and the fruit extract make the variety almost irrelevant: the character of the grape is based on its concentration. However, some exciting wines are waiting here in the wings.

Major varieties in Laconia include Kidonitsa, Petroulianos, Thrapsa, and a local kind of Mavroudi, on top of Assyrtico, Roditis, Agiorgitiko, Mandilaria, and Monemvasia. Kidonitsa is a white variety, mildly vigorous, productive, and sensitive to arid conditions. It ripens in late September, giving low sugar levels, moderate acidity, and an exquisite aroma of ripe quince. Petroulianos is a white variety, vigorous, but only moderately productive, and resistant to drought. Its wine is not as aromatic as Kidonitsa's, but it gives high alcohol and low acidity. Thrapsa is a red grape, and as a vine it is vigorous, productive, but very sensitive to leafroll virus. Diseased vines have light-coloured berries and are sometimes called White Thrapsa by local *vignerons*. It is harvested by mid-September and gives high alcohol and low acidity, as well as very low colour. There is also the rare red Skilopnihtis, a dark-coloured variation of White Skilopnihtis, planted in Lefkada and Aitoloakarnania. Both colours are harvested by late September and give high alcohol and moderate acidity. The same characteristics are shared by Smirneiko, another uncommon variety that is occasionally found around Monemvasia. Kipreiko is only found in Kithira, being vigorous, productive, and resistant to drought. It ripens in early September, giving intense fruity aromas, high sugar levels, and moderate acidity.

Laconia has two TOs – one prefectural and one awarded, deservedly, in the Monemvasia area. Both TOs came in after 2000, making them some of the most recent additions to the regional wine list.

Laconia TO

White still: dry.
White varieties: Roditis; Athiri; White Aidani; Assyrtico; Kidonitsa; Petrouliano; Monemvasia.
Rosé still: dry.
Rosé varieties: Agiorgitiko; Mavroudi; Roditis; Mandilaria.
Red still: dry.
Red varieties: Agiorgitiko; Mavroudi; Thrapsa; Mandilaria.

Monemvasia TO

White still: dry.
White varieties: Roditis; Athiri; White Aidani; Assyrtico; Kidonitsa; Asproudes; Petrouliano; Monemvasia; Fileri.
Red still: dry.
Red varieties: Agiorgitiko; Mavroudi; Thrapsa; Mandilaria.

PRODUCERS

KYTHIRA WINERY

Thesi Markesakia, Kalokairines, 801 00 Kythira.
Head office: 6 Chrisostomou Smirnis, 151 21 Pefki. Tel: +30 210 612 5430; Fax: +30 210 802 6500; Website: www.cerigo.co.gr; Email: info@cerigo.com.gr
Vineyards owned: 1.5ha; under contract: 6ha; production: 400hl.

The only commercially active winery in Kythira, this was established in 1996 by the Raikos and Stratigos families. Unfortunately, the two key partners passed away a few years ago. Filio Stratigos is now in charge. The winery's own vineyards are planted mainly with Petroulianos. This is bottled as a varietal and is slightly on the heavy side. The collaborating vineyards in Nemea provide Cabernet Sauvignon and some Corinthiaki, and their fruit is used for Arikaras Red, which has a pleasant, spicy character. Unfortunately, the wines are more expensive than they should be.

KOUTSOYIANNIS ORGANIC VINEYARDS

Thesi Sarkokaliva, Githio, 232 00 Laconia. Head office: Thesi Mavrovouni, Githio, 232 00 Laconia; Tel: +30 273 302 3930/3931; Fax: +30 273 302 4436.
Vineyards owned: 3ha; production: 240hl.

Although Ksenofon Koutsoyiannis was one of the first people to start a winery in Githio back in 1993, his annual production is still low. He works exclusively with his own organically farmed vineyards, planted with Agiorgitiko and the local Mavroudi, and has succeeded in promoting a relatively upmarket image for his wines, which are relatively difficult to find. Only two labels are produced. One is a varietal Mavroudi, which is made in very small quantities, with a light but pleasant structure. The top *cuvée* in both quality and in price, is Melanas, a pure Agiorgitiko aged in French oak for over a year. The wine shows a ripe character, full of warmth, while it has the most distinctive packaging – the bottom half of the bottle is enclosed in a clay pot.

MONEMVASIA WINERY

Velies Monemvasia, 230 70 Laconia. Tel: +30 273 205 3096; Fax: +30 273 205 3119. Website: www.malvasiawines.gr; Email: malvasia@hol.gr

Vineyards owned: 20ha; under contract: 20ha; production: 2,000hl.

Monemvasia Winery can be considered Laconia's leading winery and its founder, Giorgos Tsimpidis, one of the most promising *vignerons* in the Peloponnese. Active since 1997, its portfolio came into full bloom in 2000. Tsimpidis is one of those people who feel that the winemaking is the least exciting part of making wine; what fascinates him is the vineyard.

One of this venture's main aims is to unlock the vast varietal potential hiding in Laconia and, specifically, in Monemvasia. Tsimpidis also wants to go one step further – he wants to recreate the Malvasia wine of old as closely as possible, and then to give it a modern and personal twist. He is not alone in this quest. Vitro Hellas, the country's leading nursery with its research centre based in Naoussa, is helping with the huge number of varieties that Tsimpidis is unearthing. There are also major viticultural research projects with the Agricultural Universities of Athens and Thessaloniki.

Sometimes, it seems that the portfolio is more directed towards this research than towards optimum commercial development. Tsimpidis has his own, organically cultivated vineyard in Velies, but collaborating vineyards extend to other parts of Laconia and Achaia, Mantinia, and Nemea. Tsipmidis usually works with yields around fifty hectolitres per hectare, sometimes going down to forty.

The winery produces a complex portfolio of thirteen products, many of the wines being a blend of three, four, or even five varieties, with the relative percentages changing almost every year. Alcohol levels are very restrained, rarely exceeding 12.7 per cent. Anthosmias is an interesting medium-sweet rosé blend of Agiorgitiko from Nemea, Moschofilero from Mantinia, and Roditis from Achaia. The last two grapes are also blended in the aromatic white Lambritsa. Kastropolitia and Maleatis are the largest-volume wines, with each one having a white and a red version. These capitalize on Thrapsa, Kidonitsa, Agiorgitiko, and Mavraki, with the oak-aged red Maleatis being a wine full of character. Mavraki is a red variety that produces low yields of concentrated, sweet, and quite acidic grapes.

The same structure can be found in the red and white pairs of Laloudi, Laconicos, and Monemvassios wines. The red Laloudi has an interesting cedary touch from thirty per cent Cabernet Sauvignon; red Laconicos is a very elegant Mavroudi,; and Monemvassios is a typical Mavroudi/Agiorgitiko blend. The best of the whites is the very expressive Laloudi, a Moschofilero-dominated blend of up to five varieties. The top wine is Petroulianos, rich but very elegant and truly different. Only 4,000 bottles are produced every year and it is well worth seeking out.

THEODORAKAKOU ESTATE
17km Sparta-Githiou Rd, 230 57 Dafnia Krokeaon.
Tel: +30 273 103 6555; Fax: +30 273 103 6550;
Website: www.estatetheodorakakos.gr; Email: gtheodor@internet.gr
Vineyards owned: 30ha; production: 3,000hl.

One of the first people to try to put Laconia on the modern Greek wine map, Giorgos Theodorakakos sources fruit exclusively from his own organic vineyards. Together with Koutsoyiannis, they are Laconia's largest organic growers. Theodorakakos grows around eight varieties and yields are kept close to fifty-five hectolitres per hectare. Alcohol levels are moderate, while winemaking is simple and kept on the oxidative, traditional side.

Likovouno white, made from Kidonitsa, Assyrtico, and Roditis, is the softer white, and its red counterpart, an Agiorgitiko/Mavroudi blend, follows the same style. Perivleptos White and Red follow broadly the same blends, with the white having a touch of Moschofilero and the red spending a year in new French oak. The three Theodorakakou Estate wines are the best of the range. The varietal Mavroudi, with a hint of Agiorgitiko, is complex and soft. Theodorakakou Estate Vareli is a barrel-fermented Assyrtico with Roditis and Petroulanos, which shows its new oak treatment. The best Theodorakakos wine is the varietal Kidonitsa, with its small addition of Thrapsa, showing the full and sweet quince character of the grape.

VATISTAS VINEYARDS
Lachio-Neapoli, 230 53 Laconia. Tel/Fax: +30 273 402 4132;
Website: www.vatistas-wines.gr; Email: info@vatistas-wines.gr
Vineyards owned: 21ha; under contract: 12ha; production: 2,400hl.

Yiannis Vatistas' winery was the area's most important investment in the early 1990s and he currently produces the most wine in Laconia. He has struck a good balance between local and international varieties, as well as introducing non-Laconian Greek varieties, like Athiri and Malagousia, into his private vineyards.

The style of Vatistas is very soft with relatively muted fruit, allowing for the development of herbs and spices. The whites have an edge over the reds. Out of fourteen wines, the most interesting are those with varying styles: a very textured and supple Petroulanos; a rich Chardonnay from Pylia, called Iliokritos, and an excellent, clean, crisp Athiri.

MESSINIA

Messinia is located in the southwest of the Peloponnese, with Laconia to the east and Arcadia and Ilia to the north. Just off the prefecture's capital, Kalamata, is the Messiniakos Gulf, while the gentle bend of the western coasts close to Kyparissia, the second most important town, forms the Kyparissiakos Gulf, a sub-part of the Ionian Sea. Messinia is one of the least mountainous prefectures of the department. There is the daunting Taygetos Mountain right in the middle of Mani and the high altitude area of Mountain Psihro southeast of Kyparissia, but the rest of the area is covered by mild hills and small plains.

The climate is influenced by the presence of the Ionian Sea and the relatively low latitude. Messinia is quite hot during the summer months, although not as hot as Corinth. Despite being on the western side of the Peloponnese, rainfall is limited during summer months. But this goes up in October, when the average rainfall is 85.3 millimetres (just over three inches), making Messinia unsuitable for varieties that are harvested this late.

In terms of vineyard acreage, Messinia is far more important than Laconia, with almost four-and-a-half times more land dedicated to vine. However, most of these 2,800 hectares are found close to the Ionian coasts or in the proximity of Messinia. In most of the sites, water management is important and vine stress can be excessive in hot vintages. Having a milder topography than Corinth and Arcadia and a lack of high altitudes makes site selection slightly easier for local Messinia growers. Soils are generally clay-dominated and are fertile enough to support good yields. Even at ninety hectolitres per hectare, good quality and maturity are attainable in most vintages.

A variety of varieties

Messinia traditionally has a complex varietal profile, with influence from the Ionian Islands, as shown by the presence of Goustolidi and the rest of the Peloponnese, with the red Fokiano, Monemvasia, and Corinthiaki. Even Aegean varieties, like Mandilaria, are present. Despite a relatively equal balance between white and red grapes, Messinia has created a good name for its red wines, as shown over the last decade with the excellent wines of Konstantinos Tsolis and Theodoros Dereskos. The reputation of this region – which, until 1985, didn't boast any bottled wine – is growing, persuading companies from other areas to invest in vineyards and wineries.

Another change that has happened over the last fifteen years is the introduction of French varieties, especially Cabernet Sauvignon. Currently, the only Greek red variety included in the Messinia list of recommended varieties is Monemvasia. Cabernet Sauvignon gives some impressive results, especially in the most important vine-growing area of Trifilia, close to Gargaliani. There is also some Agiorgitiko and Grenache Rouge, while it seems that Tempranillo has found a good home in the neighbourhood. For white varieties, mainly confined around Pylos, the main grapes are Ugni Blanc, Chardonnay, the occasional Savatiano, and some Grenache Blanc. Typically, Messinia wines reflect the warmth of the area in their intensity, showing a very New World-like personality. This is also a region where growers should aim for high levels of ripeness.

Messinia does not have any quality-wine appellations, OPEs or OPAPs, so the TO status could be seen as a bit of a let-down for Trifilia. The other two regional designations are a prefectural TO of Messinia and one for the whites of Pylos.

Messinia TO

White still: dry.
White varieties: Roditis and Fileri sixty per cent combined; Ugni Blanc up to thirty per cent Lagorthi; Chardonnay.
Red still: dry.
Red varieties: Merlot thirty per cent; Carignan; Grenache Rouge; Cabernet Sauvignon; Cabernet Franc.

Pylia TO

White still: dry.
White varieties: Ugni Blanc up to twenty per cent; Roditis; Chardonnay.

Trifilia TO

Red still: dry
Red varieties: Carignan; Grenache Rouge; Cabernet Sauvignon; Cabernet Franc; Merlot.

PRODUCERS

APOSTOLOPOULOS ESTATE

Raches, Kiparissia, 245 00 Messinia. Tel: +30 276 107 1234.

Head office: 21 Makedonias, Kalamata, 241 00 Messinia.

Tel: +30 272 102 0600; Fax: +30 272 106 2800.

Vineyards owned: 5ha; production: 800hl.

The Apostolopoulos Estate is located to the north of Kyparissia, close to Messinia's borders with Ilia. The winery has been active since 1987, when it was established by Konstantinos Apostolopoulos, whose sons – Giorgos and Thanassis – now run the company. The family vineyards are registered as partially organic.

Interestingly, the wines from Apostolopoulos are all dual-varietals. Their style is forward and supple. The white of the estate is a Chardonnay/Fileri blend, with hints of exotic fruits and honey aromas. Fileri is also used for the light rosé wine of the estate, coupled here with Grenache Rouge. Finally, there are two Cabernet Sauvignon-dominated reds. Lyrodos is Cabernet Sauvignon with Grenache, coming from the organic part of the estate, while the top wine is a Cabernet Sauvignon/Merlot blend, aged in French barriques for a year. Overall, an honest and well-made, if slightly conservative, range.

DERESKOS ESTATE

Floka Gargalianon, 244 00 Messinia.

Tel/Fax: +30 276 304 1105.

Vineyards owned: 5ha; under contract: 5ha; production: 150hl.

Together with Tsolis Winery, Dereskos Estate is the finest of Messinia's wine producers. Theodoros Dereskos started his private enterprise in 1995, based on a vineyard plot he acquired in the Agrilia area, close to Gargliani. Only Chardonnay and Cabernet Sauvignon are planted, forming the backbone of his range. Dereskos manages to craft excellent wines in a cellar that has only the most basic equipment, proving that a low-tech approach in a hot climate can give good results – provided that the winemakers knows exactly the style they are aiming for.

Agrilia White is a stainless-steel-aged Chardonnay, fermented in slightly elevated temperatures. It does not have a high-pitched aromatic fruit profile but it does have warmth and concentration, being close in style to the excellent Papaioannou unoaked Chardonnay. Dereskos Estate White is the oak-fermented version, aged in new French and American oak for five months. It is full-flavoured and intense without being overripe, but is perhaps a little less graceful than Agrilia.

The same brand names are used for the two Cabernet Sauvignons. Agrilia Red is fermented with natural yeasts and a maceration of seven days. The wine stays in barrique for about ten months, in a blend of American and French oak. Agrilia, even if it is not the most extracted Cabernet, can age gracefully for more than a decade, especially in good vintages like 1994, retaining freshness and a charming grassiness. The most remarkable wine is the Dereskos Estate Red. This goes through a longer extraction and the ageing is in new oak. The levels of grape ripeness are higher than in the Agrilia, so Dereskos uses cultured yeasts. Less elegant than Agrilia but intense, typical, and with a few years in bottle, very complex.

INOMESSINIAKI
6km Kalamata-Messini, 241 00 Kalamata.
Tel: +30 272 106 9905/9465; Fax: +30 272 106 9906;
Website: www.inomessiniaki.gr; Email: inom@otenet.gr
Production: 1,000hl.

Panayiotis Ksigoros started this business in 1998 with a modern winery located near Kalamata. The aim was the creation of a solid line of bottled products, mainly aiming at the local market. The basic wines are multi-varietal: the Messiniakos White is made from a blend of Roditis, Fileri, and Chardonnay; the Rosé is a blend of Grenache Rouge, Carignan, and Fokiano; while the Red includes Cabernet Sauvignon, Cabernet Franc, Mandilaria, and Agiorgitiko. The best Inomessiniaki wines are three single-varietals: a Cabernet Sauvignon, an oaky, yeasty Chardonnay, and an intense, rich yet firm Merlot.

NESTOR, COOPERATIVE OF MESSINIA
Chora, Trifilia, 246 00 Messinia.
Tel: +30 276 303 1264; Fax: +30 276 303 1850;
Website: www.onestor.gr; Email: onestor@onestor.gr
Members: 1,100; total production: 52,000hl.

A leader of the region in terms of volume, Nestor is almost on a par with its counterpart in Nemea. The co-op was established in 1954 and is a major supplier of red wine for big, branded table wines from most large producers. The winery crushes over twenty-one varieties, most of which are French, and sells most of its production in bulk, although there are some bottled products, mainly in one-litre bottles or larger formats.

TSOLI WINERY

Mouzaki Gargaliani, 244 00 Messinia. Tel/Fax: +30 276 302 2125.

Vineyards owned: 20ha; under contract: 10ha; production: 2,500hl.

Konstantinos Tsolis started this venture in 1993, trying to capitalize on the Cabernet Sauvignon vineyards he had planted in the mid-1980s. The winery quickly attracted Dionissis Koukis, a key figure in the Greek wine trade as well as in publishing, and his son, Philippos, then studying oenology in France. Excellent vineyard sites and a very focused winemaking approach showed from the initial vintages that Tsolis was one of the emerging greats of Greek wine. The quality of the estate improved further in 1999, when Philippos returned to Greece and took over as head winemaker. The style remained powerful and dense, but several layers of complexity were added. The Koukis winemaking style is not highly technical nor overly extracted, so the power and the density is due mainly to low yields, often below forty hectolitres per hectare.

The only white produced in this winery is Ampelou Ghis, a sixty/forty Chardonnay/Roditis blend, with three months in new French oak. There is also a red Ampelou Ghis, with an individual blend of seventy per cent Tempranillo and Cabernet Sauvignon. This is the most approachable Tsolis red, with only five days of maceration and eight months in oak, a third of which is new. The wine has a charming softness and is a very promising indication of what Tempranillo can do in the region.

The rest of the Tsolis portfolio leans towards much more serious levels of structure. The first Cabernet Sauvignon is called K of Ftelia. The must is macerated for seven to eight days and then aged in forty per cent new French oak for a year and then another year in bottle. K of Ftelia is a full-bodied, spicy, and age-worthy wine. The next Cabernet Sauvignon of Tsolis, Annie's Animus, is more expensive, so most people assume it is a better wine, but each, in its own way, is equally impressive. Annie's Animus is macerated for ten days, while the ageing in oak lasts for two years. Because of longer contact in wood, the proportion of new barriques is limited to one-third, so that all the oak is rotated every three years. After two more years in bottle, Annie's Animus has a different kind of complexity and another style of power. A recent addition is Annie's Animus Merlot, which is kept in wood for eighteen months and forms a softer, quicker-maturing version of its counterpart. Only the three top reds of Tsolis are unfined and unfiltered.

It would be interesting to see Tsolis focusing on Tempranillo, a variety that seems to have the potential for great things in the area. An Annie's

Animus Tempranillo could be the first attempt at a Greek interpretation of a Rioja Gran Reserva – the winemaking team is looking into it, as well as the possibility of an Annie's Animus Chardonnay.

ILIA

Ilia is in the northwest of the Peloponnese. Together with Achaia and Aitoloakarnania in Central Greece, Ilia is often grouped under the separate sub-department of Western Greece. It borders Achaia to the north, Arcadia to the east, Messinia to the south, and faces the Kyparissiakos Gulf and Ionian Sea to the west. The capital is Pyrgos, with Amaliada being the second most important town.

The southwest-facing slopes of Mount Erymanthos occupy a small part of the region, and the borders with Messinia are relatively mountainous, peaking at 1,344 metres (4,409 feet). Apart from these two areas, Ilia has plenty of low-lying fields suitable for many kinds of agriculture. As one might expect, most villages have developed around these more exploitable areas. The climate of Ilia is influenced by the Ionian Sea, with its high humidity and bouts of rain in the summer. High-capacity vineyards with crowded canopies can occasionally lead to problems with downy mildew and botrytis.

Vines and grapes

Viticulture in Ilia is a cross between Achaia and Messinia. The acreage of vineyards is 3,232 hectares, larger than Messinia but still just half of what exists in Achaia. The growers of the prefecture have traditionally been linked with the producers of Patras, since the latter were the only wine companies in the proximity that were able to generate some demand for their grapes. The local co-op has been established for decades but it is unable to absorb the substantial local production. In terms of private wineries, the situation is similar to that of Messinia in that twenty years ago there were no producers bottling wine on a noteworthy scale. The salvation came in the shape of the Mercouri Estate, a winery that had been active in the area during the nineteenth century and the first decade of the twentieth. In the early 1990s, the latest Kanellakopoulos generation, Hristos and Vassilis, decided to start wine production again. Their Mercouri Estate made most wine aficionados rethink the quality potential of Ilia, and four other wineries were soon established.

The varietal profile of Ilia includes Roditis, Mavrodaphne, and some Corinthiaki. The Mercouri Estate had introduced Refosco in the 1870s, which became widespread in the area and was known as Mercoureiko. There is also some Avgoustiatis, and Tourkopoula. The latter was once believed to be a clone or sub-variety of Roditis, but has since been proved to be a separate vine. Moderately vigorous but highly productive, it is sensitive to downy mildew, so quality-oriented producers must keep yields and canopy densities under control. It buds in late March and is harvested in late August. It can give high sugar levels, low acidity, and full, quality Roditis-style aromas.

There are two TOs in Ilia. The TO of Letrinoi is the designation created for Mercouri Estate, while the Pissatidos TO relates to Roditis whites.

Letrinoi TO
Red still: dry.
Red varieties: Refosco eighty-five per cent; Mavrodaphne fifteen per cent.

Pissatidos TO
White still: dry.
White varieties: Roditis; Fileri; Chardonnay; Sauvignon Blanc.

PRODUCERS

BRINTZIKIS ESTATE
Latzoi, Pelopio, 270 60 Ilia. Tel: +30 262 106 9183/202 4195;
Fax: +30 262 202 4195.
Vineyards owned: 8ha; under contract: 10ha; production: 450hl.
This small organic producer started planting vineyards in the early 1990s, but did not begin bottling wines until 1997. Dionissis Bintzikis' winery – very close to the site of the ancient city of Olympia – was initially quite low-tech, but in the last five years much investment has gone into winemaking equipment. Four wines are produced and all bar the Chardonnay are made with organically cultivated grapes. Enipeas is a Pissatidos TO, with good, melony Roditis fruit; the Chardonnay has decent aroma and body; the rosé is made with many local varieties; but Brintzikis Estate is the best wine. It is mainly Avgoustiatis, with a small percentage of Mavrodaphne, and has an excellent, intense nose and a relatively light but vibrant palate structure.

COOPERATIVE OF ILIA AND OLYMPIA
8 Kokkinou Street, Pyrgos, 271 00 Ilia. Tel: +30 262 102 9973/6; Fax: +30 262 103 5712; Website: www.eashlol.gr; Email: eashleiasolympias@yahoo.gr

Vineyards under contract: 2,000ha; production: 5,000hl.

The Cooperative of Ilia and Olympia started back in 1921, but has remained small in size, at least given the total vineyard acreage of the region. It is one of the least developed co-ops in the Peloponnese. Head winemaker is Dimitris Dionissopoulos, a skilled oenologist who has been giving valuable help to many local private wineries, including the Mercouri Estate. The winery crushes mainly white grapes, such as Roditis, the Asproudes family, and Fileri, with only small quantities dedicated to local Mavroudi versions. There is a focus on bulk wine and the only bottled product is the Pothitos White.

KOKKALIS ESTATE
Skafidia, 271 00 Ilia. Tel: +30 262 105 4069;
Fax (in Germany): +49 21 614 1046.
Vineyards owned: 2.7ha; production: 90hl.

Kokkalis Estate is a very idiosyncratic winery, even among Greek producers. Hristos Kokkalis has been making wine in Ilia since 1993, but not a single bottle of it had been sold in Greece. He lives and works in Germany, so the total production is exported to this market. However in mid-2000, an eagle-eyed sommelier spotted some bottles in Germany, and now Kokkalis Estate wines can be found in tiny quantities in Athens.

Dimitris Dionissopoulos is the wine consultant. Kokkalis produces only two red wines, the most famous of which is Trilogia, a full-bodied and quite tannic Cabernet Sauvignon, much in the style of Messinia Cabernets. Although some bottle variation has been noted in the past, the wine is seriously age-worthy. Mova, a Cabernet Sauvignon/Agiorgitiko blend, is a lot more approachable, showing more fruit and a less firm structure.

MERCOURI ESTATE
Korakohori, Pyrgos, 271 00 Ilia. Tel: +30 262 104 1601;
Fax: +30 262 104 1901; Email: mercouri@otenet.gr
Vineyards owned: 8.5ha; under contract: 5ha; production: 1,000–1,200hl.

This winery has it all: one of the most beautiful estates in Greece; two of the most down-to-earth owners in the Greek wine sector; plus some of the most elegant wines made at this latitude around the world. One of the most high-profile families in Ilia for some time, the Mercouri connection with wine dates back to 1870, when a winery was built for the grapes produced on the estate. Mercouri had strong connections with Italy, so it decided to plant the Italian grape Refosco.

Despite the winery's success, the estate lay dormant between World War II and the late-1980s, at which time Hristos and Vassilis Kanellakopoulos thought it would be a good idea to relaunch the Mercouri Estate. Dimitris Dionissopoulos, a friend of Hristos and the winemaker at the local co-op, became consultant. The Dionissopoulos style is to let every vineyard speak for itself, rather than impose his own vision everywhere.

A few thousand bottles of Domaine Mercouri were released onto the market in 1991 and it was an instant success. Many Greeks initially tried it only because they were thinking there was some connection with one of Greece's greatest divas, Melina Mercouri. But the first sip was enough to convince anyone. This blend of eighty-five per cent Refosco and Mavrodaphne had an amazing elegance, grace, and breathtaking complexity. It was understated in many ways, but the essence was there.

Over the years, Domaine Mercouri has developed, getting better and better, defying modern trends to continue evolving its own personality. The wine shows vintage variation, but this has more to do with ageing ability than character. During its first five years, there is a growing depth and a fascinating fragrance, and this bottle development made the Kanellakopoulos brothers think about making a cava. This label does not differ from the standard Domaine Mercouri; both wines are aged for about a year in a mixture of old and new French barriques. But while the standard version is released onto the market two years after harvest, the cava is out after four. It is the same great wine, but at another phase of its development.

Slowly but steadily, Mercouri's range has been embellished with more products. The only wine that has been made in any significant quantities is Foloi, a Pissatidos TO Roditis. One of the intense examples of the variety, it is full of juicy, ripe fruit. There is a barrel-fermented version of it, Foloi Fumé, but the oak is a bit too much for the grapes.

The rest of the range consists of far more imaginative products, but unfortunately, quantities are severely limited, usually less than 5,000 bottles per year. Antaris is a Mourvèdre/Avgoustiatis blend, with aromatic intensity from the Ionian grape. It is warm, rich, and deep. Kallisto is made from Tourkopoula and Ribolla Gialla, an Italian grape from Friuli: a spicy, full, and individual white. Coma Berenices is a Viognier, a touch on the full-blown side, but possibly lacking the extract and focus of the variety. Orion is an enjoyable rosé from Grenache. Finally, there is a sweet wine called Hortais made from Mavrodaphne and some Corinthiaki which is aged in oak for more than four years. This could clearly be a yardstick for where Mavrodaphne dessert wines could aim in the future. Mercouri is a great estate that deserves to be well-known worldwide.

STAVROPOULOS ESTATE
Palaiochori, Amaliada, 272 00 Ilia.
Tel: +30 262 102 6657; Fax: +30 262 103 0657.
Vineyards owned: 3ha; under contract: 1ha; production: 75hl.

Dimitris Dionossopoulos is the wine consultant at this, the most recent Ilia venture, active since 1998. The start was a bit slow, but a new winery in 2002 has given a whole new dimension to the wines. The owner, Dionissis Stavropoulos, is working towards complete organic cultivation. The main varieties are Alepou Roditis and Merlot, with some experimental plantings of Avgoustiatis and Aglianico.

The first wine produced was Ilis, a pure Merlot aged for a year in new French and American oak. Although dominated by wood, beneath this layer the wine is soft and elegant. The new winery will change things, as shown by the addition of an Assyrtico named Linon to the portfolio, which has freshness and charm, a factor evident even from the packaging. This producer is likely to get much better in quality, and Aglianico has the potential to give excellent results in the area.

ACHAIA
Achaia forms part of the northern coast of the Peloponnese, touching on the gulfs of Patraikos and Corinth. Ilia lies on its west, Arcadia to the south, and Corinth to the east. The capital is Patras, with Rio, Egio, Kato Achaia, and Kalavrita being the most important provincial towns.

Most of Achaia lies on the slopes of three mountains so steep that they almost block any communication with Arcadia. From west to east these are Erymanthos, Panahaiko, and Helmos, also known as Aroania. Apart from some coastal areas, the only low-lying part of the region is found in the western parts, towards Ilia and the towns of Amaliada and Pyrgos. This is the parcel with the richest soils, as well as the warmest meso-climates. Higher elevations escape much of the summer heat, but low winter temperatures can be a potential problem. In addition, summer rainfall is quite high by Greek standards, but not quite high enough to rule out irrigation. Due to the proximity of Patras, infrastructure for irrigation is in place and water is not scarce. There are, however, some humidity traps in the area that can potentially lead to fungal diseases in sensitive varieties.

Achaia is another viticultural powerhouse, with a total vineyard acreage of 6,703 hectares. This makes it slightly larger than Corinth and one of the largest prefectures in Greece in terms of grape production. Vine-growing has always been a strong part of the local culture, as well as a major occupation for people living outside Patras and its important port. Key factors in this have been the flourishing Corinthiaki raisin production; the presence of a large company, Achaia Clauss; a strong cooperative; and finally a prosperous bulk wine trade.

Quality and sweetness

In the last three decades Achaia has been blessed with no fewer than four quality-wine appellations, one of which has proved to be a gold-mine. There is one OPAP related to dry whites from Roditis, called Patras (*see* Chapter 4 and Appendix 1). The rest of the Quality appellations are OPEs and relate to sweet wines: Mavrodaphne of Patras; Muscat of Patras; and Muscat of Rio of Patras. All these appellations allow a maximum yield of ninety-four hectolitres per hectare. Sweet Muscat wines can be produced using three methods, namely *vin doux*, *vin doux naturel*, and *vin naturellement doux*, with the most popular being the first two where fortification takes place at some stage of the process (*see* Glossary). Only the very best producers go for the third, a totally natural alcoholic fermentation of overripe or sun-dried grapes. Mavrodaphne is only made as *vin doux* and *vin doux naturel*.

Patras OPAP is the appellation where the Roditis variety, or varieties, should be at their best, and in many cases they are. Well-made Roditis from high-altitude, low-yielding vineyards can be the epitome of Greek white wine. Rich, lemony, intense on the nose, broad on the palate, and full of volume, from the first whiff to the last note of the aftertaste. The fruit is ripe, melony, and honeyed. The top Patras wines develop in bottle for two to four years into more restrained but honeyed aroma profiles.

The Patras appellation covers a variety of locations, starting with the slopes of the surrounding mountains, the valley floors, and finishing close to the coast. This area is made up of a vast number of different sites, soils, and meso-climates, and a proportion of the designated region might have difficulties laying claims to quality-wine production. Even among top-quality sites, there are vineyards able to produce excellent fruit, but that are not suited to Roditis. To accentuate the problems, much potential is lost due to widespread plantings of Gaidouroroditis ("donkey Roditis"), the high-yielding, large-cluster Roditis clone that was favoured during the latest Achaia replanting programme. Its grapes attain the characteristic pink tinge only with difficulty.

Given the lack of uniformity within the Patras OPAP region, there is not much discussion about *cru* designations or Super-OPAP status – at least not as much as in Nemea. The reason is the different nature of Patras producers, which tend to be slightly larger than average and to use much more cross-commune blending than their counterparts in Nemea. Nevertheless, mountainous regions like the villages around Kalavrita and the slopes of Mounts Panahaiko and Tritea, have vast potential with their exquisite granite, silicone, and sand soils. The declassification of some low-altitude, more fertile sites, and the creation of some TOs (regional wine appellations) within or outside the Patras OPAP area would surely assist improvement in quality, as well as encourage experimentation with alternative grapes. Vine-growers across Achaia, cultivating "proper" Roditis, Roditis Alepou, or other varieties like Vertzami or Santamariana, a rare white variety full of power and aroma, should be promoted and protected by law.

Fame and fortune

Mavrodaphne of Patras is the most famous appellation in Greece, both within and outside her boundaries. The style of this sweet wine from the charismatic Mavrodaphne variety was probably first established by Gustav Clauss, the founder of the pioneering Achaia Clauss winery. Clauss had been visiting Douro, studying port, just before he came to live in Greece in 1861. On encountering Mavrodaphne, a variety that had been imported into the region from Cephalonia, he decided to try to make a port-style wine with it. Nearly 150 years later, Mavrodaphne of Patras is one of Greece's strongest wine export products. Today, more than fifteen wineries produce Mavrodaphne of Patras.

Even if the initial inspiration for Mavrodaphne was port, wineries soon started experimenting, which resulted in a number of variations in methods of making and ageing of the wine. Some producers stayed loyal to the initial inspiration, allowing a short fermentation before fortification. Others went for a different approach, with the addition of spirit shortly after the grapes have been pressed, so that fermentation is not conducted at all. Both methods lead to fifteen per cent alcohol, but there is a difference in the residual sugar levels. *Vin doux* wines have at least 200 grams per litre, while *vin doux naturel* wines usually have around 160 grams per litre.

During ageing, everything relates to cost, quality aspirations, and philosophy. Cheap Mavrodaphne will be left to age in stainless-steel or cement vats. Good-quality wines will age in oak, usually old, large barrels, sometimes exceeding a capacity of 2,000 litres. So far, only Nikos Karelas (*see* below) has experimented with new oak, and the results have been promising. Some small growers are said to have left their Mavrodaphne barrels in the sun, trying to get some degree of maderization.

Another factor determining the character of the final product is the topping-up of barrels. While some winemakers will allow a head-space to develop, leading to a degree of oxidation and higher levels of volatile acidity in the final product, others will meticulously keep their barrels full. In the former style of ageing, the volatility can be excessive, but in wines full of extract and density, the oxidation can add complexity rather than subtract quality. Usually, the wine used to top up the barrel is from younger vintages, if not the latest, so there is a kind of short *solera*, with very few *criaderas*. Subsequently, most Mavrodaphne wines on the market are non-vintage and any vintage-dated wines must be in the oxidized style if their vintage date is to be believed. Length of ageing is also a key element, with at least five years needed in oak for the wine to develop its typical dense patina.

At the moment, the Mavrodaphne of Patras OPE is seriously under-performing. This is not to say that there are not plenty of good to excellent wines on the market. In my view, this appellation has the potential to belong to the premier league of the world's sweet wines, together with port, madeira, and sherry. Sadly, this potential is rarely encountered. The first reason is the size of the appellation, including in it land that is evidently not suitable for top-quality grape-growing. There are three zones of cultivation: one around Rio; another on the low fields of the western part of Achaia, and a central part in high-altitude land, with many calcareous elements. Only the last part can be considered prime land, followed to a lesser extent by the Rio zone.

Another factor is that Mavrodaphne does not reach the high Baumé level it does in Cephalonia, so an ameliorator is needed. The handiest solution used to be the addition of some Corinthiaki, since there was a surplus. Today, legislation allows the addition of up to forty-nine per cent of

Corinthiaki, a curse for quality. On the other hand, it is encouraging to see top producers like Antonopoulos disregarding such easy options and starting to make Mavrodaphne with genuine respect for its potential.

Muscat

The two Muscat appellations of Achaia, Muscat of Patras and Muscat of Rio of Patras, are not as popular as the Aegean Muscats, possibly because they are eclipsed by the success of Mavrodaphne. Both were established in 1982 with four different sub-categories: the three methods of production plus a *grand cru* designation for wines coming from the higher parts of the region. The usual method of production is through fortification: it is cheaper; less labour-intensive; and gives cleaner, sweeter, and far more commercial wines. Due to their close proximity, Muscat of Patras and Muscat of Rio may seem as though little differentiates them. However, this is not true: Most of the Patras appellation area is on clay, leading to richer, more intense, and fruitier Muscats. In contrast, the coastal Rio is milder during summer months, leading to more supple, less forward, but more floral wines. Only the Co-op of Patraiki and Achaia Clauss produce wines from both appellations.

Beyond the quality designations, Achaia has two TOs. The TO Côtes de Petrotou has been developed for Château Clauss, the Achaia Clauss blend of Mavrodaphne and Cabernet Sauvignon. The second TO, Côtes de Aigialias TO, was established after the persistence of Angelos Rouvalis and the late Yiannis Karabatsos, co-founders of the Oenoforos winery (*see* below).

North and south

Aigialia is one of Greece's few major northern-facing regions to cultivate vines. In warm climates, many vine-growers believe that by planting vines on slopes with a northern aspect, the unwanted effects of blazing sunlight can be avoided. This is not true if the ambient temperatures on these vineyards are high – the vine, in a hot environment, needs more energy and therefore more sunlight, to both sustain itself and to ripen fruit. Nonetheless, the "balconies over the Gulf of Corinth", as Aigialia is often referred to, have quite a unique meso-climate.

The land of Greece flows from a mountainous spine formed by the Pindos range and several other mountains of the north to the southern tip of the Peloponnese. Because of this, the vast majority of vineyard sites face from west to south to east. Most regions with a northerly aspect have less sunlight but high temperatures. The only significant exception to this is a strip of sea formed by the gulfs of Corinth and Patras. This body of water has a cooling, moderating effect on the surrounding areas so that Aigialia, being on the south side, escapes the heat and sunlight reflected by the water.

In addition to this, winds accelerate around Aigio, since it is so close to the narrow meeting point between the gulfs of Patras and Rio. The surrounding mountains, just to the south, break the hot winds coming from Africa. All these factors combine with altitudes of 600–900 metres (1,968–2,953 feet) to create a meso-climate in Aigialia that is remarkably cooler than Patras, Corinth, or the central Peloponnese. Cabernet Sauvignon and other varieties grown on Côtes de Aigialia can reach 13.5 per cent potential alcohol with ease, coupled with acidities of nine grams per litre, out of which a full four grams per litre can be malic acid, an acid that decomposes in the grape in hot environments, especially when the temperature exceeds 25°C (77°F). In the Nemea region, a couple of hours drive to the southeast, most Agiorgitiko grapes are harvested at 12.5 per cent potential alcohol, but have only traces of malic acid.

Côtes de Aigialia, overall, has enormous potential for quality. The key architect of the modern Greek wine scene, Stavroula Kourakou-Dragona, was impressed enough to call it "one of the best terroirs around the world".[1] Unique climate aside, it is a region with an exceptional homogeneity of sites. In addition, growers have shown an unusually high level of technical dexterity and commitment to high quality and low yields – even Gaidouroroditis is relatively hard to find. When the short list for the next new OPAP classification is drawn up, Côtes de Aigialia must be one of the prime candidates.

Patras OPAP

White still: dry.
White variety: Roditis.

Muscat of Patras OPE

White still: naturally sweet (*vin naturellement doux*); fortified sweet (*vin doux naturel*); fortified sweet from selected vineyards (*vin doux naturel grand cru*); fortified sweet (*vin doux*).
White variety: Muscat Blanc.

1. *Ampelooinika Nea* ("Wine & Vine News"), October–December 1996.

Muscat of Rio of Patras OPE

White still: naturally sweet (*vin naturellement doux*); fortified sweet (*vin doux naturel*); fortified sweet from selected vineyards (*vin doux naturel grand cru*); sweet (*vin doux*).
White variety: Muscat Blanc.

Mavrodaphne of Patras OPE

Red still: naturally sweet (*vin naturellement doux*); fortified sweet (*vin doux*).
Red varieties: Mavrodaphne, Black Corinthiaki.

Côtes de Petrotou TO

Red still: dry.
Red varieties: Mavrodaphne (at least sixty per cent of the blend); Cabernet Sauvignon.

Côtes de Aigialia TO

White still: dry.
White varieties: Lagorthi (at least sixty per cent of the blend); Chardonnay, the balance being other local recommended and permitted grape varieties.
Rosé still: dry.
Rosé varieties: Volitsa (at least sixty per cent of the blend), the balance being other local recommended and permitted grape varieties.
Red still: dry.
Red varieties: Cabernet Sauvignon (at least forty per cent of the blend), the balance being other local recommended and permitted grape varieties.

PRODUCERS

ACHAIA CLAUSS

Petroto, Patras, 265 00 Achaia. Tel: +30 261 036 8100;
Fax: +30 261 033 8269. Email: achaia@clauss.gr
Head office: 184 Kanakari & Gounari Street, Patras, 262 21 Achaia.
Vineyards owned: 10ha; under contract: 80ha; production: 15,000hl.

One of the most historic wine companies in Greece and the first major private investment in the sector, Achaia Clauss was established in 1861 by German Gustav Clauss. He is also credited with initiating the sweet style of Mavrodaphne, as well as its successful promotion throughout Europe (*see* page 351). After World War I, the company was bought by Vlassis Antonopoulos, a trader of Corinthiaki grapes.

Over the decades, the company gradually became less proactive and faded out of the spotlight – until the 1970s, when Demestica was introduced. Demestica was a high-volume, value-oriented product and, at the same time, it was the first Greek wine bottled under cork. Demestica totally dominated the Greek market for fifteen years, while it also won fame and notoriety in export markets and among ex-pats around the globe. Even in the late 1990s, many UK wine-drinkers will cite Demestica as the first Greek wine they ever tasted.

At its peak, during the early 1980s Demestica is said to have sold close to twenty million bottles annually. At that point, Achaia Clauss entered a troubled era, with fierce economic problems that sadly pushed the Antonopoulos family out of the business. The company was taken over by banks and financial institutions. Nevertheless, the winery in Clauss Hill, outside Patras, is still one of the most impressive establishments in Greece.

Sweet Mavrodaphne owes a lot to Achaia Clauss, but at the same time the reputation of the winery relied on this wine. Achaia Clauss uses Corinthiaki at a much lower level than the allowed forty-nine per cent. The desired oxidation is controlled by topping-up the barrels. Given that the majority of Achaia Clauss Mavrodaphne is released onto the market at eight years of age, the wines taste youthful and are still fruity.

There are three standard bottlings. The basic Mavrodaphne Imperial is a good entry point and excellent value. Mavrodaphne Reserve 601 is a step up in quality, but remains reasonable in price. The Mavrodaphne Grande Reserve is a lot higher in price, but this is more than reflected in its quality. It is usually released around the fifteen- to eighteen-years mark, each bottle is numbered, with the last two digits signifying the vintage. The elegant style of wine suggests frequent topping-up, so a small percentage of younger wine must have been included at some stage. Regardless of vintage, Grande Reserve is what is needed to place Mavrodaphne in the same ranks as other, better-known fortified wines.

But Achaia Clauss' involvement with fortified Mavrodaphne goes much further. The company's cellar contains an amazing library of barrels said to go back for the last seventy years. Despite its significant financial difficulties, this cellar remained untouched. The apogee of this collection is found in two barrels with wine from the 1882 vintage. A few bottles of wine are produced each year from these barrels and the wine is sampled on special occasions.

Beyond Mavrodaphne, Achaia Clauss remained focused on traditional, high-volume products until some recent additions to its portfolio, aimed at younger consumers. The company produces more than sixty products, but the most important dry wines are Cava Clauss and Château Clauss. Cava is a blend of Mavrodaphne, Cabernet Sauvignon, and Agiorgitiko, while Château Clauss, the first Greek wine to bear such a designation, is Mavrodaphne and Cabernet Sauvignon. When first released in 1978, these wines created quite a stir.

ANTONOPOULOS VINEYARDS
101, 25 Martiou Street, 265 00 Patras. Tel: +30 261 052 5459;
Fax: +30 261 0526762; Email: neadris@hol.gr
Vineyards owned: 20ha; under contract: 45ha; production: 4,125hl.

A great name and a great Greek wine estate, Antonopoulos Vineyards was started in 1987 by Konstantinos Antonopoulos, after his family began losing control of the Achaia Clauss winery. The heart of the venture was a private vineyard in Vassiliko, Achaia, where Antonopoulos planted many French and rare local varieties that he wanted to explore. His first releases showed an approach that was light-years ahead of his time. Unfortunately, in 1994, Antonopoulos died in a car accident and the future of his enterprise was in jeopardy. The Halikias cousins, Nicos and Yiannis, owners of Santa Maura, the distribution company for Antonopoulos, decided to buy the operation to try and give it a second chance. After a few vintages, Yiannis was left in charge of Antonopoulos Vineyards while Nicos returned full-time to Santa Maura. Antonopoulos would always have been a hard act to follow, but over the years Halikias has proved himself a worthy successor.

The winemaking team has always been key to the company's success. Tassos Drossiadis, a gifted oenologist currently working for Oenoforos, started his career here. Now the winemaking team has five members, including a viticulturalist, and is headed by winemaking prodigy Mihalis Probonas, who seems able to perform the most complex processes with great ease. Most importantly, every grape gets individual treatment. For example, every red variety is cold-soaked before the start of the alcoholic fermentation which ranges from three days at 8°C (46°F) for Vertzami, to five days at 5°C (41°F) for Cabernet Sauvignon, and seven days at 12°C (54°F) for Merlot. Some musts are pressed at the end of fermentation and the skins are then added back to the finished wine, while other varieties go through more conservative post-fermentation extractions. Length of macerations vary according to the vintage, and oak-usage is carefully controlled. The second-fill barriques for Syrah have to be from Cabernet Sauvignon, but for Cabernet Sauvignon they must be from Chardonnay.

The portfolio illustrates this obsession with detail. The workhorse wines of the winery are the Idiotiki Sillogi pair: a fruity and juicy unoaked Chardonnay from a vineyard in Ilia and a soft Mavrodaphne/Merlot blend. Antonopoulos Mantinia is one of the best-selling premium Moschofilero wines in Greece. Adoli Ghis, a blend of Lagorthi, Asproudes varieties, Roditis, and Chardonnay, has won many fans, including noted UK wine writer and critic Steven Spurrier. Stylistically opposite, Antonopoulos Chardonnay is a powerful but balanced wine that has been compared with Comte Lafon Burgundies by leading UK journalist Jancis Robinson MW.

The top Antonopoulos wine produced in quantity is Cabernet Nea Dris, meaning "new oak". The seventy/thirty blend of Cabernet Sauvignon and Cabernet Franc is aged in seventy-five per cent new oak. Nea Dris is a red akin to top-quality Barossa Cabernet. Meanwhile, a small-volume range called Gerontoklima Rematias is earning top honours for pure individuality. A Moschofilero Gris de Noir – ultra-ripe grapes macerated for twelve hours at 5°C (41°F) and kept *sur lie* for three months, gives a most exotic example of the variety. The Sauvignon Blanc of the range is closer to the Loire in style than anything else made in Greece. Finally, there are two monumental blended reds: a unique Vertzami, sourced from Lefkada, blended with Cabernet Franc, plus a more conventional Merlot/Syrah.

Finally, there are two sweet wines made from overripe grapes. They are classified as OPEs, while all the others are basic EOs. Antonopoulos Muscat of Rio is honeyed and floral, while Mavrodaphne of Patras is truly excellent. It is kept for six years in old oak, with no topping up, yet the complexity of its raisiny fruit puts all the oxidation into a great framework.

CAVINO

Thesi Gefira Meganiti, Aigio, 251 00 Achaia. Tel: +30 269 107 2003/4;
Fax: +30 269 107 1201; Website: www.cavino.gr; Email: cavino@otenet.gr
Vineyards owned: 30ha; production: 40,000hl.

One of the larger private companies to be found in the north Peloponnese, Cavino was established in 1958, with production stepping up a gear from 1969. Known throughout the 1980s and 1990s as a producer of rather bland, high-volume wines, Cavino did not enjoy a particularly good image among wine-drinkers in Greece. Lately, the company has started investing in new vineyards in Aigialia and in new, fresh, modern packaging. The quality is now there and the new-era Cavino wines should see the company's profile develop in a more positive manner.

Cavino produces over thirty different wines, from retsina to négociant bottlings of OPE Samos and Muscat of Limnos. The recent developments, however, can be seen primarily in a small section of the portfolio. Oionos Chardonnay and Merlot are two TO Peloponnese varieties with a forward, almost Chilean approach and striking packaging. General manager Yiannis Anastassiou wants to expand the product range into organic products, and Aegiohos is a good starting point. It is an OPAP Patras Roditis, sourced from vineyards at 700 metres (2,300 feet), and fermented in new oak barriques. A good line of attack, although it would be interesting to have the percentage of new oak toned down.

There are also two Côtes de Aigialias TOs, which hint at the excellent potential of this terroir: a buttery, barrel-fermented Chardonnay and a firm, reserved Cabernet Sauvignon. Finally, the Cavino Nemea Réserve remains a classic, being restrained and not flashy, but velvety and charming.

FLERIANOU COLLECTION

Kidonies, Patras, 250 08 Achaia. Tel: +30 269 402 2676. Head office: 31 Bacogianni, Vrilissia, 152 35 Athens. Tel/Fax: +30 210 804 5730; Email: fleri@hol.gr Vineyards owned: 2ha; under contract: 1.5ha; production: 200hl.

Mary Flerianou has been one of the most active female winemakers over the last two decades, with an impressive track record at Achaia Clauss and Domaine Hatzimichalis. Mary has been joined by her son Yiannis, a well-travelled, highly educated winemaker in his own right. As well as their individual consultancies, mother and son have joined forces in the Flerianou Collection, a kind of sideline started by Mary in 1994. The portfolio has remained quite small over the years – a varietal Chardonnay, a Nemea, a Mavrodaphne of Patras, and a Sillogi Flerianou White, which is a Robola. All wines are, as expected, very competently made and possess a certain grace rather than power. However, it seems like a spark of excitement is missing both in the wines and in the way they are promoted.

OENOFOROS

Selinous, Aigio, 251 00 Achaia. Tel: +30 269 102 9415; Fax: +30 269 106 0380. Vineyards owned: 8ha; under contract: 150ha; production: 3,000hl.

Oenoforos was founded in 1991 by the oenologist Aggelos Rouvalis and the viticulturalist Yiannis Karabatsos near the town of Aigio. Both men believed that the surrounding Aigialia region had enormous but unrealized potential. From the first vintages it was clear that they had the ability to produce a top Patras OPAP wine. A new winery in the mid-1990s, a wisely expanding portfolio, increasing commercial success, plus the presence of the talented oenologist Tasos Drosiadis, confirm that Oenoforos winery will be one of the high-flyers of the Greek wine industry.

Sadly, in early 2004, Yiannis Karabatsos died, resulting in half the company being put up for sale. Vassilis Kourtakis, a key figure in the wine industry and a friend of Rouvalis, came to the rescue. Kourtakis is managing director of leading Attica-based company, Greek Wine Cellars, formerly known as Kourtaki (*see* page 238).

The Oenoforos claim to fame is its basic product, the white Asprolithi (meaning "white stone"), an OPAP Patras Roditis. Asprolithi is a classic example of what OPAP Patras can be and is one of the best varietal Roditis wines in Greece. Made in a straightforward way, the focus is on the fruit. Despite its popularity, the style is constantly refined. Since 2000, a data-bank has been established from Roditis clones planted in contracted vineyards in order to source a higher proportion of the classic Roditis Alepou, avoiding the sites planted mostly to the Gaido> Gaidouroroditis clone.

The small proportion (eight per cent) of grapes currently put through pre-fermentation maceration is likely to increase to about a fifth, but not above that, in order to preserve the style of the variety. In the 2004 vintage, a Bucher pneumatic press was bought, giving more control over pressing and enabling higher but finer levels of extraction. This increased the proportion of juice that could be included in the Asprolithi from fifty-five to sixty-five per cent, and added extra layers of aromas. The oak-aged version of Asprolithi is a bit more demanding and shows a different approach – gross lees contact in oak, forty per cent new Burgundy 228-litre barriques, and up to fifteen per cent American oak, with no fining or stabilization. There are plans for a reserve version of this, to be released three to four years after the harvest.

Beyond Roditis, Rouvalis and Drosiadis are keen to capitalize on the unique climate of Aigialia with other varieties. The slow ripening and cool temperatures of the area inspired Oenoforos to plant Chardonnay and Cabernet Sauvignon. Both varieties show a compact yet lean personality, coupled with a restrained fruit character. However, the wines bloom after a few years in bottle, the Chardonnay towards a Burgundian style, and the Cabernet Sauvignon into an herbaceous, crushed raspberry leaves, expression. A slightly different style was developed with the Riesling varietal, which displayed a richer character than one might expect.

The range of Mikros Vorias ("little north") is very different in approach. Mikros Vorias Lagorthi retains the cool-climate personality of the variety, but adds more exotic fruit notes, especially on the warmer vintages. Mikros Vorias Syrah vividly shows Drosiadis' cutting-edge knowledge of "fragmental extraction" for reds. The three parcels of Syrah all mature at different times, showing different styles of maturity at harvest. Drosiadis plans what he wants to get from each plot and tries to take the best out of his grapes by varying temperatures, lengths, and methods of maceration. Mikros Vorias Syrah is one of the freshest examples of the grape yet its structure is not heavyweight. Rouvalis also planted a small parcel of Viognier, which is harvested at about the same time with at least one plot of Syrah – the Viognier is pressed and its must added to free-run juice of Syrah, creating Esperitis Rosé.

Finally, Oenoforos and Kir-Yianni have a joint project, Ianos, where Xinomavro from Naoussa, selected by Yiannis Boutaris, plus Cabernet Sauvignon from Rouvalis' Aigialia vineyards are blended and aged at Oenoforos. Initially, Greek wine writers hailed the venture as "the Greek Opus One", but excitement faded quickly. A shame, since the wine has been getting better and better.

PARPAROUSSIS WINERY

1 Ahileos Street, Proastio Patron, 264 42 Achaia.
Tel: +30 261 042 0334; Fax: +30 261 043 8676.
Vineyards owned: 10.5ha; under contract: 6ha; production: 1,000hl.

Dijon graduate Thanassis Parparoussis established his winery in 1974. At the time he was one of the most modern winemakers in the Peloponnese and was the first to use refrigeration for fermenting white wines. As the region started to develop, Parparoussis began to take a more back-to-basics approach, trying to make pure yet complex wines. Rare Greek varieties were added alongside Cabernet Sauvignon, and the use of oak became much more considered.

Today Parparoussis makes two different Nemea wines. Oinari is the higher-volume, more simple *cuvée*, full of sweet red-berry fruit; while Epilegmenos Nemea is the *réserve*. It has an opulent structure but with a rather traditional aromatic profile – no overt, jammy fruit character here, just spicy complexity. For many, this wine is the best old-guard example of the appellation. But the same could be said about Drossalis, the OPAP Patras, which is in complete contrast to Oenoforos Asprolithi – a wine with muted fruit though it is layered on the palate.

Parparoussis has now been working with Cabernet Sauvignon for years and has even planted some vines on sand, right by the coast, to explore the vine's behaviour in such extremes. So far, his only varietal is sold under the Oenofilos label, showing a charming cedary complexity. Perhaps the most individual Parparoussis wines are made from Sideritis, a rare, local white variety that falls into the textured, rich category. Dora Dionyssou is the stainless-steel version, and is a good starting point for those who are unfamiliar with this variety. Dora Dionyssou Fumé is oak-fermented, not as pure, but far more complex. The portfolio is concluded by a Muscat of Rio, which is more of a tenor than a soprano in style. Thanassis also crafts small quantities of a good, aged brandy.

PATRAIKI COOPERATIVE
38 Anthias, Patras, 263 32 Achaia.
Tel: +30 261 032 2644; Fax: +30 261 033 0391.
Head office: 3 Pantanassis, 262 21 Patras; Email: coopatra@otenet.gr
Vineyards under contract: 1,000ha; Members: 7,980; production: 30,000–10,000hl.
The cooperative of Achaia, Patraiki, takes full advantage of the vast quanti-ties of grapes produced in the prefecture. It was one of the first co-ops in the country, established in 1918, and has held an important role in the local community for the last five decades. The people behind Patraiki, especially head winemaker Giorgos Flingos, try hard to keep a good level of quality, something that is presumably not always easy. It is not just the name of Patraiki that is at stake, however, since most of the producers that sell Mavrodaphne use the co-op as a supplier.

When compared with other co-ops, the portfolio of Patraiki is relatively small, considering the volume. However, a key for Patraiki's success is the production of a few, high-volume lines that are great value. The basic line is called Santa Laura, available in white, rosé, and red, followed by a strong retsina and a Cabernet Sauvignon-based cava. Patraiki produces one wine for every quality appellation in the prefecture. While Patras is quite full and rich, and Muscat of Patras has good *typicité*, the fascinating product is the Mavrodaphne. It is a good-quality wine, which happens to be about forty per cent of the appellation's total output. Since it is not aged as long as the one from Achaia Clauss, it has a higher level of primary fruit and also a higher level of tannins. Given the volume of total production per annum, Patraiki is doing a fine job.

PATRAS WINERY/KARELAS WINERY

18km Patron–Pirgou, 252 00 Kato, Achaia. Tel: +30 269 302 3340.
Head office: 41–43 Skagiopouliou, 262 22 Patras, Achaia.
Tel: +30 261 032 1000; Fax: +30 261 031 5858;
Website: www.gkarelassa.gr; Email: info@gkarelassa.gr
Production: 6,800hl.

The Karelas family has been making Mavrodaphne since the mid-1930s. Giorgos Karelas, the current family member in charge of the business, has done much to improve the image of the winery and to expand exports. Oenologist Nicos, Giorgos' brother, keeps the traditional lines running while also developing more exciting products. The core of the Karelas brothers' wines consists of a basic Esperia Patras, an Aiolos Nemea, and three EOs (table wines). Beyond these, there is a dry, floral, crisp Muscat. Nicos has introduced a premium Patras, exclusively from the Violento clone of Roditis – a fine-quality wine that shows density and extract on the palate. The Karelas Muscat of Patras is very idiosyncratic, with its muted varietal character, low residual sugar level, and good palate structure – all signs of a later fortification than usual.

Karelas Mavrodaphne does not include any Corinthiaki and is aged for six years and belongs to the volatile genre of its appellation. In 2005, Karela introduced a Mavrodaphne Fumé, aged for two years in highly toasted new oak, which proved to be a successful, modern interpretation of the grape. Finally, the Karelas family has one barrel of the 1944 Mavrodaphne vintage. Every so often a few bottles are released at a steep price. This, again, belongs to the madeirized school of thought, but the extract and the complexity are still there, undisrupted.

8

Cyclades islands

The Cyclades are the islands that fill the southern part of the Aegean. The Dodecanese Islands are further east, Crete is to the south, and the Peloponnese to the west. Most of the Cyclades are confined within a triangle formed by Andros in the north, Milos at the southwest tip, and Astypalea in the southeast to the east of Santorini – or, if you prefer, a circle or *cyclos*; hence the name. There are around eighteen islands in all, plus numerous inhabitable islets. The largest or most significant ones are Andros, Tinos, Syros, Mykonos, Delos, Paros, Naxos, Serifos, Sifnos, Milos, Ios, Amorgos, and Santorini.

In some ways, the Cyclades are the least isolated of all the Aegean Islands. The Dodecanese and the North Aegean Islands are on Greece's eastern border and very close to the Turkish coast; transport and communication with the Greek mainland is not always easy, especially during the winter – from Rhodes to Piraeus, the port of Athens, it is nearly twelve hours by sea. The Cyclades, however, are mostly less than four hours by sea to Piraeus. It can be quicker door-to-door to Paros or Naxos by ship than by plane – and at a fraction of the cost. This guarantees a steady stream of both tourists and Athenians with holiday homes. On the Cyclades viticulture is of secondary importance to the hospitality industry.

THE RISE OF TOURISM
Probably because of this proximity, the Cyclades followed the political history of the mainland much more closely than either the Dodecanese or the Ionian Islands. They were a part of the Aegean wine trade boom of antiquity – although not as important as Hios or Ikaria in the North Aegean – and prospered during the Malvasia trade of the Middle Ages. Later, when

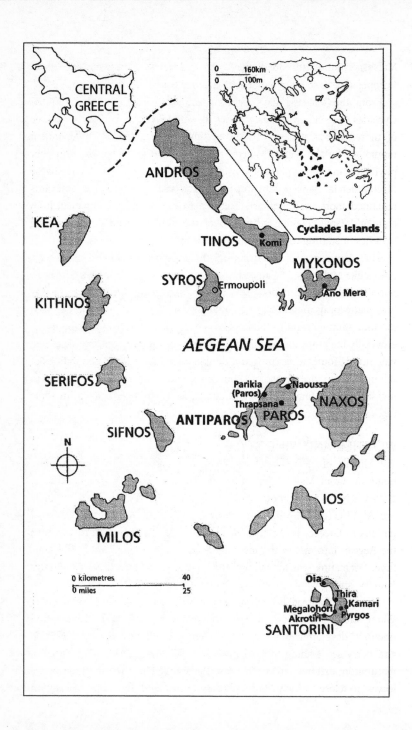

Malvasia's popularity faded, they had to develop other wine exports to Europe, and, as so often happened, Venetian traders played a major part.

From the Malvasia days right up until phylloxera, wines from the Cyclades were either sold as generics or were used to augment the volume of more famous wines. This did nothing to establish an independent reputation for the region. When France returned to full production after phylloxera in the first part of the twentieth century, there was a total collapse of commercial wine production in the Cyclades, although the vineyards remained more or less intact. This led to many major companies from mainland Greece taking advantage of the situation and either creating wineries or starting to work with local co-ops.

The second part of the twentieth century brought a flood of tourists: places like Mykonos, Ios, and Santorini suddenly became some of the most popular holiday destinations in Europe. From being close to the poverty line, many locals found that they could generate a good annual income from the four summer months alone. As a result, agriculture was pushed aside, especially the crops that required most work during the tourist season, like viticulture. Tourism has proved a double-edged sword: the possibilities of selling wine to visitors are vast, but fewer and fewer people are willing to invest the land, time, money, and effort that viticulture requires. In some cases viticulture seems destined to be a thing of the past.

WEATHER AND WINE STYLE

The climate of the Cyclades is, as one might guess, perfect for summer holidays. From May to September rainfall is almost nil, the number of cloudy days is rarely more than ten, and average temperatures routinely exceed 27°C (81°F). A minor drawback is wind: this is one of the windiest regions in Greece. In August, for example, the Meltemia winds can turn the Aegean into one of the most dangerous, demanding, and at the same time, fascinating seas for sailing. The mildest months are from October to January; spring winds can be severe on these islands.

This type of climate is rarely associated with high-quality wine production. Water stress is a major concern, and maturity – especially flavour and phenolic development – can be hindered. Wind can disrupt flowering and berry set, leading to unviably low yields. During the final stages of maturation, extreme stress can cause the stomata on the underside of the leaves to close, which slows photosynthesis and thus the maturation process. Beyond a certain point, sugar levels increase because of dehydration rather than ripening. Picking takes place early, sometimes before August 15, and in most vintages the decision to pick is not taken on the basis of optimum ripeness, but because the growers fear that leaving the fruit any longer will be too risky.

This environment usually leads to what is typically thought of as a Mediterranean wine style. Whites can be very low in aroma and fruit, with a tight structure. Reds are typically light and "burned" in colour, and go brown relatively quickly; they have hot fruit on the nose, moderately low but dry tannins, and high alcohol. Nevertheless, when these almost inhospitable terroirs are matched with the right vines and with producers who are not afraid to take risks, then some exceptional wines can arise.

Phylloxera has never invaded the majority of the islands. The bug can only infect new vineyards in the crawling stage of its lifecycle, and then only if the soil contains at least five per cent clay. Most of the islands have extremely infertile topsoils with little clay. So the average age of the vines is possibly the highest in Greece. They are a kind of viticultural Jurassic Park, especially those on Santorini.

New vines are planted through layering – burying a shoot while still attached to the vine, and then cutting it off the mother plant when it has grown roots. Vines are never uprooted because of low productivity; the only reason for replacing a plant is death. White grapes are dominated by Monemvasia and Assyrtico, while Mandilaria is the principal red.

Out of the whole Cyclades group, the most significant wine-producing islands are Santorini, Paros, Tinos, Mykonos, Naxos, and Syros. There are two OPAPs, Paros for whites and reds, and Santorini for fabulous dry and sweet whites. Paros also has a TO, Thrapsana, which both stylistically and varietally is very close to the islands' quality appellation. Strangely, there is a TO on Syros as well, although there are no significant producers there.

Aegean Islands TO

White still: dry.
White varieties: Assyrtico; Aidani; Athiri; Monemvasia.
Rosé still: dry.
Red still: dry.
Red/Rosé varieties: Black Aidani; Black Athiri; Mandilaria.

SYROS

Syros is one of the northern Cyclades, south of Andros and off the southwest coast of Tinos. It is one of the smaller of the important islands within the group and its principal town, Ermoupoli, is the political capital of the Cyclades. Syros has a low average altitude and the only hills, up in the north, are less than 400 metres (1,312 feet).

Wine production is extremely limited and there are no noteworthy bottlers. The vineyards are mainly south of the capital. On a varietal level, the local specialities are Kseromaherouda and Kseromaherouda Mavri (Black), both of which are occasionally found in other parts of the Cyclades. White Kseromaherouda is the workhorse, a low-vigour, low-yielding vine that is relatively resistant to dry conditions. Its growth cycle starts relatively early, in mid-March, and it is harvested before mid-August. It can produce wines with high alcohol, however its acidity is low. The red version, Kseromaherouda Mavri, ripens a few days later, producing berries that are inky-black. Syros has a TO for still whites that must be a fifty/fifty blend of Monemvasia and Assyrtico. Both of these varieties are commonly found in Syros, but at a commercial level the wine is obsolete.

Syros TO

White still: dry.
White varieties: Monemvasia fifty per cent; Assyrtico fifty per cent.

TINOS

Tinos is in the north of the Cyclades, between Andros and Mykonos. The three islands are essentially descending peaks of the Evia mountain range. The southern part of Evia is Mount Ohi, standing at 1,399 metres (4,590 feet), Andros is 995 metres (3,264 feet) at its highest point, and Mykonos is the flattest of the trio. Tinos is fairly hilly, with a gentle rise on its eastern part, and a second, steeper system of hills in the west. Only rarely does the land rise above 500 metres (1,640 feet).

Tinos is considered by the Greek Orthodox Church to be a Holy Island, and the celebration of Tinos' Panayia, the Festival of Our Lady, on 15 August each year, is one of Greece's most important religious events. Most Greeks go on a pilgrimage to Tinos at least once in their lives. There are numerous monasteries, most of which have substantial land holdings. There are some restrictions on tourism, such as nightclubs having to close early. However, the quietness of the place and its proximity to Athens have tempted many upper-class Athenians to buy houses here.

The climate of Tinos is hot, dry, and windy. Wind stress in summer is extreme, even more so than on Santorini. Another problem is aridity – not just low rainfall, but also water availability. Vines are trained low, with growth directed in a spiral, so that after a few years there is a basket of old canes. Young shoots develop on the outer part of the plant. This shape develops naturally, with no pruning or other human intervention, apart from harvesting. Picking here is very difficult, since the picker has to kneel by each vine, search carefully through it for the clusters, and then struggle to cut and take them out of a dense framework of shoots and canes. Nevertheless these "basket vines" have two very important advantages: their low position protects them from wind; and their dense structure of canopy and wood shields them from too much heat or sun, while preserving any traces of moisture. They do not, however, protect against rabbits, which are an additional problem here. Fencing of vineyards is a necessity.

Soils in Tinos are infertile but are not as hostile as the volcanic soils of Santorini, and they have better water retention. Vineyards are terraced to minimize erosion. One study has suggested that Rhône varieties might do well here, although even they would need water during the hottest periods. Non-local varieties might be a solution, since indigenous vines don't seem to promise much in the way of quality.

Potamisi is a major white grape and is supposed to be one of the oldest in the Cyclades. It is a vigorous, productive plant that buds in mid-March and ripens in late August. It is used locally for retsina and it can give high alcohol levels and decent acidity, but its aromas are restrained. There is a black version, Potamisi Mavro, which has a deep colour, ripens about twenty days later, and is sun-dried to produce a sweet, rather strong red. Potamisi Mavro is usually blended with Koumari, or Koumaria, another red variety. Koumari is vigorous, productive, but very sensitive to aridity. It ripens in late August, can reach high sugar levels, and is very flavourful, so it is also used as a table grape.

Local wine production remains mostly artisanal, and until 1997, when Hristos Fonsos started his winery (see below), there were no commercially oriented wineries on the island. Nevertheless, more and more people are now taking an interest in Tinos. Alexandros Avatangelos started Tiniakoi Ampelones a few years later; this was one of the most substantial investments of the turn of the century, not only in Tinos, but possibly the whole of the Aegean. The Levantis family, well-known in the Greek wine trade, is also interested.

PRODUCERS

FONSOU WINERY

Komi, 842 00 Tinos. Tel: +30 228 305 1718/1048; Fax: +30 228 302 4289.
Vineyards owned: 1.2ha; under contract: 0.5ha; production: 45hl.

In 1997, Hristos Fonsos was the first to invest in winemaking in Tinos. He focused mainly on the most widely available varieties such as Potamisi, Potamisi Mavro, and Koumari, with some Monemvasia and Mandilaria. All the estate vineyards are certified organic.

His red wine, called Mathioulis Red, is a blend of Mandilaria, Potamisi Mavro, and Koumari. Mathioulis White is Potamisi and Monemvasia. The top wine is Beloni, a rare varietal Potamisi. All the wines are quite modern and well-made, but possibly lack a bit of excitement and character.

TINOS VINEYARDS

65 Vassilissis Sofia Avenue, 117 28 Athens. Tel: +30 210 729 5713;
Fax: +30 210 729 5712; Email: piniaki.ampelones@mail.com
Vineyards owned: 12.5ha.

Tinos Vineyards could be a paradigm for future investors. Alexandros Avatangelos was a partner in Sigalas Winery in Santorini and joined with Paris Sigalas and Yiannis Tselepos to create a winery in Nemea, Driopi Estate (*see* page 308). Then Avatangelos decided to look at the possibilities of his homeland, Tinos.

The main emphasis was placed on Mavrotragano, the obscure but promising grape of Santorini, and a few parcels were also dedicated to Assyrtico and Malagousia. There have been trials of different pruning and training systems to see which is best for the extremely windy conditions. Drip irrigation is essential, even if expensive.

In the 2002, 2003, and 2004 vintages grapes were harvested, but no wines were made. In 2005, the fruit will be experimentally vinified at Tselepos. Building a winery on the estate has started, but there will be no commercial releases before the 2007 vintage, in 2008 or possibly 2009. The first wines will thus be released almost a decade after the company's establishment.

MYKONOS

Viticulture in Mykonos is almost a contradiction in terms. In the latter part of the twentieth century the island has been one of the most expensive holiday destinations in the world. It has been estimated that on Mykonos from June to September more First Growth Bordeaux and *grand cru* Burgundy are consumed than in all the restaurants in Athens, all year. Owning land or a house in Mykonos is a passport to a very comfortable way of life. But establishing a wine business poses a number of difficulties. One part of the island is completely devoted to tourism and very crowded. Most of the rest is full of luxurious villas, where regulations are aimed at keeping businesses away, in order to preserve the tranquillity of the place. So starting a new winery is either impossible or extremely expensive.

Mykonos is also a difficult place to grow grapes. It is one of the flattest, windiest, and warmest islands of the Cyclades, with water in very short supply. In addition, finding vineyard workers during the peak summer season is tricky. On the other hand, a Mykonos wine would have a great advantage and a unique selling point in export markets.

PRODUCERS

MYKONOS WINERY

Ano Mera, 856 00 Mykonos. Tel: +30 228 907 192;
Website: www.mykonos-wines.gr; Email: info@mykonos-wines.gr
Vineyards owned: 9.3ha; production: 503hl.

In 1994, Nicos Assimomitis decided to do what was locally considered unthinkable: he replanted a family vineyard in Marathi, together with a plot that used to belong to the monastery of Panayias Troulianis, and started Mykonos Winery. The vineyard switched to organic cultivation swiftly after its establishment, embellished with some vintage Assimomitis overtones – for example, vineyards are equipped with hi-fi systems that fill the air with Mozart concerts, since Nicos believes that vines respond to beauty, harmony, and serenity. The vines are a typical Aegean blend of Monemvasia, Assyrtico, Athiri, Aidani, and Mandilaria, together with small parcels of Cabernet Sauvignon, Syrah, and Malagousia.

In 2000, a collaboration began between Assimomitis and Federico Lazaridis, son of Nicos of Château Nico Lazaridi in Drama, with Lazaridis fine-tuning the vineyard. A new winery is also underway and will probably be ready for the 2007 vintage.

Commercially these wines are far from achieving their potential, but the quality is there. The basic "Paraportiano" range, including a white, a rosé, and a red, sells well locally, but beyond that, market response is not what it could be. The top *cuvée* is Polistafylos Methidotis, forty per cent Cabernet Sauvignon, plus equal parts of Mandilaria and Monemvasia. The result is one of the lesser-known triumphs of the Aegean. Unfortunately, only 2,500 bottles are produced each year.

PAROS

Paros is located near the centre of the Cyclades, close to Naxos in the east and the much smaller sister island of Antiparos to the west. It is part of a different system of underwater ridges from the one forming Andros, Tinos, and Mykonos. The central part of Paros is the most mountainous, with a peak reaching 724 metres (2,375 feet). The capital is Parikia, a small town on a gulf in the northwest. The local population is prosperous. Tourism is important but Paros is also famous for its marble. Finally, agriculture and specifically viticulture are relatively profitable.

The climate is not as extreme as on the other Cycladic islands. Paros is less windy than Tinos or Santorini and there are higher levels of humidity, even if rainfall is still extremely limited during the summer. Water stress can be high, but in general, water availability is above the Cycladic average. Soil salinity can be a problem on low-lying vineyards near the coast.

Vines grow low and unsupported, but instead of the basket shape of Tinos, the old wood extends horizontally, almost touching the ground, and the young shoots grow down vertically, creating a "floor covering" of vines, a system known locally as *aplotaries*. Old plants can cover a surface of six square metres or more.

Paros and Santorini are the most important islands of the Cyclades as far as the volume of wine is concerned. The vineyards on Paros are scattered around the island, but the higher-producing regions are in the low plains near the slightly more humid coast to the west and north. Arguably, the best vineyards are on the slopes of central Paros, on altitudes ranging from 250–400 metres (820–1,312 feet).

Antiparos is not included in the Paros OPAP appellation, but some of the best Mandilaria grapes are produced there. In general, Antiparos vineyards are totally dedicated to red grapes and the two producers of Paros use these in some EO or TO blends.

Grapes and classifications

Paros was one of the first islands to develop a significant wine industry in ancient times and it retained its importance up to modern times, almost without interruption. Some suggest that Monemvasia, the traditional grape of the island, is a leftover from the "Golden Malvasia" period of the Middle Ages (*see* pages 296 and 334). Mandilaria is presumably a later introduction, although locals claim that it has been cultivated for at least 100 years. In the twentieth century, Paros wine became much used by producers of high-volume pink blends, for which growers needed a more productive white variety to blend with Mandilaria, instead of Monemvasia. Savatiano was introduced after World War II and Monemvasia was slowly superseded.

In 1981, following years of effort, the Paros OPAP was established. Paros white was defined as pure Monemvasia while the more common Paros red is a blend of one-third Mandilaria and two-thirds Monemvasia. The standard practice is to add freshly crushed Mandilaria to fermenting Monemvasia must. This is the only exception in Greece to the general rule forbidding the blending of white and red varieties for rosé or red appellation wines, but Mandilaria is so rich in anthocyanins that Paros red can still be one of the deepest-coloured wines of the Aegean. The only problem relating to the co-fermentation and maceration of the two varieties is that Mandilaria reaches full ripeness at least three weeks after Monemvasia, so the usual solution is to use overripe white grapes and slightly underripe red. Typical sugar levels at harvest time are twelve degrees Baumé for Mandilaria and fourteen degrees Baumé for Monemvasia.

The mandatory percentage of Monemvasia in the red blend imposed a severe restriction on quantity, since the variety had a limited acreage at that point. So the authorities allowed blends of half Mandilaria and half Monemvasia for the OPAP up until the 1989 vintage. At the same time, any new plantings of Savatiano were forbidden. The best examples of Monemvasia, either pure or blended with Mandilaria, suggest that the grape has great potential.

The varietal profile of Paros must have been a lot more complex in the past, but these days most vineyards are dominated by Mandilaria, Savatiano, and Monemvasia. Savatiano is heavily criticized for adding nothing to a blend apart from volume, and its price has consistently fallen, with most producers abandoning it in order to return to Monemvasia. Mandilaria, according to some growers, is not ideal for Paros, since it is a late-ripener and is prone to disease in humid years. Monemvasia from low-altitude, high-yielding vineyards can be excessively alcoholic, easily reaching fourteen per cent potential alcohol, but cooler sites can give excellent quality. A minor variety is Aidani Mavro, a black version of Aidani, and the Moraitis Winery is putting serious effort behind this rare plant. In addition, some plantings of Assyrtico can be found around the island.

Paros red can be excellent, provided that the angular structure of Mandilaria and the tendency of Monemvasia to oxidize are dealt with. Pure Monemvasia has very distinctive aromas and a rich palate. High alcohol can be a problem but, if produced from yields well below the legal limit of seventy hectolitres per hectare (ten tonnes per hectare), it has sufficiently high extract to give good depth and balance.

Paros OPAP

White still: dry.
White variety: Monemvasia.
Red still: dry.
Red varieties: Monemvasia sixty-six per cent of the blend; Mandilaria thirty-three per cent.

Thrapsana TO

White still: dry.
White variety: Monemvasia (at least seventy-five per cent of the blend), the balance being other local recommended and permitted grape varieties.
Red still: dry.
Red varieties: Mandilaria (at least sixty per cent of the blend), the balance being other local recommended and permitted grape varieties.

PRODUCERS

COOPERATIVE OF PAROS

Thesi Aghiou Georgiou Paroikias, 844 00 Paros.
Tel: +30 228 402 2179/2235; Fax: +30 228 402 2189.
Vineyards under contract: 650ha; Members: 1,300; production: 8,000–12,000hl.
The Paros cooperative was one of the first to be established in Greece, in 1929. However, with just under 1,300 members, and a production of around 10,000 hectolitres per year, it is relatively small. Boutari, Paros' biggest supporter at the national level, at least as far as volume is concerned, buys wine here.

The winery crushes the three major varieties of the island, Mandilaria, Monemvasia, and Savatiano, and some minor grapes as well. The core of the portfolio is the EO wines which, along with a red and a white TO of the Aegean Sea, are used to quench the thirst of tourists. The best wines are the three OPAP bottlings, a Paros red, a Paros white and a varietal Monemvasia. The wines show ripeness and warmth, coupled with some raisiny and oxidative character. They are very versatile food wines, but most foreign wine lovers would consider them a bit old-fashioned.

MORAITI WINERY

Naoussa, 844 01 Paros. Tel: +30 228 405 1350;
Fax: +30 228 4051193; Email: moraitis@par.forthnet.gr
Vineyards owned: 16ha; under contract: 15ha; production: 6,500hl.

The Moraitis family has been involved with Paros and its wines since 1910. The current owner is Manolis Moraitis, with Maria Moraitis as general manager. Under their guidance the winery produces a good portfolio, one of the best in the Cyclades. Moraitis works with low yields, around forty hectolitres per hectare, and always tries to identify the cooler spots for planting. There are many styles and quality levels, but prices remain firmly anchored to the ground, making Moraiti wines some of the best value-for-money offerings in Greece.

The winery produces four different OPAP Paros wines. The basic red is a typical blend of Mandilaria and Monemvasia, co-macerated for thirty-six hours, and aged in oak for six months. While Moraitis believes that Monemvasia is essential for achieving the true "red Paros" character of his wines, he thinks that two-thirds is too high. Thus some tanks are filled with slightly different proportions, ranging from fifty to sixty per cent red grapes. After six months in oak the best barrels are put aside for ten more months, while the rest are blended into the basic Paros red. The barrel selection is matured for a year in bottle and then released as Paros Réserve. The Réserve is clearly the best example of the OPAP produced at the moment, being rich, complex, and not at all aggressive.

White OPAPs are, again, a basic bottling of straightforward Monemvasia, and a Paros White Vareli. The latter is an oak version, with maturation in new French oak and *batonnage* for four months. Moraitis thinks that Monemvasia has great quality potential and a good affinity with oak, but overripeness can be a problem. For his best Monemvasia, he uses fruit from the high villages of Strompoula and Aghios Ioannis, both exceeding 400 metres altitude (1,312 feet). There have been attempts at pre-fermentation maceration but the equipment needed to drop the temperature to 4–6°C (39–43°F) was not available. In 2004, a new refrigeration unit was bought suggesting that quality will be even better in the future.

Arguably the most exciting wines are Syllogi, a pair of Aegean Sea TOs from vineyards owned by Moraitis. The white is a high-altitude single-vineyard Monemvasia that shows the potential of this variety. The red is a blend of eighty per cent Cabernet Sauvignon with the rare black version of Aidani, Aidani Mavro. This is mainly found in Paros, where it used to be interplanted with Mandilaria, to lift the aroma and alcohol and to give some ripeness of texture. Aidani Mavro is moderately vigorous, productive, and resistant to drought. Moraitis believes that it can add certain nuances to a blend, but is best not used as a single-varietal in its own right. In Syllogi red, the Cabernet tightness is blended excellently with the vivacious but light character of Aidani Mavro, while a year in oak adds depth. The two Syllogis, both made from organic grapes, belong in the top rank of Aegean wines.

NAXOS

Naxos is, along with Andros, the largest Cycladic island and one of the most mountainous. The western part is flat, but in the east there is a vertical block which peaks at 999 metres (3,278 feet). If revenues from the tourist sector were excluded, Naxos would be one of the richest islands of the group. It has some of the most famous marble in Greece, although it is not as highly regarded as that quarried in Paros. Food is good here, too: the local potatoes and vegetables are sought-after in Athens. Some of the finest cheese-makers of Greece are here, while meat is top-quality: animals are grown by the seaside and fed on wild greens that soak up seawater, giving their meat a distinctive saltiness. Naxos also produces spirits like raki and Citron of Naxos, a flavoured liqueur.

Viticulture is not very important here, since the locals have other, more profitable options. There has been a steady decline during the twentieth century and very few growers produce grapes for commercial reasons. Even certain local wine styles have been eliminated, like the sweet wine made from sun-dried grapes around the village of Aperathou. Currently, most vineyards are concentrated around Apollonas, in the northern tip of the island, and are planted with red varieties, mainly Mandilaria.

PRODUCER

PROBONAS WINERY

84 300 Naxos. Tel: +30 228 502 2258/2104; Fax: +30 228 502 3783.
Vineyards under contract: 20ha; production: 500–600hl.

Probonas Winery is one of the oldest estates in the Aegean Islands, founded in 1915. Probonas wines are mainly available locally. The winery crushes Mandilaria and a small quantity of Assyrtico. The wines produced are Probonas White, Rosé, and Red, while the Retsina is clean and soft.

SANTORINI

Santorini is one of the most remarkable and beautiful places in the world. Its wines are also among the best in Europe, and it is almost a sad fact that these two qualities co-exist on the same plot of land. People travel from all around the globe to see the beauties of Santorini and watch the sunset. Sometimes people actually applaud when the sun disappears, as if thanking Nature for the spectacular performance. There are no words to describe Santorini's magnificence – one has to see it, and most of all, feel it for oneself.

Santorini and its small sister island of Thirassia exist on a dormant volcano. During its last eruption, in 1500 BC, much of it collapsed, forming an inverted cone that starts from the cliffs of Santorini and plunges under the sea: this is the caldera. This eruption was connected to the destruction of the Minoan civilization in Crete, which is located over 100 kilometres (sixty-two miles) to the south. Tsunamis and earthquakes created a catastrophe of epic proportions, leading many to speculate that Santorini could have been the Atlantis of legend. Two small islets have been created over the centuries in the space between Thirassia and Santorini, called Nea Kameni and Palea Kameni. Palea Kameni, "Old Burnt", was formed less than 2,000 years ago, while Nea Kameni, "Young Burnt", or "The Volcano" as locals refer to it as, started becoming visible around 1580 AD.

Volcanic evidence

There have been constant signs of activity since, but without the violence of twenty-five centuries ago. There were small-scale eruptions in 1649 and 1650, and as recently as the 1920s. In 1956 there was some activity, followed by a devastating earthquake that made many locals seek refuge in Athens. During this eruption, new lava was added to Nea Kameni, making it the youngest volcanic earth in the eastern Mediterranean. The volcano has never been completely silent, and sulphurous smoke can be seen coming out of Nea Kameni every day. The Greek Army has an organized plan in place, enabling the complete evacuation of Santorini in less than forty-eight hours, even at the peak of the summer season.

The island has very complex, young volcanic soil, superimposing schist, limestone, lava, and ferric dusts. There is little organic matter or water; even *Vitis vinifera* finds it difficult to live here. Rainfall is next to zero during the summer, and springs are so rare and precious that they are usually not used for irrigation. To decrease competition between vines, the average density is very low, less than 2,500 vines per hectare. Even weeds are inhibited by the dryness and infertility.

Wind is another serious problem. It can disrupt flowering and berry-set, or increase the water stress in July and August. Basket vines are the only form that offers protection from the wind and preserves humidity. In the early 1990s a local grower decided to defy convention and establish a Royat-trained vineyard. After the first serious wind of the spring he went to check on the vineyard. It is said that he drove past his land without noticing, until he reached the next village – the posts, wires, and vines had been completely torn apart and gathered, like a huge hay ball, several hundred metres away.

The eastern side of the island, facing away from the caldera, is fairly flat; it is the only side where beaches can be found. Moving westward, the island starts a steady incline and then reaches a plateau, which in turn is cut off abruptly by the cliffs forming the caldera. Vineyards can be found in most areas but are more usual in the central and western parts. Ripening patterns vary across the island, and quality-oriented producers must follow these closely and be able to harvest fruit at very short notice.

Santorini has its own quality-wine designation, OPAP, the legal maximum yield for which is about fifty hectolitres per hectare, making it the lowest in Greece. However, in reality yields are much less: only a few vineyards, in the most plentiful vintages, manage over forty hectolitres per hectare, and most producers are content with half this. Roughly two years in every decade, most vineyards produce seven to ten hectolitres per hectare. But these low yields don't necessarily make for higher quality. On the contrary, most growers believe that increased yields of around thirty hectolitres per hectare would give better quality – as well as being more financially viable.

Grapes

The vineyards are dominated by four varieties. Assyrtico covers about seventy per cent of the total area and Mandilaria about twenty per cent, followed by the white versions of Athiri and Aidani. Yet the remaining small proportion of the island's vineyards contains a remarkable diversity of vines. It is commonly stated that a century ago, the total number of varieties cultivated was approaching 100. At that time, vineyards covered an area of around 4,000 hectares, but as the population gradually turned away from viticulture, that fell to the current level of around 1,200 hectares. A lot of varieties became obsolete.

Along with the loss of varieties went the loss of expertise. Yiannis Paraskevopoulos claims that, in his first days as a winemaker on the island in the early 1990s, old vine-growers could walk with him around the vineyards and identify the most obscure varieties from ten paces, while no obvious differences were discernible to the uninitiated eye. In addition, these people, in their late eighties, were able to suggest particular ways of getting the best fruit from these vines. Most of these people have gone by now, and young people tend to be better at differentiating between styles of Margaritas than at knowing their Platani from their Mavrathiro. Currently there appear to be around thirty varieties in fairly common usage. How many have been lost will never be known.

Assyrtico is arguably the best white variety of Santorini and one of the finest in Greece and the Mediterranean. It is not aromatic but it can produce an excellent combination of steely structure, minerality, extract, depth, high alcohol, and high acidity. In Santorini, a wine with 13.5 per cent alcohol, a pH of three or less, and an aromatic expression that is closer to the Loire than to a hot climate is not uncommon. This intense balance is mainly achieved because vine stress inhibits maturity, wind dehydrates the berries, therefore increasing the sugar levels, and low yields lead to very high dry extract. This intense personality is toned down by the roundness of Aidani and the more expressive Athiri.

The list of local varieties makes interesting reading. Platani is another white vine, lesser in significance than those already mentioned, but still of high quality; it ripens in late August and can reach high sugar levels with moderate acidity. Thrapsathiri used to be considered a clone of Athiri but has been proved to be a separate variety. It ripens late, close to mid-September, and is one of the most aromatic to be found on the island.

FlaskAssyrtico was considered, also incorrectly, to be a clone of Assyrtico. It is a grape that ripens in mid-August, with high sugars, and acidity below 4.7 grams per litre. Flaska is not related to FlaskAssyrtico, and is less productive, ripening a week later and giving higher acidity.

Gaidouria is one of the oldest varieties of the Cyclades and one of the most vigorous vines of Santorini, but it is still only moderately productive. Harvested in mid-August, it gives high sugar levels and moderate acidity. Kritiko declares in its name that it comes from Crete, but so far there is no evidence that it is grown beyond Santorini and a few other Cycladic islands; it matures in late August, producing sweet grapes with very low acidity. Glikadi is possibly Glikerithra, found in the Peloponnese. In Santorini it is rare, producing high sugar readings and very low acidity. Agrioglikadi – "wild Glikadi", might well turn out to be genetically linked to Glikerithra and Glikadi. It is a very rare vine, matures in the second week of August, and produces high sugar and low alcohol. Katsano is close in style and habits to Agrioglikadi. Finally, very few plants of Santorini's Asprouda must exist by now. It's a moderately vigorous and moderately productive vine that reaches high ripeness levels and is harvested in mid-August.

Mandilaria covers about twenty per cent of the cultivated area and is used for dry rosés, dry reds, and some rosé dessert wines made from sun-dried grapes. There are a number of other red varieties, but they're not as numerous as the whites. Aidani Mavro is present, together with Mavrathiro, a high-quality grape that matures in the first half of September and gives rich colour, high sugar, and moderate acidity. Voidomatis is grown in other Greek regions as well, and in Santorini it matures in mid-August, at least twenty days earlier than it does elsewhere. It produces deep colour, high sugar levels, and low acidity. Stavrohiotiko is one of the most rare red varieties in Santorini; it is productive and very resistant to drought. It ripens in mid-September, giving rich sugars, but very low colour and low acidity.

Mavrotragano covers less than two per cent of Santorini's vineyards, but merits a special mention. It is one of the most promising new red varieties to have been "discovered" in the last decade. A number of producers have been dealing with it for several years, but it was Paris Sigalas who, in the mid-1990s, produced a few hundred experimental bottles that created quite a stir (*see* Sigalas Winery, page 392). It was a new breed of Greek red: deep, dense in colour, concentrated, "old-viney" on the nose but without a single hot note, while the palate was rich and coated with graceful tannins. The quality stirred up excitement among both consumers and producers, and Mavrotragano became a rising star. Currently more than half of the active wineries in Santorini produce small quantities of it, and there are efforts from producers outside the island, like Tiniakoi Vineyards.

Mavrotragano is traditional in certain parts of Santorini, mainly in Thirassia and Profitis Ilias, but new plantings are extending it beyond these areas. It is a vigorous vine, moderately productive, and relatively sensitive to aridity, suggesting that interesting results could be obtained in less dry regions of Greece. Full maturity comes during the latter half of August, but harvesting a sufficient quantity of Mavrotragano at the same stage of ripeness is tricky. Different vineyards might reach ripeness as much as ten days apart, so it can take days to fill a whole vat. New plantings will eliminate such problems and increase quality. A remarkable depth of colour is achieved after five to seven days of maceration and the tannic structure of the wine encourages most producers to age it for up to two years in oak.

Heritage

The island has no lack of traditional styles of wine. The oldest, and currently the most famous, is vinsanto, not to be confused with the Tuscan speciality, *vin santo* (*see* below). Assyrtico and Aidani are left on the vine to reach high levels of ripeness, ideally above sixteen degrees Baumé. After picking, they are sun-dried for between six to fourteen days. Sun-drying increases the volatile acidity and some producers – for example the Argyros Winery (*see* page 384) – tried drying the grapes on stacked trays, so that half the fruit was dried in the shade. But controlled volatility can add complexity to vinsanto without being a fault. A more traditional approach to minimizing the negative effects of sun-drying is to harvest the fruit as late as possible. The sugar level is higher and fewer days are needed in the heat of the sun to reach the desired concentration.

After the drying, the grapes are crushed and fermented, mostly on their skins. It takes ten kilograms of raisins to produce a kilogram of vinsanto. Fermentation is usually finished before Christmas, and the usual levels of residual sugar are between 200–240 grams per litre. A vinsanto has to be aged by law for two years in oak before release, but many producers age it for longer. New oak has yet to make a strong statement in vinsanto, but older barriques are being added to the traditional 500-litre or larger casks. Topping-up is done with care, sometimes with wines from younger vintages, while racking is rare. Each barrel is usually treated as a separate personality. Many old-style vinsantos finished their alcoholic fermentation at low strengths, below nine per cent, and some producers used to fortify it with high-strength tsipouro (the grape spirit), to thirteen per cent. In the last decade, however, most high-quality producers have preferred to use yeast strains that will continue fermentation to give a natural strength of over thirteen per cent.

It is difficult to compare vinsanto with Tuscany's *vin santo*, especially since the latter can vary from fino sherry-like dryness to highly oxidized sweetness. Most of the volatility in *vin santo* comes from the barrel-ageing, while vinsanto develops it mainly through sun-drying. *Vin santo* is dried in the shade, more gently, but for longer. A telling difference is the high acidity of Assyrtico; Malvasia on the other hand adds a more pronounced, primary fruit intensity to the Italian *vin santo*.

Mezzo is a style close to vinsanto. It is produced much in the same way, but only red grapes are used, mainly Mandilaria. Mezzo clusters are sun-dried for less time; usually less than ten days. Sugar levels are not high, since there is less dehydration, and Mandilaria grapes at harvest are not as sweet as Assyrtico. Most mezzos are aged in oak for more than a year. The alcohol level is over thirteen per cent and residual sugar is below 200 grams per litre.

It seems remarkable that vinsanto sometimes had trouble in fermenting to higher alcohol levels, since the island's other two traditional styles were highly alcoholic by any standards. The first, brusco, derives its name from the Venetian period, from the word for "coarse". And coarse it was: because vineyards were fragmented, yields were low, and picking grapes was physically demanding, the locals were not able to gather large quantities of fruit in a day. Each day's crop was put into a shallow vat, on top of the previous day's harvest. When enough had been picked, the grapes were trodden and the must drawn off. The whole process could take up to a week, during which time the juice would start fermenting and macerating of its own accord. The oxidation and extraction of phenolics were intense. Brusco could be white, rosé or red, but was always fiercely tannic and acidic, with alcohol levels over fifteen per cent, sometimes up to seventeen per cent.

Brusco can still occasionally be found in Santorini these days, but not commercially. The style could easily be Greece's answer to the idiosyncratic whites from Josko Gravner in the Italian Collio region, near the Slovenian border. Gravner is famous for resuscitating extremely old winemaking techniques, like macerating white grapes for weeks, or ageing wines in large clay pots. His whites emerge brown in colour, throw as much sediment as vintage port, and have high tannins, high alcohol, and evident oxidation. A technically oriented winemaker could easily find dozens of faults in Gravner whites, as well as in brusco. However, these wines can be rich, intense, very complex, full of concentration, and indeed, balanced. It would be interesting to see a top Santorini producer try their hand at brusco.

If brusco was the product of a lazy winemaking approach, nykteri offers a complete contrast. The grapes destined for nykteri had to be ripe, but not as ripe as for brusco, and they had to be picked before dawn and pressed and drawn off the must within a day. Presumably it was a long day, since the name means "working the night away" in Greek. This passionate effort was aiming at the creation of the finest wine, with minimum extraction of colour and contact with air. nykteri had to be aged in oak for long periods, sometimes for as long as vinsanto. Traditionally there is some slight madeirization, but usually the character is not obtrusive.

Nykteri is increasingly popular, with a rising number of producers making it. Most use oak and many use new oak, although some do make a distinction between oaky and non-oaky examples. Alcohol levels in modern nykteris range from 13.5 per cent to fifteen per cent or more.

Modern times

What has made Santorini famous among Greek wine-lovers is not these traditional styles, but a more modern approach championed by Boutari and the pioneering co-op, Santo Wines (*see* page 391). Picking is done earlier, bringing potential alcohol down to around twelve per cent. Pressing is faster, with pneumatic presses playing an important role, and the fermentation temperature is cool, in stainless steel. This "new era" Santorini might lack some of the character of the more traditional styles, but displays the grace of Assyrtico in a less extreme form.

Another turning point was the creation of the white wine Kallisti by Boutari in 1988, the first attempt to give the modern style of Santorini a coating of oak. It was a breakthrough for Greek white wine and remains one of the best. Many producers tried to copy the method, but most initial efforts had a very crude oak character and no interaction between the wood and the fruit. There was little understanding of barrel fermentation; most fermentation was done in steel, followed by oak maturation. There has been a steep learning curve. Alcohol levels have risen, and nowadays most oaky Santorini wines have well-married fruit and wood. Some producers have moved their oaky whites closer to the style of nykteri, while others have placed them as a stepping-stone between unoaked whites and nykteri.

There is only one appellation on the island, OPAP Santorini, which encompasses all styles, from dry to sweet. The appellation includes the Thirassia islet. Sweet wines can be called vinsanto and can be produced by all three methods to become *vin naturellement doux*, *vin doux naturel*, and *vin doux* (*see* Glossary). The second approach, where grape spirit is used to arrest fermentation, is less common than the first, even if some producers can occasionally add spirit after fermentation has stopped naturally. Assyrtico and white Aidani can be used for vinsanto, but white Athiri can be included only in dry wines.

With the tourist sector in Santorini going from strength to strength and viticulture being financially unattractive, the steady decline of vineyard acreage seems inevitable. The co-op has done much to protect growers, but it does not have the power to guarantee a decent, secure future for all. Private producers starting their own ventures have been and will be the only hope. The signs of change have been evident since the mid-1970s. Boutari's major investment has been key to securing the future of growers, as well as promoting local wines to visitors. Yet pessimists argue that the not-too-distant future could see viticulture here becoming a distant memory. This would be an immense loss. The real aim today should not be not just to preserve Santorini but to realize its full potential.

Santorini OPAP

White still: dry; naturally sweet (*vin naturellement doux*); fortified sweet (*vin doux naturel*); sweet (*vin doux*).
White varieties: Assyrtico; White Aidani; Athiri, the latter allowed only in dry whites.

PRODUCERS

ANTONIOU WINERY

Megalohori, 847 00 Santorini. Tel: +30 228 602 3557; Fax: +30 228 602 2633; Website: http://antoniou.santorini.net; Email: antoniouk@otenet.gr
Vineyards under contract: 30ha; production: 900hl.
Kostas Antoniou is a successful jeweller. In 1992 he decided to start a wine

business, mainly as a hobby, and it turned out to be an expensive one. He bought one of the best-known old Santorini wineries, right at the brow of the caldera, and in 2001 it opened as a conference/function centre, museum, and tourist attraction. There are plans for a modern production plant nearby.

Antoniou wines are still made in the local cooperative, under the guidance of consulting oenologist Professor Dimitris Hatzinicolaou, a Bordeaux-trained winemaker and one of the key figures in Greek wine. The range of products begins with a basic OPAP Santorini, with Assyrtico accounting for more than ninety per cent of the final blend. It is a slightly phenolic but very complex wine, firm and racy. There is Vareli Santorini, aged in new oak and trying to emulate the nykteri style (*see* above). Its colour is extremely deep and the nose is usually overwhelmed with nutty, toasty oak, while the extract on the palate cannot balance the wood. The Antoniou Vinsanto is much more successful, going for about a week of ageing and a week of sun-drying, hence achieving a drier character with more primary fruit than most.

ARGYROS WINERY

Episkopi Gonia, 847 00 Santorini. Tel: +30 228 603 1489;
Fax: +30 228 603 2285; Email: margiros@otenet.gr
Vineyards owned: 3ha; under contract: 18ha; production: 3,000hl

There are a number of wine professionals in Greece who consider Yiannis Argyros to be both the best sweet-winemaker and the best white-winemaker in Greece, the former for his vinsanto and the latter for his Assyrtico. Coming from a family whose involvement in wine production dates back to 1903, Argyros has been responsible for the winery since 1974. He has worked hard to ensure that the quality of fruit is as good as possible. The winery remains traditional but his style does not need high technology to shine.

His basic line is the Atlantis range, including white, rosé, and red EOs. The basic OPAP bottling is Canava Argyros; fifty per cent is from the first light pressings and the rest is free-run juice. It is stainless-steel-fermented and bottled after a few months of lees contact. It is not flashy or ultra-clean on the nose but there is a low-key complexity and an impressive dry extract on the palate that sets the scene for the other two more upmarket labels.

Argyros Estate Vareli is a pure Assyrtico from Episkopi vineyards, aged in new oak for eight months. One of Greece's best wine writers, Simos Georgopoulos, named this as the nation's finest wine across all styles. It is indeed beautifully crafted, with pronounced but very well-integrated oak, serious concentration on the palate, and immaculate balance. Nevertheless, it is more an excellent oak-aged white than a typical Santorini. The latter is far more convincingly achieved by Argyros' standard Argyros Estate, where half the wine comes from the light pressings and half the initial blend is aged in stainless steel, thirty per cent in old oak and twenty per cent in new oak barriques. The result retains all the raciness and individuality of the terroir, but wraps it in a fine-grained patina.

The most famous wine of Argyros and one of the most expensive in Greece is his vinsanto – and justifiably so. First of all, it was a masterful move to start releasing his vinsanto at seventeen to eighteen years of age. It is a blend of Assyrtico, Aidani, with just a drop of Athiri, aged in old oak for fifteen years and then racked into younger oak for the finishing touches. The long ageing and the careful and constant topping-up of the barrels means that Argyros uses a kind of short *solera* system for his vinsanto. Once a year, he goes to his vinsanto warehouse, an old monastery that used to belong to the Catholic Church, and assembles the different barrels to create his new vinsanto. The very few people that have had the luck to be invited there claim that the process is almost a spiritual experience.

BOUTARI

Megalohori, 847 00 Santorini. Tel: +30 228 608 1011; Fax: +30 228 608 1606; Website: www.boutari.gr; Email: santorini.winery@boutari.gr
See also pages 130, 144, 150, 232, 449.

The Boutari company decided to invest in Santorini in the early 1980s, believing that the island had high viticultural potential which was, at that time, underdeveloped. The company was then established in traditionally red wine regions and wanted to gain a foothold in a white appellation. The Boutari presence in Santorini was multi-faceted and worked on many levels. As a private investor, the company poured substantial capital into the local community and increased the local appeal of viticulture. In 1988, it created Santorini's first winery that also served as a tourist attraction; it is also an impressive architectural feat.

But the influence of Boutari in Santorini was not only social and financial. The basic Boutari Santorin bottling was the one that became known on a national level, with a fresh character, light alcohol, and a crisp, well-defined palate. The next step was Kallisti, a barrel-fermented Santorini that other producers needed almost a decade to challenge. Even if nowadays there are more extracted and sophisticated oaky Assyrticos, Kallisti remains unsurpassed in its understated elegance and its ability to age – leading Greek sommeliers, like Giorgos Floudas from the prestigious Elounda Beach Hotel in Crete, will confidently age and serve ten-year-old Kallistis. A more concentrated and intense Assyrtico was later added to the portfolio.

Another Boutari initiative that somehow escaped wide attention was the establishment of Selladia Estate. This six-hectare property is on the southern tip of the island, in Faros, close to the village of Akrotiri. Varieties planted include Assyrtico, Athiri, Aidani, and Mandilaria, as well as smaller amounts of Mavrotragano, Voidomatis, Platani, and Katsano. The estate's range of altitudes – from 105 to 140 metres (345–460 feet) – allow an interplay between plants, soils, and terroirs. Planting densities started at 2,500 vines per hectare but selected parcels have gone up to 3,500. The wine produced, Selladia Estate, is made in a straightforward way, and shows a typical Santorini character with several layers of mineral extract on top.

Boutari's Santorini wines conclude with a barrel-fermented Nykteri reaching up to fifteen per cent alcohol, and a traditional Vinsanto, aged in oak for two years. Both are admirably priced and are perfect entry-level examples of the more esoteric styles of Santorini. Generally speaking, the Boutari offerings from Santorini are some of the most undervalued wines on the island, if not in Greece.

CANAVA ROUSSOS

Episkopi Mesa Gonia, 847 00 Santorini. Tel: +30 228 603 1349.
Head office: 22 Zisimopoulou, Palaio Faliro, 175 65, Athens, Attica.
Vineyards owned: 4ha; under contract: 10ha; production 3,000hl.

Ioannis Roussos, or Capetan ("Captain") Roussos as most people call him, is a larger-than-life figure. His personality is unstoppable and his approach to life, love, food, and wine is the epitome of optimism. Behind him there is a family wine tradition going back to 1836, beating everyone else in Santorini by a margin of fifty years. A good part of the company seems to be lingering in that century – some aspects of production, for example, or a couple of the wines – but not in an off-putting way. Nevertheless, hiring Panayiotis Korniotis, a promising wine-trade executive, in 2003 gave Roussou Winery a much-needed breath of fresh air and the company turned to a more modern approach for its dry whites.

The Santorini is now fresh and vibrant, without the phenolic style of previous vintages. Roussou Nykteri is one of the lighter versions of the style, aged mainly in large old oak barrels. The varietal Athiri, aged in oak for a few months, is a bit closed in aromas but could be a good food wine. Rivari is a basic rosé from Mandilaria and Assyrtico, and Caldera is a tannic, age-worthy, serious Mandilaria. It is an EO, allowing the blending of different vintages. The core is aged for two years in oak and older parcels are usually added.

Yet Roussos' forté is his sweet wines. His Nama (the name generally used for Holy Communion wine) is the best and one of the most popular. It is made like vinsanto but sun-dried for less than a week and aged in oak for less than a year. The best wine in the range is Mavrathiro, a blend of Mavro Athiri, and Mandilaria. The grapes are sun-dried for about ten days and barrel-maturation lasts about three years. Bottle age is deemed important for the required style and the wine is released at seven years old, but keeping it for another decade will only improve it.

GAIA

Ekso Vrahies, 847 00 Santorini.
Website: www.gaia-wines.gr; Email: gaiawine@acn.gr
Vineyards under contract: 55ha; production: 1,000hl.
For full details, *see* Gaia entry on page 309.
After working for a number of years for Boutari in Nemea and Santorini, Yiannis Paraskevopoulos decided to start his own business with the viticulturalist Leon Karatsalos in 1994. At the time it was difficult to establish a winery in Santorini, so Paraskevopoulos accepted Yiannis Argyros' offer to use Argyrou Winery's facilities for making his wines. Initially there was only one wine, Thalassitis, which was a basic Santorini.

Even if Argyrou Winery was low-tech, Paraskevopoulos managed to create an expression of Assyrtico that was very modern, very defined, and most of all, paid tribute to the variety's intense, clearly defined nature. Thalassitis is one of the most individual dry Santorini whites: the nose is not intense or fruity, but full of compact minerality. On the palate there is a steely and salty structure – once again not broad, but very extracted. In the last decade this has probably been the wine with the lowest average pH, steadily below three and sometimes close to 2.80. By local commercial standards it is so minerally and acidic that many Greeks would never take a second sip. Nevertheless, Paraskevopoulos managed to turn it into one of the most popular labels in the country.

Although the character of Thalassitis has remained unchanged over the years, its quality has never stopped improving as Paraskevopoulos gains experience with the variety and access to better equipment. The whole game has been about finding Assyrtico's limits; it is a vine which is both phenolic and prone to oxidation. Better refrigeration allowed for longer pre-fermentation macerations – up to eighteen hours – as well as longer fermentations that lasted four weeks or more. The must used to be clarified to the limits, but now Paraskevopoulos is willing to use hazier musts to gain more complexity. The same goes with lees stirring, with more gross lees retained every year and kept in contact with the wine for longer.

The breakthrough came in 2001, when Gaia created a winery in Ekso Vrahies, close to Thira. This became a platform for Paraskevopoulos to further expand his work with Assyrtico. Currently there are micro-vinifications to identify promising yeast strains for Assyrtico. Small quantities of Thalassitis are fermented and matured for six months in new Nevers oak and released as Thalassitis Oak-Fermented. The first vintages had a slight lack of wood and fruit integration, but more recent vintages have been more balanced and display the ability to develop in bottle for up to four years.

An attempt to uncover another facet of Assyrtico is the five-year-old Gaia Assyrtico vinegar, fashioned in the traditional Greek vinegar style rather than the sweeter, heavier, popular Balsamico.

GAVALAS VINEYARD
Megalohori, 847 00 Santorini. Tel/Fax: +30 228 608 2552. Head office: 200 Palaias Kavalas Street, Peristeri, 121 36 Attica. Tel/Fax: +30 210 571 1978; Website: www.gavalaswines.gr; Email: info@gavalaswines.gr
Vineyards owned: 3.5ha; under contract: 25ha; production: 800hl.

The Gavalas family established this wine-producing and trading company in 1895, making it one of the oldest in the Cyclades. During the 1970s and 1980s, Giorgos Gavalas collaborated with other leading wineries, producing certain labels for them, like the first vinsanto vintages for Boutari. In the last decade the company has focused entirely on its own products.

The best *cuvée* of the dry whites is a plain Santorini, typically ninety per cent Assyrtico and ten per cent Aidani. They are fresh and crisp, low in aromatics, with quite a phenolic finish. The winery's Vinsanto is one of the more traditional, lower in alcohol than most but showing good balance. The most controversial wine is Ksenoloo, a blend of Mavrotragano,

Voidomatis, and Athiri. Aged in oak for five to six months, the wine is a very light ruby-red, bordering on rosé. The structure is very delicate and there is a certain understated sweetness. People expecting a rich, tannic, deep Mavrotragano style will be disappointed, but the numerous fans of Ksenoloo adore it for its freshness and lightness.

HATZIDAKIS WINERY
Pyrgos, 847 01 Santorini. Tel: +30 228 603 2552; Fax: +30 228 602 8395; Website: www.hatzidakiswines.gr; Email: hatzidakiswinery@san.forthnet.gr
Vineyards owned: 1.5ha; under contract: 8ha; production: 550hl.

Oenologist Haridimos Hatzidakis established this winery in 1997 as a low-budget, competent production facility with no intentions for high-volume production. Since then, the equipment is constantly improving, there are plans for a whole new winery, but Hatzidakis has remained true to his belief that the size of his operation must remain relatively small. Currently he produces around 6,000 cases, spread over six different labels, all of which grow more exciting with every new vintage. The style of the house is not as high-pitched as Gaia or Sigalas, leaning closer to the Argyros style, although it is a little more playful with oxidation. Hatzidakis wines are rich, complex, and individual – not for the uninitiated wine-lover.

The basic Hatzidakis Santorini is from the earliest-picked fruit and usually reaches 13.5 per cent alcohol. Over eighty per cent of the grapes have a few hours of pre-fermentation maceration, and the wine rests *sur lie* for at least four months after fermentation. The sister wine is a blend of thirty per cent Aidani, seventy per cent Assyrtico, but Hatzidakis wants to emphasize the Aidani character, so it appears as Aidani/Assyrtico on the label. The Assyrtico starts fermenting, while the Aidani is added little by little over a period of a week or so. The result is much more aromatic than the standard Santorini, but still with some density. The Aidani/Assyrtico fruit is produced from certified organic vineyards and there are thoughts of pushing it into the biodynamic sphere in future vintages.

The Santorini Vareli offers a step up in ripeness and extract, being mainly Assyrtico that has been harvested at above fourteen per cent potential alcohol. The wine is fermented and aged for six months in French oak, sixty per cent of which is new. The oak character is surprisingly integrated, given the high proportion of new wood. The top dry white from Hatzidakis is his Nykteri, picked above 15.5 degrees Baumé and aged for six months in old oak barrels, ranging from 225–500 litres. Hatzidakis is aiming for a very traditional style in Nykteri, seeking a slight maderization on the nose. This wine is one of the most adventurous and convincing examples of the style.

Hatzidakis Vinsanto is possibly the only wine that, on a blind tasting, could be mistaken as a young release from the Argyrou Winery. The fruit is harvested extremely ripe, well above Nykteri levels, sun-dried for about ten days, and aged in oak for no less than five years. It is remarkable on release, but a few years ageing in bottle adds even more dimensions. The sole red wine from this producer is an experimental Mavrotragano, macerated for five days and aged in oak for a year. A very interesting wine that needs some time in bottle to soften up.

ILIOPOULOU VINEYARDS

Megalohori, 847 0 Santorini. Tel: +30 228 608 1796;
Fax: +30 228 608 1798; Website: www.vedema.gr; Email: vedema@hol.gr
Vineyards owned: 7ha; under contract: 5ha; production: 225hl.

The Iliopoulos family owns the Vedema Hotel, one of the most prestigious establishments of its kind in Santorini. Iliopoulos started this wine venture in 1995 and for the first vintages made his wines at the cooperative. There is now a winery in Megalohori and the vineyard holdings are being seriously developed. The range of wines is small, including a Santorini, an oaky dry version, and a vinsanto. The style is low-key, consistent over the years, but possibly lacking a bit of drama.

PETRA WINERY

Kamari Episkopis Gonias, 847 00 Santorini. Tel: +30 228 603 1332.
Vineyards owned: 1.5ha; production: 50hl.

Petra Winery was established in 2000 by Hristoforos Karamolegos, the long-serving chief winemaker of the co-op, Santo Wines (*see* opposite), as his boutique project. The initial plans were to focus on a small number of labels and to take grapes almost exclusively from his own vineyards. The first releases, Stroggili Santorini and Petra Vinsanto ("*petra*" meaning "stone") have been exceptionally promising.

In an unexpected twist of events, Karamolegos decided to become a priest. It is doubtful if any wine has been produced and bottled in the last few vintages. One can only hope that Karamolegos' soul-searching will bring him back to winemaking in the future.

SANTO WINES

Pyrgos, 847 00 Santorini. Tel: +30 228 602 2596; Fax: +30 228 602 3137; Website: www.santowines.gr; Email: info@santowines.gr

Vineyards under contract: 1,200ha; Members; 2,360+; production: 25,000–30,000hl.

Santorini's co-op, Santo Wines, is the Cyclades' largest wine producer and one of the most important in Greece. It has been instrumental in promoting Santorini in a number of ways. Firstly, it is a local source of very good dry white wines, imported from all over Greece. Promotion of Greek wines to tourists is essential and the winery's tasting room is flooded with visitors almost every summer day. Secondly, the co-op's wines are produced in substantial quantities and have managed to spread the reputation of the island in mainland Greece and well beyond. Most of all, the organization has provided full support to young and emerging wine producers by renting cellar space, bottling facilities, and freely giving advice and expertise. Many producers could not have started their business without this support.

Santo Wines was founded in 1947 and all the growers of the island are members. There are 2,361 registered associates, but the active growers number around 1,000. Hristos Kanellakopoulos is the competent chief winemaker. The co-op works closely with all growers, particularly in trying to coordinate the timing of the harvest. For example, some growers are advised to pick slightly underripe fruit, preserving acidity, in order to use their wines as an acidifying agent for the more alcoholic, heavier wines picked towards the end of the season. Currently, a programme for converting vineyards to organic cultivation is underway, with more and more growers becoming involved.

The number of wines made is large and includes many low-quantity, almost experimental bottlings, like some single-varietals of Voidomatis or Aidani. The brand names used for the basic EOs are Meltemi and Vedema, and the wines are produced in a variety of colours and levels of dryness. The retsina is fresh and not too heavy on the resin. The appellation wines start with basic Santorini, an almost pure Assyrtico coming mainly from the higher-elevation vineyards in the northwest of the island. Taking into account volumes produced as well as price, this is a good ambassador of Santorini.

Santo's nykteri is released in two versions, both made in a relatively light manner, but with Nykteri Vareli being aged in oak. Santorini Fumé is closer in ripeness to the standard Santorini, but fermented and aged in partially new oak. Quite understated, it is also the most significant organic label of the co-op.

Santo Wines also releases two vinsantos, a *vin doux* at fifteen per cent alcohol and 290 grams of residual sugar, and a *vin naturellement doux* with just eleven per cent alcohol and a sweetness level of about 220 grams per litre. *Vin doux* grapes are allowed to reach higher concentrations, fermentation stops naturally with alcohol reaching about eight per cent, and then spirit is added to reach fifteen per cent. Both Vinsantos are aged for two years in old oak barriques. There is also a mezzo, aged in oak for more than six years; this is sweeter than most, with a residual sugar level of about 260 grams per litre. The last sweet wine of the portfolio is Nama, an enjoyable Holy Communion wine.

SIGALAS WINERY

Oia, 847 02 Santorini. Tel: +30 228 607 1644; Fax: +30 228-607 1645;
Website: www.sigalas-wine.gr; Email: sigalw1@otenet.gr
Vineyards owned: 20ha; under contract: 30ha; production: 1,100hl.

A mathematician by training, Paris Sigalas started his winery in 1991 as a hobby and, within fifteen years, has managed to transform it into one of Greece's most successful wine businesses. This success has been accompanied by an equally impressive rise in quality. The initial small-scale winery was replaced in 1998 with a winery in Oia. Sigalas realized that the business needed a serious injection of capital as well as commercial expertize and, in 2003, decided to take Alexandros Avatangelos on as a partner. In addition, the highly regarded Thanassis Fakorelis joined the team as consultant winemaker.

The wines of Sigalas are the stylistic opposite of Gaia's Thalassitis. While the latter shows extreme austerity, Sigalas Santorini is about breadth and intensity, without masking the grape's minerality and raciness. In the last few vintages, the portfolio of Sigalas has moved decisively towards higher alcohol levels, with the top wines being constantly above 13.5 per cent. The OPAP Santorini is the epitome of the Sigalas style: very intense but not fruity, rich but not fat. His Santorini Vareli has benefited radically from both Fakorelis' contribution and the higher alcohol levels, since the initial versions lacked a balance between fruit and oak. Nevertheless, Sigalas claims that these wines developed excellently in bottle for over four years, absorbing the wood and letting the fruit emerge. It remains to see whether the much more integrated new Vareli wines will develop as well.

Sigalas could also be held responsible for bringing Mavrotragano to the forefront of the Santorini wine scene. Deeply coloured, this variety is very tannic and has a great affinity for oak – Sigalas ages it in barriques for almost two years, but on release, the wine seems a year younger. The first vintages in the mid-1990s were promising, but a bit shy on ripeness levels and extraction. Current releases show that the variety has top-quality potential. Sigalas works with Mandilaria, but thinks that the grape is not capable of playing more than a good supporting role. Most of his Mandilaria is bottled as Niampelo Red, a blend which includes thirty per cent Agiorgitiko from Nemea to soften and broaden the palate.

The Sigalas portfolio of sweet wines is of high quality, but possibly lacks the intense personality of his dry offerings. His vinsanto has more primary fruit, less raisiny character, and lower volatile acidity than the average and is aged in barriques for two to three years. Mezzo, a sweet red wine, is a pure Mandilaria, sun-dried for eight to ten days and then aged in barriques for about a year. It is one of the drier examples.

VOLCAN WINES
Vothonos, 847 00 Santorini.
Tel/Fax: +30 228 603 1322; Email: waterblu@otenet.gr
Vineyards owned: 2ha; production: 1,800–2,000hl.
Volcan Wines, one of the oldest wineries in Santorini and currently one of the largest, is owned by the Koutsoyiannopoulos family. The winery has traditionally kept a low profile, while shifting noteworthy quantities either to Athens or Sweden, its main export destination. However low-profile and traditional, current general manager Giorgos Koutsoyiannopoulos has been following the unfolding of trends and developing new labels. Lava Santorini and two Koutsoyiannopoulos Vineyards wines, one of which is aged in oak, are made from the family's vineyards. There is also a nykteri and two vinsantos, the best of which is simply called Koutsoyiannopoulos. All the Volcan range is reliable and typical of its respective style. The overall style is middle-of-the-road, neither old-fashioned nor overly modern.

9

Dodecanese islands

The Dodecanese are a group of twelve islands situated on the southeastern corner of the Aegean Sea (*dodeca* means "twelve" in Greek and *nissos* is "island"). These islands are the most remote part of Greece, notwithstanding the overshadowing presence of the Turkish coast lying just a few kilometres to the east. This isolation has caused problems for the Dodecanese, but at the same time, there has always been a distinct self-containment – the people of these islands decided to become part of the Greek nation after World War II not because they needed to, but because that was where they felt they belonged.

The history of the Dodecanese is typical of the Aegean Sea islands – from the glories of Ancient Greece to the periphery of the Roman and Byzantine Empires, then on into Ottoman rule. Apart from Rhodes, which was punished for being too tough to conquer, the rest of the islands enjoyed a milder form of Ottoman occupation. Due to their strategic location, Turkish officers decided to apply a less obtrusive way of governing the local societies. This was underlined and reinforced by emigrating populations from the Turkish coast.

CLIMATE, VINEYARDS, AND WINE CULTURE
The weather in this part of Aegean Sea is predictably warm and there are no extremes of temperature. Winters are relatively mild and quite short: in February it's not unusual for the northern parts of Greece to be covered in deep snow while the Dodecanese are enjoying excellent, sunny spring days. Aegean winds can be a problem for wine-growers, though flowering is usually uninterrupted and summer winds arrive late in the season, by which time the vines have developed enough to forego damage. Rainfall during the final stages of ripening is very limited, but plentiful during winter and early spring. Wind and water stress are common and carefully

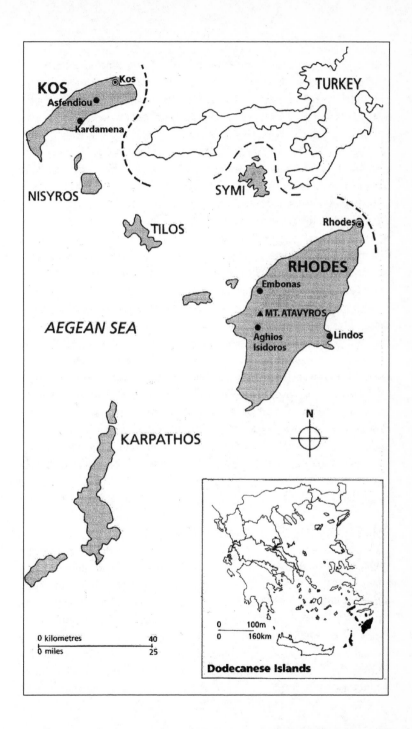

KOS

Kos

Asfendiou

Kardamena

NISYROS

TURKEY

SYMI

TILOS

Rhodes

RHODES

Embonas

▲ MT. ATAVYROS

AEGEAN SEA

Aghios
Isidoros

Lindos

N

KARPATHOS

| 0 kilometres | 40 |
| 0 miles | 25 |

| 0 | 100m |
| 0 | 160km |

Dodecanese Islands

monitored irrigation could well make a significant contribution to the cultivation of better-quality grapes.

Rhodes is the biggest island in the Dodecanese, as well as the most significant in terms of wine production. Vineyard area on the island is 1,143 hectares, while the rest of the Dodecanese combined have an acreage of just 302 hectares. Kos has a relatively organized viticultural sector, although the overall scale is very small. Beyond Kos and Rhodes, few islands of the group can claim any sizeable wine production and, in most cases, there are only isolated spots of vineyards. Patmos, Nisyros, Tilos, Astypalea, Kasos, Simi, and Karpathos have scattered vineyards and some artisan wine producers; while Kalymnos, Lipsi, and Leros have only minor production. Rhodes and Kos are also the only islands attempting to promote their wines outside the local market – in the rest of the Dodecanese, local homes and tavernas are the only places where the indigenous wines can be found.

Wine culture in the Dodecanese has been further affected by low taxes on spirits. The region enjoys a reduced alcohol duty rate as well as lower VAT rates – a perk established by the Greek government to keep the islands financially vibrant, despite their isolation from the mainland. (A few years ago the islands were totally duty free, but that status changed recently.) As a result, hard liquor is significantly cheaper to buy here than in mainland Greece and the Dodecanese has become a destination for shoppers seeking cheap spirits. Most traders catering for this market focus on sales of whisky, vodka, rum, and gin, leaving little space for wine sales and devaluing the local wine-drinking culture (though this situation seems to be changing).

CLASSIFICATIONS

Aegean Islands TO
White still: dry.
White varieties: Assyrtico; White Aidani; White Athiri; Monemvasia; Muscat Blanc.
Rosé still: dry.
Red still: dry.
Red/Rosé variety: Mandilaria.

Dodecanese Islands TO
White still: dry.

White varieties: Athiri (at least eighty per cent of the blend); Assyrtico and Ugni Blanc (combined to make up other twenty per cent).
Red still: dry.
Red varieties: Mandilaria (at least eighty per cent of the blend); Grenache Rouge and Syrah (combined to make up other twenty per cent).

KOS

Kos is one of the most fertile islands in the Aegean and is often referred to as "the garden of the Aegean". The fact that vine-growing is usually not very profitable, combined with the hardy nature of vines which can survive on soils where most crops would not stand a chance, means that any vineyards on Kos are naturally restricted to the less-forgiving parts of the island. The land is fairly flat, with Mount Dikaios at 843 metres (2,765 feet) being the only high point on the island. The majority of the best-quality vineyards are located in its foothills up to an altitude of 300 metres (984 feet).

There is evidence to suggest that Kos enjoyed a far more illustrious past as far as viticulture is concerned. Wine production was an important local asset, but never the prime source of income – fertile soils had other, more profitable uses even in antiquity. The high quality of Kos wine was well-documented by several writers, but exports never reached the levels attained by Hios, Samos, and Limnos in the north, or Rhodes and Crete further south. It seems that however good the local wines were, they were destined to remain imprisoned on the island.

During the years of Ottoman rule, Kos was considered a strong financial centre with much potential. As a result, a significant number of Turkish people immigrated to the island, mainly to take control of its resources. This core has remained remarkably stable through the centuries and, even today, there is a strong Muslim element in local society. This created a limited local market for wine and demand fell to levels that were unable to sustain the number of people who wanted to be involved in wine production.

Yet despite these difficulties, vine-growing in Kos never became obsolete. From the period of Ottoman rule until the present day, wine has had at least some significance for local people. Many landowners continued cultivating their vineyards to supply their own needs, although there was no significant trade in wine. The situation changed briefly in the late twentieth century, when Vinko emerged as the local cooperative. It did a very good job promoting Kos wines within the island – and there were even attempts to expand sales into the rest of the Dodecanese. Today, sadly, Vinko has faded into oblivion and vine-growers have lost the sense of structure and purpose that a co-op always provides. Nevertheless, it seems that all hope is not totally lost.

PRODUCER

INAMBELOS
Thesi Miniera, Asfendio, 853 00 Kos.
Tel: +30 224 204 1012; Fax: +30 224 206 9622; Email: info@inambelos.gr
Vineyards owned: 10ha; production: 450hl.

Kos is heading back into the vinous spotlight with this promising new entry. The Triantafillopoulos family began Inambelos in 2001. Considerable investment has been made in the vineyards, with vines planted in Kardamena and Asfendio, the two sites considered best for viticulture. Kardamena is near the coast, and benefits from sea breezes, while Asfendio is located at a higher altitude near Mount Dikaios.

Initial vintages were vinified in the family home, but the 2005 vintage was processed at a substantial, new state-of-the-art winery. If the quality of the first vintages is anything to go by, Inambelos could become one of the most exciting wineries of the Aegean Islands. The wines are modern, full of extract, body, and intensity, while the fruit flavours are clean and powerful.

Yet the family may have a difficult job promoting their wines. Kos is not commonly associated with wine production, let alone high-quality estate wines. In addition, Inambelos labels are old-fashioned, using names and symbols from Byzantine and Ancient Greece. This is somewhat surprising – it's more usual for wineries to spend enormous amounts of money designing fashionable new labels, even if their wines are old-fashioned. But labels can easily change – and they will, according to general manager Mary Triantafillopoulos – what's inside the bottle is more important.

The basic line of wines is the Epiloges ("selections") range. The white is an interesting fifty/fifty blend of Malagousia and Sauvignon Blanc, not dissimilar to an early Domaine Gerovassiliou white (*see* page 152). Epiloges Rosé, based on Grenache with up to twenty per cent Cinsault and Syrah, is fresh, fruity, and simple. The red is a split, co-fermented blend of Syrah and Tempranillo. The Spanish variety adds a notable dimension of elegance to the blend and planting it in Kos is almost a stroke of genius.

Top of the portfolio are the red Deipnos ("dinner") and white Eorti ("feast"). Deipnos, the only Inambelos wine to receive any oak treatment, is made from equal amounts of Merlot and Cabernet Sauvignon, finished off with twenty per cent Cabernet Franc. Rich, soft, and full of charm, it seems more Merlot than Cabernet, and its ageing for one year in 100 per cent new French oak is marked but not obtrusive. The broad and textured Eorti is predominantly Chardonnay, with small amounts of Malagousia, Athiri, and Assyrtico. All Inambelos wines – especially Deipnos and Eorti – deliver fruit and density, but curiously, given the climate of Kos, the alcohol rarely exceeds 12.5 per cent. Developments in future vintages are eagerly awaited.

RHODES

Rhodes has one of the longest wine-producing histories in the world and it was an important part of the Aegean's global wine production powerhouse in antiquity. The island's wines were so important that their distinctive amphorae were imitated by rival producers including Crete and Cyprus. Rhodes is the easternmost island of the Dodecanese and was used as an intermediate port by ships travelling from the east to the west, or vice versa. Known as "the gateway of the Aegean", it may have been one of the very first regions of Greece that planted vines.

This prosperity declined somewhat during the first centuries AD. In 1522, the island was captured by the Ottoman Empire. Prior to that, Rhodes had been occupied by the Knights of Saint John for nearly two centuries. At that point, it was an important supplier of Malvasia wine and both the knights and the Ottoman rulers were keen to preserve such a valuable resource. For that reason, the Ottomans respected the business of viticulture in Rhodes slightly more than elsewhere in mainland Greece, although a lack of long-term planning and willingness to invest led to a slow but steady decline. In the twentieth century, the Italians occupied Rhodes from 1912–45. During this brief period, viticulture developed on a small scale alongside attempts to upgrade the economy and improve standards of living.

The climate on Rhodes facilitates viticulture to a significant degree. Although limited during summer and early autumn, rainfall during winter is usually sufficient to fill water reserves and overall levels are among the highest in the Aegean. The climate is warm to hot, though air currents have a cooling effect throughout the year – from May to September these take the form of gentle sea breezes and sometimes violent winds. Within these parameters, vines in many high altitude sites around the island can still be subject to heat or wind stress or aridity – though not to the extent of those in Crete or Santorini. This is reflected in the styles of wine produced – including a sizeable proportion of sparkling wines – which display more elegance than one would expect at this latitude.

Vineyards and viticulture

There are roughly 1,200 hectares of vineyards on Rhodes, separated into two distinct zones. Zone A comprises the lowland vineyards, while Zone B covers the slopes of Mount Atavyros, which peaks at 1,216 metres (3,990 feet). Vines are trained on a low, double-Royat system, in order to preserve moisture, while Zone B is mainly terraced to avoid erosion. Soil is a mixture of small pockets of sand, clay, limestone, and gravel. It is difficult to determine a dominant soil type, though Zone B has higher levels of limestone than Zone A. Vineyards in Embonas, on the slopes of Mount Atavyros, are among the best sites on the island for Athiri, mainly because the grape's maturity is significantly delayed. In other regions white grapes are harvested in mid-August, but in Embonas the Athiri vintage doesn't begin until early October.

Viticulture is benefited by, if not shoehorned in, the demarcation of the island's appellations, since more than ninety per cent of the vine-growing areas fall within the existing OPAP and OPE boundaries. Only forty per cent of the total wine production is bottled as such, but the figure still exceeds the national average by more than 400 per cent.

The quality-wine appellation, OPAP, of the island is simply called Rhodes and includes dry white wines from Athiri and dry reds from Mandilaria, locally called Amoriano. The permitted yields are sixty-three hectolitres per hectare (nine tonnes per hectare) for the white and seventy hectolitres per hectare (ten tonnes per hectare) for the red. Although both Athiri and Mandilaria are mainly used as blending varietals in most wine-growing regions of the Aegean, in Rhodes they are allowed to shine alone. Athiri is planted in higher-altitude vineyards, and some Oreina examples (literally, "coming from the mountains") are impressive. Low and flat land with lighter soils is reserved for Mandilaria, since it is a variety that needs both heat, to synthesize anthocyanins and sugars, and infertile soils, to control its extreme vigour.

Sweet Muscats of Rhodes can be released under the OPE classification, and legislation covers all styles from sun-dried to fortified. The permitted yield is eighty-four hectolitres per hectare. The traditional Muscat of Rhodes was Muscat Blanc, but Muscat di Trani is a later introduction that is supposed to be of Venetian origin – it is not certain whether this is a different Muscat variety or simply a clone of Muscat Blanc. What is certain is that growers and winemakers working closely with it do observe a higher aromatic intensity, as well as greater density. In most instances the Muscats from Rhodes lack the breathtaking complexity of Muscats from Samos, but they do have a much richer, less monotonous fruit than those from Limnos.

Beyond Muscat, Mandilaria, and Athiri, the varietal composition of Rhodes vineyards is relatively straightforward. There are very few Greek varieties to be found and almost none are exclusive to the island. Diminitis, a black, thick-skinned, and small-berried variety, may have been the only grape to qualify as such, but now it is almost extinct. Only a few growers have a notable number of Diminitis vines and they tend to keep the fruit for their own wine. French varieties account for an increasing proportion of the plantings. These include Ugni Blanc, Chardonnay, and Sauvignon Blanc, but the main emphasis is on red grapes such as Grenache, Cinsault, Cabernet Sauvignon, Merlot, and Syrah.

Growers and producers

A common concern for quality-oriented winemakers who source their grapes from individual growers is that viticulture on the island is difficult to control. The invasion of French varieties has become a reality in the past years, even if traditional varieties find a unique and remarkable expression in the island's terroir. Most growers opt for seriously high yields, frequently above the permitted levels, despite strong evidence that Rhodes could produce world-class wines if production was curbed at thirty-five hectolitres per hectare or lower. Instead, many growers practise irrigation and yields of 200 hectolitres per hectare are not uncommon. In the last couple of decades, many vineyards have been planted with Grenache, which can give higher yields and is easier to grow. Nevertheless, growers still demand top prices for diluted Grenache fruit. Late harvesting is fiercely resisted, due to fears of losing the crop in the event of early autumn rains. The whole situation becomes more depressing if you take into account the excellent state of the base materials – phylloxera never invaded Rhodes, so the old vines have been preserved and the average age of traditional vineyards exceeds fifty years. However, some large producers, such as CAIR, are taking the matter in hand and quality could soon reach higher levels.

The island's production is dominated by two producers: CAIR and Emery. By Greek standards, Emery is considered a medium-sized producer whereas CAIR, the unofficial cooperative of Rhodes, produces almost ten times as much wine. Both producers are particularly well-known throughout Greece on account of their sparkling wine production, which has great commercial significance nationally. For decades, Rhodes was the main source of "Greek Champagne", which was consumed mainly at wedding receptions, for celebrations like New Year's Eve, and in nightclubs around Greece. Most Greeks were introduced to sparkling wines by drinking a bottle of CAIR or Emery – and quite a few rarely tasted anything beyond that. When standards of wine production and wine culture around Greece started developing, some consumers began to look down on these wines, preferring imported "Champagne" labels – which most of the time were not Champagne at all. This is unfortunate since the quality of "Rhodes Brut" and "Demi-Sec" products is far superior to many non-Greek sparkling wines that can be found in the marketplace. The style is extremely charming, soft, and easy-drinking, combining warm-climate fruit ripeness with freshness. Sparkling wines from Rhodes have yet to rival top Champagnes, although some bottles of Emery traditional method brut, and the CAIR Ten-Year-Old Rosé Brut Réserve can be stunning.

Rhodes OPAP

White still: dry.
White variety: Athiri.
Red still: dry.
Red variety: Mandilaria.

Muscat of Rhodes OPE

White still: naturally sweet (*vin naturellement doux*); fortified sweet (*vin doux naturel*); fortified sweet from selected vineyards (*vin doux naturel grand cru*); fortified sweet (*vin doux*).
White varieties: Muscat Blanc; Muscat di Trani.

PRODUCERS

CAIR

2nd km Rhodes–Lindos Avenue, 851 00 Rhodes. Tel: +30 224 106 8770; Fax: +30 224 106 2575; Website: www.cair.gr; Email: info@cair.gr

Vineyards owned: 2.5ha; under contract: 1,100ha; production: 50,000hl.

If the CAIR winery had not been founded in 1928, wine production on Rhodes would have been very different. Almost single-handedly, this company made viticulture a financially viable option for landowners on the island. The company expanded quickly, converting successful sales into good returns for all involved. It worked hard in the late 1960s to persuade authorities that Rhodes was worthy of not just one quality appellation, but three – almost ten per cent of those granted across Greece at the time. By the late 1990s, more than two million euros had been spent to create a cutting-edge production unit, but it seems that even that was not enough. Close to thirteen million euros have been allocated for relocating parts of the operation to a new one-hectare site by 2007. CAIR is one of the very few examples in modern Greek times of prosperity and viticulture going hand in hand.

Although technically CAIR is not the official cooperative of Rhodes, essentially it functions like one. There is an obligation to buy the harvest from a certain group of growers representing around 1,100 hectares of vines. Winemakers do try to select different parcels and isolate interesting sites but there are restrictions – most vats are bulky, twenty-five tonnes or larger – and separating small parcels is impossible. In addition, the harvest across Rhodes is pretty condensed in terms of timing, with ninety per cent of the white grape vineyards being harvested in one week, meaning that grape loads from most regions arrive at the winery at the same time. Still, there are criteria in place and selection does produce significant distinction within the product range.

The CAIR portfolio consists of around seventy different products, not counting the various packaging formats, from airline bottles to bag-in-box and even bulk wine. Thanks to that, sales can cover most sectors of the trade, not only on Rhodes or in Greece, but also in most important export markets, like the USA, Germany, and Japan.

Despite this success, Alexandros Glynos, production manager and managing director of the company, was aware of the limitations of the current production system and suggested that CAIR develop its own vineyards. By 2005, there were already 2.5 hectares under this plan, with more acquisitions along the way. This CAIR-owned land is not intended to act as a substitute for the vineyards of local growers under contract. The project's main aim has been to draw conclusions about best viticultural pratice and use these to help local farmers to achieve better results – as well as to ensure some top-quality crops for the premium CAIR wines. A viticultural team has been formed to work on these plots, but so far, any influence on other vineyards under contract has been minimal.

CAIR's quality-wine products, its OPEs and OPAPs, are very important in the national market, while the local market takes up a large proportion of the company's regional and table wines, its EOs. Ilios White and Chevalier de Rhodes Red are both entry-level OPAPs. The latter is the only red OPAP produced by CAIR and is fresh, light, and simple. Ilios is the lesser selection from OPAP Athiri vineyards, but it is by no means low-quality.

The top Athiri, selected from the best parcels of Embonas, is saved for two bottlings. The lower-price, higher-volume wine is called "2400" and has far more definition and character than Ilios. It is made from fruit in vineyards located at up to 600 metres (1,968 feet) altitude. Fruit from higher plots is kept separate for the Athiri Oreinon Ampelonon (literally, "Athiri from mountainous vineyards"), which is one of the best expressions of varietal Athiri, full of elegance and grace. Both wines are made in a straightforward way, with cool, stainless-steel fermentations, short maturations, and early bottling. The exception is lees contact: while Athiri Oreinon Ampelonon always receives up to one month of lees contact in vats, 2400 gained a bit of body but lost a lot of aromas when aged *sur lie* in the 2003 vintage.

Paraskevi Hatzistamatis, winemaker at CAIR, believes that more work is needed on Athiri. Most people working with it accept that the potential of the variety is still untapped. It is of prime importance to develop yeast strains that could embellish the character of the grape without mimicking other varieties, as is the case when it is fermented with Sauvignon Blanc strains. It has been noted that some parcels work well with lees, but others do not. Hatzistamatis claims that Athiri works well with oak, as shown by the excellent Oinofos, a complex wine from ungrafted forty-year-old vines and aged for four months in barriques. Whether it is easy to sell all 7,000 bottles produced annually is another story.

CAIR rosés have been bestsellers, epitomized by the fruity Moulin Sec, made from Mandilaria with a bit of Athiri, and the aromatic Moulin Demi-Sec, where Athiri is substituted with Muscat Blanc. Reds are, again, a difficult sell, but CAIR has been putting serious effort behind Knight's Cellar – a Cabernet Sauvignon aged for a year in new oak, part American and part French – and the rounder, faster-developing Arhontiko, which is a blend of Mandilaria and twenty per cent Grenache, aged nine months in French barriques.

As mentioned above, CAIR was instrumental in developing a popular image for Rhodes sparkling wine. Boheme Brut and Demi-Sec are Charmat-method wines with freshness and soft acidity. Cair Brut and Demi-Sec are a distinct step up. Both are Athiri-based, fermented in bottle, and aged on lees for about a year, after which the wines are transferred into vats, filtered, and bottled under pressure. The top sparkler is the Cair Rosé Réserve. Based on Athiri, but also with Mandilaria rosé wine for colour, 3,000 bottles are made every year. It used to be aged for ten years on lees, resulting in a very pale hue and a breathtaking, yeasty, floral but not fruity nose. But this style only appealed to connoisseurs, so CAIR decided to include a proportion of three-year-old wines during the transfer phase. The new style is still good and more vibrant in fruit, but it seems to have lost a few layers of complexity.

CAIR also produces an OPE Muscat, sold simply as Muscat de Rhodes. It is made from Muscat Blanc and Muscat di Trani, harvested at around 13.5 degrees Baumé and fermented up to 8.5 per cent alcohol, at which point alcohol is added to fortify it to fifteen per cent. The aromatic first pressings of both Muscats are included. Hatzistamatis thinks that Trani is a more interesting Muscat than Blanc, but finds it difficult to combine both. Muscat Blanc needs bottling as soon as possible, while Trani develops a whole new array of flavours if kept in the vat until at least mid-spring. The logical step forward would be a varietal dry Muscat di Trani. The closest CAIR has got to that is Idinos: a fresh, aromatic, very promising Athiri/Muscat di Trani blend.

Other noteworthy products include Amandia, a *vin de liqueur* Mandilaria aged in old oak for a year, and the million-bottles-a-year Retsina – a good example of the style, showing both a careful use of resin and the fresh wine underneath.

EMERY

Embonas Kritinis, 851 08 Rhodes.
Head office: 28 Australias, 851 00 Rhodes. Tel: +30 224 1029 111;
Fax: +30 224 102 2716; Website: www.emery.gr; Email: emery@aias.gr
Vineyards under contract: 70ha; production: 6,000hl.

Emery is actually an older enterprise than CAIR, established five years earlier, although many people might not believe this, as it is a much smaller, family-owned business that has followed a very different path over the years.

Emery started out in 1923 with the aim of producing several types of alcoholic drinks, including flavoured liqueurs. The company then started producing pure alcohol, initially to meet its own needs. At that time the alcohol market was not saturated, so after a few years, spirits developed into Emery's main product.

In the 1960s, the Triantafillou family decided to move into wine production, partly as a hobby and partly because of increased competition in the ouzo and liqueur market. CAIR had already started making waves with sparkling wines, so Emery used that success as a stimulus. Before too long, a full range of wines across all styles was successfully developed. The small size of the venture allowed Emery to create a modern winery right at the heart of the best Athiri-growing region, Embonas. Even if the current production has significantly increased since the early vintages, most grape supplies are still gathered from neighbouring vineyards, either in Embonas or Aghios Isidoros, on the opposite side of Mount Atavyros. Emery has shown little interest in developing vineyards, but instead, has focused on developing close relations and long-term agreements with local growers.

Given its size, Emery produces a remarkably large number of products. Almost all types of wine are represented, reflecting several aspects and trends in the market – from the popular sparklers and the OPAPs of traditional varieties to the occasional venture with Cabernet Sauvignon or oak-aged whites and *demi-sec* bottlings to satisfy local tastes. The overall style of Emery wines is close to that of CAIR, with evidence of a shared terroir underlying the wines. However, in many cases, Emery wines reveal more extract, polish, and depth.

There are several layers of OPAP wines. The basic brand is Mythiko ("legendary"), available in both white and red. Going up in price and down in volume (and yield levels) one finds Rhodes Athiri and Rhodes Amoriano, Enoteca White Demi-Sec, White Sec, and Red. All of the whites in the range are vinified in stainless steel, with very little, if any, lees contact. Reds are all aged in oak and bottled for varying amounts of time, ranging from a few months in barriques and bottle up to three years total maturation time in Emery's cellar.

Nicos and Mary-Irene Triantafillou, the cousins who are in charge of Emery, are keen to develop the premium side of their portfolio and are sticking to Athiri and Amoriano with impressive dedication. Top Athiri is expressed with three different labels and three different styles. Rodofili Fumé is fermented in new French oak and then transferred to older oak for six months. Although the oak is integrated and well-balanced, the clarity of fruit achieved in the two other wines makes the oak influence seem unnecessary. Athiri Vounoplayias ("mountain slope") is a single-vineyard wine from Embonas at 600 metres (1,968 feet) altitude, which was planted in the mid-1980s. There are hints of ripeness and spiciness on the nose, but acidity remains dominant on the palate and the alcohol is a very modest twelve per cent. While the style of Athiri Vounoplayias is widely admired, Villaré Blanc de Blancs is an excellent statement of Athiri's reserved elegance. Grapes are selected from higher vineyards, approaching the 750-metre (2,460-feet) mark. The grapes are harvested a little later than the Athiri Vounoplayias crop, but the alcohol is lower due to the cooler temperatures. Nevertheless, longer hang-time gives a different aromatic intensity and lower acidity. The result is not as expressive as some other Athiri wines, but still top quality.

While Emery reds are very good illustrations of Mandilaria, they do not achieve the same heights as the whites. Mandilaria can be too tannic, but still remains low in alcohol, so most Rhodes reds might have the skin and the backbone, but usually lack the flesh. Oak- and bottle-ageing help to round off the palate and Emery puts a lot of emphasis on that side of the cellar. Zacosta is the most modern Mandilaria red, with four months in French oak, one month in large, used Cognac barrels, and then a few months in bottle before release. The Amoriano Vounoplayias is the most age-worthy Mandilaria but, on release, also the most tannic and unforgiving. The reverse is true for Cava Emery, a developed and quite traditional style of Aegean red.

The final Mandilaria style in the company's portfolio is the first-rate Granrosé. When Mandilaria is used to produce rosé wines, some of the potential drawbacks of the variety become distinct advantages. Low alcohol and high acidity retain freshness, the deeply pigmented grape gives a lovely colour, and a short maceration allows very little tannin extraction. For this wine, Emery chooses some of the highest Mandilaria vineyards in Greece, at 700 metres (2,460 feet) altitude, and aims for a short carbonic maceration. Granrosé has more than a touch of cool climate structure, but is still an attractive and forward wine.

Emery produces only two sparkling wines: Grand Prix Brut and Grand Prix Demi-Sec. There is a standard policy of bottle-ageing on lees for at least two years and, as a result, Grand Prix is more yeasty and floral, but less fruity than CAIR Brut or Demi-Sec. The winery does not produce any OPE wine, since the naturally sweet Efreni is Muscat Blanc-based, but still contains considerable portions of Athiri. The only Emery wine made from non-traditional varieties is Rodon – a 100 per cent Cabernet Sauvignon from Kalavarda vineyards, aged in new French oak for six months. It is certainly a good wine, but Rhodes – and Greece in general – needs more wines like the rest of the Emery portfolio, not just another good Cabernet.

10

North Aegean islands

The North Aegean Islands are one of the four groups of isles that fill up the Aegean archipelagos, alongside the Cyclades, the Dodecanese, and the Sporades. The North Aegean Islands are not as northern as their name might suggest. The most southerly island, Ikaria, is on the same latitude as Nemea in the Peloponnese, while Limnos, the most northerly island, is level with Thessaly. There are five main islands, from north to south: Limnos, Lesbos, Hios, Samos, and Ikaria. In addition, there are smaller islets scattered around the area, like Aghios Efstratios just south of Limnos, Psara, and Andipsara on the northwestern corner of Hios, and between Ikaria and Samos lie Fourni, Thymena, Thymenaki, Alatonissi, Makronissi, Aghios Minas, Samiopoula, and even the tiny Megas Anthropofagos, meaning the "Great Man-Eater". There are three prefectures: Lesbos, comprising both Lesbos and Limnos; Hios; and Samos, the latter of which includes Ikaria.

The North Aegean Islands are closer to the Turkish coast than to mainland Greece. The relationship between the two nations has greatly improved in recent years, but for many periods of the last century, such proximity was chilling. When the weather prevents ships or planes reaching the islands, a sense of isolation can set in. The islands' strategic position is well-known, and most of them have a strong military presence, especially Samos, Limnos, Lesbos, and Hios. Tourism is of importance, but nowhere near the extent found in Santorini, Crete, and Rhodes, and so military personnel and students provide the local community with a reliable source of income.

CLIMATE AND CLASSIFICATIONS
The climate of the region is very typical of the Aegean Sea. The summers are hot and dry, with August being especially windy, and the winters are

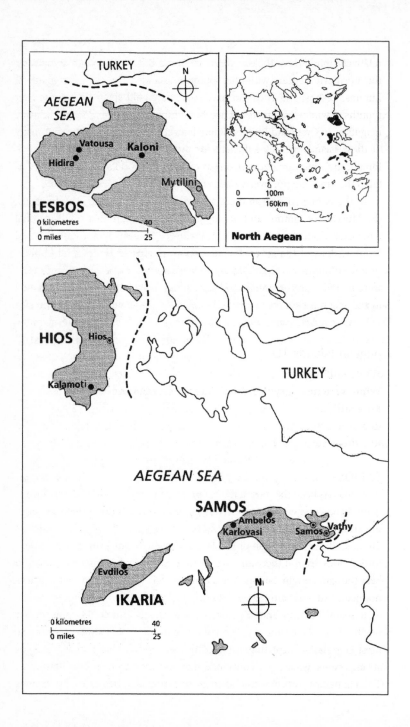

relatively mild. Nevertheless, there are some differences when comparing the northern Aegean with the southern islands. The northern parts of Limnos, Lesbos, and Hios can have some very cold spells during the later months of winter. Summers are hot, but temperatures do not reach the same heights as in Crete and Rhodes. Rainfall levels are roughly similar, but many of these islands are self-sufficient for water, especially Samos and Ikaria. Finally, the winds are not as strong as in Santorini and Paros, so in most vintages the vines are not overly stressed.

In the Northern Aegean there are two OPE quality-wine classifications, the Muscats of Limnos and of Samos. In Samos there is a small regional wine classification, the Côtes de Ambelos TO, and in Limnos an OPAP of Limnos. Both of the latter designations were created to cover dry whites produced on the respective islands. The Limnos OPAP and the Samos OPE were included in the initial 1971 legislation; the Limnos OPE was created in the second wave, between 1979 and 1982; and the Côtes de Ambelos TO was established in 1990.

Aegean Islands TO

White still: dry.
White varieties: Assyrtico; Athiri; Muscat of Alexandria.
Rosé still: dry.
Red still: dry.
Red /Rosé varieties: Limnio; Mandilaria.

SAMOS

If retsina has been the most famous Greek wine export, while Mavrodaphne is the better-known indigenous variety, then Samos must be Greece's most illustrious appellation. All the other Muscat-related OPEs of Greece, such as Limnos, Rhodes, and Rion of Patras, include the words "Muscat of" in their formal titles, even if there are no other alternative grape varieties that could bear the same origin. Samos, like a famous rock star or football player, does not need that – a plain "Samos" on the label will do.

It seems that, in antiquity, Samos was not as famous as some of her neighbours. Maybe the style of wine produced at that time was not the most popular – surprisingly, Samos did not follow the market trend for strong, sweet wines, but continued making dry and relatively light reds. The change of fortune came after an unexpected series of events. Samos had been extremely popular among pirates for centuries. In the latter half of the fifteenth century, a sizeable part of the population decided to seek protection in nearby Hios. Samos became more or less deserted and most forms of cultivation needing human input were destroyed. A hundred years later, the Ottoman rulers offered benefits for Samos people willing to return to their homeland. Vineyards were once again planted with new stock, this time including more white varieties, and specifically, Muscat Blanc.

The rise of Muscat

Phylloxera arrived on the island in 1892 with growers needing more than a decade to recover. New vineyards gave even more preference to Muscat over other varieties. The final blow for red varieties came in 1934, with a law stating that only Muscat wines were allowed to be named as Samos wines. Currently, Muscat plantations account for close to ninety-five per cent of the vineyard area. Varieties that can be found in isolated spots include Ritino – which produces wines moderately deep in colour, with high alcohol and balancing acidity – and Fokiano. This variety, probably originating from the Near East, is moderately vigorous, productive, and very tolerant to drought. It ripens in early September and produces wines with low colour, and moderate alcohol and acidity, making it more suitable for rosés than reds.

Samos wine exports have always been exceptionally strong, even during the years of the Ottoman occupation. The locals are proud to say that, for centuries, ships destined for the most prestigious locations in the world were lining up to fill their holds with sweet Muscat wines. Although much has changed in the last forty years, at the time the national market was not developed enough to absorb any substantial proportion of the production, so these exports were a blessing.

However, in regions where exports are the main source of income, joining the trade comes with many challenges, including language, cultural and financial barriers. In contrast, strong local demand creates an accessible market. In Samos, the strong exports benefited the traditional, long-standing traders, who had total control over the island's growers. This situation increasingly frustrated the local population, and in 1934, the Samos growers requested and finally succeeded in creating a cooperative monopoly. Ever since, vineyard owners have been obliged to provide their whole harvest to the Samos Union of Winemaking Cooperatives, which is the sole supplier of Samos wines for buyers all over the world. The venture has the right to sell

Samos wines to other bottlers to sell under their name, or to brand alongside the Samos designation.

So far the cooperative seems to have been doing an excellent job. Not only has it safeguarded the interests of co-op members, but it has also raised the profile and increased sales of Samos wines, both at home and on the export market. Even the Catholic Church has designated Samos UWC as a communion wine supplier. Its success is illustrated by the fact that, more than seventy years later, every grower is happy to appear under the co-op banner. There is a fair pricing structure, and prices paid by Samos UWC are among the highest in Greece. Ripeness is rewarded over quantity. A kilo of grapes around fourteen degrees Baumé could fetch 0.70 euros, while higher levels of sugar concentration, or fruit from selected vineyards meeting more rigorous specifications, could increase that price by at least seventy per cent.

Degrees of sweetness

The sweet wines of the island are made using three distinct production methods: *vin doux*, *vin doux naturel*, and *vin naturellement doux* (*see* Glossary). For a *vin doux* wine, Muscat is harvested, pressed, and the juice is fortified almost immediately. Sugar readings therefore remain around 200 grams per litre. The alcoholic strength reached after fortification is fifteen per cent with almost no fermentation taking place, therefore all the alcohol is spirit-related. This means that the quantity of spirit added is the highest and dilution is a bit more evident. In addition, the lack of aromatic fermentation by-products leaves the spotlight on the primary, intense, Muscat-derived terpene compounds, giving freshness, but being a bit short on complexity.

For *vin doux naturel*, fermentation takes place for the initial degrees of alcohol, and is then stopped by the addition of alcohol. For a *grand cru vin doux naturel* – *grand cru* vineyards are selected parcels above 400 metres (1,312 feet) in altitude – yields are below thirty-five hectolitres per hectare and, in general, only top quality fruit is used. The grapes from *grand cru* sites are harvested riper, but consumption of sugar by the yeast leaves the final wine with a sweetness level below 150 grams per litre. The amount of spirit needed is lower and the aromas are more compact and expansive.

A *vin naturellement doux* is made in a completely different way. Grapes from the best high altitude vineyards are harvested when they are fully ripe. Then selected healthy bunches are sun-dried for seven to ten days, pressed, and the must slowly starts to ferment. Selected alcohol-tolerant yeasts are used, since sugar levels can be around 360 grams per litre. Even so, these yeasts get dehydrated and die at about fourteen per cent, leaving about 130 grams per litre of unfermented sugars.

Not all of Samos is allowed to bear the OPAP designation and the western side is largely excluded. Viticulture is mostly confined around Mount Ambelos (1,150 metres, 3,773 feet). There is one higher peak on the island, Mount Marathokampos, just west of Mount Ambelos at 1,434 metres (4,705 feet). The low-altitude fields are confined to the east side of the island – also the hottest. Most vineyards are terraced, and located between 150–800 metres (492–2,624 feet) on north-facing slopes, as producers deliberately seek out the cooler spots.

Even if this is essentially a one-grape island, the harvest is extended because of the wide differentiations in altitudes, exposure, soils, and meso-climates. The first grapes are harvested in the hottest, lowest vineyards, before mid-August, while the highest parcels might not reach the winery until well into October. Given that the Samos UWC produces a vast array of Muscat wines, from dry to fortified to naturally sweet, the prolonged harvest and the complex patterns of processing the grapes is a blessing. The co-op's winemakers are able to get to grips with the various terroirs, identify the island's best parcels, and work out how they should be handled to provide the optimum quality for any of its given brands. The outcome is, in short, one of the finest cooperative portfolios around the globe.

Samos OPE

White still: naturally sweet (*vin naturellement doux*); fortified sweet (*vin doux naturel*); fortified sweet from selected vineyards (*vin doux naturel grand cru*); fortified sweet (*vin doux*).
White variety: Muscat Blanc.

Côtes de Ambelos TO

White still: dry.
White variety: Muscat Blanc.

PRODUCER

SAMOS UNION OF WINEMAKING COOPERATIVES
Winery One: Thesi Malagari, 831 00 Samos. Tel: +30 227 302 7297. Winery Two: Karlovasi, 832 00 Samos. Tel: +30 227 303 3173; Fax: +30 227 303 0002.

Head office: Thesi Malagari, 831 00 Samos. Tel: +30 227 308 7510;
Fax: +30 227 302 3907; Website: www.samoswine.gr; Email: info@samoswine.gr
Vineyards under contract: 1,500ha; Members: 4,000+; production: 60,000–80,000hl.
For many, the modern wine history of Samos is represented by the Samos Union of Winemaking Cooperatives. Founded in 1934 with the exclusive responsibility of producing and selling all Samos wine, it took until the 1950s for sales to really take off, and it was the 1970s when Samos became the most successful Greek wine export. Sales continue to be strong, with the French market taking more than seventy per cent of the whole production, and the United States and Japan developing fast.

Four thousand members belonging to twenty-five preliminary co-ops contribute fruit from 1,500 hectares to Samos UWC's operations. Growers are directed to send their grapes to one of two wineries: one in Karlovasi on the western part of the north coast, the other in Malagari, close to Vathy, on the eastern side. Both wineries take full advantage of the highly fragmented harvest pattern, managing to identify the most promising plots for the best possible method of production. Not only is the structure of the different brands remarkable, but also the consistency of the products across vintages, both in the sweet and the dry styles.

Samos dry Muscats are a relatively recent phenomenon and the grapes for these are the first to be harvested on the island, although a proportion of later-maturing, higher-altitude fruit is used for power. The key word here is freshness, and early harvesting aims to keep the Muscat character relatively light and vivacious. "Early harvesting" on Samos means sugar levels of around 12.5 degrees Baumé. The main wines produced from these grapes are Samaina and Golden Samaina. Neither are bone-dry, having about five grams per litre of residual sugar, displaying a rich but clean Muscat nose. Stainless-steel, cool-fermentation is used for both whites, the only difference being that Golden Samaina is a blend of selected batches of higher vineyards and therefore shows riper, but at the same time finer, fruit. A striking feature of these wines is their price. Giorgos Loukas, a sommelier at the Michelin-star Spondi restaurant in Athens and 2003 winner of the Greek Ruinart Sommelier Competition, admits to using a higher mark-up than usual because "it is so cheap that no-one buys it".

The range of dry whites also includes Aegeopelagitikos, an Aegean Islands TO made from higher vineyards and the driest and most expensive of the range, and Doryssa, a lower-priced product but still vibrant and full of varietal character. An extremely charming Selana rosé is made from Fokiano and Ritino. The fabulous Samos Retsina should not be forgotten either. The synergy of elegant resin and the flowery Muscat nose makes this one of Greece's best, most individual retsinas.

For the rest of the Muscat fruit, sugar levels are left to soar up to at least thirteen degrees Baumé. Fermentations for all sweet Samos Muscats are made with the yeast *Saccharomyces bayanus* because the winemaking team believes that the resulting aromatic profile and the fermentation by-products are better than the more usual *Saccharomyces cerevisiae*. The standard sweet Muscat is Samos Vin Doux. For this wine, grapes from the lower slopes are chosen. Although the wine is a bit short on complexity, the ripeness and sweetness of its fruit are so intense that it justifies completely the huge commercial success of the wine – and it is superb value for money. The other young sweet wine is Samos Grand Cru Vin Doux Naturel. Overall a far more elegant personality than Samos Doux, the Grand Cru has taken over the number-one export spot for the French market, and is also the Samos style chosen by the Catholic Church for its communion wine. The remaining sweet wines are oak-aged Muscats. New oak and even barriques have yet to invade the cellars of Samos UWC and older barrels are used with confidence. The main sizes are 2.5 tonnes and 500 litres. The high alcoholic degree of the wine and the residual sugar levels make matured Samos a most stable product and large wooden vats are not in danger of developing acetic bacteria. The point here is not to give oak flavours to the wine but to give it a chance to infuse the intense Muscat theme with the spices and the complexity of time.

The first step is Anthemis, which is a *vin doux*. The best and most promising *cuvées* from the basic wine are separated and cask-aged for five years. The basic readings of acidity, alcohol, and sugar are identical to the young Samos Vin Doux, but the maturation process manages to envelope the evident spirit and powerful primary flavours of the young wine with an excellent multi-faceted density. The colour, the nose, and the palate turn a bit heavier, going past the ultra-clean Muscat expression, but the whole structure and integration are first-rate.

All of the above Muscats are made by using freshly gathered grapes with fortification during the production process. The flagship Nectar, a *vin naturellement doux*, is different. After the natural end of fermentation, the wine is transferred into oak. Nectar starts off so complex that it does not need the same length of ageing as Anthemis, so it stays in barrels for three years. The dry extract of this wine is exquisite and the fruit displays a lovely spiciness without lacking any freshness – a cross between Rivesaltes and Rutherglen. The wine is not just a very good example of a sweet Muscat aged in oak; there is a grace in the way the wine fuses grape, method of production, and ageing that can be attributed only to a terroir dimension.

The commercially available Samos wines end with the delights of Nectar. Nevertheless, the Samos staff are occasionally persuaded to bring out and even give away single bottles of old Nectar. These vintages could go as far back as the early 1950s. Selected barrels of Nectar are earmarked for prolonged ageing that can go on for as long as the winemaker considers feasible. There is a very strict policy regarding the topping-up of vats, and wines used to fill empty spaces are, whenever possible, taken from vintages that have more or less the same age. These *cuvées* exhibit further development compared with the standard releases, but, remarkably, a total lack of coarse oxidation. It is highly debatable whether barrel age for Nectar has an optimum duration and, beyond a point, what is lost is a bit more significant than what is gained. Nevertheless, Samos UWC reserve Nectars belong to the first division of any sweet wine classification, matching excellent depth and concentration with the marvellously charming, floral, sweet character of Muscat Blanc.

When looking at the sound Samos UWC set-up, its sensible product range and the excellent quality of the wines across all price-points and styles, it is difficult to understand why this formula has not been copied elsewhere in other Greek wine-producing regions.

LIMNOS

Limnos is the second most important wine-producing island in the northern Aegean. It has volcanic, infertile, light, and mainly calcareous soils, but the main difference from the mountainous Samos is that most of Limnos is almost at sea level. If a small part of the northwestern corner of the island is excluded, about ninety per cent of the surface area is below the 250-metre mark (820 feet). This is the main reason why most vineyards are located on the cooler western part of the island. Even if Limnos is the most northern island of the group, it is, on average, one of the warmest during the summer months.

Limnos used to produce red wines and, like Samos, the variety that made the island famous was a later introduction. Limnio is the famous local red grape, with Hesiod mentioning a Limnio vine originating from the island of Limnos in his seventh-century BC writings. The variety still survives on the island, but is not at present living up to its fame. The majority of red Kalambaki wines, the local name for Limnio, seem thin and lacking in extract, especially when compared with wines produced in Thrace and Macedonia from the same variety. Although the reds of Limnos do not tend to reach the heights of the whites, some good, clean, refreshing Limnio rosés are produced by the co-op. Other red varieties of the island are Fokiano, Mandilaria, and Vaftra, a variety that is one of the deepest-coloured varieties to be found in Greece, and is used to add alcohol and pigments to local blends.

Nowadays, Limnos vineyards are dominated by Muscat and justifiably so, since the quality is excellent. The Muscat of Limnos OPE classification is an exception among the other Muscat-related appellations in Greece in its choice of Muscat. While all other OPEs are dedicated to Muscat Blanc á Petits Grains, or, in the case of Muscat of Rhodes, Muscat Blanc and Muscat di Trani, Limnos prefers Muscat of Alexandria. This sub-variety of Muscat is generally regarded as a lesser grape for wine production, not reaching the extract or the character of Muscat Blanc. It is multipurpose and can be used for raisins and table grapes as well as making wine.

When analyzing Limnos Muscats it is inevitable to compare them with Samos wines. The latter are usually more complex and more extracted, while in aged versions, maturation seems to suit the grape. Limnos Muscats are by no means less serious; they are profound, youthful, more floral, and far more forward. Apparently, flavour development versus sugar accumulation in Muscat of Alexandria grown in Limnos is slower then Muscat Blanc grown on the higher Samos vineyards. Another factor might be that the legal maximum in Limnos is eighty-four hectolitres per hectare, twenty per cent more than the Samos' limit. Still, Limnos makes very appealing wines which, in most cases, offer good value for money.

Limnos has two different appellations. OPAP Limnos is reserved for pure Muscat dry whites, although there is an allowance for off-dry and semi-sweet styles. All sweet wines have to go under the OPE Muscat of Limnos umbrella, which engulfs all possible options: *vin naturellement doux*, *vin doux naturel*, and *vin doux*. For *vin doux naturel* wines that are produced from selected vineyards, a *grand cru* designation can be used. This sub-appellation is seen only in the local cooperative's bottlings and, as in Samos, it is reserved for less sweet, lower-fortification wines. There are fewer examples of barrel-aged sweet Muscats and almost none is matured for more than a few years. Possibly, just another fact confirming that Muscat of Alexandria is more about fruit than depth and complexity.

The Limnos co-op was founded just three years after its counterpart in Samos, but exclusivity was not granted to the organization. As the local and national market started to improve, some growers decided to start their own ventures. Hatzigeorgiou was one of the pioneers in Limnos in the early 1980s, and Petros Honas started a decade later. In 2005, Honas was in the early stages of setting up a joint venture, Limnioi Ampelourgoi, (Vine Growers of Limnos), with two other local wineries: Kremmidas, a traditional producer, and Tzaneros, a recent enterprise, although all three growers will keep their own individual product portfolios.

Limnos OPAP

White still: dry; semi-dry; semi-sweet.
White variety: Muscat of Alexandria.

Muscat of Limnos OPE

White still: naturally sweet (*vin naturellement doux*); fortified sweet
(*vin doux naturel*); fortified sweet from selected vineyards (*vin doux naturel grand cru*); fortified sweet (*vin doux*).
White variety: Muscat of Alexandria.

PRODUCERS

HATZIGEORGIOU WINERY

Karpasi Petros, 814 00 Limnos. Tel: +30 225 403 1082; Fax: +30 225 403 1155.
Vineyards owned: 2.5ha; under contract: 10.6ha; production: 700hl.
Hatzigeorgiou is the smallest Limnos winery commercially active on a substantial scale. Established in 1982, it is a family-run business, with Petros the general manager, Themistoklis the production manager, and Polikseni the oenologist. The business owns vineyards that cover less than twenty per cent of its needs, but Hatzigeorgiou has devised a sensible way of securing top quality fruit from collaborating growers: he pays cash for the best vineyards, while the usual credit terms for the local co-op are six months or longer. This selection of grapes results in an excellent range of products, focusing on Muscat of Alexandria and Limnio.

Hiring the talented Professor Giorgos Kotseridis of the Agricultural University of Athens as consultant winemaker and buying a top-quality pneumatic press in 2004 will raise the standards even higher. The dry whites deserve a special mention and it would be interesting to see him working with the finer Muscat Blanc.

Hatzigeorgiou produces two *vin naturellement doux* sweet wines, with Muscat grapes dried in the sun for about a week. The basic Muscat of Limnos is made in stainless steel, while Ifaistou Gnosi is aged in oak, a proportion of which is new French barriques. Limnios Ampelourgos ("the vine-grower of Limnos") is an off-dry, fresh, flowery Muscat. The very best *cuvées*, coming from cool, high vineyards located on the northeastern side of Limnos, are reserved for the bone dry Limnia Ghi, a very typical, fine Muscat. Kaveiro is a rosé predominantly made from Limnio, with a small proportion of Muscat added for aromatic lift. Pyroessa concludes the range: a pure Limnio that is macerated for ten days and aged for twelve months in partially new oak, and is possibly the most convincing expression of the grape in its native land.

HONAS WINERY

Kaminia Moudros, 814 01 Limnos. Tel: +30 225 409 1100/210 97 1846; Fax: +30 225 409 1355/210 971 8464.

Vineyards owned: 2.5ha; under contract: 7ha; production: 3,000hl.

Before starting his winery in Limnos, Petros Honas was already a seasoned vintner, having worked during the 1980s for Boutari. As a senior member of the winemaking team, among other projects, he was responsible for Lac des Roches, one of Boutari's most successful brands. Still on very good terms with his past employers, he makes but does not bottle any Muscat of Limnos OPE under his own name, since Boutari buys his entire sweet Muscat production.

Honas is well aware that to achieve good quality with a variety like Muscat of Alexandria, attention is needed in the vineyard. In the Limnos terroir, a key priority is keeping fruit-load per vine to sensible levels. He works closely with several growers to keep yields low and to orchestrate picking times so that acidity remains reasonable.

The portfolio consists of two wines: both dry, pure Muscats. Ilinoi is the top label, from selected parcels, and uses only the free-run juice. A second selection is called Filonoi and is not as bone-dry as Ilinoi, but still cannot be classified as a *demi-sec*. The two wines are some of the most individual dry Muscats produced in Greece, going beyond the clean, rose-petal *typicité* of the variety. The style here is richer but not heavier, bringing through much darker shades of fruit and more developed floral aromas. The broad palate structure coupled with very good acidity makes them excellent food wines. Honas Muscats are more Honas than Muscats, in an utterly appealing way.

LIMNOS UNION OF AGRICULTURAL COOPERATIVES

Mirina, 814 00 Limnos. Tel: +30 225 402 2212; Fax: +30 225 402 3409;
Website: www.limnoswines.gr; Email: easlim@otenet.gr
Vineyards under contract: 700ha; production: 35,000hl.

The Limnos Cooperative was established in 1937, just three years after its counterpart in Samos. The structure of the vine-growing sector in Limnos developed in a different way, and the co-op does not enjoy the same monopoly that exists in Samos. Nevertheless, it has proved that competition can be a good thing. While private enterprises started appearing in Limnos, the co-op completely restructured and repackaged its products. Until then, many consumers had been considering Limnos Muscats as the poor relatives of those produced in Samos. In the last decade, the Limnos Co-op has managed to position its wines much more clearly, aiming for fresh, easy-drinking styles and targeting younger, less wine-oriented consumers. Sales success in Greece and the foreign markets suggests that the move was correct.

The co-op continues to work closely with many producers to improve standards and to develop new projects. For example, there is a move towards organic viticulture, and so far over 100 hectares have been certified organic. The wine appears under the Aroma label in two versions. The basic bottling is a refreshing, straightforward, clean, dry Muscat, at twelve per cent alcohol. The second, Aroma Limnos Driinos, is essentially the same wine but aged in barriques for three to four months. This is the most adventurous Limnos co-op white to date, but time will tell whether a dry, pure, fresh Muscat can blend successfully with oak, or if the palate structure is dense enough for barrique maturation. So far the oak expression in this wine is not excessive.

The dry whites include two other labels: a fresh, vibrant Muscat OPAP Limnos and Aegeopelagitikos, an Aegean Islands TO. The latter has fifteen per cent Assyrtico added, providing a lift on the acidity without interfering too much with the necessary aromatic *typicité*. The portfolio also includes one rosé and one red, both made from pure Limnio and named after the local synonym for the variety, Kalampaki. The rosé Kalampaki is fresh and shows red-berry fruit aromas, while the red has a relatively light structure, making it a good red for summer drinking.

The high point of Limnos co-op is its sweet wines: Muscat of Limnos and Muscat of Limnos Grand Cru. The first is a *vin doux* where the spirit is added before fermentation starts. The wine shows an intense Muscat character, while sugar levels, usually around 220 grams per litre, and moderately low levels of acidity, typically around 4.5 grams per litre, make this wine extremely easy to drink.

For the second, the best higher-altitude parcels, classified as *grand cru*, are harvested a few days later, the cooler meso-climate keeping acidity at the same level as in the basic *vin doux*, but alcohol levels are at least one degree Baumé higher. Grand Cru Muscat of Limnos is a *vin doux naturel*, so fortification takes place when the fermenting must has about 120 grams per litre of residual sugar remaining. This is a more complete wine, expanding on the Muscat character, while the palate is more balanced and the finish appears drier. Neither of the sweet wines spends any time in oak, underlying the fact that one of the main points for Muscat of Alexandria must be its freshness and youth.

LESBOS

Lesbos is very close to the Turkish coast, less than two kilometres (1.2 miles) at the village of Molyvos on its northern coast. The capital is Mytilini, near the southeastern tip of the island. The unusual shape of Lesbos is caused by the merger of three peninsulas, and is determined by two gulfs. The Kaloni Gulf is the biggest, almost cutting the island in two, while the second, smaller gulf enters Lesbos from the southeast, almost separating the leg of Mytilini from the rest of the land mass.

If the area near the Kaloni Gulf and its inland extension are excluded, then Lesbos is pretty mountainous. One mountain range runs from the northern point of the island to the west, while the southern peninsula is dominated by a peak reaching 968 metres (3,176 feet), and even the Mytilini strip has slopes rising to more than 500 metres altitude (1,640 feet).

Lesbos is another Aegean Island which had an illustrious wine-producing past that overshadows its present situation. The wines from Lesbos were famous from ancient times up until the fifteenth century. Production was predominantly red and Limnio probably played an important role. Thereafter, the importance of viticulture, and specifically Limnio, have faded significantly.

Ouzo

One of the main reasons that Lesbos' wine gradually disappeared is because locals found ouzo to be a much more successful and less risky product. ouzo, the alcoholic beverage produced by the maceration of pure spirit and seeds, mainly anise, is relatively easy and cheap to produce, starting costs are not huge, there is no ageing period, and most of all, it is not strictly an agricultural product. That means it can be manufactured to order, unlike wine, where production takes place once a year. Over the years, the local community developed a strong culture around ouzo in the same way that most Greek regions approach wine, with many artisan producers aiming to cover their own needs and then trade on a local scale.

A combination of luck, skill, and circumstances made Lesbos the ouzo centre of Greece. Today there are more than fifty companies producing, trading, and exporting ouzo, while there are numerous small distilleries selling their outstanding products only in the vicinity. The diversity of producers is remarkable, ranging from drinks giant Pernod-Ricard and its offshoot "Ouzo Mini", down to small enterprises that export their entire production to one market.

Current vineyard plantings in Lesbos are less than eighty hectares. Limnio, Athiri, and Assyrtico are the three recommended varieties, while permitted ones include Savatiano and Fokiano. In the heart of the island, around the town of Kaloni, the local Kaloniatiko black grape variety is dominant. Scattered plants of this variety, also on the permitted list, can be found in other regions of Lesbos. Moderately deep in colour, moderate in sugar levels, and with a low acidity, it is likely that it appears under a different name on a much wider scale throughout the Aegean. So far, the research has not been carried out to locate the true identity of Kaloniatiko.

The island's commercial wine production sector is almost non-existent, excluding one winery called Methymnaios. Most of Lesbos' wine is sold in bulk or consumed locally.

PRODUCER

METHYMNAIOS

Hidira Vatousa, 811 03 Lesbos. Tel: +30 225 305 1518; Fax: +30 225 305 1642; Website: methymneos.gr; Email: info@methymneos.gr
Vineyards owned: 2ha; under contract: 0.5ha; production: 110hl.
Methymnaios winery started in 1995 and is owned by the Lambrou family. It is the only winery in Lesbos to sell any quantity of bottled wine beyond the island's boundaries, even if the size of the enterprise is small – the average annual production is less than 1,500 cases. Nevertheless, the calibre of the whole effort is remarkable. In the early years, the skilful Ampelooiniki team took care of oenological matters while Haroula Spinthiropoulou, the guru of lesser-known Greek varieties, was vineyard

consultant. In addition to these excellent specialists, Methymnaios is one of the best-designed and equipped wineries of its size in Greece.

Methymnaios is decisively linked with Lesviako Krasostafilo or "the wine grape of Lesbos", the only variety that is grown and crushed in the winery. The Lambrou family have substantial stock of the variety, but there are very few, if any, plants to be found elsewhere on the island. Giannis Lambrou has tried – but failed so far – to register the variety as Lambrino. There is no doubt that the vine is a distinct variety and, most probably, is confined to Lesbos. In the cellar, Lesviako Krasostafilo behaves in a similar way to Limnio, having difficulty in achieving deep colours or high levels of primary fruit aromas. The nose is unique. There is a tendency to develop reductive notes, but if handled carefully, the wine shows more elegant and charming aromas, although still within the leather/animal spectrum.

Methymnaios Red Wine is the only label produced and it is made from organically cultivated grapes. The wine shows quality, has a total lack of old-fashioned character, and could probably develop over the course of two to three years. It will be interesting to see how this promising winery will build up in the future.

HIOS

It is a great misfortune that the legendary island of Hios, home of the famous and highly sought-after *Ariousios Oinos* and, later on, desirable Malvasia wines, currently has about 11.3 hectares of vineyards, and only one registered winery. While the neighbouring islands of Limnos and Samos have been going from strength to strength over the last centuries, the image of ships lining up in the port of Hios frantically requesting local wine, is a memory from an almost forgotten past.

The main vineyard area used to be called Ariousia, and Ariousian wine was one of the most famous vinous products of antiquity. There are accounts suggesting that Ariousian production survived until the fifteenth century, albeit on a smaller scale. During the Ottoman occupation, viticulture was attacked by the Turks and neglected by the Greeks. The final blow came in 1822, where the Hios massacre took place, as depicted by the famous artwork by Delacroix that hangs in the Louvre in Paris. The Turks decided to punish the Greeks for their 1821 revolution and killed about 8,000 people: almost a quarter of all inhabitants. At the same time, the vines of Ariousia were almost completely uprooted. Hios finally joined Greece after the end of the first Balkan War in 1912, but viticulture was never restored to its previous importance.

Hios is a croissant-shaped island, with its capital, also called Hios, at the centre of its eastern coast, overlooking Turkey. It takes less than forty-five minutes to get over to Cesme in Turkey by ship and, on a clear evening, car lights from across the border are clearly visible. Hios is linked with two small groups of islands located just off its northern tip: Inousses to the east and Psara and Antipsara to the west. Central and northern regions are mountainous and the southern part is completely flat. Most soils are calcareous and infertile, excluding the low-altitude area called Kambos. This is the only part of Hios with rich and deep soils suitable for nutrient-demanding cultivations. There is a marked difference in climate between the north and the south side, with the former being much cooler and far more humid. Most of the existing vineyards are still situated in the original Ariousia region, nowadays called Kourounia.

Wine never had a chance to regain its former significance in modern Hios because of the stiff competition from other local products. Apart from a healthy ouzo-producing sector, Hios is the exclusive producer of one of the most successful agricultural commodities, at least in Greece: mastic. The small mastic tree grows in the southern, flat part of the island. It produces a form of white resin, which is extremely flavourful and even deemed to have medical properties. There have been attempts to transplant mastic trees to other regions in Greece, in Turkey, Lebanon, and even Japan, but success was minimal. Mastic exports have boomed for more than two decades and the raw material is now used for manufacturing a vast array of products, from chewing gum to toothpaste and shampoo. The other fact that kept Hios people away from investing in vineyards is the affinity the locals have with seafaring. Today, Hios is home to some of the most powerful ship-owning families in Greece and the Mediterranean.

Most of local wine production is sold in bulk and, overall, winemaking is neither popular nor developed. Although still treated as an important product, wine is almost rare – you have to be well-connected to find local wine in Hios. The recommended varieties in the region are Athiri and Assyrtico, but strangely, white wine is an extremely small proportion of the overall amount produced. The largest part is vinified in a semi-commercial rosé style that could be classified as dry, but frequently has some residual sugar. These rosés are low in acid, moderate in alcohol, and have a sweet but oxidative fruit expression. The most interesting type of wine is the red, a potent style made from sun-dried grapes. Drying lasts from seven to ten days and some locals are not afraid to macerate them for two weeks or more. The result is very close to a primitive *recioto*, with high-pitched, raisiny fruit oxidized in a charming way, broad and alcoholic on the palate.

Mandilaria is the backbone of both the red and the rosé wines, but complexity is added by two grapes, Fokiano and Agianniotiko. A few Agianniotiko vines survive scattered around the Hios vineyards. It has a relatively long growing period, from mid-March until very late August or early September, grapes are moderate to large, thick skinned and deeply coloured, while they separate from the stems with difficulty. There are signs that Agianniotiko could be a good quality variety and it could be wise for growers to pay more attention to it.

PRODUCER

IASSOS WINERY
Kalamoti, 821 02 Hios. Tel: +30 227 107 1253;
Fax: +30 227 107 1276; Email: kalamoti@otenet.gr
Vineyards owned: 4.5ha; production: 150hl.

Iassos is currently the only substantial winery in Hios, which is sad for an island with such a celebrated past. Iassos is not located in the famed Kourounia region, but lies on the southern end of the island. Owner and winemaker Mihalis Triantafillou seems to be the only person to keep the Hios wine-flag flying high – but in a way that is not confined to tradition. Vineyard holdings, which are substantial by Hios standards, are focused on French varieties, including Cabernet Sauvignon and Merlot for reds, and Sauvignon Blanc, Chardonnay, and Semillon for whites. There are no off-dry rosés or semi-sweet reds produced, just two blended whites, Iassos and Triantafillos White, and a blended red, called Triantafillos Red. The wines are rarely available outside Hios but are worth seeking out when visiting the island, being the most modern ambassadors of such an historical wine-producing region.

IKARIA

Ikaria lies less than twenty kilometres (twelve miles) off the southwest coast of Samos. Between the two, there are a number of smaller islands, with Fournoi being the most significant. The formation of Ikaria, Samos, Fournoi, and the rest is, in essence, the same underwater mountain, so soils

– mainly granite – topography, and meso-climates in this group are very similar. The main terroir differences between Ikaria and Samos are the slightly higher water availability of the latter and the lack of any low-altitude plains in Ikaria, in contrast with Samos' relatively flat east side. Ikaria is very mountainous, though less steep than the western part of Samos – yet most vineyards are terraced. The strong ties between the two islands are underlined by the fact that these two islands are clustered by the Greek state under the prefecture of Samos.

The wine history of Ikaria shares more similarities with Hios than nearby Samos, since it is another island with a celebrated past, a gloomy present, and an insecure future. Ikaria can claim a first in wine history, where a wine from a specified origin became famous and highly sought-after. This happened with *Pramnios Oinos* produced from the site of Pramnia Petra, near the ancient village of Oinois, today's Evdilos. Many authorities suggest that this could have been the world's first "appellation", however this is not entirely true. There was no legislational framework imposing restrictions or offering security to local producers, just the widely held acclaim of the nobility for the wines originating from Pramnia Petra. Pramnios Oinos would have enjoyed export success from at least the eighth century BC. Nevertheless, five centuries later, the name was extensively used by many other Aegean Islands, and even in regions of mainland Greece. It seems that, within this time, Pramnios Oinos had developed from the first geographical designation to an ill-protected brand and then a generic wine style.

Local people quickly turned to maritime trading and, as in Hios, became very successful. Viticulture remained the main form of agriculture, but over-all, the sector continued to be limited in significance. In the seventeenth century there were some plantings of vines for raisin production. Raisins from Ikaria achieved a certain commercial success and it is this product that kept vine-growing alive on the island. Before the invasion of phylloxera in 1910, vineyard acreage was almost 1,000 hectares. Today, current plantings are about a tenth of that, although vines dedicated to raisins are now a small proportion of the overall size. On the whole, the current state of Ikaria wines is far from vibrant, but still not quite as depressing as that of Hios. There are only three noteworthy wine producers releasing, on average, fewer than 50,000 bottles of wine annually.

Mandilaria is the main red grape variety, locally called Koundouro or, in the female form, Koundoura. The list of permitted and recommended varieties is short, including Athiri, Assyrtico, Agianniotiko, Fokiano, Kotsifali, and Ritino. A variety that could be considered native, although a few plants have been found in Samos, Hios, and Lesbos, is the white Begleri. It is a vigorous vine, sensitive to aridity, producing thin-skinned, medium-sized grapes that ripen in mid-September with moderate alcohol and acidity levels.

PRODUCERS

AFIANES FINE WINES
Hristos Rahon, 833 01 Ikaria. Tel: +30 227 504 1556;
Fax: +30 227 504 1352; Email: afianes@otenet.gr
Vineyards owned: 1ha; under contract: 1ha; production: 80hl.
Nicos Afianes established Afianes Fine Wines in 1997, focusing entirely on local varieties. Begleri is used for Nicaria White, while Mandilaria and Fokiano are used for both Nicaria Red and the more upmarket Icarus red. This is an extrovert producer, trying to promote his wines well beyond Ikaria, building distribution in both Thessaloniki and Athens.

All three labels have a distinct warm-to-hot-climate note, but lack any old-fashioned tones. The reds are more notable than the white and, stylistically, they are very close to Rhodes reds.

IKARIA WINERY
Pigi Ikaria, Evdilos 833 02. Tel: +30 227 503 1151; Fax: +30 227 503 1945;
Website: www.ikarianwine.gr; Email: gkarim@otenet.gr
Vineyards owned: 1.5ha; under contract: 1.5ha; production: 200–250hl.
Ikaria is the biggest commercially oriented producer on the island, being responsible for close to fifty per cent of bottled wine production. Giorgos Karimalis is the owner and winemaker, while the wines are released under the G Karimali Estate label.

The winery has two wines, Ikariotikos White and Ikariotikos Red, available locally and, albeit infrequently, in Athens. The white is a pure Begleri and has charming primary fruit character, especially when enjoyed young. The red blend includes all the local varieties, like Mandilaria, Fokiano, and Ritino, but also a notable proportion of Cabernet Sauvignon. It is evident that the addition of Cabernet provides the traditional blend of Ikaria red grapes with extra backbone and more layers of fruit.

PIROUDI WINERY

Thesi Akamatra, Evdilos, 833 01 Ikaria.

Head office: 4 Lazaradon, 113 63 Athens. Tel/Fax: +30 210 883 6248.

Vineyards owned: 3ha; under contract: 3ha; production: 90hl.

Piroudi Winery was the first winery to be established in Ikaria, in 1992, putting the island back on the Greek wine map. Leonidas Piroudis is the owner and winemaker, and investments made in the vineyards suggest that the current annual production of slightly more than 10,000 bottles is likely to increase substantially in the coming years. Since Piroudis was the first to start such an enterprise, it was relatively easy to decide a brand name for his wine, also taking into account that the winery was built near Evdilos, purportedly the home of the world's first "geographical" wine, Pramnios Oinos. Piroudis produces only one label, the red Pramnios Oinos. This modern version is predominantly Kountoura (Mandilaria) with some Fokiano. It has warm fruit and well-integrated leather notes, while the palate structure is lean, possibly lacking a bit of extract, but definitely having character and complexity. Some Begleri is also grown on the estate, but, so far, no white wines have been produced.

11

Crete

Crete is the largest and most important Greek island. It forms a natural barrier separating the Aegean Sea from the Libyan Sea, and is an impressive land mass. With a mountain range as its spine, Crete is a thin 256 kilometre (159 mile) strip of land running from west to east, its maximum width is sixty kilometres (thirty seven miles), while its average is about thirty five kilometres (twenty three miles). Only a small percentage of land is flat, and this is mainly coastal, though there are a few flat mountain passes that lead from the north coast to the south. The morphology of the island is slightly tilted on one side, with the eastern tip being mostly below 900 metres (2,953 feet), while the western part is much higher. In the centre of the island, halfway between Rethymno and Iraklio, is Crete's most famous peak, Mount Psiloritis, at 2,456 metres (8,058 feet). Lefka Ori ("White Mountain") situated south of the town of Hania, stands only two metres (six feet) lower. Mount Dikti, just west of Aghios Nikolaos, is 2,148 metres (7,047 feet).

Because of political and economic links with mainland Greece as well as the mountain ranges that cut the island in two, most of the important cities were established on Crete's north side. Iraklio and Hania are the largest, followed by Rethymno and a far smaller Agios Nikolaos. These are the four capitals of the respective prefectures: from west to east, Hania, Rethymno, Iraklio, and Lasithi. The only important towns on Crete's south side are Ierapetra, by the coast just south of Aghios Nikolaos, and Paleohora, on the southwestern tip.

HISTORY
Crete was one of the very first places develop a culture around wine, as the plentiful archaeological evidence from the Minoan era (3000–1500 BC)

shows. Crete was invaded by Dorian Greeks in around 1500 BC, signalling the end of the Bronze Age. It remained under Greek control until the rise of the Roman Empire in the first century BC. The succeeding Byzantine era began in 330 AD and lasted for almost a millenium, including a short spell of Arabian occupation from 824 to 961 (though this left the local population largely unaffected). The end of the Byzantine Empire came two centuries later when the Venetians invaded Crete in 1204. Culture and local economy flourished at this time, together with the Malvasia export wine trade. Any developments came to an abrupt halt in 1669 when the Turkish army took control of the island. In sharp contrast with the Venetians, the Turks had no intention of mixing with the local people or respecting traditions, so reactions from the inherently free spirited Cretans were immediate. There were upheavals as early as 1692 and the situation became more tense as mainland Greece won her right to independence in 1830. Almost a century of anguish and turmoil eventually ended in 1913, when Crete finally became a part of Greece.

During the twentieth century and particularly after the Second World War, Crete began developing at a fast pace, far higher than the national average. Today, agriculture and the hospitality sector are both important and, most significantly, in balance with each other. There is a notable military presence, providing a valuable source of income. Overall the economy is in good health, with a high degree of self sufficiency. It is said that in the event of war, Crete, with no connection to or communication with the mainland, could last almost indefinitely – the only limiting factor being oil reserves. Crete could almost function as a separate country.

CLIMATE AND MOUNTAINS
The climate of Crete should be the hottest in Greece, since it is the country's southern most land, but it has a slightly cooler environment than could be expected at such a latitude. Santorini and most of the Cyclades Islands have an average temperature at least 2°C (3.6°F) higher than Iraklio and Hania. In the last six months of the year, there are, on average, thirty six days of rain in Athens while in Hania there are 36.5 days. There is a gentle grading of the climate in Crete, with higher humidity and rainfall but less heat as one moves westward. For example, Hania has an average rainfall of 21.4 millimetres (0.84 inches) and average temperature of 25.3°C (77.5°F) from July to September, while Sitia has 19.2 milllimetres

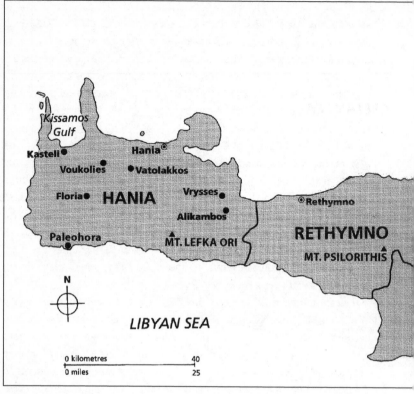

(0.76 inches) of rain and a temperature of 27.9°C (82.2°F). A closer look at the weather patterns reveals that the south side of Crete is much warmer than the north. The mountains that divide the island in two easily explain this difference in temperature between north and south. The latter side is exposed to the hot winds coming up from Africa. In contrast, the northern areas are sheltered by the mountains and receive only the cooling effects of the northern winds. There is no reliable data to hand but it is estimated that a north facing district will be, on average, over 1°C (1.8°F) cooler than its southern equivalent.

Mountains are vastly important for viticulture in Crete, and not just for contributing to the milder northern climes. Vine growers have the option of planting high altitude sites and thus securing much cooler meso climates, an advantage that is not available in most Aegean Islands. Consequently, most vineyards in Crete are found on north facing slopes. Winds can be a minor problem during fruit set, but not to the same extent as the Cyclades.

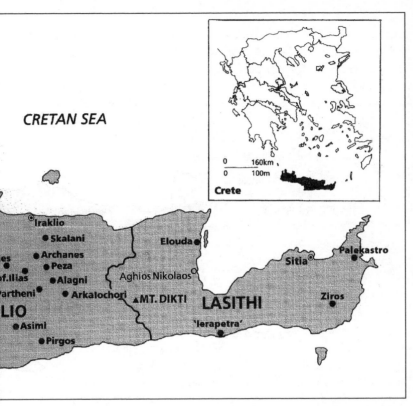

According to the Ministry of Agriculture, the acreage of vineyards is 10,098 hectares, but many sources claim that the overall land dedicated to the vine, including non registered vineyards, is as much as twice that. Even using the official figure, Crete is home to approximately fifteen per cent of the nation's vineyards, the lion's share being in the prefecture of Iraklio, with 5,895 hectares, followed by Hania (1,700 hectares), Rethymno (1,550 hectares), and finally Lasithi, at 953 hectares.

APPELLATIONS AND SOILS
Crete has four quality wine appellations, OPAPs, three of which are in the prefecture of Iraklio, the fourth being Sitia OPAP in Lasithi. The latter includes dry whites and dry or sweet reds. The three Iraklio appellations are Dafnes, dedicated to dry and sweet reds; Archanes, only for dry reds; and Peza, by far the largest appellation, which includes dry whites and reds. Sadly, apart from Peza and specific producers within this appellation, the

other three OPAPs of the island are largely irrelevant to the modern trends and developments of the Greek wine sector. There are also four regional wine appellations, TOs: one departmental (TO of Crete), two prefectural (TO of Iraklion and TO of Lasithi), and, close to Hania, the TO of Kissamos.

The majority of soils in Crete are argilo calcaire, with a high proportion of clay in many sites. Soil fertility follows a general pattern, with slopes being less rich than plains. There are very few parcels where soil infertility is as extreme a problem as in the Cyclades. Water availability is good by Mediterranean standards. Snow melt off Psiloritis and Lefka Ori produces a steady supply of creeks and wells, a source of some of the best water in Greece. This combination of climate, topography, water availability, and soil makes Crete an excellent region for viticulture. Vines thrive more often than struggle, to a point where high yields are the norm rather the exception.

Phylloxera invaded Crete in 1972, starting to make an impact in the late 1970s and spreading slowly but steadily since then. One unfortunate consequence is that a number of extremely old vineyards, some over a century old, have been lost. Ironically, a number of indigenous varieties, including Mandilaria, Liatiko, and Kotsifali, do benefit from old age and the fruit obtained from young vines can lack extract and character. So far, the worst hit appellations are Archanes and Peza. It is fortunate that the slow pace of the infection has offered advance warning, giving most growers time to replant with phylloxera resistant rootstocks, such as 110R and 41B.

GRAPES: INDIGENOUS AND INTERNATIONAL

The quality of wines from Crete is closely related to the history of wine production on the island. Viticulture entered the twentieth century in a very poor state. There were few commercial bottlers and wine traders, despite the fact that many locals were still cultivating vineyards to cover their own needs. In addition, in Crete, cultivating a vineyard to cover one's own needs does not always mean making wine. By far the most popular alcoholic drink is tsikoudia, a grape distillate. Most people will not even drain the must from the grapes to produce wine and spirit, but will just leave the must with stems and skins, and distil them together.

Given the size of the island and its long viticultural history, Crete has a surprisingly low number of key varieties. Vilana is the principal white grape, with Kotsifali, Mandilaria, and Liatiko the major reds. Varieties that have so far gained less commercial recognition than they deserve, are Thrapsathiri and Romeiko. Thrapsathiri was long considered a clone of Athiri but has now been proved to be a separate, white skinned variety. It is a vigorous, highly productive vine, resistant to drought and sensitive to downy mildew. It buds late, in early April, and reaches full maturity in early September. Thrapsathiri responds badly to high yields, but if the yield is below fifty six hectolitres per hectare, it can produce wines with an interesting aromatic intensity, full of peach and melon flavours, which are high in alcohol yet with moderate acidity.

Romeiko, sometimes called Mavroromeiko, is a vigorous vine, sensitive to downy mildew and resistant to aridity. It buds in mid March and ripens in mid September. Romeiko could possibly give wines of good quality but, with the usual yields, it produces high alcohol, low acidity, and an unstable colour that quickly turns to brown. There are also some other minor grape varieties to be found around Crete, most of which are quite localized, and commercial examples are rare or non existent.

There is a long-standing debate about high quality varieties on Crete. Many people suggest that if the terroir is ideal for viticulture, but most of the wine produced fails to live up to expectation, then something could be wrong with the varieties. A large number of growers rushed into planting foreign varieties – mostly French – some of which were totally unsuitable for warm climate viticulture. Among the more unusual choices is Sylvaner, which is presumably grown to add acidity to a blend without interfering too much with its aromatic character. Chardonnay, Semillon, and Viognier are faring well, Bordeaux varieties have been producing some good wines, while Rhône vines show true potential. It seems strange that, so far, almost no one has tried to exploit the possibilities of Spanish or Italian varieties or grapes that can withstand very high levels of ripeness, such as Zinfandel or Negroamaro.

On the indigenous variety front, it is still widely felt that Kotsifali and Mandilaria are rarely able to achieve good results in their respective blends – and the mono varietal wines from these grapes are definitely condemned to oblivion. Liatiko and Romeiko appear to produce average wines, with the exception of the very good but not commercial style sweet wines of the former. The whites are good only when made in a modern style, employing very cool fermentations, selected yeast strains, and extensive use of enzymes or lees contact. All the same, these practices can still produce characterless wines. But luckily, the situation has improved recently and an increasing number of producers are beginning to understand that the trouble might not be the vines, but how they are treated. The key to better quality could simply be found in low yields and very careful cultivation.

THE COOPERATIVE MOVEMENT

As elsewhere in Greece, the official way to secure the future of vine growers was the establishment of cooperatives. Crete managed to come up with six, possibly the highest number per grower or per vineyard area in Greece. Central Greece, a much larger region, has almost as many. Co ops were, as usual, obligatory and growers had no option but to become members and sell their entire crop to them. Most of the co ops were established before World War II and, at the time, it was easy for them to accumulate great power. This environment pushed the growers to adopt an approach of "the more the better", aiming for the highest yields in order to earn the highest income. People working in the co ops swear that they regularly came across yields above 420 hectolitres per hectare. This state of affairs ruined potential for quality for the local highly abused varieties.

In the 1950s and 1960s, a number of large producers appeared in Crete, providing growers with an alternative choice. Although the move was positive, the situation created very high standards for would be new entries. Major change had to wait until the 1990s, when traditional vine and wine families decided to have a go at commercial wine production on their own.

All parts of the wine industry in Crete have realized by now that the modern wine trade is highly competitive and that the only way to survive is to adopt a proactive stance. All the same, major reconstruction of the sector is needed to achieve its full potential, which will only take place if growers and producers start functioning outside the traditional patterns and give up long established rights. At least, it is clear that today's Cretan wines are better than ever, and quality has no option but to improve in the future.

Crete TO

White still: dry.
White varieties: Vilana; Muscat; Athiri; Thrapsathiri.
Rosé still: dry.
Red still: dry.
Red/Rosé varieties: Thrapsathiri; Kotsifali; Mandilaria; Liatiko; Ladikino; Cabernet Sauvignon; Carignan; Grenache Rouge; Syrah.

HANIA

Although the northern part of Hania in the west of Crete is fairly flat, the whole prefecture is dominated by the imposing presence of the Lefka Ori mountain range. The climate is potentially the island's coolest and most humid, due to the condensation of clouds blowing in from the central Mediterranean. Water availability is high, even well into the summer months. Viticulture is mainly confined to low fields and north facing slopes, with a significant proportion of vineyards planted in relatively rich, deep soils. Very few plots are planted above an altitude of 500 metres (1,640 feet) or on mountainous sites between 200 and 400 metres (656–1,312 feet). Yields can be very high, with flat irrigated sites easily accommodating figures of 250 hectolitres per hectare.

The predominant grape in Hania is Romeiko, though there are some minor plantations of Fokiano and Tsardana. The latter is a red variety, which is also cultivated in the Rethymno area. Tsardana is moderately vigorous, productive, and mildly sensitive to aridity. It was probably more popular in the past, but now few plots can be found. Tsardana can give wines with moderate colour, high alcohol, and far better acidity than most Kotsifali examples. Romeiko is used for red, rosé, and a quite peculiar, phenolic style of white wine. It is harvested very ripe, and most artisanal wines found in growers' cellars are above fourteen per cent alcohol. (Indeed, any wine below that level is locally considered too weak and not worth drinking.) Naturally occurring yeasts are extremely tolerant to alcohol, and many oenologists in the area find wines that have fermented to dryness at 16.2 per cent alcohol or above.

The quality potential of Romeiko is debatable and most winemakers dismiss it as "too Mediterranean": *i.e.* too hot, too alcoholic, too flat, and likely to brown in colour far too quickly. Part of the problem is high yields as well as bad propagation materials. Old *vignerons* claim that "good" Romeiko vines existed, with far better colour and more extract, but most growers discarded these better quality plants, since they were not able to achieve the required – read sky high – yields. So far, no research programme has tried rigorously to examine better clones of Romeiko, let alone preserve and promote them. It seems that Romeiko will need a pioneering visionary to rectify its image. The fact that Ted Manoussakis bought a plot of sixty year old Romeiko can only be good news (*see* page 441).

On the other hand, Romeiko might be the Palomino of Greece: a variety that has difficulties in producing modern style wines but can provide a good platform for styles where winemaking or ageing are at least as important as the character of the grape. The way that traditional winemakers were using Romeiko is quite telling. Grapes were picked ripe – above fifteen degrees Baumé – macerated for a few days, and then racked into barrel to finish fermentation. Old barrels were highly sought after, mainly made from chestnut wood. These barrels were sealed, possibly using dough around the bunghole, and left aside for a minimum of four years. No topping up was done during this period (though some people used a *solera*-type system). The result was a fierce, dry, alcoholic, highly oxidized wine with nuances of honey, nuts, and dried fruit creating an impressive depth of complexity.

This wine was called marouvas and was consumed at the end of a dinner, usually accompanied by apples. Very traditional marouvas is a statement against any sense of globalization in the wine world, but it is a dying product. In essence, it is not a product at all. Local fans would never touch a bottled marouvas – they would drink their own and, if they needed more, obtain it from a trusted friend. The few examples of commercially available marouvas are just a shadow of the real thing and are usually treated by tourists as off the wall souvenirs from Crete.

The only appellation of the Hania Prefecture is a TO of Kissamos, encompassing dry wines of all colours. The red regulations are particularly complex (*see* below), making everyone wonder whether each producer takes note of all these permutations when blending a Kissamos TO.

Kissamos TO

White still: dry.
White varieties: Romeiko (up to seventy per cent of the blend); Vilana; Athiri; Thrapsathiri; Grenache Blanc; Sauvignon Blanc.
Rosé still: dry.
Rosé varieties: Romeiko (up to sixty per cent of the blend); Grenache Rouge.
Red still: dry.
Red varieties: Romeiko (up to sixty per cent of the blend); Carignan (at least fifteen per cent); Grenache Rouge (up to twenty five per cent); Mandilaria and Alicante Bouschet (up to ten per cent combined).

PRODUCERS

COOPERATIVE OF HANIA

Kolimvari, 730 06 Crete. Head office: 118 Kissamos, 731 31 Hania, Crete.
Tel: +30 282 109 3034; Fax: +30 282 109 5967.
Vineyards under contract: 700ha; production: 9,600hl.

Established in 1952, the Cooperative of Hania is one of the later additions to the Crete group of co ops. Nevertheless, it grew at a much quicker pace than the Kissamos Cooperative, its sister establishment, quickly reaching almost double the size. Bulk wine makes up a large proportion of its sales, with bottled wine aimed mainly at the area's tourism industry. Its Clos de Creta used to be one of the most popular white wines of Crete but now it seems quite old fashioned. The co op also produces a small quantity of Marouva, bottles of which can be difficult to find beyond Hania. It gives a glimpse of this unusual wine's *typicité* without revealing the full character of the "amateur" examples.

COOPERATIVE OF KISSAMOS

734 00 Kissamos, Crete. Tel: +30 282 202 2011/2125;
Fax: +30 282 202 3402; Email: easkisam@telia.gr
Vineyards under contract: 250ha; Members: 4,000; Production: 4,000hl.

Established in 1930, the Kissamos Cooperative is Crete's smallest co op, and this could explain why no quality wine appellation was awarded to Hania, just a regional wine TO at a much later stage. The winery crushes Romeiko exclusively and this variety made the Kissamos co op famous, albeit in an unexpected way. In the 1980s, Stavroula Kourakou Dragona, the inspiring architect of Greece's appellation system (*see* page 31), visited Madeira and returned to Greece fascinated by its wines and the way they were made. At about the same time, she was concerned with what could be done with the general region of Hania and the Romeiko variety in particular. On arrival in Athens, she discussed how her new ideas could be adapted, with the winemaker at Kissamos, Manolis Karavitakis. She suggested a variation of the Marouvas theme, incorporating some Madeira tricks along the way.

The result of this discussion was Ostria. The best Romeiko vines from plots around 400 metres (1,312 feet) were left to overripen on the vine, reaching at least fifteen degrees Baumé. The must was left to ferment dry with the potent local yeast strains attaining, on average, 15.5 per cent alcohol.

After the end of fermentation, the wine was fortified to twenty per cent, racked into old oak and aged for five years in a greenhouse at 75°C (167°F). During this interpretation of *estufagem*, each barrel lost about thirty per cent of its volume due to evaporation and there was no topping up, since oxidation was regarded as desirable. Evaporation caused many problems since the authorities would only accept a seven per cent loss throughout this period and the rest was deemed as an attempt to forego paying alcohol duty to the Greek State.

Ostria was one of the best Greek wines and a bargain by worldwide standards. The burnt character of *estufagem* was not as evident as in many cheap Madeiras, with Ostria closer to the classic varietal examples. It was close to a bual in colour, a verdelho in flavours, and a sercial in dryness, together with more than a hint of oloroso. Sales have never really taken off but the serious, adventurous wine lovers around the nation loved the wine. It is a shame that the co op no longers makes this wine, but on the other hand, it is great news that Karavitakis will be reviving the style at his own winery (*see* above).

The co op's current range consists of average wines, in a variety of colours and sweetness levels. As far as commercial activity goes, promotion is directed towards the local markets.

DOURAKIS ANDREAS WINERY

Alikambos Vrison, 730 07 Crete. Tel/Fax: +30 282 505 1761.

Vineyards owned: 0.7ha; under contract: 0.7ha; Production: 3,500hl.

A family owned business, founded in 1988, the winery's vineyard holdings are small, but Andreas Dourakis also sources fruit from a number of organically cultivated vineyards. The higher end whites are mainly Vilana, although Romeiko plays an important part in the basic lines. There are some varietal TOs, a rosé from Grenache Rouge, and a red from Carignan. The most interesting wines in the portfolio are the two cava EOs, with the white being mainly Vilana and the red predominantly Cabernet Sauvignon.

KARAVITAKIS VINEYARDS

Pontikiana Voukolion, 730 02 Crete. Tel/Fax: +30 282 103 3326.

Vineyards owned: 4ha; under contract: 3ha; production: 700hl.

After years working at the Hania and Kissamos co ops, including a period as head winemaker at the latter, Manolis Karavitakis founded Karavitakis Vineyards in 1998. While he was at Kissamos, he oversaw development of its benchmark Ostria wine (*see* pages 439–40), and Karavitakis already has plans to release his own version of this fortified, madeira style Romeiko. There is also a plot dedicated to Vidiano, a promising white variety from Rethymno that needs some support to secure its place in the future of Greek wine. The winery not only revives glories of the past but also has designs on the future. For example, the current plantations of Vilana, Cabernet Sauvignon, Merlot, Grenache Rouge, and Syrah have been coupled with small parcels of Sangiovese and Nebbiolo. The Italian varieties will be vinified, aged, and bottled separately before being released onto the market after 2007.

The basic line, Lithos, includes a white and a red. There are two Ampelones Karavitaki wines. The white is an interesting blend of fifty per cent each Vilana and Chardonnay, with Chardonnay providing structure and Vilana contributing aroma. The red is a blend of equal parts Cabernet Sauvignon, Carignan, and Grenache Rouge, with the latter two co vinified. The best Karavitakis wines are the three French red varietals, Syrah, Merlot, and Cabernet Sauvignon, all of which are aged in French oak for eight to ten months. Half the barriques are replaced yearly, but the new oak dimension is well integrated with the fruit. All three wines have good varietal, with the Cabernet Sauvignon having an edge over the other two.

MANOUSSAKIS WINERY
Vatolakkos, 730 05 Crete. Tel/Fax: +30 282 107 8015.
Production: 125hl.

Until 2002, the Manoussakis winery was one of the best kept secrets in the Greek wine world. The venture started in 1993, when Ted Manoussakis returned to Greece to start producing wine, having spent most of his life in the USA. He was not interested in following local traditions for old times' sake, but rather in making his land in Vatolakos reach its potential. He gathered an impressive team of high calibre consultants from France and the USA to help him set up the vineyard and winery. After much analysis and discussion, a brave decision was taken: to focus entirely on Rhône varieties. Planting Syrah and Grenache was not unusual, but Mourvèdre was rare and deciding to work with Roussanne was a stroke of genius.

The first wines came from the 1997 vintage, made under the supervision of French Canadian Pascal Marchand, who, surprisingly, has a Burgundian, not Rhône, background, mainly through his work with Clos des Epeneaux and Boisset. The first three vintages were sold on allocation to the USA, mainly in Washington DC, where Manoussakis had good connections and well respected friends in the wine trade. In 2003, Manoussakis decided to release small quantities of his wines in Greece. Guided by Greek Sommelier champions like Giorgos Floudas and Giorgos Loukas, the prestigious Elounda Hotels were quick to buy most of the available stock. Soon their rich and famous guests were drinking "stunning Roussanne from Hania" and, in just two summers, Nostos, the Manoussakis brand name, turned from a secret into a cult.

The basic bottling of the winery is Nostos Red, a blend of Syrah, Grenache Rouge, and Mourvèdre, with five to seven per cent Roussanne added in. All red grapes are cold soaked for four days. Syrah is macerated for up to two weeks, Mourvèdre for about eleven days, and Grenache for the same period, but at slightly warmer temperatures, close to 33°C (91.4°F), to gain extra aromatic complexity. The final blend of Nostos varies from vintage to vintage but Syrah is always the major component, reaching levels of up to forty per cent, and five to seven per cent Roussanne wine is always added. An exception to Syrah's dominance was the excellent 2002 vintage, which had thirty eight per cent Mourvèdre.

The wine is aged for ten months in eighty per cent Nevers barriques and twenty per cent American oak, a quarter of each type being renewed every year. The oldest parcel of Syrah is kept aside and, at the end of oak ageing, the best four barrels are selected and released as the ultra rare Nostos Syrah. Occasionally, like in 2001, there might be varietal bottlings of Grenache or even Mourvèdre. All Nostos reds are extremely Rhône like, showing leather and dark spice rather than obvious, clean fruit. Their structure, density, and character sets them apart from every other Greek blend of these varieties.

Nostos White is pure Roussanne. A quarter of it is macerated before the beginning of fermentation, which takes place in French barriques. Again, a quarter of the barrels are renewed each year. The wines spend six months in wood, with constant *batonnage*, while malolactic fermentation is blocked. The structure of the final result is remarkable: matching extract, 14.5 per cent alcohol, and seven grams of acidity per litre, with a balance most French Roussannes would envy. In the initial vintages, the oak presence seemed quite dominating, leaving the fruit in the background, but this has been noticed by resident winemaker, the extremely skilled Kostis Galanis, and future vintages should see some developments.

The future of Nostos is bound to become more exciting, with a nine hectare plot coming into production in 2006. The viticultural team decided to go for high planting densities, such as 5,000 vines per hectare, which is twice the local average. A small part was taken to extremes, going up to 10,000 vines per hectare. Some Assyrtico vines proved very promising while Agiorgitiko less so. As the new plantations become productive, a new winery will be needed, possibly by the 2008 crush. Galanis is determined to keep the quantities of the present labels unchanged and to introduce a second line, Nostos Alexandras, that will include new parcels and anything else in the cellar that is not absolutely top quality.

RETHYMNO

This prefecture is named after the picturesque town of Rethymno, one of the most important medieval centres of the Aegean. There are two natural borders – the Lefka Ori mountain range to the west and Mount Psiloritis to the east – and very few areas are at sea level. In certain spots in the centre there are some humidity traps, but overall, the climate is very close to what can be found in Iraklio, to the east, and not as cool as Hania. Being between two mountains, water supplies are almost plentiful.

In wine terms, Rethymno is the least developed prefecture of Crete. There are no registered wineries in the area and the only wine designation that is applicable is the general TO of Crete. Still, a significant amount of land is dedicated to viticulture, even if this has declined substantially over the last twenty years. The grapes are used either to cover the wine needs of the growers or they are bought by the island's big firms and added to the high volume TO or EO blends.

Despite the lack of important producers, Rethymno has no shortage of interesting vine varieties. Most varieties cultivated in Hania are found in Rethymno and vice versa, but the proportions can vary widely. Romeiko remains important but there are some rare local specialities. Valaitis, also called Ampelaitis, is a disappearing white variety, because it gives relatively low yields. It buds in mid March, ripens in early September, and reaches high sugar levels. Dermatas is another white variety that used to be cultivated in low pergolas, locally called *krevatines*. It is a vigorous and highly productive vine that is highly resistant to aridity. Grapes have quite thin skins and reach maturity late, in the last days of September, while sugar levels are high and acidity is moderate. The red Tsardana is moderately vigorous and productive but is sensitive in water stress. It produces large bunches, exceeding 350 grams each, and retains notable acidity levels even at high levels of ripeness.

Vidiano is possibly the most highly regarded variety of Rethymno. A white variety, there are about ten hectares in Rethymno and a few vines further east around Iraklio. It is a vigorous and productive plant, resistant to downy mildew and moderately sensitive to botrytis, powdery mildew, drought, and high summer temperatures. It prefers calcareous soils that are moderately infertile. The growth cycle starts in late March, while it reaches full maturity in early to late September. Vidiano can give wines with high alcohol, a healthy level of acidity, around five grams per litre, and a very lifted, individual, aromatic intensity. Many believe that this is a grape with serious potential for quality, and growers must invest in it. Viticultural guru Haroula Spinthiropoulou claims that Vidiano has all the hallmarks of a top variety, however the current plantings are in areas that are too hot for the physiology of the plant. A possible solution is to aim for higher altitude vineyards in Crete, while another option would be to abandon the island completely and plant it in mainland Greece, moving further north. Either way, it seems that Vidiano will make a claim to fame in the next decade.

IRAKLIO

The city of Iraklio is the financial centre of Crete, its most important commercial port, and the capital of the same named prefecture. Iraklio stretches from Psiloritis in the west to Mount Dikti in the east. Just south of Iraklio there is a major rich plain, suitable land for a variety of agricultural ventures. In the centre of the region there are a few low mountains, forming a complex topography. The Messara Gulf is located on the southwestern corner of the prefecture, the only substantial gulf on the south side of the island. From Messara, a valley spreads from west to east, running between Pyrgos and Asimi. This passage borders the central mountain range on the north and, on the south, a thin, high block of land that sharply cuts off the coast from the rest of the mainland.

Iraklio was blessed by the Greek wine legislation: it is the prefecture with the most OPAPs around the nation – only Ahaia can claim more quality wine appellations, and even then it only has one OPAP. Iraklio's three OPAPs are Archanes, Peza, and Dafnes. All of them are confined in a small area just south of Iraklio, on the slopes overlooking the Aegean. It is a shame that at the moment all these appellations lack any commercial appeal and, according to many local producers, quality standards are lower than they could be. Only the growers of Peza can argue that their wines have any significant presence around Greece but, even if this is true, the name of Peza does not always conjure up the most positive image in quality terms.

These image problems stem from mistakes made by those who governed these appellations in the past. High yields, low quality clones, very low winemaking standards, out-dated equipment, and a tendency towards high volume/low quality production aimed at local tourists have been (and still are) major concerns. Nevertheless, in the past two decades, many people in the region realized that the "Golden Era" for their wines, if there ever was one, was over, and the only way to survive was to become much more competent. Part of the local production still remains stuck in the past, but at least others are moving ahead.

The classified areas

The Archanes demarcated OPAP region is made up of seven villages, with vineyards covering 500 hectares. The area is a basin overlooking the Aegean, starting from low altitudes and going up to 700 metres (2,297 feet), although most vines are planted below 450 metres (1,476 feet). The north facing slopes are sheltered from the hot south winds and there are frequent cool breezes that lower the high summer temperatures. It is one of the earlier ripening appellations in Crete, with most Kotsifali being harvested in the second half of August. Most areas have argilo calcareous soils, and red grapes account for ninety per cent of the region's plantings.

Archanes OPAP encompasses only dry red wines made from Kotsifali and Mandilaria, with the former being at least seventy five per cent of the blend. Mandilaria is used to enrich colour, to add tannins, and to moderate alcohol. According to legislation, the two varieties have to be co macerated, but usually maturing patterns differ, and most of the production is made with the two grapes vinified separately. The legal yield limit is seventy hectolitres per hectare, but most vineyards are far more productive than this, and irrigation is commonly practised. Most growers say that any wine with less than thirteen per cent alcohol must have been made chiefly from irrigated parcels. Early ripening makes most Archanes wines seem hot, but quite reserved and firm at the same time, with flavour development and tannin maturity being common problems.

If Archanes is largely homogenous in terms of soils, Peza is a region where there is a wide divergence in terroirs. The demarcated Peza region consists of fifteen villages, with about half of them characterized as "higher altitude". The appellation covers about 800 hectares and its vineyards start at 350 metres (1,148 metres) altitude, reaching up to 800 metres (2,624 feet). Traditionally, Archanes was thought to have more potential as a source of finer wines, but Peza is currently proving that wrong. A potential problem of the OPAP is its size, with certain regions producing much better fruit than others. Higher sites are sandy and relatively infertile, with slightly cooler temperatures than those below. Most growers are planting Vilana in these sites, but Kotsifali can give excellent results in the same areas. Lower vineyards have much heavier soils and the yields are higher.

OPAP Peza is the only appellation of Crete that includes a white wine. White Peza has to be 100 per cent Vilana and some winemakers criticize the grape heavily, saying that it has no character or quality potential. This could have been the case in the past, but modern Vilana, if handled reductively, can be aromatic, full of ripe and spicy fruit, fresh and not heavy at all. Perhaps it is not the easiest variety to spot in a blind tasting but it can be a very good example of what Crete can do with white wines. Nevertheless, some adventurous winemakers blend Vilana with other elements, like oak or other grapes, and make some excellent whites – for example, the Nobile White from Creta Olympias (*see* below). As always, a reason for the lack of character of many Vilana wines is yields. The legal limits are quite hefty, at twelve tonnes per hectare, eighty four hectolitres per hectare.

Peza is also a red wine appellation, with an identical prescribed varietal blend to that of Archanes. It can be difficult to differentiate in style between the two OPAPs, since the producer's philosophy, standards, and know how often override any terroir contribution. Still, many Peza wines seem to have an added fragrance and elegance when compared to most Archanes. Yield limits are somewhat lower than for white wines, at ten tonnes per hectare, seventy hectolitres per hectare. Ideally, Kotsifali and Mandilaria have to be co macerated but, again, it is not possible for all parcels. The initial reaction of many winemakers who start working in the region is to dismiss this legal directive. It is claimed that separate maceration vats give greater control and flexibility on what the producer wants to take out of each variety. However, it seems that Kotsifali, a grape with low colour, has some non coloured phenolics that can aid the stabilization of the Mandilaria anthocyanins, something that is not achieved by just blending the finished wines of the two varieties. This approach is much in line with discussions regarding the co extraction of Syrah and small quantities of Viognier. It is speculated that, apart from an extra aromatic lift, the white grape improves the final wine by stabilizing the bonds created between Syrah's anthocyanins (colourants) and tannins, making a Syrah/Viognier wine appear deeper and much more youthful than a control example of pure Syrah.

Dafnes is the final OPAP to be found in the Iraklio prefecture. The most western of the three, the area is close to the other two OPAPs. Located on the northeastern slopes of Mount Psilorotis, the altitude of the appellation ranges between 150 and 500 metres (492–1,640 feet), and encompasses twenty villages. On average, the soils of the region are deeper than those of Peza, with a slightly higher proportion of clay. There is also a homogeneity of terroirs across all sub regions of this OPAP. On a commercial level, Dafnes is relatively unknown and its impact on a national level is insignificant. There are only two wineries producing OPAP wine: the Iraklio Cooperative and the very capable Nikos Douloufakis.

Despite its geographical proximity to Peza and Archanes, appellations dedicated to Kotsifali and Mandilaria, Dafnes has a totally different varietal composition. Wines in this OPAP have to be 100 per cent Liatiko and some growers believe this has been a curse for the region. Dafnes has a great potential as a terroir but, so far, Liatiko has not been able to produce more than a few serious reds. In contrast, people who try other varieties in the region, with Douloufakis being the key pioneer, yield excellent results.

Even when producing much less that the legal limit of seventy hectolitres per hectare, Liatiko is rarely able to give modern style reds. It lacks colour, tannins, and ripe, bright, sweet fruit flavours. In addition, it is too delicate to take up substantial amounts of oak, which is an important hallmark of quality for many modern wine consumers. These characteristics have led some producers to reconsider a traditional way of making sweet wines from very ripe or sun dried Liatiko grapes. So far, few examples are commercially available, but experimental bottlings from Boutari suggest a promising style. Yet, if just one visionary made dry varietal Liatiko wines worthy of note, that would be enough to change the situation.

The appellation framework is completed by an Iraklio TO, with the dry whites being mainly Vilana, the dry reds being predominantly Kotsifali, and the rosés allowed a greater degree of freedom for local or French varieties.

The most notable examples of local Iraklio varieties are Dafni and Plyto, two vines that owe much to Lampros Lyrarakis, the producer that has put them back on the map with his varietal bottlings (*see* page 454). Dafni is a white variety, which is vigorous, moderately productive and resistant to dry conditions. It buds in mid March and ripens in late September, managing to produce full flavours at remarkably low sugar levels (for Crete), at a potential alcohol level of 12.5 per cent or less. The same style of wine is produced by another white variety, called Dafnato, that behaves very similarly to Danfi, both in the vineyard and cellar, but is deemed a separate variety. Full ripeness at moderate levels is also a feature of Plyto, even if its aromatic intensity is not as high as Dafni. The vine is vigorous, highly productive, and sensitive to botrytis and aridity. It buds in mid March but it ripens about two weeks earlier than Dafni, giving grapes with moderate sugar level and excellent balancing acidity.

Archanes OPAP

Red still: dry.
Red varieties: Kotsifali; Mandilaria.

Dafnes OPAP

Red still: dry, sweet.
Red variety: Liatiko

Peza OPAP

White still: dry.
White variety: Vilana.
Red still: dry.
Red varieties: Kotsifali; Mandilaria.

Iraklio TO

White still: dry.
White varieties: Vilana (up to eighty per cent of the blend); Athiri; Thrapsathiri; Sylvaner; Sauvignon Blanc.
Rosé still: dry.
Rosé varieties: Kotsifali; Mandilaria (up to five per cent of the blend); Liatiko, Ladikino; Carignan; Syrah.
Red still: dry.

Red varieties: Kotsifali (up to eighty per cent of the blend); Mandilaria; Liatiko; Ladikino; Carignan; Syrah.

PRODUCERS

BOUTARI

Domaine Fantaxametoho, Kato Archanes, 701 00 Iraklio, Crete.

Tel/Fax: +30 281 073 1617; Website: www.boutari.gr; Email: crete.winery@boutari.gr

Vineyards owned: 7ha; under contract: 5ha; production: 410hl.

See also Boutari entries on pages 130, 144, 150, 232, 385.

The Greek wine giant Boutari has been casting its eye over the Aegean Islands for many decades, as shown by investments in both Santorini and Iraklio. The venture in Crete started in the 1980s, when nine hectares were bought in Skalani in the Archanes appellation, seven of which have since been planted with vines. A striking new winery and visitors' centre opened in 2004 at Domaine Fantaxametoho, making it one of Crete's top wine tourism destinations.

The vineyard is relatively flat for the area, ranging from 170 to 215 metres altitude (558–705 feet). The majority has been devoted to varieties needed to produce the estate's basic revenue earning wines, while specific areas have been allocated to the creation of a viticultural research site. Over twenty different vines have been planted there, split between minor local varieties and French ones, including Romeiko, Liatiko, and Thrapsathiri, together with Syrah, Viognier, Merlot, and Riesling, among many others.

The basic white is called Domaine Fantaxametoho and is predominantly Chardonnay, with smaller proportions of Vilana and Thrapsathiri and limited quantities of Sauvignon Blanc and Sylvaner. Half the Chardonnay is fermented and aged for six months in 250 litre barriques, giving an elegant, well integrated oak presence for the final product. The rest of the varieties add excellent complexity of character, giving the wine a fresh, forthcoming style, making it stand out from most other whites on the island.

The main red of the estate, Skalani, is an Archanes OPAP that truly deserves its quality wine status. This Kotsifali/Mandilaria blend is aged in oak for a year, a small proportion of which is new, plus an additional year in bottle. Even if Skalani is not a wine for long ageing, this extra time in the cellar before release adds many dimensions to the fruit character on the nose, lifting the aromas and augmenting its complexity. The Boutari wines from its Cretan domaine are two of the island's best and most modern.

However, the most exciting facet of Fantaxametoho is not found in its standard bottlings but in the small quantities of experimental wines released every year. Some of these lines appear only once while others continue, although production remains small. Among these is a promising version of Liatiko, picked very ripe, with more than fifty per cent raisined berries, and aged for up to seven years in oak.

In 2005, another sweet wine was added to the range, this time a white from Muscat of Spina. In the commune of Seliniou, on the slopes of Mount Psiloritis, there are two villages where two variations of Muscat Blanc can be found. Named after those villages, Muscat of Spina and Muscat of Maza are very close to Muscat Blanc but the berries are slightly different and the skins are much thinner. Boutari decided to work with the more promising Muscat of Spinas, letting it overripen on the vine to create a very aromatic wine, slightly less flowery when compared with Muscat Blanc. In the same year, a dry Malvasia Aromatica was released. Without doubt, Fantaxametoho's experimental wines are some of Crete's most adventurous offerings.

COOPERATIVE OF ARCHANES
701 00 Archanes, Crete.
Tel: +30 281 075 1834/2644; Fax: +30 281 075 1474.
Vineyards under contract: 400ha; Production: 50,000hl.

Excluding its counterpart at Peza, the Cooperative of Archanes is Crete's largest wine producer and one of the first to be established on the island, in 1917. The winery's products are widely distributed throughout Crete but not much further. The co op focuses on low price/high volume wines, and its philosophy is value for money rather than premium products. The main brand is Armanti, available in white, rosé, and red, in both dry and semi sweet versions. There is also a single Archanes OPAP. The wines are simple and, in most cases, relatively old fashioned.

CRETA OLYMPIAS
Kounavoi, 701 00 Archanes, Crete. Tel: +30 281 074 1383;
Fax: +30 281 074 1323. Head office: 330 Thisseos Street, 176 65 Athens.
Tel: +30 210 948 3112; Fax: +30 210 942 6744;
Website: www.cretaolympias.gr; Email: info@cretaolympias.gr
Vineyards under contract: 50ha; production: 7,000–10,000hl.

Creta Olympias was founded in 1973 in an effort to create a relatively large private company in the Peza region dedicated to selling either wine in bulk or fresh grapes. A turning point came in 1997, when the company was bought by Michalis Kasfikis, a wealthy businessman who wanted to expand his investments in the wine production sector. In the years following the buy out, Kasfikis has built a highly respected team, both on the production and marketing side, making Creta Olympias one of the most vibrant companies in Crete. There was a definite change of tack, with more and more emphasis on quality and less on volume. Now that the corporation is reaching a certain degree of maturity, Dimitris Kontominas, an extremely wealthy, gifted entrepreneur, decided to buy Creta Olympias in 2005, giving it a whole new lease of life. There are plans to expand current production to two million bottles, with talk possibly growing production of OPAP wines, either in or outside of Crete.

And it seems as if the quality of the company's wines will go from strength to strength, the main reason being the talented chief winemaker, Sofoklis Panayiotou. Still in his early thirties, Panayiotou is already highly regarded throughout Greece, and has been doing tremendous work at Creta Olympias, constantly improving every wine through hard work in both cellar and vineyard. For example, he has been trying to identify parcels of vines containing the best clones of many traditional varieties. According to experienced growers, Vilana and Kotsifali are ancient vines, and many vine variations exist. Some people call them different "clones", but this has not been proved definitively. Vilana has two very promising alter egos. The one with brown spots on its berries is the more aromatic, while another with intense green berries provides more structure but less finesse. On the other hand, Kotsifali has an old small berried, loose bunched "clone" that has both colour and aromatic intensity but gives very low yields – usually around thirty hectolitres per hectare.

All these promising sub varieties are incorporated into the best wines of Creta Olympias. Xerolithia is a white OPAP made from a strict vineyard selection of Vilana. Yields range from fifty to seventy hectolitres per hectare, ninety per cent of the plots are dry farmed, and each of the two best "clones" makes up about half of the final blend. Xerolithia is handled completely reductively and is one of the most aromatic Vilanas produced. The top white wine of the portfolio is Nobile OPAP Peza White, a two vineyard *cuvée* with seventy per cent of the fruit coming from the aromatic "clone". Half of Nobile

White is fermented in new French oak, with *batonnage* for six months. This wine is quite a remarkable achievement for Vilana, with very good structure and oak integration.

The Nobile range also includes a red, an OPAP Peza, with thirty per cent Mandilaria and three parcels of old Kotsifali. Aged in fifty per cent French new oak for about a year, it is one of the most polished Peza reds. The lower priced red Peza of Creta Olympias is named Myrambelos shows bright, sweet but fresh primary fruit rather than the raisiny character of most of the region's reds. The winery's basic lines include Nea Ghis, or Meditérra for the export markets, together with Vin de Crete, all of which offer great value for money.

Like the experimental bottlings of Boutari, Creta Olympias is releasing a series of small volume trials, called Curriculum Vitae. For Panayiotou, this is his "Formula 1" project – he uses these wines to research and explore production or market related issues that underly new ideas and concepts. For example, his CV Vilana 2001 resulted in the basis for the fermenting strategy adopted in the production of Xerolithia. In the same year, a separate bottling of "old" Kotsifali proved that there was good potential on this variation of the variety. On the contrary, a dry Muscat/Sauvignon Blanc blend made in 2002 was not warmly welcomed by the market, so this was substituted by a much more successful Vilana/Sauvignon Blanc wine. CV wines are difficult to find but worth seeking out.

DULOUFAKIS WINERY
Dafnes, 700 11 Iraklio, Crete. Tel: +30 281 079 2017; Fax: +30 281 025 6549; Website: www.cretanwines.gr; Email: wines@cretanwines.gr
Vineyards owned: 6ha; Production: 1,000hl.

Nikos Douloufakis is one of the most interesting new Crete producers and surely a leading light in the OPAP of Dafnes. The Douloufakis family has been involved in winemaking since 1930, but the present company has only officially been in existence since 1991. Nikos Douloufakis, a qualified oenologist, is currently charged with running the estate and every new vintage shows an increasingly refined style. The family owned vineyards are now completely organic and varieties planted range from Liatiko and Vilana to Barbera and Malvasia Aromatica.

The lower priced range, Enotria, consists of a crisp Vilana and Sauvignon Blanc blend, a rosé Grenache Rouge with an added lift from Muscat Blanc, and a red made of Kotsifali, Liatiko, and Syrah. The most important wine of the winery must be considered the OPAP Dafnes: a pure Liatiko which is macerated for six days and aged in oak for about five months. This is a very good example of the appellation's potential: focused on fruit and spices rather than on structure.

The two single varietal whites of Douloufakis, Sauvignon Blanc and Chardonnay, are made in a crisp, unoaked style, typical of the varieties. The Syrah and Cabernet Sauvignon are aged for about a year in oak and both have good varietal character while also being some of the softer Cretan examples of the two grapes.

The winery's portfolio concludes with two small volume but thrilling labels. Sangiovese/Cabernet Sauvignon is a serious red wine, which comes close to what a Cretan "Super Tuscan" might be. The final product is a pure Malvasia Aromatica, sun dried for a week and then fermented up to fourteen per cent alcohol. The result is an intense, sweet but balanced wine that can be a very good alternative to dessert Muscats.

DOZES WINERY
Kounavoi, 701 00 Archanes, Crete.
Tel: +30 281 074 3755/5004; Fax: +30 281 074 3755.
Vineyards owned: 35ha; production: 4,000–5,000hl.

Winemaker Dionysis Dozes deserves to be far better known than he currently is. Dozes is one of the people who knows Peza and the region of Iraklio extremely well, and has great experience in working with the local vines. He was with Creta Olympias through the organization's difficult early phase, leaving in 1994 to create his own business. At the moment, his venture is focused mainly on the local market. Only Vilana, Kotsifali, and Mandilaria are crushed, together with the occasional Sultanina, while the range of wines includes a white and red Peza and a white and red TO of Crete.

COOPERATIVE OF IRAKLIO
Winery One: 700 11 Dafnes, Iraklio, Crete. Tel: +30 281 079 1280.
Winery Two: Thesi Koroni, 715 00 Iraklio, Crete. Tel: +30 281 025 0212.
Head office: 62 Martyron Avenue, 711 00 Iraklio, Crete.
Tel: +30 281 025 4502/4603; Fax: +30 281 026 1150;
Website: www.agrunion.gr; Email: info@agrunion.gr
Vineyards under contract: 1,800ha; production: 18,000hl.

The Iraklio Cooperative is one of the most proactive co ops in Crete – if not the whole of Greece. With offices in Athens, there are healthy exports to the USA, Germany, Finland, and Canada. Apart from wine, olive oil sales are a significant source of revenue. The co op has two wineries, with the one in Dafnes dedicated primarily to the production of the local OPAP red wine. Beyond quality wine appellations, the co op produces a significant number of products of all colours and styles. Ones to highlight include the Malvicino semi sweet range, allegedly reintroducing the Malvasia wine style, and the Domenico dry range, a relatively famous wine brand in the tourist resorts of Iraklio. Overall, the wines are quite old fashioned in style.

LIDAKIS WINERY

701 00 Archanes, Iraklio, Crete. Tel: +30 281 075 1815/2281.

Vineyards owned: 3ha; production: 150hl.

A small venture based on the energy of Vaggelis Lidakis, general manager, viticulturalist and winemaker. The winery produces some of the best OPAP Archanes in a traditional but charming style. Red wines top the portfolio, with a high extract Kotsifali/Cabernet Sauvignon TO of Crete as well as a blended Bellena Red that includes small amounts of Syrah. The only white wine is Bellena White, an unusual blend of Thrapsathiri, Plyto, and a little Muscat of Spina. The quality can be very good across all the wines, although there have been some cases of significant bottle, or batch, variation.

LYRARAKIS ESTATE

Alagnio Arkalohoriou, 703 00 Crete. Head office: 92 G Papandreou, 713 05 Iraklio, Crete; Tel: +30 281 028 4614; Fax: +30 281 028 8515; Website: www.lyrarakis.gr; Email: gea@lyrarakis.gr

Vineyards owned: 8ha; under contract: 4ha; production: 8,000hl.

This is one of Crete's most historic, premium estates and it is exciting to see that the Lyrarakis family is not resting on its laurels. For more than four decades, Lyrarakis has been instrumental in preserving tradition as well as suggesting new ways forward. In 1966, the first form of the Lyrarakis Estate was established, making it one of the first attempts in Crete to make a family wine producing estate commercially significant. In 1977, the company became more focused on creating new vineyards in the Alagni village and started one of the first modern, organized Vilana sites. These plantings were the main source of parent stock for most local growers before the arrival of phylloxera, and for nurseries after many areas started succumbing to it.

Vilana is not the only local variety that owes a lot to Lyrarakis. The Alagni site, at an altitude of 470 metres (1,542 feet), is now fully planted with the traditional Kotsifali and Mandilaria varieties, the popular Syrah, Cabernet Sauvignon, Merlot, Carignan, Chardonnay, and Sauvignon Blanc and, most importantly, Plyto and Dafni. The two vines are some of the oldest in Crete. Plyto used to be widely planted in the general Iraklio region and Dafni was always one of the minor grapes. However, both have been neglected since World War II and were saved from extinction, commercial if not actual, by the efforts of Lyrarakis. The two wines have quite similar palates, with a good combination of moderate alcohol, moderate acidity but good overall ripeness of flavours and texture. However, Dafni is a lot more aromatic on the nose, a factor helped by the ten hour skin contact.

These two varietals form the most esoteric side of the Lyrarakis whites but the rest are very competently made. Lyrarakis White is a balanced blend of Vilana and Sauvignon Blanc, with a drop of Sylvaner to increase acidity. A varietal Vilana is made in two different *cuvées*, one OPAP Peza and one TO of Crete. Neither are the most aromatic examples of this variety, but they have good structure on the palate. A new bottling line in 2004 and a new cellar in 2005, as well as a HACCP quality control accreditation gained in the same year (*see* footnote on page 178), is likely to push quality to even higher standards.

Without a doubt, the high point of the Lyrarakis portfolio is the domaine's red wines. Lyrarakis Red is a blend of Kotsifali, Mandilaria, and Carignan, with an impressive youthful colour – something that can be obtained only when non irrigated sites are used, according to Lyrarakis. There is a Lyrarakis TO of Crete, which is an excellent varietal Kotsifali. Very few people are confident enough to produce a good, pure example of the variety. The Red OPAP Peza is the least modern wine in the portfolio, following a slightly more traditional path, whereas the opposite is true for the winery's top red labels: a Syrah/Kotsifali and a Cabernet Sauvignon/ Merlot. The first wine is a high extract Syrah with thirty per cent Kotsifali added for aroma and spice, while the second label is a fifty/fifty blend of Bordeaux varieties that has huge density and power. The two wines are aged in predominantly new French oak for about ten months and both belong to the top class of Aegean Island wines, even if it would be difficult placing them as such when tasted blind.

MICHALAKIS VINEYARDS

Winery One and Head office: D'Tetragono, 714 08 Iraklio, Crete.

Tel: +30 281 038 1303; Fax: +30 281 038 1183.

Winery Two: Metaxohori, 700 10 Monofatsiou, Crete. Tel: +30 281 074 1222;

Fax: +30 281 074 3753; Website: www.michalakis.gr; Email: info@michalakis.gr

Vineyards owned: 44ha; under contract: 120ha; production: 14,500hl.

Michalakis Vineyards constitutes possibly the most significant investment programme of the last decade for the wine industry of Crete. The Michalakis family became involved with wine in the 1960s, being among the first to deal in bottled wine when bulk was more the norm. Growth has always been an important part of the Michalakis strategy; in 1980, the company moved to new premises, while in 2000, a separate entity was formed in order to run the forty four hectares of estate owned land, all of which is organically cultivated. The whole investment is likely to total ten million euros, making it one of the highest ever in the private Greek wine sector.

The winery's basic lines offer reasonable quality and value for money. The brand names Lato EO and Le Manoir TO of Crete are competitive in their respective market and price segments. The white and red Peza OPAP labels are solid parts of the portfolio, offering good, typical expressions of their origin. The company also trades in some OPAP wines produced elsewhere, namely some wines from Mantinia, Nemea, and Mavrodaphne of Patras.

Since the late 1990s, the Michalakis Vineyards has been going beyond the traditional styles to develop a series of premium products. The varietal range includes a more modern Vilana, a fresh and simple Kotsifali as well as an easy drinking, bone dry rosé blend of Kotsifali and Grenache Rouge. The three top of the line wines are Evanthis, a blend of fifty per cent Vilana and fifty per cent Sauvignon Blanc; Atarahos Rosé which is Kotsifali with Syrah; while Atarahos is a blend of fifty per cent Cabernet Sauvignon and fifty per cent Kotsifali. The varieties for the Atarahos wines are harvested, macerated and aged separately in new Alliers oak. In the beginning, this premium range of Michalakis wines was not convincing, lacking fruit and clarity. Now, it seems that the winemaking team has begun to better understand the requirements of the genre, mastering extraction, cool fermentation, and the use of oak, and, as a result, the last few vintages have much improved. It seems that the quality should reach higher levels in the future.

MINOS WINES CRETE

701 00 Peza, Archanes, Crete.

Tel: +30 281 074 1213/1265; Fax: +30 281 074 1597;

Website: www.minoswines.gr; Email: info@minoswines.gr

Vineyards owned: 5ha; under contract: 20ha; rented: 25; production: 4,000hl.

Minos Wines is a private business, owned by the Miliarakis family with roots dating back to 1932. It was one of the major powers in the Cretan wine trade up to 1990, but since then, a series of personal and financial problems have taken their toll and the company has been curtailing development as well as sales growth. However, it would seem logical to assume that Minos Wines will sometime in the future reclaim its place in the premier league of Aegean wine production.

Minos Wines adopts a traditional approach to both its wines and their labels. This, by itself, is not a problem, especially when more than seventy per cent of sales are directed at local markets selling low priced products. In this sector, being modern is not always a positive asset. Nonetheless, Minos has a range of limited production products that do show imagination and a more modern approach. For example, the winery makes about 8,000 bottles a year of an oak aged blanc de noirs Kotsifali, which is a most interesting, individual white. A Vilana Fumé has just a kiss of oak but does display some of the grape's aromatic character. The Minoiko OPAP Peza is released in both a white and a red version and has for years been among the most prestigious offerings of the Peza appellation. Today both wines might seem a bit tight and in need for some extra ripeness.

UNION OF PEZA COOPERATIVES

Kalloni, 701 00 Archanes, Iraklio, Crete.

Tel: +30 281 074 1945/6; Fax: +30 281 074 1528;

Website: www.pezaunion.gr; Email: marketing@pezaunion.gr

Vineyards under contract: 750ha; members: 3,000+;

production: 80,000–115,000hl.

The Union of Peza Cooperatives was established in 1933 and now consists of 3,000 grower members and nineteen cooperatives. Currently the biggest producer in the Aegean Sea, the Peza union has for decades been responsible for the profile of Cretan wine throughout Greece. For many Greek wine drinkers, their acquaintance with wines from Crete starts and ends with the products of the Peza Union. Retail outlets around the country become a neighbourhood's "wine centres", where the locals would buy everyday jug wine in plastic one and a half litre bottles, a bottled wine for Sunday lunch, and, possibly, an OPAP Peza Red for a special occasion dinner. The people behind the organization have been very active in promoting its wines, pursuing exports in numerous markets, from China to Bahrain.

The Peza union never claimed to produce the most refined, elegant or top-quality wine. Its philosophy was to make affordable wines that people would like to drink. The OPAP bottlings do not have a great emphasis on primary fruit but are easy drinking and relatively light in structure. Beyond these wines, there are numerous labels, including the TOs of Crete, or EOs in almost every style of dry, or semi dry, non fortified wine imaginable.

Logado has traditionally been a strong brand name, focusing on the drier side of the portfolio. A huge success in the last few years has been To Krasi tis Pareas ("the wine of the party"). Capitalizing on the trend towards bag in box formats and Tetra Pak litre containers, this wine has gained huge market share with its imaginative and innovative packaging. Many Greek producers would argue against the Peza union's products, philosophy, and methods. Few could argue about its success.

LASITHI

Lasithi extends east of Mount Dikti, with its slopes flowing down to the narrowest part of Crete, less than twenty kilometres (twelve miles) wide, with the Gulf of Mirabello to the north and the beautiful, tourist region of Ierapetra to the south. The area east of here has a moderate altitude. The capital of the prefecture is Aghios Nikolaos and, apart from Ierapetra, the only provincial town is Sitia, close to the northeastern tip of the island. The climate of Lasithi is generally the driest and warmest of Crete; in half of the vintages the last rain falls before the end of April. Lasithi is one region where organic cultivation is extremely easy and, indeed, is the cheapest option. The only disease that appears occasionally is powdery mildew.

Lasithi is the smallest prefecture of Crete in terms of vineyard acreage, with less than a tenth of the total area. However, most plantings are located in its sole quality-wine appellation boundaries; out of a total of 953 hectares, 689 are entitled to produce OPAP Sitia. The Sitia zone engulfs a large part of the eastern prefecture and is made up of two relatively low mountain ranges. Most vineyards are located between 250 and 650 metres (820–2,133 feet), but occasionally vines can be found in lower plots. The soils are mainly limestone, and yields in non-irrigated vineyards are much lower than the Cretan average: as low as eighteen hectolitres per hectare.

The Sitia OPAP designation can be used for dry whites and dry or sweet reds, all of which have a legal yield limit of seventy hectolitres per hectare. White Sitia must be at least seventy per cent Vilana, together with Thrapsathiri, which adds some complexity but lowers the aromatic intensity. Varietal composition for the red Sitia OPAP was defined as 100 per cent Liatiko, when it was established in 1971. This variety has very low levels of phenolics, and it is not ideal for creating modern red styles. As a result, many local growers sun-dried Liatiko grapes to make sweet wines – some of which were excellent. However both sweet wines and pale, dry reds fell out of fashion, with sales becoming increasingly difficult. To address this, in 1998, the Sitia Union of Cooperatives requested an amendment to allow the addition of twenty per cent Mandilaria. As is the case with Peza and Archanes, Mandilaria is used to deepen the colour of a blend, to increase acidity, and to moderate high alcohol. This adjustment was passed, and now OPAP Sitia reds have to follow an eighty/twenty Liatiko/Mandilaria rule.

It is debatable whether this change was in the appellation's long term interests. There are fierce opponents, like Yiannis Economou (*see* page 461), who believe that Sitia producers must respect and persist with Liatiko, instead of succumbing to easy solutions. The quality of Economou wines does illustrate the varietal's potential. In addition, it seems that Liatiko behaves differently in Sitia to Dafnes, the other Liatiko dominated OPAP. Many growers speculate that this could be a clone- and not a terroir-related matter, but whatever the cause, it is certain that the best Sitia Liatikos have an extra dimension when compared with their counterparts from Dafnes.

Another point of concern is the fact that Mandilaria vines are rare, if non existent, within the Sitia OPAP region. In 1998, although the varietal composition was modified, the boundaries were not. Therefore, producers wishing to follow the letter of the law have to source Mandilaria from other regions – for example non OPAP Lasithi vineyards or areas outside the prefecture – effectively breaking another aspect of the law.

Apart from Sitia OPAP, the prefecture was awarded a TO of Lasithi for dry wines of all colours. Curiously enough, there is not a single producer at the moment producing a TO of Lasithi.

Sitia OPAP

White still: dry.
White varieties: Vilana (at least seventy per cent of the blend); Thrapsathiri.
Red still: dry; naturally sweet; fortified sweet.
Red varieties: Liatiko eighty per cent; Mandilaria twenty per cent.

Lasithi TO

White still: dry.
White varieties: Vilana; Athiri; Thrapsathiri; Ugni Blanc.
Rosé still: dry.
Rosé varieties: Mandilaria (up to five per cent of the blend); Kotsifali; Liatiko; Ladikino; Carignan.
Red still: dry.
Red varieties: Kotsifali; Mandilaria; Liatiko; Ladikino; Carignan.

PRODUCERS

DIGENAKIS WINES

Sitias, 74 Myssonos, 723 00 Sitia, Crete. Head office: 7 Katakouzinon, 713 07 Iraklio Crete. Tel: +30 281 032 2846; Fax: +30 281 021 1466; Website: www.digenakis.gr; Email: info@digenakis.gr Production: 3,500hl.

A family owned company established in 1992 and mainly aimed at trading own branded wines bought from several producers and co ops around Greece, most notably from the Sitia Union of Agricultural Cooperatives (*see* page 462). Some interesting varietal bottlings are released, most notably Chardonnay and Cabernet Sauvignon.

ECONOMOU WINERY

Ziros, 72059, Sitia. Tel: +30 284 309 1235.
Head office: 102 E Stavrakaki, 723 00 Sitia, Crete. Tel: +30 284 302 2232; Fax: +30 284 302 5268; Email: domaineconomou@yahoo.com
Vineyards owned: 12ha; production: 200hl.

Yiannis Economou is one of the best and most underestimated winemakers in Greece. His CV is impressive, with an oenology degree from Alba, cellar work in Germany and Bordeaux (Château Margaux and the difficult 1993 vintage) as well as Piedmont, under the guidance of Nebbiolo maestros such as Ceretto and Scavino. Upon his return to Crete in 1994, he resurrected the family wine business, immediately making waves in the area.

Eoconomou works with ungrafted, traditional vines from the Ziros plain, most of which are at least forty years old. Cultivation is totally organic, though this is not stated on the label. Yields are extremely low, with an average of fifteen hectolitres per hectare. Overall production is limited and can fluctuate widely, with some vintages producing less than 10,000 bottles. With strong demand from Germany, few cases of Economou wines are sold and drunk in Greece. New plantings and acquisitions are under way, with the aim of reaching a production of 60,000 bottles per annum.

Economou is a great believer in Liatiko. "I enjoy the old French school [of winemaking] where depth of colour is not related to the quality of a red wine," he says. "Red wine is about complexity, finesse, and aroma. The world should not be full of Cabernet, or Cabernet-like wines. I hope my Liatikos show some people that there are alternatives." He makes three different Liatiko wines. A deep, extracted rosé is possibly the easiest to appreciate, but it is still far from the simple, refreshing style advocated by many producers. Economou Sitia Red is a pure Liatiko. The grapes are harvested above 13.5 degrees Baumé and the wine is aged for a year in 350-litre oak barrels. Barriques are not used, since these would be too heavy for the elegance of Liatiko. The wine is released when it is three years old, having been carefully cellared at 18°C (64°F). This late release does wonders for the complexity of the wine, which is an example of what less popular Greek varieties can achieve when handled correctly. The final Liatiko is a sweet wine, made from grapes left on the vine to reach about 18.5 degrees Baumé, then naturally fermented up to 15.5 per cent alcohol, and aged for two years in oak.

The same method of sweet winemaking is used for a blend of Vilana and Thrapsathiri, the only difference being a shorter oak-ageing of about eight months. The same white grapes are harvested much earlier to make a dry, but rich, Sitia White. Both of these wines are more about complexity and texture than aroma. As well as preserving old treasures, Economou intends to try some new projects. A recently acquired site has been planted with Grenache Rouge, Syrah, Chardonnay, Viognier, Merlot, together with – presumably he could not resist – Nebbiolo and Barbera. Apart from wine, Economou dedicates his free time to olive oil, honey, and vinegar production, trying to make his estate a more complete agricultural proposal. Definitely a producer with great potential.

SITIA UNION OF AGRICULTURAL COOPERATIVES

Head office: 74 Misonos Street, 723 00 Sitia, Crete. Tel: +30 284 302 2211;
Fax: 284 302 3222; Website: www.sitiacoop.gr; Email: info@sitiacoop.gr

Vineyards under contract: 500ha; members: nearly 9,000; production: 20,000hl.

The Sitia UAC is one of the oldest and most important cooperatives in Crete.
Established in 1933, it currently consists of forty-three co-ops and close to
9,000 member-growers. The organization splits its efforts between wine
and olive oil, with the latter being among Greece's best.

Unfortunately, the vinous offerings of Sitias are not as high-flying as its
olive oil. However, the wines are better than adequate, and do show good
quality. The basic Myrto range, offered in white, rosé, red, dry, and semi-
sweet versions, is extremely well-made, showing fruit and clarity. The value-
for-money TO of Crete range has three wines: the white is a blend of
Thrapsathiri, Vilana, and Muscat; the rosé and red are both blends of Liatiko
and Mandilaria and have a remarkable balance for their respective styles.

The Sitia UAC bottles three different OPAPs, all of which are produced
from selected higher altitude sites. Sitia White is moderately aromatic, finely
textured, and complex; Sitia Red shows an impressive Liatiko character,
reinforced with Mandilaria's colour; but the winery's best product is the sweet
red Sitia, a fortified 100 per cent Liatiko that seems to balance somewhere
between a Mavrodaphne and a sweet oloroso.

TOPLOU MONASTERY

723 00 Sitia, Crete. Tel: +30 284 302 9630/1226;
Fax: +30 284 302 9635; Email: biositia@otenet.gr

Vineyards owned: 16ha; Production: 200hl.

The historic monastery of Toplou is one of Crete's most important. Lying six
kilometres (3.7 miles) north of the village of Palekastro, its involvement
with wine production can be traced back decades, but it was in 1999 that
Archbishop Theofilos decided to start a wine business. The Sitia UAC came
to the monastery's assistance, helping with vine cultivation, by renting out
winery and cellar space, and agreeing to distribute the wines produced.

Varieties planted include some white grapes, but only red wines are
released. The sweet Ktima Toplou is made from sun-dried Liatiko with a
little Black Muscat, while the dry version is Cabernet Sauvignon, Merlot, and
Kotsifali. The wines can lack clarity and have oxidation problems. However,
it is early days and Toplou Monastery deserves support, particularly at the
commercial level.

Appendices

I

Greek wine legislation

Official title	Date introduced	French equivalent
QUALITY WINE		
OPE Wines of Appellation of Controlled Origin; famous Greek wines needing protection.	1971–2	*appellation contrôlée*
OPAP Wines of Appellation of Origin of Higher Quality; for regions that "show potential for quality".	1971–2	*vin de limite de qualité súperieur*
Amendments Ageing terms: *epilegmenos* and *eidika epilegmenos*.	1988	*réserve* and *grande réserve*
Young wines: *neos oinos*	2005	*nouveau*
TABLE WINE		
TO Regional Wines of Origin; three quality levels, rising as demarcated region becomes more specific.	1989	*vin de pays*
EO Local wine.	1971–2	*vin de table*
Amendments *Cava*	1989	
OKP Wines of Appellation by Tradition		

Demarcated area	Factors	Number
Yes: zones normally follow commune lines. Production must be withiin area, but bottling can be elsewhere.	Varieties and varietal composition; yield; alcoholic strength; viticulture; vinification.	8
Yes: as above.	Varieties and varietal composition; yield; alcoholic strength; viticulture; vinification.	25
	Minimum timespans for ageing both in barrel and in bottle. Differs for red and white wines.	N/A
	Can be sold before December 10 after harvest	N/A
a) Whole department. b) One prefecture. c) One commune.	Region; variety; vintage. Stricter than EO, but not as strict as OPAP/OPE.	c.80
None	Yields.	
	Minimum timespans for ageing.	N/A
Retsina: throughout Greece. Verdea: Zakynthos.	Like EO with "tradition".	2

SWEET WINE

Greece has a remarkable array of sweet wines, both red and white, and a varied range of procedures to make them. Below is a brief summary. For more on these sweet wines *see* Part II, Chapters 7, 8, and 10.

Style	Description	Factors
vin naturellement doux	naturally sweet	Overripe or sun dried grapes, no spirit added.
vin de liqueur	fortified sweet	An umbrella term used for all sweet fortified wines.
vin doux naturel	fortified sweet	Fermentation started as normal, spirit used to arrest fermentation at the appropriate moment, depending on alcoholic strength desired.
vin doux naturel grand cru	fortified sweet from selected vineyards	As above, but using grapes from key vineyards; *e.g.* in the OPE Mavrodaphne of Patras, these are from the higher vineyards.
vin doux	fortified sweet	Spirit added before or right at the beginning of fermentation.
vinsanto (white) mezzo (red)	Now generally not fortified, but can be.	Sun dried grapes used. Legally can be made with or without fortification, but usually made using *vin naturellement doux* methods.

VINES AND REGIONS

Numbers of hectares of land under vine in each department according to the 2001 Ministry of Agriculture census. (Figures given to the nearest ten.)

Thrace	400
Macedonia	7,210
Epirus	700
Thessaly	4,410
Central Greece	20,900
Ionian islands	3,560
Peloponnese	21,850
Cyclades	4,100
Dodecanese	1,450
North Aegean	2,810
Crete	10,100

II

Native Greek varieties

Greece has arguably the richest selection of indigenous varieties of any wine producing country. In addition to the grapes featured in Chapter 5, listed below is a selection of other native grapes, with a note of where they are mentioned in the main text.

WHITE GRAPES
Agrioglikadi *see* Glikerithra, below.

Ampelaitis *see* Valaitis below.

Asproudes a collective term describing a mixture of white vines planted – and often vinified – together. Singular, Asprouda. *See* Glossary.

Avgoustiatis *see* Zakynthos, Ionian Islands.

Batiki *see* Trikala, Karditsa, & Dougos, Larissa, Thessaly.

Begleri *see* Ikaria, North Aegean Islands.

Dafnato *see* Iraklio, Crete.

Dafni *see* Iraklio, Crete.

Damiatis *see* Bellas Winery, Evros, Thrace.

Dermatas *see* Rethymno, Crete.

Flaska *see* Santorini, Cyclades Islands.

FlaskAssyrtico *see* Santorini, Cyclades Islands.

Glikerithra sometimes called Glikasprouda, one of the most important Asproudes varietals *see* above.

Goustolidi *see* Zakynthos & Cephalonia, Ionian Islands; Messinia, Peloponneseaka Vostilidi and Goustoulidi.

Mavroudi *see* Thrace.

Migdali *see* Zakynthos, Ionian Islands.

Moschatella *see* Cephalonia, Ionian Islands.

Kakotrigis *see* Corfu, Ionian Islands.

Katsakoulias *see* Zakynthos, Ionian Islands.
Katsano *see* Santorini, Cyclades Islands.
Kritiko *see* Santorini, Cyclades Islands
Kseromaherouda *see* Syros, Cyclades Islands.
Kidonitsa *see* Laconia, Peloponnese.
Kontokladi *see* Fthioda, Central Greece
Muscat di Trani *see* Rhodes, Dodecanese Islands.
Opsimo *see* Bellas Winery, Evros, Thrace.
Pavlos *see* Zakynthos, Ionian Islands.
Petroulianos *see* Laconia, Peloponnese.
Platani *see* Santorini, Cyclades Islands.
Plyto *see* Iraklio, Crete.
Potamisi *see* Tinos, Cyclades Islands.
Skiadopoulo *see* Zakynthos, Ionian Islands.
Sklava *see* Zachiarias Wines, Corinth, Peloponnese.
Tsaousi *see* Cephalonia, Ionian Islands.
Thrapsathiri *see* Santorini, Cyclades; Crete.
Thiako White *see* Cephalonia, Ionian Islands.
Tourkopoula *see* Ilia, Peloponnese.
Valaitis aka Ampelaitis, *see* Rethymno, Crete.
Vidiano *see* Karavitakis Vineyards, Hania, and Rethymno,Crete.
Zakinthino *see* Yiannikostas Metaxas, Cephalonia, Ionian Islands.
Zoumiatiko *see* Thrace and Serres, Macedonia; aka Dimiat in Bulgaria,
Smederevka in Yugoslavia. .

RED GRAPES
Agianniotiko *see* Ikaria & Hios, North Aegean Islands.
Aidani Mavro *see* Santorini, Cyclades Islands.
Arahovitikos *see* Fokida, Central Greece; Bekari and Vlahiko, Epirus;
aka Mavroudi Arahovas.
Corinthiaki *see* Korinthiaki below.
Diminitis *see* Rhodes, Dodecanese Islands.
Fokiano *see* Messinia, Peloponnese; Samos, Limnos, Ikaria,
and Lesbos, North Aegean Islands.
Fraoula Kokkini *see* Holevas, Magnissia, Thessaly.
Galano *see* Kazani, Macedonia; Rapsani,Thessaly.
Georgina, Krassato *see* Tsantali, Larissa, Thessaly.
Hamburg Muscat *see* Holevas in Magnissia, Co op of Tyrnavos; and
Vasdavanos in Larissa, Thessaly.
Kalambaki *see* "Limnio", page 72.

Kaloniatiko *see* Lesbos, North Aegean Islands.
Katsakoulias *see* Zakynthos, Ionian Islands.
Karampraimis *see* Evia, Central Greece.
Karnahalades *see* Bellas Winery, Evros, Thrace.
Koumari *see* Tinos, Cyclades Islands.
Koundouro *see* Ikaria, North Aegean Islands; "Mandilaria" page 73.
Korinthiaki *see* Zakynthos, Ionian Islands; Messinia,Ilia, and Ahaia, Peloponnese; also known as Corinthiaki.
Kseromaherouda Mavri *see* Syros, Cyclades Islands.
Lesviako Krasostafilo *see* Methymnaios, Lesbos, North Aegean Islands.
Limniona aka Limnio in Thessaly, not to be confused with the Limnio found elsewhere.
Mavrathiro *see* Santorini, Cyclades Islands.
Mavro Messenikola *see* Karditsa, Thessaly.
Mavroromeiko *see* Romeiko below.
Mavrotragano *see* Tinos & Santorini, Cyclades Islands.
Mavroudi *see* Laconia, Peloponnese; *see* Glossary.
Moschomavro *see* Kazani, Macedonia.
Neroproimia *see* Bellas Winery, Evros, Thrace.
Pamidi *see* Cellars of Evros, Thrace; also called Pamiti, aka Pamid, Bulgaria.
Petrokoritho *see* Corfu, Ionian Islands.
Potamisi Mavro *see* Tinos, Cyclades Islands.
Prekniariko *see* Chrisohoou Estate, Imathia, Macedonia; has several synonyms, such as Prekna, Preknadi or the more usual Priknadi.
Refosco *see* Ilia, Peloponnese.
Ritino *see* Samos, North Aegean.
Romeiko *see* Crete; aka Mavroromeiko.
Rosaki *see* Karditsa, Thessaly
Sikiotis *see* Holevas, Magnissia, Thessaly.
Stavrohiotiko *see* Santorini, Cyclades Islands.
Stavroto *see* Kozani, Macedonia; aka Ampelakiotiko Mavro, and when virus infected, Ampelakiotiko.
Thiako Red *see* Cephalonia, Ionian Islands.
Thrapsa *see* Laconia, Peloponnese.
Tsardana *see* Crete.
Vaftra *see* Limnos, North Aegean Islands.
Vergioto *see* Kozani, Macedonia.
Voidomatis *see* Santorini, Cyclades Islands.

III

Other recommended producers

MACEDONIA

Arabatzis Estate
Gefyra, 570 11 Thessaloniki.
Tel: 30 231 071 3402.

Avlagas
591 00 Trifolo Beroias.
Tel: +30 033 109 3281.

Diamantakos Estate
Thesi Mantemi,
592 00 Naoussa.
Tel: +30 233 202 8623.

Hatzivaritis
Olybou 115,
546 35 Thessaloniki.
Tel: +30 231 021 5259.

Kastaniotis Winery
9 Georgiou Kirtsi,
592 00 Naoussa.
Tel: +30 233 202 2516.

Messimvria Winery
Nea Messimvria,
570 22 Thessaloniki.
Tel: +30 231 071 3981.

Vlachopoulos Winery
Thesi Nea Drosia,
570 04 Nea Michaniona.
Tel: +30 293 203 2540.

CENTRAL GREECE

Adanoglou Estate
Thesi Olympos,
Anavissos190 13, Attica.
Tel: +30 229 105 3432.

Andreou Winery
Isidorou Ghika 4,
Paiania 190 02, Attica.
Tel: +30 210 664 3324.

Andris Estate
Thesi Panormos,
Nea Makri 190 05, Attica.
Tel: +30 229 401 0001.

Angelou Wines
Makrigianni 16,
Kalivia 190 10, Attica.
Tel: +30 229 904 8621.

Avros Nikolou
Nikolaou Ntouni 8,
Koropi 194 00, Attica.
Tel: +30 210 662 3046.

Bassis Estate
Georgoula 28,
Athens 115 24, Attica.
Tel: +30 210 692 7072.

Bekas Estate
Nea Odos Spaton Loutsas,
Spata 190 04, Attica.
Tel: +30 229 408 6255.

Biosystem Stratus
Thimari, Anavissos 190 13, Attica.
Tel: +30 229 104 0879.

Daremas Winery
Thesi Poleme, Vravronos Avenue,
Markopoulos, 190 03, Attica.
Tel: +30 229 9025744.

Diamantis Vineyards
351 00 Komma Lamias.
Tel: +30 223 103 9227.

Dimakis Estate
Xiou 62, 153 43 Agia Paraskeui.
Tel: +30 210 600 8334.

Dromos Aeroporias
Ifanti 15, Koropi 194 00, Attica.
Tel: +30 210 662 2486.

Davaris Winery
Thesi Mandra Bekiri,
Paiania 190 02, Attica.
Tel: +30 210 602 9422.

Ergastiri
Iroon Polytehniou 7,
Elefsina 192 00, Attica.
Tel: +30 210 556 0375.

Evoinos Kouloheri
Plateia Xenofonta,
Spata 190 04, Attica.
Tel: +30 210 663 2542.

Haniotis Winery
Thesi Plagia, 350 04 Elatia.
Tel: +30 223 403 1637.

Isaias Estate
350 09 Komnina Molou.
Tel: +30 223 506 1512.

Katselis Estate
Asopia, 322 00 Thebes, Viotia.
Tel: +30 222 108 2590

Liberis Winery
Askri Thivon, 320 02 Askri
Thebes, Viotia.
Tel: +30 226 206 7650.

Nikolaou Winery
Halkidas Karistou Highway,
345 00 Aliveri, Evia.
Tel: +30 222 302 2905.

Papachristos Vienyard
16 km Athens Spata,
Pallini 153 44, Attica.
Tel: +30 210 603 2510.

Papakonstantinou Vineyards
Koukouleza 301,
Shimatari 320 09, Viotia.
Tel: 30 226 205 8359.

Papoutsis Estate
Androutsou 10,
352 00 Atalanti.
Tel: +30 223 302 2508.

To Patitiri
181 Marathonos Avenue,
Pallini 153 52, Attica.
Tel: +30 210 603 1020.

Pavlidis Winery
Mossaiou 6,
Nea Makri 190 05, Attica.
Tel: +30 229 409 1275

Pikermi Cooperative Winery
58 Ippokratous,
Athens 106 80, Attica.
Tel: +30 210 360 9539.

Sinis Winery
Kekropos 4,
Keratea 190 01, Attica.
Tel: +30 229 904 2161.

Sokos Winery
Manoli Blessa 15,
Athens 114 76, Attica.
Tel: +30 210 643 6664.

Tripodakis Winery
Thessi Zafiri Kalatha,
Elefsina 192 00, Attica.
Tel: +30 210 554 5666.

Tsakanikas Winery
Alkiviadou 24, Athens 104 39.
Tel: +30 210 881 2233.

Voulgaris Vineyards
Sideri 43, Spata 190 04, Attica.
Tel: +30 210 639 4564.

Zarogikas Estate
Bathi Aulidos,
341 00 Halkida, Evia.
Tel: +30 222 103 4991.

PELOPONNESE
Boultadakis Iakovos
46 Gravias, 161 22 Kaisariani.
Tel: +30 210 725 2317.

Dimitra
241 00 Laiika Kalamatas.
Tel: +30 272 108 0175.

Douros Winery
Aerodromio Argous, 212 00 Argos.
Tel: +30 275 102 4908.

Giannakopoulos Vineyards
205 00 Asprokambos Nemea.
Tel: +30 274 605 1353.

Grillas Winery
6th Parodos Monastras,
272 00 Amaliada.
Tel: +30 262 202 9385.

Kalogris Traditional Winery
221 00 Kapsia Tripoleos.
Tel: +30 271 024 3409.

Kaltsis Winery
205 00 Archea Nemea.
Tel: +30 274 602 4151.

Kimothoi
Karaiskaki 85, 265 00 Patras.
Tel: +30 261 036 8100.

Kissas Winery
202 00 Diminio Kiatou.
Tel: +30 274 202 8811.

Klaros Estate
200 08 Agios Vasilios Chiliomodiou.
Tel: +30 274 109 7204.

Koliperas Vineyards
250 08 Farai Chalandritsas.
Tel: +30 269 406 1962.

Korkas Winery
22 Mesogion,
200 06 Poullitsa Vrachatiou.
Tel: +30 274 105 5856.

Kotrotsos Winery
Karaiskaki 120,
26 500 Akteo Patras.
Tel: +30 261 099 2160.

Mantinias Winery
221 00 Zevgolatio Tripoleos.
Tel: +30 271 057 2272.

Miragias Vineyards
Dorieon 54, 231 00 Sparti.
Tel: +30 273 102 8290.

Nikolaou Winery
11 Eustathiou Maniati,
205 00 Nemea.
Tel: +30 274 602 3005.

Olympos Winery
6th km Eparchiakis odou
Tripoleos Spartis,
220 12 Tegea.
Tel: +30 271 055 7055.

Orino Ecological Estate
221 00 Zevgolatio Tripoleos.
Tel: +30 271 057 2501.

Panousopoulos Vineyards
240 01 Pidasos Pilou.
Tel: +30 272 302 9404.

Papargiriou Estate
202 00 Laliotis Kiatou.
Tel: +30 274 202 2745.

Politis Winery
220 04 Kandila.
Tel: +30 279 603 1333.

Sarantos Wines
200 06 Poullitsa Vrachatiou.
Tel: +30 274 105 6540.

Smirnis Estate
220 21 Leodari Arkadia.
Tel: +30 279 106 1788.

Stratus Biosystem
11 Solomou, 175 63 Palaio Faliro.
Tel: +30 210 984 8680.

Tetramythos
Eparchiaki odos Poudas Kalavriton,
250 03 Ano Diakopto.
Tel: +30 269 109 7242.

Theodorou Estate
200 20 Stimaga Velou.
Tel: +30 274 206 1620.

Tourgelis Winery
205 00 Asprokambos Nemea.
Tel: +30 274 605 1378.

Trichilis Estate
230 56 Pappadianika.
Tel: +30 273 2083093.

Vakchos Winery
200 02 Stimaga Velou.
Tel: +30 274 206 1605.

Varelas Winery
200 05 Athikia.
Tel: +30 274 103 9520.

Venus Winery
250 06 Akrata.
Tel: +30 269 603 1403.

CYCLADES ISLANDS
Kasteli Wines
847 00 Vothonas, Thiras.
Tel: +30 228 603 2047.

Reklos Winery
847 00 Exo Gonia, Thiras.
Tel: +30 231 027 8296.

CRETE
Foudoulakis Winery
700 10 Asimi Pyrgou,
Iraklio Crete.
Tel: 30 289 303 1460.

Mandre Winery
731 00 Gerolakkos, Hania.
Tel: +30 282 106 5375.

Ieronimakis Vineyard
Profitis Ilias, 715 00 Iraklio.
Tel: +30 281 087 1107.

Papadodimitrakis Wines
Georgiou Georgidadou 46,
713 05 Iraklio, Crete.
Tel: +30 281 023 7653.

Paterianakis Estate
Zografou 7, 712 01 Iraklio, Crete.
Tel: +30 281 028 4689.

Venianakis Dimitris
106 Kazantzaki Avenue,
731 00 Vamvakopoulo, Hania.
Tel: +30 282 109 8302.

IV

Further information

BIBLIOGRAPHY & RECOMMENDED READING

Athinaios *Deipnosophistis*, Ikaros Publishing House, Athens, 1992.
Dalby, A *Bacchus: a Biography*, British Museum Press, London, 2003.
Franke, P & Marathaki, E *Oinos kai nomisma stin Archaia Ellada*, Ktima Hatzimichalis, Athens, 1999.
Hatzimichalis, D *Ampelourgein*, Ktima Hatzimichalis, Athens, 1995.
Hesiod *Works and Days*, Oxford University Press, Oxford, reprint 1999.
Johnson, H *The Story of Wine*, Mitchell Beazley, London, 1998.
Lambert Gocs, M *The Wines of Greece*, Faber & Faber, London, 1990.
Manessis, N *The Illustrated Greek Wine Book*, Olive Press Publications, Corfu, 2000.
Robinson, J *The Oxford Companion to Wine*, Oxford University Press, Oxford, 2nd edition 1999.
Spinthiropoulou, H *Oinopoiisimes Poikilies tou Ellinikou Ampelona*, Olive Press Publications, Corfu, 2000.
Tsakiris, A *Elliniki Oinognosia*, Psihalos Editions, Athens, 2003.
Vinetum *To Evretirio Tou Krasiou*, Vinetum, Athens, 2003.

ORGANIZATIONS

Agricultural & Technical Professional Educational Institute of Nemea
37 Mathitikis Estia, 205 00, Nemea, Corinth.
Tel: +30 274 602 3072; Fax: +30 274 602 3032
Agricultural University of Athens
75 Iera Odos, 118 55, Athens. Tel: +30 210 529 4522;
Fax: +30 210 529 4525; Email: ceaz2emn@aua.gr; Website: www.aua.gr
Ampeloiniki
Technologiko Parko Thessalonikis, 4th km Thessalonikis Thermis, 57001, Thessaloniki. Tel: +30 231 047 6244; Fax: +30 231 049 8280;

Email: ampelo@filippos.techpath.gr;
Website: www.ampelooeniki.techpath.gr
Aristotle University of Thessaloniki
Agriculture Department / Chemistry Department
541 24, Thessaloniki. Tel: +30 231 099 5187/9 (Agriculture Dept) and
+30 231 099 7640 (Chemistry Dept); Website: www.auth.gr
Athens Wine & Vine Institute, National Agricultural Research Foundation
Sofokli Venizelou Street 1, 141 23, Athens.
Tel: +30 210 281 6978; Fax: +30 210 283 2456 / +30 210 2844954;
Email: insampel@otenet.gr / wineins@otenet.gr
Attican Vineyards Wine Producers' Association (ENOAA)
Eleftherios Venizelos International Airport, 190 19 Spata, Attica.
Tel: +30 210 353 1315; Fax: +30 210 353 2310;
Email: enoaa@ath.forthnet.gr; Website: www.enoaa.gr
Greek Sommeliers Union
113 Leoforo Pentelis, 152 34, Halandri, Athens
Tel: +30 697 741 8686; Fax: +30 210 623 0000;
Email: contact@greeksom.gr; Website: www.greeksom.gr
Greek Wine Association (SEO)
Nikis 34, 1005 57, Athens. Tel: +30 210 322 6053;
Fax: +30 210 332 7942; Email: seo@wine.org.gr
Greek Wine Journalists (ELDOIN)
PO Box 65049, 154 01, Athens.
Tel: +30 210 933 9250; Fax: +30 210 932 8036
Greek Women of Wine
PO Box 78533, 176 02, Kallithea, Athens.
Tel: +30 210 821 6102; Fax: +30 210 821 6102;
Email: info@womenofwine.gr; Website: www.womenofwine.gr
Hellenic Export Organisation
Marinou Antipa 86 88, 163 46, Ilioupoli Athens.
Tel: +30 210 998 2100; Fax: +30 210 996 9100; Email: info@hepo.gr
Northern Greece Vineyards Wine Producers' Association (ENOABE)
c/o Helexpo, P.O. Box 1529, Egnatias 154, 540 06, Thessaloniki.
Tel: +30 231 028 1632; Fax: +30 231 028 1619;
Email: wine roads@the.forthnet.gr; Website: www.wineroads.gr
Organic Growers' Unions Federation
62 Solomou, Nea Ionia Athens.
Tel: +30 210 282 0207; Fax: +30 210 282 0207
Organic Products Control & Certification Organisation (DIO)

Aristotelous 38, 104 33, Athens.

Tel: +30 210 822.4839; Fax: +30 210 821.8117; Email: info@dionet.gr

Peloponnese Vineyards Wine Producers' Association (ENOAP)

Patriarchou Grigoriou E' 18, 221 00, Tripoli, Arcadia.

Tel: +30 271 022 275; Fax: +30 271 022 1275

Technical & Educational Institute of Athens (TEI)

Aghiou Spiridonos & Dimitsanas, 122 10, Aigaleo, Attica.

Tel: +30 210 538.5504; Fax: +30 210 531.3874;

Email: oenology@teiath.gr; Website: www.teiath.gr

University of Athens

Chemistry Department, 157 71, Panepistimioupoli, Zografos.

Tel: +30 210 727.4342; Fax: +30 210 727.4097;

Website: www.chem.uoa.gr

Vine and Wine National Interprofessional Organisation (EDOAO)

Louizis Riankour 73, 115 23, Athens, Attica.

Tel: +30 210 692.3102; Fax: +30 210 698.1182

Vini/Viticultural Centre of Cephalonia and Ithaki

Vallianos Agricultural School, P.O. Box 281 00, Argostoli Kefalonia.

Tel: +30 267 102.6878; Fax: +30 267 102.6878; Email: valliang@otenet.gr

Vitro Hellas

Niseli, Alexandrias, Naoussa, 59300 Imathia, Macedonia.

Tel: +30 233 302 7281; Fax: +30 233 302 6417;

Email: vitro@alfanet.gr; Website: www.vitrohellas.gr

WEBSITES

Websites for individual producers appear with their entries in the main text. Below is a selection of other more general sites.

www.allaboutgreekwine.com

North American-based website representing 23 Greek wineries.

www.atheneeimporters.com

US importer of Greek wine.

www.greekwinemakers.com

Superbly informative website from a US-based Greek wine consultancy.

www.thegreekwine.com

Athens-based commercial site for Greek wine products.

www.biology.uch.gr/gvd/contents/index.htm

The Greek Vitis Database, genetic database of Greek indigenous varieties.

www.vinetum.gr

Athens-based wine communication company, organises "Oenorama".

Glossary

Acidity levels – In this book, acidity is expressed as tartaric acid. Winemakers can artificially increase or decrease the acidity of a specific wine during or after fermentation. According to viticultural expert Haroula Spinthiropoulou, a low acidity level in grapes is below 4.5 grams per litre; moderate acidity is 4.6–5.5 grams per litre; good acidity is 5.6–6.5 grams per litre; and high acidity is above 6.6 grams per litre.

Aghios – Greek for "saint." Female is *aghia*.

Ampelones – Greek for "vineyards." Can be used on labels only when the wine in question is made entirely from vineyards owned by the producer and located in the same commune. Vinification must occur in the same prefecture. It can be used only with OPAP, OPE, and TO wines.

Aplotaries – A distinctive way of training vines, commonly used on the island of Paros. The trunk of the vine grows over-ground at a sharp angle and extends horizontally on the ground. Young shoots develop vertically but still touching the ground, creating a floor covering of vines.

Asproudes – General term for various local white varieties grown together and usually harvested together. The singular is *asprouda*.

Cava (Kava) – Label term indicating a table wine that has been aged for longer-than-average. White cavas are aged for one year, with a minimum of six months in oak and six in bottle. Cava reds are released after three years with at least one year in oak and one in bottle. Al

Chora – "Land". The Ancient Greeks used this word in a much broader sense (very close to the French notion of terroir) than modern Greeks do.

Cru – The French term for "specified site". In Greece, usually loosely used for parcels that are deemed to be of superior quality and/or producing wines with distinctive character.

Cultivars – A term used by ampelographers, botanists, and horticulturalists to describe different varieties within the same species.

Eidika Epilegmenos – "Specially selected" or *grande réserve*; used on labels to denote quality-wines that have been aged for longer than *epilegmenos* (*see* below). Whites are released after two years, with a minimum of one year in oak and six months in bottle. Reds have a minimum eighteen months in oak and the same in bottle, and are released on the market after a total maturation period of four years. (*See also* Appendix I.)

Epilegmenos – "Selected" or *réserve*; used on labels to denote quality-wines that have been aged for longer-than-average. Whites are released after one year of ageing, with a minimum of six months in oak and three in bottle. Reds have to be aged for a total of two years, with a minimum of twelve months in oak and six in bottle.

FYROM – Acronym of the Former Yugoslavian Republic of Macedonia.

Kapilia – Wine tavernas; the establishments that made retsina popular.

Krasi – "Wine." In Ancient Greek the word for wine was *oenos/oinos*, while *kratistos oenos* was wine diluted with water. *Krasi* is the development of *kratistos oenos*, even though now Greeks do not mix wine with water.

Krevatines – Low pergolas found in Crete.

Ktima – "Estate" or "domaine". A label term which can be used only for OPAP, OPE, and TO wines made from a minimum of fifty per cent estate-grown fruit. The vineyards must be in the same commune and vinification must occur in the same prefecture.

Mavroudia – A blanket name for a number of dark-skinned varieties found throughout Greece, most of the time interplanted with other vines or other types of Mavroudi. The dark-skinned equivalent of *Asproudes*.

Mezzo – Sweet wine from Santorini, principally made from sun-dried Mandilaria grapes. The red equivalent of vinsanto (*see* below).

Monastiri – The Greek word for "monastery".

Nama – Sweet wine, destined for Holy Communion use. There are no legal restrictions on its composition. The commercial viability of such wines is influenced by the connections of the producer with the Church.

Neos Oinos – "Young wine". A relatively new term used for wines released on the market before December 10 following harvest. It is recommended that these wines are all sold by the end of the coming April.

Oinopoiio – The Greek word for "winery".

Oreinoi Ampelones – "Mountainous vineyards". Generally this term is used to describe wines made from grapes sourced from altitudes above 300 metres (984 feet). The use of the term on a wine label must follow the same rules as *ampelones* (*see* above). Only used for OPAP, OPE, and TO wines.

Plagia – The Greek word for slope or *côte*. Plural: *plagies*.

Potential alcohol – Measurement denoting total alcoholic strength of a wine if all the sugar was fermented. Based on the convention that 16.7 grams of sugar per litre will produce one per cent alcohol. However certain factors, like the yeasts used or the method of fermentation, may alter the final alcoholic strength. In grapes or musts, potential alcohol is a way of measuring technological ripeness (as opposed to physiological or phenolic).

Prefecture – A term used by the Greek government mainly to describe administrative regions. The Greek State is divided into departments, these are divided into prefectures, and these in turn are split up into communes.

Pyrgos – "Château." Term used on labels, similar to *ktima* (*see* above). A building that resembles a château must exist within the vineyards.

Rootstock – The part of the plant that forms the root system to which the trunk of the fruiting variety, called its scion, is grafted. In most cases, the rootstock is from an American species or a hybrid, used to overcome problems related to soil pests, diseases or specific soil compositions.
The most important rootstocks used in Greece are:
110 Richter: a high vigour, drought- and phylloxera-resistant rootstock, but it can delay maturing in fertile soils.
140 Ruggeri: a drought- and phylloxera-resistant rootstock, but it is also extremely high in vigour, so it should be avoided in prolific sites or with certain varieties.
161-49 Couderc: A highly phylloxera-resistant rootstock that is also tolerant to lime. However it is more sensitive to arid conditions.
1103 Paulsen: A vigorous rootstock, very resistant to drought and phylloxera, but moderately tolerant to soils with a high lime content.

Stremma – The Greek unit of measurement for land. Equal to 1,000 square metres, a tenth of a hectare or about a quarter of an acre.

Sugar levels – A measurement of grape ripeness, and in direct relation to potential alcohol (*see* above). The total sugar content of grapes determines the must weight. Around the world, sugar levels are measured in many units, such as Brix, KMW or Oechsle. In Greece, the most popular method is using degrees Baumé, which indicates the degrees of potential alcohol.

Symposium – An important form of social gathering in Ancient Greece, when men met and exchanged views. Wine drinking was a major part of a *symposium* and it is fair to say that this occasion was instrumental in the development of a wine-drinking culture. Plural: *symposia*.

Terpenes – Highly aromatic compounds, associated with distinctive, floral aromas. Terpenes are commonly found in specific varieties such as Muscat or Gewurztraminer, as well as in, mainly American, oak.

Tsipouro – The spirit obtained by distilling the grape solids and stems left over after the grapes have been pressed. Greek equivalent of grappa.

Vareli – The Greek word for "barrel".

Vin de liqueur – A fortified wine, usually, but not necessarily, sweet.

Vin doux – A sweet fortified wine. Fortification takes place in the very first stages of fermentation, or before the fermentation has been initiated.

Vin doux naturel – A sweet fortified wine, where fortification has taken place after the initial phases of fermentation.

Vin naturellement doux – A sweet wine made with no addition of spirit at any stage of the production. Grapes used have to be very ripe, either left on the vine or dried. As a result, the yeasts cannot fully ferment the must, resulting in a high alcohol level and a significant amount of residual sugar.

Vinsanto – Famous sweet wine from Santorini. It is unrelated in style to the Italian wine of the same name. Vinsanto is based on Assyrtiko, with White Aidani. Grapes are left on the vine to reach a high level of ripeness, and sun-dried for a week to fifteen days. Fermentation stops naturally, but some producers will add spirit if the alcohol level is considered too low. Vinsanto must be aged for at least two years in oak prior to release.

Yield – In much of Europe, yield is commonly measured in hectolitres per hectare. Yet Greeks use kilograms per *stremma* (*see* above). The two entities are in fact measuring slightly different things – the former is the volume of liquid produced per unit surface of vineyard, while the latter is weight of fruit per unit surface. However, taking as a given that 100 kilograms of grapes produces 0.7 hectolitres, then hectolitres per hectare can be calculated by multiplying the kilograms per stremma figure by 0.07.

Index